The trial of Col. Aaron Burr on an indictment for treason : before the Circuit Court of the United States, held in Richmond (Virginia), May Term, 1807 : including the arguments and decisions on all the motions made. Volume 3 of 3

Aaron Burr

THE

TRIAL

OF

Col. Aaron Burr,

ON AN INDICTMENT FOR

TREASON,

Before the CIRCUIT COURT of the UNITED STATES, held in
Richmond, (Virginia), May term, 1807:

INCLUDING THE

ARGUMENTS AND DECISIONS

*On all the Motions made during the Examination and Trial, and on
the Motion for an Attachment against Gen. Wilkinson.*

TAKEN IN SHORT-HAND BY T. CARPENTER.

VOL. III.

Washington City:

PRINTED BY WESTCOTT & CO.

1808.

Circuit Court of the United States.

TUESDAY, *September* 1.

MR. HAY observed to the Court, at its opening, that he had neither argument nor evidence farther to offer to the Jury on the indictment. He had examined the opinion of the Court, and must leave the case with the Jury

The Jury accordingly retired to their chamber, and in a short time returned; when Col Carrington, their foreman, read the verdict, which was endorsed on the indictment as follows

" *We, of the Jury, say, that* AARON BURR *is* NOT *proved to be guilty under this indictment, by any evidence submitted to us. We, therefore find him* NOT GUILTY "

Mr *Burr* Wherever the verdict of a Jury is incorrect, in point of form, or in words, it is improper, and ought not to be placed on any record. the Jury have no right to travel out of the course the law has assigned them. I hope the Court will direct the verdict to be given in the usual way.

Mr *Hay* It certainly, and in fact, is a verdict of acquittal The Jury have thought proper to state it in certain words, and surely the Court ought to record it in the words they themselves have used There is no precise practice, or form, that ought to govern the Jury in making a verdict: it is the verdict of a Jury, and if the Court received it, it must be entered in their own words

Mr. *Burr* The Jury have no right to return a written verdict at all. they have no right to depart from the usual form; the Court ought to suppress it. The Jury ought to be sent back again, and to return with an oral verdict, simply of *guilty* or *not guilty*, and if they choose to make a speech to the Court, or the audience, they have a right, if the Court permit them

Mr *Martin* They say, that they have not evidence before them to prove that he is guilty and, therefore, find him not guilty. This is exactly the reason why all Juries return their verdict, because they have, or have not evidence. I can see no reason for a preamble to the verdict in this particular case. Do the counsel wish to make it appear, that the Jury censure the decision of the Court, in not giving them irrelevant testimony ?

Mr *Burr* called for the recital of the common direction given to the Jury by the Clerk. [It was read, and ends in the following words " if you find him guilty, you are to say so; if not guilty, you are to say so—*and no more.*"]—The Jury *cannot* be indulged they have defaced a paper belonging to the Court, by writing upon it words that they have no right to write.

Mr *Hay* If there is any effect to be obtained by an opposition to the form of this verdict, it is done: the Jury, without looking at the indictment, can answer in these words, *ore tenus*

Col Carrington, one of the Jury. It was understood as a full verdict of acquittal.

Mr Parker, another of the Jury. If I am sent back, I certainly shall give the same verdict as is now returned, and in the same words. We all know that the verdict was not strictly consistent with the usual form, but as this was more satisfactory to us, so we have returned it, and I cannot agree to alter it.

Mr Burr I shall insist that the verdict shall be given in such a way as is prescribed by law, and no otherwise. The Jury must alter it, to bring it within the forms of law, they may write whatever they please upon any other paper, but let it not be made a matter of record. I pray that they may have the privilege of altering it, or, if not, that the words may be erased from the indictment

Mr Hay mentioned a circumstance in which some words were written on an indictment in addition to the bare verdict. The Jury insisted upon their continuance, in opposition to the arguments of counsel; and the Court directed that a general verdict should be entered on the record.

The *Court* decided that the words should remain on the indictment, and that the general verdict of " not guilty," should be entered on the record. If the Jury insisted upon their verdict retaining the form in which they had inserted it, the Court could not reject it.

Proclamation was then made by the Clerk, but Mr Burr observed, that he should not move for his discharge until to-morrow

Mr Hay informed the Court that the counsel for the United States had not determined on the course which they should pursue—whether to proceed to the trial of Aaron Burr on the indictment for misdemeanor, or whether they should now move the Court to commit him for trial in Kentucky, in which State an overt act is said to have been committed, (at the mouth of Cumberland) It was necessary to take time to consult on that subject.

Jonathan Dayton (against whom a bill for treason committed on Blannerhasset's island was returned by the Grand Jury; and also another for misdemeanor at the same place) appeared in Court An affidavit was exhibited to prove that he was not at the island at the time charged in the indictment *a nolle prosequi* was entered on the indictment for treason, and he was held to bail with two sureties in 10,000 dollars, to appear from time to time to answer the indictment for misdemeanor if it should be called up.

WEDNESDAY *September 2*

Mr Hay I have examined the opinion of the Court, Sir, and I am desirous of conducting myself in conformity to it but I wish to know whether my understanding of it is correct or not. According to my construction of that opinion, it amounts to this—that the evidence of the transactions on Blannerhasset's island does not come up to what is denominated levying war against the United States I consider that opinion as settled, and, if so, it

is not necessary to go on with the prosecutions against Blannerhasset and Smith, upon the indictments as they now stand. I
shall not encounter the opinion of the Court, nor press upon a
Jury what the Court says does not amount to levying war. I
shall therefore consider it necessarily my duty to enter a no-
lo prosequi on each indictment for treason, as it will be improper for
them to go through a trial here and elsewhere, under these circumstances. I presume an application, for their being sent to the
place where they did commit the overt act will be correct.

Chief Justice. Undoubtedly the Court intended to decide, in
that opinion, that the particular acts proved to have been committed on Blannerhasset's island, did not amount to the overt
act of levying war; but the Court did not intend that the opinion
should apply to the facts in *any* particular case; they only wished
to give such a statement of the law as to enable the Jury to apply
the proper facts proven, and it was then the province of the Jury
to say whether the treason had been committed or not.

Mr *Hay.* That being the case, Sir, I consider it my duty to
regulate my conduct in conformity with it. I shall therefore
move the Court to commit them (Blannerhasset and Smith) and
also the person who now stands before the Court (Burr) in order
that they should be tried in that place where the crime can be
established and proved on them. I move that Mr. Blannerhasset and Mr Smith be brought into Court, and that the whole
evidence may be gone into, as the facts will affect them all.

The Court agreed that they should be brought up

Mr *Burr.* Before the court make any order upon the subject,
I beg it to be observed, that it is proper a distinct motion should
be made against each individual, at least, that the motion against
me may be taken up separately; for otherwise a confusion must
necessarily be produced; the testimony against one may be said
to be testimony against another, and thus one will be charged
with what may be called another man's crimes. Again I wish
also, that there should be a specification of the place to which
these charges are meant to be applied, that I may have the better
opportunity of meeting the testimony.

Mr *Hay.* I do not know that I am *bound* to afford this specification, but I am willing to do it as far as I am able. I have
not been very minute in the examination of witnesses, but I am
told that there was such an assemblage of men at the mouth of the
Cumberland, as, by their numbers and their acts would constitute
an overt act of levying war. That all along down the river
Ohio and the Mississippi, their forces, their military array,
and warlike position were kept up, and that their numbers and
accoutrements were gradually increasing till the time of their utter dispersion. It also appears that Mr Burr was there with them,
and that he was the very *soul* of the expedition. It will be the
province of the Court, after the evidence is examined, to say
whether he has committed the overt act or not, and whether
such proof shall be produced as to justify their being sent to Kentucky, if the crime was committed there, or wherever the crime
was committed. I confess, Sir, that I make this motion with
great reluctance, but from the evidence which has come to my
view, it is a course which my conscience has pointed out as a

very proper one, and one which I am bound to make, having a proper regard to the opinion of the Court

I understand, Sir, the form of the motion is objected to, and that Mr. Burr thinks he ought not to be blended with the other two, but certainly there can be no difficulty in separating the testimony in such a way as to distinguish each man's acts, and to appropriate them to him solely The propriety of examining the cases at once is obvious if the motions are made separate, the evidence must have to be three times given, which will occasion immense delay It is apprehended that it will be attended with confusion, but this is not likely, for however chaotic and mixed the testimony will be, the Court can make the proper application to the several persons, and the trouble and difficulty will be less than if there is a separate examination. I have chosen this as the most expedient way, I may, however, be mistaken I believe that the evidence given respecting one will bear much about the same on the others, because they were all present; all engaged at the same time, and having all the same object in view Col Burr was at the mouth of Cumberland where he was joined by Blannerhasset and Smith, and they all departed down towards their destination together If it be the pleasure of the Court to require distinct motions, I shall submit

Mr *Burr*. There will be no occasion of repeating the evidence thrice times, nor perhaps at all; because, the same evidence after the case is gone through in the motion on one, can be taken out, so far as it might apply, to another, and be applied by the Court. There may be much of the evidence that might bear upon the other gentlemen which might not at all bear upon me, and *vice versa* It certainly would be more clear and easy to examine separately.

Mr. *Botts*. If I understand Mr Hay aright, his proposition extends to no less than this· that he should have the whole range of the river presented to the Court, to support his prosecution, and no less than three persons to be the subject of the same motion? Now, Sir, if there is no law, no precedent to be found, to regulate the Court, yet it certainly is the duty of the Court to enquire whether the cases are analagous; and, upon investigation, I am confident, that it will appear obvious, that they do materially differ They differ both upon legal ground, and upon the ground of evidence If the case should be brought forward, in the distinct acts of the individuals, each will know to what charges he has to answer; but, if they are combined, I think the evidence itself will subject Mr Hay to ridicule, even to the acknowledgement of himself, because, instead of an *overt act* of treason, in levying war. it will be discovered to be a *covert act* of peace. Added to this, it is a fact, that there are separate Counsel concerned in the several cases, and the examination ought to assume the same shape as any regular prosecution. The unity of the assemblage has not been made to appear, and a number of collateral objects will present themselves Applying this principle, Sir, what would the Court say to the prosecution? " You must charge each one specifically · the cases cannot be united without the consent of all "

Mr *Wickham* Col. Burr has been tried for treason against the United States, and a Jury have given a verdict of *Not Guilty* He is consequently entitled to his discharge, although he has not yet moved for it. But there are still indictments pending against the other gentlemen. The charge against *him* has been falsified by the verdict of a Jury, and he is to be considered as an *innocent man* He has not complained loudly, to be sure, of the situation in which he finds himself placed, but it must be obvious that he would not feel himself in a pleasant situation, when a motion is made to embrace *him* with the other gentlemen The circumstance of his being found not guilty, varies the case immensely

Again There are different counsel employed There is learned counsel employed for Mr Smith, who, has not yet appeared, and who, for ought we know, may take a very different ground from what we have taken for Col Burr Added to this, is the different circumstances of the cases the whole length of Ohio, and other extent, amounting to fifteen hundred miles, is embraced by the prosecutor, as the scene of action, as a part of which, it has been proved, one of the parties was not present. If any person is charged with a high crime, such as treason, or felony, the prosecutor is always obliged to specify some place, as well as time, where and when the crime is alleged to have been committed, and the combination of persons differently situated, cannot be admitted

Chief Justice With respect to any distinction, which is produced by a verdict of not guilty, that is a question of law, and not of fact, and consequently cannot blend the cases, because that verdict only extended to one of the persons it is, so far, unimportant whether the facts are blended or not, because that distinction can, at any period of the examination, be discussed Upon the question of a general charge, I conceive the law to be, that any specific charge might be made against any individual or he might be charged generally, and if a crime shall be found against him within the United States, he may be committed by the examining Judge; and it is, afterwards, the duty of the district Judge to remove him for trial to the place, where it shall appear the crime was committed.

With respect to the question of examining into the three cases at once, or distinctly, depends upon the analogy of the cases themselves; and of the applicancy of the testimony to each case. It may, in some circumstances be proper, and is sometimes done: for instance, the Grand Jury often find a joint bill, but I do not know that more than one has ever been tried under one indictment, without their own consent [*Mr Randolph—never.*] I rather suppose not In every case of examination, the testimony must be applied to the person charged, otherwise he cannot be affected by it, let its weight be what it might. It would be a wanton waste of time to repeat the same testimony, and, if all the persons accused are in Court at the time of its relation, I can see no possible disadvantage either one can sustain, for the whole being gone through in relation to the three, but the Court would incur disadvantage by a repetition of the same evidence.

Col Burr said there could be no doubt but that there could no be a joint trial without consent of parties

The *Chief Justice* mentioned a difficulty which he did not know how the Court could get over. Col Burr was now in custody of the marshal, and bound to answer an indictment for a misdemeanor. He did not know how he could be taken out of that custody and sent to a foreign jurisdiction for trial of another offence.

M *Hay* I shall make the motion to the Court, and leave it to the Court to decide

Chief Justice said he did not know how he could do it

Mr *Hay* I know how to do it. When the Court is called upon to decide, and the difficulty presents itself, I will remove it. I do not expect to untie the knot, but I can cut it

Mr *Wickham* contended, that the difficulty should be removed in the first instance. Col Burr was now in custody

Mr *Hay* observed, that it was obvious the question did not occur till the Court was called upon to transmit the accused. Then the difficulty will present itself, and not before

Mr *Botts* said, the subject presented two questions, one to *commit*, and the other to *transmit* to a foreign Court. Which was the most regular, in the order of proceedings? Surely the commitment. Suppose Col Burr had been in custody, and bound to answer in another Court—Could this Court act upon him till he was discharged from his prosecution there?

Mr *Wirt* When the motion comes on, we shall be able to answer to the gentleman's observations

Chief Justice The motion is, he being already committed and in custody, to charge him with the crime of an high misdemeanour

Mr *Hay* It appears to me, Sir, that it is your province to commit, but if there is a removal called for, according to the act of Congress, it is the duty of the *district Judge* to transmit to any other place, where the crime might have been committed, upon a motion made to that effect. If he should decide that he cannot transmit the prisoner, circumstanced as he is, we are prepared to argue upon it

Mr. *Wickham* The process is to arrest *Col Burr* He is here in Court. The motion is made to commit, when he is already committed, and in custody, and whilst he stands here, charged with a crime, he cannot be removed. Suppose he is acquitted in the place where he is sent to, is he to be discharged? No, Sir he is to be sent back to Virginia, to be tried for the charge yet remaining

As to the district Judge, I do not know that he has any directions whatever. it is for this Court to judge. this is the prior jurisdiction; the motion is made to commit; he is committed, and here he stands, amenable to the charge. The Court have jurisdiction over the offence. It might be nothing to the government to keep a man here, who has, at their pleasure, been detained, month after month, and forced to travel from the Mississippi Territory to this place; because it was, perhaps, thought the *fittest* place to try him. I will not say, that such a length of imprisonment, a journey of twelve hundred miles, or the verdict of a Jury, could be a death to Col. Burr. but I will say that it would be death to any gentleman, whom the government might choose to prosecute ; for they can find a bill of indictment, upon these principles, against any man

Chief Justice I should think that the bill charging with misdemeanor, ought first to be disposed of, before he is removed out of the custody where he now is, into another custody The Court know not how to commit else, since he is already *in custody*

Mr *Hay* The application to you, Sir, is to commit If the district Judge should find any difficulty, upon enquiring into the circumstances, it will be removed

Chief Justice The only doubt is whether this Court is not bound to hear the whole case, before a decision is made Suppose the motion had been made before the district Judge, might he not require a decision upon the present indictment, before he committed? (After examining the law,) the Chief Justice said, that when a person was to be transmitted to a foreign Court, if the offence was bailable, the Court was to take a recognizance of bail Now, can the Court take a recognizance to appear in another Court, when the party is bound to appear in this?

This Court is bound to certify the Court to which the accused is to be sent, and the district Judge is bound to send him

Mr Blannerhasset and Mr Smith were brought into Court by the Marshal

Mr *Hay* observed, that the three persons then before the Court, all stood in the same situations, and the same difficulty applied to all He regretted, that the Court had not expressed an opinion, before the prisoners had been sent for He was not disposed to disturb the opinions of the Court, but would go on with the trial for a misdemeanor against Col Burr

The Clerk was about to read the indictment for a misdemeanor, when he was interrupted by Col Burr, who said, he was not to be arraigned, but might plead by attorney He said that he was not in Court upon that indictment He was only in Court, because he had not moved to be discharged from the first indictment He hoped that nothing which had passed, would prevent a full consideration of this subject In this case, he wished to set up certain land marks, by which others might be guided, who were to follow, and he feared there would be many

Mr *Wirt* enquired as to the effect of the proclamation which was made by the Marshal, after the Jury had returned their verdict The usual course was (and the one which had been adopted in this case) for the officer to make proclamation if any person "knew of any treasons, felonies, or other misdemeanors committed, or done by the prisoner at the bar, let them come forth, and they shall be heard The prisoner at the bar stands upon his deliverance," that is, his *discharge*

Mr *Hay* It was at first objected that Col Burr was in custody, and therefore he could not be transmitted to any other Court We are now told that he is not in custody

Mr *Botts* went into a very lengthy argument, to prove that although Col Burr was *corporally* present, he was not *legally* in Court He produced a number of precedents from the records of the General Court of this State, as well as of the Federal Court, to shew that after an indictment for a misdemeanor, the regular process was a *summons*, and not a *capias* by which the body could be arrested. He relied particularly on the opinion of Judge *Iredell* pronounced in *Mundell's* case, in which he considered the practice of the State Courts, as adopted throughout, by the judicial act of Congress, and on the practice in Sinclair's case, which was a prevention under this very act. In the latter case, the process was a summons.

The cases referred to, were from the order book, No 36, page 75, 79 and 76, 97. Sect 34 Jud act. 5 Bl 280, and in the appendix. Caul's Mss 115, 232, 217, 129, 130. Act 2nd March, 1793. Order book A. 358, 398, 401, 459. Calender's trial, Chase's impeachment, page 5, 17, 35. 2 Hawk 402, ch. 9, sect. 27. 4 Bl 301, &c.

Col *Burr* observed, that his Counsel considered it a question of policy, not to move for his discharge immediately. In submitting to give bail as to the misdemeanor in the first instance, it was never his intention to admit the right to demand it.

The *Chief Justice* said, that he had determined, in the first instance, that bail was demandable, without considering the subject fully. He thought the law was clear. but he was open to conviction. He did not think himself precluded from a full examination of its propriety.

Mr *Hay* said, he was not solicitous as to the result of the motion. The question now was, whether the prisoner should appear to the indictment for a misdemeanor without bail. Whenever a motion should be made to discharge him altogether, he should object to it, on the ground that treason had been committed elsewhere. He relied upon the act of Congress, which said, that for any *crime* or *offence* against the United States, the prisoner upon an arrest should be committed, or give bail. He also relied upon the practice of this Court in the case of Logwood. He had no doubt as to the application of the law of Congress, to the practice of the State Courts in civil cases. His only doubts were, whether it applied to criminal cases.

Mr. *Wickham* considered that the act of Congress, declaring that the *usual mode of process* of the several states in criminal cases should be adopted, was conclusive upon this question. The act of Congress fixes the punishment, but the proceedings are to be according to the laws of the several states. He had no objection to state the motives which governed the Counsel of Col Burr, in submitting to bail as to the misdemeanor. Such was the infatuation of the public mind, that if the Grand Jury had not found a true bill as to the treason, it was believed that Col Burr would have been taken with or without process, and sent to some other place. He therefore gave bail, as to the misdemeanor, in order that he might be under the protection of the Court.

The *Chief Justice* said, that when he gave his opinion on the question, of entering into an examination of evidence, with a view to send the accused to Cumberland, or to some other place, it was predicated on the idea, that he was actually confined by the process of this Court. The precedents of this Court, which have been quoted, seem to settle the practice very differently from my ideas of the law of Congress, in relation to criminal prosecutions. The question deserves consideration, and if I should be of opinion, that I am bound by those precedents, then the foundation on which I gave my opinion fails

Mr *Hay* enquired, where would be the propriety of issuing a process, to bring a person into Court, who was already before it

The *Chief Justice* said, that if a *capias* should be determined to be the proper process, he should consider the state of the party as sufficient, and might direct the Marshal to take him into custody but if a summons should be considered the regular process, he could not make such an order, and a *venire* must be awarded. If a venire issues, it will involve a question, whether the party is not entitled to a continuance

The Court took time to consider, and adjourned till to-morrow

---

THURSDAY, *September 3*

The *Chief Justice* delivered the following OPINION of the Court, on the proper process to be employed for bringing AARON BURR before the Court to answer the indictment for the misdemeanor

The question now before the Court is, whether bail be demandable from a person actually in custody, against whom an indictment for a misdemeanor has been found by a Grand Jury As conducing directly to a decision of this point, the question has been discussed, whether a summons or a capias would be the proper process to bring the accused in to answer the indictment, if in point of fact he was not before the Court.

It seems to be the established practice of Virginia, in such cases, to issue a summons in the first instance; and if by any act of Congress, the laws of the several States are adopted as the rules by which the Courts of the United States are to be governed in criminal prosecutions, the question is at an end · for I should admit the settled practice of the State Courts as the sound construction of the State Law, under which that practice has prevailed

The thirty-fourth section of the judicial act, it is contended, has made this adoption

The words of that section are · " That the laws of the several States, except where the Constitution, Treaties or Statutes of the United States shall otherwise require or provide, shall be regarded as rules of decision in trials at common law, in the Courts of the United States, in cases where they apply

It might certainly be well doubted, whether this section, if it should be construed to extend to all the proceedings in a case where a reference can be made to the State Laws for a rule of decision at the trial, can comprehend a case where, at the trial in chief, no such reference can be made Now in criminal cases, the laws of the United States constitute the sole rule of the decision, and no man can be condemned or prosecuted in the Federal Courts on a State Law The laws of the several states, therefore, cannot be regarded as rules of decision in trials for offences against the United States. It would seem to me too, that the technical term, "trials at common law," used in the section, is not correctly applicable to prosecutions for crimes. I have always conceived them to be, in this section, applied to civil suits, as contra-distinguished from criminal prosecutions; as well as to suits at common law, as contra-distinguished from those which come before the Court, sitting as a Court of equity or admiralty.

The provision of this section would seem to be inapplicable to original process for another reason. The case is otherwise provided for by an act of Congress. The fourteenth section of the judicial act, empowers the Courts of the United States, " to issue all writs not specially provided for by statute, which may be necessary for the exercise of their respective jurisdictions, and agreeable to the principles and usages of law."

This section seems to me to give this Court power to devise the process for bringing any person before it, who has committed an offence of which it has cognizance, and not to refer it to the State Law for that process. The limitation on this power is, that the process shall be agreeable to the principles and usages of law. By which I understand those general principles and those general usages which are to be found, not in the legislative acts of any particular State, but in that generally recognized and long established law, which forms the substratum of the laws of every state.

Upon general principles of law, it would seem to me, that in all cases where the judgment is to affect the person, the person ought to be held subject to that judgment. Thus in civil actions, where the body may be taken in execution to satisfy the judgment, bail may be demanded. If the right of the plaintiff is supported by very strong probability, as in debt upon a speciality, bail is demandable without the intervention of a Judge. If there be no such clear evidence of the debt, bail is often required upon the affidavit of the party. Now reasoning by analogy, from civil suits to criminal prosecutions, it would seem not unreasonable where there is such evidence as an indictment found by a Grand Jury, to use such process as will hold the person of the accused within the power of the Court, or furnish security, that the person will be brought forward to satisfy the judgment of the Court.

Yet the course of the common law appears originally to have been otherwise. It appears from Hawkins, that the practice of the English Courts was to issue *venire facias*, in the first instance, on an indictment for a misdemeanor. This practice, however, is stated by Blackstone, to have been changed. He says, (vol 4, p 319.) " And so in the case of misdemeanors, it is now the usual practice for any Judge of the Court of King's Bench, upon certificate of an indictment found, to award a writ of capias immediately, in order to bring in the defendant."

It is then the English construction of the common law, that although in the Inferior Courts, the *venire facias* might be the usual course, and although it had prevailed, yet, that a Judge of King's Bench might issue a capias in the first instance.

This subject has always appeared to me to be in a great measure governed by the 33d section of the judicial act. That section provides, that for any crime or offence against the United States, the offender may, agreeably to the usual mode of process against offenders in that State where he is found, be arrested, and imprisoned or bailed, as the case may be.

This act contemplates an arrest, not a summons, and this arrest is to be, not solely for offences for which the State laws authorise an arrest, but, " for any crime or offence against the United States." I do not understand the reference to the State law respecting the mode of process as overruling the preceding general words, and limiting the power of arrest to cases in which, according to the State laws, a person might be arrested, but simply as prescribing the mode to be pursued. Wherever, by the laws of the United States, an offender is to be arrested, the process of arrest employed in the State shall be pursued; but an arrest is positively enjoined for any offence against the United States. This construction is confirmed by the succeeding words. The offender shall be imprisoned or bailed, as the case may be. There exists no power to direct the offender or to bind him without bail to appear before the Court, which would certainly have been allowed, had the act contemplated a proceeding in such a case which should leave the person at large without security. But he is absolutely to be imprisoned or bailed as the case may be.

In a subsequent part of the same section, it is enacted, " that upon all arrests in criminal cases, bail shall be admitted, except where the punishment may be death."

There is no provision for leaving the person at large without bail, and I have ever construed this section to impose it as a duty on the magistrate who proceeds against any offender against the United States, to commit or bail him. I perceive, in the law, no other course to be pursued.

This section it is true, does not respect the process upon an indictment. But the law would be inconsistent with itself, if it required a magistrate to arrest for any offence against the United States, if it commanded him, on every arrest, to commit or to bail, and yet refused a capias, and permitted the same offender to go at large, so soon as an indictment was found against him. This section, therefore, appears to me to be entitled to great influence in determining the Court on the mode of exercising the power given by the fourteenth section in relation to process.

On the impeachment which has been mentioned, this point was particularly committed to Mr. Lee, and the law upon it was fully demonstrated by him.

The only difficulty I ever felt on this question was, produced by the former decisions of Judge Iredell. If the State practice on this subject had been adopted, I should have held myself bound by that adoption. But I do not consider the State practice as adopted. Mundell's case was a civil suit, and the decision was, that the State rule respecting bail, in civil actions, must prevail. Sinclair's case was, indeed, a case similar to this, and in Sinclair's case a venire facias was issued. But I am informed by the Clerk, that this was his act, at the instance of the Attorney—

not the act of the Court. The point was not brought before the
Court

In Callender's case, a capias, or, what is the same thing, a
bench warrant was issued. This was the act of the Court, but,
not having been an act on argument, or with a view of the whole
law of the case, and of former decisions, I should not have considered it as overruling those decisions, if such existed. But
there has been no decision expressly adopting the State practice;
and the decision in Callender's case, appears to me to be correct

I think the capias the more proper process. It is conformable
to the practice of England at the time of our revolution, and is,
I think, in conformity with the spirit of the thirty-third section
of the judicial act. I shall, therefore, adopt it

To issue the capias to take into custody a person actually in
custody, would be an idle ceremony. In such a case, the order
of the Court very properly supplies the place of a capias. The
only difference between proceeding by capias, and by order,
which I can perceive, would be produced by making the writ
returnable to the next term

As soon as this opinion was delivered, Mr *Hay* observed that
he would then proceed to the trial of the indictment for the misdemeanor

Chief Justice The issue must be made up, I suppose.

Mr *Burr* A letter has been demanded from the President of
the United States, which has been often promised, but never
produced. I wish to know if that letter is in Court, and whether
it cannot be put into the hands of the clerk

Mr *Hay*. I believe that it is not in my possession, for I have
not been able to find it among my papers after a minute search.
It is possible that it may be among them. Perhaps it may not be
necessary to produce it, as there is a copy of it, which is ready to be verified by the oath of more than one person

Mr *Burr* I cannot admit a copy. It is certainly strange,
that after the President's promise, this letter is not here

Mr *Martin* It is within my knowledge, that Mr Rodney has
been to the City of Washington since the application was made
for this paper

Mr *Hay* I have made a minute search among the large bundles of papers, which Mr Rodney has transmitted to me, but I
have not yet found it. General Wilkinson has a copy of the letter verified on oath

Chief Justice Unless a loss of the original be proved, a copy
cannot be admitted

Mr *Burr* then observed, that he should now call the attention
of the Court to the subject of bail, as the opinion just delivered
by the Court demands bail. that since bail was demanded of him,
on a former occasion, circumstances had considerably varied.
and some had occurred which ought to mitigate the amount of
bail. that it was useless for him to mention those circumstances, as they were well known, and it would consequently be understood that he was not as able to give as much bail. that it
should also be recollected, that the prosecution for treason had
failed, and that, under such circumstances he conceived that half
the sum which was demanded on a former occasion, was sufficient for the present

Mr. *Botts* repeated the same idea He observed, that in this country the state of a man's property was a criterion for the amount of bail; and that it could not be expected that a man of no property should give high bail Col Burr's circumstances were well known

Mr *Hay* differed in one respect from the opposite counsel. Col Burr had certainly been acquitted on the charge of treason; but it was not after a full exhibition of the evidence. A small portion indeed had been produced but the greatest part of the most interesting evidence had been excluded It was proper that the charge for treason should be fully investigated some where, either in Kentucky, Tennessee, or the Mississippi Territory; and that Burr's person should be kept safe, until he himself could have an opportunity of moving for his commitment, which he should certainly do, as soon as the trial for the misdemeanor would permit him

Mr. *Wickham* hoped that bail would not be taken in reference to a future motion Col. Burr has been tried, and acquitted. And what has been proved with respect to the misdemeanor? Nothing, that was done in the state of Virginia

Mr *Botts* hoped when this motion was made, that the Court would see in it an attempt most alarming, and they would consider it as a germ, which, if not crushed in time, would hereafter grow up to the extreme danger of the rights and liberties of American citizens It was best, however, to say at this time as little about it as possible The government had selected a particular place for Col Burr's trial, and from the success of that prosecution, the Court will easily argue the fate of those which might come after As to the motion which was menaced by Mr Hay, it would not be forgotten that inquests had been already held on these acts in Kentucky and Tennessee

The *Chief Justice* observed, that in demanding bail on the present occasion, he would not make any reference to any charge which may be made hereafter—that, on the former occasion, he had not taken into view the charge of treason, nor ought he to do it on the present occasion, that he thought, and does still think, that his former bail was a very high sum, for to bail a man in a sum six times higher than the fine to which the punishment of that offence *could* subject him, was certainly a high sum, particularly in a country whose Constitution forbids the exaction of excessive bail, but that he was disposed on that occasion to require as high a bail as he could reconcile with his ideas of propriety Circumstances however had varied since that occasion Debts of a civil nature had come against the accused, which would necessarily increase the difficulty of his giving bail Under all these considerations, he should be content with the sum of five thousand dollars.

Mr *Wirt* suggested, whether the taking of bail would not entangle the prosecution in their motion for commitment, and whether this motion could not be heard before the present measure was adopted Would not this recognizance impede the motion for commitment?

Mr *Burr* I hope that the Court will not proceed by anticipation, upon a motion, not yet made

Chief Justice. The motion for sending to another district for trial, might be heard immediately, if there was not an indictment for misdemeanor now pending before this Court. But, the Court has already declared, that this indictment holds his person here, by law, until it shall be disposed of by course of law; he is here ready to abide the judgement of this Court, and it is out of the power of the Court to send him any where else for trial, for any other offence, whilst he is held under recognizance to meet this indictment. The gentlemen can bring on the motion for removal when they please, by getting rid of the misdemeanour, but not without.

Mr *Wirt.* I should suppose that the removal itself would exonerate him from his recognizance, because he would be in custody.

Chief Justice. I cannot conceive its operation: the Court wishes not to commit itself by expressing its opinion. I cannot imagine how, being in *actual confinement*, and in *legal custody*, this Court can have power to discharge it. It is known that the Court has not the right to transmit him to any other place.

Mr *Wirt.* I must beg pardon of the Court for speaking so often; but, as in a recognizance for misdemeanor, or trespass, &c bail is given to a small amount, proportioned to the crime, and the party is permitted to go at large till trial; but shall the party be permitted so to go at large, where there is a case of murder, treason, or felony, yet pending upon that person, under the small bond of five thousand dollars? I can see it in no other view, Sir, than exoneration, because a person guilty of a crime of magnitude, will be influenced to escape in such a situation.

Chief Justice. Those who prosecute, are not bound to prosecute for a small offence, if they have one of greater magnitude in view. They can set it aside, if they please, and proceed with the motion to commit for a larger crime.

Mr *Wirt.* I should be glad, if the Court would not make up its mind too soon. Suppose a prisoner not to be discharged from his recognizance here, in the charge for misdemeanor. He goes into another district, and commits some heinous crime, (such as murder, &c.) it being known, that he is held to appear here, in a small sum for misdemeanor, would the Judge not consider himself bound to hold him in confinement, merely because of his recognizance here? Is the recognizance here to exonerate him from a responsibility for a large crime? This, Sir, is a question of importance.

Mr *Burr.* Let the gentleman state a case, where there is but a single act charged, supposing it to be levying war, or whatever. The government having selected their very *spot* and *time*, as well as the *crime*, makes the essence of the charge. How can two indictments grow out of this single act? In England there was but one example of it, and there the Court told the attorney to suppress the indictment, and it was discharged. Am I to be pursued, Sir, from place to place? The district where a crime is stated to be committed, can take measures, through their ministers of justice. If the gentleman does not choose to proceed with his charge, he ought to enter a *nolle prosequie* on the present case.

Mr Martin There is no analogy in the two cases If a man has two charges against him, undoubtedly, that of the greatest magnitude will hold him until it is discharged in due course of law The present question however, is, whether he shall be sent away, before the present indictment is disposed of, either by *nolle prosequi*, or by trial. He now stands indicted of a crime.

Ch f Justice The case put, is inapplicable to this, because there is no doubt but that if a man was to commit murder or treason, that this prosecution could not prevent his being apprehended and tried, where such a crime was committed The whole difficulty of the case is this the Court which already has the cognizance of the charge is called upon, during the operation of that charge, to remove the prisoner to another state for trial, to answer for a crime, said to have been committed in that State.

Mr Hay I will not pretend (at present) to say where it can be tried, but I consider that the first question is, whether there can be a removal at all or not? I wish, Sir, to make a motion to commit the person of the accused to prison, in order to his being tried where the crime was committed Here are many witnesses who have been waiting for a long time I want to dismiss them as soon as possible Now, suppose I make this motion, and the Court is of opinion that the prisoner ought to be committed in order to be transmitted to another district, then, and not till then, the difficulty would occur, as to the execution of the motion, when the Court shall hear the grounds of our motion We can then enter an *exoneratur* upon the recognizance, and he can be transmitted for trial, if the Court should see occasion, but, before that, I want the Court to understand the true ground of the motion

Mr. Wickham. The Court have already determined upon the motion of Mr Hay without going into the testimony for he makes his motion in the present state of the case He may consider himself entitled to make a motion whenever he pleases Let him do it, and we will endeavor to be ready to meet them, but let him first be prepared to remove difficulties out of the way

Mr Botts The gentleman's proposition is nothing less than bargaining with the Court if the Court are satisfied that Col Burr ought to be committed, then he will put it in the power of the Court to commit him! So that unless your honor enters into an engagement with Mr *Hay* upon certain propositions to be made by *him*, nothing is to be said! The question now is, whether you shall have power to grant? "They will exonerate if the Court would only commit" Now, Sir, who brought on this difficulty? Not the Court, nor us, but the counsel for the prosecution Now was this motion a meritorious one? Was it a necessary one? The prosecutor has both the questions—one at his disposal, the other at the pleasure of the Court He well might have said that it was important, since one trial for treason has already passed, and another pending, and besides that, an indictment for misdemeanour in this Court, yet untried Sir, I will present you with a more comprehensive view of the evil it is certainly, as has been stated, without example, for a prosecutor to make out of *one* act two offences, of an immensely different nature. It must be obvious to you Sir, that if he could make two he could make more, first, he charges levying war, failing in that he comes in with an indictment for a riot; failing in that, (if there were any lives lost in the war) he charges with murder for every man's life lost; and failing in all these, he comes to the charge of an unlawful assemblage, or even something inferior to that, in order to bring the accused in somewhere, or somehow, as often as he pleased, through the whole catalogue of crimes. In the English rebellion, we know that if the crime charged, was not proved upon the man, he was acquitted, and no other charge of the same rebellion was brought against him. Then, Sir, will you break down legal barriers in order to find the same offence under different names? We hope not.

Mr. Wirt. I thought the question we were discussing was upon the propriety of taking up the motion to commit, and it was to that I was applying my remarks, but Mr. Botts' remarks were applied to the question as though regularly made, the prisoner charged and acquitted, and therefore that it was impossible for us to renew it hereafter. Sir, we ask the previous point to be settled, to wit, have we the *right* to make the motion? We can then answer *all* objections.

Here a long and desultory conversation ensued as to the state of the motion, in which Messrs. *Martin, Burr, Botts, and Wick-ham* spoke on one side, and Messrs *Wirt* and *Hay* on the other. At one period it was thought they had got hold of the true question for discussion, but it was almost immediately turned into its original vortex. On the one side, the trial for misdemeanour was called; on the other, whether the Court would commit for trial to another district if sufficient evidence should be produced.

Chief Justice. I am *bound* to try the misdemeanour, and I have not *power* to suspend the removal, if the *district Judge* should choose to remove the prisoner. I am therefore not so much at liberty to divest myself of the case as another magistrate would, because he would not be under that controul that I *must* be: and perhaps it is not in the power of the attorney to relieve me.

Mr. Martin. The attorney can enter a *nolle prosequi*, even out of Court.

Mr. Wirt. The question is not quite so optional with us as has been represented by the Court, and some of the counsel think it is a question of vast moment—no more nor less than this, whether a man standing charged here with a small crime, may with impunity commit a great crime, or having committed a great crime beyond your geographical line, he shall be sheltered from prosecution, because he stands bailed in a small sum here to appear to answer for a small, (comparative) crime? There is this also, which, notwithstanding all the arguments which have been used I cannot give up, that if he should or has committed ever so great a crime in another state, he is sheltered under the charge of misdemeanour, now made, unless the Court should consider that he may be committed for those greater crimes. The accused might move a continuance of the cause, and I consider his attempt to obtain a certain letter as the harbinger of such a motion: he has not thought proper yet to mention such an intention however.

Mr. *Burr.* When a public prosecutor is about to pursue a man, he has his electieri what denomination of crime he may choose to charge him with; and where he may take him for trial, (if within the rules of the law.) But here the prosecutor has thought proper to make two descriptions of crime out of the *same* offence; and has produced two indictments; this, even, they ought not to have done; much less, having failed in one, ought they to carry the accused person to another place, to be tried for the offence, which he has been acquitted for. This difficulty might have been foreseen by the gentleman. Although there is nothing very alarming in the measure, except their violence, yet all ought to have been foreseen by the prosecution. It is oppression, to be giving so many faces to one chance, because a government might try in this place, in another, and then in another without end.

Mr *Wirt.* There certainly could be nothing extremely alarming, neither in the transactions of the prisoner, in his making so many faces to this transaction, as is said he did? If one of his faces bore towards the *North.* (as is said,) and another towards the *South;* another to a central revolution as it is called; and another towards the Spanish territories, how can it be wondered that the government should be alarmed? Sir, is it a wonder that we have undertaken this case? It is not one of those things that we ought not to have done, but it is one of those things that we were *forced* to do, and what our duty did not permit us to avoid, as to the prosecution for treason?

Are we baffled, Sir, under that indictment? If so, all the consolation that we have, is, that we know how it was; it was not from want of evidence, but he was sheltered under *principles of law.* We depend upon the construction to the law given by the Supreme Court, and in this, we were preceded by the Grand Jury; who were a collection of men, the most enlightened in the State. And we, as well as they, have been misled by such an interpretation of that opinion, as most men in the State would have given it. The Court, however, have said, that the opinions of the Supreme Court, have been misconceived. But, Sir, it is not upon the charges, nor upon the evidence that have been produced to *this* Court, for much less than half of the evidence has been permitted to be disclosed.

As to the duty of the Attorney for the United States, he holds in his hands evidence of the treasonable *acts* of the prisoner. Then, Sir, were he to permit that man to go away, without *every* effort in his power, to bring him to due justice, what would be the opinion of the people of the United States, for whom he is prosecutor? Would he act, then, as a faithful prosecutor for the United States, to permit such a case to go off in silence?

Mr *Martin.* Sir, we deny that Col Burr ever gave two faces to this transaction, and we are prepared to prove, whenever the question shall be in order, that the government, on the 27th December last, charged him with nothing but an expedition against the Spanish colonies. How it is turned into *treason,* since that time, I know not.

A farther conversation of some length, ensued between Mr. Botts and Mr *Hay:* after which, the *Chief Justice* declared his unwillingness at present, to decide upon the suggestions made. He wished not to divest himself of, or shrink from any act of duty, but he should not be disposed to enter into the question, until it was ascertained, whether it was intended that the trial for misdemeanour was to go on. On that ground he should reserve any determination upon *previous* propositions.

Mr *Burr* then observed, that he had lately discovered that a letter of General Wilkinson's of 12th of November, was material to his defence. He had made an affidavit to that effect.

Mr *Hay* observed, that he had that letter; but he would beg leave to state, that in General Wilkinson's letters, there was a great deal of matter which ought not to be made public; among the rest, several strictures upon certain characters in the Western country, which were freely imparted to the government, in the strictest confidence. Would it not be better, to trust the Court with the selection of such parts, as it might deem necessary, to the defence of the accused?

Mr *Martin*. Are we to have a secret tribunal? Let the argument be in writing.

Mr *Hay* then proposed, to submit those letters to the inspection of either Mr Randolph, or Mr Botts, or Mr Wickham; the man so selected, to pledge himself upon honour, not to divulge the confidential contents. If there was any difference of opinion, as to what were confidential passages, the Court were to decide.

Mr Burr's Counsel objected to inspecting any thing, which was not also submitted to their client, as they acted only as *Counsel*.

The subject was waved for the present, on Mr Burr's suggesting, that the opposite Counsel might perhaps, come to some understanding on this point, during the recess of the Court.

Chief Justice determined, that he would proceed upon the trial of the indictment for a misdemeanour, to-morrow, if Col Burr should be ready.

Col Burr was declared by the Court, to be discharged from the indictment for treason; and the following order was entered.

"Ordered, that *Aaron Burr*, against whom an indictment was lately depending in this Court for treason, and upon which the Jury, on Tuesday last brought in a verdict of *Not Guilty*, be acquitted and discharged of the said offence, and go thereof without delay. And it is ordered, that the said Aaron Burr, enter into a recognizance himself, in the sum of five thousand dollars; and give two or more sureties, in the sum of five thousand dollars for the said Burr's appearance, before this Court to morrow, then and there to answer an indictment against him, for misdemeanour. Whereupon the said Aaron Burr, acknowledged himself to be indebted to the United States, in the sum of five thousand dollars, of his lands and tenements, goods and chattels to be levied, and to the United States rendered. Yet upon this condition, that if the said Aaron Burr, shall make his personal appearance before this Court to-morrow, at twelve o'clock, then and there, to answer the said indictment for misdemeanour, and shall not depart thence, without leave of the said Court, or until discharged by due course of law, then this recognizance to be void."

[*William Langborn* and *Jonathan Dayton* were his securities.]

The *Chief Justice* observed, that the Court was willing to hear the argument, on the motion for removals, if the case of misdemeanour did not come on. The prisoner would, therefore, be remanded to custody under the civil process, by which he was confined, and be consequently brought up by habeas corpus to this Court.

General Jonathan Dayton appeared in Court, and Mr. *Wickham* observed, that if it was the pleasure of the prosecution to proceed upon the indictment for treason, found against General Dayton, some steps would be necessary, preparatory to a trial.

Mr *Hay* said, that after the decision of the Court, upon the doctrine of treason, he did not see the propriety of incurring the expense and trouble of a trial, especially as he did not know of any act charged against him, which would amount to treason, under that decision. He, therefore, thought it the most correct course to enter a *nolle prosequi* as to that indictment, which was accordingly done.

Mr *Wickham* then, as Attorney for General Dayton, pleaded *not guilty*, to the indictment for a misdemeanour; and recognizance was entered into, for his appearance in Court from day to day.

FRIDAY, *September 4th*

Col *Burr* renewed the subject, of the two letters from General Wilkinson, to the President of the United States, one of the 21st of October, 1806, and the other of the 12th of November, of the same year, for the production of which, a writ of *subpœna duces tecum* had been awarded. He said that he had a right to process of contempt, but as this mode of proceeding would be very unpleasant, and necessarily produce delay, it might perhaps be avoided, by obtaining a copy of that of the 21st of October, which was said to have been lost or mislaid, if such copy could be satisfactorily authenticated. With respect to the letter of the 12th of November, which was stated to contain certain confidential communications from General Wilkinson to the President, and which the Attorney for the United States, had expressed a willingness to produce, with the exception of those parts which were said to be confidential, he was not at present disposed to accede to the proposition. He had reason to believe that the whole letter had been shewn without disguise to others, and had been used against him.

Mr *Hay* said that he could assure the accused, that the letter had never been seen by any human being to his knowledge, except the person to whom it was addressed, the counsel for the United States, the Chief Justice and some of Col. Burr's counsel, to whom it was confidently communicated with a view to ascertain whether an arrangement could not be made for its production with the exception of those parts, which in his judgment ought not to be disclosed.

Col *Burr* said that he would be more explicit. He would ask whether the letter or a copy had not been produced to the Grand Jury.

Mr. *Hay.* I do not know that either the original or a copy were ever laid before the Grand Jury. I believe that they were not. But I am not so well acquainted with what passed in the Grand Jury as some other gentlemen *are.*

There could be no doubt of the accuracy of the copy. Before he was certain that he had the original letter of the 14th of Nov. he obtained a copy from General Wilkinson, which he found, in comparison was correct, in the most remote particulars. He mentioned this circumstance merely to show the strong probability that the copy of the letter of the 21st of October might be relied upon as equally correct.

In order to verify the copy of the letter dated the 21st October. Mr *Hay* called Mr. Duncan, who was sworn.

Mr. *Hay,* Please Sir, to look at this paper and say what you know of it?

Mr *Duncan* This is a true copy of the letter spoken of, the original of which was shewn me by General Wilkinson.

Q. Do you know in whose hand writing it is?

A. I think it is all in the hand writing of Captain Walter Burling, who acted as *Aid-de-cong* to General Wilkinson whilst he was on the Sabine expedition. I am well acquainted with the hand writing, having often seen him write.

Mr *Botts.* Is that all the evidence which you have?

Mr *Hay.* It is, and we do not consider more to be necessary. I will be upon oath, if required, that I have not been able to find the original letter: I have examined among my papers as well as I can. Mr Rodney informed me that he sent all the letters, but I cannot find that identical one among the packet that was sent.

Mr *Wickham.* Do you suppose that you have lost it?

Mr. *Hay.* I imagine not, but I know not where it is. Are you satisfied with the authenticity of this copy which is undoubtedly a fair one.

Mr. *Botts* Certainly not, for how can we know it is an exact copy without seeing the original. We did hope that it would have been produced. As it is, I see no other way than to adjourn, that the gentleman might have the opportunity again to examine his papers. We have been charged, and want to avail ourselves of public documents for our defence. You recollect Sir, that the President has put a construction on certain parts of this letter, which we do not know of.

Chief Justice Perhaps after the reading of this copy you may know what is alluded to.

Mr *Botts* I do not know that we wish to compare.

Mr. *Martin* It is impossible for Col. Burr and his counsel to have a communication on the spot; after adjourning we may form a definitive idea.

Chief Justice to Mr *Hay* Is there any difficulty in going forward with the trial for misdemeanour against General Dayton?

Mr. *Hay* wished to get forward with all possible speed; but he was not at present ready with materials for the trial of General Dayton. I do not precisely know how far he was concerned, nor where, as to his *acts*

Chief Justice. Do you expect to be able to prove any thing of the kind?

Mr. Hay. I cannot say that I do

Mr. Botts As the gentleman does not suppose that he can get proof farther about this letter for the present, I hope he will agree to the trial of General Dayton

Mr. Hay I confess that I cannot, because I have not heard all the evidence, nor do I know on what ground the Grand Jury found their bill; perhaps I may be able by to-morrow to know, but at present I cannot conjecture

Chief Justice The attorney must certainly judge for himself if it is too soon to know whether so much of this case has not already been opened, or whether he has yet to examine whether he can or cannot support the indictment As it is evident that General Dayton was not at Blannerhasset's island, but in Jersey, there may be a question, how far he could be connected I do not say that it is impossible that he should have been connected ; but I do say it is necessary for the attorney to produce evidence of this connection or assistance rendered I do not think he ought to be pressed to go to trial until he has made himself acquainted with his case ; still he ought to examine soon, in order to give the defendant an opportunity of returning to his home if there is no chance of a trial.

Mr. Hay My opinion will be much governed by that of the Court respecting the law If the prosecution is restricted to the acts of General Dayton, done in Virginia, I do not suppose there will be a chance of producing a conviction ; but if we may bring forward evidence generally *connecting* him with the parties engaged, even a letter written by him might be evidence perhaps

Mr. Wickham. This is mooting a point of great magnitude.

Mr. Hay I cannot go into this case now, because we have others of the same nature that will come first.

Mr. Martin expressed his desire that Israel Smith should be arraigned, in order to ascertain the measures the attorney would take on the subject

Mr. Hay said he would go through all the cases as soon as he could, but he could not at present

Mr. Botts I have run my eye over this copy of the letter, referred to, but I cannot make up my mind, that it tends to remove the difficulty which I had conceived respecting the difference between a copy and the original But there is another matter, which the Court can deliberate upon It will be recollected, that yesterday Col Burr mentioned the letter of the 12th November, 1806 That letter is in possession of the attorney of the United States Col Burr has made affidavit that he believed that letter to be material to his defence. There is only one way that I know of, by which we can get at that letter, if he persists in refusing it : and that is, that a *subpæna duces tecum* be directed to Mr Hay I suppose that this will be objected to, because of the public situation of a prosecutor ; but I contend that there can be secrets which the prosecution ought not to disclose, in order to assist a man in making his defence However, lest it might be said that I am taking too broad a ground ; I will say, that there is no documents in the possession of the public functionaries that ought to be withheld when considered by us important. If we have a right to summon the President of the United States to produce this letter, (as was ruled) we have certainly the same right to demand it from the attorney, in whose hands the President deposited it. It was suggested that this letter might be of a very delicate and confidential nature: and perhaps developing names and connections, which ought not to be exposed, because, it was not meant to be made public. If we examine this argument, we shall see, that it is such a one, as in our country, at least, ought to be abandoned. Here is a high military officer, in troublesome times, makes a communication to the government; but, why should that government be fearful to disclose that communication, when the storm is over? Are not the energies of the government sufficient to suppress any evil designs, which a faction can raise? But suppose a number of characters should have been maligned, and denounced one by one, as they should fall in the way of the officer; ought they not to have the opportunity of proving their innocence, and not be locked up in executive knowledge? How should the executive know the justness or falsity of the charge? If it is a just accusation, the characters ought to be avowed; if unjust, the men ought to know their enemies. It would be an act of injustice and impropriety in the President himself, to shield the accuser, and condemn the accused without a hearing!

But, Sir, take our case in another view: the rule of law is, that no man shall be condemned, without being allowed to produce the *best evidence*, which the nature of the case will admit of, even, if it be from the coffers of the government. I remember the time, when I abhorred the idea of *state secrets*, under another administration: it is equally abhorred now, in every aspect which I can view it. He moved the *subpœna duces tecum.*

Mr. *Hay.* I have nothing to say, but I do wonder at the misapplication of things by Mr. Botts.

Mr. *Burr.* The right of an accused-person to claim evidence cannot be denied, nor abandoned. The client of the prosecutor is the people of the United States in this case, and with them there ought not to be any such thing as *state secrets.* But, at all events, if we put it upon that ground, and it is right to withhold any thing, it must be limited to that species of secrets, which regards the *public good*; and not to make a secret of individual denunciations. If a man has made secret denunciations of individual characters, the public ought to know who that man is, and by what means he has so acted.

Mr. *Hay.* The Court certainly cannot misunderstand our motive, although the gentlemen all seem to do it. It cannot be believed, that I have the smallest desire to withhold any thing that would serve the accused. It seems to be taken for granted, that my wish to withhold it, is from a desire expressed by General Wilkinson. It is not. I am not satisfied, from the observations which I have heard made by the accused, that this application is made for the sake of any evidence which could serve himself: if it were, I should have no objection to afford him all the opportunity of every force of evidence in my power, consistent with my duty; but I want him to ask no more than will be serviceable to his case   Sir, it cannot be right that he shall have liberty to have access to a letter, merely for the purpose of making it public, to betray the confidence of man to man, or, if he pleases, of an officer to the government, respecting private characters, by which private controversies would be produced. I could wish the Court to look at the letter, and say whether it does not contain such things as ought not to be exhibited to pub he view.

Sir, we can very easily suppose a state of things, when every man ought to be looked upon with caution   He may live in a part of the country where he may be suspected, from his situation, of mal-deeds, when he is not, in truth, guilty of any   He may discover that the public functionaries in that part are tainted, and the public welfare requires of him to disclose to the executive, something about certain persons, whilst the damage meant to be fabricated, is yet undone   Now, Sir, ought such a communication to be made public? Suppose one or two persons mentioned in this letter should be of that description; can it be believed that Mr. *Burr's* defence requires the exposure of their names?   Can the Court encourage any measures that shall make a difference between General Wilkinson and those persons, when his object was merely the public good?   I never will be instrumental in putting into his hands any information which cannot be used for his defence, to the injury of others   I do not say that he will use it so   he may be above such a pitiful act, but I am rather surprised at his anxiety to obtain such information. Suppose that other persons should fall in consequence of any denunciation by General Wilkinson; what would it be to Col Burr?   Would this be a circumstance that would be of service to his case?   He may say that it would impeach General Wilkinson's character but it cannot do it, as to his evidence at least, then why should he be the friend of those who were denounced? (if any)   He may have all the advantages that belongs to his defence, without, as well as with it ; in short, it is not his business : he may have all those parts of the letter for his assistance, if he can find any, which relate to his defence : of this, I wish the Court to judge · but when the Court examine it, they will find that there is not a single syllable that can belong to it.   In short, the passages in the letter, which it would be improper to expose, are only *opinions* of the writer, respecting certain persons at New Orleans, &c which opinions, may have been since changed, and, indeed, with respect to one of them, I know it has changed.

It was said the other day, that there was in my possession an affidavit of Jacob Albright, and the gentleman declaimed, because I would not produce it   Rather however, than subject Albright to inconvenience I did produce it: but what use was made of it?   None at all   And, notwithstanding all the clamour, this would be the same as to the defence of the prisoner. There is not one single word from the beginning to the end of this letter, that can go towards his favor. I cannot say, however, that the gentleman's ingenuity can do, since I know it to be very great   Mr Wickham might look at the letter if he pleases, and if he can say there is any thing important to the case, I will let it be seen

Mr *Wickham*. I cannot do that: I only act here as the counsel for Col Burr, and can receive no secrets which shall not be subject to his inspection.

Mr *Hay* There are two passages in the letter, which I can not allow to be seen, except extorted by the Court Indeed, I do not know that any thing could extort it from me, under any circumstances whatever All that can be done, is, that I may be committed to prison, and that I would submit to, rather than betray a sacred trust

Mr *Burr* We may be of different judgments, as to the applicability of a piece of evidence I know of no other way to obtain it, than by reference to the Court

Mr *Wickham* After this defiance from the counsel on the other side, it only remains for us to refer to the Court to know whether or not, they shall direct the paper to be produced Mr Hay has been pleased to suggest that he is influenced alone by his own judgment, as to the disposal of the letter.

Mr *Hay* I only said that the objection did not originate in General Wilkinson, or the President In one of the letters from the President, he expressly empowers me to hold back any part of any communication which I may suppose it would be improper to produce By virtue of that power and my own judgment, I withhold this letter, or so much of it as has been expressed

Mr *Burr* The President of the United States is no more privileged than Mr Hay, for, if he was to be brought into this Court, any documents which he possessed, or any evidence which he could give, could only be withheld upon the principle of public good

Mr *Wickham* The *subpœna duces tecum* has been regularly awarded to the President, who has empowered Mr. Hay to deliver that letter whenever the Court shall direct it, upon the discretion of the President, it has been transmitted to Mr Hay for that purpose There is an officer in England denominated the keeper of the king's conscience; but I have never heard that Mr Hay was keeper of the conscience of the President If he was so, it would be an office of delicacy indeed; but motives of delicacy, it has been long ago settled, are not sufficient to suppress evidence which may be deemed essential to a case, for the purposes of justice We all know the history of the Duchess of Kingston's case, A D 1776, in which evidence of a most *delicate* nature was enforced, and which related to subjects, which the parties had solemnly promised to conceal. But Courts of Justice know none of these particular rules of delicacy. all men in all stations, must yield to the settled rules of justice If the President of the United States were himself to come forward, and under the sanction of an oath, to declare that the public good required that the letter should be withheld, because its exposure would bear upon the dearest interests of the country, it certainly would deserve notice. But Mr Hay does not even say, that it can have any public operation

Sir, let us suppose that *all* this letter is composed of calumny, (I do not know that it is, but,) would it not weaken, very much weaken the testimony of General Wilkinson? Surely it would be a very good argument indeed for us. Again. Suppose it to be an act of slander, would not an evidence of calumny in the party, have an operative effect in the decision? I do not know that it is, but this may be the fact, and it is essential for us, that nothing of this kind should tend to enhance the charge, or have a bearing on the case of our client. Mr. Hay supposes that General Wilkinson acted with candour and patriotism, in sending this letter; and it seems that he thinks so from the eulogies he has spent on General Wilkinson. It may be so, but of this we want to be acquainted, by access to the document which we consider material to our defence, and which it is our right to have.

As to the reference to Albright's affidavit, we wanted it in order to prove what we have fully ascertained, that his parole testimony and his affidavit, is not only a prevarication but a direct contradiction; and, being under the impression that it would be so, we called for the affidavit and evidence taken by the Clerk, at the first examination. Supposing this contradiction to be so palpable, we made no use of the affidavit. But does that destroy our right to examine it? We know not what use we might wish to make of it. This is, however, brought as a pretext.

Sir, there is but one ground upon which the letter can be withheld, and that is, that it contains such State secrets as that the public good would be compromitted by its exposure. We will remember that some time ago it was said that a government in this country, ought to have no State secrets. to this I did not agree, nor will I now advocate the doctrine. If General Wilkinson has acted right, no man will blame him for what he has done, but if he has acted wrong, no man ought to shelter him.

Mr. *Hay.* I am directed by the President, in his letter, not to disclose any parts of this letter which are not connected with the purposes of public justice, and therefore I am determined in no event to do it.

Chief Justice. The writ of *subpœna duces tecum*, is sometimes awarded upon motion, but it is more frequently a matter of course upon the suggestion of the party. Any argument as to the propriety of calling for the paper, for the production of which it was awarded is reserved for the return. The writ must issue agreeable to the motion.

The writ was accordingly awarded (returnable immediately) commanding George Hay Esq. to produce the letter from General Wilkinson to the President, dated 12th November, 1806. To which Mr. Hay made the following return, after some farther conversation on the subject.

" I hereby acknowledge service of the above Subpœna, and herewith return a correct and true copy of the letter mentioned in the same, dated 12th November 1806, excepting such parts thereof as are, in my opinion, not material for the purposes of justice, for the defence of the accused, or pertinent to the issue now about to be joined: the parts excepted, being confidentially communicated to the President, and he having devolved on me the exercise of that discretion which constitutionally belongs to himself   The accuracy of this opinion, I am willing to refer to the judgment of the Court, by submitting the original letter to its inspection   I further certify, in order to shew more clearly, the irrelevancy of the parts excepted, to any defence which can be set up in the present case, that those parts contain a communication of the opinion of the writer concerning certain persons, about which opinion, or the fact of his having communicated it to the writer, if a witness before the Court, could not legally, as I conceive, be interrogated and about which no evidence could legally be received from other persons   *George Hay*"

The *Chief Justice* enquired if there was any objection to that part of the letter being received ?

Col Burr said, he should have no objection to a copy of the *whole* letter, but he could not be satisfied with a part

Mr *Hay* refused, under any mode whatever, to give the original, or a copy of the whole, for the reasons before adduced He hoped the Court would not take it in the view which Mr Wickham had, that it was setting them at defiance, for he had no such idea   He wished, however, to know the opinion of the Court upon it

Chief Justice   The operation of the subpœna is to bring *the letter*, not to *send* or *bring* a copy of it

Mr *Wickham*   We consider that as the gentleman's return, and shall take the course that is proper on such an occasion.

Mr *Botts*   I should certainly feel the deepest regret, if it were necessary to move an attachment against Mr Hay. But if it were really necessary, no considerations of friendship—even if he were my brother, or my father, would deter me from it, after his announcing to the Court, that he would go to prison sooner than surrender the letter   It would be particularly painful to me to make such a motion.   This being the unpleasant situation, another course may be taken, which, I am sure, must be much against the disposition of all concerned, since that alternative would cause a delay, when a speedy decision on the business must be extremely desirable ; and nothing but this wish could possibly excite me to depart from this course

Sir, we have two resources for compelling the production of this paper one is to move an attachment against Mr Hay, who holds, and has refused to produce the letter   the other is, that the case may be continued until the letter is produced, which would be inconvenient and oppressive but inconvenient and oppressive as it might be, we must either submit to it, or call for a measure which would hurt our feelings. He has stated in his return, that it is not pertinent nor necessary to our defence, to have this letter produced ; but this I am not willing to trust to the judgment of the prosecutor in, nor to submit it to the inspection of the Court for its decision ; we wish to judge of its irrelevancy ourselves Who can judge of the applicancy of the letter to our defence, when it is yet unknown upon what grounds we shall defend our client?   If we know not its purport, how can we know what new sources of defence it might open to us ?

The attorney's return makes points worthy of our investigation.   It first intimates his discretion as to the prosecution ? It supposes, that he is worthy of trust.   Now, this embraces the general principle, that it is the officer and not the particular man who fills the office itself, that is worthy of trust. This is not to be conceded, for on the part of the accused, the *attorney for the United States is not* to be trusted as an *officer*, whatever we may think of him as a *man*. Because, that office will always imbibe with it all the zeal, the jealousies, the feelings, and the inclinations to support prosecutions in favour of the State with vigilance. This is natural to the infirmities and fallabilities attached to men, however virtuous and humane they may be. Indeed, the moment in which the accused person has to depend upon the friendship of *that* officer for his protection, would be an injurious æra to the liberties of the country. Whilst it is an office of trust to the government, it is incompatible that it should be confided in by the defendant.

Then, Sir, as to his judgment on our case, are we to depend upon his arbitrary discretion, to determine whether this paper is proper for us or not? Shall we be forced to depend upon that gentleman's judgment, who has been singled out, by his office, to contest all our proof, to carry on, with all his possible vigour, the prosecution against us; to stop all our witnesses, if possible; and, in fine, to do every thing against us that a prosecutor could do? The proposition is monstrous! It goes to vest an arbitrary discretion, not in a Court, for this would even be dangerous, except all were good and upright Judges: but it would vest it in an attorney when the case does not entrust him with it. It is a sacred principle of truth and law, that the defendant shall not be forced to disclose his ground of defence, no, not even to a Judge himself, and much less ought he to put himself at the mercy of the prosecutor. Are we then to be called to give our reasons for wanting this letter, and to disclose the use we mean to make of it? And yet we are asked what use we want to make of the letter! Is this Court to be transformed into a tribunal of inquisition, without hearing the accused, or go through the mockery of a trial, and require of us to shew the materiality of a letter to our defence? Is he placed there to withhold from us our means of defence, upon the mere suggestion that it is of a *delicate* nature? We have heard much of treason stalking abroad through the streets of New Orleans, and of Gen Wilkinson's successful efforts to stop its direful ravages. We are told, that Gen. W feels no delicacy upon the exposure of the letter, and yet, you are immediately told that you are called upon to expose the secret transactions of Orleans; and the danger of the exposure of certain persons is spoken of. Well, if Gen. W is not interested, what sort of State secrets can protect the persons mentioned in this letter?

Mr *Hay*. What Gen Wilkinson's opinions are upon the subject I know not. I said that he had not made objection.

Mr *Botts*. Then, Sir, the objection must come from Mr Hay as the guardian of Gen W and if so, why may he not endeavour to remove what has been termed a false and malicious accusation upon the General; and permit two more laurels to crown his venerable brow, by shewing, in that letter, some farther traits of his patriotism, and expose those two characters to prosecution:

I cannot express myself sufficiently strong to shew the detestation which I have, and which every body must have, of this *domestic* State secrecy. It never can do any good; but it may be used to shelter designing characters who may seek the downfall of any persons of whom they are jealous, and who may be marked for destruction. There ought to be very few secrets in a government where every person is responsible to the people for his conduct · nay, there ought to be none. The people of the U. States have a right to know every public act, except in the diplomatic department. in the domestic department nothing ought to be kept secret. Principles of justice do not yield to *delicacies* of state. It must be disclosed, however confidentially communicated.

We do believe, Sir, that the part of this letter which is withheld, is of the greatest importance in this accusation; and that without it, the part which Mr. Hay is willing to expose will be of little or no avail to us. We say, Sir, that the Court ought to let us look at that letter and apply it to our defence we say, that the letter itself must be in the power of the Court before the Jury is impannelled. It has been offered to the counsel of the accused, but we want it not for the purpose of curiosity, so that no human eye should light upon it, we want it for the benefit of our client before this Court; and as a document which must bear discussion in public.

I will again predict, that if there can be such a secret, inquisitorial tribunal, established by you, and it shall receive the sanction of your name, (from which there can be no appeal) that you may preclude written, or (even upon the same principle) oral testimony, of which the public prosecutor is to judge, it must go down to posterity with that sanction, and whenever a man may become the subject of executive vengeance or jealousy, a denial of the public documents, subject to his pleasure, or that of the prosecuting officer, might promote his destruction.

The question now, Sir, is for a rule, that this prosecution should stand, and be continued until that letter shall be in the possession of your Clerk

Mr. *M'Rae*. Sir, there can be no ground for this motion for a continuance. The affidavit made by the defendant is, not merely, that the letter *is* material, or that he *believes* it to be material; but that it *may be material* to his defence. Now, there is no ground for any belief, that it *may be* material to him. The attorney, in his return, goes to shew, that it is material for him to state reasons why it is so, whilst he has stated, that he does not believe it to be so, and yet they oppose this statement by the affidavit of the defendant, who has never seen this letter? How does this question stand? Is there now any ground upon which the Court may believe that this is material, or ought to be considered so by the Court, by themselves, or by any body. The only proper ground upon which we are to consider this question is, whether it is material or not, before an indefinite postponement shall be ordered. Now, I say, that the affidavit cannot give the Court any ground to believe that it is material.

I beg leave to submit to the Court the propriety of the motion, under the pending circumstances. The attorney informs the court that the President delivered it to him under certain restrictions of secrecy. Can he violate his pledged faith? Can he divulge what is committed to his care? The attorney of the United States ought to be regarded, with respect to this letter, in the same view as the President would if he were present. Gentlemen have been pleased to consider this as a mere question of delicacy, but this is placing it upon a ground that we have never placed it. I regard it, Sir, as a question of importance, which may affect the whole country at some time or other, whenever a question of the kind shall be submitted to a Court. I consider that a confidential communication made by a respectable citizen to the executive, to be on the guard against what would endanger the government, respecting persons who never have been prosecuted, ought not to be made public. If the Court should sanction such a capricious demand, and order a paper of this nature to be given, it would have a right to demand any paper whatever, under the pretext, that the public good required it. and thus every paper in the possession of the government, might be demanded at the pleasure of any applicant, even if it should endanger the public peace, and implicate innocent characters. If characters are mentioned in it, I beg to know whether it should not be kept from the public eye? (at least till those persons should demand so much of such paper as respects them particularly) I beg to know whether every person shall be permitted through caprice to demand what he is not implicated in, and what does not respect him? Even if his life was in danger, it would not be permitted. Does not sound policy require that private communications should be kept secret? and justice requires that names should be withheld from public view, when those names cannot serve the public, or any private good.

Now Sir, from a full and impartial view of this subject, who can be a better judge of what the public good requires should be kept secret, than the President of the United States? This Court I am sure, will not say that they have a right to examine every communication of any nature whatsoever, that might be made to the President of the United States. This Court will surely admit of the right of the President, as well as the right of any other individual when it is called upon. it will not call for any paper which the public good requires should be kept secret. I understood the Court to have expressed this opinion at the time the *subpœna duces tecum* was called for, wherein reference was made to the case of *Marbury versus Madison*. General Lincoln, acting as Secretary of State, the Court determined that he should not be compelled to disclose what the public good required should be kept secret. Then, Sir, if the Secretary of State might withhold confidential communications, surely the President of the United States, (even if standing before this Court) might also. I presume that in the confidential manner the President has given this letter to the district attorney, it may well be compared to a communication made by the executive to the Secretary of State, and is equally a "State secret," and it ought, in this Court, to be treated with the same respect as the Supreme Court treated the case of Marbury vs. Madison.

Mr Botts says that General Wilkinson cares nothing about this communication, but that Mr Hay is his *guardian* Of this we know nothing but whether general Wilkinson does or does not, the communication was made confidentially to the President, and he is bound to keep the secret, even so far as it respected his correspondent, independent of the persons mentioned

Then, Sir, as the public good requires that this communication should not be disclosed, I beg to know upon what principle gentlemen can call for this, unless they go upon the principle that the President ought not to keep any communication secret This *bold* ground they have not taken yet

Mr Botts has said *much* as to the persons who may be said to have been calumniated, and upon that ground has seemed to have demanded who they were That question is not now before the Court, nor are the persons concerned before the Court but it is an unquestionable fact, that they do not demand a sight of this letter to meet any accusation which might be brought against the defendant Justice does not require him to have any testimony or letters which are not pertinent to the case, and particularly what does not at all relate to it The Court can never agree to continue the case, unless they can believe the evidence to be material it can only be material to enable those gentlemen the more effectually to utter their abuse against General Wilkinson Upon examination, it will not be in the power of the Court to perceive how information of this kind can be made to promote their defence, and I trust that the gentlemen will not wantonly call for papers that they do not want, under such circumstances. Now Mr Botts has said, that those parts of the letter which do not refer to the defendant, and are not pertinent to the issue, but relate to other people, are the parts which he most materially wants What Sir, is his ground? Is it not to divulge what ought not to be made public, and which ought not to be granted? If the letter cannot be material to his defence, it ought not be exposed The Court yesterday said, that it would not be their disposition to call for papers which could not be material to the defence Now, Sir, if instead of being material to the defence, it can only tend to embroil Gen Wilkinson in personal disputes to no possible advantage, will the Court call for such a paper? I cannot suppose that they will It certainly cannot, except first it be proved that the production of those parts of the letter which we wish to withhold, can be material to the defendant in some possible way and secondly, that the power now attempted to be exercised by us to withhold it, is not what the public good requires to be withheld when it has been stated by the attorney that the refusal was upon that ground, I think that at least the attorney might be confided in as to the tendency and nature of the document in his possession. I hope, Sir, that the Court will see this application to be unreasonable, and therefore say that the rule shall not be made

Mr *Hay* Surely the Court never will agree to continue the case, if the purposes of justice do not require its continuance This is a question to the sound discretion of the Court. This is not a common question of the suppression of evidence, which the trial cannot progress in without. This is of a peculiar nature, the subject of which ought not to be disclosed. However, I am willing to leave it to the judgment of the Court; but I presume that if they do order a continuance, at least that they will expect a sufficient reason to be adduced; and not such a one as has been given the non-production of this paper cannot possibly be considered as a sufficient reason.

Mr *Burr*. The character of the President of the United States, as President, does not divest him of the claims which can be made upon any citizen. He has his channels of communication as the chief magistrate of the country; now if the letter is not of a public, but of a private nature, his official capacity cannot cause his responsibility to disclose it, as he would be obliged to do, as a citizen, any other private communication: and it is evident that this can be no official letter if it is so, we have not heard it.

Again The President is not the keeper of the public papers; he cannot retain a public paper in his possession without committing a criminal act these powers are distributed to the different public officers in the various departments

Again When the President retires from office, the succeeding President succeeds to all those papers which are termed official—*State secrets*, and every thing in short which belongs to the public. I ask then what belongs to the public? Private letters do, if he files them in his public capacity as from a public officer. will he do this for the benefit of his successor? But General Wilkinson could make no communication to the President in his official capacity but through a public officer, (the Secretary of War) and then it would become an official paper of the government

General Wilkinson may, from his patriotism and zeal, communicate to the President this, or any thing else he may as well disclose a conspiracy to the President, as any one individual might communicate any thing within his knowledge, or ideas, to another person; but is that a reason in a Court of justice, why a communication should not be made public when purposes of justice require that it should The President says that this is a State secret this is denied by *his* possession of the letter and not depositing it in the archives of State. this is not an official document; it is a private communication The case of Marbury and Madison is of no weight, because that was an application for a public document.

The remainder of the argument refers to the contents of the letter That we cannot argue upon, because we have not seen the letter; we are refused the cognizance first. But there has been one great secret developed here to-day that is, that there is a great State secret adopted in the system of *espionage*, which I am sorry to say has been productive of secret denunciation, and that it is not only made but strangely invited

Mr *Hay* I do not know how far the gentleman may be right, as to his general observations; but there is one part in which I must declare him to be totally unwarranted in saying as to denunciation or even information being invited, I am sure it is not.

Mr. *Burr* I should be glad to be convinced that I was in an error, but it does not seem to me that I am. The only way to satisfy the public that they are not invited, is to expose the names of the men, by submitting the letter

Mr Wickham spoke at considerable length in support of the motion for a continuance of the case if the letter was not submitted Mr Wirt replied to the charge of espionage, and insisted upon the rights of the attorney to withhold the paper under the circumstances in which it was confided to him he expatiated much on the affidavit of Colonel Burr, when he called for the letter, which he contended was too vague to admit of the idea of absolute necessity, although it allowed the *possibility* of its usefulness to his defence With his usual eloquence he supported the right of the government to withhold papers of public secrecy under such circumstances, and most particularly when nothing but unwarrantable and vexatious curiosity was exhibited to call for it, and not an argument could support it as a matter of necessary defence This was particularly evident from the offer of the attorney, (who had exhibited it to the private investigation of several gentleman of the Court and amongst the rest the Chief Justice) to make affidavit that it could in no possible way serve in the defence of the accused The affidavit therefore that it *might be useful,* could by no means be compared with arguments which had been used to shew that it *could not possibly* be useful to the defence He presumed that this Court would never agree to continue a case for ever, upon the mere conjecture of the accused, that something might possibly be in the possession of the executive that would serve him, without any pretence of saying what bearing it could have on his case

Mr *Botts* replied He contended that the affidavit could not have been formed on any other terms than it was, when the contents of the letter could, at most, be only guessed at upon the exhibition of it, its applicancy could only be discovered, but that the defendant believed it to be pertinent was exemplified by his oath He contended that this was the usual way of procuring a paper, the contents of which were not precisely known to a defendant As to the comparison of the affidavit of the attorney and that of the defendant, it might as easily be supposed that the attorney could not know in what way it might be used in the defence, as that he could, since he could not know the course of the defence He could not at any rate be robbed of the benefit of it, because it belonged to him as much as any other paper did. He took a view of the executive department, and again urged that the bureau of the President was no more a repository of secrets than that of any other individual, and that no secrets of any nature could be withheld when called for by a Court of Justice to vindicate the cause of innocence He hoped that whoever the characters might be that were mentioned in the letter, the Court would not consider that as a sufficient excuse for withholding it, when its exhibition might promote the purposes of public justice

The *Chief Justice* delivered his opinion to the following purport

It is not without regret that I feel the necessity of delivering, an opinion on the present application, because on the one part there may appear to be something like hardship, and on the other, a delay upon a case which it must be desirable to terminate.

It is extremely probable that the letter, or the parts of the letter called for, and which has been the subject of much debate, is of infinitely less importance, if it should be looked into, than gentlemen suppose, and that the objections which have operated to a refusal, would vanish at its production; because it is probable, that, if it *was* produced and read, very much of the suspicion now entertained, would be wiped away, and the allusions perhaps be not such as they now are. I cannot (certainly) say that this would be the case—not only because what I may have heard, (which I never ought to have heard at all, and which I must treat as though I never had heard. I cannot, therefore, speak from any knowledge I have of the letter,) but I think it extremely probable that much of the suspicion entertained, has been excited in the bosoms of a great number of persons by this letter, which would be removed by making the letter public.

There has been an affidavit produced, upon which a *subpœna duces tecum* was awarded to the President of the United States, directing him to produce this letter. a communication was made upon the subject to the Attorney, upon which, it seems, he thinks it proper to withhold certain parts of the letter, because he believes them to be confidential, and therefore, that they ought not to be shewn to the public. If this might be likened to a civil case, the law is express upon the subject. it is that the powers of any Court of the United States, on a motion to require the party to produce books or papers, are under the same conditions as a Court of Chancery. and it should be the same, if the Court has power to order a nonsuit.

Now, if a paper be in the possession of the opposite party. what statement of its contents or applicancy can be expected from the person who claims its production, he not knowing its contents? it cannot be expected of him. It has always been thought sufficient to describe the paper, and identify its general nature and authenticity, and state its materiality to the case, in some degree, when its contents are fully known. But it being in the possession of the opposite party and in his power to produce it or not, leaves the question in a very different situation.

It is necessary, before the Court could order a continuance of the case, that it should be well satisfied of the materiality of the evidence asked for and refused; and how far it necessarily relates to the case in hand. In a case where a piece of testimony is in possession of the opposite party, and he cannot produce it, from whatever cause, the law goes a great way indeed—even to a nonsuit by default. Criminal cases, however, are not provided for, but with respect to the defence, Courts are always as tender as the case will admit. The prosecutor is the representative of the government, and the government act as a party through the agency of the Attorney, who particularly directs the process of the prosecution. in behalf of the government; and he is a party on no other view. If there is any paper in the possession of the executive, which is not of an official nature, he must stand in nearly the same situation as any other individual who possesses a paper which might be required for defence If then the executive possesses a paper which is really believed by the accused to be material to his defence, ought it to be withheld?

The question here will occur whether it is material to his defence? All the evidence that we can receive upon this subject is from the party himself he has made his affidavit to its materiality But that is stated not to be good: and why? Because it is stated that the letter "may be material" in the defence. There were two separate charges brought against him, one for treason and one for misdemeanor that relating to treason is at an end, and therefore it cannot relate to it, but must apply to the indictment for misdemeanor indeed the affidavit was made since judgment was given on the treason.

It is stated that the particular passages required, are not pointed out, but how can this be done, or how could the applicability of the parts withheld by the Attorney, be stated by the accused when he was not certain of its contents, but merely believed that they would be so, having seen the letter himself? Now the Court cannot know of its materiality, without it is somehow informed of the way in which it is intended to be applied; and this cannot be done without the defendant discloses his defence

Let it be supposed that this letter may not contain any thing relating to the person now before the Court, it still might, as has been stated, relate to a witness who is material in the case and thus become important, by withholding his testimony, because of its bearing on that testimony Different representations might have been made, or conduct used by that witness, which would vitiate his testimony. How then is it possible to judge upon the particular applicancy of a paper without a knowledge of its contents and the applicancy, if known by the defendant, would not be exposed. It cannot be expected that he could describe the nature of the paper, and if he could, it could not be demanded of him agreeably to the principles of law

That the President of the United States might be subpoenaed and examined as a witness, and called upon to produce any paper which might be in his possession, is not controverted indeed, that has once been decided There may, however, be an inducement to prevent his production of such a paper, and the same inducement might operate upon the Court not to force it I do not think precisely with the gentlemen on either side, on a case of this sort I can very readily conceive, that the President might receive a letter which it would be very improper to require for public exhibition, because of the manifest inconvenience of its exposure. There ought, in such a case, to be an extremely strong occasion for its demand, and, within the knowledge of the Court

I admit that very much reliance must be placed on the declaration of the President in such a case as this; and I do think that a privilege does exist with respect to a private letter to the President of a certain description The reason is this—letters to the President, in his private character, are often addressed to him in consequence of his public character, and perhaps might relate to public concerns, and yet be only private letters, the same as any other individual might receive on such a subject. Now, it is a very serious question, when such letters may be supposed to contain something very material to the defence of any individual, that he should not be able to avail himself of the advantage of it, as well as of any other paper.

It is a very serious thing to proceed to trial in such a state of things. I cannot precisely say what ought to be done; perhaps the Court ought to consider, that the reasons which induced the President to refuse the paper as a governing principle to induce them to refuse its exhibition, except it shall be made to appear to be absolutely necessary in the defence. The President may state the particular reasons which might have induced him to withhold the paper, and the Court would then undoubtedly give credit to those reasons. The Court, at the same time, cannot avoid paying proper attention to the affidavit of the defendant, but it could not proceed without that affidavit. The Court would be very glad to hear farther testimony on the subject, in order to determine properly upon the materiality of the paper called for, but that is not offered.

I suppose it will not be alleged, in such a case, that the President ought to be considered as having offered a contempt to the Court, in consequence of his not having attended, notwithstanding the subpoena was awarded agreeable to the demand of the defendant. the Court would, indeed, not be asked to proceed as in the case of an ordinary individual. On the question for withholding the paper, its materiality ought to be shewn, and without that being shewn, it does not appear to be in the power of the Court to take such measures as it would for the production of this paper, if reasons sufficient were given. The President, however, in this case, has assigned no sufficient reason, or. that any reason whatever operated upon his mind of sufficient weight to make this letter an official letter. It, therefore, belongs to him, particularly, and no body else can judge as to his motives for withholding the letter · they may be sufficiently strong, but of this we cannot say: for a reason given by the attorney cannot be supposed to emanate immediately from the President, without he gave a direct authority upon the subject. If the President, when he sent it, had subjected it to any certain reservation, or had made such parts of it, as his judgment should direct, to be kept private, when he transmitted it, he would have given such a recommendation, but we have no knowledge of such reservation.

Now, with respect to the letter, it is impossible that either the Court or the attorney can know in what manner it is meant to be used. I must, therefore, consider declarations made upon that subject, as though they had not been made. Any argument on its materiality, or the contrary, does not appear, since no sufficient reason is adduced, except that in the affidavit of the accused, and upon that, the Court must suppose that the paper ought to be produced; and if that is refused, the Court must take the proper means of ordering the continuance of the case, until it is produced.

With respect to the secrecy of these parts which it is stated are improper to give out to the world, the Court will take any order that may be necessary. I do not think that the accused ought to be prohibited from seeing the letter: but, if it should be thought proper, I will order that no copy of it be taken for public exhibition; and that no use shall be made of it but what is necessarily attached to the case. After the accused has seen it, it will yet be a question whether it shall go to the Jury or not. That question cannot be decided now, because the Court cannot say, whether those particular passages are of the nature which are specified. All that the Court can do, is to order, that no copy shall be taken, and if it is necessary to debate it in public, those who take notes may be directed not to insert any part of the arguments on that subject. I believe myself, that a great deal of the suspicion which has been excited will be diminished by the exhibition of this paper.

Mr Hay said, that he was not particularly acquainted with the wishes of Gen Wilkinson on this subject, but he would consult him; he hoped that consent would be given under the restrictions made by the Court, since the purposes of public justice would not admit of a delay.

The Court ordered a Jury to be summoned, and that the prisoner should be furnished with a copy of the *venire*.

SATURDAY, September 5

Mr. Hay wished to extend the terms of the return which he made yesterday. There was one passage in Gen Wilkinson's letter, which he was certain the President himself would keep back.

Mr M'Rea. As the President is now at Monticello, is it not practicable to send an express to him, with a *subpœna duces tecum*? It is advantageous on every consideration, to have the trial completed at this term. Almost all the witnesses are present; and perhaps it would be impossible to collect them here again. An express might, perhaps, return in four days from Monticello; and is it not far better to postpone the trial for that period, than to the next term of the Court?

Mr Hay here read the following,

"*Additional return*

"I hereby certify, that upon a more minute examination of the letter above mentioned, I have observed other passages, which are entirely of a public nature, and which, according to my best judgment, ought not to be disclosed; and which, I conceive, would not be disclosed by the President himself, if the return were to be made by him.

"GEORGE HAY"

Mr Hay then observed, that he did not conceive himself at liberty to put this letter into the hands of the defendant; but that he would immediately send an express to Monticello for instructions, and that the return would probably be made by Tuesday evening.

Chief Justice. Is there any objection then, to the Court's adjourning till Tuesday?

Mr Marton said that he proposed to bring the case of Israel Smith before the Court on Monday.

Mr. *Burr* observed, that some agreement might be made between his counsel and the prosecution, respecting the letter, and that they might go to trial on Monday.

The *Chief Justice* then observed, that the Court would meet on Monday, as some arrangement might be, in the mean time, made, respecting the letter

Mr *Hay* I can consent to no arrangement, but for me to furnish such parts of the letter only as I may deem material to the defence

Chief Justice If there are any state secrets in that letter, the Court would be extremely unwilling to call for its production

Mr *Martin* Gentlemen need not be so scrupulous, Sir, upon this subject, for we can compel the appearance of the President before this Court, with that letter.

Mr *Hay* Shall I furnish such parts, in the mean time, as I am disposed to surrender?

Mr *Burr.* Yes; under the reservation, that such a step does not impair my right to demand the remainder

---

MONDAY, September 7.

Mr *Botts.* The Court will recollect, that when the order was moved for the continuance of the trial for misdemeanor, we deprecated the serious inconveniencies of delay. It is much to be regretted we should now be driven into the trial, without the letter, which we have required, but as that letter may probably be received in the course of the trial, we are willing to enter into it

Mr *Hay* observed, that he should not wish the trial to be gone into, with such a declaration on the part of the accused; that he had sent an express to Monticello, agreeably to his promise, and that he expected him to return by to-morrow 12 o'clock He therefore did not wish the Jury to be fully sworn to day.

The *Chief Justice* did not see any necessity for delay on that account The paper would probably be here by the time when it is wanted, as it will not be required until the defence is opened

Mr. *Hay* wished every preparation for the trial to be made to day, but hoped that the trial would not be gone into, until to-morrow He expected some communications from the President, which would have considerable influence on him, with respect to his conduct on the trial

At this moment, Herman Blannerhasset appeared in Court. when Mr *Botts* observed, that Mr. Blannerhasset had attended for the purpose of understanding his true situation. He could obtain bail for the misdemeanor, and it was obvious, that under the opinion of the Court, the indictment for treason could not be supported Will you, Mr Hay, enter a *nolle proseque* to the prosecution for treason?

Mr *Hay* acquiesced

Mr *Martin* Will you not adopt the same course, as to the case of Mr Israel Smith?

Mr *Hay* acquiesced again

Mr Martin. I will mention the case of John Smith of Ohio, would it not be better to save the expence of bringing him here as a prisoner, by entering a *nolle prosequc* in his case?

Mr *Hay* His case is not before the Court

Mr *Botts* then requested the Court to fix Blannerhasset's bail for misdemeanor. It was already ascertained that he is not rich

The *Chif Justice* determined that he should give the same bail as A. Burr, five thousand dollars The same was also fixed for Israel Smith.

Mr *Botts* observed, that as Mr Blannerhasset would find some difficulty in getting two securities; he hoped it was not an inflexible rule with the Court to insist upon it, when one alone w deemed sufficient to cover the amount of Bail Mr D Woodbridge had offered himself to be Mr Blannerhasset's bail

Mr *Hay* I can have no objection, if the Court deems one security sufficient

Mr Woodbridge was accepted

Some conversation then ensued about the Jury when it was determined to examine, but not to swear them to-day

When *Orris Payne* was called, Mr Hay mentioned that motives of peculiar delicacy induced him to wish that Mr Payne might be excused from serving, as he was extremely intimate with him, and was in the constant habit of conversing with him on this subject

Mr. *Burr* I may perhaps get a worse man

Mr. *Hay.* You cannot get a better

Mr Payne was suspended for further examination

2 *Thomas Underwood*—Mr *Burr* I challenge you, sir I do it, because I understand you have expressed opinions unfavorable to me Mr *Underwood* It is true that I have, Sir —
Mr Underwood was accordingly set aside

3 *Nicholas Hallan* was excused on account of his indisposition

4, *James Bootright* was accepted

5 *Obadiah Gathwright* wished to be excused, on account of the indisposition of his family —Mr *Burr.* Perhaps your family may be better to-morrow

6 *John Murphy*—Mr *Burr* Have you not expressed unfavorable opinions about me?—Mr *Murphy* I do not recollect any time or place, where I have done it, but it is more than probable that I have Mr Murphy was accepted

7. *Byrd George* wished to be excused on account of indisposition. He was directed to attend to morrow, if he was better. If not, his non-attendence would not be noted

8 *William Nice* had expressed very unfavorable opinions of Aaron Burr—*Set aside*

9 When *J M‘Rae* was called, Mr M‘Rae (counsel for the prisoner) observed, that if motives of delicacy had suggested a late application to the Court, he thought that still stronger motives of delicacy would apply to *him* on the present occasion After a short conversation between Mr John M‘Rae and the accused, which we did not distinctly hear Mr M‘Rae was excused

10 *Francis Walker*—Mr *Burr* I challenge Mr Walker —
Mr. *Walker.* I intended to have stated my objections to serv-

ing. I believe the plans attributed to Col. Burr, were such as as he had really formed; that he contemplated the separation of the Western from the Atlantic States, and after seizing on New-Orleans, he intended to attack Mexico

11 *Benjamin Harris* had received, and still retained an opinion that Aaron Burr had been guilty of something   Set aside.

12 *Jacob Ege* had formed and expressed strong prepossessions against the accused   Set aside.

13 *Tarlton Williams* was not a freeholder.

14 *Robert Adams* had made declarations against the accused.

15 *Nathaniel Wilkinson*   Mr. *Burr*   Mr Wilkinson will be good enough to declare whether he has not formed and expressed opinions against me?   And very strong ones?   Mr. *Wilkinson*   Yes *very* strong ones indeed   Set aside

16 *Abraham Gowley* had formed and expressed opinions unfavorable to the accused   Set aside

17. Col *Wm.* Bentley was accepted

18 *William Austin* had expressed very unfavorable opinions of the accused   Set aside

19 *Joseph P. Owens* was detained on the Jury in the District Court (now sitting in the other wing of the Capital.)   Mr Burr observed, that Mr Owens might perhaps be at liberty to attend to-morrow

20 *Thomas Pulling* was indisposed; but suspended till to-morrow

21. *Daniel Wiseger* was suspended for a similar reason.

22 *James Whitelaw* had formed, and expressed very unfavorable opinions of the accused   Set aside

23 *Yeaman Smith* was accepted

24 *Richard Young* was excused, on account of his indisposition

25 *Carter Page* was extremely indisposed, suspended till to-morrow

26 *Robert Randolph* was indisposed, and wished to be excused   Mr. *Burr* requested him to be suspended until to-morrow. Mr *Randolph* urged his extreme anxiety to be excused from serving   Mr. *Hay*. I do not wish to object to you, Sir; but there is one ground on which you may get off   Have you not formed and expressed some opinion on this subject?

A I have Mr. *Wickham*.

If Mr. Randolph will deliberately declare that he cannot give an impartial verdict on this case, we wish him to be discharged.

A. I must repeat that I have formed an opinion on this subject, without intending to say, on which side that opinion leans   Mr. Randolph was discharged.

The *Chief Justice* then instructed the Deputy Marshal to summon twelve additional Jurymen by to-morrow.

Mr *Burr*. The Marshal can hand me the list of them, this evening

The Court adjourned till to-morrow, 10 o'clock,

TUESDAY, *September* 8
No measure of importance was adopted this day.

Mr *Hay* informed the Court, that his messenger had not returned from Monticello.

Mr. *Israel Smith* appeared in Court, and was bailed on the indictment of a charge of misdemeanor; himself in the sum of five thousand dollars, and his securities, John B. Walton and John Alcock, in twenty five thousand dollars each.

WEDNESDAY September 9

The names of the jurors who had been previously selected, were called over; some of them were absent. The Court then proceeded to fill up the vacancy

1 *Charles Spencer* had formed and expressed an unfavorable opinion of the accused *Set aside*

2 *Robert Gordon* upon being asked by the Chief-Justice whether he had formed or expressed any opinion on the subject, replied, that like most other people he had conversed about it, but that he was not concious of any fixed prejudice for, or against the accused *Accepted*

3 *James Taylor* had formed and expressed an opinion that Col Burr was guilty of something *Set aside*

4. *John Glinn* had also formed and delivered an unfavorable opinion *Set aside*

5 *John New* was in the same situation *Set aside*

6 *William Rowlett*, observed, that he lived in Richmond, and was in the same situation *Set aside*

7. *James Penn* had been occasionally engaged in conversation on this subject; but he had not made up any positive opinion *Accepted.*

8 *Heath Jones Miller* was decidedly of opinion that the accused was guilty *Set aside.*

9, *Jourdan Harris* had made up a positive opinion to the same effect. *Set aside*

10. *James Harris* was in the same situation *Set aside.*

11 *Samuel Woodson* had formed a very unfavorable opinion of the accused *Set aside.*

12 *Benjamin Wolfe* had formed and expressed his opinion a thousand times His mind was fixed as to the guilt of the accused *Set aside,*

13 *Jessee Bowles* had said, that if common report was to be believed, Colonel Burr had been guilty of something, but he had not made up a positive opinion on this charge *Accepted.*

14 *Daniel Holloway* was excused from indisposition.

15. *John Price* was excused for the same reason

16. *Thomas Lewis* had, in general conversation, expressed an opinion unfavorable to Colonel Burr; being asked by the Chief Justice, he said that his opinion on this charge was not fixed *Accepted.*

17. *Richard Young* was excused from indisposition.

Carles B. Berkeley, one of the selected jurymen, wished to be excused from serving, on account of his business

Mr *Hay* Have you Mr Berkeley formed and expressed no opinion on the subject?

Mr. *B* I have seen, Sir, different publications about it; I have thought that Col. Burr might have been guilty of something ; but I have formed no positive opinion. Mr B's excuse was overruled by the Court.

Mr *Hay* was solicitous to have Orris Payne excused, and asked him whether upon his conscience he had formed no opinion on the subject ? Mr. Payne observed, that he had formed an opinion

Mr *Barker*. Is it a fixed opinion on this particular charge or has it fluctuated according to circumstances ? Mr Payne observed, that he had no fixed opinion as to this particular charge. Mr. Payne was retained

The Jury were then sworn and consisted of the following individuals :

Orris Payne,	*Carter B Berkely,*
James Bootright,	*Robert M'Kim,*
Obadiah Gorthright,	*Robert Gordon,*
John Murphy,	*James Penn.*
William Bentley,	*Jesse Bowls,*
Yeamans Smith,	*Thomas Lewis*

The clerk then rose to read the indictment, to which Mr Botts objected He said it was the province of the attorney himself to read his own indictment. Mr Hay replied that such was not the usual practice, and after a short conversation it was read by the clerk in the following terms.

Circuit Court of the United States of America, for the fifth Circuit and District of Virginia

District of Virginia, *to wit* :

The grand inquest of the United States of America, in and for the body of the district of Virginia, now on their oath, do present, that *Aaron Burr*, late of the City of New-York, and district of New-York, Attorney at law, did, on the tenth day of December, in the year of our Lord one thousand eight hundred and six, within the jurisdiction of the United States, to wit : at a certain island in the river Ohio, called Blannerhasset's island, in the county of Wood, within the district of Virginia aforesaid, and within the jurisdiction of this Court, with force and arms, begin a certain military expedition, to be carried on from thence against the dominions of a foreign Prince, to wit. the dominions of the king of Spain ; the said United States then and there being at peace with the said king of Spain, against the form of the statute, in such case, made and provided. to the evil example of all others, in like case offending, and against the peace of the said United States and their dignity . and the Jurors aforesaid. upon their said oath, do, farther present, that the said Aaron Burr, afterwards, to wit : on the said tenth day of December, in the year of our Lord one thousand eight hundred and six, and within the jurisdiction of the said United States, to wit. at a certain island, in the river Ohio, called Blannerhasset s island, in the county of Wood, in the district of Virginia aforesaid, and within the jurisdiction of this Court, with force and arms, did set on foot a certain military enterprize, to be carried on from thence against the territory of a foreign Prince, to wit the territory of the king of Spain, the said United States then, and there being at peace with the said king of Spain, against the form of the statute in such case, made and provided, to the evil example of all others, in like case offending, and against the peace of the said United States, and their dignity,—and the Jurors aforesaid, upon their oath, do farther present, that the said Aaron Burr, afterwards, to wit on the said tenth day of December, in the year of our Lord one thousand eight hundred and six, within the jurisdiction of the said United States, to wit at a certain island in the river Ohio, called Blannerhasset's island, which is in the county of Wood, in the district of Virginia aforesaid, and within the jurisdiction of this Court, did, with force and arms, set on foot a certain other military enterprize, to be carried on from thence, against the territory of a foreign Prince, to wit: against the Province of Mexico, in North America, the said Province of Mexico, then and there being the territory of the king of Spain, and the said king of Spain then and there being at peace with the said United States, against the form of the statute in such cases made and provided, to the evil example of all others, in like case offending, and against the peace of the said United States, and their dignity. and the Jurors aforesaid, upon their oath, do farther present, that the said Aaron Burr, afterwards, to wit on the said tenth day of December, in the year of our Lord one thousand eight hundred and six, within the jurisdiction of the said United States, to wit at Blannerhasset's island, in the river Ohio, which island is in the county of Wood, in the district aforesaid, and within the jurisdiction of this Court, did, with force and arms, provide the means, to wit. boats, men, provisions, fire-arms, gun-powder, bullets, leaden bars and other military munition, for a certain other military enterprize, to be carried on from thence against the dominions of a foreign Prince, to wit. against the dominions of the king of Spain, the said United States then and there being at peace with the said king of Spain, against the form of the statute in such case, made and provided, to the evil example of all others, in like case offending, and against the peace of the said United States, and their dignity and the Jurors aforesaid, upon their said oath, do farther present, that the said Aaron Burr, afterwards, to wit on the said tenth day of December, in the year of our Lord one thousand eight hundred and six, within the jurisdiction of the said United States, to wit: at an island in the river Ohio, called Blannerhasset's island, in the county of Wood and district of Virginia and within the jurisdiction of this Court, did, with force and arms, prepare the means, to wit, boats, men, provisions, fire-arms, gun-powder, bullets, leaden bars, and other military munition, for a certain other military expedition, to be carried on from thence against the Province of Mexico, in North America, the said Province of Mexico, then and there being the territory of a foreign Prince, to wit. the territory of the king of Spain, and the said United States, then and there being at peace with the said king of Spain, against the form of the statute in such case made and provided, to the evil example of all others, in like case offending, and against the peace of the said United States, and their dignity; and the Jurors aforesaid upon their said oath, do farther present, that the said Aaron Burr, afterwards, to wit: on the said tenth day of December, in the year of our Lord one thousand eight hundred and six, within the jurisdiction of the said United States, to wit at an island, in the river Ohio, called Blannerhasset's island, in the county of Wood and district of Virginia, aforesaid, and within the jurisdiction of this Court, did, with force and arms provide the means, to wit boats, men, provisions, fire-arms, gun-powder, balls, leaden bars, and other military munition, for a certain other military expedition, to be carried on from thence against the dominions of some foreign State, to the Jurors aforesaid yet unknown, with whom the United States, were then and there at peace, against the form of the statute in such case made and provided, to the evil example of all others in like case offending, and against the peace of the said United States and their dignity; and the Jurors aforesaid, upon their oath, do farther present, that the said Aaron Burr, afterwards, to wit: on the said tenth day of December, in the year of our Lord one thousand eight hundred and six, within the jurisdiction of the said United States, to wit. at Blannerhasset's island, in the river Ohio, in the county of Wood, and district of Virginia aforesaid, and within the jurisdiction of this Court, did, with force and arms, set on foot a certain other military enterprize, to be carried on from thence against the dominions of some foreign state, to the Jurors aforesaid, yet unknown; with whom the United States were then and there at peace, against the form of the statute in such case made and provided to the evil example of all others, in like case offending, and against the peace of the said United States, and their dignity

GEORGE HAY,
Of the City of Richmond, in the State of Virginia, Attorney of the United States for the Virginia District, Prosecutor.

A TRUE BILL,

JOHN RANDOLPH.

A Copy Test,

WILLIAM MARSHALL, CL'K

The Clerk was then proceeding to charge the Jury

Mr *Botts* contended that this was the province of the attorney for the prosecution.

The *Chief Justice* observed, that there was no charge necessary

Mr *Hay* All that the Clerk had to say, was, that to this indictment the accused had entered *not guilty*, and that the Jury were to try the validity of that plea In saying this, however, I have delivered the charge

Mr *Hay* then stated to the Court, that his express had arrived from Monticello, and had brought back the return of the President of the United States, which he was now prepared to read.

The *Chief Justice* did not know whether there was any necessity for it, if there was any difficulty on the part of the bar.

Mr *Hay* None at all, I assure you.

Botts　*We* wish, Sir, to hear the return

Mr *Hay* then read the following certificate from the President, annexed to *his* extracted copy of Gen Wilkinson's letter

" On re-examination of a letter of Nov 12, 1806, from Gen Wilkinson to myself (which having been for a considerable time out of my possession, is now returned to me,) I find in it some passages entirely confidential, given for my information, in the discharge of my executive functions, and which my duties and the public interest forbid me to make public I have, therefore, given above, a correct copy of all those parts which I ought to permit to be made public Those not communicated are in no wise material for the purposes of justice, on the charges of treason or misdemeanor, depending against Aaron Burr : they are on subjects irrelevant to any issues which can arise out of those charges, and could contribute nothing towards his acquittal or conviction The papers mentioned in the first and third paragraphs, as inclosed in the letter, being separated therefrom, and not in my possession, I am unable, from memory, to say what they were I presume they are in the hands of the Attorney for the United States

Given under my hand this 7th day of September, 1807.

Th · Jefferson "

Mr *Hay* observed, that in *his own* and in the President's extracted copy from Gen Wilkinson's letter, there was not a variation of more than ten or fifteen words, the omitted passages were, indeed, so manifestly improper to be submitted to the Court

Mr *Hay* then rose to open the charge of the misdemeanor ·

May it please your Honours, and Gentlemen of the Jury.

The defendant, before you, is charged with a violation of the law of Congress of the United States, passed in the year 94 As it originally stood, the existence of this law was limited to a short period ; but experience having proved its salutary tendency, it is now made permanent The defendant stands charged with violating the fifth section of this act, and no other That section is in the following words

" If any person shall, within the territory or jurisdiction of the United States, begin or set on foot, or provide or prepare the means for any military expedition or enterprize, to be carried on from thence against the territory or dominions of any foreign Prince or State, with whom the United States are at peace, every such person so offending, shall, upon conviction, be adjudged guilty of a high misdemeanor, and shall suffer fine and imprisonment, at the discretion of the Court in which the conviction shall be had, so as that such fine shall not exceed three thousand dollars, nor the term of imprisonment be more than three years."

You will observe, gentlemen of the Jury, that an offence against this law may be committed by beginning, or setting on foot within the territories of the United States, any military expedition or enterprize against the territory of any foreign Prince or State with whom the United States are at peace The law declares, that if a man begins or sets on foot, or provides or prepares means for any such offence, he shall be liable to punishment

The indictment filed in this case contains seven counts, between which there is some slight difference — These it is incumbent on me to state

The first count in the indictment, charges the defendant with *beginning* a military expedition at Blannerhasset's island, to be carried on from thence against the king of Spain, with whom the United States are in a state of peace

The second, charges him with *setting on foot* a military expedition against the territory of the king of Spain.

The third, is the same as the last, except, that the Province of Mexico, is stated as *the* territory of the king of Spain, against which the expedition is intended

The fourth count, charges the defendant with *providing the means* of a military expedition against the *dominions* of the king of Spain

The fifth is the same as the fourth, except that Mexico is particularly mentioned, as the Province against which the expedition is intended

The sixth is the same as the fourth, except that the foreign territory is said to be unknown.

The seventh, charges him with *setting on foot* a military design against the dominions of a foreign State, to the Jurors unknown

If the evidence produced, proves him guilty on any count in this indictment, you must find him guilty — This is all that you are bound to say. The fine and imprisonment belong to the Court. I shall trouble you with no remarks upon the enormity of this offence, nor upon the consequences which were likely to have resulted from this expedition, had it been carried into effect. The Court will consider these circumstances in estimating the fine and imprisonment It is only your province to determine whether he is guilty or not of the facts charged in the indictment

It is not necessary for me to enter fully into the evidence which will be exhibited before you. The case is shortly this:—It is believed, and it will probably be proved to you, that the accused, with several others, had formed a scheme to dismember the Western from the Atlantic States, and that for this purpose preparations were actually made But the design did not terminate with the separation Their object was to make war upon the territories of the king of Spain To effect this scheme, New Orleans was to be seized, and Mexico was to be invaded both by land and sea During that period, and ever since that time, Spain and the United States have been in a state of peace To accomplish this object, men, arms, and provisions were prepared. About thirty-five or forty men assembled at Blannerhasset's island, under the direction of the accused It will be proved to you, that they left that place and descended the Ohio, on his apprising them of the danger of interruption from the civil, perhaps the military authority. It will be proved to you, that after they had arrived at the mouth of Cumberland river, they were joined by the accused, who took the command of all the force there assembled; that they descended the Mississippi to a considerable distance below Natchez; that at Bayou Pierre he received the first intimation that the first part of his project could not be accomplished, that he fell into the hands of the civil authority, from which he is said to have escaped, and that he was arrested and brought here.

I have only one additional remark for your consideration. The act of Congress is not intended to operate upon those who have accomplished their plans. Success is not necessary. It operates on those, who prepare and set on foot a military expedition. It is not necessary they advance far in the enterprize. If means are already accomplished, and their destination certain, it is sufficient. You, gentlemen of the Jury, are to inquire, whether the accused did prepare these means with the view of making such an attack. If you conceive that such was his intention, you must pronounce him guilty.

Mr. Hay then called over the names of the witnesses on the part of the United States.

Mr. John Graham was summoned to the book, and was about to be sworn, when Mr. Burr requested the attorney for the prosecution to state the substance of Mr. Graham's testimony, and whether it related to the acts done on Blannerhasset's island.

Mr. Hay observed, that he could give a very rough outline of Mr. Graham's evidence, as he had not frequently conversed with the witnesses on the subject. He believed, however, that Mr. G. would prove that the military expedition down the river was under the direction of the accused, that he had set on foot and provided means for the expedition; whose object was to invade the Spanish territories, after the preliminary object of taking possession of New Orleans had been accomplished.

Mr. Burr. It would save time if gentlemen would state the contents of Mr. G's testimony with more precision. It is within their knowledge, that Mr. Graham has never seen me but once, and then only for a few moments, at the town of Washington and that he was not at the island at the time when the military expedition is said to have been there, nor any other which is expected to be proved. We shall ask the Court to confine the counsel for the prosecution to proving the facts first.

Mr. Graham was sworn. when Mr. Hay observed, that he hoped he was at liberty to bring out the evidence according to his own discretion; but that not having the advantage enjoyed by others, of understanding the evidence, it was impossible for him to state the substance of each witness's testimony. He believed, that Mr. Graham would prove the setting on foot of a military expedition.

Mr. Burr. In the district of Virginia?

Mr. Hay. Yes; begun in the district of Virginia.

Mr. Burr conceived, that the opposite counsel should either restrict themselves to the bringing out the evidence in the order which they proposed on former occasions, or that they should be called upon to prove first, the fact laid in the indictment.

Mr. Wirt. Part of the fact laid in the indictment is the destination of this very enterprize.

Mr. Botts. When we wished them, on a former occasion, to begin with the proof of the overt act, they urged, that their course was the local order of nature. Will the gentlemen then, depart from it in the present instance? It is either right to pur, sue this course, which they themselves recommended, or to prove first the act laid in the indictment. Rather than disturb them in the course which we had supposed they had selected, we had made up our mind to submit to all inconveniencies The gentlemen had surely better begin at the island itself, and after they have proved the existence of their military expedition, they may then search all the world over for stuff and nonsense enough to fill up the vacuum which they have imagined

Mr *Hay* then observed, that he would not waste the time of the Court in useless disputations, that he would take the gentle men at their word, and begin at the island, and then he would look out for other nonsense, as the gentleman called it, to fill up the chasm of his statement. Then Sir, as we are confined to the district, we will begin at the island.

Peter Taylor. whose general testimony was before given, was again called. He now stated, in addition, that there were about thirty men there, who appeared to be under the command and direction of Comfort Tyler, (with whom they had come) before they arrived there he did not know how many arms or how much powder there was, but there was some, and there were some provisions and bullets. Mr Blannerhasset and Mr. Love were all that he knew of their having taken with them from the island.

A question here occurred by relating to his interview with doctor Bennett, to whom application was stated to have been made for the delivery of the public arms for the service of the expedition; upon which some conversation ensued. when Mr. Hay stated that the witness (Dr Bennett), had been attending here for some time, but, that in spite of all his admonitions he *would* go home, and therefore they must lose the benefit of his testimony.

Question by Mr *Wirt* Do you know any fact that connects Blannerhasset and Burr in this affair charged?

Witness All that I know is about the letter, and what Blannerhasset said to me about going to take Mexico He wanted all the single and orderly young men that he could get to go with him Col Burr wanted to be king, and his daughter to be queen after he was dead.

Col. Burr What time did you see me at Blannerhasset's island?

Witness It was in the beginning of September that you were there, but I never did see you there at all I well remember that, because I buried my wife while you were there. My business in Lexington was done in October; the object of which was to inform Mr Burr not to come back to Blannerhasset's island for danger.

The evidence before given was in many parts repeated, and in no instance differed from the former

Evidence of *Maurice P. Belknap*

Mr *Burr* wished to know what was to be proved by this witness. Mr Hay stated that his evidence related to a letter and other particulars relating to the island.

Witness Do you mean me to give evidence as to the conversation which passed?

Mr *Hay* Every thing which relates to the transactions on the island.

Col Burr The gentleman has already acknowledged my absence from the island. I shall certainly object to any evidence which does not relate to the precise spot. I am charged with a particular crime committed at a specified spot, but they are going to charge me with a crime at a place where I was not. If they shall fail respecting time and place, or cannot prove that I was present, they must fail in their indictment. What took place out of the district, nor the words of any body can be received. I will, however, permit the witness to go on, in order to afterwards prove that he is mistaken as to his evidence.

Mr. *Hay* The witness will prove that he took a letter, which will prove the connection of Mr. Burr with the transaction on the island.

Question to the Witness Were you on Blannerhasset's island, —at what time, and what did you see there?

Witness I was there on the evening of the 10th December, 1806, I had been employed by Mr Blannerhasset. He required me to take a letter to Lexington in Kentucky, to a Mr *John Jordan*, and in that letter there was one inclosed to Col Burr. Some short time previous to Mr Blannerhasset's asking me to go to Lexington, in consequence of reports that were going on, I stated to him, that I believed that the expedition was an unlawful one, but he assured me that it was not. On that, I shewed him a letter, which I had had from one of my friends, and told him I would have nothing to do with the business, if that was the case. I suppose that that was the reason of his reading the letter directed to Mr Burr to me, before he sealed it, which he did. The letter acquainted Col Burr of his acquittal at Lexington, for that the Jury did not find a bill. It also mentioned the state in which the boats were on the Muskingum, though I do not recollect what he said respecting them. This, I think, was about the middle of November 1806, or a little later. The letter also mentioned the quantity of provisions that he should probably want, to take him down the river. He mentioned *corn meal* as one article ; and he mentioned that he should probably take his family with him. The letter was very long, and I cannot recollect above a half of it. This letter I delivered to Mr Jordan, who broke it open, and requested me to take the inclosed letter to Frankfort to Col Burr. I carried it to him, and then returned back again with a letter from Col Burr to Mr Blannerhasset.

Question by a Juror Did Col Burr hold any conversation with you?

Witness No Sir, not that I recollect. Before he closed his letter he handed it to me to read. I read a part of it, and asked him the explanation of some words, upon which he took it out of my hand and read it himself. The substance of it was that he thanked Mr. Blannerhasset for his exertions in preparing the boats, and stated that he should probably leave that place in about eight days, I believe for Nashville. He said that he should probably go down the river before Mr. Blannerhasset would; and that he was glad to hear that his family were coming on with him, and that he would procure a situation for them at Natchez, or at New Orleans, until they should be better situated at the Washita.

M. *Hay.* Was there any mention made as to speed?

A Yes, he desired him to make all the speed he could, because perhaps the river would soon close with ice.

Q Did he state any other reason?

A No, not that I recollect.

Q Did you carry no verbal communications?

A Yes, Col. Burr requested me to mention to Mr. Blannerhasset, to have the boats that were going down the river, to have in the day time, the signal of a white flag, and in the night time, a lanthorn or lamp.

Q Believing that the expedition was lawful at first, had you not agreed to go with it?

A Yes, I had proposed to go. I do not know that he ever said that the government were engaged in it. He said that he expected there would be a war with Spain, and that those people who went with him, provided there was a war, would join with the regular army on the frontiers, against the Spaniards. If there was no war, then they were to go and make a settlement on the Washita. He mentioned that General Eaton, Mr. Gallatin and General Wilkinson had been acquainted and joined in it.

Q By a Juror. Were they civil or military officers that he meant, when he said that the officers of the government had joined it, or knew it?

A I do not know, as he mentioned both.

Mr. *Wirt.* Did you go down the river with him?

A I Did not.

Q What prevented you?

A On my return I found in the post-office, a letter from young Mr. Danelson, General Eaton's son-in-law, with Gen. Eaton's testimony. Finding then that General Eaton was not engaged in it, as I had been led to suppose, and that we had been deceived, I communicated the deception to my friends, and a number of us abandoned the expedition altogether.

Mr. *Hay.* Had you any conversation with Mr. Burr on the subject?

Q No. He only asked me some particulars respecting the state of preparation of the boats, and what number of men would go down with the boats, but he did not mention the number that he expected would go.

Mr. *M'Rae.* You mentioned that some others besides yourself withdrew from the expedition, how many were there?

A There were three or four, several were gone. I remember that Mr. Cushing and Mr. Dana's brother forsook the expedition.

Mr. *Hay.* Did you carry no message from Burr to Blannerhasset, to hasten the departure of the boats?

A No, Sir, no otherwise than I have stated, except that I recollect once, Mr Burr stated that from the common report and from the newspapers it appeared that the public mind was very much agitated, and incensed, but that he hoped there would be no opposition made by those who had the management of the boats to the civil or military authorities. I think his expression was the constituted authorities. I suppose that the people he meant were those that were afterwards on the island.

Q. Were the men armed after you got to the island?

A. When I got to the island, I went into the hall, and was struck with some surprize at the number that was there. There appeared to be about 20 there, and they appeared in much confusion: some of them had guns and were cleaning them.

Q Did Col. Burr speak of those boats and men as though he had authority over their movements?

A. He spoke as one concerned, but not as though he had authority: he thanked Mr Blannerhasset for the exertions that he had made in expediting the enterprize.

Mr. *M'Rae.* When he spoke of the people descending the river, and said that he hoped they would not resist the lawful authorities, did he speak of them as *his* people?

A. Not particularly. "*they*," I think was the word that he used. He did, as I understood, before speak as though he had connection with them.

Q When you delivered the letter, had you heard nothing of the measures instituted by the legislature of Ohio, to suppress the expedition?

A No, nothing, till after I returned.

Col *Burr.* The legislative measures were on the 4th or 5th December, and the departure appears to be on the 10th. Chillicothe, the seat of government is 200 miles from the place where I saw Mr. Belknap, and therefore he could not have heard.

Mr *Hay* I did not know the date of Mr Burr's letter.

Mr *Belknap.* It was dated about the last of November or the beginning of December, and I returned to the island about the 10th December.

Mr. *M'Rae.* When you returned to the island, had you any conversation with Mr Blannerhasset before he started.

Witness Yes, but I do not particularly recollect any thing particularly of it. he made some small enquiries concerning Col Burr.

Q Do you particularly recollect what it was?

A Why. Sir, he asked about his health, I believe; and asked if there was a probability of his going away. I said, I think, that there was another Grand Jury summoned, and that I returned soon after I heard it. I think it was between 8 and 9 o'clock in the evening I got there, and he said he was going away before day.

Q Did it rain that night?

A. Not that I know, but it was very dark and cold.

Q Did you ask him, or did he inform you of the reason for facilitating the departure?

A. He said he expected the people of Kenawha he said he had enraged them against him; and he was under some appre hensions that he should meet with some difficulty if he did not depart immediately and besides, he said that he had detained there for a long while

Q Had you any other communications with Mr. Burr?

A No, Sir, I never saw him before or after until I saw him here

Q Did you understand from both of them, that there was a connection between them?

A Yes, from both of them

Q Was there any public rumors or report before you went to Lexington?

A Yes

Q What were they?

A Why, it was about the Spanish invasion, and there were various opinions concerning it

Messrs *Martin* and *Burr* objected to evidence of this sort

Mr *M'Rae.* My object is to ask the witness whether Col Burr did not enquire as to the state of the public mind Did he not enquire something about it?

A Yes, Col. Burr asked me what was the news abroad I think I told him that the public mind was much agitated, and that the people thought there was something on foot, which was not legal

Q No other enquiry or remark?

A He asked, I recollect, whether I had seen any thing in the papers from the government, on the subject?

A I told him I had not.

Q. What was his reply, as to the public opinion?

A He answered that the public were under a wrong impression, that he had no illegal intention, but he did not state what intention he had

Q What were the offers made to you, to induce you to join the enterprize?

A Nothing in particular Mr Blannerhasset told me that if I did not find it as he had stated, after we descended the river; and that if I did not find that General Eaton and General Wilkinson, and others were there, and that if there were not a Spanish war, he would bear my expences back

Q Then when you thus engaged, it was to engage in a war.

A Yes, if a war took place. I remember that was always mentioned.

Q And Mr Gallatin was to have joined?

A Yes, so Mr Blannerhasset said.

CROSS EXAMINATION

Col Burr Do you remember, in my letter, my offering a specific quantity of land to Mr. Blannerhasset?

Witness No, Sir I think there was something mentioned of this nature that he might offer to young men, one hundred acres each

Q Did I not mention giving him forty thousand acres?

A. No, Sir.

Q Did I not show you a map of the land?

A. Yes

Q Did I not show you some deeds of the land ?

A I do not recollect it

Q Did I not speak of the expedition, as rather doubtful , and speaking as to the advantages and disadvantages of it, say, that if he could not live in peace with his neighbours, he had better come down ?

A Yes, I have some such impression. the impression that is on my mind, however, is, that you did expect him down the river

Q Did I not ask you whether he could live in peace amongst his neighbours ?

A Not that I recollect , but I think you asked me if he was coming down

Q Did I ever mention any thing to you, about Tyler's party ?

A No Sir.

Q Where were the boats building, of which you speak ?

A At Muskingum, in Ohio

Q How many guns do you suppose there were with Tyler's men ?

A I do think there were more than three

Q Did I ever speak of any people or party as *mine* ?

A No, not that I recollect your expression in general, was, " they "

Q Had you any officers from me ?

A No, not from you.

Col Burr having done questioning

Mr *M Rae* Did you communicate to Mr Blannerhasset the cause of your not going ?

A No, Sir, I did not , but I did to Mrs Blannerhasset . he had gone. I got my information from young *Danielson*, son-in-law to General Eaton

Chief Justice Did he say any thing there about going to Washita, and of your going with him, in case those things should not happen, as you expected ?

A No, Sir, not that I recollect , he only spoke of bearing my expences back

Mr *M'Rae* You spoke of others, besides the names you mentioned , do you recollect who he spoke of besides ?

A He mentioned Mr Dayton, Mr Devereux, and Mr Smith of New-York

Q Did he mention Col. Burr too ?

A Several times he did

Q Did he mention him, as being at the head of it ?

A I asked him if Mr Burr was concerned, and he remarked that he did not know what Mr Burr was going to do . he said he supposed I knew that he was not very high in the confidence of the country. Afterwards, whenever he mentioned him, I did understand that he was to be at the head of this business ; and so I understood him in all his other conversations.

Mr *Wirt* Were you at the boats ?

A No, I landed some rods above them.

Mr *Burr.* Were they rifles that you saw ?

A I think they were

Mr *Berkly* (a Juror) In the communication you had, did Mr. Blannerhasset speak of these men, who came to the island, as though they came at the instigation of Mr. Burr, or that they were drawn there by himself?

A I do not recollect that he ever did say any thing upon that subject any way

Q When he spoke about these men, what did he say?

A. He said that there were a number of men coming down to go along with him*

Testimony of Richard Nul.

Mr *Hay* requested the witness to proceed to relate all he knew on the subject before the Court

Witness Last year one of my sons lived on the island, conducting Mr Blannerhasset's business I have another in the neighborhood, who came backward and forward About the first of September, Mr Blannerhasset sent for me I went, and when I got there, he appeared to be very busy writing After a while, he asked me, if I could keep a secret, he said he had a parcel of writing to do, and that he wanted me to copy; that he had sent the first number, † which the printer did not understand

Mr Burr. I was willing to permit the gentleman to show any thing that tended to look like a military undertaking, as was charged in the indictment, if he could, and I have for some time indulged evidence to be given of conversations held with other people but since there is an evident and wide departure from even that species of evidence, it is time to stop them · it is not that we did not long before this see the impropriety of the length which witnesses have been suffered to take

Now, this witness seems to be about relating a conversation with his son, and with Mr Blannerhasset, at different periods : and conversations which did not occur in my presence I shall object, Sir, to any evidence of this nature I am perfectly willing, and, indeed invite the gentleman to bring forward any testimony which goes to shew any thing like a military expedition, or military preparation

Mr Hay I could have brought forward our witnesses in almost any order whatever, if they were all in Court, but, with all the efforts I have been able to make, I cannot get them here as I could wish I think, Sir, that we ought to be at liberty to prove the connection of the parties concerned in the expedition This, I have not the least doubt, I shall be able to do, and it cannot signify in what *precise* order our witnesses are introduced.

Mr. Burr If the gentleman means to prove his charge by any acts that were done out of the district, there certainly will be objection made to it I see several persons in Court who were examined on a former occasion, and who were present at the island, if the gentleman was to call forward those persons, I should not object

---

* See *Mr Belknap's testimony on August* 20, p. 346: *also see September* 20

† *It is presumed this was a number of the paper called the* "*Querist*"

Mr *Hay*. Then we never shall agree as to the introduction of testimony.

Mr. *Burr* If they do not go to the point, I shall certainly object to all irrelevant testimony; or to their going to the Jury

Mr *Hay* Sir, we shall prove by this witness that there was a connection between the accused and the persons on the island, and that the expedition had a military appearance; and we have more witnesses to the same purport I presume we may proceed

Mr *Burr* wished the gentleman to say, in candour, whether he meant to proceed in this kind of testimony? We have a variety of grounds upon which we shall object to the testimony of Mr Niel, or of any other witness of a description whose testimony must be totally irrelevant We have a number of law points to contest, and it would be better for the gentleman to produce all his testimony, relating to the nature of the military expedition, before we commence our argument

Mr *Hay*. Is there any objection, then, to going down the river, to prove the character of the expedition?

Mr *Martin* Certainly there will be

Mr *Botts* I regret exceedingly, that Mr Hay should show so uniform a predilection for this little island, which he has singled out as the spot where to lay his indictment, which was not merely manifest, but expressed, and his reluctance to go to any other place was equally clear We could have really wished, that the public should have been made acquainted with the military expedition We have no idea of one act being split into a thousand parts, and existing, at the same moment in different places with relation to the same individual I presume that this case might be productive of the same altercations and delay, as we have experienced in the case of treason, except the Court at once require the evidence to the facts charged to be given, and not go into an idle parade of two months evidence to hear nothing pertinent to the case.

Upon a view of the act of Congress, defining the crime now charged, a question must arise whether any *accessorial* offence *can* be committed or not We shall contend that no person can be brought within the pains and penalties of the statute, but a person who shall have been proved to be present, at the time the act was done, and not only present, but concurring in, and acting at the fact. You have settled this question, Sir If he can be guilty, here, he not being present, it must be under the common law. Now, the common law is a creature, and a *creature* cannot exist without a *creator* This then applies itself to the question, whether the common law can exist in the United States, so as to attach itself to the statute. Upon the acknowledgement, therefore, that he was not present at the time of the act, I must conclude that he cannot be guilty. because the statute only speaks of offenders who were present, and not of accessaries. This doctrine your own opinion strongly supports and you go on farther to say. that if there is an offence to be made out within the limits in which the accused falls, it must be by the operation of the common law and not of a statute I conceded however, that the creature does not exist. I need no remind you, Sir, that it was one of the favorite principles of the worthy prosecutor, that this creature (the common law,) had never arrived on this side of the Atlantic. Then if the creature pre-supposes a creator, and the ocean is a bar to its emigration here, I must take it for granted, that this prosecution cannot be supported upon principles of common law.

I do not mean Sir, to travel over the former ground of argument, in any of the positions necessary to lay down at this time, but I consider our doctrines tenable under the following positions.

1. That under the act of Congress (on the third and fourth sections of which this indictment is formed,) there can be no accessorial offender, i. e. none are within the pains of the statute but such as are acting in the fact charged.

2. If this point be not sustainable, we shall say that no act of Col. Burr, done *out of the district*, can be given in evidence against him.

3. If the first point be not sustained, we shall prove that no act of accessorial agency can be given in evidence on this indictment, which charges the offence of *acting* at the island, and not charging specially that the person indicted did the accessorial act.

Upon the two last points, I have little more to do than to read extracts from your own opinion upon the subject. " The place in which a crime was committed is essential to an indictment, were it only to shew the jurisdiction of the Court, &c." (See opinion of the Court, on the motion to stop the evidence,) Hawk. B. 2. ch 25. sect 84. and ch 25. sect 91. are referred to It would compel a man to go through the acts of life, to be prepared to make a general preparation for meeting the specific act laid in the indictment, were it otherwise, other parts of your opinion; if I have a true understanding of it, intend similar doctrines; and from all which it appears to me, that there can not be an offence made out against Col. Burr on the present indictment, because the evidence does not say that *any* act was done by him upon Blannerhasset's island, which could connect him with a military expedition there and that if he did any thing at all, it was at a distinct time and at a distinct place, and in short, in a different State. Therefore, whatever his acts were, it could be no more than the *procurement*, which is not charged in the indictment. The gentlemen must, therefore, feel themselves in an inextricable perplexity from the mere words of the indictment and the law on the subject. It will be unnecessary to trouble your honours with all the seven Counts in the indictment, nor indeed with many of them, because the crimes charged in them never had an existence. But however, it might be supposed, the *venue* was laid at Blannerhasset's island, when he was two hundred miles from it at the time: and in the place where he was, it is not proved that he did any thing conducive or tending to the operation of any unlawful expedition.

The enquiry then closes on this single point. his absence and the physical impossibility of his acting on the island when he was so far from it.

4. The fourth point is, that, if the foregoing points be not sustainable, still no evidence of accessorial agency could be given until a record of the conviction of some *actor*, in the expedition, be produced. Here I recur again to passages in your opinion. (Mr Botts read some parts of the opinion to elucidate his position, and expatiated on them in application to this case,) under all the admissions that could be made, still, as the guilt of the accessary must solely depend upon the guilt of the principal, he contended that accessorial guilt could never be made out in a Court of Justice, until that guilt on which it depended for its existence was made to appear, and therefore, the argument must necessarily be brought to this, that no man is to be charged with an offence, until that offence is actually performed and if the pretended performer of the offence cannot be brought forward, the procurer surely cannot be, since the commission of the offence cannot be taken for granted, but must be proved, he not being specially cognizable with the offence

The rules of law on this subject have been read, and need not to be repeated. Upon the whole, he conceived that argument would consume time unnecessarily, since the opinion given by the Court on the other occasion, furnishes as strong language in support of the position as could be given.

5. But should gentlemen at any and every stage of this proceeding, say, that we are not in a state of maturity sufficient to support our positions, they may uniformly be told that it is in their power, if they are able to prove any thing and we say that the acts on Blannerhasset's island do not, and cannot amount to a providing or preparing the means, or a beginning or setting on foot a military expedition *there*

This point resolves itself into two others. The first is, that there was no military expedition in maturity there. Secondly If there was a military expedition in progress there, it was not " begun" nor " set on foot" there nor were the means for its progress or beginning provided there

In discussing this question, it will be necessary to carry along with us the application of the principle of *construction* to penal statutes. Penal statutes are not only to be construed strictly and in favor of the accused ; but, wherever from the particular structure of the statute, there shall be a doubt of its meaning, it must be liberally applied to his benefit. See 1 Hawk p 116, ch 30, sec 8, 1 Bl p 88, in the note. There are some examples illustrating this principle, and which shew how rigidly this rule was carried into practice. Stealing money was as great an offence as stealing goods, yet, it was held that money was not included in the word " goods." There is one exemplification of this in Leech 23. The statute made it larceny to steal a cow. the fact was proved upon the culprit, but although he stole what looked like a cow, yet it was found out that she never had a calf, and therefore she was an heifer. This was under St 12, Edw 6, but it was afterwards altered, so as to read " or other cattle," by statute 14, Geo 2, ch. 6 But although the legislature had erred in not making the crime of theft so particularly understood in this case, yet the Court thought it was better that the person should not be punished, than to wrest a word out of its meaning in order to punish. In Taylor's reports, p. 446, you will find a case of this kind of ambiguity, where the Court supported this principle of lenity, and would not construe law to the detriment of a prisoner. Apply this principle to this question, and I then will ask, what constitutes the offence charged by the act of Congress. At another time, and upon another occasion, in which there had not been so much excitement, I think I should have been able to prove that these sections are not capable of the explanations put to them on the other side, but I have conceded, and shall continue to concede every doubtful point but with respect to one thing there can be no doubt, that to "begin and set on foot a military expedition, or "to provide and prepare" the means of a military expedition, intends that there shall be the *whole and complete* means of a *military expedition* provided and prepared. The natural import of the words will furnish an answer to every question upon the subject, and it is not an half, or even nineteen twentieths of the means prepared that makes the *whole* means.

Applying the same language, Sir, to any other subject sup pose it, for instance, to be said, that *means* had been prepared for building a state house : it is not to be understood that even the most material parts are provided, but that the full means are prepared for building that house. So with respect to a contract, if the *whole* of it is not completed, there will be a breach of contract. If it were not so, what would it lead to ? We will suppose that a perfect state of preparation of means is the thing required by the act of Congress, can you suppose that an imperfect preparation of the means will satisfy the impositions of that act ? The moment that you recognize such a doctrine, you throw yourself on the ocean of uncertainty, for the means are undoubtedly the first thing that entered the mind of the projector ; because it cannot be ascertained, by the number of men, the quantity of means, of guns, of powder, shot, &c by them, what constitutes prepa ration, &c they go down to the very first steps, or even the very first thought that entered the mind of the projector. It may be supposed to exist in the purchase of some guns, or in the employ ment of some men, or it may be taken in its simplest and most unconnected form, and thus, Sir, you must be at a loss to say at what stage the statute would intend to fix the crime intended *Men*, are said in this indictment to be the *means* Men are free agents to be sure Well, if *men* would be sufficient to constitute the *means*, under the act of Congress, a collection of men must be such a proportion of the means (met for whatever purpose) to come within the limits of the act—indeed any thing short of the whole would be sufficient I am forced to make this amplization, because I really should be at a loss to know how far the matter might be carried · I should fear that it might be brought down to even the meeting of two or three individuals for a purpose unknown to any I know of no other means towards this supposed expedi tion, than that about twenty-six young men met at Blannerhas set's island

Mr *Hay* interrupted Is this meant for argument against the admission of farther testimony ? If so, it is strange that it should be admitted as such

Mr Botts Why, Sir, certainly we have a right to shew that the meeting of men on the island could not be called sufficient means under the provisions of the act. The means we say, upon principles of *law*, must not only be sufficient for an expedition, but in a state of *complete preparation* for a *military* expedition The word " military" is in the law, and that word must be satisfied to its full meaning Men may collect together, to go upon an expedition, (and this is not unusual in this country) but it must be for a military purpose, it cannot else be a military expedition Even an *hostile* expedition may not be sufficient to satisfy the words of the law, because it may not be sufficient to assume a military form agreeably to the prerequisites of the case, to have a military expedition, the word " military" cannot be satisfied without having a military character infused into the means prepared and provided There may be all the materials provided, but the law requires that there should be a military end in view, and military means prepared Every military assemblage is necessarily a warlike assembly, but contrarywise, every warlike assembly is not necessarily a military assembly. Persons assembled together with crow-bills and other such weapons might constitute a warlike assemblage, but, when you have these, you must put something more to make a military character there must be a military *posture* as much as in treason, there must be a warlike posture and the means must be, in some measure commensurate to the end to be produced If I am not correct in this respect, one man may form a military expedition ! Why Sir, was it that you were asked, why *one* man setting off to New Orleans could not commit war ? It was because there was nothing in it that looked like it So in this case no number of men short of a reasonable computation, in some measure, (at least) commensurate to the object, can possibly form a military expedition

There is one point in this case upon which I might draw an argument, and which the prosecutor has not disclosed in opening his case, nor has he exhibited it in his evidence, but he has left it to be inferred We are told that Col Burr assembled a parcel of innocent men, who met down the river without being informed of any project whatever but now an inference is to be made, that they meant to overturn a great government without knowing any thing of it, by the personal energies of this individual ! Well These people, twenty or thirty in all, knew nothing at all of it—how then could the means be prepared to do this great work by the assembling of them, with all the powder and ball which we have heard of ? I have heard of a poor man travelling through the country and not being disposed to beg, he set up a little advertisement in all public places, that at a particular time he would shew some great sight the people came and he received his money presently, the poor man let a little pig out of a bag, and the great curiosity was exposed Our case, to be sure, differs somewhat from that, for according to the account that has been given to us, our boar pig has never yet got out of the bag, so that we have not had the opportunity of shewing the people our wonderful sight

Mr Botts concluded the argument of this day by declaring, that *intention* could not aid *facts* and that *organization* could not make a war, nor a military expedition, and concluded, that let it have been what it would, still Col. Burr must have been present at it, else he could not be answerable for its consequences.

THURSDAY, September 10.

Mr *Botts* this day continued his argument: he contended that nothing which was on the island, from any evidence which had been or could be given, tended to shew any military appearance—that the boats, the few men, and the small quantity of powder and balls, even added to the few rifles and pistols which they had heard of, could afford even such an idea. He recapitulated some of the arguments which he had used upon the subject, and took a view of the evidence which had been given by Taylor, Allbright, and others. Nothing like officers, nothing like soldiers, and nothing like discipline or subordination appeared, nor any thing like military character. The term "military" then must go unsatisfied, or else it must be satisfied by appearances entirely contrary to its own meaning and character. If the means of a military expedition were not there, it is impossible that a military expedition could have been "begun and set on foot" there.

I have spoken much on the ambiguity of this law of Congress. Mr Hay was utterly incapable to define, or to explain it, as it was the duty of the attorney to do, when he framed an indictment on it; he could not say what the offence was which was intended to be punished by it—he could not say, what was the meaning of a "military expedition." Indeed it was of such a perplexing nature, and the Supreme Court was so thin at the time, that they did not think proper to embarrass themselves with so great a difficulty. Laws of ambiguity require all the strictness, and at the same time all the liberality in their explanation in favor of the prisoner, that it is possible to give them: the result of a contrary doctrine, in arbitrary times, is evident from example. Indeed, Sir, when I take a view of the case in its truest colours, I can scarcely treat it with that gravity which the presence of the Court requires, but it would be doing injustice to the person I represent, not to say that it is a *frivolous* subject, and the best I can say of it is, that it is founded on an *ambiguous statute*. If I should depart from the usual course of argument, or treat this subject in the light which *I think* it merits, I hope no offence will be given, and that the Court will receive apology as flowing from my duty to my client. I will state the result of an old act under the colonial legislature, which inflicted a penalty of 25 dollars on a person who should kill a deer within a certain precinct. If the person was unable to pay the twenty-five dollars he was to receive thirty-nine lashes; the concluding clause of the act directed that one half should go to the informer. A man was taken, carried before a magistrate, and convicted according to law: the money was demanded, but he was unable to pay it, he was therefore ordered to be lashed, but the magistrate finding that half must go to the informer had him lashed also, so that they had to receive nineteen and an half each, as the penalty in default of making payment. The inflictor in that case, and the prosecutor in this, might be taken in upon equal terms by the application of this rule which is contended for.

We have got on the island, Sir, and what do we see there? You will recollect that formerly the same subject was under consideration. At that time it was thought convenient and natural to begin at the *head* at another time the same reason was advanced why they should begin at the tail, and so they went on; but we were not surprized that they were weary of any one place, since, whether they were above or below the island, they could discover no crime whatever, that had been committed upon the island, where we are charged with the commission of a crime We ask what they mean to prove: but the attorney tells us he does not know what he expects to prove, nor what witnesses he has? Now, Sir, after announcing to the public that a crime was committed, and that he means to prove it on my client, at last comes out that they do not know what they can prove It is, in fact, that they do not know where or how to prove any crime

When this business first came out, it was made to appear by them, that Col Burr was endeavoring to get the Spanish provinces, next to that it was, that in order to do that, he attempted or intended to take New Orleans, and now it comes out in the indictment, that he intended all the things therein recited against two nations, unknown. After all, they take up the evidence, go on with it, and then tell us that they do not know what they may prove, but want the liberty to search here, there, and every where for testimony They might have got out a search warrant, while they were about it, to find out the facts that would amount to their charge, as it appears awhile ago, a magistrate in this city granted to a man who had lost his cow, they would find a greater difficulty in discovering a military expedition, and in fact, I am sure, that with all their researches, they never will be able to find it out

Again, Sir If there were such means in progress as are charged, they were not begun or set on foot on the island, or prepared there If any means were prepared there at all, it is certain that there were greater preparations by far made elsewhere We therefore object to this mode of proceeding If it was begun in Pennsylvania, and increased as it went down the river, that is no argument that the accused should be subjected to a multiplicity of trials Where it was begun, (according to the words of the law) is the place, (and the only place) to institute a prosecution Your own reasoning on this subject will be sufficient to meet every objection, as exemplified in your opinion, which I need not read but you conclude that upon the same principle of constructive presence, he might be tried in any state; but you conclude that this would be "too extravagant to be maintained, certainly it cannot be supported by the doctrines of the English law." Sir, Col Burr has done no act, as we know of, any where, but certainly he has done none in Virginia I take it for granted that the gentleman will not pretend to urge constructive presence in opposition to the reasoning of the Court

Sixthly and lastly No declarations of Mr Blannerhasset, or of any other person, of conversation said to have taken place between any persons can be given in evidence against Col Burr, unless he was present at the time the conversations passed, and approved of them.

Mr. *Botts* drew several inferences and analogies from this position He quoted 2 M'Nally 611, to 618, in which reference is had to Stafford's case, 3 St. Tr. 109; Lovet's case 9 St Tr 615 to 630; Hardy's case, vol 1, p 815, 6 and 7. He contended that any man might be subject to the pains and penalties of a prosecu tion at the discretion of a government, if this doctrine was sub- stantiated ; and indeed the case at bar was one of that nature To one witness, he wondered what the people could have got into their heads, to another he declared his determination to set- tle the Washita lands, and that it was near the frontier ; *in case of a war with Spain* he should, by all *laudable* means, enter into it. He also decla ed that the persons engaged in it ought not to resist the constituted authorities, indeed he expressly requested that they would not Now suppose that all which was jocosely said had been gravely spoken, what could have been effected by these twenty-five or thirty men ? Does it look like converting our government, or like going against the Spanish government and making him *king*, and his daughter his successor ? It has as much desire in it as the Arabian Tales, and as little of probability.— Is it to be supposed that Col Burr, with all the caution, reserve, and artifice ascribed to him, could have proceeded on an expedi- tion of this sort with so slight and uncertain means.

So, in all these points of view, I must contend that the Court ought to arrest the subject ; for there is not a particle that has or can be given in evidence, that can in the least affect Colonel Burr

That all these questions are questions for the Court, and not the Jury to decide, has been amply illustrated , the Jury powers never could extend beyond what you have laid down , and that opi- nion more expressly and emphatically applies to this case. It is a question of law and not of fact, and a man's liberty and pro- perty is no more to be subjected to the caprice or ignorance of jurors in this case, than was his life in the former.

Mr *Martin* entered into a few additional remarks, and eluci- dated the observations of Mr Botts He contended that the sta- tute was ambiguous, for that although the word " beginning " was known in the English language, yet the words " setting on foot on expedition " was a phrase known no where, and its true con- struction could not be found. He examined the history of the law of April 30, 1790, under which this indictment was framed, and said that it would be found that it never was meant to be carried into execution Indeed there never and been an instance of punishment or. prosecution under it ; it was an American word, and in American use, and was not in English diction Indeed it passed under great opposition, and by the casting vote of the Vice-President, in the Senate ; and had Mr Gallatin taken his seat (which was declared to be vacated) it would not have passed into a law at all. After it got through the Senate and sent to the House of Representatives, it received violent opposi- tion Indeed Mr M believed that its inaccuracies were so great that it never could be carried into execution. To shew that un certain words and ambiguous terms ought not to affect an ac cused person, he quoted 6 Coke 42.

Again The law required that the party charged must be the person who did the act. He must " begin, carry on," or " provide," and not another person This is the case where there is an *act done* by the person, and where there can be no possible accessary Accessorial guilt is a crime at common law , and attaches itself to offences above that of misdemeanor It attaches itself to such crimes as treason, murder, routs, riots, assault, and even in felonies, where there may be accessaries *before* the fact but in crimes of inferior magnitude, such as profane swearing, Sabbath breaking, extortion, &c &c there is no such thing known in law as an accessary indeed, in the whole class of offences known in law by the name of *mala prohibita*, there is no such thing known as accessaries before or after the fact

Now, Sir, it is not even pretended, that Col Burr was on the island, and consequently he cannot be made answerable for any offence committed there, if there was any committed and it is not a case where any man can be *accessorially* guilty

But from viewing the indictment, he is not charged rightly Authorities were offered upon this subject, in the treason case but in addition, see Moore, 787, Lady Russel and Countess Nottingham's case.

Chief Justice. Was that a case at common law ?

Mr Martin Yes, Sir, it was in the Star-Chamber, and it is in confirmation of the doctrines laid down in Vaughan's case, which has been so often quoted. It shews, indeed, that the principal must be first indicted, before the accessary can be called to answer. See also, 27th year book of assizes, 4th case and to prove another point which has been contested, see 2 Hawk. ch 25, p 25, sec 19 , ib 214, ch 45, sec 34, 5.

As to the last point laid down by Mr Botts, to wit that the declarations of Mr. Blannerhasset cannot be given against us, I cannot suppose that the gentlemen can seriously contend it because it is among the first principles of law, that declarations or confessions of one man cannot be used against any other person Authorities are universal upon this subject, and need not our elucidation

Mr *Hay* I should have liked to have had a little more time to have reduced the arguments of the gentlemen to some system but, being sensible how much of the time of the Court has been consumed, I must proceed, without asking more time of the Court, because so much has already been consumed

I will not, however, follow the example of the gentleman who has gone before me, in the light and ludicrous manner in which he has treated this subject, because trifling and humour but ill becomes a subject so serious to the United States as this must unquestionably appear.

Why this solicitude of the accused to repress the evidence? Is it because its introduction would overwhelm him beyond the possibility of redemption ? Why treat the subject with this extraordinary levity ? Is it to impress the public mind, that it is not worthy of a serious consideration ? With what is A Burr charged ? One of his counsel had asserted that the accomplishment of his scheme would have been honourable to him and to his country. And what were those schemes ? They were con

trary to every principle of an honest man and a virtuous citizen
They consisted in violating the laws of his country in a point
the most materially interesting to her foreign relations. They
were such as a man of ambition, disposed to delude ignorant
people, might be disposed to conceive. They have alarmed and
exasperated the whole country. And so difficult has it been to
obtain a complete Jury for the trial, that nineteen out of twenty
men have been excluded; and yet in a case thus interesting to
the public mind, have the opposite counsel had the hardihood to
stand up here and declare, that it was so farcical he could not
treat it with serious consideration. If these gentlemen had
but one moment reflected upon the consequences which must
have resulted from the military expedition, they would have
shrunk from this course. Perhaps the ambition of this party
would have been gratified, and their hope of plunder would have
been satisfied perhaps the mines of Mexico would have been
theirs, but little would it have been to them, that France and
Spain should have exhausted their revenge in devastating the
Eastern coasts of our country. Had the gentlemen considered
it in this light, they would have viewed it as every other man
would, as a scheme formed by an ambitious man to effect his
own aggrandisement, and they could not have treated the subject with such unwarrantable levity

The object of this motion is to exclude the evidence

The ground taken by Mr. Botts, is, that no person can be
found guilty under the act of Congress, who was not present and
concurring in the offence charged. But this point was already
decided even in the treason case; it was there determined, that
a man may be guilty of levying war, without being present at the
scene where the war is levied, if he be properly indicted.

The true ground of objection to the evidence meant to be taken by Mr Botts is this, that Aaron Burr not having been present at the time of the offence charged, the evidence offered
must be *irrelevant* This indeed is the only ground on which
the evidence can be excluded; for mere variance will not justify
its exclusion. If A be indicted for killing B with a hammer,
would the evidence be considered as irrelevant which goes to
prove that the instrument of death was a broad axe? Must not
the whole of the evidence necessarily go before the Jury; and is
it not for them to decide, under the instructions of the Court?
It is only in a case where the evidence does not bear upon the
subject at all, that the Court may exclude it

Assuming this, then, as the basis of his remarks, Mr. Hay
stated, that the enquiry would be, whether the evidence now
offered be relevant to the indictment. The defendant is charged
with beginning, setting on foot, providing and preparing the
means of a military expedition at Blannerhasset's island against
Mexico. These are the charges to which his plea relates, and
which we are bound to establish. The evidence offered, goes to
prove, that the men *were* assembled and means *were* provided for
an expedition against Mexico, on the island, and that Burr was
the projector of the plan, and provider of the means. Is not this
testimony relevant? And if it is, how can the Court exclude it?

In the treason case, the indictment charged the prisoner with being present at the acts done on the island.

There is a manifest difference between this and the indictment in the treason case. In the latter, the indictment charged the prisoner with being present. But in this indictment, there is nothing which either expressly or by imputation proves him to be present. Burr might begin or set on foot, provide or prepare the means of a military expedition at Blannerhasset's island without being present. Thus a merchant in Philadelphia might prepare the means of an expedition in New York; he might enlist men by bounty, and even equip a vessel for carrying them to the West Indies, without once stirring from his compting house.

Presence, therefore, not being expressly stated, nor even alleged by inference, there is not even a variance between the case and the evidence. If there was, it would be no good ground for exclusion. If it be said that the indictment is defective in not stating expressly whether he was present or absent, it might be a good reason for a motion in arrest, but not for the exclusion of evidence. This objection as to the variance is entirely new. In the cases of indicting a man for keeping a gaming house, of retailing spirituous liquors without a license, or for providing meat and drink for voters, it is not necessary to prove the presence of the accused; and such a defect is no ground of objection. But even if the defendant was charged expressly to have been present, in this case, still he might be convicted, though the evidence proved him to be absent, because in this case no proof of an overt act is required.

As to Mr Botts's second proposition, that no evidence of facts done out of the district was admissible, this had even been settled in the treason case, for if after giving evidence of an overt act of treason on Blannerhasset's island, you can give explanatory and confirmatory evidence from another district, a *fortiori* can be done in the present occasion.

The 3d proposition is, that no evidence of accessorial agency can be received, unless the guilt of the principal is proved by the record of conviction. True, such is the law, and such is the principle laid down by the Court; but there is an essential difference between a case, such as the gentleman supposed, and the present case. Where a number of men met together and levied war upon their government, all concerned are traitors; persons who are not present may be leagued in the general conspiracy, and perform their part at a distance. In such case, the law says, that the principal must be convicted first; but in the present instance, the persons who were assembled at Blannerhasset's island, are supposed not to have been guilty. We consider them as guilty of nothing, but that they were the means provided by the defendant, who was the principal, though not present. He is charged with preparing a military expedition, and his collecting a number of men together is a part of that expedition. Can he say that he is only an accessary, because he was not on the spot. Sir, he is not charged with being there, but he is charged with having provided the means, and with having provided those who were present with all that they had towards the expedition, wherever they might have been.

Chief Justice There can be no doubt of the correctness of your argument, but you seem to misunderstand the argument of the gentlemen on the other side—their argument is this that the person who did provide those means, or by whose advice or instance they were provided, did employ some person to provide them, who must have been a principal—for instance, if the means was men, somebody must have enlisted those men if provisions or arms, somebody must have purchased them Such an one they consider as principal, and not the men enlisted

Mr Hay I should be very sorry, Sir, to see such a doctrine as that established, both upon principles of law and of propriety I should regret it upon principles of common sense, that such a rule should be laid down, for by it, many an innocent and honest man might be deluded to become an agent in such procurements, for able, artful and designing men, who themselves would escape punishment, although the projectors and chief in the mischief This is a bold error indeed, and I hope I may be excused when I express my surprize, if such an idea ever did occur to the able and learned gentlemen Here, Sir, is a volume which demonstrates, not only the learning, but the zeal with which Smith and Ogden were defended Now, I think that they did very little, if any thing, themselves, but they employed persons to purchase guns and other military stores for them, and yet such an idea was never thought of by the learned counsel [Mr Hay read p 102, and 104 of that trial, where such a thing might have been mentioned]

Mr Botts here stated his argument He never meant to concede. that one man alone could ever set on foot a military expedition; nor if he could, would he say that all who were concerned were as guilty as himself Where there is a free agency, undoubtedly the agent is as guilty as the projector but here, how could there have been a *military* expedition if the people on board the boats could have discovered nothing of it, which it appears they did not ?

Mr Hay Who, Sir, can be the principal, if Burr was not ? Let him undertake to tell the Court There was an agency, to be sure, employed, for the purpose of getting the people to the island, but I deny that the men employed, although doing particular acts, and all tending to one point, can be regarded as principals, because it was all done by his special direction Besides, what did the agents do ? Burr says. " I want ten boats built on the Muskingum to be sent down to Blannerhasset's island," Mr Woodbridge, without knowing his scheme, has the boats built ; and procures certain articles of pork, &c But will any man suppose that Mr Woodbridge is the principal, or indeed, guilty of any thing whatever ? He asked nothing about it, and it was not necessary to the conspiracy, that the men employed should know any thing about it, or if any thing, they have not been apprized of the extent of it. No, Sir, the principal knew the human disposition better than to reveal his whole scheme to them He spoke to some intelligent men, who could keep a secret, to get men for him. He knew full well the extent of his whole calculations, and the influence he could have, as well as the deceptions he could work with He told the men engaged, that he was engaged in an honourable scheme, and which would turn out profitable to adventurers ; and that he was willing to hazard all he had in it · that the scheme was known to and approved of by the government

Now, Sir, can individuals thus engaged be said to be principals, or be charged with having provided the means of a military expedition ? They might have supposed different things : one might have supposed, that the conquest of New Orleans was the object · another might have supposed the Spanish Provinces to be the primary object—and others might have supposed, that the humble and inoffensive settlement on the Washita, was the ultimate object ; these various things he had told to *some* of them, and indeed one grew so out of the other, that it might appear feasible ; but in whatever point it is viewed, the accused cannot point out any other principal but himself.

But in whatever view it is taken, I ask you, Sir, whether it be not a question of *law* and *fact*, and, therefore, a proper subject for the Jury to decide upon, and not the Court ? And yet the gentlemen are continually calling upon the Court to arrest evidence Now, Sir, I call upon this Court to arrest this attempt of theirs to stop the evidence ; and, as a reason, contend, that it is *only* the province of the *Jury*, and not of the Court, to decide and I can see no ground or principle to the contrary

The fourth proposition, the Court will discover, is only a repetition of one which was made in the case of treason. It was then contended, that there was no treason, because there was no military expedition or appearance on Blannerhasset's island it is now renewed as respects the misdemeanor. Now, Sir, I think it was expressly stated by the Court, that the question, whether there was or was not a military expedition in progress to operate there, was a question of law and of fact, and therefore was a proper question for the examination of the Jury

Whether, therefore, under this act of Congress, a man may be said to provide the means of a military expedition , or, in the language of Mr Botts, whether they provided *adequate* means, for he says, that according to a bare and evident exposition of this law, the means must have been adequate to the object, otherwise the offence was not committed This he illustrated by a man building a house ; he supposed that a man could not be supposed to have provided the means for that object, when he had but one brick towards it Why, Sir, this is very far fetched, indeed But, suppose a man was seen with a number of carts loading, pursuing some supposed object ; and he was to be asked what he was doing . he would answer—" I am preparing the means for building a house, could it be doubted that he was doing so—even if he had but two carts ? If he could not, where will you draw a line of distinction according to Mr Botts, a man cannot be supposed to be providing the means for building, if there be even one shingle wanted.

Mr *Botts* said, that under the act of Congress a man providing the means for an expedition was not guilty : there was a material difference between *provided*, and providing.

Mr *Hay.* It is impossible, under this construction, for any Court or Jury to say what are adequate means the adequacy of the means depends upon the object to be obtained but here the object was to be kept a secret from the world, and even from those engaged the possession of New Orleans—the division of the Union, and the acquisition of the Spanish Provinces were all spoken of, and these may be sub-divided into the intentions of conquest, of plunder, and of revenge, or either of them All that the law requires is to know, whether it was his intention to set on foot any expedition against a foreign country. the adequacy of the means cannot be ascertained without the object is ascertained

Every law is to be taken by conspiracy of its parts, and by examination of all the whole law, and all laws on the same subject The construction given, would be found to be inconsistent with the law itself, because adequate means were not required by the law. What shall be done with a man, who begins a thing of this sort and sets it on foot in the words of the law, if the full means are requisite? He must escape, who provides the means, and he who does the act, must be punished! There can be no reason given, why so small a degree of guilt should rest on the principal perpetrator and mover of an expedition of this sort.

Yesterday the court were informed that the word " military" was a very important one. It is so, but it is not so in the way in which he treated it If a man sets out for the purpose of a trading voyage, enterprize or expedition to another country ; or for a speculation in land, he could not come within the meaning of this law for the word " military" can never be construed to mean pursuits of a peaceable nature.

But he says, that to characterize it " military" there must be a *military* origination, such troops and an assemblage otherwise no offence can be committed I do not admit of that position. a man may be collecting men to the very last moment of an expedition, ships may be provided and every thing put on board for the service, but it is not till the very eve of sailing that the men go on board, and yet, according to the doctrine the man who provides the means with this express view is not an object of punishment, because the means are not compleated! Unquestionably, upon the principles of common sense, such a man would be guilty of a violation of the law For instance, one thousand men may be directed to meet at Blannerhasett's island at a certain time; and one thousand guns may be provided and sent there, but before the men are capable of getting there in a state of military array, the scheme is discovered, and the projector of the plan is discovered, every thing is done, but bringing the army together, but yet, there is no violation of the law, say the gentlemen, because there is no military organization, this is truly making the law a dead letter

As the 5th objection, that the expedition was not commenced on Blannerhasset's island; however every thing of late have became a question of *law*, yet, I cannot suppose but this *must* be considered as a question of fact, to be decided by evidence, and consequently if nothing else did, this would belong to the jury. But as to the local commencement of the expedition, it is not of importance, if the means were proved at that island for carrying on the expedition.

The 6th point is, that no evidence can be given of what Mr Burr said or done by Mr. Blannerhasset. The proposition taken singled is unquestionably law—but there is a limitation to this general rule. It was truly said, that wherever two persons were engaged in the prosecution of the same enterprise, the acts and sayings of the one, may be received as evidence against the other. Mac Nally 613, might be consulted on this subject. but, sir, we mean to say and shew that there was a most intimate connection between these parties. indeed, Mr. Belknap has shewn that he understood from Burr and Blannerhasset themselves that there was an enterprize going on under Burr's control. We mean to prove the union between them, not merely by declarations, but by incontrovertible facts. In the trial of Smith and Ogden p 10' there are acts of the whole of these men engaged brought in evidence against Smith, and why? They were not leagued with him. But, Sir, they were *employed by him to make purchases*. Every thing that these men said or did was offered and permitted to go to the Jury, notwithstanding the zeal and intelligence which were manifested. I think every objection was overruled by the Court. Now whether you consider Blannerhasset as a conspirator, or as an agent of Burr's, he certainly was engaged in the purchase of boats and providing for the expedition, and consequently Burr's agent. What he did or said, therefore, in the case, testimony might be given of.

FRIDAY, *September* 11.

Mr *Martin* produced some authorities to the Court in favor of the positions laid down, to prove that the confession of Mr Blannerhasset could not be made use of to affect Mr Burr. 8 St Tr 474. and p 506 vol. 4 p. 195. vol 6 p. 218 Kelynge 18 1 Gib 280 Mac Nally 621, and p 37, 40 2 Hewes s abridgment 860 placite 6

Mr *Martin*, also laid down a new position, which was a conspiracy for killing the king, under the laws in England; and if that conspiracy was to continue for five years, it would be but one single act of treason or conspiracy, or however long it might continue. He quoted 4 St Tr 570. 1 Hawk p 11, ch sect 2. note He made some few observations on Smith and Ogdens case, and referred to p 113 of the trial in proof of his position. He made some few observations pointing out the difference in the cases between the expedition of Miranda and the ideal expedition of Burr

Mr *Botts* continued his observations without producing much new argument, he quoted 1 Hale 623 and 4 Bl 342. on the subject of locality of crime

Mr. *Mac Rae* was sorry to trouble the court and jury, and, indeed he said he would not were he not perfectly convinced that justice to the public, required that the whole truth respecting the guilt of Aaron Burr ought to be laid before the Court, the Jury and the country at large. I believe, said Mr Mac Rae, that, if the *truth* can come out, there will not be found, within this room, nor upon the face of the *globe*, an individual who can entertain a different opinion from that which we have contended for or but will be convinced that there is every effort making to stop the truth from coming out. However feeble, therefore, my efforts may be, I should consider myself unpardonable, were I to remain in silence, or not endeavour to bring out the *whole* truth. He hoped to be excused for using *strong* language at *any* time, because it arises from those feelings, which, what he heard and observed necessarily must occasion, rather than from any predisposition to do wrong Of that he said he was innocent He declared that he never would have consented to appear against the accused, if he did not believe him to be guilty, and guilty of the crimes attributed to him and this he supposed must be the universal belief This he thought proper to say in answer to what had been advanced as to the futility of this prosecution, and to declare that it was from a conviction in his own mind of the strong ground they had, he had willingly engaged to endeavor to give things and circumstances their just color (for he believed that the former prosecution failed, owing to the advantage taken of a small point of law) He could not avoid being urgent against *an* effort to take every advantage of, and every endeavor which was made to arrest the most important part of the evidence. It was enough to satisfy every candid mind that the defendant and his counsel were afraid to meet the testimony If they choose to make his innocence appear, why do they not invite, rather than repress the evidence, offered by the prosecution?

Mr *Botts* here interrupted, and reduced his six points to four, on which he made some observations

Mr *Mac Rae* continued his remarks he observed, that it was not on common law, but on the act of Congress that this prosecution was built and therefore the prosecution could not be conducted upon common law doctrines, whether he understood the law or not he would not be vain enough to say, but he must cherish a belief that there could be no doubt but that the defendant could be convicted under it of the offence charged

Mr *Mac Rae* here read those sections of the law upon which the indictment is founded; and expatiated on the terms " beginning, setting on foot, and preparing means for a military expedition or enterprize, if either of which could be proved, although he was not upon the spot charged, but at a remote distance, yet as was yesterday said, he must come within the *spirit* of the law. All the principal part might be affected through the medium of the post office, enclosing to *agents* sums of money sufficient to purchase provisions, arms, &c. and enlist men in the plain meaning of the act of Congress : and the plain understanding of mankind would consider such an one as the principal. He contended that if they could shew that he was the principal actor or instigator, his conviction ought to follow · and every positive fact ought to be adduced to the Jury, to shew the circumstances of his connection. Mr. Botts says, that a man must not merely begin, but he must *complete* his enterprize. Well, Sir, I will say that in September, he was there and *began* it : it is true that the indictment says the 10th of December ; but the Court know that the date is not important · it will be sufficient if we shew that the crime was committed *there* about that time, even if it was in September.

Mr *Burr* I was on Blannerhasset's island at the latter end of August, on the first of September I was at Marietta

Mr *M'Rae* I shall contend upon this law, that we have a right to go elsewhere, for proof of the object and transactions of this expedition, and if I have not a right to do so, I am most egregiously mistaken indeed in the import of the law. I say, that when he was there in August, he began what was afterwards carried on, and that he made contracts in Marietta to carry on his plans, whatever they might have been This will appear from the testimony of Albright and Woodbridge, already given, and it is corroborated by Mr Belknap. Indeed the whole connection is so evidently to be seen, that it need not be pointed out to a Jury There can be nodoubt but that the enterprize was commenced, at least, as early, nay, I would say at a much earlier period than the first September, and of this I conceive the Court and Jury must be well satisfied, even from what they have already heard.

If I understood Mr Botts, he said, that the acts on the island were not cognizable under this law, for that the man who begins and sets on foot an expedition of this sort, does not *commit a crime*, because to commit a crime the means must be commensurate to the object This language, perhaps, might suit his purpose, but he could not be serious, or at least, I cannot suppose the Court or Jury will receive such a doctrine A mere reading of the act itself will afford a sufficient answer to every argument of this nature, as to the quantum of means, or the period of commencing an expedition of a military nature; in five hundred men there may be five hundred opinions, but if there was not a designatory character to such a crime, in the understanding of men, (as indeed appears in the act of Congress) there could be no such a thing as an offender discovered

But, he says, that no act done out of the district is to be given in evidence: by his own argument, Sir, he has shewn the necessity of going out of the district for evidence, for he has called for facts, from whatever quarter, to ascertain the crime Sir, in order to discover the crime of Aaron Burr, it would be necessary not only to go out of the district, but out of the *United States* to discover his means to carry on this expedition Besides this, he has pleaded the smallness of the numbers engaged Why, if we examine into this charge, that will admit of a strong argument in our favor, since, although the force was inadequate at one place (say Blannerhasset's island) yet it increased, and became growingly adequate to a military enterprize This, although partly discovered by evidence, yet requires more, and therefore enhances our claim for obtaining evidence to be heard to prove it a military assemblage, even if we were to follow it to Mexico if he had gone so far. Thirty men assemble at this island, one hundred at the mouth of Cumberland, one hundred and fifty at Natchez, and as they descend the river their increase continues, until their numbers become adequate to their purpose When it is shown, Sir, that the men and means provided were sufficient to begin with, or "set on foot" a military enterprize I do suppose there ought to be no bounds set to our evidence even were it to come from our extreme limits of territory.

On the fourth point, the Court heard arguments which I did, when they were offered, and do now deem conclusive. The cases which have this morning been urged, I have heard and considered; but it does not appear to me that one of them applies to the case now before the Court. Those cases go to prove that the confession of a principal offender will be good evidence against himself, but not against third persons. No doubt but this is sound law. But when the fact is proven and fixed upon one, and the connection of others with that fact is likewise proven, surely the conversations and acts of that person, who is so intimate in the connection, might be given in evidence. East 96, holds the doctrine that whatever is done by one conspirator, although unknown to others at the time, is to be considered as the act of all who are concerned in the conspiracy. The conspiracy and connection must first be proved, but then, acts though not done in his presence, may be charged upon him. In the present case, the connection of Blannerhasset and Burr is proved to have existed, and consequently what was said by Blannerhasset to a third person upon the subject charged, of intention or acts, must be good evidence.

Here Mr. M'Rae reminded the Court of Smith and Ogden's case, p. 102 and 104 to prove that it was not necessary that he should have been present in person, to commit such a crime as that charged, and to prove that the prosecution was rightly conducted, notwithstanding what Mr. Botts had said, and to which he presumed it was unnecessary to consume the time of the Court to reply, since it did not belong to the case. He concluded with expressing a wish, that the Court would permit that transaction to appear in its true character, to which the defendant would have every opportunity to make answer and produce counter testimony, if any he had to produce.

Mr. *Burr*. We have at no time refused the power to give evidence of any act of mine on Blannerhasset's island; nay we invite them to show it.

Again. We invite them to shew that there was any military expedition " set on foot" any where. It was said by one gentleman, (Mr Martin) that the words " setting on foot" was not to be found in any English authority. That gentleman was mistaken in his exposition, for there are such words relating to the establishment of lotteries.

Mr. *Wirt* commenced by complaining of extreme indisposition, (occasioned by a want of health;) but he did not think that the subject admitted of such ludicrous treatment as Mr Botts had given it. he considered the transactions to which the conduct of the prisoner might have led, as of the most important, as it might have been of the most direful nature. He examined the cases of *mala prohibita* and *mala in se*; and referred to the Smith and Ogden's trial, and to the *wool* case, in answer to Mr Martin, who he contended, had not correctly represented the cases, and in which, truly no accessaries could be discovered applicable to that before the Court; on this subject, as well as the opinion of the Court, he should think proper to reserve himself for a future part of the discussion; but still he must contend that the opinion did not prove what had been attributed to it. The *mala in se* were those who carried on the expedition against the party or nation, and must be principals in the nature of the crime, but by whatever names the persons might be called who began and set on foot a military expedition against a nation with whom the United States were at peace, yet the crime, though in some respects, accessorial, was in its nature principal, because the principle guilt was in the performance of acts towards the promotion of a purpose where he was not present, but had made all the preparations for and exertions in. Need a man to be *present* in levying war, who did *actually* levy war? By no means, and yet here is a crime of an inferior nature, in which it is contended that he must be *present*, on the spot! Indeed this simple *setting on foot* had extended itself so far as to alarm the whole nation, and so far to alarm the executive of the United States, as to call out the power of the country to repel it.

The particular reason for the act being passed, it appears, was the circumstances which took place under *Genet*, formerly minister from France: the crime itself was never pretended to be more than *inceptive*; and yet its tendency in the extreme would have been related to the balance of power; and to peculiar foreign connection. The essential sub-stratum of the offence is, that the nation would be thereby embarked in a foreign quarrel.

What is the second clause of the law? it relates to the enlistment that still concerns a *foreign* service that is, the leading idea of the offence (and it not only extends to those who enlist, but to those who procure others to enlist.) it embraces the proper policy of crushing the crime in its bud.

The third clause directly contemplates the offence, but still considers it, in its nature accessorial, as fitting out an army, &c. It is not the individual who embarks himself on board of a ship, or the man who fights the battles against a foreign nation, but he, who procures those acts to be done, that the guilt of doing them lies, and not on him who does it.

The fourth clause, certainly indicates the mere furnishing of means for a foreign service in hostility to a friendly nation; but it is under the fifth section particularly, that the indictment is drawn, where "beginning or setting on foot," or "providing and preparing the means" are made to constitute the crime. Now all these descriptions of crime are accessorial in their nature, and reason. A man might stay at home and not strike a blow, and yet his offence, although *simply* that of a procurement, might be *principal*, because he is the principle operator, although the crime itself, (by law) is accessorial. The sixth, seventh, and eighth sections Mr Wirt ran through, with a very few observations, except enforcing to the Court, that the nature and policy of the law were such, as were calculated to bring *criminals* and only criminals to justice.

But, he supposed that the *words* of the law were sufficient to meet *this* case. Gentlemen attempted indeed, to screen their client, Aaron Burr, by splitting the case into two parts, and make him appear as an accessory, and therefore not guilty of the charge but what was the opinion from the bench, and the case put? Why, that if a man enlists a soldier, (even an as agent) he is guilty of the crime charged to the principal, because he carries on the expedition so far as he is engaged But these were inferior agents, it was true. Tyler, in Pennsylvania, and Blannerhasset on the island, to depict this *paradise* in Washita, who, by their *other* agencies, slipt about from State to State, to " carry on" the business, while the prime mover was kept out of sight.

Mr. Wirt then contended that it did not require numbers to " levy war" even, and much less to *set on foot* a military expedition, since all the objects of the law only contemplated that there should be a " setting on foot" towards the execution of a certain enterprize; and thus, the agency itself must shew the object, from what had appeared, were it only an agency, but it was more

But is " *presence*" the principal, or only ingredient to the commission of crime of this sort? *Presence* appears to be the main requisite! But what establishes the guilt? Doing the thing, *they* say, but *we* say, that agreeable to law it is " beginning or setting on foot," &c. Cannot this be done without actual presence? Suppose a case For instance, suppose Mr. Blannerhasset (who is said to be an eccentric gentleman, having, in the language of that country, every sort of sense but " common sense," and with all the perfections of his musical talents) should have been discovered to have turned his mind more into the ideas of commodore Trunnian Suppose he had procured five hundred cannon, and magazines of powder comparative to them. Suppose he had stored his graneries with all kinds of provisions, suitable for such an expedition, and that he had invited from his own country, a set of desperadoes to assist him in his pursuits And again Suppose that Mr. Burr had, in Mr Jordan's room at Lexington, enclosed to him a letter full of bank notes to assist in achieving the object which Burr himself was proved to be at the head of, would this amount to nothing on the account of Aaron Burr

Here Mr. Wirt made some pertinent observations on the *quo animo*, and of the *objects* intended by the words " beginning and setting on foot" a foreign expedition, and which he contended did not mean the act itself, but might *waft* itself from " pole to pole," A letter could be an active agent; it could procure soldiers, weapons, provisions, and all that would be necessary to promote and carry on any powerful expedition. Thus, were Burr in Lexington or any where else within the power of acting, he *might* act with effect in a military expedition against the U. States in any part, for he could multiply himself to be any and every where, *ad infinitum*, by letters and agencies: and yet *himself* escape, because *he* is not on the spot! Thus might a general of an army escape from doing any wrong action, because he was at a distance, and did not strike the blow that did the harm imputed to him A man might procure means; he might draw together his army, and, from the remoteness of the parts, he might appoint a place of rendezvous, and yet, from the doctrines here held, he might be an innocent man!

Here Mr. Wirt took another and a more extensive view of the coincidence of this case with that of Smith and Ogden, on the Miranda expedition he quoted pages 121, 127, and 229 of the report of that trial, in comparison with the *agencies*, so said to be exhibited in this case, and contended that *Col Burr* must be considered as *much a principal* in this case as *they* must have been in that, where it appeared that they were the sole movers : as the whole expedition seemed to be under their controul, although they had agents to purchase provisions, enlist men, and make other preparations

Again It is said, that no evidence of an act done out of the district can be given in evidence against the defendant   But this charge consists not in the *completion* of an expedition, but in "beginning and setting it on foot," and, therefore, if the act was done in Lexington, still the *venue* might be laid in another district, if the assemblage was there to commit the act   Suppose Burr levied in New York, and set on foot means to execute an expedition through New Orleans against La Vera Cruz, by sending *money, men,* provisions, &c would he not be as liable, or properly answerable in New Orleans, although he began to set it on foot in New York, as though he began it there ? It is not the mere writing of a letter, but the carrying on measures such as Aaron Burr has done, of which the government have so justly complained, and for the discovery of *his* guilt, they have the right, by reason, and by *law* to draw evidence from any State where he commenced and carried on his measures, and exhibited his intentions   Now, how can this intention, or his destination, be so well shewn as by producing evidence of his conversations and measures as he descended down the river ? Indeed this evidently is the *intention* of the act   Suppose a contrary construction to be just—suppose Burr to have such an enterprize in view as is charged, numerous preparations are made in various parts of a State or of several States, at none of which is *he* present, but he appoints a place of rendezvous without the boundaries of the United States, where he meets his men to execute his plan   Would not a doctrine like this, indeed, give a full scope to such a man as Aaron Burr to do every species of crime   He is clear from punishment

As to the acts of Blannerhasset which are refused to be received in evidence, if the Court hould so say. Mr Wirt observed, that it must divide itself into two points of argument—whether the crime charged, should be treason, conspiracy or whatever   First, the existence, the nature, and the extent of the crime must be ascertained   and then, secondly, the part which the accused took in it, must be produced in evidence   but it could not be so produced, if that evidence was refused to be heard

Mr *Wirt* went at some length into a view of the authorities of Mr Martin, contending that he had produced but one which could have any effect in the promotion of his doctrine, (Mac Nally 611, 635) and even that, if he had quoted it with proper candor, would have appeared in another point of view ; because Baron Eyre, in that opinion, stood opposed to every member of the bench in the principle now contended for   Hardy was on his trial, Thelwall, who was not, having taken a paper to be printed, this paper was produced against Hardy, because the connection was first proved   Here was an act of Thelwal's done in the absence of Hardy, given in evidence but yet the solitary autho rity of Baron Eyre is here the *mouldering prop* of Mr Martin, upon which his argument stands The profound learning and reasoning, however, of Justice Buller, brought all the Judges over to him, and, at last, Eyre himself gave up, and admitted the evidence of letters which were before rejected. (See Hardy's trial) Letters were invariably produced, and every other species of evidence of the sort where the connection was established, also in the trial of Tooke Why then *a fortiori* can the letters of Blannerhasset be received in evidence against Burr, and the connection of Burr with him be rejected? If the prisoner consented to the design, and was connected with it, the evidence of others also concerned, may be given, although it relates to mere conversa- tions between the parties and the case being *only* for a *misdemean or* does not impair the obligation to procuring it, more than as though the charge was of greater magnitude, as treason, &c This position is proved by the authorities themselves Even M'Nally who has been quoted, will not controvert it and East, 96, states the very position, that in *all* matters of controversy you have a right to prove a charge by the writings and sayings of the party; but to be sure he goes on, like the others, and states, that you *must* prove the connection of the party, if it were not so, a man might carry on his dark and intricate designs, however dangerous to community, in his own way, without means of law to molest him, and particularly a man of the ex- traordinary enterprize and genius of Burr His *all* depends upon exculpating himself now, and we want to produce proof of his being the life of every embarcation that was made towards his object This, however, it is attempted to shut out.

Chief Justice. Have you ever met with a case where testimony of this kind has ever been admitted; where the indictment does not charge a conspiracy? If there be such a case, I could much wish to see it

Mr *Wirt* answered, that he had not such a case *at present* in his knowledge, but he doubted not there were such He was encouraged to suppose so, from the heading of M'Nally's chap- ter on conspiracies, p 610 Yes, it occurred to him at that mo- ment, that there was such a case in Salkeld, but he did not re- collect where, but it was a case where one family endeavoured to break up the peace of another family, and the indictment was for a conspiracy *Co-operation* he conceived to be the main in- gredient in conspiracy, because it required *others*, besides the first *projector* to understand and embark in the general plan Indeed it had been confessed, that the " choice spirits," and the ' best blood in America" were embarked in this enterprize, whatever it might be ; but it was evident that it was designed to be against a nation at peace with us. (Indeed they appeared to be " choice spirits,"—some of them at least)—and this appear ed from the circumstances combined with the *reason* of the law

Referring to the case of Smith and Ogden, Mr Wirt observed that although the *counsel* had endeavoured to disunite the con- nection, yet, the *Court* had overruled it, and permitted evidence from the whole of those who had bought and paid for articles for the expedition, to be given in evidence because it was considered in the true light of a conspiracy, and therefore, applicable to the case. He further contended, that the generic *quality* of a crime was to be observed by a Court and Jury, in preference to the technical finesse used too commonly, which neither common sense nor justice could calmly admit of. This over nicety produced from the mind of even the benevolent and feeling *Hale*, (2 Hale, 193,) a reflection which expressed its abhorrence at the "nicety" which must inevitably disgrace the law, too commonly exposed in indictments, which promoted the escape of offenders, and however nice Mr. Botts had been in making distinctions between "beginning" and "setting on foot" a military and *warlike* expedition, their distinctions were of little importance, since both of them were opposed to the peace and happiness of society but it was one consolation, that the gentleman had only his own *ipse dixit* to support him.

Mr *Wirt* here made several observations on a position of Mr Botts, that there must be a sufficiency of means to accomplish the object; for that, without such a "sufficiency," the act of Congress was not violated, and, in addition to that, he requires a completion of the object, for, he says, if it is crushed in the bud, it cannot meet the anticipation of the law But what does this doctrine amount to? Why nothing less, than that he should have provided men enough to subdue the thirty millions who inhabit the Spanish American Provinces, backed by their rich mines Now can this, by any thinking man, be supposed to be the object of the law—can it be supposed that the executive is to wait for final consequences before he can move towards the suppression of a measure of this nature? Such a doctrine must, indeed, be replete with the most monstrous consequences.

Having amused the Court with such kind of argument, the gentlemen had next proceeded to contrast the small force of thirty men on Blannerhasset's island with the magnitude of the expedition supposed to be on foot We're thirty men capable to overthrow such a mighty empire! *He* reasone upon it, and so have many other *people*, but is the evil *design* to stop here? Are the thirty men on the island to be all that will be collected? look to the immense distance of three or four thousand miles before he could have reached his port of destination, and also to the scenes of his actions He took this silent wilderness and this silent river to march with this *embrio* of his army. Even at Cumberland, assistance flowed down the stream to him so that his thirty men at the island, where the expedition was begun and set on foot, was increased to one hundred But, however great the means or however numerous the men, if we cannot prove it on the island, we are to be foiled in our attempts to bring the defendant to justice! It has indeed been stated that he had six or ten thousand at command when he wanted them His means were sufficient, his ambition continued fired; and he still continued hungry for his prey, until the commander and chief of our army took such measures as to baffle all his ambitious and direful attempts to destroy the harmony and if possible, the government of his country.

But Mr. Botts says, that this offence cannot be tried any where, but where it was *begun* How will this hang with the rest of his argument? Before he said that a man was not answerable except the crime was *compleated!* So that if the crime is begun (of however serious a nature) in New Hampshire, and is compleated in Georgia, the objects of the law can never be carried into effect, nor the culprit tried at all. But Mr. Wirt contended that *where ever* there was an appearance of "military" enterprize, and any accession made towards compleating the object in view, (since an expedition of this nature must be "begun" in one place, "carried on" in another, and "compleated" in another) and each part was cognizable and at every *place* where an act was done. Were there not additions received at the island; men, ammunition, arms? Tyler's phalanx, and what took place among them there, will compleatly satisfy the phrases of the law, if one step can afterwards be adduced to shew the *quo animo,* the beginning is the least thing to discover where the *insertion* can be evinced.

But Burr was not at the island when these things were transacted! Sir, we can, and will, if you permit us to prove his *instrumentality* and *agency* in every thing that was done there.

Mr. *Wirt* would not say any thing respecting trials by Jury, and the propriety of Juries being provided with evidence, but he could not avoid expressing his astonishment at any attempts to defeat the introduction of evidence to a Jury; but this was a point with the bar, by art to turn a criminal trial of consequence into nothing.

Mr. *Randolph* commenced with some strictures on the mode with which this prosecution had been continued, and the misrepresentations which he had observed on the subject of exclusion of evidence, which reiteration he could ascribe to no other motive than to take hold of the ear of the people. He said he came not there to make answer, however, to such a species of argument, but to argue it upon principles of law, which were calculated *only* to a Court of justice. In order to meet these numerous anathemas Mr. Randolph said that he found more than ever the necessity to see that there should be a fair trial, and to require what the law required and that alone: for beneath that, the opinions of men must vanish like a mist before the sun. They had, to be sure used language which was not grateful, but it was extorted.

It is the *power of government*, said Mr. Randolph, and that only which we fear, and I will dare to say that the clamour against colonel Burr originated from the executive authority, who ought not to have made it. Another thing was, that there was a certain perceptible feature in every address: there was one word to the Court and another to the Jury, and whenever this trial should be *faithfully* reported, it must appear to the world. *Exclude evidence, break down Jury functions, a mere mockery of trial.* This was the constant theme, Sir, I wish all those on the outside of this bar did attend to the *true* statement of the case. *We do not ask the Court to take this case from the Jury*, but the rights of a Jury are not to ride triumphant over the rights of a court. There are certain points which the Court *must* prescribe, and the Jury *must* obey. This may be considered as a little irritating, but I am not afraid to declare it, since it is sound law.

Mark the facts, which cannot be varied. Col. Burr was not at Blannerhasset's island on the 10th of December, nor within a hundred miles of it, and this *absence* gives a death wound to the indictment. Here Mr Randolph read the seven counts in the indictment, upon which he made a number of inferences in application to the *absence* of the defendance, much in the same train as was before taken by Mr. Botts &c. He also referred to words "set on foot" and quoted Johnson's dictionary for its meaning, observing that so vague and uncertain was its acceptation that not less than 73 definitions were given of it. Indeed, he said it was one of those laws which did not apply so much to our own country, and perhaps less care was taken in its complication than is usual with laws. It was a law enacted to gratify a foreign nation that this indictment was wholly built upon. Now, if penal laws were to be construed strictly in any cases, all those that were made to gratify foreign nations must be peculiarly so. The history of the world would furnish abundant lessons of this sort. Mr Randolph here called to view the reign of Louis XIV and his power over the feeble Hollanders. But, he declared that he was afraid of Buonaparte, and indeed of every nation who were to be gratified by laws made by us in their favour. But these remarks and fears, he declared to be excited from a view of human nature, history and the relative situation of nations, powerful and defenceless, and not in reference to any particular case. The meaning of the law, he contended, ought to be restrained to what *must* be understood, and always to be constructed in favour of an accused person. He quoted 6 Bacon, 292, to elucidate the necessity of the most liberal construction, so that if there was a doubtful meaning in the words of the law, it ought not to injure the accused by interpretation.

What, say the gentlemen, will you suffer a great offender to escape, and one of less importance, or indeed, a little one in the transaction, to be involved? What would the world think of such a thing? Why, Sir, I will tell you what the world will say some time or other, when the public mind shall become cooled from its present inflamed state: it will say that the man ought to have a fair and unprejudiced trial. it will say, that those who were concerned in his defence ought not to be intimidated from their duty, or any apprehensions of what the world would say: it would say, that it must be far better that Burr and a thousand more should escape, than you should establish a precedent which would open an inquisition into every man's private transactions. Transpose this *animalcula*—this embrio—this insipient existence of an action, "beginning and setting on foot," into a crime, when no definitive meaning can be fixed to the words, and there will remain no man safe at his own fire-side. No latitudinary he believed could extend himself so far. The gentlemen concerned had surely the full view of the evidence and all the extent necessary; and they had all the time and means to examine and prepare which could be desired.

To "levy war," Mr *Randolph* contended, was an act which *absence* must render impossible. This was the sense which the Court affixed to the words, and whether it related to treason or misdemeanors of this kind, the action must appear, however dif ferent the nature of the offences: some *act* was necessary in both cases; and, therefore, in that sense they were alike Beginning and setting on foot an expedition at a certain specified place, he contended, must require the presence of the person charged with those acts, as well as an actor in treason would require his presence. When a man was said to do an act at a certain place, was it not to be supposed that he was at that place at that time ? *Presence only* could produce an effect, upon philosophical principles, when the charge of *presence* and *time* were each mentioned in the indictment He contended that to punish a person under a law made merely to satisfy a foreign nation, (especially when he was absent) and where the law was vague and uncertain, would be too absurd an intrusion, upon all principles of law and justice, If, he was, not there, let conjecture and idea extend itself where it pleased, still the respect due to an opinion of the Court must call forth an argument which nothing could destroy or defeat *Inference* could not be permitted to exist. " Beginning" and " setting on soot" a foreign expedition, he supposed to be synonymous; but were equally vague terms; and were such as he considered in all their nature and full extent, too indefinite to meet this case, or to support this indictment.

Here Mr *Randolph* took some review of the arguments of Mr. Wirt and Mr M'Rae, on the subject of Col Burr's presence; but he contended that none which he had heard could produce in him the least conviction, which would possibly support an indictment under such circumstances. Indeed, he should suppose, that if an indictment could be supported any where, it must be in Kentucky where the defendant *was*, and not at a place where he was not; and where he could have committed *no* offence.

On the article of *absence*, Mr. Randolph concluded this day's session of the Court.

SATURDAY, September 12

Mr *Randolph* continued his observations. To bolster up this indictment, he contended a plot, and contrivance of misdemeanor was attempted to be proved. Now, as to the idea of plotting and contriving a misdemeanor, it is the same as that of plotting or contriving a treason: for the principle is the same, and nothing but the words can change its appearance. Advising and procuring a misdemeanor—what was it?—Was it not misdemeanor itself? Could the phrase change the ground? There was not a single proposition, nor attempt towards it on the last of August, or the 1st of September, at that time he was at Marietta, and then he talked with Woodbridge about boats; or whatever business else he had to transact; but there was nothing on Blannerhasset's island, but was, in its own nature, innocent in its effects, and nothing like military in its appearance: Indeed these provisions were totally disqualified for a military expedition.

He could not admit of the imputation of constructive " beginnings," nor of misapplied " carrying on," since his absence was evident. He here referred to the opinion before given by the Court, as to legal presence. Gentlemen had referred to the effects, which a great genius commanded, when his single letter

must sink the Alps and Pyrennees, and create an army at pleasure, whilst the innocent actors must suffer. Such a case, Mr
Randolph insisted upon must be assimilated to one of murder, as
to advising and procuring, and he must as much be termed an accessary as one at fifty miles distance from where the murder was
committed. But they say, " why do you ask for the presence of
the man where the act might be done without him and it is not
necessary?" We answer, that it is necessary, and we so say, be
cause the law says so : and it is not the peculiar talents or efforts
of Col Burr, that are to produce his conviction more than that
of any other man, if his guilt cannot be legally established He is
not to receive the honor of talents for his conviction, which, per
haps, would be withheld from him on other occasions Take men
as they are, Sir, little and big, in law, let not the nature of the
crime or *public policy* vary the thing, the law embraces every
man alike—if it is rotten, be it so, but let not one *iota* be added
to it *here.*

The affair of Miranda had been assinated with this, and al
most, he had heard the same, with respect to the ships under com
modore Douglass at Hampton Roads, but this was too trifling
as to its distance and probable effects, he believed to require a
serious answer.

It was said, that all the law upon which the defence had rested
contained accessorial offences, and were so in their nature What
was meant by this expression he could not understand. It must
mean one of two things. either, that there was a real " principal"
who had put in motion men, who were capable of committing such an offence, who could act though absent, and there
fore was impeachable or else that the *actual* perpetrators
were principals. The latter we say, we say that the actual
perpetrators, are principals in law, and that it is a down-
right error to affix the character any where else. But as be
fore observed, *procurement* is not an offence within the law. By
what *modus* can *he* be transformed into a principal under this
indictment, who merely procures and directs? He is said to be an
actual perpetrator at Blannerhasset's island ; and that he there
did, on a certain day, such and such acts Now, the plain sense of
words tells me that if he was not there, he could do no act on a
certain day This I think is a sufficient reason to put an end to
the whole of the argument on that head.

" A military expedition "—What is a military expedition?
Your honor has given me an ample definition of it in your opinion
" a warlike assemblage, &c " an expedition of this sort as I under
stand from Dr Johnson's dictionary, is a martial or military march
or voyage ; to do an action by force of arms, attended by suitable
military apparatus, (and not such as would change boats loaded
for agricultural objects, into implements of war) and intended
for purposes of hostility It is not enough, that a few bushels of
flour or corn meal shall be collected together, and that conjec
tures shall be formed on the existence and probable consequence
—but it must exist in sufficient *force*, so that in the judgment of
observers it shall be believed to mean and obtain the evident
object from their hostile appearance. Will the transactions of
Blannerhasset's island, in one single feature, resemble this?
must be " a military expedition" on this particular island, *the*

" begun and carried on," and to this our attention must be particularly leant.

This was said to be a *mecuus*, round which, at some time, hosts
were to assemble, but this does not relieve the indictment from
the entanglements absolutely attached to it. That *spot*, and the
presence of the person charged, is inevitable to its support.

Smith and Ogden's case is brought in comparison, but there
every thing was military in its nature and manner, and thus is
entirely different from this, where nothing martial in matter or
manner could be discovered, and no infringement of the law
whatever was distinguishable. To " provide and prepare" means
for a military expedition are personal acts, and so are to " begin
and set on foot," and persons must be a component part, where it
is of a military nature; but where are the soldiers? Smith and
Ogden he thought however, might very well be considered as
principals, without touching the present case, because the indictments were of different form. Smith was indicted, not only
for doing an act in New York, but in a particular ward of that
city; he was in New York at the time, and had it been a case of
felony, it might have been said that he was within " striking
distance," capable of giving *any* assistance. But, suppose he had
been at *Boston* at this time, would Judge Talmadge, (this mirror
of justice) have considered it possible for him to do an act in the
first ward in New York, and therefore a principal in the act?
By no means. At any rate the indictment should have exhibited
the case *quo modo*

Mr Randolph said he should not be so critical as to go into the
distinction between the article *a* and *the*, but he could not help
observing the words which the legislature had affixed to their law,
they had not said *any* means, but they had said " *the* means"—
the *very means*, and not the breath, the inception, or the embrio,
as it was called. Then the means must be at least adequate to
make the attempt, under the prospect (at least) of success, so as
that it might be supposed, that the party thought he could do
something. It would be modern chevalry in the extreme, however to suppose that his means were adequate to the object, as specified in this indictment, by looking at the few men on the island
and the three or four muskets possesed by these thirty men.

As to the necessity of evidence being given to the *spot* charged as the seat of the offence, the books were specific, where place
was a part of the charge the law was universal and uniform on
that subject, and needed no comment, but a reference to precedents

But what was expected most to be gained from the declarations
of Mr Blannerhasset, were, they say, that he was a fellow conspirator, and therefore all that he uttered went to shew the nature and extent of the conspiracy Why, as to the *conspiracy*,
Sir, said Mr. R. there is no charge laid, and you, as a Judge, can
make no enquiry into the subject; and *we* are not called upon to
defend ourselves against a charge of conspiracy. But here the
gentleman asked if it could not be brought forward in evidence?
Yes, he answered, Thelwall's declarations were produced against
Tooke. Here he had forgotten the nature of that indictment,
for it was Tooke, Hardy, Thelwall and others did conspire a-

gainst the king's life, &c and therefore the language of judge Buller was just They received notice to come and be prepared to answer a joint accusation in which they were *all* concerned It was the same combination and the same action Hale and all writers require that a man shall be charged specifically, so as to come prepared for defence to the utmost of his power ; and not, as in this case, have charges, law cases, and arguments applied, which are not hinted at in the indictment. To what avail then, would be such evidence, and how could it apply to the indictment?

Mr *Martin*, in rising, appologized for his extreme hoarseness, but could not avoid making some additional remarks on a subject, which to him appeared momentous He complained of the gentlemen on the part of the prosecution, for having spent so much time, which he considered as having a tendency to excite public clamour , and giving an improper impression to those who heard them, against the accused ; but, he would wish to know wherein that solicitude appeared He believed they had not exhibited it. but it was true, that they had wished to avoid a conviction of crimes which *could* not be attached to them · and that they still would contend against Here Mr. Martin referred to the law as to the proper district where a crime should be tried, &c but certainly it was in vain for the prosecution to have supported their indictment or have said that they could try the case any where else — Whatever evidence they may have relating to any other place, we will say that we have come forward *solely* to answer the charges made against us, upon constitutional principles. The government never can complain, for they have had a full opportunity, and advantages which we have never had—they might have selected Kentucky or any where, but they have brought *my friend* to this *spot,* where they have charged the offence to have been committed Why, Sir, was *this* district selected ? Sir, the prejudice of this district we have found to be so great, that we have been scarcely able to try at all We have, indeed, found one of the first officers of the government of this state so far brassed as to have said, that if he had not been convinced of the guilt of the prisoner, he should not have engaged himself to support the prosecution Thus is the attrocity of *Burr* held up — All this while they seemed to have forgotten the foundation of their charge . and they appeared also to forget that there was any expectation of a Spanish war, to which, their own witnesses have amply testified ; as have also the reports of the expedition to the Sabine, which the Spaniards have crossed, contrary to our treaty. (Patterson's opinion, p 85 Smith and Ogden's trial)

Here, Mr Martin went into some lengthy remarks on the motives, which the gentlemen concerned in the prosecution, had expressed for their ardent engagement therein ; motives which in his view were no less extraordinary and unjustifiable than those which induced them to bring forward improper and irrelevant evidence. And yet their loud cry now was " you want to stop the evidence " Irrelevant evidence, however, they have admitted cannot go to the Jury, yet variant evidence might Why, of its variance, or relevancy, the court are to decide ; and it is to the court that we wish to commit it · for instance, the difference of a day, as in the case of Lord Balmerino, *the court* decided to be non-important In a case of murder, suppose it was laid that a man was killed with a weapon, would a witness be permitted to come forward and prove that he was poisoned ? By no means . and who but the Court is to decide upon the relevancy of such testimony ? It would be in vain that counsel should argue that a man had been guilty of this, that, and the other, atrocious crime, if they could not prove the crime charged. The court would not permit such evidence to go to a Jury

But, the gentlemen say, that we will not let them get off from Blannerhasset's island . that if they could once get away from there, they could make such a display of his actions in Kentucky as must convict him ! Why did they not bring him there at first ? But what is the case ? Was he not brought there ; and was there not a Grand Jury there summoned on his case, as well as witnesses, as many as the attorney of that district thought proper to have ? Col. Burr appeared there like a gentleman to answer to his country The result was, that he was honorably discharged with a most explicit declaration from the Judge that there did not appear to be one single idea formed by him injurious to the United States It was not from a want of enemies there that he was discharged, but from the want of an atom of proof that could tend any way towards his conviction.

Afterwards, in the Mississippi Territory, where the government had determined to have a full examination made, and where the father of the attorney general of the United States sits as Judge There was the spot for obtaining witnesses to prove every thing that was done, but nothing could be proved, and he was discharged with honor by that Grand Jury, in a country where we may fairly suppose there exists a peculiar attachment to government ; (so says the President of the United States in his communication) They were never able to find out the crime of Col Burr , and yet, all this while, Gen Wilkinson was picketting the City of New-Orleans, and repairing its garrisons to. receive this arch enemy He was preparing the minds of all the people to meet a powerful enemy, who was coming to take their city with a powerful military force He called the merchants and others together to prepare for what was never feared or even expected, more than was an earthquake to shallow up the city ; and what never come to pass nor even contemplated Here M Martin branched into some observations on the laws on gaming and nuisances, as to their specification ; and also referred to Vaughan's case as to the locality of the crime. On this subject he referred again to a former opinion of the court as to principal and accessorial guilt and extended his observations thereupon to a considerable length : he also referred to a period when, instead of endeavoring to keep back testimony, they had invited the prosecution to produce testimony, and when it would have been no loss of time, because a great number of days (13) were to spare This might have removed the mighty prejudices since exhibited against Col Burr, had they so thought proper, but they did not . then might they have decided to what district he was to be sent, if he could not properly be tried here. That was the time for the Court to exercise its legal discretion as to the proper place for him to be, and, yet *now*, a charge is brought of a desire to keep back testimony.

Mr. Martin has made some lengthy remarks in answer to Mr. Wirt, and some authorities which were produced, which related not to the charge now exhibited, but to conspiraces. He also referred to some of his former observations and authorities from McNally 621, and 616. but contended that the inferences deduced, were far from being correct as to their application to Blannerhasset. This common declaration of a person, might be made very carelessly and imperfect, because of their seeming of trifling importance; and therefore are liable to considerable misrepresentation, but the correspondence of persons being in writing is not committed to the hazard of memory, and consequently not so likely to err. What is a conspiracy? It depends not upon the amount of the crime, for it may be treason or any other crime and is not the act done, but the act intended to be done, when the indictment charges a particular *action*. How is a person to be punished for the indesirable intention of the mind? The guilt of this offence is intention, What is *intention?* It is not *action*. Mr Martin referred to his former observations and authorities produced early in this case, as to accessaries; and elucidated them by some application to the present motion; he referred to Hale 178 and supposed that the case referred to by a gentleman in behalf of the prosecution must have stumbled upon it from misconception and mistaken memory, or he would never had so erred as to the applicancy of his argument, because it was unfortunate for him as it could possibly be.

But the gentleman had most ingeniously made a distinction by an argument, that the act of Congress intended acts of an accessorial nature, for that those only who carried war into a country were principally guilty. therefore those who carried arms were principals, and all concerned must be accessaries. What is the natural inference upon this? Why, that no offence can take place under this law unless the principal offence has taken place, and consequently no punishment can ensue.

Mr *Martin* then took a review of the argument of gentlemen on the principle of common law, when they themselves had so strongly inveighed against its introduction here. He also took a review of the circumstances under which this law was passed and its intended short and confined duration? it was passed, he said, under an administration, and in times commonly termed *Federal*, and much clamor was made against it by those very persons who were now so extremely solicitous of carrying it into effect against the accused. But how amazingly are time and thing changed! Mr. Martin made some observations on Smith and Ogden's case, and pointed out a different circumstance attending that and this case, for, in that, both presence and action were conspicuous, but in this, neither. His doctrine, he said, was supported by the illustrious authority of Judge Tucker or Blackstone in note B. He also referred to Coke, sec. 3. to shew that such unmeaning terms as were expressed in this law of " beginning setting on foot" &c. were synonymous to " attempting" or " going about" a thing which might be merely the act of the mind, and therefore could not be criminal in itself, because it must remain forever undefined, unless by *construction*. Various opinions had been uttered on this subject, and it certainly must at last become evidently necessary, that the question should be forever settled by the solemn opinion of the Court He never could indulge the idea however, that the framers of this law meant every " insipient" act, to assume the character of the act in its maturity. To " begin," we know, is to do the first part of something; to " set on foot" appears to be synonymous with beginning; this is nothing of itself. But I can conceive that " providing and preparing means" is something that may be specified by witnesses But is this providing and preparing means in themselves criminal? By no means it must be proved that it was to carry on a war &c that this was done Means adequate to the object must be intended, or the law is futile That the means must intend the full success and accomplishment of the end intended, we do not argue but that there must be a probability of success, is an indispensable requisite Many expeditions among warriors are undertaken and fail

Mr Martin here indulged himself with some severe animadversions on the conduct of the executive in ordering out the military to stop this expedition, which was not of a military nature, nor, he contended augured any thing terrific, or what could be possibly embraced in the law authorizing the President to employ a military force to quell. Before the military can consistently, be called out, there must be an expedition on foot, for then the civil authority may be too weak to quell it. The intention of the law could not be to call out the military power at the beginning and setting on foot what cannot be known the law does not say a word about conspiring or advising to do an act, or procuring the act to be done, those expressions, and consequently their intentions are left out

One person, it is said, might begin and set on foot, a military expedition ; and yet it must be denominated a conspiracy ! Mr Martin extended his remarks to show, that it was not the person who advised and procured, but he who had *done* the act, ought to be punished ; and contended again, that if it was he who had done the act that was punishable, where there was no act done, and when the person charged was absent, he could not be guilty of any thing. Acts done at the spot were admissible evidence, but no other

He then contended, that there was no accessorial guilt, of any kind, in the person who procured, (under this law) nor did the common law know of such a thing Some statute must make it a crime, or it could not be one The question then, must inevitably be, whether these men violated the law, which is produced to charge them with a crime, on Blannerhasset's island ? if there was any guilt committed, it must rest on those who did some unlawful act there . there can be no accessorial guilt by common law, and by statute law it appears there is none created ; where then is the evidence to convict Col Burr, who was two or three hundred miles off. The very act which they before called *treason*. is now transformed into *misdemeanor* , and no evidence of either can be produced. A distinction had been attempted between the nature of evidence in a charge of levying war and a charge of misdemeanor, but it was in vain; for if the evidence respecting *presence* failed in the one charge, it must fail in the other.

Qui facit per alium, facit per se, was a principle in civil law; and would apply equally well in this case. How could a partnership exist, he would ask, for who had a right to bind him at hundreds of miles distance? Consequently, whose acts could be laid to his charge? If fifty men were combined, and one of them only killed a man, but it was proved to be their conjoined object; and that they were within such distance as that they could give him " aid," they must be considered as equally guilty with him who struck the blow. but if they are not so near, and their connection in the murder cannot be proved, the law would not charge them principally or accessorially, for no person is answerable for the criminal act of another, unless he is, at least, *legally* present. In this then is a distinction between the criminal and civil law, but this distinction was not drawn in the arguments on the other side.

Mr. Martin again referred to Smith and Ogden's case, as to the indictment, and contended that whatever number of counts there might have been laid, still it was clear from the decision, that there was but one crime. He is charged with preparing means, &c. for carrying on a war with a nation at peace with us; this was but one act, if an act had been done by him, as appeared by evidence to have been done in the other case; but yet that was determined in favor of the defendants. He referred to the motion: and contended that the Court must decide upon it, if no pertinent evidence could be adduced. Col. Burr and Gen. Dayton he insisted could not be convicted in this charge of misdemeanor, even if there had been one committed, because they were at a great distance. There must have been *an act committed,* and there must have been the presence of the parties to support the indictment. With these observations he should submit the case to the Court.

Mr. *Wickham* observed, that he commenced his observations under the disadvantage of having been absent during the discussion; but, however, he felt it his duty to address the Court on the subject of the motion, from information of what had passed, and from his impressions of the nature of the case. If he was capable of feeling surprise at any thing which has occurred, or which could occur in this prosecution, which was surprising in itself, he must now express it at this indictment being at all tried after that of treason, which was stranger than this, and yet this proceeded upon the very same ground. It was laid down then as a ground on which they fully expected to succeed, that in the highest and lowest offences all were principals, and the same argument is now attempted to be made, but with a different feature. When arguments of this nature were advanced by such learned gentlemen, Mr. W. thought it his duty to oppose them; and especially as one gentleman had boldly came forward with a declaration that he was so fully convinced of the guilt of the accused, that he felt it his duty to engage in his prosecution. As a matter of delicacy, he might, however, have been excused from declaring this his willingness to procure conviction. Upon what ground was that gentleman convinced—upon a knowledge of the facts? No, for they have all told the Court that they were not possessed of the facts, and did not know what their own witnesses could prove, and cannot know what the witnesses of the accused can prove. They must pardon me, said Mr W, when I say that they are entirely *ignorant* of the law of treason, for the course of their study has not gone that way Indeed they have not only confessed their ignorance of it, but have given sufficient evidence of it, however eloquent may have been their arguments. But, Sir, I have no doubt but they have a solid reason for entering into this prosecution—the remuneration they are to receive from the United States If they had told us this was their reason, we should have been better satisfied than with the one advanced.

Another fertile topic of declamation (for it was not argument) has been used—that of invading the rights of the Jury Because we are not willing to permit the conversation of third persons to be given, we are charged with attempting to take from the Jury their right to hear testimony! How is this to be judged of—can they lay their hand on one solitary law or precedent where any other than the Court is to decide this point? They cannot. The Jury have nothing to do with irrelavant testimony: we must address ourselves to the Court on it, and they must judge; otherwise a witness or a prosecutor would be tolerated to say any thing, and the Jury be condemned to hear it. There is one seeming fact: gentlemen have been satisfied that they must convict the accused, and they have supposed every means to be lawful for the attainment of that desirable end! And is an accused person to be judged guilty (as is insinuated) because he does not choose to sit still and let the attorney go to every length that he pleases? Where is a case in the books like it? I trust that this will be held up as a beacon to shew to what a situation the counsel on the other side have endeavored to run the country into

As to one of the general propositions that Col. Burr began, set on foot, and procured the means of a military expedition. Mr. Wickham thought, the proof ought to be exhibited in his procurement of powder, balls, ammunition, &c. after which let it be shewn how far he was a principal in any transactions. This sort of testimony will not be rejected; nay, it has been earnestly invited again and again. But no, they say all this was done in Kentucky in Mississippi terri ory, &c To what purpose is all this—is this Jury competent to near what was done in those districts? By no means. He is guilty or not guilty of committing the crime charged on *Blannerhasset's island.*

But, Sir, said Mr. Wickham, for what is this evidence attempted to be forced upon you? Is it to please the public? It may be so. But are we to set here to perform a *farce* or *comedy* to entertain the public? This Court has no right to hear an iota of evidence which does not relate to the transactions laid in the indictment; and if there was positive proof of the acts charged, but if they occurred out of the district (Virginia) the Jury would be obliged to find a verdict of *not guilty:* consequently one title of testimony of transactions of the district, cannot be received here. Let not a Court of Justice be made the author of newspaper amusement to the public, but let law and justice hold their sacred seat.

Gentlemen had talked about consequences, &c. if Col. Burr should get clear. Let them take the consequences. How came he here for trial? Was it easier to convict him here, than in Mississippi territory or elsewhere? They had the advantage of a Virginia Jury* here it is true, where prejudice enough, as we have seen, prevails universally against him. To which it may not be improper to suppose there might be added a little executive influence. The fact is, that they suppose it to be easier to convict him here, than elsewhere. From whom this sprang, Mr Wickham would not pretend to say: the President and the attorney had both disclaimed it; he could wish however to detect the author. He was brought here, and that without a cause, but the people of the Western country, where these occurrences happened, and who are stated to have had all these proceedings before their eyes, cannot be entrusted with the case? But it was the situation of those gentlemen, as good soldiers, to obey orders, for knowing the alternative of disobedience, they cannot be blamed. However, let them not blame Col. Burr for refusing to hear irrelevant testimony here. He was brought here by a military power, and here they thought proper to commit and to try him, by some authority or other, and for some reason or other.

Mr. *Wickham* next went into the question of a military expedition, and asked whether there had been such a thing " begun and set on foot" on Blannerhasset's island? If there had; he had heard of no evidence to substantiate it; its beginning must have been at a higher place, if there was any thing existing there: but these twenty or thirty men arrived there, stand there a short time, and sat off as they arrived, without the least acquisition of strength! Thus it appeared. It was an expedition truely, but was it military? Nothing like it. The emigration of Mr Blannerhasset with his servant and a couple of guns, are too ridiculous to mention. What were the means provided? None. There is not an iota of evidence to prove that a military expedition was begun, set on foot or carried on at that island.

But this, they say, is a question for the Jury to settle; they must hear the evidence. Not so in this case: they are not to hear evidence out of their own district and charge.

Here, Mr Wickham went to some length into the nature of *derivative* guilt and it's applicancy to the present case. If the guilt was derivative, he insisted that, before the accessary could be tried, there must be evidence that the principal had committed some offence. Blannerhasset and Burr could not be connected in the commission of a crime, if no crime was committed. The guilt of one, if it was of a derivative nature, must depend upon the guilt of the other.

But it was said that Col Burr was on the island. When? Once in the time of his life? Yes he was there, but what it was not then nor on business as we know of, relative to this expedition. No evidence appears of his having done any thing there, or of any thing having been done there at his instigation or to his knowledge.

---

* *Wait for Mr Hay's explanation of the cause at a future period of this case, which must convince the public on this subject*

But Col. Burr's having written a letter to Mr. Blannerhasset on the subject, seems to be enough. This, Mr. Martin has sufficiently answered and illustrated: the principle cannot answer in *criminal* cases. If a criminal act was done by another, by the instigation of a letter, *he* only who did the act would be punishable If the present case could be maintained in any form whatever, it could only be upon the principle of derivative guilt, and, in that view, Mr Burr not having been present, Mr. Blannerhasset must be convicted before the other could be tried. But, being a statuary offence, that person *only* who did the act is punishable He only, who goes on the expedition and commits the act of violence is guilty of hostility, and it would be an absurdity to consider him as an accessary, whilst he, who provides the means or is distantly connected shall be considered principal. Mr. Martin has proved the absurdity of this doctrine. But admit that the act of Mr. Blannerhasset was accessorial, what must Col Burr be? Why the accessary of the accessary, a character unknown in law?

As to the law, Mr. Wickham insisted that if it was incorrectly drawn, or insufficient to its object, it was not the fault of that Court, nor could a Court of justice sit to make laws, it belonged only to Congress But it was well known to all, that laws were continually amending to embrace cases which at first were not seen It would be in vain for a Court of justice to put a case into a law which it did not embrace, as was now attempted to be done he must not escape punishment, the gentlemen think. we say he ought not, if he can be proved to be guilty.

Mr Wirt had relied much on the difference of this case from that of levying war: levying war he had supposed to be an act of a very different nature from preparing the means for a military expedition. Mr. Wickham said that the term, "levying war" was as variegated, and as liable to produce perplexity, *ad infinitum*, as any crime that could be charged, and in what could differ the preparation of means for levying war and the preparation of means for effecting the cruize charged? If force was required in one, force was necessary in the other.

On the subject of the *presence* of the party, being necessary, Mr Wickham made some observations, and quoted 2 Hawkins, 443, ch. 29, Sect 11, where a just principle was laid down. He referred also to deductions drawn from the quotations used from Smith and Ogden's trial and Judge Talmadge's opinion, which he treated with much severity, sarcasm, and derision

The acts and declarations of others are said to be good evidence in cases of this sort. I ask, said Mr. Wickham, if there is a single criminal case, except conspiracy, in which such evidence could be received? No, Sir. We can produce numerous authorities in our favor, when, we say there cannot be evidence of this kind given, and no conspiracy is laid in the indictment. Mr. Botts has justly stated on the subject of preparing a military expedition, that means, mean *means*: that is, the whole means, and not a part, or an insufficient part of the means. They say that unless their construction is taken, the law will lead its provisions to absusdity Be it so, but that would not warrant the Court to alter it We must take it as it is.

What are the means of a military expedition? Military preparation must be made. the law does not say "some of the means," or a " beginning of the means," it is " the means " But whatever means were prepared, or whatever intentions formed for an object, since there was a *locus pænitentiæ*, and he had determined not to do the act, there could be no crime, according to the true genius of our laws, and sound rules of construction. A statute must, according to rule be construed strictly, and certainly not to the injury of an accused person in a criminal case. Let those gentlemen address Congress on the subject, and tell them what an insufficient law they have made, but let not a Court of justice be troubled with what it cannot amend, and not exhibit their anxiety about the escape of a person accused under such a law. I do *yet* say that the party must be able to go on in a *military* character, and it would be mockery to make any thing else of it, or to call in Blannerhasset's aid to assist the prosecution

There is one principal that runs through our whole criminal code, and that is, that no man can be punished for *intention*, or any thing but plain unequivocal *acts*. This is the doctrine of treason in our constitution—*open* and *palpable* acts must be committed

Mr. Wickham then proceeded to his concluding remarks, he must mention one thing which had been very much dwelt on by the counsel on the other side, and that was, respecting *public opinion*, and the feelings of the people How these had been raised it was not difficult to define The eloquence used on this occasion was conspicuous, and could not but make its impression It was not intended, he said, for the Court nor for the Jury, but for the people Mr W hoped the counsel would pardon him, when he declared that he knew the people of this country better than they did, and it was a painful subject to reflect on, that they had so plainly evinced their impressions, not only before the Court but elsewhere

He concluded by referring to the selection of Jurors which had been made, (not that he would even insinuate that the marshal had not faithfully executed his duty,) but certainly there was a selection of some of the most violent men in the country placed on the pannels, indeed many of them came forward and disqualified themselves by their own declarations This was a lamentable state of the justice to be expected in this case, and it therefore requires all the exertion that could be made to do that justice, which the nature of the case required He assured the counsel on the other side that he meant no disrespect to them in any thing said or done

Mr *Hay* I certainly did not invite the observations which have been so profusely bestowed This severity was unprovoked. Some of the remarks which have fallen from the gentleman last up, were of such a serious nature, that I will venture to say, that they were not what I think *justice* and *propriety* make necessary I did believe, and do believe that every thing said of a personal nature was *unwarrantable* and *unjust*

Mr *Wickham* Not a single remark was intended to apply to the gentleman personally, but I will remark on such part of the

gentleman's arguments as my business leads me to It is their *arguments* and not their *motives* that I attack, so far as decency will
permit

MONDAY, *September* 14.

Mr Hay made some few remarks in allusion to what had dropt
from Mr Wickham, immediately after which the Chief Justice
delivered the following opinion Judge Griffin was absent.

The United States,	}	*On a Misdemeanor*
vs		
Aaron Burr,	}	

The present motion is particularly directed against the admission of the testimony of Neale, who is offered for the purpose
of proving certain conversations between himself and Herman
Blannerhasset It is objected that the declarations of Herman
Blannerhasset are at this time inadmissible on this indictment

The rule of evidence which rejects mere hearsay testimony,
which excludes from trials of a criminal or civil nature the declarations of any other individual, than of him against whom
the proceedings are instituted, has been generally deemed all essential to the correct administration of justice I know not why
a declaration in Court should be unavailing, unless made upon
oath, if a declaration out of Court was to criminate others than
him who made it; nor why a man should have a constitutional
claim to be confronted with the witnesses against him, if mere
verbal declarations, made in his absence, may be evidence against
him I know of no principle in the preservation of which all are
more concerned I know none, by undermining which, life,
liberty and property, might be more endangered It is therefore
incumbent on Courts to be watchful of every inroad on a principle
so truely important

This rule as a general rule is permitted to stand, but some ex-
ceptions to it have been introduced, concerning the extent of
which a difference of opinion prevails, and that difference produces the present question.

The first exception is, that in cases of conspiracy, the acts,
and it is said by some, the declarations of all the conspirators,
may be given in evidence on the trial of any one of them, for the
purpose of proving the conspiracy, and this case it is alleged,
comes within the exception

With regard to this exception, a distinction is taken in the
books between the admissibility and operation of testimony,
which is clear in point of law, but not at all times easy to practice in fact It is, that although this testimony be admitted, it is
not to operate against the accused, unless brought home to him
by testimony drawn from his own declarations or his own conduct

But the question to be considered is, does the exception comprehend this case ? Is this a case of conspiracy according to the
well established law meaning of the term ?

Cases of conspiracy may be of two descriptions.

1st. Where the conspiracy is the crime, in which case the crime is complete although the act should never be formed, and in such cases if several be indicted, and all except one be acquitted, that one cannot, say the books, be convicted, because he can not conspire alone.

2d Where the crime consists in the intention, and is proved by a conspiracy, so that the conviction of the accused may take place upon evidence, that he has conspired to do an act which manifests the wicked intention.

In both these cases an act is not essential to the completion of the crime, and a conspiracy is charged in the indictment as the ground of accusation If the conspiracy be the sole charge, as it may be, the question to be decided, is, not whether the accused has committed any particular fact, but whether he has conspired to commit it Evidence of conspiracy in such a case goes directly to support the issue It has therefore been determined that the nature of the conspiracy may be proved by the transactions of any of the conspirators in furtherance of the common design; the degree of guilt however, of the particular conspirator upon trial, must still depend on his own particular conduct

In the case at bar, the crime consists not in intention but in acts The act of Congress does not extend to the secret design, if not carried into open deed, nor to any conspiracy however extensive if it do not amount to a beginning or setting on foot a military expedition. The indictment contains no allusion to a conspiracy, and of consequence the issue to be tried by the Jury, is not whether the conspiracy has taken place, but whether the particular facts charged in the indictment have been committed.

I do not mean to admit, that by any course which might have been given to the prosecution, this could have been converted into a case of conspiracy, but most assuredly if it was intended to prove a conspiracy, and to let in that kind of testimony which is admissible only in such a case, the indictment ought to have charged it

I have not been able to find in the books a single decision, or a solitary dictum which would countenance the attempt that is now made to introduce as testimony the declarations of third persons, made in the absence of the person on trial, under the idea of a conspiracy, where no conspiracy is alleged in the indictment. The researches of the counsel for the prosecution have not been more successful But they suppose this case, though not within the letter, to come clearly within the reasoning of those cases where this testimony has been allowed

It has been said, that wherever the crime may be committed by a single individual, although in point of fact more than one should be concerned in it, as in all cases of felony, the prosecution must be conducted in the usual mode, and the declarations of third persons cannot be introduced at a trial, but whenever the crime requires more than one person, where from its nature it cannot be committed by a single individual, although it shall consist, not in conspiracy, but in open deed, yet it is in the nature of a conspiracy, and evidence of the declarations and acts of third persons connected with the accused, may be received whether the indictment covers such testimony or not

I must confess that I do not feel the force of this distinction. I cannot conceive why, when numbers do in truth conspire to commit an act, as murder or robbery, the rule should be, that the declaration of one of them is no evidence against another, and yet, if the act should require more than one for its commission, that the declarations of one person engaged in the plot would immediately become evidence against another. I cannot perceive the reason of this distinction; but, admitting its solidity, I know not on what ground to dispense with charging in the indictment the combination intended to be proved. If this combination may be proved by the acts or declarations of third persons made in the absence of the accused, because he is connected with those persons; if in consequence of this connexion the ordinary rules of evidence are to be prostrated, it would seem to me that the indictment ought to give some notice of this connexion.

When the terms used in the indictment necessarily imply a combination, it will be admitted that a combination is charged and may be proved. And where A. B. and C. are indicted for murdering D, yet in such a case the declarations of one of the parties made in the absence of the others, have never been admitted as evidence against the others. If then this indictment should even imply that the fact charged was committed by more than one person, I cannot conceive that the declarations of a *particeps criminis* would become admissible on the trial of a person not present when they were made, unless those declarations form a part of the very transaction charged in the indictment.

If in all this I should be mistaken, yet it remains to be proved that the offence charged may not be committed by a single individual. This may, in some measure depend on the exposition of the terms of the act; and it is to be observed that this exposition must be fixed. It cannot vary with the varying aspect of the prosecution at its different stages. If, as has been said, a military expedition is begun or set on foot when a single soldier is enlisted for the purpose, then unless it be begun as well by the soldier who enlists, as by the officer who enlists him, a military expedition may be begun by a single individual. So if those who engage in the enterprize follow their leader from their confidence in him without any knowledge of the real object, there is no conspiracy, and the criminal act is the act of an individual. So too, if *the* means are *any* means, the crime may unquestionably be committed by any individual. Should the term be even so construed as to imply *that* all the means must be provided before the offence can be committed, still all the means may, in many cases, be provided by a single individual. The rule then laid down by the counsel for the prosecution, if correct in itself, would not comprehend this case.

2dly. There are also cases in the books where acts are in their nature joint and where the law attaches the guilt to all concerned in their commission, so that the act of one is in truth the act of others, where the conduct of one person in the commission of the fact constitutes the crime of another person: but this is distinct from conspiracy.

If many persons combine to commit a murder, and all assist in it, and are actually or constructively present, the act of one, is the act of all, and is sufficient for the conviction of all So in acts of levying war, as in the cases of Damane and Purchase, the acts of the mob were the acts of all in the mob whose conduct showed a concurrence in those acts, and in the general design which the mob were carrying into execution But these decisions turn on a distinct principle from conspiracy The crime is a joint crime, and all those who are present aiding in the commission of it participate in each others actions, and in the guilt attached to those actions The conduct of each contributes to shew the nature of this joint crime, and declarations made during the transaction are explanatory of that transaction, but I cannot conceive that in either case declarations unconnected with the transaction would have been evidence against any other than the person who made them, or persons in whose presence they were made If, for example, one of several men who had united in committing a murder should have said, that he with others contemplated the fact which was afterwards committed, I know of no case which would warrant the admission of this testimony upon the trial of a person who was not present when the words were spoken. So if Damane had previously declared that he had entered into a confederacy for the purpose of pulling down all meeting houses, I cannot believe that this testimony would have been admissible against a person having no knowledge of the declaration and giving no assent to it

In felony the guilt of the principal attaches to the accessary, and therefore the guilt of the principal is proved on the trial of the accessary In treason, all are principals, and the guilt of him who has actually committed the treason does, in England attach to him who has advised, aided or assisted that treason Consequently the conduct of the person who has perpetrated the fact must be examined on the trial of him who has advised or procured it But in misdemeanors by statute, where the commission of a particular fact constitutes the only crime punished by the law, I believe there is no case where the declaration of a *particeps criminis* can affect any but himself

3dly The admission of the declarations of Mr. Blannerhasset may be insisted upon under the idea he was the agent of Col B How far the acts of one man may affect another criminally, is a subject for distinct consideration, but I believe there is no case, where the words of an agent can be evidence against his principal on a criminal prosecution Could such testimony be admissible, the agency must be first clearly established, not by the words of the agent, but by the acts of the principal, and the word must be within the power previously shown have been given

The opinions of the circuit court of New-York in trials of Smith and Ogden have been frequently mentioned Although I have not the honor to know the Judge who gave those decisions, I consider them as the determination of a Court of the United States, and I shall not be lightly induced to disregard them, or unnecessarily to treat them with disrespect I do not however in the opinions of Judge Talmadge, perceive any expression indicating that the declarations of third persons could be received as testimony against any individual who was prosecuted under this act If he has given that opinion, it has certainly escaped my notice, and has not been suggested to me by counsel He unquestionably says in page 113 of the trial " that the reference which was made to the doctrine of conspiracy did not apply in that case " The reference alluded to was the observation of Mr Emmet who had said " that if the object was to charge Col Smith with the acts of Capt Lewis, they ought to have laid the indictment for a conspiracy " The opinion of the Judge that the doctrine of conspiracy had no application to the case, appears to me to be perfectly correct

I feel therefore no difficulty in deciding, that the testimony of Mr Neale, unless he can go further than merely stating the declarations made to him by Blannerhasset, is at present inadmissible.

But the argument has taken a much wider range The points made, comprehend the exclusion of other testimony suggested by the attorney for the United States, and the opinion of the Court upon the operation of testimony As these subjects are entirely distinct, and as the object of the motion is the exclusion of testimony supposed to be illegal, I shall confine my observations to that part of the argument which respects the admissibility of evidence of the description of that proposed by the attorney for the United States

The indictment charges the accused in separate counts with beginning, with setting on foot, with preparing, and with providing the means for a military expedition to be carried on against a nation at peace with the United States Any legal testimony which applies to any one of these counts is relevant — That which applies to none of them must be irrelevant

The expedition. the character and object of that expedition, that the defendant began it. that he set it on foot, that provided and prepared the means for carrying it on, are all charged in the indictment, and consequently these charges may be all supported by any legal testimony But that a military expedition was begun and set on foot by others, or that the means were prepared or provided by others, is not charged in this indictment, is not a crime which is or can be alledged against the defendant, and testimony to that effect is therefore not relevant.

All testimony which serves to show the expedition to have been military in its character, as far, for instance, testimony respecting their arms and provisions, no matter by whom purchased, their conduct, no matter by whom directed, or who was present, all legal testimony which serves to show the object of the expedition, as would be either actually marching against Mexico, any public declarations made among themselves stating Mexico as their object, any manifesto to this effect, any agreement entered into by them for such an expedition, these or similar acts would be received to show the object of the expedition

In trials of Smith and Ogden they were received Whether the particular acts of the accused on which his guilt or innocence depends, must precede this species of testimony or may be preceded by it, is a question which merely respects the order of evidence There can be no doubt but that at some stage of the prosecution, either before or after the particular part performed by the accused has been shown, the character and object of the expedition may be shown. and that by any legal testimony caculated to develope that character and object. Whether this testimony is admissible before the proof which particularly applies to the part performed by the accused, or ought to be introduced by first proving that part, is a question which is not made in this case and which was not made in the case of Smith and Ogden In that case it was certainly entirely unimportant, and it is probably not less so in this

It has been also contended that the acts no more than the declarations of third persons can be given in evidence on this indictment

It has been already said that those acts of equipment which go to show the character of the expedition may be given in evidence If, for example, Blannerhasset, Tyler, Smith, or any other persons provided arms, amunition or provisions which were applied to the armament, this would be evidence because it would show the character of the expedition This was done in the case of Smith and Ogden without enquiring who provided the arms, for they belonged to the expedition Captain Lewis for instance, purchased several military equipments It was not deemed necessary to show that Smith was connected with Lewis, for these purchases were made for the expedition, and Smith was not charged with providing them. He was charged with providing other means, and the means provided by Lewis served to show the character of the expedition

But although the acts of all persons providing means applied to the expedition may be given in evidence upon the same principle that the state of the expedition may be shown, it does not follow that other acts of third persons may be given in evidence

It has also been contended that no transactions out of the district are testimony.

This position is correct to a considerable extent, but not to the extent in which it is laid down A declaration of Mr. Burr for example made in Kentucky or elsewhere, that he did set on foot a military expedition on Blannerhasset's island to be carried on against the dominions of the king of Spain while the United States were at peace with that power, would I think be evidence, so would the actual marching of the troops proved to be raised by him against the province of Mexico Testimony which goes directly to prove the indictment, may I think be drawn from any place

But I do not understand this to be the point really in contest. I understand the counsel of the United States to insist that providing means in Kentucky, that enlisting men in Kentucky, that joining the expedition in Kentucky, may be given in evidence to to show that the accused did begin and set on foot the expedition in Blannerhasset's island, or did provide the means at that place as charged in the indictment. This I understand to be the great question which divides the prosecution and defence

It is I believe a general rule that in criminal prosecutions a distinct crime for which a prosecution may be instituted cannot be given in evidence in order to render it more probable that the particular crime charged in the indictment was committed. If gentlemen think me wrong in this, I will certainly hear them upon the point, but I believe the position to be correct. Now providing the means for a military expedition in Kentucky to be carned on against the dominions of a prince with whom the United States are at peace, is certainly in itself a distinct offence upon which an indictment may be well supported as it can be or providing means for the same or a similar expedition in Virginia— According to the rule laid down then, this testimony cannot be received unless it goes to prove directly the charges contained in the indictment   But how can it go directly to prove those charges? Does it follow that the man who has provided the means in Kentucky has also provided the means in Virginia? Certainly it does not follow, and consequently the acts alleged in Kentucky do not prove the charges contained in the indictment — They would prove the defendant to have been connected in the enterprize, and gentlemen argue as if they thought this sufficient for their purpose   I shall be excused if I employ a few moments in stating my reasons for thinking it not sufficient

I have already said, and surely no man will deny, that two distinct persons may, at different places furnish different means for the same enterprize   It will, I presume, not be contended that one of them may be indicted for the means provided by the other.   So too, if the same man shall provide means for the enterprize at different places, as in Virginia and Kentucky   I do not imagine that an indictment for providing arms in Virginia, could be supported by proving that he provided ammunition in kentucky   They are distinct offences for either of which he may be punished, and the commission of the one may render more probable, but does not prove the commission of the other

How then do gentlemen mean to make this testimony more relevant?   It is by making the acts of Blannerhasset, Tyler and Smith, the acts of Burr, by insisting that their acts show an unlawful expedition to have been begun by him in Virginia, or that the means for that expedition were provided by him in Virginia   This being accomplished, his acts in Kentucky may be adduced to corroborate or confirm the testimony which discloses his conduct in Virginia.

As preliminary then to this testimony, such proof of the specific charges contained in the indictment must be given, as may be left to the consideration of the jury

This proof relates to place as well as to fact.—" Of whatsoever nature an offence indicted may be," says Hawkins B 2. Ch 25 Sec 35 " whether local or transitory, as seditious words or battery, &c   it seems to be agreed that if upon not guilty pleaded it shall appear that it was committed in a country different from that in which the indictment was found, the defendant shall be acquitted."

This rule is the stronger in the United States where it is affirmed by the constitution itself, and where the jurisdiction of the court is limited to offences within the district.   Its obligation therefore is complete

If there be any direct testimony that an expedition was begun, or set on foot, or that the means were provided or prepared in Virginia, that testimony has not yet been heard so far as I recollect   If there be such testimony it must also be shown that the expedition was begun or that the means were prepared by the accused   No single act of his in Virginia has been offered in evi dence —He made a contract in the state of Ohio for boats and provisions, which may have been intended as a part of the expedition, but no contract appears to have been made in Virginia, nor were the boats constructed or provisions procured in Virginia — How then is it to appear that he begun or set on foot a military expedition in Virginia, or that he provided or prepared the means for such an expedition.

It is said, that if he gave orders from Kentucky or elsewhere, and in consequence of those orders, the means were provided in Virginia, the accused is within the letter of the act, as well as its spirit, and has himself provided the means in Virginia

If these orders were in proof, the Court as well as the counsel would be enabled to view the subject with more accuracy and to treat it with more precision. Since those orders are not adduced, nor accurately stated, and the question has been argued without them, the Court must decline giving any opinion, or consider the orders as offered, and say what orders would be admissible and what inadmissible. The latter course may save the bar the trouble of another argument

To whom are orders supposed to have been given, and who are supposed to have executed them?

They must have been given to accomplices or to those who had no share in the expedition

The accomplices, under the direction of Col Burr, have provided the means. Can their liability to the penalties of the law be doubted? I presume not. If persons engaged in the expedition have provided the means for carrying it on, it will, I presume be admitted, that they are within the letter and the spirit of the act. Each man has himself provided and prepared, those particular means which he has furnished. If Col Burr, as was the case with Col Smith, has supplied money for the expedition, then money may be charged as the means provided by him, but if that money was advanced to an accomplice, its investment in means for the expedition is the act of the accomplice, for which being a free agent, he is himself responsible. The accomplice has committed the very act which the law furnishes. Has the accused by suggesting or procuring that act, also committed it?

I will not say how far the rule, that penal laws must be construed strictly, may be carried without incurring the censure of disregarding the sense of the legislature. It may however be safely affirmed that the offence must come clearly within the description of the law according to the common understanding of the terms employed, or it is not punishable under the law. Now to do an act, or to advise or procure an act, or to be connected or leagued with one who does that act, are not the same in either law, language, or in common parlance, and if they are not the same, a penalty affixed to the one, is not necessarily affixed to the other. The penalty affixed to the act of providing the means for a military expedition, is not affixed to the act of advising or procuring those means to be provided, or of being associated with the man who has provided them. The distinction made by the law between these persons, is well settled, and has been too frequently urged to require further explanation. The one is a principal, the other an accessary. In all misdemeanors punishable, only by a statute which describes as the sole offender, the person who commits the prohibited act, the one is within and the other not within the statute. In passing the act under consideration, Congress obviously contemplated this distinction. I presume that in a prosecution under the 3d section, for fitting out a privateer, it would not be alleged, that a person who was concerned with the man who actually fitted out the privateer, but who performed no act himself, could be convicted on an indictment, not for being concerned in fitting out the privateer, but in actually fitting her out. These are stated in that section as separate offences.

This distinction taken in the law is well understood, and cannot be considered as overlooked by those who frame penal acts. They cannot be considered as intending to describe one offender when they describe another, and if experience suggests defects in the penal code, the legislature exclusively judges how far those defects are to be remedied.

While expounding the terms of the act, it may not be improper to notice an argument advanced by the attorney for the United States which was stopped by my observing that he had not correctly understood the opinion delivered in the case of treason. He understood that opinion as approving the doctrine laid down by Keeling and Hale, that an accessary before the fact might plead in bar of an indictment as accessary, that he had been acquitted as principal, whence it was inferred that on an indictment for doing an act, evidence of advising or producing that act might be received. I was certainly very far from approving this doctrine. On the contrary I declare it to contradict every idea I had ever formed on the subject. But if it were correct, I endeavored to show that it could not effect that case. My disapprobation of the doctrine induced me to look further into it, and my persuasion that it is not law is confirmed.—Hale v. 2. p. 292, says " if A and B be indicted of the murder of C, upon their evidence it appears that A committed the fact and B was not present but was accessary before the fact by commanding it, B shall be discharged."

In H. 2. ch 85 sec 11 Hawkings discusses the subject, shows in a note the contradiction in those authorities which maintain the doctrine, cites the opposing authorities, and obviously approves the opinion which i. here given. It is apparent then, that the law never considers the commission and the procurement of an act, even where both are criminal, as the same act.

I cannot therefore consider means provided by those who are his accomplices in the expedition, as means provided by Col Burr.

If the means were provided by order of the accused, by persons not accomplices and not guilty under the act, the law may be otherwise. I shall not exclude such testimony. There is, however some doubt whether the place of trial should be where the orders were given, or where they were executed.

At common law, if an act was procured or advised at one place, and executed at another, it was doubted whether the procurer could be tried at either place because the offence was not complete at either. This difficulty was removed by a statute made in the reign of Edward 6th. If there be testimony showing by orders from the accused, means were provided in Virginia by a person not an accomplice, it may be received, and the question respecting the scene of trial put in way for a final decision.

The question whether all the means must be provided before the offence described in the statute has been committed, relates to the effect rather than to the exclusion of the testimony. I shall certainly not reject any evidence which shows that any means *were provided by the accused in the place charged in the indictment*

Upon the subject of beginning and setting on foot a military expedition or enterprize, it would be unnecessary at this time to say any thing, were it not on the account of the question respecting the introduction of testimony of the district

What is an expedition? What is an enterprize?

An expedition, if we consult Johnston is "a march or voyage with martial intentions" In this sense, it does not mean the body which marches, but the march itself The term is, however, sometimes employed to designate the armament itself, as well as the movement of that armament

An enterprize is "an undertaking of hazard, an arduous attempt" The proper meaning of this word also describes the general undertaking and not the armament with which that undertaking is to be accomplished.

The first count in the indictment charges, that Burr began the expedition in Blannerhasset's island The 2d and 3d, that he set on foot the enterprize on Blannerhasset's island

If the term expedition is to be taken in its common and direct sense, that is to mean a march or voyage with martial intentions, it began where that march or voyage begun, and it must have been begun by the accused to bring him within the act

If the term be taken in its figurative sense to designate the armament instead of the movement of the armament, then I cannot readily conceive an act which begins an expedition, unless the same act may also be said to provide the means of an expedition The formation of the plan in the mind, is not the commencement of the expedition within the act Our laws punish no mental crimes not brought into open deed The disclosure of that plan does not begin it If it did, the first disclosure would be the beginning, I find a difficulty in conceiving any act which amounts to providing the means for an expedition However if there can be such an act, and it has been committed in Virginia, it may certainly be given in evidence

The same observations apply to setting on foot an enterprize

These remarks are made to show what it will be necessary to prove in order to let in corroborative proof

It is then the opinion of the Court, that the declarations of third persons not forming a part of the transaction and not made in the presence of the accused cannot be received in evidence in this case.

That the acts of accomplices, except so far as they prove the character or object of the expedition, cannot be given in evidence

That the acts of the accused, in a different district which constitute in themselves substantive causes for a prosecution can not be given in evidence unless they go directly to prove the charges laid in the indictment

That any legal testimony which shows the expedition to be military or to have been designed against the dominions of Spain may be received

Gentlemen well know how to apply these principles. Should any difficulty occur in applying them, the particular case will be brought before the Court and decided.

After the opinion was delivered, Mr Hay requested a copy of it, and made some observations as to its effect upon the future progress of the trial. He considered that the man who had the supreme command and direction of this military enterprize, (which they could prove it to be) did provide the means and set it on foot. This was a question he thought proper for the consideration of the Jury, and this idea would be strengthened by evidence which could be produced, if permitted.

Mr *Wirt*. The fact is, that Mr. Belknap can prove (as well as others) that he sent orders and did other acts shewing that he was at the head and command of the whole.

Chief Justice. But suppose the connection was proved, (which I have no doubt could be) and suppose the enterprize originated with Col. Burr, (which is very probably the case) others might have provided the means from what could be made to appear. He is not indicted for being connected with the enterprize, but for providing certain specific means.

If the party under Tyler is to be considered as of a military nature, and that an expedition began at Beaver, or where not, if the movement is to be considered as an enlistment of men, then wherever the first movement was made, *there* the expedition began.

I do not think that his taking the command at Cumberland, can be considered as a count in the indictment, it might go to render it more probable, (if there was any doubt as to the transaction) that what was done under his controul; but the act itself must be proved on Blannerhasset's island, and there the intention with which that act was done would come in by proving that he took the command afterwards. But how can he be charged with beginning there, if it should appear that he began in Pennsylvania?

The question of "*beginning*" I do not mean to take from the Jury, of the place of beginning and of the acts themselves, they must decide. An abstract independent question will arise however, which is, whether the witnesses proved the indictment or not? Now I do not think that they did prove the indictment. What might be done is a future question.

Mr *Wirt*. Am I to understand, Sir, that the acts of accomplices, out of the district, tending to prove the acts laid in the indictment, may be given in evidence?

Chief Justice. Any act which shews the character of the transaction *itself*, in my opinion may be given.

Mr *Wickham* I understand the opinion of the Court to be, that he cannot be liable for the acts of others, though done within the district, no auxiliary acts can be given against us, and they are not entitled to go out of the district to show acts done elsewhere, against us?

Mr *M'Rae* If we shall offer evidence, that will be proper to submit to a Jury, to prove where he did commence this enterprize, at any period whatever, it is not necessary that we should show that he remained on Blannerhasset's island all the time

But seeing the enterprize was actually commenced, we shall be able to satisfy a Jury, that when Burr was on the island, he did there actually project it, and did agree with Blannerhasset as to its progress, which was afterwards carried on, we ought certainly then to be at liberty to go out of the district to show that he was the principal person concerned in it; I do not suppose it necessary for us to show that *all* the means were provided by him

Chief Justice. There is one doubt which I had at the commencement of this case (which I do not now suggest to make a question of) it relates to the indictment, and consequently to a particular part of the evidence, particularly to the words of the statute " beginning and setting on foot an expedition " I do doubt whether it is not necessary to show in the indictmen how the expedition was begun I do not know that it is necessary to set forth the principal means in the indictment It is, in itself, an extremely vague term, but if it is a necessary one, surely the particular manner of beginning must be showed. I think however it ought to be laid in the indictment, and if so, that is a strong reason why it ought to be shewn by evidence.

The counsel on both sides were ordered to be furnished with copies of the opinion, and the Court adjourned to Tuesday ten o'clock'.

TUESDAY, *September* 15

Mr. *Hay* said, that the counsel for the prosecution had agreed to go on as well as they could, for that they had drawn such a construction from the opinion as to excite them to suppose that they had sufficient evidence yet remaining, to produce a conviction of the person accused, without interfering with the opinion of the Court He was stating some of the points laid down by the Court, as far as we were able to hear him, (which was extremely difficult) when

Mr. *Botts* interfered to explain what were the limits set by the Court, upon which he dwelt at some length, and repeated most of the arguments before used, as to the absence of Mr. Burr, and the evidence offered respecting conversations held between him and others. Indeed he took a brief review of the whole opinion, and concluded upon the whole, that the absence of Mr. Burr rendered all evidence, which it appeared could be produced irrelevent, none had been offered, and he defied the prosecution to offer a particle —for from the whole review of the opinion, it was not within the compass of the heart of man to produce a conviction.

Mr. *Martin* offered a few observations favorable to the production of any evidence which the prosecution *could* produce if they exceeded the bounds which the Court had justly prescribed, it would then be due time to make objections, on which the Court would determine.

Much desultory conversation ensued, when Richard Neale was again called, and asked whether he was on the island on the night of Blannerhasset's departure

A I was not, I left that country in October, and know nothing of it.

James M'Dowell was then called and sworn

Mr *Burr* stated that this witness was introduced for the purpose of proving an interview between him and the accused at the mouth of Cumberland river, when the accused stated to him the object of the expedition

The witness commenced his evidence by saying that he should begin up at Wheeling and proceed downwards to Cumberland where he first saw Col Burr, when

Col Burr interrupted him by observing, that he understood that this was offered as corroborative or auxiliary testimony, but auxiliary to what? They ought first to demonstrate acts done at the island, before they attempt to prove what was done, or (what is worse) said, out of the district

Mr *Wirt* went into a review of the opinion to support the propriety of offering this species of evidence, and contended, that before they could come to the substantive charge, they ought to be permitted to shew the parts so nearly attached as this was On this ground was Gen Eaton's testimony admitted, because it bore direct on the charge laid in the indictment, and equally intimate were the acts at Cumberland Under the act of Congress, the charge is providing means, &c Now, was not the assumption of the command of those engaged in this expedition a material article in the means provided or providing? Here was the right to command acknowledged It is not our meaning to say, that there he began the expedition, he provided most of his means elsewhere, but there he met with his men, and there he headed them, (he referred to Vaughen's case) The mouth of Cumberland transaction was one link in the great chain, it commenced perhaps with what occurred between him and General Eaton, and proceeded by degrees till men, arms, &c. were procured, but the superintendence of Burr was discoverable every where; he projected and hastened on the scheme, as will appear The transactions at Cumberland cannot be abstracted more than others of equal importance Such corroborative testimony as that now offered, he contended was even let in in capital cases, and could not be excluded without manifest injustice to the prosecution, because of its very intimate connection with the whole There was a wide difference between a mere connection, and a man having the sovereign command of a criminal transaction, (as was now attempted to be proved) The beginning was with General Eaton —the consummation was to be some where else It would be proved that Burr not only began, but brought the thing about so far as it went; he was the life and prime mover of the whole Mr Wirt went into some reasoning and elucidation of the propriety of this evidence, though it was no positive proof of his guilt under the indictment, yet he insisted it was strong circumstantial evidence, that these means were his means, and that the evidence was within the meaning of the Court as far as he understood the opinion

Mr *Botts* expressed his extreme surprize at the light in which the gentleman had represented the opinion of the Court: he made some strong strictures on Mr. Wirt's representations of it, and admired the Judge's patience to sit there and hear it He then quoted some parts of the opinion and made some strong eulogistic remarks upon it, after which he compared it with the point in dispute: as to Burr's presence, &c (which has so often been the topic)

It was stated to be one continued act Be it so ; let it be supposed to be an act of unanimity and continuity, and how would it then stand ? a distinct offence was charged to have been committed by Col Burr on the island, but instead of its being done by him, on the island, it appeared to have been done by others, and evidence of words used elsewhere were brought as corroborative, to prove what was done where he was not ' by what kind of ingenuity could any thing done at Cumberland be transported to Blannerhasset's island, where the act, though laid there, was already disproved ?

Chief Justice I certainly should not have sat so patiently to hear the elaborate arguments which were offered, if I had not had a hope that the opinion which was afterwards delivered would have settled the point · an opinion which I thought was given so clear as to render it unnecessary to give another opinion upon the same point It appears to me now that it would be unnecessary were it not for the vaguity of the law, and different understandings of gentlemen as to the terms " beginning and setting on foot" an *expedition* They vary in opinion amazingly on those terms

Now what is " beginning ?" there must be some definitive meaning affixed to the word, or I do not know how a Court is to act upon the law It means something, or else it is too vague for a Court to punish those who have committed the act, or are the subjects of prosecution As I before stated, an *expedition* must mean one of two things, it must indicate the march of a military force or army from one place to another, or it must be considered as a military armament substantively Now its natural and direct meaning must be the *movement* of a military armament, and not the *armament* itself Now when this movement takes place the expedition is said to begin ; the march is said to have commenced

But the word also means an *armament that moves*, rather than the movement of that armament However, I did not undertake to decide this question of the meaning, because I wished not to fix a positive meaning to terms when they relate to a law that may possibly undergo a revision, particularly when I had no precedent nor assistance in it

But if it be the movement of an armament itself, when that armament existed as such, then, I said before I could not distinguish between providing the means of that armament and the beginning of it I cannot conceive what it is, nor can I conceive any *fact* that will amount to a " beginning" this armament, unless it is in the provision of *the means*, or of *some* means Furnishing money or enlisting men may be considered as providing means This, then, must be beginning the expedition

It *must* either mean this, or it must mean the march If it means the march, then the expedition was brought down by Mr Tyler from Beaver where they first assembled and afterwards rested at Blannerhasset's island whence they proceeded lower down If it be expedition and the meaning of the word is the march of the armament, then the proof is positive that it did not begin at Blannerhasset's island. If the meaning is the *provision* of the armament, then the beginning of the expedition is the place where the first means were provided. Taking then, the word in one or the other meaning, it certainly appears to me that the testimony produced by the attorney of the United States disproves his own charge for that it was not begun on Blannerhasset's island, where the charge is laid in the indictment. The beginning, then, is out of the question.

The question then is, whether the means were *provided* or not on Blannerhasset's island. If there be any testimony that go to prove this, I certainly am not at liberty to refuse it. But gentlemen will consider whether they are not wasting the time and money of the United States, and of all those persons who are forced to attend here, whilst they are producing such a mass of testimony which does not bear upon the cause.

Any arguments on the principle which was stated, that the testimony respecting means provided elsewhere, supporting this charge, I am willing to hear. If the opinion of the Court before given can be proved to be erroneous, I shall be very happy to hear it pointed out, because I wish to be as correct as possible : but if these principles are not erroneous, why do gentlemen bring witnesses forward in direct opposition to them? I can ascribe no other reason to it, than because the law does not give definitive ideas on the subject of its own provisions.

The truth is, the words of the law must be taken to retrospect to the origination of the plan. For instance, General Eaton states that in Washington the accused laid before him a certain plan, when he said that he had sufficient means, &c. Now, if those means could be discovered, it certainly shews that the beginning of this expedition was in Washington, but the indictment states it to be on Blannerhasset's island.

Now, unless the fact itself shall be proved, how can there be evidence given of motives, yet undiscovered?

Mr *Hay* seriously regretted that he had not understood the opinion of the Court, but he had one consolation that opinions and arguments were daily misunderstood. Some difficulty, however, he begged leave to observe was foreseen on this head. He did not mean to censure the Court for it.

This he observed, was a new law, on which there had been no judicial decisions, and therefore he possibly might be incorrect in his opinion of its provisions, but yet, none of the arguments which he had heard, had shaken his first ideas, that under its provisions a prosecution could be maintained in any part of the United States, where means were found to have been provided for an expedition of the nature charged, against the person who was providing those means. The assembling at Cumberland he had thought ought to be given in evidence, to prove that Burr was the actual provider of the means which were obtained at Blannerhasset's island.

Mr. Botts had used strong expressions as to his observations, Mr. Hay said, of the opinion of the Court. He could assure the Court, that he meant no disrespect, and shew to the Court how far he was disposed to submit to its opinion, he should enter a *nolle prosique*

The *Chief Justice* observed, that he did not take any observa tions made to be disrespectful, but he certainly must express his surprize, that he had been misunderstood. The fact is, gentlemen, have mistaken those vague terms in the law "beginning and setting on foot," for the very instant they came to apply the facts to the case, they are under the absolute necessity of flying to these words

Col. Burr I understand that the gentlemen on the part of the prosecution proposes to enter a *nolle prosique* It is a principle that I do not understand, when a Jury is sworn I feel myself entitled to the verdict of a Jury

Mr. Hay This is not the time for either

Mr. Wickham confessed that he was incapable to offer any argument on the subject, because the opinion of the Court had completely absorbed it already, after a very lengthy discussion, the Court had already said, that for the acts of Blannerhasset and Smith, Col. Burr was not answerable, and that he, not being on the island, could not be a participent in their conduct Admit then, that he was the prime mover of the whole transaction, and that all that was provided and done on the island was at his in stigation, still, except he *himself* did provide the means *there*, though done by procurement elsewhere, it would not do

Chief Justice If there are any testimony to be given as to pro viding means for the expedition on Blannerhasset's island, let it come forward.

Mr. Hay then called *Dudley Woodbridge*. He asked him to state what were the provisions specified in the contract, as to the boats, provisions, &c

Mr. Botts asked where the contract was made.

Mr. Woodbridge. In Marietta

Mr. Botts That is enough—not a word more

Mr. Wickham If Mr. Woodbridge can state any act done on Blannerhasset's island, or in Virginia, then the Court will have it as testimony, but if the counsel for the United States go to acts done *out* of Virginia, the exception falls within the opinion

Chief Justice I understand that Mr. Woodbridge was not concerned at all in the expedition, but an agent of Mr. Burr. How far Mr. Woodbridge acted in that agency, and how far he acted respecting the contract in Blannerhasset's island, as well as the question whether and how far Mr. Burr is answerable from the evidence, are questions yet left open. The reason was, that under the common law, if any man procured an act to be done, in one place, (or district) and it was done in another, there was a dispute as to its application (see statute 2, and 3, of Edward 6) For instance, if Burr had written a letter in Kentucky, directing provision to be made for a military expedition on Blannerhasset's island, the opinion has not determined to refuse such testimony. it will afterwards be so placed, perhaps as to suit the indictment,

Mr. Hay Who composed the company in Marietta, of which you were a part?

Mr. Woodbridge Mr Blannerhasset and myself?

Q. Did not Mr. Burr provide some kiln dried meal?

A. Yes, he had a quantity sent to where these boats were built. it was brought down with the boats, and was taken with the boats.

Mr *Burr.* Who was it taken by?

Witness It was taken by Gen Bewell, I believe. It was sent to mill as I understood, near where the boats were built. It was dried I believe, on the island; some of it was purchased, but it was some of it of his own raising?

Q Were yourself and Mr Blannerhasset equally authorized and engaged in the purchase of kiln dried meal?

A Yes, we were in partnership, and what we did was so far connected

Chief Justice Where was the meal taken?

A On the Muskingum

Mr *Burr.* Was the corn carried into the company books?

A No Sir, not that I know of, I never had any thing to do with the corn.

Q Was you not the ostensible person as to purchases, &c.?

A I was, but I understood he had purchased some corn, I kept the books and general transactions of the business

Q Was this corn brought into the account at the close of your business with Mr Blannerhasset?

A No, Sir, I only kept the accounts of our partnership transactions, this was not a concern on the partnership account

Peter Taylor, was then called to prove what he knew of the purchase, &c of the corn by Blannerhasset

Mr. *Botts* Well, suppose Mr Blannerhasset did purchase some corn, this purchase is irrelevant to our present case· we have nothing to do with *his* transactions, unless it was a part of the charge now made

Chief Justice Perhaps it is not very important. For the acts of Blannerhasset, he himself only is answerable. I suppose that the intention is to make out that this purchase was made for the purpose charged and therefore not specially his own

Witness Mr. Blannerhasset did buy some corn, and I took some corn after that to some mills on the Muskingum and on the Kenhawa, and the Muskingum, both of them, and it was afterwards brought back from both mills to the island?

Mr. *Burr* What become of this meal?

A. Why it was left at the island, and the Kenhawa to it, as I suppose

Q Did those who went down the river take any meal along with them in the boats?

A. I cannot tell—I was otherwise employed.

Mr. *Hay* observed, that he perceived it to be impossible to proceed without meeting at every turn, such opposition as it was impossible to combat He saw no other way to get rid of the difficulty than by discharging the Jury, since the opinion of the Court had precluded him from managing the case in his own way. If the law was incomprehensible in its nature, how could it be expected to be comprehended here He well knew that it was a rule of law for the Jury to give a verdict, but he had also known a case where a Jury had been discharged, even where the life of a person was at hazard. He referred to a case He believed that the vaguity of the act of Congress, as it was represented, must arise more from a want of its being well understood, than from the insufficiency of its words to explain itself, and yet the prose cution was charged with ignorance of the law under which they prosecuted ! The opinion of the Court met them every where they turned, and it seemed to be impossible to proceed He quoted Foster p 327, 8. to shew that after a Jury was impannelled, it might be drawn or discharged at the discretion of the Court

He was led to this mode of proceeding by the consideration, that the law under which this indictment was formed, was vague in its terms, in some measure It may be replied that it was our business to understand it Now, if the law itself is vague and uncertain, how can we be supposed to understand it better than others ?

The present Jury might be discharged, and if any thing more can hereafter be discovered, the prosecution may be recommenced at a future day He would submit the subject to the Court

Mr *Burr* spoke a few words in opposition to the wish of the attorney to withdraw the Jury.

Mr *Martin* also made a few comments on the quotation of Foster, respecting a *nolle prosique*, observing, that it was entered in consequence of a false charge in the indictment This would not apply upon the present occasion, where the case had gone on

Mr. *Botts* then went into a review of several cases, and made some lengthy remarks on the subject of entering a *nolle prosique* Kinlaw's case, p 28, 30 Locke's Gilbert, 38, 39, 40 and lord Grey's case, were quoted, where a number of reasons and occasions were exhibited for the practice, conjunct settlement, absense of witnesses, &c &c

Mr *Randolph* commenced his argument by an examination into the motion for a *nolle prosique*, which he did not suppose could be entered consistently with rule indeed the Court had decided, that there must be more than ordinary reason for it, after a Jury had been impannelled these reasons he enumerated—Did justice require it? Were the witnesses not to be found? Did the case require it? If it would not be promotive of principles of justice in a particular manner, it ought not to be indulged. He enlarged his argument, but not to public interest.

Mr *Martin* spoke upon the same uninteresting subject of *nolle prosique*, without much elucidation

The *Chief Justice* observed, that he should be willing to discharge the Jury, if he did not see it improper so to do The attorney had a right to do it previous to the Jury being sworn He believed that after the Jury was sworn, both parties in this country, (and he believed in England) had a right to their services, and consequently was entitled to a verdict, particularly in criminal cases This was the common practice, whether it arose from law or not, he had not had time to examine : it was however uniformly the practice in criminal cases, that a Jury could not be withdrawn without mutual consent Indeed he conceived, that the Court could not exercise a discretion on the subject, because the Jury had the case If the attorney failed in his charge or not, it must remain for the Jury to decide The Jury must give a verdict.

The Jury then retired with the indictment, and after an absence of about twenty minutes Mr Orris Payne, their foreman, returned with the verdict of " *not guilty.*"

Mr. *Hay* then announced the course which he was now to pursue, Mr Burr was not yet discharged from his recognizance for misdemeanor, that it was his intention to move for his commitment to that place for trial, where the military expedition is said to have been completed, that he should combine in the same motion Messrs Smith and Blannerhasset, and that he should have no difficulty in entering a *nolle prosique* to their trials for misdemeanor

Mr *Burr* requested the attorney to alledge the place where the act is said to have been committed

Mr *Hay* replied, that the evidence he should introduce would cover a vast extent of territory, that he would name if he could the very spot

Mr *Burr*   The district then

Mr *Hay*   I do not distinctly recollect the opinion of the Court, but I believe it will be proved that troops were assembled at the mouth of Cumberland river, and down the Mississippi to Bayou Pierre, in a warlike posture   It is not my business to locate the scene   It will be the province of the Court, after they have heard the evidence, to fix the place where he is to be tried   I wish to produce the evidence

Mr *Martin* mentioned the case of John Smith of Ohio   but an arrangement was made.

Mr *Wickham* mentioned the case of Jonathan Dayton   Mr. Hay observed, that he did not think himself justified in entering a *nolle prosique* as that would discharge him from his recognizance and he was not certain but some evidence would occur in the course of the examination which would induce him to combine Mr Dayton in his motion for commitment   that he had no doubt that Mr D was leagued in the general conspiracy, and if he had any, the similarity of the hand-writing of the letter he had in his hand (Gen Dayton's) with some he had previously seen, would have satisfied his mind

Mr *Wickham* then proposed, that Mr Hay should enter a *nolle prosique* and that Gen D should continue his recognizance: which Mr Hay acquiesced

---

WEDNESDAY, *September* 16

Col Burr commenced this day by expressing a wish, before the enquiry farther was proceeded in, lest he should either appear ignorant of his rights, or as having abandoned them, to state that it was now in his full power to put an end to all further enquiry in the case, because there was nothing legally against him   but as it was yet stated that there were acts of war, &c. committed somewhere, and that others were concerned in it, he was willing to wave his right, and indulge the gentlemen to pursue their enquiry if they pleased, to give all *relevant* testimony, which they had boldly said it was in their power to produce — if they should, however, wander from the line drawn by the court, and the subject before the Court, they must indulge him bringing them back   But he must give notice that in the farther proceeding, he should enquire for the two letters, of which so much enquiry had been made, of the 21st of October and 12th

November , the former, he believed, had been put in the hands of the clerk, but with respect to the latter, he was not satisfied the Court ought to make no question how to proceed on it

Again. It appeared to be intended to bring on the examination of three persons at once (himself, Mr Blannerhasset, and Mr Israel Smith.) This must evidently tend to produce confusion. he had a right to demand a separate examination, otherwise the inconvenience would be manifest, in as much as one man's charges might be placed to the account of another Now the cases were so palpably different ; the charges so remote, and the circumstances so variant, that each must involve different principles, and must consequently consume time, instead of saving it, which was the object professed

Further, he had a right to demand a specification of the charges intended to be laid Where was the right, by the law or constitution, to detain him, he asked, without some specific charge Suppose, said he, I had demanded my discharge last even g, you could not have kept me here to answer to any thing without a warrant , and that warrant must specify some supposed crime and place where committed It is to be supposed that I am to travel in my imagination, from Maine to Orleans ? No sir, I demand a specification of my charge

Mr. Martin and the Chief Justice entered into some remarks on the subject of specification, which is of little importance for the public eye.

Mr Hay said that he had some difficulty as to locating the offence. some had appeared as to jurisdiction, as he had understood, of the mouth of Cumberland river, that spot never having been ceded by Virginia to Kentucky He hoped therefore, that the Court would examine the subject generally If the offence were to be located, it was in the power of the Court. if wrong to send the accused to another district, where there was no doubt of his having levied war.

The only question then was, whether they could be at liberty to introduce the enquiry as to the whole three, or whether they were to be taken one by one , and the examination of the same circumstances to go three times over, which was inevitable in considerable part of it. He did not see the difficulties which Mr. Burr had pointed out to balance this in any degree : since the Court could very easily apply the different testimony to the different persons, and save very much time, both to the Court and to the witnesses who had been so long attending, and who were very much complaining for being so long detained from their homes and their business.

Mr. Wickham declared that the very same motives expressed by Mr. Hay to carry his point, would influence him to make a different conclusion He thought there would be less time taken by separate examinations, because the cases varied so much, and because they had different counsels , a vast many circumstances which must occur in Col. Burr's case, would not require any notice in Mr Blannerhasset's and Mr. Smith's

Mr Hay. The very first witness I shall introduce will implicate the three, and show their connection in the transaction , and that they all embarked in the same undertaking, whatever it might be proved to be

Chief Justice I must be very strongly inclined to save time I think time might be saved by going into the examination of the the three together. I cannot however pretend to know so much as the gentleman who prosecutes ; nor how far the cases can afterwards be divided Let the case however go on as is proposed ; and if it is found in the examination that any confusion is produced, they can be decided At present I do no think it necessary

Mr. *Martin* I must call the attention of the Court to the necessity of a specification before the case can proceed, upon principles of law, and rules of Court, of Justice

Chief Justice That is necessary , and it must be in writing

Mr *Hay* then produced and read the following paper

" The attorney of the United States for the Virginia district, charges Aaron Burr, Herman Blannerhasset, and Israel Smith with treason, in levying war against the United States ; and charges that an overt act of levying war was committed on an island, whose name is not known, at the mouth of Cumberland river, in the state of Kentucky , and that other overt acts of levying war were committed at Bayou Pierre, in the Mississippi Territory and on the Mississippi river, between the places above named

Mr *Burr* I now remark that there will be objections arising to some of this, but at present we will not take notice of it I do not know how far the testimony might be carried I hold my right however to object to the competency of Gen Eaton as a witness at another time

Chief Justice After the testimony is gone through, objections to any part of the testimony will be open to either party, on a motion for that purpose

The attorney then called James M'Dowel, who gave the following testimony ·

In December I was at Wheeling. and engaged with one William Dean to go down the river to New-Orleans to take down a boat loaded with Flour and Whiskey. We went down the river with the boat from Wheeling to Shawnee-Town . and here I saw Mr Blannerhasset, Smith, Tyler, and many others From that place we went down to the mouth of Cumberland river in company with these gentlemen [Mr Hay Where is Shawnee Town ? A It is below Blannerhasset's island.] It was at the mouth of Cumberland I saw Col Burr for the first time We all went up to the beach where he was introduced to us all, and there we formed a ring or circle, where he told us it was not a proper time to divulge his secrets · there were too many bye-standers

Col Tyler and Mr Smith, and Mr Dean and Blannerhasset stood together, and he told Col. Tyler he might tell the gentlemen engaged what he thought proper, and Col Tyler said he would inform the captains of the boats ; for each boat had a captain — Col. Tyler said he would let them know where they were going, when they got to Nautz de Grace (New-Madrid, as some call it) —Mr. Dean sold the boat we went down in to Comfort Tyler and Israel Smith Then we proceeded in going down, till we got to New-Madrid, where we expected to hear some encouragement for going down ; and there we were told by Comfort Tyler, that when we got lower down, they would tell us. They appointed two or three places, but they never saw one fit for it We went down to Bayou Pierre.

Mr. *Burr.* We are now enquiring into an act done at the mouth of Cumberland, as it is stated, and we shall insist that they be confined to it. They have set out to prove an act of war done at the mouth of Cumberland, or some where in Kentucky— let them prove that act agreeably to the charge if they can

Some desultory conversation here occurred (of no interest) between Messrs Burr and Wickham.

Mr *Hay* declared that they could not, with consistency, separate the evidence—and that there was no object in view but consistency in the management of the examination

Mr *Wickham* said he had nothing to do with motives, but that no Court ought to hear testimony that was illegal and irrelevant, the rules of the Court would stand opposed to it, if one of the parties objected to its being produced. There is a manifest reason against it We know very well that every word that is droped in this Court by the witnesses, or by the counsel or by the Judge, is taken down, and published to the world—it circulates every were

This prosecution, we may suppose (from what we have seen) will never be dropt while they can carry it on, in any way that they can assume Although it has failed in this Court, every thing that has occurred will appear and be published in Kentucky, to the prejudice of any trial that can be held there, and Col Burr cannot have a fair trial by Jury there, because the Jury there cannot be unprejudiced after what has and what may be publish ed in Newspapers

This Court has not the power to receive illegal testimony, and, I contend, that we have a right to object to it in the same manner as though the case was before a Jury. But, if I am wrong in this, if usage is to be the rule, there are many manifest reasons that would operate to promote our argument. If they were necessary they may be adduced.

Mr *M'Rae* wished the Court would take the charge into its own hand, and say when the counsel were going wrong

Chief Justice. I do not think that inadmissible testimony can be received at any time, but I do not see that this testimony is inadmissible. To be sure it ought to relate to the " overt act "

Mr *Burr* We are ready to hear every thing that relates to the " overt act" if the gentlemen will confine themselves to Kentucky, to save time and confusion : but, if they do go down the Mississippi, there will be objections made, which the Court cannot avoid hearing.

Mr *Martin* expressed the same sentiment ; but, he observed that first they must prove an overt act in Kentucky, or somewhere It was impossible, he said, to mix overt acts in different places to make one crime Any departure from Kentucky would make a different ground of argument. Down the Mississippi, for instance

Chief Justice If the gentlemen choose to go down the Mississippi, I must hear their testimony, or any objections that may be made to such testimony.

Mr. *Hay* wished the gentlemen to take notice that the charge was not confined to a particular spot, but to the river at large — Very possibly gentlemen might satisfy him of the incorrectness of this course, and surely the inconvenience to witnesses and the Court could not be unobserved by him, but he had not yet seen any impropriety in the course taken

Mr *Wirt* observed that the expences of the government from witnesses on both sides was a matter of serious consideration to the government, since it might consume some weeks He supposed that it would be agreeable to the Court that they should, that evening, or, at some other time, take affidavits, as a substitute for oral testimony, in this case

Chief Justice I have no objection

Mr. *Burr* I presume that the gentlemen will ask my consent, before they do that. I must give my answer to them

The *Chief Justice* declared that he was determined to hear all witnesses who were present, and those who were absent, *their* affidavits might be read If the witnesses were present, he should think it wrong to discharge them

Mr *Martin* I will venture to say that there was never such a position made before

Mr *Burr* Do I understand the gentlemen as insisting on going below the line into the whole Mississippi territory ?

Mr *Hay* Yes.

Mr *Botts* commenced a long argument on the admissibility of evidence on such a subject Saving of time had been argued for by the prosecution but what they were about to do would perhaps save the time of one hundred witnesses who were waiting here Here Mr Botts went through some of the arguments and declarations of the prosecution of what they meant to have proved, but not an atom of it had they proved, or were likely so to do, and the perplexity must recoil upon themselves.

Here Mr Botts took some review of the opinion of the Court, and laid down a position that no evidence of acts done in the Mississippi territory was admissible, under the judiciary act, under which the charge was exhibited, and drawn, this had been since recognized by decisions—(see 33rd sect)

It may be charged that you assented to our proposition You did so: you declared, Sir, that evidence of facts in the first instance must be given, and, after that, any collateral matter might be produced This you said on the motion to commit, and this you have strengthened by your recent observations.

One branch of the charge is respecting acts done in the Mississippi territory this we must object to being given in evidence We affirm, Sir, on this point, that neither in your capacity of a circuit Judge of the United States, nor in your magisterial character, can you take cognizance of an act of treason, or any other act done within a *territory* of the United States Whatever authority you have, Sir, is given to you by the 33rd section of the judiciary law, vol 1, laws United States. p 72 Mr. Botts here went into some argument on the *examining* powers of a Judge and how far the laws enabled him to transport an accused person to another district but, he contended that there existed no powers to send to a *territory* of the the United States in its integral character. No territorial Court, or any Court but a circuit Court could have cognizance of the offence charged. No Court in the Mississippi territory could be in the meaning of the law, and there fore not a Court of the United States, but a Court of a territory be longing to the United States In the 2nd section of that act, p 47. there is a designation of what should be denominated the United States, and there are laid out thirteen districts

The rules of construction, in all acts of parliament and legis latures, were, that no words in the act should be rejected as senseless, if the proper sense could be found out Now, as a de pendency of the United States could not, by this act, have cogni zance of a crime of this nature, it must necessarily follow, that if you give to one of these dependencies a cognizance of this of fence, you must abrogate the sense of the law, and render the 33d section meanless The words of that section, he contended, were as imperious as though Congress had said in so many words that no Court but a Court of the United States, proper, to wit, one of the districts before designated in the 2nd section, should take cognizance of this offence This word " district" occurs no less than nine times in the 33rd section, and must have an imperative meaning, especially when to it is added, that no Judge but the district Judge can commit for trial in another state or district.

Mr Botts then went into an examination of the word state and the word district, and to draw the distinction between them . also as to the territories of the United States, &c—[Of no importance] He enforced his argument and conclusions by saying that though the Chief Justice was a Judge of the United States in some way and for some purposes, yet his jurisdiction did not extend beyond itself it could not extend to the territories of the United States Every word and every line of the law would speak for itself and prove Congress only contemplated the law to comprehend often ces committed within the body of the United States, and not in the territories He produced, as a reason for their reluctance to go into the Mississippi territory, that they would have to meet rank perjury at the very threshold of the case ; and this must be enough to produce a terror to any man of prudence

We care not to meet a fair enquiry into this case, but we do fear to meet perjury. We therefore think proper to avoid all en quiry into acts where you have no cognizance, because there you cannot have the opportunity of knowing what is brought for ward

Another reason why we object is, that the verdict of acquittal for treason must operate as a bar to any future enquiry about the same act.

Chief Justice That point had better be reserved until so much of the testimony as may be proper on the other subject shall be brought forward I did not know until to-day that it was meant to prove an overt act in the Mississippi territory. That question in my opinion is of a constitutional nature, and can only be deci ded by the Supreme Court of the United States, and I would not as a committing Magistrate, pretend to act upon it, unless it should be absolutely necessary.

Mr. *Martin*. It is a case that your honor *must* meet it is a case that we have a right to call upon you to meet , and our situ ation and charge require that we should call for your decision upon it

Chief Justice Suppose it be a case upon which I should feel a doubt, and cannot make up my mind, what would then be consequence? I do not say that the point shall not be argued, but I say that it is best not to argue it at present, until we see what evidence can be produced to the charge

Mr *Botts* In the manner that we are driven, it might be proper and advantageous to avail ourselves of every ground applicable to our object, and among these grounds is this. It is much to be regretted that the testimony is not gone through, as we have invited it. We mean not however to trouble the Court with our objections in *detail*, but upon the *principle*

Farther I have thought it my duty, in the course of this prosecution, to bring to the view of the Court every point which might possibly occur in such a case, that there might be established, by such a decision, land marks for our future guide. This does not relate to myself particularly, but it may be of some future use. Such occasions do not always occur, and very often a Court might want the benefit of such an opportunity

If they will go into the territory, I will oppose it

Mr *Hay* It is my wish not to meddle with the subject now, but it is my wish that it should be taken up, discussed and decided upon. If I could withdraw or suspend the motion, I should rather do it, because I want the opinion of the Court to guide me in what I call the great question of transmission

Mr *Burr* It is a new species of doctrine, that I am to be brought up here to be charged with treason in one place, and again and again charged in other places with the same act? When is this species of conduct to stop?

Mr *Hay* I have no objection except on the account of the witnesses, to meet the question now

Some loose conversation occurred here between Messrs Wickham, Burr, Hay and Martin

Mr *Botts* proceeded, he wished to accommodate his argument as much as possible to the opinion of the Court. He proceeded into an elaborate argument respecting the locality of an overt act, and called into view the history of the rebellion of '15 and '45, where crimes were committed every where, but it was only considered as one continued act, and wherever its location was fixed, it was but the same offence. There was the best of opportunity to multiply offences, *ad infinitum*, for overt act might have been found every where, but they did not think proper to pursue that vexatious spirit of prosecution

The case of lord George Gordon, Mr Botts also quoted, in that case, the nation was extremely eager on his acquittal. He was acquitted, but, upon the principles of law now laid down, he might have been charged with the act of levying war in Moorfields, in St George's fields, in Bloomsbury, in Fleet Street, in Lincoln's Inn fields, &c. &c successively, until the prosecutor had gone through the whole of London, and have hazarded him to forty, or to a hundred chances for his life. Besides, if they could take those advantages, he contended that they could take others, they could have charged him with Arson, Homicide, Burglary, &c.

&c. and thus multiply offences as well as places, *ad infinitum* Any attempts, however, he believed, to have tried a man twice for the same *war*, in '45 or '80, in a different place, would have been in vain, because it never had been a sacred principle with the British Juries prudential government, and to put a man to hazard more than once for the same crime This was a principle of law that grew out of experience, and the sacred principles of justice which could not be evaded, and the boldest magistrate or attorney general that ever was known would not have dared to make the attempt, this was a law, settled of old England, and transplanted into the United States *Justice* wafted it over those seas, and here it became a favorite principle to guard our rights and cherish every thing that would promote them By the constitution and the laws, no man was to be twice put into jeopardy for the same offence, if the United States had made a a wrong selection, as they had the whole selection before them, it was no reason why an accused person should be subject to an infinity of prosecutions And therefore, Mr Botts contended that the verdict of acquittal must forever operate as a bar to any charge for the same offence, how variegated soever might be its introduction or location Time, he contended, would be spent in vain in branching out into all the arguments and precedents of so clear a position, " common sense" would fix it beyond all the power of art and argument to defeat If the attorney would not agree to take up any actually unnecessary time, he would be bold to say that the witnesses would not be long detained, nor the case be long suspended

The third point which Mr Botts mentioned, was the acquittal of Col Burr by a Grand Jury in the Mississippi territory (See appendix D.) A discharge or a commitment, he contended, was inevitable if he was discharged, he could not be recommitted for the same charge, if he was committed and tried, he could not be again tried for the same offence, and therefore, he could not be again returned for trial in that territory

Besides, If there was any offence committed there, what was since become of the civil authority—had it slept ever since? No, every thing had been going on as usual, and not only the government of the United States but its territories had even since remained unmolested He inferred at large on the manner, expence and cause of the removal to this district, but observed that it was a politic thing in the government to remove him to a place where the name of *Jefferson* must have an influence, which, instead of being operative to guard the people's rights and standing up to support the citizen, would evince how far the weak was inferior to the strong, and how unable to withstand its power But it was not to the government that he could look for protection: it was to a Court of justice, as the executors of law, and the guards of the people against the oppression of a government that they were to look to know whether a man was to be brought from place to place, at the will of the government, and go through all the hazards of a criminal trial day after day, and in places unknown to him If this Court could send him to Kentucky, Mr Botts wished to know whether that Court could go through the solemn mockery of a trial with him, or whether they would not send him back again; that might be done as easily as sending him away, if the prosecutor should choose so to do, and there would be no end to the case whilst they choose to repeat the motion

Was there nothing to be done, he asked, to stop prosecutions of this kind, if it was determined to carry them on with relentless hand? Yes, your judicial discretion, Sir, must, in some degree at least, interpose against executive power, which (under some future administration) might become arbitrary Without this check, our liberties are not worth a groat, for we yet remain slaves to the will of any administration to transport a prisoner from place to place until a suitable one is found to convict him This is a most singular case—in Kentucky, in the Mississippi territory, and twice in Virginia are crimes sought for, but none can be found, they have sought in vain, yet that will not satisfy them The bitterest enemies of the administration (to which I am attached from principle) would rejoice at the success of the present motion, because the object must inevitably fail?

The next point, Mr Botts observed, related to the testimony produced by the attorney himself already, respecting what was done at the mouth of Cumberland, even if evidence was permitted to be given of acts done there All the argument necessary in that point would consist in asking questions which must grow out of the opinion delivered by the Court, and which must necessarily relieve the Court of all the trouble of farther examination on the motion to commit Was there any war there? Was the party in a condition to make war against the United States there? Were they armed and arrayed in a warlike manner? Were they in a warlike posture? Was it a warlike assemblage and in a warlike character, appearance and situation?

Mr Botts concluded with a reference to Judge Chase's opinion in the case of Fries, and a declaration which had been proved, that the assemblage knew not for what they had assembled, and therefore could have no conspiracy or treason in view, more than they had committed, which was none

Mr Martin rose to refer to Cornish's case in the State Trials, wherein the Lord Chief Justice observed, that if the conspiracy continued for seven years, it was but one continued act, and must be treated as such on the trial of one of the traitors

Again he referred to Hawkins's, as to the profanation of the sabbath. if twenty acts of profanation were committed on the same day, there could be but *one* charge of profanation · if the prosecution should fail in that one charge, it cannot be renewed under any other act of profanation committed on that day.

Mr M'Rae commenced in answer to Mr Botts He wished to mark, that the favorite object of the gentleman, that of saving me, had been too much disregarded he was desirous of avoiding his example of prolixity, and to reply with all possible brevity, although it must be necessary to consume too much time on a question so replete with importance He descanted pretty largely on Mr Bott's observations and others, of what was meant for the public ear in the article of bringing the accused *here* for trial in preference to the place now proposed to remove the case and explained the reason why he was brought to Richmond.

Mr Perkins, he said, at a place very far distant from this State, brought him, without any consultation, knowledge, or direction, of the President, brought him here but, when he was brought here, the President acted as he ought to do—he directed that he should be put into the hands of the proper authority. He could not silently pass by the observations which had been made respecting the interference of the President as to the place of trial, because he did not believe that the President had any knowledge of it, nor did he direct or wish it Notwithstanding, however, that Mr Botts and disclaimed any wish to excite the public mind on the subject, there could be no doubt but he had endeavoured to do it, and as it was not the first time that the public mind had been attempted to be raised against the President, it would be criminal to be silent whilst a vindication of good actions was necessary. However it might be looked upon in itself, the President had nothing to do with bringing him here for trial

But Mr Botts had joined on this and other grounds with the other counsel on his side, and called this a persecution carried on by a relentless spirit This he had hoped not to have heard

Mr *Botts* interrupted If he had said so, he declared it to be without his recollection, and what he ought not to have said.

Mr *Martin*. If you had, you need not to apologize

Mr *Botts* Yes, I will apologise I do not think that I ought to judge actions—I am obliged to speak of their actions, but will not of their motives My words did not apply to motives but I must still say that this prosecution has been carried on with more zeal and relentless energy than I have ever experienced

Mr *M'Rae* Then though our motives are good, the prosecution is a very cruel one I am sorry that, instead of examining witnesses to support our positions, I am forced to turn aside and answer the remarks of those gentlemen He would ask the Court and the counsel to say whether there had appeared in the whole course of this examination, any thing which looked like the character given it by Mr Botts ? These observations were intended for the people, but he was sure that the people nor the Court could discover any savoring persecution Wherein could the impropriety be made to appear, if two trials had been had and failed for their attempting to bring on another trial where it would not fail ?

To examine this subject, it would be proper to follow the ground marked out by Mr Botts

Two more enquiries had been made, one respecting treason against the U S. and the other respected misdemeanor under certain law Now he would ask the candor of the gentlemen to answer whether in the course of these a wish had been discovered in the counsel for the United States to convict the accused contrary to law ? the *people*, to whom those observations were addressed, must see at some future period, and appreciate their true character

Mr *Botts* had objected for four reasons The first, Mr M'Rae took up, respected the evidence from a territory, but this did not go to establish the innocence of the accused, nor to to the merits of the case. He clings to the word of the statute " States," however guilty he might be of levying war in the territories, he must be discharged, because it was not done in one of the States enumerated in the law. This was an objection which never could have been dreamt of or anticipated till the present day, but he thought there could be no reasonable doubt entertained that this Court had the power to commit a person for an offence, to wherever such offence was committed within the United States

Mr M'Rea took a review summarily of the constitution and creation of the Territorial Courts, and of the State Courts under the laws and constitution, which he contended were so nearly assimilated as to render their cognizance the same

But, fearing that he might be wrong in this position, and that the Court might have the power to send the accused to a territory as well as to a State, and that the guilt of the accused should require such a transmission, he had taken the ground of the former two trials and acquittals.

If I understood the Court, it did express an unwillingness to bring the question of *auterfois acquit* up at this time, because such a plea was generally put in upon the trial of the party accused, during the pendency of an *indictment*, and not on an enquiry founded on a motion to commit   It must then depend upon a question of fact on which a man has been tried and acquitted, and the plea made at the moment of the indictment for a crime for which the party has before been tried   Now, Mr Botts contends it upon this ground, to be a question of fact, as triable before this Court as it would be before a Jury, as to the question of fact.   Then, *a fortcori*, it will be proper to consider whether the ground charged in the present offence, is the *very* ground which has been before tried or not.   I consider, that by a reference to the opinion of the Court, it expresses that no crime was committed on Blannerhasset's island, within its cognizance, but that opinion was given upon the idea that he was not present on the island, and therefore could have committed no act there, yet it does not prove that he committed no offence at all at any place.

But, take the charge to be that of levying war on Blannerhasset's island, he is tried and acquitted of that charge; but does it follow that he must be acquitted for acts done any where else, at another time ? Besides, the argument before was, that he was not present, and not concerned · but does it follow, that, at a distant time and at a distant place he should be innocent of a charge made against him ? he may be innocent in the district of Virginia (according to the opinion,) but that cannot acquit him for a continuance of the same crime in another district   This question has not been urged, nor any evidence given upon it, but, if he is innocent, let it appear from the testimony which can be produced ; and it would be preposterous to suppose that the prosecution could so well point a spot for a continued act of treason, as the evidence itself would designate.

Mr. M'Rae referred to 4 Blackstone 335 and to Tucker's note upon the subject for an explanation of the plea   Here he was charged and acquitted; and here he is charged with crimes committed under another jurisdiction. The want of jurisdiction here is an evidence that he cannot be brought here again and tried for what he has been tried, because it proves that no overt act has been committed in Virginia by him, but we say immediately after leaving this district he did commit it. Can an acquittal here then operate, if we prove that in the continuance of the same act he committed the crime elsewhere? The operation of such a doctrine would effect the escape of many a culprit who should be taken in another place, and, by mistake be tried were he did not commit the crime. He continued in a strain of argument and referred to a quotation of Tucker's, 2 Hale 245. Some conversation closed his observations on the 2d point.

The third point of objection was grounded on the acquittal in Mississippi territory by a Grand Jury The authenticity of the paper read: Mr. M'Rae said he had not been very nice in examining into, nor did he think it necessary, since the acquittal by a Grand Jury was grounded only on an exparte and very partial examination into facts this idea must be strengthened by the consideration that but a very small proportion of the evidence could be brought there A future Grand Jury when more proof shall be produced, might be able to find a bill

A few more observations closed Mr M'Rae's remarks, when he was followed with some remarks by Mr Burr.

Mr Burr stated that as he wished the gentlemen to be fully aware of their ground, they had produced their points to the view of the Court As to the first point, he observed, that it really appeared to them a matter of surprize and astonishment, and as a subject worthy of enquiry, whether there could exist a power in any Court of the United States to send a citizen out of the United States for trial, to where their laws were not made by the congress of the United States, but by the President, and indeed where the Judges themselves were legislators in a great degree If there was any authority to sanction such a removal, they were desirous to know it. It may be possible indeed, that there was no appeal from the judgment of that Court, on a subject of this nature Now, if there was no power to transmit to a territory, it would be worse than a waste of time to go into evidence relative to any act done there

With respect to the verdict of acquittal, it was not pretended to plead them as though the case was now at trial, because the Chief Justice he now considered in the capacity of a committing magistrate, with whom rested a decision of the case at bar upon a sound discretion; to do as circumstances, and an exception of this kind would not admit of a general rule, say the gentlemen in support of the motion for commitment. This in some degree might be just, but where is the limit? Now as to evidence before objections is made, or when made, we want to know our land marks—the time, the spot, the circumstances our due charge.

Farther In England there had been numerous recent examples of charges for treason, where the parties were acquitted, although, upon principles similar to that now existing there might have been a succession and continuity of charges in different countries No instance had occurred of a man being pursued, after one verdict of acquittal for the same crime.

The effect of a former Grand Jury examination, he contended, was of the same nature: it was pleaded in bar, subject to the sound discretion of the Court; and all the pretended grounds of alarm, held up as a reason for the conduct that was pursued must revolve itself into the same submission

This argument must bear upon the whole of the testimony that is to be offered—and we regret that it will, because it is my wish to have heard all that could be produced in that district. I deny the whole, however, and we shall be obliged to take the whole into our review, if offered.

A few uninteresting remarks occurred between Mr Hay and Mr Burr, and then an adjournment took place.

THURSDAY, September 17.

The proceedings of this day commenced with desultory conversation between the Chief Justice and Mr Hay, on the subject of transportation to a *territory* of the United States, in which the *Chief Justice* declared his opinion that the law bound him to commit any person to a state, and did not authorize him to order a commitment to a territory: on this subject however, he was willing to hear farther argument, as he was not yet of a decided opinion: when he was satisfied he could commit there, he should be willing to go on with evidence respecting the crime charged to have been committed there.

Mr Hay. I think I can satisfy you, Sir.

Chief Justice. Then, indeed, it might go on.

Mr. Hay. I wish to go on with the witnesses: they are continually going out of town, and therefore if we do not go on immediately, we shall be left without testimony. I cannot detain them here so long.

Chief Justice. I cannot hear any evidence about what was done in the Mississippi territory, until I am satisfied that the Court can commit there for trial.

Some farther conversation, of no interest, ensued, respecting the circumstances that occurred in the Mississippi territorial Court, after which Mr *Hay* took up the main argument and observed, that, on the first point he was totally unacquainted with the circumstances: it was possible that the attorney did not present a bill to the Grand Jury of that district, but that, from the prevalent report, they had taken up the subject themselves, perhaps not to disprove the acts of Burr, but for the purpose of shewing their extreme disapprobation at the disappointment which had attended the project. To some men this was undoubtedly a source of deep regret.

In the argument of Mr. Botts, he said there was no force employed, nor any thing done which could denominate this new act of treason. This argument requires very little answer, because it assumes the point in dispute: for we are stopt at the very first (and at every) of our propositions; and, consequently, the evidence that we want to bring forward to prove them *cannot* be heard. We want to bring forward all our evidence, and after that, the character of our evidence (whether it be auxiliary or not) can be estimated. Suppose a Judge, on a trial, in this place was enquiring into a case, certainly the evidence would be let in from the mouth of Cumberland, or any where in the United States, after the facts at the place charged had been heard. The question before a Court is not whether acts done at the mouth of Cumberland do or do not amount to treason: this is a question exclusively belonging to a Jury.—the question now presented to the Court is, whether such facts have been or can be proved as will authorize a Jury in another district to give a verdict

[He drew a parallel between the situation of the Chief Justice and a district Judge in Kentucky, and referred to the opinion of the Court on the subject of commitment; at the same time enforcing, that if they were permitted to produce evidence as to acts done at the mouth of Cumberland, &c there could be no doubt of *direct* proof to produce a conviction, without the aid of what was denominated " collateral testimony."]

Mr *Hay* then proceeded to the second point—that of the plea of a former acquittal in bar The simple question on this position was, whether this was, or was not the *same offence* for which he had been before indicted, and from which he was acquitted. There is an essential difference, both in reason and law, when we take into view the difference between an examination before a magistrate, and a trial before a Jury. When a man is indicted for treason (or any capital crime) the indictment must specify the overt act, and the time of its being committed, as well as the place, but here is a charge laid without a specification, subject to the sound discretion of the Court to commit where it shall find the crime has been committed The line of Blannerhasset's island, in Wood county, Virginia, was heretofore made the line of distinction, but if a crime has not been committed there, but the same crime charged has been committed somewhere else, what is the reason, in common sense, or common justice, that that mistake in the indictment and information, should prevent a future enquiry ? If that rule should be established, no matter how common or how enormous offences would be, because a violation of them would be inevitable, wherever there was a design so to do.

A question had been asked by the accused, where was the line at which the prosecution would stop ? No line is necessary, where a crime of this magnitude has actually been committed. He drew a supposition, and upon it contended that an error in the charge would always support a renewal of the charge, upon that *error* being exhibited to a Court of discretion, and the innocence or guilt of it being produced to the examining magistrate or Judge Ignorance of law nor of right could be pleaded, because every man knew how to do right He feared not any attempt of the government at judicial persecution, because he believed that the people knew too well how to ascertain the weight and consequences of acts of violence and persecution—indeed sufficiently so to ruin any administration. How far intrigue and corruption would answer, he would not precisely say, but he believed even they would prove inefficient to promote executive influence in these days Violence and persecution he believed never would be operative

Mr Hay next went into the question of the former acquittal, and the reason why such should and should not be brought in bar against a further examination. He referred to 4 Bl 335 : Hawk. ch 35 sect 3. and 2 Hale. 244 from all which, and the true nature of a case of this sort he adduced an opinion that the plea might properly be enquired into, if it arose from any misapprehension of the laws in any prosecutor, where facts could be produced to promote the prosecution for an offence. Whether a committing magistrate could make such an enquiry or not, he would not say, because he had not examined the subject He would draw a supposition that the Court had the power to commit for the crime which was charged—even place it upon the footing of a trial of an overt act, before the Jury· say that he is charged with an overt act of levying war at Cumberland, but he pleads in *bar* that he was tried and acquitted for the same offence before· would that plea be received, when the variances of places is so very evident?—A man might be connected with a treasonable expedition at the mouth of Cumberland, when he had not even joined in it at Blannerhasset's This plea could not be in bar, he contended, because though he was charged at a place where it appeared, no treason was committed, it could not result therefrom that he was not guilty any where. In support of this idea, it was even urged by the accused, that the second indictment was illegal.

Mr *Burr*. I did state that such a thing never had been done in England, and that it was insupportable

Mr *Hay* answered that no such rule or precedent was laid down, but, there was an immense difference between the comparative population and extent of Great Britain and the United States One was small and covered with an immense population, where every thing could be known of every person, and the other was of such immense extent and so thin a population, that a man might travel from Philadelphia to New-Orleans and no one know him on the journey Neither upon principles of sound policy, sound sense nor law, could he see a sufficient reason for supporting the position The solicitude of the government to convict lord George Gordon, he very much doubted, but at any rate it was inapplicable to the present case. He read some of the conclusive arguments in that case

As to the second position—let it be admitted for a moment, that in the enquiry into the probable cause for commitment, a committing magistrate could exercise the same rigor in the examination as though he was a Judge having a Jury before him to decide the case ; what would such an exclusion of evidence lead to ? The Court only could exclude evidence on the ground of its irrelevency, whether in itself strong or weak : what harm then can irrelevent evidence produce when it comes before a court for trial ? Here a charge is made of an overt act committed, upon which evidence is offered, but this evidence is refused on account of location and not of the crime Were it irrelevent, a committing magistrate would have the power to object to it

But here, gentlemen had said, that the judicial law only mentioned and meant a State—not a territory, and it was not in the power of a district Judge to transmit to a territory. Upon this subject Mr Hay dwelt at some length, he contended that the power of the Judges of the United States, extended on the subject of commitment, to every part and territory of the United States, in the strict meaning of the law, although territory was not mentioned, because the United States were divided into judicial *districts*, and there the judicial power must extend

The words of the law wrested on were these " such Court of the United States as by this act has cognizance," &c when this Mississippi territory did not then, (1789) exist, except as forming a part of Georgia. But Mr Hay contended that it was a sound principle of law and justice that all the acts of the government were to be taken together to form one general code for the great purposes of that government. If therefore under this law of '89 this Court could not have cognizance of this offence, but that that cognizance was given by some other law, it would be sufficient to denominate the Court of that territory, a Court of the United States, and consequently having cognizance of crimes committed against the peace of the United States. At the time of its separation from Georgia, it was established as " one district," to be denominated the Mississippi territory; and the act of Congress establishing it, providing for its separation, directed all causes to be tried in it the same as in any Circuit Court of a State, and therefore he contended that offenders could be as well sent there as to any State, for the trial of crimes committed *there* against the U States In this view he considered a district, territory, and State to be synonymous, and the power of transmission in a district Judge he considered to be the same in each, if there were a violation of the laws of the United States committed there By the sixth section of this act it would be seen, that the Mississippi territory was to have the same sort of government, which was granted by the ordinance of Congress in 1787, to the people north west of the Ohio, and if there were no other clause in the laws of the United States, this would be sufficient to establish the principle contended for. See 137, Graydon's digest This " colonial" government could not injure the accused, as the laws amply provided him with means to prove his innocence It is true the Judges there were appointed by the President, but it was precisely in the same way, that the others were by the consent of the Senate, and continued in that high station during good behaviour only. There could not be possibly any difference between one of these territories and the States, except that their population did not yet entitle them to a representative admission into the union as a State; but they equally formed an integral of the union in every other capacity, and were equally entitled, except in their representative capacity, to the benefit of its laws

Some conversation here occurred as to the proceedings in the Mississippi territory of the Grand Jury, &c. which Mr. *Burr* here explained

In fact there is a mistake which it might be proper here to correct. It was said that the Grand Jury at Natchez, might not have been charged with the offence against me, but that they might have taken it up of their own accord, rather to favor me, (it was insinuated) than otherwise So far from that there was a stipulation between Mr Meade, (then acting as governor) and myself, that a Grand Jury should be summoned for the purpose of examining my case They were summoned and designated by the Judge, seventy or more, and the Judge gave them a charge. Depositions were taken, which I consented might be taken in, and witnesses were examined in the usual way,

It is also alleged that I was not brought here by the order of the government. I was surprized to hear this. I do not know whether this will be insisted upon, but it is well known from the depositions which were taken, that there was a military party sent by General Wilkinson, (not in uniform) to seize and carry me on board the gun boats, and to do with me as they pleased. I was afterwards taken by the order of Gen. Wilkinson, and brought on by the person who had me in possession to Fredericksburg, on my way to the seat of government, and there a letter was received from the Secretary of State to convey me to this place, where I arrived under escort for examination.

Mr. *Hay* did not believe the last part of the statement was correct, for he did not think that any intelligence of his progress towards the seat of government could have been received by any member of the administration, or that they knew it until he was brought here.

As to the selection of this place particularly, for trial, it was a mistake, and any assertions respecting the influence or interference of the President on the subject were unfounded, and if the circumstance of the arrest made by Mr. Perkins was rightly viewed and the time of travelling also, it would clearly appear. It was true they were met at Fredericksburg, but it was only to bring him to a suitable place for examination and commitment for trial, as he supposed. The Marshal took possession of him, he was indicted by a Grand Jury, and appeared to trial, where he was acquitted, and yet after all, it was solemnly averred, that his was a place selected for his trial, because the influence of the President was supposed to be greater here than any where else, and his conviction more sure! For myself, said Mr. Hay, if I am considered as implicated in any part of this affair, I view the charge with indifference as to myself, but I do not view it so with respect to the government, or of its officers, because I know that they are not concerned in it. It seems to me impossible for them to have done otherwise than they have done, and that those who sent the order to detain him here, did it from principles of justice and propriety, because it was here that they viewed the case proper to be decided.

And, Sir, after he was brought here, it was your business to elect the place for trial, or the examining magistrate. It therefore could not be conformable to the wish of any one that he was tried here, but as the evidence should appear to direct, so the Chief Justice might point out the place of trial, as he has done. How then can the government be charged with it?

Admitting then, this district to have been selected, it was not a selection made by the government, but by the first judicial officer of the United States, whom it is certain the government could not control, and whose independence of mind is sufficient to resist any influence whatever.

Mr. *Hay* next made some observations upon the degree of warmth and fervor which had appeared, but he was willing to abide it on his part, because he believed it to be a justifiable warmth, which he was willing to exhibit to the country in its true colors—he was satisfied with having done his duty to the most of his ability, and he should not be deterred by any censure whatever which might be cast on his conduct, nor by any language that might be used, however strong the denunciation might be. He was willing to meet every censure at his individual hazard.

It was avowed that there were some persons behind the curtain, unknown, whose influence was considerably felt. He could not understand who those unknown characters could be, he knew that if there were such, it was equally unknown to the counsel for the prosecution, and he had no doubt, to the executive. He wished the gentlemen, if they had any knowledge of it, to be so obliging as to state who were those persons and what they were doing, as a source of interesting information. He solemnly declared upon his honor, that he believed it was a total mistake in the gentleman. As to the President's interference, he would say that he had never received any instruction or communication from him, nor could he be governed by any "orders" on the subject from the executive. He could not but feel hurt at such an unjustifiable insinuation, when placed in so public a situation. This situation he would endeavor to discharge with faithfulness and without any spirit of persecution, of which spirit he believed the government to be as incapable as he knew himself to be. Indeed were it not so, he should be unworthy of filling the station of a States Attorney, and public prosecutor

Chief Justice. Col. Burr having been committed to this place for trial, I feel it necessary to state, a second time, the principles upon which I have proceeded. It is not my idea, by any means, to cast an imputation of censure upon any person, nor to countenance any one, but I think it proper to state the reasoning which passed in my own mind

With respect to treason, nothing need be said, because it is well known that I did not commit him for treason: for I did not think the evidence was sufficient to warrant a commitment for that crime. Indeed, I did not commit him at all, but I bailed him to appear for trial at this place. Indeed, the offence was not located at all, but it did appear to me from the circumstances that there was sufficient cause to suspect that he did set on foot a military expedition against Mexico, from somewhere. This opinion was formed principally upon the affidavit of Gen. Eaton, and Gen. Wilkinson's letter. This letter was laid before the Supreme Court, and I think the opinions of the Judges coincided with mine, but where to fix the seat of this military expedition yet remained a question undefined. That letter did not contain one syllable that could enable us to locate the offence, or in the least to say where it was begun or where carried on.

If there was a just cause to suspect that there was a crime committed in any part of the United States, which was triable in some Court of the United States, I could readily conceive that I must either commit or discharge the person if brought before me for commitment; and knowing that some Court must have the jurisdiction. Otherwise, I must leave it, which I could consistently do to the Court, where more testimony might be obtained.

From all these, and other considerations of the same nature, I bailed him, to be tried in the state of Virginia, and I would have bailed him to have been tried any where, if I had been satisfied that he ought to have been taken there. I had not one iota but that of right, to govern me as a committing magistrate. I had no alternative, in my opinion, but to bind him over to appear here.

Much conversation here occurred (but of no interest) between the Court, Col. Burr, and Mr. Hay, as to the interference of the government in assigning Richmond as the place of trial, where it was stated presidential influence existed to the extreme, and that it was meant to bear down the accused This declaration was denied, as to *motives*, by Mr Wickham, who was charged with saying it He replied with his usual warmth on this topic at some length, and much warm, confusing, and serious conversation occurred between Mr. Hay and Mr Wickham, (but of no public concern, nor relevant to the case) at length it arrived nearer home, to the point in argument, and Mr Martin produced some new authorities Act of parliament 23 Geo. 2. ch 20 sec 11, and 2 Hawkins, 55 ch 8. sec 29 He also referred to Graydon's digest, 68 a law of the United States, 1793, respecting fugitives from justice This was intended to apply to the question of jurisdiction in the Mississippi territory for trial.

Mr. *Hay* answered to a number of loose and uninteresting observations in objection to the location of the crime in the Mississippi territory

The *Chief Justice* observed, that the difficulty appeared to him to arise from the territorial cognizance of any commitment that could be made—the question was, whether a district or circuit Judge could commit to a territory for any crime ? The power must be conferred by act of Congress, but if it was not conferred, no Court could arrest under such a motion, if it was not conferred he could have no business to hear argument upon the subject

Mr *Hay* thought that the law of 1798, gave the power to the territorial Court to try

Mr *Burr* said, that they had never doubted the power of a territorial Court to try for any crime committed within its jurisdiction, but they did doubt whether the law authorized any magistrate in another place to transmit to that territory for the trial of a crime suggested to have been committed there

On the word "district" he must say one word It was a very vague and uncertain phrase, he observed, in one instance he remembered it to be particularly applicable to a county, but it was also used in our revenue laws as applicable to a larger extent of country. Judicial districts were designated by the judiciary law to mean States, but territories were not mentioned.

Mr Martin insisted, that the 33d clause of the judicial law must inevitably govern the question, and exclude every territory from State rights, and if a crime was committed out of the State, and in a territory, he contended that a Judge of the United States out of that territory had no more right to enquire into a crime than had any other person in society, much less to swear witnesses, to arrest, and to recognize to trial Every such proceeding would be totally invalid If Col Burr had committed often against the United States, in the Mississippi Territory, why and not the proper authorities in that territory send for him by their own proper authority? The answer was clear, upon a fair review of the whole case: and that was, that no open war had been committed any where. If war had been committed it would be an easy thing to establish the fact, (for war could not be an ordinary and hidden circumstance.) They have projected unsurmountable difficulties—they are endeavoring to find out war where war has never been, and they are locating a war where a war has never been committed, nor even the likeness of it, except it be on paper. Where were the army seen? Where the battles fought? It will be ever found to be a non-entity, for it never has been found, nor never will be. They may go to the Mississippi territory or any where else that they please, but they can find nothing to support the charge in what way soever they please to bring it forward.

It certainly was very severe that a pretended offender should, after being set at large in a certain place, when he got a thousand miles from that place, be taken up, examined and committed for the same crime, and afterwards sent back to the same place for trial. Upon a whole and full view of the case, it appeared that the law was not fitted to meet it.

But was it even thought or heard of, that when a crime was committed in a different state, and that when the offender was suffered to go at large, and got a thousand miles from the place, he should, upon the information of any person, be taken before a magistrate, and sent back to that place, after an examination and acquittal there? I admit that the examination of that Grand Jury does not prevent any future Grand Jury from indicting for any offence, if there be cause shewn, to produce the true crime but was it ever contemplated in a Court of Justice, that a man should be liable to perpetual and successive prosecutions for one and the same crime? If there be a change in the circumstances, let them come forward and shew it otherwise let them submit to the disabilities which their own want of evidence must inevitably produce. It was stated that he was guilty of some practices, injurious to the happiness of the Union, but no person there, that we hear of, had an idea of a war against the Union. Even severing of the Union would not be " levying of war," if there was no war levied ; and consequently it would not be an act of treason.

It was suggested, Mr Martin said, that persons were sent down there to find out what Col Burr was doing, and to look after him every where, and try to find out his crime if possible when all this was done, an officer of the United States, whose bread was dependant upon his doing his duty, under the influence and direction of the government, discovered something, as he supposed, and thence arose the whole judicial examination? Those inflamed citizens were not capable of trying a case under such a prepossession as must have been raised

Besides, there was presidential authority that those people were warmly attached to the present administration it could not therefore be supposed, that their attachment would permit them to clear Col. Burr, and thus censure the administration who had already denounced him , that these warmly attached people had declared that they did not find him guilty of planning or plotting or endeavoring to carry into execution any offence against the United States But they went farther , they expressed a pointed disapprobation at the measures that were used against him. Should he then be sent back to the same place upon no new facts being shewn ? He saw no reason or justice in it.

On the point of a former acquittal, which Mr. Martin had observed the desire of the Chief Justice to avoid, until he could obtain the opinion of the supreme Court, he should say but little . but he did hold it to be a clear principle that it was out of the power of the government (even if they would wish) to convict Col Burr a second time, or even to commit him after a judgment had been passed upon the charge of levying war Here Mr Martin made several observations, during which he quoted 2 Hawk. 525. p. 2 ch 35 sect 3 He contended upon the propriety of considering the act already examined into, as in continuity, and as not capable of being split into a thousand pieces . if it was an act of levying war against the government and of preparing, &c. an expedition against another government, what more could be made of it this had once been tried, and an acquittal had taken place, although government had the power, through all their information and advantages, to select a suitable place, if they could find one And what, he asked, was the reason of his not being found guilty of levying war ? Nothing, but because the evidence which the government had thought proper to bring forward had failed , and it must fail, when it was so inapplicable to the charge, because the charge did not embrace the evidence Mr Martin here went into a view of the comparison between this case and of the quotations respecting murder before referred to

With these observations and authorities respecting territorial cognizance of a crime said to have been committed within the United States , and the powers of a Judge of the United States to commit to a territory , and also with the submission of the two former acquittals for the same continued act, he should submit his argument to the sound discretion of the Court, and the principles of law, without any farther observations, in this stage of the argument.

Mr Wickham commenced by observing, that the few observations which he had heard adduced relative to the particular questions whether this Court has the power to commit to Kentucky after the verdict of an acquittal here , and the question respecting the power of this Court submitted to a territory, he must, without intending to shew any disrespect to the gentlemen, declare that he had not heard an observation which bore any semblance of an argument , and he hoped in God that there never would in this country exist such usages, as had been so much eulogized

The system of government in this country, he observed, had emanated from the people immediately in the states, but he asked, could it be considered so of the territories ? No, they emanated from Congress, and every enjoyment they had must be considered as a boon They were as much slaves as though under

the power of Bonaparte and at his nod. What share had the
people in the ten miles square, or the district of Columbia, in the
article of liberty? They were not governed by themselves, nor
had they the semblance of political liberty, nor rights, more than
is granted to them by those who represent them not and merely
because their numbers were not sufficient to entitle them to re
presentation. He trusted that no citizen of the United States
held his liberties at such tenure as to be sent away to any place
and at any time for trial to a dependency of this country

Independent of every thing else, however, and as a sufficient
argument to support and carry this motion, Mr Wickham contended for the former acquittal, in bar of any future trial for
the same crime The Counsel had supposed that there existed
in the Court a discretionary power to pass by the plea of *auter
foits acquit*.* There existed no such power, he contended, when
he was acquitted, more than there would if he had been convicted; and it certainly would be absurd to try a man again,
when he has been once convicted, because he is then subject to
the punishment which the law could inflict. Were this legal,
the moment a man had received his punishment for an offence in
one place, he would be subject to be tried again for a continuity
of the same charge There would be the same propriety in a
motion, after the acquittals which have taken place here, to re
commit, even in this Court for trial for the same offence, but
what would be the plea? The same, and with no stronger reason
than present—the plea of *auter foits acquit*; and no Judge would
hesitate in that, more than in this instance to admit it. If the of-
ence was the same as a former Jury had determined upon, there
could not be a question about the determination of any Jury, or
Judge. this was a question of identity which could only be settled by the fact; and, he contended that it was no matter where
the crime was committed. It was said that the Court would not
decide the question, but on this subject he must differ with gentlemen, for he would say that the Court must and could not re
fuse to decide it, and that, by law, against the motion for a removal of the party If he had not been tried, there would be no
necessity to send him on there for trial, because he could not be
tried here; but, if he had been tried here, the sound discretion
of this Court must be exercised to prevent any trial for the same
offence, upon that identity of offence being established. The
question is, is it one treason—is it one war against the United
States? The authorities say, that war might consist, in a variety
of acts, and yet it be but one war now, if each act were to be
charged separate, there would be no end to the prosecutions a

---

* *A plea of* auterfoits acquit *is a former acquittal, and is a spe
cial plea in bar of an indictment, when a person hath been formerly in
dicted for the same offence, and acquitted for no man shall be brought
into jeopardy for the same offence more than once. Of the like sort is*
auterfoits convict, *a former conviction for the same identical crime,
tho' no judgment was given thereupon, &c* Auterfoits attaint, *a for
mer attainder, either for the same, or any other felony, is another plea in
bar: for the offender having forfeited all he had by the attainder, it
would be absurd to endeavor to attaint him a second time*

man would have to undergo; and he would never be able to know when he is safe. Why does the law require all the acts to be concentrated, but that a man should be able to meet the charges against him, by being apprized at once of their amount. Thus, if a prosecutor chose to make an hundred charges under the single name of an overt act, he might vexatiously teize a man times without number

Now suppose there were twenty overt acts laid, and a man were tried and acquitted upon one, then upon another and so on, say for nineteen times, and they all fail but the twentieth, but of this last, by the determination of the prosecution to convict, he is condemned, would not this appear oppressive in any civilized country? On this subject Mr Wickham enlarged, and called in to view the opportunities which occurred to the British government in the rebellion of 1745, and 1780, had it been determined to follow the accused persons from place to place, but no such opportunities were sought, nor advantage taken He also referred to the custom universally used in England as to jurisdiction, under the rules of the Court of Oyer and Terminer, which was a local jurisdiction in each county, and from whose adjudications, he believed there was no appeal, from which he drew a conclusion, that a case tried in one county was not a sufficient bar to the trial of the same case in another county. But if it were not so, the argument of former trials would be of no avail, since it must be denominated treason against the country

But here it was asked, whether if a man had committed a number of distinct treasons, an acquittal for one would operate as a bar to the trial for others? Certainly not A man might have been tried for the rebellion of '15 and '45 also, and his acquittal for the first could not operate to procure an acquittal in the second instance; but merely for the *rebellion* of '45, no man could be again tried after being once acquitted So with respect to the western insurrection in Pennsylvania, a man might have been indicted for the whiskey insurrection, but, that could not clear him of a connection with the hot water insurrection, although he might not have been guilty of the first The plans and periods were so distinct that no connection could be formed between them, which could not be the case with one continued act of insurrection, for there an acquittal for one act of the transaction would operate upon the whole.

The question must then rest upon the character of the act, and be resolved by this principle, to wit whether it was in the execution of *one general* design or project, and whether that was of the nature now suggested? If it was, the verdict of discharge in one case would certainly operate as an acquittal in all other

But it was said, that the acquittal which took place was an acquittal of the Court and not of the Jury, because of the direction given by the Court How far this observation was correct it was easy to decide, because the acquittal was upon the verdict of a Jury, and that for want of legal testimony, applicable to the case, after every invitation was made by the Court, and all possible patience for its production The Court thought that there was no crime committed, it was true on Blannerhasset's island; but this did not alter the nature of the plea of *auterfoits acquit*, because it inevitably was proved that the accused was innocent from the acquittal, and no declaration of the attorney respecting additional evidence, if he were to say now, that he had twenty witnesses which he could before produce, could govern the Court to re-try the case which had been already tried and discharged

The accused had denied any guilt in any act *done* by him, or charged to him on Blannerhasset's island and had taken his trial upon that denial, a Jury had pronounced the verdict of innocence upon all the evidence that could be produced to them, it was presumed. Now how could he be tried again by a declaration, that the prosecution had some new witnesses?

It was said however, that the Court would not admit of acts in Kentucky to be given in evidence else they could have obtained his conviction. It was true that this argument appeared very plausible to a man unlearned in the law, but if the gentleman would view it as a professional man, and analize it as a lawyer, he must discover his mistake. But here strikes in the common argument " He must be acquitted and escape from justice without a trial!" Yes, he must, but whose fault would it be? There could be no hardship in it, since it could not violate a single principle of justice, as the government had the selection of their own spot for trial, and all the means to execute their own pleasure as far as justice would permit them. He chose this spot without Col Burr having it in his power to exercise any will of his own: and here he is brought for trial at the pleasure of the attorney, without even the slightest appearance of a crime committed in the district.

Mr Wickham continued his discant upon the jurisdiction and plea of former acquittal. He also referred to the form of the former indictment which had been spoken of before, and defended some of the observations made in allusion to the second trial of Fries at that time He concluded by observing, that there could be no possible ground upon which the motive for removal could be sustained

There never was a second charge of the same offence in all the wars, even of red and white roses, when, like vultures, the creatures of government were hovering round the head of every man, numbers were acquitted notwithstanding He also said the same of the capricious reign of Henry 8th—the time of the Stuarts, the commonwealth of Cromwell, when every opportunity was eagerly clutched at to procure a conviction of those that were pointed out as the objects of persecution He also made some allusion to the case of Horne Tooke and others, where, upon the principle now contended for, there might have been twenty conspiracies hatched up He disclaimed any allusion to motives in this prosecution, he meant to speak of acts which must be handed down to posterity As a citizen of this country he should feel much hurt, if it were not recorded on the books of this Court that the attorney had failed. It must fail

Mr Hay referred to Logwood's case, who was indicted for counterfeiting one indictment was for counterfeiting a particular bank note; another, a different one, so that he was tried not less than five or six times, and convicted and punished for them all

It was my object, in my former declarations, to say, that though Col Burr had been acquitted, he was not acquitted for the same offence as he is now charged with, because it was an offence committed in a different district

Mr *Wickham* That will resolve itself into the main question of identity of crime. If the Court should think it to be the same crime, he must be discharged

Mr *Martin* There is no such thing as continuity, in a case of counterfeiting a number of bank notes, they are all distinct offences. But in levying war, suppose a person to kill fifty men, or to burn several houses, it is not denominated murder or arson, because it is in the continued act of levying war, and there called the same levying war

Mr *Wirt* commenced in answer to Mr. Wickham's arguments of the identity of the offence, on which ground he could not be tried twice The English statute of Mary declares, " That all trials of treason shall, from henceforth, be according to the course of the common law " Now, in order to discover this, application must be made to the common law books on the subject, 2 Hawk P C ch 25 sect 1 It was necessary, Mr. Wirt said, to analize the description of it as given by Hawkins, in order to come to a right understanding of him. In order to make a former acquittal at bar, there must be at least three things occur. The indictment must be from error, the case must be well commenced, and it must be tried before a Court which has jurisdiction of the offence Several cases were put, by way of illustration In answer, Mr. Wickham had referred to Sect. 8 But on that, it was certain that the error would have been discovered and discharged by the Court before the acquittal

It must be tried " before any Court which had jurisdiction of the case " On this it was necessary to rest a little He would remark on Mr Wickham's idea of the meaning of Hawkins, that if this Court had a right to enquire into the treason, it could not be again enquired into here. It was proper to advert to the 10th sect, which proves the jurisdiction to be upon local ground, and not with a general view to the subject In the margin here, it is, that an acquittal in Wales is a good plea in bar, to a trial in England The article of *variance* relied on by Mr Wickham, Mr. Wirt also examined. A man is indicted for the murder of A in the county of B, but the evidence proving nothing, he must be acquitted. But he is afterwards indicted for the very same murder in the proper county the question then will be, whether proof of a former acquittal will avail? Stanford thinks it, but Hawkins does not think it will Now then, how stands the reason of the law ? Why, a man shall not be twice put in jeopardy of his life for the same crime. Why, he is not put in jeopardy of his life at a place where the offence was not committed, because he could not be convicted there By the reasoning of the law then, a man may be tried twice for the same crime But suppose it was so that Mr Burr did levy war in Kentucky and in Virginia too, certainly they must be considered as widely different crimes, and the reasoning of the law must yield to the principles that he might be again tried, or where else Is the holding of a castle in Virginia the same crime as fighting a battle in Kentucky? They are both levying war, and distinct ones; as in the case of forgery every act is a distinct forgery. And so it is in piracy every act bears the same generic name

But in cases of treason, the gentleman says, that if it be composed of different acts, yet it is but one war against the United States. that the crime is a general one, for that it was as much against the people of Maine as those of Georgia, or any other state. True, but that could be no reason that the prosecution should be prevented from beginning with the beginning, and failing in that, to follow him down to Bayou Pierre. the indictment tied them down to an insulated spot, that of Virginia, and that was the boundary which was made to the evidence. Now could it be said that they were trying this whole treason, which was denominated a *general* charge? By no means. this charge did not cover the union, although the crime extended to some other parts of it which they were not permitted to touch. When we go into a review of the trial which we have had here, said Mr Wirt, if it deserves the name of trial, it must surprize us that it should be held up in bar to a motion of this sort. The acquittal here does not prove that there was no war in Kentucky, or at all any where, but only that we could not prove one in Virginia

As to the power to send to the Mississippi territory, Mr Wirt would only make a remark. If an offence had been committed before the Mississippi territory had been separated from Georgia, it would have been an offence within that state, but certainly against the United States. And certainly there was no dismemberment of that country, (4th art old ordinance.) They had the liberty, as well as the Judges here, to take cognizance of offences, and their Juries act upon the same principles. the Judges have their functions in the same way. How then is this country dismembered.

Mr. *Wickham* I do not wish any expressions of mine to be construed more strongly than I intended them. particularly as I dare say that the people there, are as well off as they are in the district of Columbia, and their practice the same. I say that there is no political liberty in that country—civil, I know there is.

Mr. *Wirt* said that he supposed if the accused went there to be tried, it would be of no consequence whether those people were represented in congress or not, since what he would have to regard would be, whether the Court and Jury were governed by such usages as they are in Virginia

The act of congress he contended had used the word " *district*" as a general word for jurisdiction. The principal question for the Court to enquire was, whether there were crimes committed by him sufficient in that district for him to be sent there, as to any other district for trial? The act of congress which separated this district from that of Georgia, only intended to make two of what was before but one—the district of Georgia. The ordinance of 1787 expressly provided that all the acts of congress should be of a general nature, from this ordinance, the act of congress was nothing more than an act of supererogation, in order to assure the people that their former privileges were continued to them. Could it be supposed that they were to be deprived of their judicial rights when they were separated? Again could it be supposed that it was ever intended by congress that crimes should be committed with impunity within the territorial line, because the culprit could overstep that line and successfully escape justice?

Mr Wirt concluded with some observations respecting the judgment of the Supreme Court, and a misunderstanding of which had led to the errors the prosecution had fallen into, by which they had failed. But it was not the attorney alone which had misunderstood that opinion, but a Grand Jury, who were truly denominated of the most enlightened men in Virginia.

Some conversation of little importance occurred between Mr Wirt and Mr *Wickham;* when Mr. Wirt made some remarks, merely enforcing his observations as to the confidence which they had placed in the opinion of the Supreme Court; and that if the accused was innocent of the crime, he ought to have made it appear. His guilt or innocence remained as undecided in view of every body, as it was, before there was an examination. There remained therefore but two courses to pursue. either to set him at large without enquiry as to his general guilt, or else to take a course to send him to some place where his guilt could be made to appear. For this purpose he had risen to make the foregoing desultory observations.

Mr *Botts* was sorry that the gentleman had thought it necessary to rise for the purpose of making these desultory observations, because he might have taken another time and occasion for some of them. But if he had committed an error, all that they could do, would be to take the usual course of answering to them. Mr Botts then proceeded upon some supposed observations of Mr Wirt on jurisdiction, which Mr. Wirt rose and denied.

Then the identity of crime was a point that he would make some remarks upon, which could not be supported but on the point of continuity. If it was not a disjointed offence, then it certainly was a continued offence, and consequently the same He supposed a case—that the United States was divided into counties for Courts of Oyer and Terminer, from Maine to Georgia, and that a rebel army had passed through the whole of them, would it be reasonable that a man, for being with that army, and acquitted in one county, should be dragged through all the counties and tried? The absurdity of this practice would have been acknowledged, but this would merit an odium of the same precise nature.

But now the gentlemen are willing to acknowledge that there was nothing done on Blannerhasset's island. Now before this, while the case was pending, it was said that we were ridiculous for supposing that they could not prove the crime We have all along believed, that there was nothing done there that could be called a crime of any kind; and we aver that a trial having been held on that charge he cannot be carried from state to state for a continuity of the crime, more than for a charge from county to county.

What would be the consequence, if an acquittal was to take place in Kentucky if he was to be sent there? why they would make their efforts to take him to some other state or territory. But what does the law say? Why, you have made your selection and to that selection you must abide still they would contend that no trial had been held, and thus would it be from place to place, if this court shall give them permission

It was denied that it was by the influence or knowledge of the government Mr Botts expressed his joy that it was, and it was now for the first time announced to the public, that it was not one of the acts of violence which had been charged But a question must yet remain to satisfy the public, why Mississippi territory or Kentucky was not at first selected? The fact is, that from where the greatest offences were committed, they have removed him to where none appears, and that without a motive being urged Gentlemen must be in an unfortunate condition indeed to be forced to subscribe to the confession. They removed him however from his witnesses (but this he would not ascribe to motive and design) Mr B continued his argument on the continuity and identity of the expedition

But this trial (if it deserved the name of one) Mr Wirt had said was not a bar In some respects to be sure it did not deserve the name of a trial It began with a truly tragical appearance, but it eventuated as some comedies do, with a farce, whoever were the principal actors in it he would not say,) but he wished it to be remembered that neither comic farce, nor after piece originated in them for they had not appeared in it from choice, but necessity, and yet it was an all serious trial, brought before the highest jurisdiction in the United States.

The next thing they came to was the question of *district*.

Mr Hay certainly deserved the credit of discovery, he said, to find out that there was such a thing as a judicial district in the Mississippi territory It was necessary, he contended, when gentlemen were talking about a district, that they should examine what the legislature meant by the word When the congress was speaking of a juridical district, that and no other was meant, that would be seen in the second *section*, but what juridical district was there in Mississippi territory? Collecting districts there are. When the word *district* is used, it is invariably applied to states, but this is not a case with a territory.

But this *casus omissus* is a serious thing. It certainly is so for them, because it inevitably disables you, if you were so disposed, from sending Col Burr to a second trial for the same crime and particularly when it is proposed to send him to the same spot he was sent from And if there be a construction to be put upon the statute, Sir, you are to construe it with the greatest liberality in a penal case. Mr. Botts trusted the Chief Justice would not permit his mind to be searching out for meaning of laws to draw Col Burr into eternal prosecutions.

But the judgment of the Supreme Court had been employed to promote the removal To this he answered in a few words; but he said it was clear that this argument was used for the purpose of conviction; because the application was to the Chief Justice himself, who had delivered that opinion He referred to some parts of it in reference to the opinion of Judges Chase and Iredell. (See the appendix.) He also went over the old ground of error into which the prosecutors had fallen from a misunderstanding. He confessed that they knew the gentlemen must commit errors, and he would yield so far to them as to say, that if the intentions of the Supreme Court were what the attorney, &c. had supposed, he must confess himself to be perfectly blind, and not know A from B, and force from no force.

Mr *Botts* then referred to the additional support, which besides the Supreme court, they had the corroboration to their opinions of a most enlightened Grand Jury. He did not know how it got into that body, nor how far they had been misled; but if they had been misled, it might have occurred from the public argument which occurred previous to their bringing in their bill. The prosecutors then must have led them into error, if they were in an error, as to the opinion of the Supreme Court.

Again. The 6th section of the act establishing the Mississippi territory, declared that that territory should be entitled to the benefits of the territory in 1787, and it was attempted to be proved by legal reasoning, that under the operation of the extension of that right, a man might to be taken up, tried there, and executed. Mr Botts said he never before knew that it was a benefit to a man to be taken up and executed. This could only be implied. He took the real meaning of it to be, that if there were any benefits to be derived to the people from the territorial ordinance of Ohio, they might enjoy them, but if there were any whose operation would injure them, they might refuse them.

To evade the continuity of this action, there was another idea presented by Mr Hay, which he conceived to bear as much perplexity on its face. Any immunities of taking away a man's life, those immunities were sought to be applied to Col Burr. This indeed, would be a benefit for which he ought to be thankful. How he intends it, Mr Botts said he did not know, but he did seem to wonder how Col Burr could so suddenly have disappeared in Pennsylvania, and appeared in the Mississippi territory. That he should have sunk on Blannerhasset's island, and rose twelve hundred miles off with such facility, and if that could be the case, then there would the connection of the whole appear evident. Whether it was possible to make this an immunity for taking away life by proof belonging to himself, remained to be unfolded. If there should be such a case, the gentleman might argue it, that Aaron Burr became a mole, and committed war under ground; and afterwards landed safe and victorious, to recommence afresh. There would be really as much justice and propriety in such, and war in such an act, if war must be performed, as there has been in any war that can be proved to exist between those two when Col Burr was above ground.

Mr *Burr*. It was hoped that this argument would have been concluded before now : but the question is an important one, Sir; very important indeed. This is the sixth trial which I have had to encounter, and it seems really desirous that I should know how many trials a man may undergo for the same thing. The gentlemen have been invited to shew whether there is cause, but they have not produced it. We wish them to produce evidence, precedent, or authority. They notwithstanding call on you to give your weight and sanction to their wishes I trust that if any other gentleman should be desirous of speaking, he will be indulged, but it is now too late for this day.

Chief Justice. There is one fact necessary to be examined, and that is, whether by the act under the former government, there was really a Court created in the territory north west of the Ohio. The ordinance was passed under the government of the former congress: I do not recollect whether that provision was made or not.

Mr. *Martin* There is one fact; that at the period when the judiciary law passed, much of what is now the Mississippi territory was claimed by, and actually was in possession of the Spanish government

Mr. *Burr* hoped the gentleman would go more into it to-morrow.

Mr. *Hay* said that he had not heard of any trial in that territory. There was one examination in Kentucky, and another here.

Mr. *Randolph* observed, that to-morrow he should endeavor to take up the subject, though he was fearful that he could not convince the gentleman.

Mr. Randolph had hoped, that with the second verdict of acquittal there would have been an end to every attempt at our liberties, but it seemed that the gentlemen were not satisfied without a double defeat. But I am mortified, that, on my part, I shall have to confront the invasion of the rights of our citizens, and the violation of the spirit of our constitution, for both these things are involved.

To transport a man from Virginia to the Mississippi territory, does at the first mention of it, sound harsh in an American ear — When I look back, Sir, to the magna charta, I find that an opposition to this very measure of transportation, was purchased with the sword. When I advert to the numerous instances which called for American vengeance against British tyranny, I find one of its prominent incitives to be, in the transportation of persons to another country.

Mr R then adverted to the law of 1789, but this ought to be construed strictly, because strictness of construction was necessary in a penal code, in order to prevent it becoming the engine of oppression. And civil precedents once established, would cause a thousand more He would not call this a *casus omissus*, though even that would be a sufficient reason why a Court should not act But the constitution was enough: that instrument speaks of " *States*" and " *territories* ;" and in distinction, the one from the other It speaks of thirteen States; and upon them all that great act of legislation seems to have been intended to operate, as well as such as might be thereafter made States. With relation to the territories of the U. S. they were to be provided with all needful regulations by Congress. Here the regulations are distinct. States existing; States which might thereafter exist; and territories different from States, and which may be denominated a kind of colonies

Why then if the word States comprehended every thing which belonged to our citizens, was this power specifically provided for: that Congress should make all needful regulation relative to territories of the United States? The name "State" cannot comprehend a territory in any respect, otherwise why was this power particularly given?

Here Mr Randolph adverted to the arguments and feelings exemplified on the extension of powers, and the fear of creating treasons, &c in the convention of Virginia on the formation of the constitution of the United States.

On the first session, immediately after the formation of the Congress met, when each member might be supposed to have brought with him all the feelings of his constituents, after their recent debates and jealousies of their privileges in their several conventions. Immediately a law passed on the subject of the judiciary, and there is not in that law, in spite of the ingenuity of gentlemen, who have endeavored to discover one, a single word that applies to a territory as to their prosecution of crimes against the United States (He read the law in part, and the marginal heads, p. 45 to 75. laws U. S vol. 1 ch. 18) He demanded of gentlemen to point to the place.

A "district" it was contended must apply to this particular case, because this territory was a district A district, it was urged had various senses, one only was mentioned, and that was a revenue district; but there were two others A district for the temporary purposes of government, (such as collections, and a judicial district.) Now the word temporary is used at the same time the word territory is spoken of, and the term district then cannot comprehend the judicial district. it means for the temporary purposes of government; and at the time the law divided that territory into two districts, (Ohio and Indiana) it meant two governments, and not judicial districts Laws U. S. May, 1800.

Mr Randolph next went into a review of the private inconvenience and public expence attending binding one hundred and twenty or more witnesses at this place, to attend at such a distance ; and provision would undoubtedly have been made to avoid this grievance, if Congress had thought it possible, that a man could thus be transported to a territory. But this was contended for, because that territory was once a part of Georgia | If it was once so, it has since been severed into a territory. Again. If any power is to be claimed on this score, it ought to be in the name of the State of Georgia, because it was a part of itself once. But this cannot be, more than those parts of other territories could by the States to which they may have once belonged. At the time of the formation of the Ohio territory in 1787, the judiciary act was not formed nor thought of Subsequent laws have since to be sure been formed, in which it has been declared, that the Superior Court of Ohio, shall take upon themselves certain powers, under the laws of Congress, but these relate not to the cognizance of crimes, such as relate to the present case ; as that of removal for trial.

But what a serious and lamentable thing it would be if this was a *casus omissus*, and there was no power to transmit Reason, justice, and humanity would be infringed upon. Yes, they would, bacause no man would be beyond punishment! Every man would be forever open to persecution, by the presentments of different States, unless he should shew the record of his acquittal, which we contend closes the whole business Congress never intended to surrender this right by their provision of any jurisdiction by any homogeneous law. They meant to be uniform in their code

Humanity In criminal cases it means *oppression* and *power*. What is oppressive, if forcing a man to go twelve hundred miles for trial after he has been acquitted here, is not?

But what if there be no such power, it was asked, would this Court exclude testimony to be heard, whilst sitting as a committing magistrate? Yes Mr Randolph said, the Court had more than once declared he would exclude irrelevant testimony, and consequently if there existed no power to order to a territory for trial, every thing must be irrelevant, and the Court had no right to receive such testimony.

If there was danger, that suitable notification would not be made on this transaction, he would observe, that it would not be from the want of industry, power, money, or disposition to collect and transmit testimony from one end of the United States to the other How many depositions are in the port folio of the attorney for the United States? How much testimony can their agents produce? What part of America has not been ransacked for information? Even the contents of the executive bureau has been transmitted Do not then spend your time, Sir, of which too much has already been spent, merely to be informed of what has been done in the Mississippi territory, respecting which you have no cognizance.

But there is no danger of oppression to an individual, by any composition between the government and an attorney, Grand Jury, &c our government is too pure Sir, we have not lived so long in the world as not to know that political purity will not remain forever Although I am confident of the greatness and purity of the man who is now at the helm of our public affairs, I *may* have reason to change, with respect to others who may not have been tried I will never be an engine to save from acts of oppression, while it is put in the power of government, as a great mammoth, to create devastation : unless it is watched carefully by the people, least it should rise too gigantic to be coped with.

I will not trust the president with power, nor any man who is capable of becoming *corrupt*, and that *every* man is

Next Such power was not supposed to belong to Congress according to the constitution when this law was passed. The strict letter of that instrument, and the imminent danger that accompanied a deviation from it in this respect, opened to their view. This however Mr R would leave to the discretion of the Chief Justice.

The next, and most important point which affected this case is, that of *auterfoits acquit.*

A former acquittal, he said, was a principle at common law, and incorporated into our constitution in both, this splintering of offences into various acts was strictly prohibited It was like the radii belonging to the same circle: all arising from the same identical centre, and belonging to the same figure It was like the

Ohio in its full continued course, divisable, perhaps, by little land marks; but still the water below and the water above, only constitute the Ohio He knew of no attorney that could create a omnipresence of action in one man It would seem then, that when natural justice was to be applied to, public vengeance is to affect every part of the administration of it, if the prosecutor was right

Here Mr R asked for precedents—whether ever reiterated attempts had been made to promote the conviction of a man acquitted before for the same crime? History gave no intelligence on the subject

There was an observation of Mr Hay, which Mr R would take some notice of—it was, that there was a difference between the situation of England, and this country, inasmuch as that England covered but a small spot of ground, and there the prosecutor might see the whole spot and extend with accuracy He believed there were as many hiding places and refuges in England as there were in Virginia, if the comparison was made. But in neither had there ever been exhibited a scene of second prosecution.

By resorting to the common law, he found that the first motive was, " let there be an end to the dispute at some time or other " And how strong must this maxim appear when the life of a man is at stake? He would not admit that any English cases could counteract the doctrine for which they contended, but on the contrary in affirmance of it. A man may be indicted for burglary in stealing the goods of A, and acquitted, and afterwards he may be indicted for larceny in stealing the goods of B ; but he could not have been twice indicted for the same burglary. And why? Because the great generical crime has already received a verdict of acquittal This Mr R compared to the case of treason The very authorities which were read by Mr. Wirt, he contended, were against himself, (Hawkins) because here there was no veiled misapprehension or mistake could be pleaded—the question then must be, whether the substance of the offence was not really the same as before tried?

M. Randolph observed that Mr Wickham's argument was construed to be founded upon a very wrong basis, because he had said that no man was to be brought in jeopardy twice for the same offence Here Mr Randolph went into an enquiry of what was the " same offence." The definition must rest on the word same. An offence created by the same words of the same law . integrality as to authorities to support its character to the same, the same facts, the same parties; supported by the same integral charge This he elucidated by some supposed cases. He would ask whether an instance occurred where evidence was divided and subdivided into different offences, when there was but one charge? He had examined every civil, criminal and penal case, but could not find the principle affirmed any where in any degree If a man exhibits an account against another, and he omits an article of 100l. which constitutes a part of the account, a verdict shuts him out forever, and no apology for his being misled, that his clerk deceived him, would operate, because the verdict is conclusive Again How many men have been acquitted, whom most men believed to be guilty ; and very shortly after, testimony has come forward that would shew their guilt but no attorney would be permitted, after the verdict, to renew the trial; because no co-existent facts can afterwards be introduced, that could have been given before.

Here came in the argument so often wrung in their ears. Mr Randolph said, of the insipiency and embryo of the transaction at Beaver, which progressed until they arrived at the mouth of Cumberland. Blannerhasset's island was before supposed to exhibit the centre and scene of the same scheme; but that failing, this resource was hit upon. Now, he asked whether this could be the same offence? He would appeal to the world to know whether that which was in complete subordination to it, can be itself? It would be an useless multiplication of words to say more on the subject. Here Mr Randolph went into a metaphysical view of identity as to person, which he compared to acts, and made some inferences applicable to his argument.

But there was no jurisdiction in this Court as to acts done in Mississippi territory. And what then? The verdict says, that he is to be acquitted of treason against the United States. To be sure it locates itself at Blannerhasset's island, but that does not alter the acquittal for the crime against the United States

Reference was made to the opinion of the Court, but he was not certain whether the Court meant what the gentleman attributed to it. It did not touch much at large on it, and indeed there was but little discussion on it. But it was asked whether it did not appear in Deacon's case, recited in Foster, that there were many acts done out of the county which might be brought in, to explain an act done in the county. You yourself, Sir, have said, that where this main act shall be proved, auxiliary acts might be brought in. I do not pretend to view the extent of this doctrine at this moment: there are cases in which testimony of this sort would be admissible; but can it be produced in a case where he was acquitted of an offence with which he was charged, for want of some other testimony which might have been exhibited.

But it was asked whether the holding a castle in Virginia was the same offence as the figting a battle in Kentucky? Are they parts of the same scheme, or are they distinct treasons? Determine me an answer to this question, and then my answer is ready. If they are distinct treasons, carried on by different leaders, with different means, and to complete different objects in view, then I should not consider them as inclusive under one indictment, of any sort: but, if they are part of the same scheme, under the same leaders, and with the same system of conduct, then I contend it matters not how wide spread they are from each other, provided their acts are all subservient to the same object.

Suppose that all the overt acts laid relative to the treason existed in the same district, and one only was charged, would the person after acquittal for that one, meet twenty more? every man must acknowledge that this could not be the case. And what would be the reason? Plainly this—That the attorney has it in his power to introduce his other acts, in some form or other if not as a substantive charge in the indictment, at least as an auxiliary

Here Mr. Randolph observed, that on the doctrine of treason, our constitution and the common law were synonimous Mr Wirt had quoted Hawkins, who said that if a case was well commenced, provision was made by common law for the future proceedings, such as a power to give in evidence, &c But if there be no power to commence a trial in a different county, which Hawkins will show it is not law to do, then how can it be " well commenced?" There may be marginal notes from other authorities, but place it on the ground of acquittal, Sir, and take a view of penal jurisdiction agreeable to his ideas, you must always say " acquit," and if you have a doubt upon the subject, you will say so I would rather say, in fact, as Mr Hay says, that the line has not yet been drawn, and that it is an original case in this country; and therefore I would wish to have our own construction, and view the consequences of the different positions, according to the understandings of the plain people of this country, without regard to the refinements of English constructions, though I say they are in my favor.

As to the constructions of the people in America, I will view the consequences on each side Suppose an acquittal be admitted, or the former verdict be supported, what harm is done to the public ? It only requires that in future, the examination should be more precise, and the tribunal to be more fitly chosen. Is it proper that we should undergo this immense hardship merely to save trouble and care to those who conduct public prosecutions ? If there be twenty parties to the same war, look well to where the most pointed testimony is, choose that, and stick to it But do you exclude, then all the other parts? No, Sir If one overt act will go directly to prove another overt act that is laid. it is possible that you may do so. there is no harm done to the public It only requires a little more attention, and the United States is secure

Mr Randolph here reiterated his remarks of the industry used by the government to obtain evidence. He supposed the whole chart had been exposed, and that there was not a town nor hovel between New-Hampshire and Orleans but had been tried to obtain testimony, in any way, or of any sort

Gentlemen speak of consequences if it should escape punishment, as if an overt act was to be treated as a branch of revenue Must all this parsimony of the government be used in order to find food for all these worms on human life ?

He then descanted on the kiln dried malt, pork, &c. that had been prepared, and the expences which must attend the accused, not merely in the circumstances on the Muskingum, but what had occurred otherwise by witnesses and yet must, besides the immense danger for want of keeping and sending them from place to place If this was suffered, he should not wonder if, at a future day, even a Raleigh might have his trial postponed until all his witnesses had perished, and he fall a sacrifice

He also spoke of article 8, amendment constitution, requiring a speedy trial, and of what policy a government would exhibit, was it not for that valuable point, and recapitulated some of his former arguments about a person's being dragged from place to place

He answered to Logwood's case, where six indictments were proved. Was not every emission of a forged bill a separate felony, and every setting of a type a separate felony? Every stroke of a man who managed the printing press was a separate felony, and not at all in subservience to the one great scheme. Each act was subservient to the amount of the several bills. But was this the case in treason, where meal, pork, boats, &c were brought to prove the one general scheme?

Mr. Randolph then referred to the opinion of the Supreme Court. It was his duty as counsel to select every argument, although it might appear to clash with so high an authority, and therefore had it upon the grounds, first, that the opinion was extra judicial. Secondly, upon a more solid ground, that the construction was different from the opinion itself. But what was this subterfuge? Was it not to lead the counsel on the other side into a second prosecution?

A mistake! A mistake in counsel to produce a rotation of indictments! How often has it happened that an attorney general has been mistaken in his indictment, but when did we ever before this, hear of a mistake in the prosecution producing cause for a new trial? But if ever it was necessary, it is not in this case. How long have we been engaged in this prosecution? The first that we found of it was, the attorney general of the U. S. acting as a general and making out the *camp*. Some other general after that, we found commanding the line of march. They marched forward from stage to stage, and at last we hear them cry out " *a mistake*." If there be a mistake it is no cause with you to commiserate it, by ordering a new trial any where else.

But the most subtle of the arguments used, Mr R said, was that case of murder, where it was said, that if a man had been indicted and acquitted in the wrong county, he could be tried again in the proper county. It was remarkable though, that none of the gentlemen produced a case of treason. Indeed none of the books did make mention of one, and the reason might be, that many overt acts in different places might be introduced into the indictment. The case of murder had no analogy. There may be distinct murders committed, for which a man is answerable distinctly. An averment would make them appear to be distinct acts, although the words, except as to place and name were the same.

Mr R. drew towards a conclusion with some keen remarks on the prosecution : they were not supported he said, by English law, nor precedent; nor by the constitution or laws of this country.

Before he concluded, he would observe, that it was said, that neither the guilt nor innocence of the person accused had been justified. What could be the meaning of that? He has been acquitted by law. They have not yielded to us one iota of law principles ; they have pushed us to all the extremity the law would admit of. And are we to perform the part of a knight errant, and surrender all the principles of law in order to gratify the world? I take it for granted that there is nothing better for society than this—seek the law and no more, and he is a good citizen that seeks the law and no more. Sir, the result of all this consideration, that the present attempt to prosecute Col

Burr must be ended in the opinion of the Court He has been acquitted of the facts charged, and it is the same case whatever they have attempted to shew, yet in all, they have but proved it to be the same case

Then, may it please your honor, when we look to the gentlemen's arguments, we must and *you* must conclude that the Mississippi is shut against them. I hold it to be one of those extraordinary energies that a Court may exercise to declare with divided language upon such an important point of law What, Sir, says Justice Hale ? " If I am called upon to exercise a power upon which I doubt, I never will act " Leave us therefore where we are. If there be a prosecution that any other tribunal think proper to institute, we shall always be within the United States, to answer it. After his acquittal this Court has no right to consider Col. Burr in any other light than any other individual

The *Chief Justice* immediately gave the following opinion

Two questions arise from the present motion

1st Is the Judge who composes this Court, either as a Court or as a magistrate authorized to commit any person for trial in the Mississippi territory

2dly Is the verdict which has been rendered in this Court a bar to a prosecution either in the same or a different state, for different overt acts of the same treason ?

On the first point I will observe as preliminary to a consideration of the act of Congress, which is supposed to give the power contended for, that I have been inclined to think the territorial Courts were erected, not under the third article of the constitution, which defines the judicial power of the United States, but under the fourth article, which enables Congress to make all needful rules and regulations for the government of their territories One reason for this opinion is, that the territorial Courts have cognizance of cases over which Congress, under the third article are incapable of giving jurisdiction to the circuit Courts of the United States. I do not mean to say, that the circuit system may not be extended to the territories. I only mean to say, that the existing territorial Courts are not created in virtue of that article, which creates and defines the judicial powers of the United States.

The act which is denominated the judicial act, passed immediately after the formation of the constitution, and appears to have had exclusively for its object the organization of a system under the third article of that instrument

Its title is "An act to establish *the* judicial Courts of the United States," and it contains no reference to a territorial Court.

The second section divides the United States into districts, no one of which includes any portion of territory not then included in some State In this section then the term " United States" designates the States composing the union in exclusion of that territory which was governed by the United States The word " district" in the same section obviously means a judicial district created by the act The term is plainly used in the same sense in the third section, and in every other part of the act where it is employed, so the term " circuit Court" is never employed but with a plain reference to the Courts created by the act: and under this construction the Supreme Court has refused to take cognizance of an appeal from a territorial Court.

The 33d section authorizes any justice or Judge of the United States, to arrest and commit for any offence against the United States, and because an offence against the United States may unquestionably be committed in a territory, it is argued that these words authorize a Judge here to arrest, and commit for trial there

If these words stood unconnected and uncontrolled by others, I should not consider the sentence as absolutely free from doubt, Although perhaps I might give it the construction required by the counsel for the United States. Some doubt would be induced by the subject matter on which the words are employed. An arrest and commitment of an offender is necessary for the purpose of bringing him to trial and an act creating particular Courts of criminal jurisdiction in order to give effect to an important article of the constitution, and authorizing the Judges of those Courts to arrest and commit offenders for trial generally, might be construed, without departing far from acknowledged rules, to authorize a commitment for trial in those Courts only, to which the constitution and the law related

But all doubt upon this subject is removed by the particular words of the act.

Every person admits that a legislative act like any other instrument, is to be taken altogether, and that general phrases may be explained, and restrained or enlarged by other words which demonstrate the sense in which those general phrases were used Now the sentence authorizing an arrest and commitment for trial proceeds to say before what Court such trial must be had It must be before the Court, which by that act has cognizance of the offence How then can the authority extend to a commitment for trial before a Court. which by that act has no cognizance of the offence ? which derives its jurisdiction from a different act, and is distinct in its character and in its powers The words " such Courts of the United States as by this act have cognizance of the offence," are not senseless There are operative words which form an important part of the description of the power given How then can they be rejected ? The words which authorize the district Judge to remove the person committed into that district in which he is to be tried, must obviously mean that judicial district, and refer as plainly as a reference can be made to that district in which the commitment expresses that the offender is to be tried On this the committing Judge decides

It has been contended, that because the Court for the Mississippi Territory has, by a subsequent act of Congress jurisdiction over all offences committed within the territory, that the grant of jurisdiction to that Court enlarges the power of the committing magistrates of other courts

The correctness of this deduction cannot be admitted. I cannot comprehend that train of reasoning by which the grant of power to one Court, can be considered as enlarging the power of magistrates belonging to another Court, having no relation to the newly created Court, and who are not in any manner contemplated by the act creating that new Court.

But if this point could have been involved in doubt, that doubt is, I think, removed by the circumstances existing at the passage of the judicial act. A territorial Court was then in being, exercising its jurisdiction over offences which were committed within the territory. The Court for the western county, as I perceive, from the journals of the old Congress, was formed soon after the passage for the ordinance for its government. If immediately after the passage of the judicial act, a Judge had been required to commit an offender for trial before that territorial Court, what must have been his answer? He must have said, Congress has empowered me to commit for trial, only before a Court created by the judicial act. On the policy of their motives for this restriction, I am not to decide: such is their will and I am bound to obey it.

If such must have been the construction of the law, with respect to the territorial Court, existing at the time, such must be its construction with respect to other territorial Courts created since, on the same model.

I am on these reasons perfectly clear, that I have no power to commit for trial in the Court for the Mississippi territory, and of consequence it would be altogether improper in me to go into an enquiry on a subject on which I cannot act.

The second question is much more doubtful. It is a constitutional question of great importance, and one which I ought not to decide, unless it becomes absolutely necessary, while a single doubt respecting it exists on my mind. I have attended to the arguments which have been urged on both sides, and doubts upon it do yet exist.

I acknowledge the force of the argument so repeatedly urged, that levying war is one continued crime; and the different overt acts of the same war, are as much parts of the same treason, as different stabs or different doses of poison given to the same individual are parts of the same murder. The difference between levying war and a felony may be in some measure this. If for felony, as robbery or burglary, a man be indicted in the wrong county, he is charged in a jurisdiction in which no part of the offence has been committed; but if he be indicted for levying war within a district through which the force has passed, he is indicted within a district in which a part of the offence has been committed. The arguments at bar formed upon this distinction have great weight with me. They deserve to be more maturely considered. So far as respects overt acts within the same jurisdiction they are perhaps conclusive.

My doubt consists in this. The overt act now charged, could not have been laid in the indictment on which Col. Burr has been tried. There is, therefore, considerable force in the argument that his acquittal does not prevent a distinct indictment for the war in Kentucky. My judgment is not decidedly formed upon this point. I shall therefore hear the testimony relative to the conduct of the accused within the United States, and shall in the mean time, reflect further on this subject. In the course of this reflection it is impossible not to allow much weight to the arguments delivered to-day, especially to that which shows the difference between murder and treason in this, that proving a murder to be committed in another county does absolutely disprove the indictment.

In the course of this argument an incidental altercation at the bar has produced some commentaries on the construction given by this Court to the opinion of the Supreme Court, in the case of Bollman and Swartwout, which I do not think myself at liberty to pass over altogether without notice

Reports may very possibly be in circulation that this Court, instead of obeying, has absolutely reversed a decision of the Supreme Court. While such reports would be entirely incorrect in point of fact, they would cast an imputation on this Court, which, I flatter myself, will never be merited   But such reports may circulate with great facility, and the labor of reading the opinion to which they refer, and which would certainly refute them, will be taken only by a few   If then a declaration made from the bar to myself, evidently purporting that my opinion, instead of construing, reverses that of the Supreme Court, should be heard unnoticed, I certainly might be understood to acquiesce in the remark, and to countenance any reports which might be circulated to the same effect   I therefore feel myself bound to declare, that I have given what I believe to be sound and true legal construction of the opinion of the Supreme Court ; and I feel myself further bound, to state to gentlemen the particular parts of that opinion on which there has been a difference between the construction made by the Court, and that made by the counsel for the prosecution

The points inferred from that opinion by the counsel for the United States, were,

1st. That war might be levied without the application of actual violence to the objects to which it was intended to be applied.

2ndly. That a man might be indicted as being present, on an overt act committed by others in his absence

On the first point, as must be recollected, this Court concurred with the counsel for the prosecution   Their construction was declared to be correct   But because war might be levied without the application of force, they had concluded that war might be levied without the existence of force, and therefore that war was levied on Blannerhasset's island.

I attended to the arguments of gentlemen with all the powers I possess   It required no effort to do this, for their arguments commanded attention , but I do not recollect one sentence from either of them, indicating the idea that the opinion of the Supreme Court dispensed with potential force, with the posture of war ; or that they had reflected seriously on this question.   The court made certainly a very elaborate investigation of this point, but it was produced not by any misconception of it stated at the bar, but in consequence of misconceptions understood to have been formed elsewhere, and because it constituted an important question then on trial

The second point, was one on which there was clearly an opposition between the construction of the law made by the counsel for the prosecution, and that of the Court.   On the part of the prosecution it was clearly understood that an absent man might

be indicted for an overt act committed by another. I am persuaded that gentlemen, if they will examine the train of reasoning by which their minds were conducted to this conclusion,
will satisfy themselves that they have been misled by ideas drawn
from other sources than the opinion to which this error has been
imputed

By the common law, accessories in treason are principals, and
they have understood a declaration that a man leagued in a conspiracy may become a traitor by performing a part distinct from
that of appearing in arms as an adoption of this common law
principle. I am persuaded that when the feelings created by
warm contestation shall subside, gentlemen will themselves suspect that this conclusion has been precipitately drawn

No sensation whatever has been excited by the remarks which
have occasioned these observations, other, than the opinion that
this explanation has been rendered necessary by them.

Gentlemen will, if they please, proceed with their testimony
relative to the conduct of the accused in the United States

James M'Dowell.

Mr *Hay.* Did you go as low as the Chickasaw Bluffs? *A* I
did Q. What number of men were assembled at the mouth of
Cumberland river? *A* About one hundred Q How many additional men joined them there? *A.* I do not recollect Q Did
you see any boxes of arms? *A.* No Q. Did you see any guns
with bayonets? *A* I saw a few Q Any pistols? *A* Six or
eight pair; and some rifles. Q Do you know of any men who
joined them at Fort Massac?

Mr. *Burr* objected to this question Fort Massac was in the
Indiana Territory

Mr. *Hay* Did you see any powder? *A* Yes. Q What quantity? *A* A couple of small casks. Q Did you see any bullets,
and what quantity? *A.* I helped to run some myself, and I saw
one barrel about two thirds full I saw those bullets below Bayou
Pierre. Q Did you see Blannerhasset and Smith? *A.* Yes
Q Did this party seem to be under Burr's command? *A* They
said, it was Col Burr's boats and party They regarded themselves as under his direction. Q Were there any other officers
apparently under Burr's command? *A* Yes. Colonel Tyler was
an officer and Mr Blannerhasset seemed to be one; but not to
have so much command as colonel Tyler

Mr *Wirt.* Did you see any agricultural tools such as ploughs
and hoes, adapted to the settlement of lands? *A* Not any. Q
Were there any families; that is, any men with their wives? *A.*
There were two families. Q. Of what description of character
was this part composed? *A* Principally of young men. Q. Did
they appear to be men, accustomed to plantation labor? *A.* Some
of them appeared fit; but most of them seemed like gentlemen.

Mr. *Hay* presumed that it would not be departing from the o-
pinion of the Court, if he asked a question concerning some
transaction out of the United States which might serve to elucidate the state of the party at the mouth of Cumberland Might
he not, for instance, enquire whether the witness had seen any
boxes of arms at Bayou Pierre; because it was perfectly fair to

infer, that if they had not been subsequently received, they must have been with the party *at* the mouth of Cumberland river

Mr *Burr* No precise inference can be drawn from that circumstance because these arms might have been received into the boats below the line of Tennessee.

The *Chief Justice* thought it a proper question if the acts attempted to be proved were done in the United States, evidence might be drawn from any place to prove them But no evidence could be produced to prove an act, that was done in the United States.

Mr *Baker* This is really a strange mode of inferring circumstances by contrast The witness says expressly that they were not at the mouth of Cumberland, and yet he is to be interrogated whether he did not see them at Bayou Pierre

Mr *M'Dowell.* I did not say that they were not at the mouth of Cumberland I said only, that I did not see them there

Mr *Hay* Was there then any fact to induce you to believe that there were chests of arms on board? A I did not see them But they took in some boxes at Blannerhasset's island Q Did they take in any boxes between the mouth of Cumberland and Bayou Pierre? A None Q Did you see any at Bayou Pierre? A Yes, I saw more in my boat, but there were more men came into it some at Cumberland, and some at some other place some of the boats leaked ; and the men left them and came to us

Mr *Wirt.* You say that there were about one hundred men at the mouth of Cumberland river Was there any accession to this party afterwards? A It was increased before we got to Coles's Creek Q What was the total amount of the party? A There were about one hundred and thirty at Coles's Creek Q Was there any application to you to join them? A Mr Blannerhasset applied to me. Q In what manner? A He asked me to go along with him ; but I said I did not wish to go without knowing where they were going He was at me two or three times. He said that many men were going, without knowing any more than I did I told him I had very little in the world ; but that I did not wish to leave it in that way

Mr *Burr* here interrupted the examination. He observed that the counsel for the prosecution were bound to prove the overt act first ; that there was no impropriety in producing circumstances explanatory of the overt act , but how could these conversations between other persons, and held in his absence, contribute to establish this act, or how could they affect him?

Mr *Hay* contended that these circumstances might contribute to shew the intentions of the party and the character of the enterprize.

The *Chief Justice* considered this as admissible testimony If the counsel for the prosecution charge a military assemblage at the mouth of Cumberland, they were at liberty to produce every circumstance explanatory of the nature of that assemblage He considered conversations among the men themselves at the mouth of Cumberland as admissible, because they contributed to show the nature of the expedition ; and why should not conversations that were afterwards held, be as explanatory as those which were there maintained? The charge too, was not confined to the mouth of that river, but was extended to any place below that. which was in the limits of the United States. It is then immaterial where these conversations passed, because they make a part of the transactions at the places actually charged

Mr. *Botts* objected that these conversations were not held within the United States, because the jurisdiction of Mississippi had never extended beyond the margin of the Mississippi

Mr *Wickham*, with all due respect to the Court, observed that he had understood the Court to say formerly that they were not at liberty to go into collateral testimony, until they proved the overt act, but they certainly do give collateral testimony when they examine into matters down the river, &c. But the gentlemen say they offer testimony about the overt act. Surely if there is not a tittle of testimony likely to prove an overt act, the Court will stop all further examination

Chief Justice There is no doubt but the overt act must be proved in the first instance, but when witnesses are called to prove an overt act, the Court cannot say that that particular testimony does not relate to an overt act, and therefore stop them

Now I suppose that the conversation at the island forms a part of the transaction; and may be heard, to prove a military assembly, in any other part of the evidence Now, I hold the conversation among the men, who were assembled at that time, to be a part of the meeting on the island, and may be given in evidence The conversation of the same company, proceeding lower down the island, (especially within the United States) to come within the rule laid down by the Court, and really as a part of the transaction

Chief Justice, to the witness Where was it that Blannerhasset made the application to you to go with him? *A* It was somewhere above the Chickasaw Bluffs. *Q* Where is Coles's creek? *A* Near Natchez.

Mr *Burr* I shall submit to the opinion of the Court, but how conversations at any other time or place can be received, I know not This may have no reference to the meeting on the island

Considerable conversation ensued between Messrs. Wickham, Martin, Burr, Baker and Botts, with the Chief Justice, as to the opinion he gave to all of whom, he answered similarly to the above explanation After which some conversation occurred between Messrs Burr, Botts, Wickham and Hay, about the jurisdiction. The contest was, whether the borders of Tennessee on the river belonged to the United States or to the Indians The map was examined, but it was not decided

Mr. M·Dowel was dismissed, and William Love, Blannerhasset's groom was called into Court.

William Love.

Mr *Hay*. Did you not go down with the boats? *A*. I went down from Blannerhasset's island. I considered myself as his servant. *Q*. Did you see any boxes of arms? *A*. I saw one chest in Mr Floyd's boat. *Q* How many men went from Blannerhasset's island? *A*. About twenty-five *Q* Did any more men join you on the way? *A*. None. *Q*. Were there any other boats at the mouth of Cumberland? *A*. Some, but not belonging to our party

Q. Did any men join you before you got there ? A. Mr. Blanner hasset did Q How many boats went from the mouth of Cumber land river ? A I do not recollect how many. Q. Were there ten? were there six ? A There were more than six altogether Q Did no one join you at the mouth of Cumberland but Col. Burr? A Yes, some more Q Who were in the other boats ? A. Mr Floyd had joined us with three boats at the falls of the Ohio one was loaded with provisions, and the rest had provisions like wise. Q How many men were in these boats ? A I do not re collect Q Were there twenty ? A There were about eight Q. How many boats were there in all ? A There were four of Col. Tyler's, two of Col Burr's from Nashville ; one of Ellis's, and two of Mr. Floyd's, who joined at the falls of Ohio , and captain Dean's boat, called the commissary's boat , and one small boat of Mr. Blannerhasset's Mr *Hay.* Tell me what you know about the arms. and recollect what you said before on this sub ject.—[Counsel for the accused objected to this mode of interro gation.]—How many chests of arms did you see at the mouth of Cumberland ? A I saw one chest and a box with rifles. There were several other chests like that one, but whether they con tained Mr Blannerhasset's books or the arms, I am not able to say. Q What was the size of the chest ? A Of course as long as the musket Q But of what depth ? A. I never measured the dimensions, but it was about as deep as my knee Q. Could you straddle over it with your legs ? A I could not Q Where did you first see this chest? A. At the mouth of Cumberland

Mr *M'Rae.* What sort of arms? A French. Q I mean of what form and nature· Were their any bayonets ? A There were Q Was this box opened ? A It was opened by the care lessness of the people, who took it in the boat. Q What kind of chest was it ? A It was rough. Q Were there any others of the same appearance? A Yes , but I know not their contents. Q. Do you recollect one thing ; were these chests heavy ? A. They were Q Did you see any other military apparatus? any bul lets ? A. I did. There were some bullets in a barrel, standing in the bow of one of Col. Tyler's boats Some said there were about six hundred in it.

Mr. *Wirt.* Did you see any powder ? A I am not certain whe ther I saw one or two , but I am certain that I saw one tin cannis ter of powder, that was put on board at Mr Blannerhasset's island.

Mr *Blannerhasset.* You said that you saw the boxes that were said to contain my books in the commissary boat , did you notice them ? A. I did not see them. Q. Did any body tell you that I had put arms on board ? A No one.

Mr. *Hay* Did you go ashore at the mouth of Cumberland ? A I did. Q. What passed there ? A. All the young men went up. Col. Burr wanted them to come up, for him to pay his addresses to them. Q Well ; and where did he receive them ? A. A lit tle piece above the bank Q. You did not see them form a cir cle ? A. No. I was not with them.

Thomas Hartley

Mr. *Hay* Were you at the mouth of Cumberland ? A. No, I was at Fort Massac when the boats were there I had left it two

weeks before. *Q.* You were with Col. Burr at Fort Massac?
A I was

Col. *Burr* objected to this question. Fort Massac was in the
Indiana territory

Q Did you descend the Mississippi, and with whom? *A.*
With M' Fort and Mr. Hopkins. *Q.* Where were you joined
by Mr Burr's party? *A* Just below Fort Massac. They passed
the fort in the night, and we joined them next morning. *Q.* How
many boats had they? *A* About eight or ten. *Q.* Do you know
whether they had any arms in the boats? *A* I saw none but
fowling pieces. *Q* Did you descend the river with them? *A.*
Yes I went to New Madrid by the directions of Col. Tyler
Q Were you not left behind to enlist men?

The counsel for the accused objected to the principle as well as
form of this question. After some discussion, the Chief Justice
decided the principle of the question to be relevant.

Mr *Hay* Will you state then for what purpose you were left
behind? *A* All the boats landed at New Madrid on new-year's
day, and staid four days. Mr. Hopkins and Mr Fort and myself
went before to get more men. We got two; and some more joined at Nantz de Grass. *Q* On what terms did they join? *A.* At
twelve dollars and a half a month, and one hundred acres of land
besides

Mr. *M'Rae* And what services were to be performed? *A.*
They were to go to this Ouachita country, and also to descend to
New-Orleans to work on Col Burr's boats.

Mr *Wirt* Was Col. Burr looked on as the head of this party?
A He was *Q* Did you and did these recruits understand that
they were to be placed under Col. Burr's command? *A.* They
were to be delivered to him, and to go on board his boats.

Cross-examined by the Accused.

Mr *Burr* Who wrote the articles, under which they were
engaged? *A* A Mr. Hopkins *Q.* Repeat them. *A* I do not
particularly recollect them *Q* But there was something in them
about the Ouachita lands? *A.* They were to go there after they
had gone to New Orleans.

Mr. *Wirt* These men who were engaged in New Madrid; did
they join the detachment? *A* They did, at the mouth of Coles's
creek. *Q* Do I understand that the sole object was the settlement of the Ouachita lands?

Mr. *Botts* objected to these questions. How could these transactions affect Col Burr, when they took place in his absence?

The objection was overruled, and Mr Hartley replied, that
the contract declared that they were to serve for six months,
that they were to settle on the Ouachita lands, but that they
were to go on to New-Orleans

Mr *Wirt* Did you see the men assembled, before they arrived
at the Chickasaw Bluffs? *A.* I did not overtake them before
they got to Coles's creek

Mr. *Burr* You say that they were to go to the Ouachita and to
New-Orleans. Were they to go in *any* event? *A* They were to
go to the Ouachita: but the articles did not specify what business they were to follow. The only service which was mentioned was, that they were to work the boats down.

Mr. *Baker* objected to this kind of evidence He contended that the best sort of evidence ought in every case to be produced; and that no *paper* ought to be mentioned which was not exhibited in Court.

The objection was overruled ; when

Mr. *Hay* asked the witness whether he was certain they were to go to New-Orleans first? *A.* I am, I recollect the articles were read after we got into the boat

Mr. *M'Rae.* And they were to serve six months? *A.* They were.

SATURDAY, *September* 19.

Examination of Jacob Dunbaugh

Mr. *Hay* Will you describe the situation of the party at the mouth of Cumberland river? Witness. Am I to be confined to the Cumberland river? Mr. Hay You may go down to the Chickasaw Bluffs. Mr. *Botts* Go down to the Mississippi river? and whether you are to go further, the Court will instruct you Some desultory conversation here ensued on this point, after which the witness proceeded

On the 26th December 1806, very early in the morning, a small skiff with four men and a Mr Hopkins, arrived at Fort Massac Some time after the arrival of this skiff, Capt. Bissell (commandant at the fort) detailed me for command, to go to the mouth of Cumberland river, to purchase a beef for him. *Q.* What were you? *A.* I was, and am still serjeant in the army of the United States. He told me I was to call on Col. Burr with his compliments ; and if Col Burr wanted my assistance, that I was to furnish it Captain Bissell told me, this Mr Hopkins, who came in the skiff with four men, was going up with me. When we got half way up to the Cumberland river, we stopt, and I asked Mr. Hopkins his business at Fort Massac, and he said it was to ask Captain Bissell whether he would oppose Colonel Burr's passing by the fort I got to the mouth of Cumberland, about half an hour before sun set, on the 26th December and landed ; Colonel Burr was then encamped on Cumberland island. After I had crossed over to the island, I saw Col. Burr and delivered Capt Bissell's message. Col Burr said he was much obliged to him, and that Capt Bissell was very good Col Burr asked me " is not this my old friend ?" I had seen him before He said he believed I drank no brandy ; and asked me if I would not have a glass of wine. When I drank, I said " here's success to Col Burr and his undertaking , and Mr. Blannerhasset (this was the first time I ever saw *him*) stamped his foot and said " Amen." Col. Burr told me that I must take breakfast with him next morning. I replied that I would. On the 27th I saw Col. Burr, and told him I was going to the garrison. He told me to bear his compliments to Captain Bissell, and asked me if I could take a barrel of apples to him I told him I would. Whilst they were getting the apples on board, the wind sprung up very fresh, and I was not able to start. In the course of that day I crossed him several times over to the Kentucky shore, and several of his men. During that day Colonel Burr asked me how I would like to go down the river with him. I replied, very well, if I could obtain the consent of my general. He said that that would make no odds. He would fix it without. This was on the 27th, and on the 28th I called on Colonel Burr and told him I was going to Fort Massac He sent his compliments to Captain Bissell, but said he expected he would get there before me I told him that he might man his barge as well as he could, I would arrive there before him. I arrived at the garrison sometime in the afternoon.

Mr *Botts*. There you may stop. It is impossible to progress without running into some impropriety, unless we ascertain the limits within which the witnesses are to be confined.

Mr *Hay* observed that he did not mean to prove any *acts* at Fort Massac. After some conversation the examination proceeded

Mr *Hay*. Did you see any military parade? A I saw the men drawn up at the mouth of Cumberland. Q. How many men? A. I did not count them ; but I suppose there were about one hundred. Q What kind of men? A. Generally young men.

Mr. *Wirt* Did they look like hard laborers? A The principal part did not Q How drawn up? were they drawn up in a line? A No they were drawn up in three wings. Q What do you mean by three wings? divisions?

The Witness here described their position, by drawing a figure on the floor with his foot. They described three sides of a square. Col. Burr was introduced by Col Tyler, beginning at the left. The party gradually fell in and formed a circle.

Mr *Hay*. How introduced? A. He went round and shook hands with every man Mr Hay. Did you not see some chests of arms?

Mr *Burr* objected to this manner of putting the question

Mr *Hay* admitted that he had put the question inadvertently? he merely wished Mr. Dunbaugh to state what he knows of the chests of arms

Mr. *Botts* State what you know of any chests of arms within the United States.

Witness. I did not see more than a few rifles at the mouth of Cumberland

Mr. *Hay* I think the Court yesterday decided, that we were at liberty to state any circumstances out of the United States which were explanatory of the acts done within the United States.

Mr *Botts* here stated their objections: he said that it was impossible to proceed without having questions relative to circumstances out of the U. States, which might be a perpetual subject of altercation, so long as it was permitted, instead of saving time. In ascertaining the limits to which they might go, not much time would be consumed. The Court knew that yesterday, contrary to the rule laid down, there were questions asked of acts without the knowledge of Col Burr, his authority, or his recognition, and yet this course is pursuing again And now, when the prejudices of the public are wearing away so fast, it certainly was very desirable that the current of retirement should not be arrested, much less turned back again.

Here he referred to some parts of the opinion delivered ; also to East 97. 2 Hawk ch 46. sec 34. Foot, 9, 10. East. 125. 1 Dall. 33, 39. which had been referred to before, as to going out of the county for evidence. He referred to all those places where the opinion of the Court had spoken of the propriety of proving the act of treason first, and then corroboration, by relevant testimony might be let in Any testimony that should go to the intention only, or to anterior occurrences, would be totally inapplicable, because they could not prove that to be an act of war, which was not an act of war, and an act of war must be proved before any confirmatory evidence can be received. As to the act of war in Kentucky, that ought first to he proved according to the opinion and the authorities Not only the war must be proved, but the march or action must be proved—not by any thing or sayings previous, or after, but in the act itself He went at some length over the ground so often trod on, as to the composition of a war levied, and compared his ideas with the events here seen.

Another principle laid down was " that declarations or confessions of the accused to make up the whole part of the character of a crime, was no evidence " Now he was to be sent, with a full knowledge that the evidence upon which he was to be sent to Kentucky, could not be received before a Jury If confessions out of Court were to be made before a hundred persons, it would avail nothing What use then would be the immense delay and expence of transportatation ? The declaration of Burr to Tyler, and of Tyler himself even were asked for ! Of what avail could these be before a Jury ? This he enlarged upon.

The attorney of the United States should confine himself, in the first instance, to evidence of a direct act of war, committed within the U. S Next—a question arises how low the judicial jurisdiction of the seventeen States should extend. This should be left to a Court to decide About the Yazoo river, instead of the title running to the bed of the river, does not run to the river, the Indian title not being ascertained.

When the United States shall have delivered their testimony to the overt act, within proper limits, then the accused shall offer his evidence in opposition or by way of impeachment, which impeachment may be reciprocal

Mr. Botts concluded by expressing his expectations of a strict adherence to the doctrines laid down by the Court

Mr *Martin.* As to whether declarations of others could be received in evidence, observed, that it had been done In Demaree and Purchase's case, declarations of the mob at that time, shewing the universality of their object were received in evidence So in the case of burning part of the city of London, but there the mob was in the flagrant acts of violence If there was a body of troops marching through the country in military array declarations might be heard, as to their object. But war may be levied without an act of treason in the United States, for to constitute treason, the military array must be to subvert the constitution, and alter the government . therefore when persons are in an act of such open violence, the character of that act must be enquired into, by the declarations of persons connected

Mr *Hay* The particular question that was asked Dunbaugh appears to me not to violate any one rule that was laid down. I do not mean to depart from these rules, because I think them correct, and shall think them so, until satisfied to the contrary. Now what is the overt act at the mouth of Cumberland? That is to be seen. Every thing therefore that relates to this assemblage may come forward, and gentlemen cannot prevent it by saying that it does not relate to an overt act of war

Now the evidence must prove the character of the meeting at the mouth of Cumberland; such as, whether there were arms or boxes, &c at that place. Now if these arms or boxes, &c. were not seen until they were down the river at some distance, and that they could not have been put on board without their knowledge, it is a strong presumption that they were on board at the mouth of Cumberland

Now, if it was proved that Burr was not at the mouth of Cumberland, and that he did not belong to the body that was there, nothing that could be said about it could be received against him, as to the character of that meeting. But if he was there, and a member of that meeting, then every thing relating to that meeting would be proper evidence. Now, after the overt act is proved, then it must be proved by two witnesses to affect him — Every thing which goes to prove the character of that meeting, the overt act having been proved by two witnesses, may be received

Now, if this body of men that sailed from the mouth of Cumberland, should say that no other boxes, &c came to them after they descended from the mouth of Cumberland, does it not go to prove that these arms were there when they were at the mouth of Cumberland? This is actually the same thing as though they had seen them there.

Mr *Burr* rose and said then, that they had misunderstood the opinion of the Court. But the witness did not see one until he had arrived at New Madrid, eighty or ninety miles down the river. nor does he yet say whether he saw the arms. Again : those arms were not in that boat, but in another, which perhaps he did not see once in three days

Mr *Hay* My object is to prove the condition and posture of those men at Cumberland. Now how is this to be done? I purpose, in addition to those of yesterday, to prove by Dunbaugh that those arms were concealed in the boat; and that afterwards they were concealed and put under the boat, and that those chests must have been with the party when they were at the mouth of Cumberland. If it shall appear from the evidence, that those arms were with the party when at Cumberland, it will shew the posture of things there

[A superabundance of conversation here occurred on the same topic, and to the same purpose, between Messrs. Wickham, Botts and Martin, who were repeatedly answered by Mr Hay]

The *Chief Justice* reiterated such parts of his opinion as respected the point in contest, respecting the evidence of circumstances and conversations, &c. not at Cumberland

Mr *Burr* at length said—We will let the examination go on, the gentleman will confine himself within the limits the Court has prescribed. Then, Sir, we will permit you to go on.

Mr *Hay*. Is this the way we are to be intimidated? They will permit me to go on? State then, Mr Dunbaugh. what you know on this subject. Did you leave Fort Massac with Col. Burr? *A.* I overtook him at New Madrid on the 1st of January. *Q.* Did you then go down the river with him? *A.* Yes, in his own boat.

Mr. *Wickham* repeated his objections to this kind of evidence How was the witness to know, whether arms might not have been subsequently put on board the boats? He was not always in Col Burr's boat; nor was Col Burr's boat with the rest Can this be good testimony?

Chief Justice. The attorney is to shew that hereafter He is to shew, that there was no connection between the boats and the shore.

Mr *Wickham* But suppose that he has no testimony to that effect?

Chief Justice Whether arms were subsequently introduced, is a mere matter of inference, dependant on the whole of the evidence on both sides. It depends on a variety of circumstances, such as the situation of the shore and the country, &c.

Mr. *Hay.* State then, Mr Dunbaugh, what you know about the arms on board the boats.

Witness Sometime in January, we left Bayou Pierre, and descended to Petit Gulph, three miles below on the opposite side Col. Burr went ashore, and returned to the Petit Gulph The boats all shoved off at once Col Burr's was rather behind. The night we left Petit Gulph, Col Burr and Wyllie went to the bow of the boat for an axe, auger and saw They went into Col Burr's private boat and began to chop. He ordered no person to go out, but I did go out I saw a skiff lying aside of Col. Burr's boat. After they had done chopping, a Mr. Pryor and a Mr. Tooly got out of the window. I got on the top of the boat, and saw two bundles of arms tied up with cords, and sunk by cords going through holes at the gunwales of Col Burr's boat. I observed to Mr. Pryor, that he must be careful to bring up the boat, or else it could not get close to shore

Mr. *Hay.* How many arms were there? *A.* There were about forty or forty-three stands I saw besides pistols, swords, blunderbusses, fusees and tomahaws.

Mr. *Wirt* Is not the coast opposite to New Madrid a part Tennessee? *A.* No; it is the Indiana territory. *Q* Were you on board any of the other boats? *A* Several. *Q.* Did they keep together? *A.* They did, when they could. *Q* Did you see arms in the other boats? *A.* I saw several stands of arms, that is, muskets with bayonets, in Floyd's boat, and about twelve rifles Were you near enough to Col Burr at the mouth of Cumberland to hear his observations to his party? *A* I was He said there were then too many bye standers to divulge his plans. *Q* Were any men obtained after you joined them? *A* One, who got aboard at New Madrid. *Q.* Were you commissioned by Col. Burr obtain men? *A* No, not citizens *Q* What do you mean the word " citizens?"

Here Dunbaugh was stopped by the opposite counsel and examination proceeded no farther on this day.

[Here the topic of the relevancy of testimony of matters of the United States, was again brought up, and conversed about and the opinion of the Chief Justice again raised.]

The *Chief Justice* said, that any testimony, no matter where, that served to shew what was done at the mouth of Cumberland, and what was the situation of things there, even lower down than the United States, might be received: but certainly any assembly of a body of men out of the United States did not prove any thing that was done at Cumberland. It may be confirmatory of the object that those who were at Cumberland had in view. He would think upon that subject, however; but he had some difficulty upon the point. He was inclined to think that that kind of testimony would be admissible.

[This produced a long discussion.]

Mr *Wirt* hoped there would be no limits to the enquiry when it related to what was done at Cumberland, or what was their object in meeting there. The enlistment and exercising of men, declaration of their object, even though below Cumberland, and to show it to be a military expedition, if any thing did. Every person had a right to bear arms, but if the arms borne were for a military purpose, the face of the thing was changed. What, therefore, could so well discover the nature of it, as the speeches and actions of Burr elsewhere. The giving orders to obtain recruits was a prominent feature. It was not the quantity being small that could change the circumstance, because the opposition to be expected was small also, and an acquisition of numbers, &c calculated on. On this account it might be necessary to enquire the numbers at each fort and garrison which they had to pass, to get to New Orleans. If it could be shewn that he, with these one hundred and forty men might be capable of taking Orleans, they ought not to be tied down to the boundary line of the United States for evidence.

Mr. *Hay* said if they could prove that although they were not then perhaps in a condition for the attack, yet by their prospects, and their military appearance, aided by their declarations, they were capable of *commencing* such a project, such evidence he thought was relevant.

Mr *Botts* said this was the old project to get at all sorts of testimony, and apply it any way they pleased, to the number of one hundred and forty witnesses, who were condemned to stay here time unknown, without any determinate scite for the overt act charged. Sometimes at Cumberland, then at Mississippi territory and then at New Orleans. What was the proper place, he asked, for a person to be indicted for making war, but where he did make war. But no war was made, even though Dunbaugh was sent down the river, and a long story told to Gen Eaton the Morgans, &c Suppose the gentlemen were permitted to prove the condition of the forts, could not this evidence be satisfied? In order to prevent such infinite, unnecessary trouble, it was proper to confine them within bounds in time.

Mr. *Wickham* also professed, that he should not object if they would stop where they were, but the immense loss of time and business occasioned by such unnecessary delay, would admit of no patience. He went over some of the transactions related, from which he concluded that nothing could avail the prosecutor to obtain his object.

Chief Justice With respect to the *effect*, the body of men on Cumberland could have on such an expedition, it is not a point at which I have not doubted. As to the *intention* of those men, or a part of them, I have not yet expressed myself; because, perhaps the *intention* might be gathered from other sources, as well as declarations, as to the place where the crime was committed (if any) I do not think I have expressed an opinion, I have always felt considerable doubt upon it. I have always said that the exhibition at the place where the war is levied, must be justified by the act itself. The act of levying war may depend upon the *intention*. That is, that the intention, as in riots, should determine the nature of the act. This *intention* must be from the appearance of the body of men at the time, aided by any other evidence. I have not given an opinion upon this.

Mr *Martin* If your honor has not, we are ready to go into argument upon it.

Chief Justice If gentlemen may prove this, it appears to me that they may afterwards go into intention, but I have given no opinion on it.

Mr *Wickham* The opinion given is, that the assembly must be unusual in intention and appearance.

Chief Justice Military.

Mr Wickham and Mr Martin went into a review of the circumstances stated by the evidence.

[As it will afterwards be more elucidated, it is unnecessary to transcribe it.]

The *Chief Justice* observed, that it was unfortunate that the counsel on both sides differed respecting what was " levying war," and the court, unfortunately, differed from both. Thus, whenever a question of testimony came forward, each party insisted on its own opinion.

The opinion of the Court is, that to attack New Orleans, for the purpose of subverting the government of the U. S. is *treason*. Also, that a body of men, assembled, and in a condition to execute it, although they have not executed it actually, is *treason*. The gentlemen in the defence say it is not. the Court say it is treason. There will, therefore, be no end to a course of argument of this kind.

I should suppose that if a body of men were to meet in any place for the purpose of subverting the government (whether a territory of the U. S. or any other part thereof,) though they did not destroy men, women nor children, or any property, even if they did go with a design to make the attempt, and were able to have effected it, this would be levying war. even as soon as there is a real army, capable of acting in a military posture, and in a condition to execute this object, formed. The first step, I take it, is levying war ; and it is not necessary to come to battle. The gentlemen say this is not war, but the court *must* be governed by its own opinion.

If this opinion is law, all the circumstances which go to prove where this body of men assembled, and whether they were in a condition, and disposed to do the act, is the question for evidence to prove.

The object in view, and the weight of the evidence already offered to support that object, is not yet decided : but that if the object and means, as above expressed, should be proved, would amount to treason, is decided

On the first, I believe I have always entertained a doubt, and therefore, I believe I have not expressed an opinion · but the last I have no hesitation to ask, how it can be doubted ?

The charge is, that this body met together with a design to take New Orleans, and to subvert the government of the U S there. Now it certainly is a proper subject of enquiry, whether this body was adequate to its object or not ? To find this, gentlemen must undoubtedly prove the situation of New Orleans. This is certainly a proper step to the enquiry, although this enquiry would prove the particular allegation

Mr *Wickham* contended, that there was no possibility of proving an *hostile* or military assemblage of men, and no avowed purpose of hostility against the U S had ever been pretended to be proved Consequently, collateral proof was inadmissible. He contended, that therefore the evidence as to his ordering men to be enlisted, must be collateral.

If the character of the assemblage was hostile, or that acts of treason could be proved, why did they not come forward and prove them, and then come in with collateral evidence. He believed this was the opinion of the Court.

Chief Justice No doubt the character of the assemblage must be proved, and something of what might be considered as an overt act must be proved also. but as to the opinion of the Court respecting the meeting at Blannerhasset's island, as well as I recollect, the Court did not undertake to say what that meeting was, but the Court did say, what the nature of the transaction would be, to make it treason

But whatever it might be, it was no matter at all, because whatever it was, the prisoner was not there. This opinion was not given on any particular question on the subject

Mr. *Wickham* observed that the question must occur at some part of the examination, and must be decided by the Court. We say, then, by way of motion, that the assemblage that the whole transaction proves nothing but a peaceable assemblage, from the testimony which has been given. (The other gentlemen say differently) If it is a peaceable assemblage, why should there be collateral proof produced, as for levying war ? Now should the gentlemen for a moment depart from what we call the overt act, we shall object to it. If they can prove an overt act, we wish to hear what they can produce for that proof. If they say they have proved it, we wish to address the Court on the subject ; and we think we have a right to go into argument, except they will produce the testimony which they say they have behind, on the overt act Enlistment out of the country, is what they mean to prove ; which we say is irrelevant, and inadmissible to their case

Chief Justice That is a point upon which I see a doubt. The *intention* must be proved in relation to what was done at the island. Now, he observed, there were two points to which the *intention* might be applied—the intention to subvert the government of the United States in New Orleans; and then, whether that intention could relate to the meeting at Cumberland Therefore such a question, in some degree is collateral. If it is necessary to prove that those who were assembled had the same intention that Col Burr himself had, there would some difficulty arise As to the condition of New Orleans to resist, and the capacity of those who were charged, that is direct testimony, bearing immediately upon the main question

[Here a considerable conversation occurred how far the treasonable intentions of one could effect others, and whether it was necessary to prove the treasonable intentions of *all*, in order to effect any one There was also some conversation about collateral testimony as applied to this case.]

Mr *Wirt* particularly, differed with Mr Wickham as to the component and relative parts of collateral testimony, because he contended, that wherever the object was carried into effect, although one thousand miles down the river, yet if the intention and military expedition originated at the island; nothing that affected that intention and military preparation there, could be opposed in the evidence respecting the spot, as direct, and not collateral proof. It did not cease to be direct, because it was not given at that spot, but afterwards; nor did that circumstance impair its force. He should, therefore, think it competent to introduce testimony as declarations, &c by him, even though one thousand miles from that island Suppose there had been an attack on a fort, or an attack on New Orleans, would not this have been a direct proof of the treason commenced at Cumberland? Surely such evidence as that would not be denominated collateral

As to the intention being known to the whole party, Mr Wirt referred to a case, the earl of Southampton did not know of the treasonable *intentions* of the earl of Essex, and yet he was adjudged to have participated in it

Mr *Wickham* explained collateral testimony to be such, as bore upon a fact already proved or not proved, but which was said to be in existence Now, he asked, would not Col. Burr's acts at any other place be collateral, if it was attempted to prove what was the intention of the party at Cumberland by those acts?

As to the state of the forts or of New Orleans, they had no objection to gentlemen's shewing their force It was not worth taking up the time of the Court, to say whether it was direct or collateral; but he must insist, that declarations made elsewhere was collateral But he contended that there had been no *direct* testimony, and they were willing to argue the law. As to lord Southampton's case, whether it was to be considered as an authority or not, it would be found that Southampton accompanied Essex to go with the forces to the queen's palace, in order to force her to change her ministry

[Some conversation of little moment here occurred between Mr. Martin, Mr. Bott's, and the Chief Justice, as to assemblage on the island, &c and the constituent parts of an act of treason· in which was explained *again* the opinion given, and which Mr *Botts* again professed to have misunderstood; and lamented much its consequences on our citizens; who were exposed, if measures were to be taken to make that of a military nature which was not in itself military; and that levying war, which was a merely innocent assemblage. He drew some analogies also to prelucidate the evils which might attend the receipt of confessions or acknowledgements made to second or third persons. But our constitution, he observed, had wisely provided, that no advantage should be taken of what the arts and designs of evil men may draw from the credulous and unoffending. He also spoke of the disadvantages under which a man labored who was dragged away to a place, and tried before a Jury who knew not his character, and where he could obtain no witnesses in his favor, but every thing was brought against him. Was not the constitution, he asked, made to defend every man against the malevolent designs of evil men, and to protect the innocent? Were it not so, in his opinion it would be a truly alarming situation that our citizens might be left in However, he would fain hope that there were not enemies enough to upright men to be found in society, to go the length that the doctrines supported by some gentlemen, would carry them But he wished the means not to remain in their power, if such did exist]

Mr. *Hay* answered—He did not recollect an instance in which a person charged before a committing magistrate, was a dictator as to the mode in which that magistrate should act to him, or how the attorney should introduce his charge He presumed that his professional duties required as much to be attended to, and his sensibilities were as great for the witnesses being detained, as any gentleman in the Court could be. but as every inch of ground which he trod, was disputed over and over again, at least ten times, by the defendant and his counsel, to whom could be attributed the blame of delay?

Treason, he contended, consisted in the *act* and *intention* to the proof of this, he wanted to introduce evidence, and he did conceive, that the evidence he was about to produce, was *direct*. Treason, he stated, consisted in act and intention. It was not sufficient to prove, merely, that one hundred, or five hundred men met together, because that meeting might be innocent, and therefore they were not to be confined to the mere meeting, but to the object of the meeting, which must be gathered by evidence of the intention It might be, that the character of the assembly could be obtained by evidence of facts at the moment of the assemblage but yet the treasonable intentions of those men may be by what shall be afterwards given by them in conversations and succeeding acts This was *direct* evidence, he declared and elucidated by a number of observations, which have been, and more which will be reported.

Unless this was admitted, there would insuperable difficulties attend a case of this sort because an assemblage of men in military array might be proved, but nothing might exist *at the moment* to prove their intention thus. nothing criminal could be attributed to them, unless the prosecution was at liberty to resort to some other place for proof of the object with which that body met

Mr. Wickham has observed, that if this was not collateral evidence, there was none I have no objection to his saying so, because it is not his business to prove the truth of his inferences, but to prove the truth of his positions Let him prove that it is collateral. Observe, Sir, the dilemma into which we should be brought. Evidence called on the spot is direct, but the same evidence collected elsewhere is not! Now does the evidence in its nature, or in its tendency, differ?

As to confession or declarations of the person, I see no reason why it should not, in such a case as this, be received after the overt act is proved. It is true the constitution says, that no person shall be convicted of treason, but by two witnesses, or by confession in open Court Now this must only relate to a *trial* in Court. A man may be convicted of treason by two witnesses, or without any evidence whatever, if he will come into Court and confess But if no evidence of the fact were to come, and twenty witnesses were to come and say what he declared respecting the circumstance, the party would be entitled to his acquittal because the constitution acquits him!

Here Mr *Hay* referred to the case of Fries, in his confession before Judge Peters, which was received as corroborative testimony, after the overt act had been proved —Fries's trial, p. 80, 81 and though he was confined, that confession was brought into Court, and read against him on trial, as explanatory of the facts The propriety of it was never doubted

The *Chief Justice* explained the difference If Col Burr had declared these sentiments at the meeting at the mouth of Cumberland, it would have affected the character of the whole meeting, and have proved its object and if declarations were made at different places, it would tend to shew the character of the meeting there, and it would not be objected to by the Court But the difficulty is, that these expressions are not what go to shew the character of the *meeting*, but the intention of *one individual* composing it therefore it does not serve to shew that that meeting levied war, because it does not shew the intention of the meeting

Mr *Martin* suggested to the Court, if it should have a doubt upon the subject, whether it would not be expedient to leave the argument till Monday when it might undergo regular discussion The party might shew their intention to go down to New Orleans, to rob and plunder the place, but this would not be treason, even if they did it that is different from going to take and hold it, and subvert the government of the United States therein It must be an act of war, or an act of open violence against the United States. It may be an act of open violence and yet if it is not with intention to subvert the government of the United States, it is no treason Again It must have a military appearance, with the avowed and open intention of subverting the government He enlarged upon this description, but as it has before been over and over explained, it is unnecessary to tire the reader with a repetition of the same sentiments He mentioned these things he said, because it had been said a confession of Fries, before Judge Peters had been permitted by Judge Chase to be read in evidence to the Jury against Fries. Had it been so, he never would have got clear of his impeachment

Mr. *Wickham* said, if this had been a question concerning a single witness, they never should have made so serious a point of it, but he had discovered that it even extended to witnesses of the whole of Col Burr's life, and most particularly as to the last three or four years of it during which time he had been constantly watched.

He then proceeded at some length of argument to prove the necessity of proving the overt act, and that by two witnesses, before the prosecution could be permitted to touch any thing that was corroboratory. This sentiment, he contended, was perfectly congenial with the opinion of the Court.

But, if there was an intention to commit treason on Cumberland island, that intention might be proved by declarations elsewhere? What is this? It is, that *intention is* " levying war " I say that levying war consists of *open deeds*, he says that it consists in *secret intentions* If this be it, I will say, that every Judge in the world has been wrong constantly If it may be proved by declarations made elsewhere, it must consist in intention, if no open deed is sought for.

He drew an analogy supposing that on a public parade day, one of the militia were to declare, that they would seize the capitol, and overturn the public functionaries, would that give a character to the whole meeting as designing to overturn the government? By no means He believed all the critical analization which the doctrine of treason had undergone in this Court, there was but one case produced where there was not actual force applied, and that was Vaughen's case, but he was in a state of open and avowed hostility to the British government, in a vessel suitable and ready to attack any of the vessels of that nation that he was able to encounter.

But if, as it was said, he had harangued his men at Bayou Pierre—if even he had gone on to New Orleans, although he might have had treason in his heart, and though it might have been supposed, that he was about to commit this hostility, yet it was no war, no open act of war, without its being begun and would by no means relate to Cumberland, where nothing appeared

But, it was asked, whether the nature of the testimony was to be changed by the change of place? Yes, it was. Testimony drawn from the act and place is direct—testimony drawn from other places, or of other sorts, is indirect, or collateral.

But a doubt has been suggested by the Court, whether an equivocal act can be considered an act of war This we shall be prepared to meet; and more, we shall prove, that this was a peaceable assembly But admitting that the act itself was equivocal, I have no hesitation in saying that equivocal acts cannot be open deeds of war, and that no testimony ought to be received, or can make it appear to be levying war It must be *public, open, clear, indisputable*. If it was not an open act of war, then the testimony must be equivocal, and consequently must be shut out If it was an open act of war, then the testimony must be produced to shew it But in the way the counsel have gone on to shew it, it is impossible to know where the evidence will stop. If they have any evidence of the overt act let them yet bring it forward

Mr *Martin* rose to acknowledge, that in the case of Fries, wherein Judge Iredell presided, the confession of the prisoner was given in evidence, [which he had before denied.] He should, however, contend, that it was a most monstrous doctrine to receive the confession of a party as evidence. The constitution required two witnesses to the overt act, if these were produced, it was sufficient, but if these were not produced, nothing could make an act of treason, but a confession in open Court

Even in the days of the state trials, the Court expressly instructed the Jury that there must be two witnesses, to be believed by them but if they were not so credited, an examination of, and confession of the person before a magistrate might be received as corroborative.

He held this construction of Judge Iredell's to be wrong, although he professed a warm affection for his memory, and regard to his judgment

Mr Mártin then went into some appeal to reason and common sense, to support his arguments

Mr *Hay* Here is the confession of Fries, which it was agreed by Judge Iredell might be read; and here are his observations on it—(Fries's trial, p 80, 81) But Mr. Martin asks, what does " *common sense*" say ? I am very glad that the gentleman is at last come into that principle, for it is, what he has heretofore avoided

Mr. *Burr* Foster quotes that doctrine as established by former precedent, but he quotes it with marked disapprobation, and extreme regret, and says, that the doctrine never ought to be carried farther. Could that be intended to permit the examination to go into collateral and corelative proof? There may be after this, a necessity to test the credit of the witnesses upon that proof

Our dispute seems to have settled itself into two points. One is a point of fact—the other, a point of law. The point of law is of the last importance

As to the ovet act, which is one point, it is acknowledged that there was no harm done ; but, on the other side, they say it was equivocal, because there was a lurking *intention* to do the act Upon the point of fact, then, we are to enquire, whether what was done be criminal, innocent, or equivocal Then, upon that fact, the question is, whether they can go to different times, places and circumstances, for information ? You have decided that you had not the right to go into the territories Then the gentlemen evade, and say they will go into secret confessions, at different times and places

This is the point to be settled , because if it is not, we are at a loss to say what makes treason, and what does not ; because would be dangerous to trust to conversations at different times and places as to intentions to do so and so This sort of evidence might be brought at any time against any person.

I think it can be proved, that there never was in England, or any where, a treason made out, where there was no particular fact or act attending the charge. There is not one instance where there was a charge of levying war, where there was no a breach of the peace, and some act of violence. If not, this the first attempt of the kind of prosecution ; and if so, it ought to be deliberately considered.

The *Chief Justice* recited the opinions of Hale and Foster in explanation of the term "levying war."

Mr. *Burr* answered. He took the term to be an army marching and crushing all before it But in this case where was the scite , where the intimidation , where the interruption of the constituted authorities? merely in imagination! there is no *potential force* proved.

Chief Justice. I do not know what testimony might be produced there may no point arise, out of that testimony if a point should arise, I should consider no time mispent to examine it.

Mr. *Hay* said, that it certainly must be unnecessary again to travel over the question of what was levying war, or what composed it , since the circuit court had decided. This question. and every concomitant one had been most elaborately discussed ; and any thing else on the subject must be superfluous

Mr. *Burr* believed that no one could possibly feel the inconvenience of delay so much as himself but still it was necessary to bring forward the motions which had been prefered, although they might have caused that unpleasant delay.

The ground of the present, was in some degree different from any former argument , and the subject required a new examination, according to the field that was taken. Equivocal acts calculated to lead the mind astray. Equivocal acts were not known in Law innocence or guilt must attend every transaction, and there could not exist that sort of medium which an equivocal act would create. The act of treason must necessarily comprehend actual voilence and though the Supreme Court in their opinion have made it a step less, yet they argued hypothetically, and without the due course which the emission of opinions or great law questions take.

Mr. *Wirt* said, that they did not wish to reproach Mr Burr with any intentional delay ; but still, he observed there was such a thing as wearying out a prosecution by the infinitive multitude of motions which might be made on a case. Whatever was the motive, the affect was the same ; and it was impossible to know when they could get on with the testimony, so as to bring the close even in prospect

Mr. *E. Randolph* contended, that this was a question which had not yet been decided.

In common law, every charge must consist of *act* and *intention* to constitute guilt . but he would venture to say, that there had not yet a case even existed, where a man was called to answer to his *intention*, until his *act* was first proved to have been illegal ; and then only could they be coupled This ran throughout the whole code of criminal law. Thus when you speak of killing a man. the *prima facia* evidence is the intention of the person who did the act ; and hence various names are given in law to the act of killing. Robberies larcenies &c. require the same legal investigation, and so with respect to treason a meeting might be treasonable—it might be harmless, or even justifiable

He only rose he said, to request that the court in its investigation of the case, would attend to the *sub-stratum* of every criminal case, and then he was sure there would be an end of the affair at Cumberland

Mr. *Hay* observed, that it was for the Chief Justice to determine, how far the act of treason had been committed, and how far their principal powers were capable, under all the circumstances which were about to be offered, to accomplish their object, was a question for the Chief Justice to decide.

We have been engaged (said Mr Hay) since ten o'clock in the partial examination of one single witness I hope, Sir, that on Monday you will permit us to go on with the witnesses, and that you will stop us whenever we go out of the tract Unless we are so permitted to do, we know not what we shall be able to do with our witnesses to keep them here I am content to acquiesce to the bounds laid down by the Court, and measure our steps by its decision It must come to this at last, let the event of that motion be what it might

Mr *Burr*. I suggest to the gentlemen, that if they want to save time, (which is not to be doubted as to either side) they ought to pursue the recommendation given on the original motion to commit: that they should first bring their testimony as to the overt act, and then progress to other acts Now, it was impossible for an innocent assembly to be construed into an act of war. In order to discover to what peculiar description the act belonged—whether it was an innocent assembly, or a warlike one, required the explanatory aid of collateral testimony. Sufficient notice however was given to the prosecutions of these distinctions, and that they would be stopped if they attempted to wander. I am willing to meet testimony any where ; but I cannot meet it at once in all places—In Virginia, Kentucky, Tennessee, &c

Chief Justice. The Court has permitted the conversation this afternoon to proceed, under the persuasion that gentlemen would not proceed to any extravagant length, but now I feel the necessity of confining their arguments to the particular position laid down There is a very material difference between arguments upon all the testimony, and arguments on one particular piece of testimony.

The question before the Court is, whether evidence of the treason charged at the mouth of Cumberland, might be collected from expressions used at other places Gentlemen have varied in their descriptions of this. Some seem to consider the overt act not to be any other than collateral testimony.

I consider the true situation of the case to be, on a question, whether this evidence may be given respecting the *intention* of the charge at the mouth of Cumberland. Now whether it proves the fact, is one thing ; and whether it might be heard, although drawn from another place, is another.

Now, suppose there was a body of men, assembled in any one State, for the purpose of attacking the government of the United States at any one point—they did not openly declare this, though it was their object. Well, they pass through several States without the appearance of hostility or violence. They do not appear armed ; but perhaps convey their arms in wagons, boats, boxes, or whatever. When they come to the point of attack, they take out these arms and attack the place. Now all will agree that this is levying war. But the question is, whether it is not levying war at the place where they first had these arms—seeing that they always had them at command, and could take them out any time.

A farther question of importance is, whether war can be levied without the employment of actual violence. Now as to potential force, they must have arms somewhere at command, to be had at any time they shall choose, for action. Whether this is not levying war, provided you can dispense with the *act of violence*, is a question. If they have the arms, if they proceed towards the march, and if they have declared themselves, I suppose it is. This is what is called an equivocal act, because they may be going somewhere for any other purpose; they may, as Mr Martin says, intend to rob and plunder a town and yet it be not treason.

But the question is, whether the overt act be treason? If the overt act is established to be treason first, then their going on to attack a place, must be an overt act in levying war at that place; and if the overt act may be committed without violence, it may be an overt act of treason before the offence is committed, and when it is commenced with that avowed intention. The relation is so exceedingly strong, that it appears evidence ought to be heard. If at the mouth of Cumberland they had formed the evident design, and had afterwards proceeded down and taken New Orleans, subverted the government there, and taken the command of that town on themselves, there could have been no doubt, but it would have been an overt act of levying war there, but if they may levy war without any particular act of violence, I do not perceive why they might not have levied war, under such circumstances, at the mouth of Cumberland.

But if, after leaving the mouth of Cumberland, that body of men had been harangued by their leader, and he had then declared his intention of levying war somewhere else, that would not have been evidence of the overt act at Cumberland, because it would not have been proof that the body of men at Cumberland intended any thing hostile there, as it was unknown to them, when they sat off. But if this harangue had shewed, from its nature, that this very same intention had been held and known at the mouth of Cumberland, it would certainly partake of the same nature and character as though the crime had been committed at New Orleans.

There appears to me no difficulty in hearing testimony explanatory of the intention of the meeting, but the question is, whether certain testimony which might be offered, is explanatory of the intention of the meeting or not? But I shall hear it, and let its weight be determined hereafter.

I doubt its applicancy, because I do not know how a single individual, unconnected with the rest, could do such an act. It is a very different thing from what it would be if the others had known it.

I do not say but a man might levy war through the instrumentality of others; although they may not know it. So much has been said on the subject, that I thought it proper to give this general view of my ideas.

The point upon which I want to be satisfied is, whether this testimony can prove the intention of the meeting, at the mouth of Cumberland?

Mr. *Hay.* That question can be decided, Sir, after the testimony has been heard. We wish to be permitted to shew the facts and circumstances. If from the general character, it shall appear that they had such confidence in his integrity and his views as to go where he was going, and take fate with him, I cannot see of what great importance it is, whether he explained himself particularly to them or not.

Chief Justice to Mr Hay. Have you much testimony as to the occurrences at the island?

Mr. *Hay.* I do not know that I have, but the character of the transaction may be gathered from other sources, which appears to me to be nearly the same.

Mr *Botkham* expressed his opinion upon the overt act as he did before.

The *Chief Justice* said he should hear every thing on the subject that was proper, either as to the *act* or the *intention.* The intention of the meeting was the part on which he had avoided hitherto to give an opinion. He was willing to hear any testimony however on that subject; and then he should enquire into its weight. The testimony, however, which he had heard, did not appear to attain to the object, however the connection with what was left behind might show it, he would not say.

MONDAY, September 21

Immediately on the meeting of the Court, the *Chief Justice* said—On a farther reflection, I have thought it best to hear the testimony which goes to an explanation of Col Burr's intention as to the meeting at Cumberland. This will embrace the operations afterwards. Every thing which bears upon that meeting, will be received as proper testimony.

Mr *Burr* said, they had come prepared to argue the two doubted and undecided points which were suggested by the Court. First, it seemed to be doubted, whether the acts on the island were criminal or innocent. This they were prepared to shew was perfectly innocent. Secondly, the question is, whether the prosecutors would be able to go out of the United States for testimony.

I have laid it down as a true maxim, that no act, in itself is innocent—where no harm is done to any one, can, by any torturing or extortion of evidence, be made an act of guilt; and we presume that no man can have the innocent acts of his life questioned.

The first enquiry is, whether the act in itself is unlawful or injurious to somebody? Until that, we say there can be no other enquiry made. If the Court do not see this, in all its latitude, we are ready to prove its truth.

I have, since the last meeting of the Court, received two letters which regard the subject now under discussion. They inform me, that testimony is on the way, which might be daily expected. The nature of that testimony is highly interesting to me and the public. It tends to show that the *public* and *myself* have been *sold*. They are of a grade and nature that would make it improper to mention, were it not that I wish (on that account) the opinion of the Court to be suspended until I ascertain the weight of that testimony, even if it sho ' 'be ten or fifteen days delay. On the other two points, we are ready to commence an argument. The first question is, whether the evidence is to be received that these men were engaged to enlist men out of the United States?

Mr *Botts* was not surprized that the Court should feel a reluctance to hear farther debate, because its patience must naturally be worn out: but it could not be a more painful task to the Court, than it was to the counsel. But, however painful, the duty must be performed. The point made, he said, had never yet been debated. He contended that it must be a matter of great regret, first to permit testimony to be heard, and after that, that the Court should declare, that testimony to be illegal. He next appealed with urgency to the feelings of the Judge on the state of the subject; but whatever was the decision, he said it was the duty of the counsel to submit to it. No time he believed would be lost by a submission to their request.

Chief Justice. I should have no difficulty at all to suspend a decision, where momentous testimony may be suspected to explain facts of importance. Nor shall I feel any dislike to hear any arguments on any part of a case which gentlemen on either side may deem important: but there is a difference as to the views of what is important—as to the nature and effects of testimony, and as to its applicability.

The points which were suggested, do not seem to belong to the testimony. There have been questions of this sort asked of some of the witnesses. I do not say what will be my ultimate opinion on the subject

If gentlemen are earnest to make their motion, I shall not silence them, but I will suggest, that a day has been already employed to no effect.

There is no great doubt of the *bearing* of the testimony; therefore, as a sitting magistrate to examine, I have a right to hear all testimony, wherever it might come from. I ought to hear *all* testimony on a motion to commit, respecting the whole transaction, and although the application of it might not be so strong as the counsel may suppose, yet its weight must be duly appreciated after it is delivered.

Mr *Wickham* said, that their position was made upon a doubt which the court had expressed, as to the equivocal nature of the act. it was their wish to remove that doubt, by an argument on the subject—for nothing could be more clear, than that an *overt act* could not be a matter of doubt. If the act was proved, nothing collateral was necessary. He said that they were not afraid of any legal testimony: but there must a serious question remain—whether Col Burr was to be prosecuted through the whole of his life? and the result of this question now rested much on the present motion.

But, he would have no objection if it were to be examined in this Court. It was to go abroad; and he undoubtedly had a right to require that such testimony should not be heard. What is the nature of the testimony? Dunbaugh is brought here. I do not know what is the character of this witness, but I know that Dunbaugh was apprehended as a deserter, and that he was brought round here by General Wilkinson, who might have put the martial law in force against him if he had pleased

Mr. Wickham then went into an examination of the testimony of Albright and Read, but as this was afterwards as strongly scrutinized as possible. we forbear to anticipate it by any remarks now made. He also received some of the proceeding of Friday and Saturday, on the comparative nature of a military assemblage at Cumberland

Here he also renewed the position that Col Burr had been already acquitted of what he was now charged with This did not merely affect him, he contended, but every citizen of the United States, and if this course was persisted in, no man in the United States, could rest with safety On these grounds they wished the opinion of the Court, but a doubt was expressed —These doubts they wished to go into argument about, but at any rate they should object to any extraneous evidence

Mr *Burr*. There may need some apology for such apparent opposition to what appears to be the mind of the Court; but I must express my great disappointment, that at the opening of the Court, there should have been such a decision given, if not the decision of the *obitu*.

We wish now, Sir, to examine the nature of the facts—it is of the utmost moment,—(not to me only but to any person) I want it to be settled upon its true principle, as one of the greatest importance—whether an act that is in itself innocent, can by any means whatever, be tortured into guilt We hoped to have been heard on the subject

Chief Justice On the question, whether " an act which is in itself innocent, can be made into guilt," is what the Court can entertain a doubt upon nor is this a question at all before the Court I will not hesitate to say, that an act which is innocent, *cannot* be turned into guilt, even by illegal testimony This position might, perhaps, at some time receive its answer I shall not now waste time to take it up The ideas which I gave in the opinion, was upon a very elaborate argument, and under all the light that it seemed could be thrown on the subject No more I think it necessary.

But, if gentlemen will go on to prove that an examining magistrate is not to examine explanatory testimony, nor hear it, then I am willing to hear gentlemen with patience. On that subject I have no doubt for my part

Mr *Burr* I wish to point out in what the Court and my counsel are at variance It is admitted that an act, of itself innocent, cannot be tortured into any sort of proof to make a crime I also say, that equivocal acts, (for act of life almost is equivocal,) cannot be brought to bear against any man on a capital charge, and no circumstances can require or call for it We shall shew, that there was no traitorous alarms at all, nor any injury done to any one although proof was sought, but that the assemblage was innocent We trust that the Court will not come to a decision without first hearing argument otherwise, it may produce, to me, immense inconvenience It will involve enquiries of principles, which ought to be well and distinctly understood

Chief Justice I am very strongly persuaded myself, that the suggestions which are made, and which certainly deserve serious consideration, are certainly suggestions which will have no operation on the testimony but however, having strong confidence in them, I will go into the argument.

Some conversation as to the point, occurred between Mr. Wickham and the Court, in which the Chief Justice *again* explained his opinion.

Mr *Burr.* If we do not mistake, we are prepared to shew the testimony offered, could under no circumstances, be received at all If I had declared my intention, even was it to overturn the government, doubtful testimony ought to be received as doubtful as the fact, but not as to the admissibility of it We do not think that it will be of any importance on the present case , but as a precedent it must be important to ascertain true principles.

Mr *Hay* The witnesses have been detained here such an extreme length of time, that I trust I shall be excused when I inform the Court, that I mean to take the affidavits of the witnesses, and discharge them The counsel on the other side, I am sorry to say, do not seem disposed to close this case [He mentioned the number attending to be thirty or forty, instead of one hundred and thirty or forty, as had been stated]

After some general conversation, of no importance, Mr. Hay went out to take the affidavits of those witnesses who were present

Mr *Burr* insisted upon his right to demand, that no witness should be discharged without notice to him.

Some desultory conversation here ensued on the subject of testimony, (of no moment) between Messrs Botts, Burr, Wickham, Martin, on the one side ; and Mr Wirt on the other. The Court made some observations The topic also turned on the opinion, and on the transactions in evidence

The *Chief Justice* insisted, that the defendant's counsel should either go on with the question, or that the evidence should proceed The counsel have said, that they have got through the testimony at the island Testimony which shows the design of the march, (or departure) may, perhaps, be carried back by relation to the meeting at the mouth of Cumberland Whether it can or cannot, is a matter of argument. I shall hear testimony before I hear the argument.

Mr *Wickham* Then we understand, that when we have got to this point, we shall be at liberty to produce our opposing testimony.

Mr *Hay* returned, when conversation ensued between the parties at some length, but of no public importance.

Mr *Wickham* here objected to the receiving any depositions as testimony ; and gave notice, that should such be offered, they should oppose their being received as evidence. It was an irregular proceeding, because it did not admit of the parties being cross examined. If they proceeded to take depositions, it would be considered as under the authority of this Court.

Mr Dunbaugh was here called forward again. He observed that Mr. Wickham had mentioned, that he was a stranger to

Col Burr I was, not, said the witness—I travelled with him in 1805.

Mr. *Hay* State what passed between Col. Burr and yourself about your getting people to join him

Witness I stopt before with saying, that Col Burr had not spoken to me to engage citizens but he *had* spoken to me about soldiers. On the 30th of December, after Col Burr had obtained Capt Bissell's consent for me to go with him, I went to Col Burr where he was encamped about a mile or two below the garrison at Fort Massac on the Indiana side Col. Burr asked me into his cabin (a private room he had) and asked me if I could not get ten or twelve of the best men in the garrison to go along with him. I asked him how it was to be done He said, "get them to desert" I told him no He asked me if I could not steal out of the garrison, arms, such as muskets, fusees and rifles. I told him that I would not, if I could, for him or any other man on earth, that I had always been well treated by the officers of the army I told him I had a rifle of my own, and he told me to bring it with me, and he would pay me for it I started then to the garrison, and prepared myself to go, that was, after Col. Burr. I had obtained liberty of my captain.

[The counsel for the accused contended that this kind of testimony was not at all relevant to the subject. After some discussion, the examination proceeded.]

At the mouth of Cumberland, Walter. Davidson engaged a man by the name of Casey. Q on what terms? *Witness* I do not particularly recollect. Q. How did you know that Davidson was the agent of Col. Burr? *Witness.* He belonged to the party and told me he was an agent for Col Burr The substance of the engagement was; he was to receive twelve dollars and a half per month for six months, clothes and victuals for six months, and one hundred acres of land, to fight against all opponents This Mr Davidson, Plumb, and Andrew Wood, were sent to New Madrid to enlist more men. [The witness here returned to that point in his narration at which he had been interrupted on his former examination] When I returned to Fort Massac on the 28th December, I gave Col Burr's compliments to Capt. Bissell, and told him that Col. Burr had sent him a barrel of apples. The next day, 29th, this Mr Davidson, Plumb and Andrew Wood, came to the garrison very early in the morning, in a skiff; this was the time when they told me that they were going to enlist more men for Col. Burr They bought a skiff of me, that was left with me to sell by a Mr Cutler, a surveyor; their own skiff was afterwards carried off by Col Burr's party That evening after sun down, a barge came to Fort Massac with twelve men in it Col Tyler and major Hill were in it, and think also major Smith. They went up to captain Bissell's quarters, where they staid about twenty minutes; and I then heard Col Tyler tell the boat's crew to return to where Col Burr was encamped, with some other instructions that I did not hear Between twelve and one o'clock that night, Col Burr's boat passed by the fort, and landed about one or two miles below the garrison

Mr *Hay*. How many men were then in the garrison? *A.* Forty-four men. Q Was that the usual compliment of men? *A*

No; some of the troops had gone to Newport, and some to other places. Q. Was there any artillery? A. None Q How wide is the river at that place? A About a mile wide Next morning Captain Bissell told me to get six men with the clinker boat, to take him down the river a small piece. While the men were getting ready, a Mr. Fort (perhaps his Christian name was John) who had been lying there several days, asked me how I would like to go along I told him I should like it very well, if I could get leave to go He told me he had been speaking to Captain Bissell the evening before, and that Captain Bissell had consented to let me go While the boat was getting ready, Captain Bissell, Colonel Tyler, Major Hill, and I believe Major Smith, came down Captain Bissell got into his own boat; the rest pushed off in a boat that had been lying there several days, and fell down in company with him to where Col Burr was encamped. Captain Bissell went into Col Burr's boat, and while there, Col Burr asked him to let me go with him I heard it, because though I was not in the same room, there was a thin partition between us, and I heard him ask Captain Bissell I did not hear captain Bissell's answer Captain Bissell came out, got into his own boat, and after going one or two hundred yards, we landed and walked up to the garrison Thirtieth December, while I was in the military store, a man came in, who brought two letters from Col Burr He gave Captain Bissell one, and the other to me. Captain Bissell went out, and after I had done in the store, he called me, took me through the Sally Port to the back of the garrison, and asked me whether Col Burr had been speaking to me about a furlough I told him no He asked me whether I wanted a furlough to go I told him with his approbation and advice, I would take one Captain Bissell said he would not advise me, but if I wanted one for twenty days, he would give me one He told me before the twenty days were out, I should see the general. He asked me if Col Burr had told me any secrets, and if he had, that I must keep them to myself I accepted of captain Bissell's offer, and he told me to get ready to go with Col. Burr I then went and saw Col. Burr, and the conversation passed about the men and arms which I have already related. That evening (on the 30th December) Captain Bissell sent for me to his quarters, and told me he was going to advise me what I was to do; he advised me never to forsake Col Burr, that he would do something for me He told me that if ever Col. Burr got on a field of battle, never to leave him on the ground. At the same time he made me a present of a silver breast-plate That evening I went to Captain Bissell's for my furlough. He gave me a furlough, with a letter to Gen Wilkinson, to be delivered by Col. Burr Col Burr had then started, and I was to give him the letter as soon as I overtook him On the 31st December, being the day for muster and inspection, I asked Captain Bissell if I was to show my clothing; I said they were all packed up and on board. He told me I must borrow some for inspection, which I accordingly did, agreeably to his orders Whilst the men were on parade, I went to his lady's quarters, to take my leave, and on my return, Captain Bissell having brought the men to a ground, he told me, " Dunbaugh, I wish you success, let you go where you will." I wanted to see Dr Tuttle, before I went, and Captain Bissell told me if I had no particular business, I had better go on, and if any one asked me where I was going, I was to say, I was only going a few miles down the river, and that I was coming back again, There was one of Col Burr's boats with eight hands to take me to him

We overtook Col Burr on the first of January at New Madrid. I handed him a letter for General Wilkinson, and he broke it open. I told him the letter was for General Wilkinson· he asked pardon, took me into his cabin, and sealed it up. I asked him what boat I was to go in, and he said, in his own, as its accomodations were better than in any other We left New Madrid about eleven or twelve o'clock that day, (first January.) Andrew Wood remained at New Madrid, and Plumb, and Walter Davidson, who had been sent on to enlist men, got on board the boats, and Mr Hopkins was left in their places to enlist. After we got into the stream a keel boat come along side, and took Col. Burr into another boat some hundred yards off I saw him on the bow of that boat giving some instructions, but I could not hear him Major Floyd had charge of this keel boat and crew, and I understood they were instructed to be at Natchez in four days When we got within forty-five miles of the Chickasaw Bluffs Col Burr asked me if I would go ahead with him to Chickasaw Bluffs, in a small boat, as I was acquainted with the river. I told him I would—We got into a small boat with twelve more men, and he gave general orders to other boats to follow on, so as to reach the Bluffs early next morning We got there between twelve and one o'clock that night, (third January.) After we landed Colonel Burr told me I must go up to the garrison, and ask the commanding officer if he could not get quarters that night for himself and men. When I arrived at the garrison I was conducted to Lieutenant Jackson's quarters—He returned his compliments, and said, he would furnish them with lodgings — Colonel Burr went up with some of his men and supped The next morning Colonel Burr asked me if I was acquainted with the men at the garrison I told him I was—He asked me if I could not get ten or twelve of the best of them to desert I told him I would not. He then said he would speak to them himself, and get two of the best men, and he asked me to name them, which I did (Upon being interrogated the witness said, that there were nineteen men in the fort ; few pieces of cannon, and the river about as wide as at fort Massac.) Some time in the afternoon I asked Col. Burr if he had got the men to go with him ; he said he had Some time that evening he told me, that Lieutenant Jackson and the other men would follow in a few days. That day Colonel Burr employed a man, one Skinner, to run him some musket balls He run him six hundred, for which Col Burr paid him one dollar. He bought three dozen tomahawks out of the factory, which Col. Burr distributed among his men, some he had helved That day all the boats landed at the Bluff, and on the fifth they all started, except a small boat left for Col. B. He soon overtook us and got into his own boat. No one came from the garrison with him. We proceeded to a place called Palmyra, thirty five miles above Bayou Pierre, on the tenth January Col Burr again asked me, if I would go down to Bayou Pierre with him

Mr. *Wickham* asked the Court, whether the witness should proceed How was this kind of testimony calculated to prove the overt act? How was it relevant to the charge? Was it not better for gentlemen to extract whatever they deemed material out of the witnesses by putting interrogatories?

Mr. *Wirt*. The witness was just coming to certain declarations of the accused, which directly related to the objects of this expedition When he has arrived at Bayou Pierre, and is about to tell something that is important, he is stopped.

Chief Justice wished the attorney to put interrogatories.

Mr *Hay*. Did you ever get out of Col Burr's boat to get into another? *A* Never, except at Chickasaw Bluffs and Bayou Pierre, when I went with Col Burr at his particular request. *Q.* Did you go ashore at Judge Bruin's?—and state what happened there

The counsel for the accused objected to this general interrogatory

Chief Justice Ask him whether any thing happened there respecting this expedition.

Mr *Hay* Perhaps the witness may omit facts, because *he* deems them unimportant, which I may consider extremely relevant — Did any thing happen at Judge Bruin's respecting a publication? and state what it was.

Witness. On Sunday, 11th of January, while we were three or four hundred yards from the shore, Col Burr told me to arm myself with a rifle and conceal a bayonet under my clothes He told me he was going to tell me something I must never relate again He then told me that General Wilkinson had betrayed him, that he had played the devil with him, and proved the greatest traitor on the earth. I told him I could never believe it, and asked him how he knew it He said he had seen published in a paper a letter, which he had some time before written to General Wilkinson in cyphers He mentioned that General Wilkinson had made oath to this letter before the Court, or in open Court, I do not recollect which. He told me he was fearful of being injured or taken; that I must keep a good look out about Judge Bruin's. Colonel Burr went into Judge Bruin's to breakfast, and I went into a cotton gin that was near the house. A boat came, and he told me to take a spyglass and see whether it was his boat I could not determine.—He then directed me to go down, and if it was his boat to fire a musket. *Q.* Where is Judge Bruin's? *A.* About a mile and a quarter below Bayou Pierre.

Mr. *Wirt*. Where did he say he had seen the paper? *A* The paper had been handed by Judge Bruin to Colonel Burr the evening before *Q.* What was the conversation at Judge Bruin's? *A* Colonel Burr asked him if he had any papers He handed him his paper, and after reading fifteen or twenty minutes, he rose up and said he must go to the boats.

Mr. *Hay* Did the troops from the boats land there? *A.* Yes *Q.* With what view did the men go ashore below the mouth of

Bayou Pierre ? *A* They landed two or three miles below, in the Louisiana territory.

The opposite counsel objected to these questions; but they were overruled by the Court

Mr. *Hay.* State what happened at the landing of the men.

Witness. Some days after the men landed, (they all landed) Colonel Burr ordered ground to be cleared for a parade ground, for the purpose of exercising the men, but I never saw the ground myself, nor the men exercising Some of the men however are here, Mr. Munholland is one of those men who assisted in clearing off the ground. There was a guard of twelve men paraded at this place Wyllie for one had a rifle and sword

Mr *Wirt* Were there any Indians at that place? *A* None *Q* What produced this guard? *A* They understood that the militia were coming to take Col Burr, and these 12 men were placed to alarm the boats *Q* Was this before or after sinking the muskets? *A* It was before The *witness,* upon being further interrogated, deposed, that a Mr Lemaster had taken potatoes out of a hhd then in Mr. Blannerhasset's boat, a barrel of potatoes, with which he said he was going to fill the box of arms, so as to make it appear like a box of potatoes; that he was asked in the presence of Colonel Burr to go and help to clear the ground, that Colonel Fitzpatrick came to take an inventory of all the goods and arms that he could see, but that *he* did not see Colonel F search for the arms

Mr *Burr* Where was I all this time? *A* I know not; but I saw you handing two or three muskets out of the cabin window of your own boat into Mr Blannerhasset's boat The *witness* further stated, that the arms which were sunk, were sunk between Petit Gulph and Coles's Creek; that Colonel Burr was looked upon as the commander in chief of the expedition that in the night his boat was distinguished by two lanterns, placed one above another, whereas the rest had but one, and that in the day time handkerchiefs were hoisted in some of the boats by way of flag.

Cross examined.

Mr. *Burr* You say your furlough was for twenty days? *A* It was *Q.* After the expiration of this furlough, were you not advertised as a deserter? *A* I was. *Q* Were you taken up? *A* I was not *Q* When you got to Baton Rouge, did you write to Gen Wilkinson? *A.* I did. *Q.* What did you write? *A.* That my furlough had been taken from me, and that if he would send me a furlough or a pardon, I would come on in three days. *Q.* Did you promise to give any information against me? *A.* I did not

Mr. *Wirt* observed, that he was authorized by general Wilkinson to say, that he had the original furlough given by Capt Bissell.

Mr *Martin* Did he send you a pardon? *A.* General Wilkinson wrote to me to come down *Q* Have you that letter? *A* No. It was taken from me at Baton Rouge Gov. Folk has it at this moment. *Q* Did you write to Capt. Bissell? *A* I did. I mentioned to Capt Bissell, that as both of us might be injured by this transaction, if he would say that he had sent me as a spy, it would clear both him and myself. Q. When were you discharged from the army? A I was discharged in 1805, when I travelled with you. Q Why were you discharged? show your hand to the court. A There is my hand (one of the fingures appeared to have been injured) I can show my discharge. I procured a substitute; many have liberty to procure them

Mr *Hay*. Hand me the discharge, the witness accordingly presented it.* Did you come round with Gen. Wilkinson? A. I did. Q Were you subpœned? A I did not know I was. Q. Who requested you to come round from New Orleans? A I came by request of Gen Wilkinson Q Did he say for what? A. He said as a witness Q You gave a deposition in New Orleans? A. Yes Q At whose request? A. At Gen Wilkinsons Q When I came down the Mississippi in 1805, by whose orders did I have the men? A. I thought, by Gen Wilkinsons Q Had they arms? A I think not Q Had they colors? A They had, and they were flying every day Q. Did you not tell me you expected your discharge? A yes Q. Do you not know that the soldiers at Chickasaw Bluffs wanted to go with me; and I refused them? A I recollect that you wanted me to get them to go, but I refused Q Did you not tell me that some of them wanted to go? A I mentioned one or two Q Did any go? A No Q Why? A You told me that the lieutenant and all would follow in a few days

Mr *Wirt* This previous voyage you took the year before; were they not troops of the United States? A. They were Q. These soldiers; were they going where their company was? A The whole company were going to New Orleans, and this barge with ten men was sent on a head. And this flag belonged to them? A. It did

Mr. *Wickham* Were they regimental colors? A. They were colors made for the barge.

Chief Justice. Did you tell Captain Bissell, that Col Burr had applied to you to get the men to desert? A I did not

Mr *Wirt*. Did you not reject the proposition? A I did.

At the request of the Chief Justice, the witness here described the particular manner in which the arms were sunk He said that they were so deep in the water, as to prevent the boat from going within fifty yards of the shore. He also related his visit to Judge Bruin's where Colonel Burr got the newspaper. He also stated, at the request of the Court, the contents of his letter to General Wilkinson, that if he would send him the furlough which Lieutenant Roney had taken away from him, or a pardon, he would be there in three days. General Wilkinson informed him, that he had behaved very wrong in leaving the man he was going down with, but if he would come down he should not be molested

Mr. *Wirt* Where did the party break up? A. A few miles below Coles's creek—Q. How far is Coles's creek from Bayou Pierre? A About twenty-five miles Q When was it, that this

---

* *The discharge states, that " having served three years and six months, and being permitted to procure a substitute in his place (J. D) is hereby discharged.*

parting speech was made at Coles's creek? About the sixth or seventh of February

The interruptions in the examination of this witness were almost innumerable, and the appeals to the Court very frequent, which produced a reiteration of conversations on the applicability of the evidence, the boundary of the United States, &c. and remarks from the Court in answer, who thought that time would be saved by letting the witness go on, and afterwards appreciating his testimony. The public could not be gratified by reading, nor could the inquisitive be informed by the insertion of every desultory conversation which occurred. The evidence will, however, be fully detailed, and every applicable argument

On the question being asked of the witness respecting the landing of people at Bayou Pierre—Mr *Wickham* wanted to know what could possibly be proved by this?

Mr *Hay* said, that he believed the answer would tend to show, more immediately, the military character of these men.

The *Chief Justice* did not know how this could be applicable. One side might suppose a lawful act, what the other side might suppose military and hostile. If it went on to prove the continuation of the intention that was held at the mouth of Cumberland, and any unlawful intention was formed there, it might be received.

Mr *Hay* said, that this was one of the stipulations made—those who had previously joined the party, at the mouth of Cumberland, when they got down to Bayou Pierre, expected some opposition—at the mouth of Cumberland they expected none, but when they got down the river, they might have expected opposition. At the mouth of Cumberland they had a military posture.

Mr *Wickham*. There is but one defect in the argument of the gentleman on the other side that is, that he has omitted to prove that the mouth of Cumberland is Bayou Pierre, and Bayou Pierre is the mouth of Cumberland, and that they were in a military posture there. Again, he had not heard of the enlistment of any men for the service of Col. Burr, nor had he heard of any place of destination for, at Cumberland, the object of the expedition was not known at all

Conversation again occurred between Mr. *Hay* and Mr. *Botts*, on the subject of *identity*.

Mr. *M'Rae* rose. He declared that he had avoided participating in argument, not because he did not think the points held up as of sufficient importance, but because the opinion of the Court had been made up.

He did not now rise with the pretension of offering any new ideas to the Court, but he would refer the Court to its decision delivered on Saturday

The Court has considered what was called an overt act of levying war, in which was included the arms that were with them in the boxes as one ingredient, which were intended for use at New Orleans that it expressly said that not only would it be an overt act at New Orleans, but that it would make the assembly at the mouth of Cumberland an overt act of levying war there, if the intention to make war and the capacity was in sufficient progress there

If then, instead of making the attempt at New Orleans, they had merely progressed towards that attempt—had cleared a piece of ground whereon to exercise; and where they had put themselves in a posture of defence; or, if not assailed, had thought proper to engage offensively at any time, what can prevent us from shewing these things to support our charge of the overt act. I understand, Sir, that although we cannot prove any thing at New Orleans, because they never got there, we can prove any thing to strengthen or corroborate what was done at Cumberland, by what was done down the river, directly relating to the circumstance at the mouth of Cumberland.

Mr *Wickham* referred to the opinion again: he also referred to the doubt which the Chief Justice had entertained, about what he called equivocal acts, but upon the points which had been laid down, they were prepared to argue. There was a very great difference, he contended, in *intending* to make war, and in making war. When an overt act was *completely* proved, then, he understood that corroborative circumstances might be given in evidence: but this he did not believe had been the case. He referred to Vaughan's case.

Mr. *Burr* spoke at some length on the subject of evidence, and applied it to the meeting at Cumberland; he drew some analogies as to the destination: and expressed his wish that the court would keep to the question. The party might, after they had proceeded to some distance, change their designated or contemplated place of action. This question ought to be settled, whether an overt act could exist until an *act* at least appeared, towards the object charged. To what purpose, he would ask, was all this, that he should be obliged to answer when and where they pleased.

Chief Justice. I did not express my opinion, that if a body of men at Cumberland should march down to New Orleans, so as to subvert the government of Orleans, that it was treason at the mouth of Cumberland. I have no doubt but that there must be sufficient evidence given to warrant me to send the accused to Kentucky. Gentlemen differ very much in their opinions, and very probably the Court might differ from both sides. Consequently the Court must look for proof. But if there was no testimony relative to the act, at the mouth of Cumberland, I should hesitate to stop the testimony. All explanatory testimony I am inclined to hear, but that which does not explain, I do not think myself bound to hear.

The case of Vaughan, which has been so often quoted, does bear, in some measure on the present case—it goes so far as this that an overt act done in one place which does not affect an overt act done in another place, is not evidence, of the latter—That cruizing in one ship is not an evidence of a man cruizing in another, although it does form a strong impression that he did so cruize.

Here the Chief Justice drew a parallel between the cases of Vaughan, cruizing in the loyal Clencarthy, and taking the customhouse boat recited in 5 St. Tr. P 22 and the present case which comparison he believed would not altogether accord; however he was willing to hear the testimony.

James M'Dowel again called in.

Mr. *Hay.* How far did your evidence go, on your former exam-ination ? Mr. *Wirt.* The Court stopt him within the limits of the United States Mr *Hay* Do you recollect any thing that passed after you left the mouth of Cumberland ?

The *Witness* replied to successive interrogatories that he saw eight or ten arms in the boat, which he sat out in the boat of Captain Tyler and Major Smith that he saw guns but not so ma-ny in the other boats ; that Colonel Tyler was the *captain* of that boat ; that he thought there were about one hundred and thirty men at Coles's creek ; that a little Bayou below Bayou Pierre the boats stopt and Colonel Burr got out ; he knew nothing of clearing ground for exercising the men , he did not see the box-es opened , that some of the boxes were four feet long and some six, that they were heavy, and he could not lift them ; he saw six or seven boxes ; that a few miles below Coles's creek, they went upon a hill and formed a circle Colonel Burr told them, he was a thorn in their side, so long as he remained with them ; that he had been taken from them two or three times ; he had been car-ried on his trial to Washington ; and that he was now about to leave them ; he told them, what was his, was their's (alluding as the witness supposes to his property,) and that they might go on and settle the Ouachita country, which he had purchased

Cross-examined

Mr *Burr* Did you see General Wilkinson at New Orleans A. I do not know whether I saw him Q Who invited you to come here ? A I was summoned in Pennsylvania.

Mr. *Blannerhasset* Do you recollect being in Dean's boat? A. I do Q. Do you not recollect, that its roof was leaky ? A. I do Q do you not recollect, that I expressed some fear's lest the leak might injure my boxes ? A. I do not recollect.

Israel Miller

Mr. *Hay.* Were you at the mouth of Cumberland ? A. I was, I went down with Mr Tyler from Pennsylvania Q Had you any communication with Mr. Burr. A. I was introduced to Mr. Burr by Mr Tyler at the island opposite the mouth of Cumberland I never held any conversation with Mr Burr. Q How many men were at the mouth of Cumberland ? A On the whole between sixty and seventy. I am certain there were not one hundred. Q What did Mr. Burr say to the party on the island ? A. He said he had something to communicate to which he would take another time for.

Mr. *M'Rae.* How many boats were at the mouth of Cumberland A. I believe ten. Q. How many men in each boat ? A. There were seven in the boat I belonged to , I know not how many were in the others.

Cross-examined.

Mr. *Burr* How many men went from Blannerhasset's island A. about thirty-one men Q. Were these men used to labor, to farming or mechanics? *A.* Most of them were fit for it

There were only a few of them not used to labor. Q. Did they not do hard work ? A They did. Q What arms did they bring from Blannerhasset's island ? A I saw only one blunderbuss, one fusee, and a pair of pistols Q. How much powder ? A. I saw only a small keg. Q How many lbs do you suppose it contained ? A. About ten or fifteen Q. Were they not short of powder to kill game ; did they not very often come into your boat and borrow some ? A. They did. Q. What kind of game ? A Ducks and turkies

Mr. M'Rae Do they kill this kind of game with bullets ? A Yes

Mr Burr I the gentleman had ever been in Kentucky, he would have known, that it was considered inglorious *there* to kill a squirrel or even ducks, with any thing but bullets.

TUESDAY, *September* 22.

Q to *Israel Miller* —How many of those were flat bottomed boats ? A I believe there were four—besides one keel boat and four batteaux. Q How came you with that party ? A I started with Smith and Tyler to go to Washita. Q Did you make any bargain to go to Washita ? A Not a bargain, nor any particular engagement Q Were you engaged to join Burr's party or expedition ? A No I knew nothing of him having a party Q Were there any conditions or promises made ? A No, Sir Q. What was proposed ? A Why, Mr. Smith asked me to go with Col. Burr to settle some lands , and told me that the first settlers would have considerable advantages

Mr Burr Did you see more men about Coles's creek than at Cumberland ? A. I never was there

Jacob Dunbaugh was again called.

Q Have you been in the habit of going up and down the Mississippi ? A. I was down, but never was up by water. Q Were you ever up Red river A. No Q Can flat bottomed boats go against a stream ? A No, it requires keel boats Q How many boats were there ? A. Five or six flat bottomed boats, two keel boats, and four batteaux. Q Did Burr never disclose all his schemes to you ? A Why, once he told me, that his first object was to take Baton Rogue, and to keep that as his home till he collected all his forces, which was between twelve and fifteen hundred. Q. Did you ever understand any thing about what the governmeent should do ? A. Yes, but not from Colonel Burr. Q. Baton Rouge is below Red river pretty far, is it not ? A About eight miles I imagine.

Mr *Wirt.* What forts are there between Massac and New Orleans ? A Chickasaw Bluffs, fort Adams, and fort Pickering. Q. Where was Burr taken from the party ? A. I do not know that he was taken at all—I believe he delivered himself up. Q. Where? A. At Bayou Pierre. The military came and agreed with Cowles Meade to meet at Coles's creek, and after that he went to the Mississippi territory. Q. Were you present at that interview ? A No, Sir. Q. Who was present at the first meeting at Bayou Pierre ? A I understood that Col Claiborne was, but I know that Col. Woodridge was, and a fair meeting was agreed to

Mr Wirt What was the impression of the party—was it considered that Col. Burr intended to go to New Orleans

Here objection was made, and some conversation occurred

Denbaugh said that he had given the same evidence before the Grand Jury

Chief Justice Was there any public conversation with the party?

Witness Not till they got to Bayou Pierre, and then Col Burr told me to tell them, that they were going to settle the Washita lands

Mr Wirt Do you know whether any of these men went to Washita lands? *A* There were some men went up the river I believe, but I do not know where they went

Chief Justice Did you mention in your affidavit* that this man (Casey) had been enlisted at the mouth of Cumberland? *A* I did *Q* Do you know what became of him? *A* I left him at Natchez, and I believe he is in Tennessee

Q What conversation passed when Colonel Burr made this communication respecting his forces? *A* I cannot recollect particularly. *Q.* What conversation had you with Mr Blannerhasset? *A* I was not in private with him; there were more in the room, and it was not particularly directed to me.

Chief Justice How far is Bayou Pierre from Baton Rouge? *A.* About two hundred miles *Q.* Had any messengers been sent down to Baton Rouge? *A.* On the first January there was a party with Major Floyd sent down to Natchez, whether he was at Bayou Pierre, I cannot say.

Mr. *Hay* here offered the affidavit of David Fisk Some objection was made to it, but Mr. Neale and Mr Hay testifying, that he was so ill, and out of town, as to be unable to attend the Court, it was ultimately agreed that the affidavit should be received with the examination annexed.

[Here follows the deposition of Mr Fisk, taken on account of his being unable to attend Court, from sickness, and read on Wednesday, but which we insert under the head of Tuesday's proceedings]

The affidavit of David Fisk, of lawful age, who being first sworn before me, Daniel L. Hylton, a Justice of the peace for the county of Henrico, saith, that some time in the month of September, 1806, a certain Davis Floyd, of the Indiana territory, came to this affiant, and asked him if he did not wish to take a voyage down the river with him during the course of the fall or winter, that he was going to settle a new country, the Washita, on Red river This happened, either the next day, or a few days after Colonel Burr had left Jeffersonville, the residence of the said Floyd At that time this affiant did not tell him whether I should go or not; but about two or three weeks afterwards he did agree to go, the said Floyd having several times mentioned what a fine chance there would be for him; that they would not

---

* This was offered to the Court on the early examination, before the trial commenced

gree to give to any one man more than twelve dollars a month, and one hundred and fifty acres of land at the end of six months, besides clothes and provisions, but as he and this affiant were well acquainted, if he would have confidence in him, he would do something very clever for him, and if they succeeded in their object there would be fortunes made for all that went. This affiant asked what other object they had beside settling the Washita land. The said Floyd answered that there was a new road to be cut a great distance, and several houses to be built, which would be a very profitable undertaking. No positive bargain was made between the said Floyd and this affiant. On the 16th of December, 1806, this affiant moved down the river from the falls of the Ohio, in the Indiana territory, with the said Floyd, with two boats and one batteaux, which the said Floyd had built there. On the same day just as they were about to start, they were joined by Herman Blannerhasset, Comfort Tyler, and Israel Smith, with four batteaux and a number of men, the exact number he cannot state, nor does he know the number that started with the said Floyd, but when the boats joined Colonel Aaron Burr at the mouth of Cumberland, (which was of a Saturday night, either on Christmas night, or the first Saturday night after) he understood that the whole number of men, including those of the said A. Burr, were one hundred and three. After the boats had left the falls of Ohio, three or four days, he discovered for the first time, on board one of the said Floyd's boats, a chest and a box, the former of which it afterwards appeared, contained muskets and bayonets, a few fusees, and blunderbusses and pistols, the latter rifles. A day or two afterwards the said Floyd enquired of the men if they did not want each of them a gun to take care of, that he had some there which he was afraid would get rusty. The chest and box were then opened and all the arms taken out and cleaned, and some of them occasionally used by the men in hunting as they went down the river. There were, as near as he can judge, between twenty-five and thirty muskets with bayonets, two, or three fusees, three or four blunderbusses, ten pair of pistols, and about eight or ten rifles. Some short time after the boats had joined Col. Burr, and before they got into the Mississippi river, while this affiant was laying sick on his trunk, he heard the said Floyd tell several of the men that they were going to take Baton Rouge and Mexico.

This affiant asked how they were going to do it with so few men. The said Floyd answered that a large party of men were to join us at Natchez, and Gen. Wilkinson and his army were to join us at the mouth of Red river. Nothing of importance occured till the boats got down to Bayou Pierre. A day or two before their arrival there, Col. Burr took a boat and four or five men and went on ahead, as this affiant understood, to do some business, which he expected to do before the boats got down. Floyd's boat, in which he went himself, and in which this affiant was, arrived there of a Sunday morning, and the other boats not till the evening. On our arrival Colonel Burr was standing on the bank of the river, about a mile above the town; some short time after the men from our boat went on shore, this affiant saw Col. Burr, and a certain Robert A. New, (who had the command of Floyd's boat in his absence, he having then gone to Natchez) talking together for some time. The said New then came on board our boat and called all the men into it, and said he understood they were all going to be stopped and enquired of them, whether they would stand by Colonel Burr and go on, or quit. Most of the men were for going on, but two or three were for quitting. In the course of that day this affiant mentioned to the said New, that he mistrusted they were going on some unlawful scheme. He assured him that they were not, that nothing was going to take place but what was lawful and countenanced by the government. After dark the boats were removed over to the other side of the river. This affiant enquired the reason of their being removed; and was answered by the said New, that there was a party of men coming to take them, and it was best for them to make their escape. The boats laid seven or eight days at that place, and then moved about six miles lower down. While the boats were lying there, they were examined by several military officers, by the permission of Colonel Burr, but the night before they were searched, all the muskets and pistols, except a few pair belonging to individuals, were taken out, the rifles were left. This affiant never knew what became of the muskets and pistols; some of the men said they were sunk in the river, others that they were hid in the woods. One night while the boats were laying at that place, a young man came and said there were three or four hundred men crossing above us and as many below us, and that we should all be taken. A guard was posted at some distance from the encampment on that night, but what their orders were this affiant does not know, as he was not one of the number. After our removal from this place, Col. Burr went to the town of Washington to stand his trial, but it not coming on he returned. He remained with the party one night, then went again to take his trial, and did not return till it was over. He remained with the boats one day; told the men that he had stood his trial and that he was acquitted, but that they were going to take him again, and he was going to flee from oppression. He said that what property there was, the men might sell and make the most they could of; and if there was not enough to satisfy them they might go to the Washita land, and take up what land they wanted and go to work upon it. The boats and provisions were taken to Natchez, and part of them sold, and part of the provisions stored, which would not readily sell, and the money divided among the men. The boats were different in their construction from any this affiant had ever seen, rather larger than were usually seen on those waters, and such of them as were sold brought seventy-five dollars a piece, the usual price of boats being from twenty to thirty dollars. But there was a great demand for boats at that time to freight cotton down the river.

Q. After the boats and men had joined Col. Burr at the mouth of Cumberland, who appeared to have the command of the expedition?

A. It was generally understood that the expedition was under the command of Colonel Burr; but I do not recollect to have heard him give any orders, except as to the sale of the boats and provisions, after we were stopped, though I often saw him in co.

rersation with Blannerhasset, Tyler, Smith, Floyd, and New.
and supposed that he communicated his orders to them

DAVID FISK

Henrico county, &c
Sworn before me in due form agreeably to law, this 22d Sept
1807

DANL L. HYLTON

Question by d ft How did you understand the number of men
to be one hundred and three? A From one of the men, I never
counted them This included the men in all the boats at the isl-
and Q How many men came with Col Burr? A I do not
know, but not more than three or four I believe. Q Do you include Dean's, Ellis's and Boyce's boats? A Yes Q Where did
the conversation with Floyd about Mexico and Baton Rouge take
place, and was Colonel Burr, Blannerhasset or Smith, present?
A I dot recollect at what place it happened, but neither of the
three gentlemen named above were present? Q Was Colonel
Burr present when the boats were searched, or was he then at
Washington? A He was with the boats Q Did Blannerhasset
have any command over any of the boats? A. None, except his
own boat which was in company Q Did you not at that time
expect a war with Spain? A I did; it was the general expectation of the party at that time Q How did you understand Mr.
Floyd as to Mexico and Baton Rouge? A I expected we were going on in the event of a war, and that we should be joined by the
army of the United States Q Were you not told that in the event
of no war, you were to settle the Washita lands? A Yes, and
after we were stopped, Colonel Burr advised us to proceed and
make the settlement

September 28—The foregoing questions were put to Mr David
Fisk by the counsel for Colonel Burr, and the answers thereto
sworn in my presence, a justice of the peace for the city of Richmond

ANDERSON BARRETT.

Jacob Dunbaugh was re-examined.—He stated there were two
keels and four batteaux, that Mr Burr had told him between
Chickasaw Bluffs and Bayou Pierre, that his first object was to
seize Baton Rouge, and make *that* his home, until he could collect his forces, which he expected would amount to ten or twelve
thousand; he stated that Mr Blannerhasset told him, that governor Foulk of Baton Rouge would order the men to take the
flints out of their guns, he said that some of the men went up
the Red River

Upon being *cross-examined*, he stated that he had made a deposition at New Orleans at the request, but not compulsion of Gen
Wilkinson that he was well acquainted with the construction
of batteaux, that they could go up stream, and that they were
built for that purpose

Stephen S. Welch
Q Were you at the mouth of Cumberland? A I was; I only
joined there. I was there with a load, and captain Berry wished
me to join and go down the river to make a settlement; for that

it was advantageous to young men. I said, that I had no incum
brance, and being a single man, I was willing to go Q Who is
Berry? A John Berry, a man I met there Mr. Burr He was
called *captain* of the *boat*. *Witness* He was appointed Captain of
the boat I went in I agreed to go down The proposition made
to me by Captain, Berry was to settle the Ouachita country; to
have a certain portion of land, besides other compensation Q
What was it A captain Berry offered me ten dollars a month,
but I said I was not for hire, and as I was a young man, would go
as a volunteer Q Did you descend the river with them? A
Yes A Do you recollect hearing any conversation from Mr Burr
to Mr Floyd, on the subject of arms A. I do not. Q Did you
go to Bayou Pierre? A I did, and also to Natchez. Q What
became of Mr Blannerhasset? A. I think that he went down
to Natchez with us I think that the boat with his family aboard
was struck on the point of an island above Natchez, and that I
assisted to get her off I did not see Mr. Blannerhasset there, but
I was told that he went to Natchez.

On being further interrogated, the witness deposed that he
was on the piece of ground cleared for exercising, that he was
stationed there with sixteen or seventeen others as a guard to
watch the boats, about two hundred yards from it, that the boats
were then on the west side of the Mississippi, that he understood
as the reason of this arrangement that militia were expected to
come and carry the boats to Cole's Creek, that the orders of the
guard were to let no one pass to the boats, without giving the
countersign "Look sharp;" and to fire if any one attempted to
pass, not with an intention of hitting them, but as an alarm to
the boats; that a Mr. Noland from Berry's boat gave the orders,
but he knew not who gave them to him; Noland was sometimes
styled lieutenant and sometimes ensign; that centinels were plac
ed out who were relieved every two hours through the night till
day-light, the guard were not. Q Were you ever better inform
ed about the object of this expedition? The *witness* said, that he
had not been from those who had any authority, or who he sup
posed were better informed than himself; but there was a talk a
mong the men, that they were going to take Baton Rouge. Q
Why did your impressions change? A. The witness said that
he did not know who was the first person that started such a con
versation, but that *he* had first heard it from two or three or
more who were talking in the bow of the boat; that he came for
ward and heard it; that it was further said, that they were going
to drag the men to Florida Some of them were very much scar
e at the time He further said, that there were somewhere a
bou 100 men at the mouth of Cumberland, that they had no agri
cultural tools, no ploughs, hoes or harrows, except edged tool
to fell timber; that the search made by captain Fitzpatrick wa
at the Bayou below Bayou Pierre; that being only in one boa
when it was searched, he does not know whether the search wa
a fair one, that he never saw, but did hear that arms had been
sunk and concealed, that he saw, not heard of the stopping a
leak produced by two auger holes and ropes in the back part o
the gunwale in the cabin occupied by Mr Burr, for that Mr Pry
or being unable to stop the leak he had called him, and he had
stopped it

Cross-examined

Mr. *Burr.* Did you know Dean's boat? A. He sailed with us in company from the mouth of Cumberland; but I do not certainly know, whether it was connected with us. Q What became of Boyce's boat? A. It went down to Natchez.

Mr *Wirt.* Who dismissed you from this party? A When the boats were stopped and the eruption took place, I went down to Natchez Mr Wirt When Col Burr left the party, was there any ceremony of parting? any speech? A He did speak to them He said, he would have to leave them, till he could see them again. I think, he said, his property was to be distributed among them Q Was any thing said about wages; about the means of paying them A I don't recollect

Mr *Burr* How did you come round from New Orleans? A I came with Gen Wilkinson Q Were you subpœned? A I was. Q Had you any communication with Gen Wilkinson? A Not till after I had received the subpœna. Q Did you receive any money there? Any from Gen Wilkinson? A Yes, I received ten dollars from Gen Wilkinson to help me to bear my expences as a witness. Q Did you give any deposition there? A. None, but some statement of my evidence, taken down by Gen Wilkinson; but I did not give my qualification to it

William Love called in again

Mr. *Hay* When did you separate from the party? A At Bayou Pierre Mr Hay. State the circumstances which induced you to leave them.

Witness. The boat was going down to Natchez, and I went down in it. Q What boat? A The boat with two horses in

Mr *Wirt.* Did you go in Boyce's boat to Natchez? A. Yes

Mr. *Hay* Did you go in consequence of any direction from Mr Blannerhasset? A. I did not Q Why did you leave them? A I was not in the party, and I thought I might as well leave them. Q. Was there no particular circumstance as to Mr. Blannerhasset, which induced you to do it? A. Yes, when I was in the boat Mr Blannerhasset ordered me out, for he wanted to speak to the men in my absence I was not pleased at this, as I thought my life as sweet as the rest of them Capt. Elliot however, came, and told me, I might join as a volunteer, and gave me a musket I went over to the party, but finding that I could not keep as high as the rest of them, I got discontented, and was determined to go to Natchez. Q In what boat did you see the chest of arms? A. In Major Floyd's boat.

Mr *Wirt.* Do you know any thing of the guard? A. I was not there at that time

Mr *Hay.* In what boat were the other chests? A. I do not say they were arms? but I saw some boxes on board of Capt. Dean's boat.

Mr. *Wirt* Did you say you had no other reason for quitting, but because you could not keep up appearances? None.

Cross examined.

Mr *Burr* Who brought you round here from New Orleans? A Gen. Wilkinson I was introduced to him by Serjeant Dunbaugh before I was subpœnaed. Every one of the party whom he could find was carried to the general. Q Did Gen. Wilkinson ask you any questions? A He asked some. Q Was this before or after you were subpœnaed? A Before. Q Did you receive any money? A I received about twenty dollars from the military agent after I was subpœnaed. Since I came here, I have refunded it to the Marshal.

Samuel Moxley

Mr *Wirt* Were you with the party? A I was. Q Where did you join them? At the falls of Ohio Q Were you at the mouth of Cumberland? A I was Q In whose boat did you descend the river? A. In Captain Berry's boat, which was built at the falls of the Ohio, and there joined the party, Major Floyds boat also joined them there, besides a small batteaux, which was not loaded with provisions as the other two were Q Did you not proceed down the river with the boats which came from Blannerhasset's island? A Yes, we were some times in company with them Q How many men were at the mouth of Cumberland? A I suppose not not more than one hundred Q Did you see these men introduced to Colonel Burr? A I did not Q Nor heard his speech? A I heard nothing about it till I got to Orleans? Q Did you conceive you belonged to this party? A I did Q With whom did you engage? A With Mr Berry of Indiana twelve miles from Jeffersonville Q. What was the nature of that engagement? A. To descend the Ohio and the Mississippi, and to ascend Red river, to settle the Ouachita lands I was not certain whether these lands belonged to Col Burr or Mr. Lynch, but I supposed the latter It was also stated, that should our frontier be invaded by the Spaniards, we were to render every assistance in our power to resist them Q How many arms were in your boat? A About eight or nine. Q. How many men? A About sixteen Q Were you at the Bayou below Bayou Pierre? A I was Q Did any thing of consequence occur there? A I do not know what you may deem important Q were there any guards stationed there? A. There were, and for this purpose—the militia were said to be crossing the river above us in rafts, and the guard were to give the alarm Q Was any ground cleared to exercise men? A There was ground cleared, but I do not know for what purpose Q. How large a ship? A About half an acre Q To what purpose was it applied? A I do not know, but the guard were stationed there. Q Was it that the guard might stay there? A I do not know, but when it was cleared, I did not see the necessity of clearing it Q What instructions were given to the guard? A I only heard from others; that if any one approached, they were to fire two guns, and then the guard were to go off in a small boat Q Did you think that the object of this enterprize *was* to settle lands?

Mr. *Burr* objected to such enquiries. How could the mere opinions of a witness have any influence to a Court of justice? Might not those opinions be formed upon idle rumors? Gentlemen have substantially asserted that four-fifths of the people of this state have been duped by such false rumors The same means of deception was used in Kentucky; but they were so easily duped, as the gentleman represents the Virginians to have been

Chief Justice. Let the question be proposed in this form Did you see any thing *in* the party itself, which induced you to think that there was a different object? A. I did not, before the arrival of the militia, when I began to entertain doubts of the object

Mr. *Wirt.* Was there any part of your engagement about a service of six months? A We were engaged for six months

Mr. *M'Rae.* What service? A I am not certain, We were to stay there to settle the land, and it was supposed the settlement would be made in that time Q What consideration were you to receive? A Ten dollars a month and one hundred acres of land?

Mr. *Wirt* Had you any manuel exercise as you went down? A We had on the roof of the boats two or three times Q The boats were roofed? A Yes, they were flat on top, the exercise was of our own accord

Mr. *Hay* Did you see the same operation in other boats? A I did not.

Mr *Wirt* Did you see any thing of the search made by Colonel Fitzpatrick? A. I was there? it happened at Thompson's Bayou Q Did Fitzpatrick see all the arms? A The muskets were taken from our boat *before* Colonel Fitzpatrick made the search Q. To what boat were they carried? A. I know not, but they were taken out of ours Q Do you know any thing about the burying or concealing of arms? A I do not Q Do you know any thing of holes boared in the gun-whales of Colonel Burr's boat? A I do not Q You were in your own boat I suppose? A. I was—we were at too great a distance from them to have seen any such occurrence? Q Do you know any thing of it from public conversation among the men? A I understood that the arms had been concealed—I heard it talked of in the company of the men, by different persons, that they were tied to a sawyer,* also, that they were taken up the Bayou and buried, and that they were concealed underneath Colonel Burr's boat

No cross-examination

Chandler Lindsley

Q Where did you begin with your voyage? A I descended the river with Mr Ellis from Pittsburg Q What was the object of the voyage? A. Mr. Ellis called it a trading voyage Q Did you join the party at the mouth of Cumberland? A I did. Q What do you suppose was the force at the mouth of Cumberland? A. I should suppose there were about seventy or eighty men—the circle to which Colonel Burr was introduced consisted of thirty or forty, and I should suppose they composed about half of the whole Q. Did you stop at Cincinnati? A I did Q Did you receive any information of the party there? A. I heard that Colonel Burr had been there a day or two before, and had excited some consternation among the people there? Q. Did you

---

* *A sawyer is the log of a tree, or a whole tree fixed to one end the bottom of the Mississippi, and plays up and down with the current, like a man who is sawing timber.*

stop at the falls of the Ohio? A The water was low and occasioned us to remain there two or three days Q. Was any of the party there? A Mr Kibby was there engaging men to settle the Ouachita land? Q Do you recollect his christian name? A I do not Q On what terms did he wish to engage? A Mr Kibby stated to us the articles of agreement—They were nearly the same as those which Mr Moxley has described Q. Were there any signatures to the articles? A There were about ten or twelve? Q What were the terms? A It obligated them to go down the Ohio and Mississippi, and ascend the Red river to the mouth of Black river and those waters up to the Ouachita river, and it was annexed that if the frontier was invaded they were to resist. Q. Did you descend the Mississippi? A I went to Natchez with Major Floyd and Ralston, and about fifteen others in a keel boat purchased by Colonel Burr of Mr Ellis Q What was in that boat? A Bar-iron, hoes, mattocks, and a few barrels of apples Q Do you know where the bar-iron and other articles were obtained? A Yes, they were purchased by Colonel Burr of Mr Ellis at the mouth of Cumberland

Mr *Wirt*. Was Mr. Ellis's being there accidental? A At the time Mr Ellis was at the falls, Major Floyd talked of making a contract with Mr Ellis, for these articles, he did not however buy them; but told Mr. Ellis, that he would see Colonel Burr on the river, and he was confident that the Colonel would purchase the whole. Q. Where were these articles from? A. From Pittsburg

Mr *Wirt* My object is to ascertain, Sir, whether Burr's meeting with Ellis, was in consequence of any previous arrangement between them, or the mere effect of accident Can you inform me as to the point? Was Mr Ellis's voyage preconcerted with Col Burr? A Mr Ellis, Sir, was on a *general* trading voyage

Mr. *Hay* How many of those articles were there? A. I know not, Mr Ellis has, I believe, an inventory of them, and he is here

Mr *Hay* Was Mr Blannerhasset at the mouth of Cumberland when the tools were purchased? A He was. Q Was any proposition made to you to join the party? A There was Q Who made it? A Col Tyler asked me I told him, that if there was nothing hostile in their views, and there was a prospect of gain I would join. He said if there was any thing hostile, he would be as far from it as any man

Mr *Hay* Did you not join? A. I did. I had a right to withdraw whenever I pleased The greater part of Col Tyler's men were, I think, on the same terms

Mr *Hay* Why did you make that reservation? A From the reports which were then in circulation

Mr. *Wirt* What were the terms? I joined on the same term as the other young men who were with him Col Tyler told me he was going to settle Ouachita land, and those who went on first were at liberty to purchase land.

Mr *Hay* For what time did you engage? A I was at liberty to leave them whenever I pleased.

Mr *Wirt* Did you hear any observations from Col. Burr at the mouth of Cumberland? A. Only a few words. He said that he had intended to have communicated his designs at that place, but that certain reasons prevented him   I understood him to say, that Col Tyler, Major Smith and Floyd, would make those reasons known to us

Mr Wirt   Do you know any thing of the transactions at Thompson's Bayou?   A   I was not there

No cross-examination

John Munnollan

Witness   Do you wish me to state where I joined the party?

Mr Hay   Yes

Witness   I joined Mr Tyler and Mr. Smith at Beaver in Penn sylvania.   Q   Was there any agreement between you; or what was your reason for joining them?   A   My first reason was, my meeting with a William Davis from the back part of the state of New York   He told me that he was going down with a party to see the country, I wished too to see the country, but Mr Davis told me he could not engage me, but he would go to Beaver and mention me to Mr Tyler   When Davis got to Meadville, he met with Major Smith, to whom he communicated my wishes, and informed him that I was at Waterford   Major Smith called on me at Waterford, presented me with Mr Davis's compliments, and informed me that Mr. Davis and himself would be pleased to see me at Beaver   There I met with Mr. Tyler, he told me that he had an idea of going up the Red river to settle land   Q   Did he mention Col Burr's name?   A. He did not mention his name while we were at Beaver   Q   And why did you go?   A   I felt much disposed to see the country   Q   Was there no particular contract made with you?   A   Not at that time

Mr *Wirt*   Was there any agency given you, to engage men or provisions?   A   I was sent back to Waterford to hurry on salt for salting provisions that were expected at Beaver   I was also to engage what men I could, they were to find themselves in clothes and blankets   Q   Did you engage any men?   A   Yes, several, about fifteen from Meadville   Q.   What terms did you hold out to those men?   A.   That they were to ascend the Red river.   Q   Were no lands promised them? no compensation?   A   None   Q   What instructions did you give them, or were they to go to Tyler?   A   They were to go to Col Tyler at the mouth of Beaver for such instructions as he thought proper   Q   Did you receive any instructions as to the kind of men you were to engage?   A. None.   Q. As to young or old?   A   I would not of course engage old men.   Q.   Any with families?   A.   Some with families did go, I was allowed to take any I thought proper.   Q   Did you go to Blannerhasset's island?   A.   I did   Q   Was it known at Beaver, that the Marietta boats were to be of the party?   A   It was not   I knew that Blannerhasset was to join, but I believe the boat I was in would not have stopped at the island, had it not been grounded   Q   Did Blannerhasset go with you from the island?   A. He did   Q   Was there any difficulty about his going with you? was any vote taken?   A   Major Tyler and Smith asked us if we were willing that he should go with us, and we said we had no objection   It was mentioned among us, that he was under some apprehension of a mob arresting him.   Q.

Was there any rumour or alarm among you about the militia of Kenawha or Wood county? A. We had heard that there was a mob coming, and we were determined to resist them. But we should not have resisted the militia with legal authority. Q. What do you mean by legal authority? do you mean that if they had a warrant from the civil authority, you would not have resisted? A. Such was our meaning; but we would have resisted a mob. Q. What do you mean by a mob? A. If the mob had come, we should have asked for the authority under which they acted, and if they had none, they should have gone away without gaining their intentions. Q. Was there any preparation made for resistance? A. Not that I know of. Q. Any bullets run? A. There were, but they were to kill game and shoot at marks, which we frequently did on the river. Q. Where were you joined by other boats? A. By two of Mr. Floyd's at the falls of the Ohio. Q. Did you see any arms? A. There were about thirty five or thirty-six muskets or stands of arms, which I saw when we got to the Mississippi. Q. Any arms of any other description, such as rifles? A. There were three or four rifles. Q. What particularly happened on going down the river? A. At Shawanee town there was an address drawn up to the Ouachita or western land speculation company, tendering our services in any legal and honorable enterprize. This was signed by all of Tyler's party. Q. Who formed that company? A. There were no names mentioned in the address, but I considered Col Burr as one, though his name was not mentioned. Q. Who drew up the address? A. Major Tyler and Smith. Q. Are the phrases "legal and honorable enterprize" repeated from memory? A. They are. Q. Was it presented by Tyler and Smith? A. It was. How many signers were to it? A. About thirty or thirty-two. Q. Had you any assurance that the plan would be disclosed to you at the mouth of Cumberland? A. None, from those who had a right to be informed. Such however was the talk among the men, as we went down. When you were at the mouth of Cumberland, were you introduced to Col Burr? A. I was, on the 27th December. We arrived there on the 26th. Q. What took place on this introduction? A. Nothing particular. Q. At this introduction did the party form any thing like the three sides of a square? A. They did. Q. Was he introduced along the line? A. He was, to the men, one by one. Q. After this ceremony, was there any speech from Col Burr? A. I was not near enough to hear what he said, but I understood that he said he would impart something at another time. Q. Did you receive any instructions to run bullets and make cartridges? A. One day, while we were in the Mississippi, Col. Burr came into our boat and asked whether there was any one there that could make cartridges? I told him that I never had made any, but I believed I could make them, and I made three or four dozen. Q. Did Col Burr act as the head of the party? A. I considered him as such. Q. Did you understand that the real object was to settle Ouachita lands? A. It was so stated. Q. Was there no occurrence or particular conversation which induced to believe there was a different object?

Mr. *Botts.* Was there any conversation in the *presence* of Col Burr? A. It was not a general conversation.

Mr *Hay* Is it a fact or is it not a fact, that many of the men did suppose there was a different object? A I do not recollect, nor did I attend to them, because I did not suppose they knew more about it than myself. Q Do you know any thing about the seizing of Baton Rouge? A I never heard it before I got below Bayou Pierre, and then there were some conversations among the men about it. But I did not hear it suggested by any person, that there was any design of invading any part of the United States, nor did I ever hear any thing from Col Burr or any of the leaders, about invading Mexico.

The counsel for the accused said that it was unnecessary to make any statement on that subject

Mr *Hay* The present enquiry relates as well to the misdemeanor as to the treason

Mr *Martin* We have never heard of such a charge before

Mr *Hay* observed that he had also reduced the charge to writing, and had notified its existence to one of the opposite counsel, though it had never been publicly read in Court

The clerk then read the paper in the following terms

"The attorney of the United States for the Virginia district, charges Aaron Burr, Harman Blannerhasset, and Israel Smith "with a misdemeanor against the United States, in beginning, "or setting on foot, or preparing or providing the means of a "military expedition or enterprize, against Mexico, a province "in North America, of the king of Spain, with whom the Uni-"ted States are at peace"

Mr *Hay* It is immaterial besides, whether this charge has been preferred, because though the charge actually alleged is treason, yet if the other crime should occur during the investigation of the evidence, it is the province of the court to enquire into it

Chief Justice It would certainly be unnecessary to re-examine the same witness a second time

Mr *Wirt* Did you then hear nothing of the Mexican invasion? A I did not from any leading characters

Mr *Hay* Who did you consider as the leading characters? A Col Burr, Tyler, Smith, Blannerhasset and Floyd Q Had you not been informed of the plan by the President's proclamation A That did not reach us before we go to Bayou Pierre Q. Were you at Thompson's Bayou? A I was Q Do you know any thing of the ground that was cleared for exercising the men? A I assisted in clearing it.

Mr *Burr* The witness does not perhaps attend to the question Was this ground cleared for exercising the men? A There was a talk that it was for that purpose, but I do not know, whether it was for that

Mr *Wirt* Do you say that the men never exercised there? A. Never to my knowledge Q Do you know any thing of the guard? A. Yes Sometime in the afternoon, a young man came up the river in a canoe and said there were four hundred militia without any authority, coming to destroy the boats that night. This was told to Col Burr, and we determined to get out of their way, if possible Major Floyd concluded to put out centinels, to give us information of their approach The signal was to be the firing of a gun.

Mr *Wirt* I understand this Bayou is below Bayou Pierre?
A It is Q I understood you also that you did not receive the
Presidents's proclamation before you arrived at Bayou Pierre?
A I said that *you* had not reached us before we got to Bayou
Pierre, But I am not certain whether it was there we received it.

Chief Justice Had you received the proclamation before the
guard was put out? A I do not recollect

Mr *Burr* Was it not afterwards? A I do not recollect, I heard
that it was contained in some newspaper, perhaps in your boat

Mr. *Wirt.* Do you know any thing of the search, A I do, I
was in our boat at that time When Col Fitzpatrick came, Col
Tyler lifted the curtain and he was introduced. We did not once
change our posture Q How many arms did he find there A
There were a couple of rifles, belonging to a Mr Lamb, and
some pistols Q Did you hear of the searching of the other
boats? A I did not trouble myself about them Q Did you hear
of the sinking of arms A I did not

Cross-examined

Mr *Burr* How many guns had you at Beaver? A Five rifles
Q Did you see any more guns at any other time? A I did not
Q Among the four boats that went from the island, how many?
A No more than five that I saw? Did you stop accidently at
the island? A I supposed so first, but I afterwards understood,
that Col Tyler and Mr Blannerhasset were connected Q How
much powder had you with you? A About twenty five pounds
Q Did you not borrow from one another? A. We did Q Was
the powder scarce among you at last? A It was Q Was there
any game killed? I believe two deers were killed at the time we
were at the island Q Was there any disturbance on the island?
A None. Q. Had you any reason to believe that any of that
party would have assisted in any unlawful design. A None
Q Did you see a printed report by Mr Fitzpatrick? A No.
Q Did you understand that the country was much alarmed
there? A They were Q And that the party was to be mob-
bed? A Yes Q That they were coming on board at night
with tomahawks and knives? A I do not recollect. Q Would
not the militia have suffered severely if I had not fed them? A
I know that you sent over provisions to them Q How many of
them were there? A About seventy Q. Did you not understand that I had made a treaty with Cowles Mead? A I did not
know it Q Who sent us word that we must move down to the
mouth of Coles's creek? A Major Fleehearty. The answer from
Major Floyd was, that he must get more militia.

Mr *Burr* This was a piece of impertinence in Fleehearty, for
it was after the stipulations entered into between Mr. Mead and
myself I was at that time fifty miles off, at Washington, (M T)
where I went to stand a trial

Mr. *Blannerhasset* Did you hear of any report about arresting
me on the night I left the island? A I did hear something a
bout it but I believe it was not before next morning Q By
whom--the militia? A No

Mr *Blan* Did you not hear of an arrest by General Tupper?
A I did not but the morning after I left the island, Mr Blan

nerhasset himself mentioned, that he understood there was a writ or warrant to do it, and asked us if we were willing to take him along after *that* was out.

Mr *Wirt*. Was Major Fleehearty a militia officer? A He seemed so from his dress.

Mr *Burr* Was there not a great deal of talk about a Spanish war? A Yes—I saw a good deal about it myself in the newspapers

Hugh Allen

Mr *Hay* Where did you embark? A I embarked at Beaver with Maj Tyler and Smith Q On what terms? A Mr Tyler and Smith told me, that they were going to settle lands, and that whatever profits they shared I should share, I bearing an equal proportion of the expences Q How many men did you see at the mouth of Cumberland? A About seventy. Q Was that the whole party? A Perhaps there might be more Mr Tyler's party was about forty, and Mr Floyd's about thirty or forty, so they were in all about seventy or eighty Q How many men came with Colonel Burr to the mouth of Cumberland? A I do not know.

Mr. *Wirt* Did Tyler's and Floyd's parties arrive there together? A We got there first by a few hours Q When did you arrive there? A On the evening of the 26th December Q. Had Colonel Burr a party like Tyler and Floyd? A There were a number of boats there, which I understood were Colonel Burr's Q Did any thing occur to make you change your opinion of the object of this enterprize? A The only ground of my changing my opinion, was, when I understood that the government designed to arrest Colonel Burr.

Mr *Hay* And do you think that men would have left the better part of the world to go and settle a wilderness? Why did you go? A I made my calculations on this subject Mr Tyler and Smith said that the object was the settlement of lands, which would be profitable.

Cross examined

Mr. *Burr* How many guns were in your boats? A. Five rifles, and one fusee gun Q Did you get any more except at Blannerhasset's island? A None Q Did you ever see muskets and bayonet's in those boats? A Never Q What was the construction of the boats—were they able to go up stream? A They were Q Did you ever see any boats that could go up stream with them? A I never the experiment tried Q Do you know whether I had a single man at the mouth of Cumberland with me, except Dunnahoe the pilot? A I do not know him, nor how many were with you Mr. Burr here stated that he had hired hands at Nashville to bring him down to the mouth of Cumberland

Mr *Burr* Were you present when I was introduced to the party? A I was, when you were introduced, you said you had intended saying something to the men, but for certain reasons of your own, had deferred it Q. Did I say that I had any thing like *secrets* to disclose? A You did not Q Had you any reason to suspect that any of the party meditated hostily against the

United States A Never Q What do you call the Captain of a boat? is it not the man who stands at the helm? A The way is this, we choose him captain who is supposed to be the best waterman Q How are new countries settled? is it not to send a party on before, to explore it and prepare it for the reception of others? A I never settled a new country, but I suppose, that is the way

Mr *Wirt*. Aye! that's an historical fact for which we had better apply to the general records of nations Q Did you see any powder on Blannerhasset's island? A I saw a quarter cask with about twenty-five pounds of powder

Mr *Burr* Did you use that continually on the river? A Those who chose, did Q Did you know of any more powder on board the other boats? A Not till latterly Mr *Burr* Were there not some kegs of biscuit? A. Yes Q Were there any bullets in barrels? A All the bullets I saw were in canisters on Blannerhasset's island.

Mr. *Wirt* Had you any reason to believe, that you were going to New Orleans? A Not before I got to Natchez, when I determined myself to go down

Mr *Hay*, To morrow we shall be ready to shew our evidence that goes to our real object, the witnesses that we shall introduce to morrow, were not present at the mouth of Cumberland, but they will shew the intention with which that meeting was formed.

WEDNESDAY, *September* 23.

Mr. *Burr* said, that before the witnesses proceeded any farther, he wished to do what he ought to have done at an earlier period, to disqualify one of the witnesses? It might have been done earlier it was true, but, although the evidence was not given through, yet he thought it proper, at this period to stop evidence so much in the power of Gen Wilkinson as evinced, that rather than be hanged himself, he was willing to hang any body

Mr *Hay* objected to this interposition these disqualifications might have been objected in due time, and before the evidence was given for by this method, there would never be an end to this examination, which it would be desirable to conclude as soon as possible Every possible benefit which the accused could, at any time receive, might be received by him now. If those interruptions must take place, there would be no getting to an end of the business

Mr *Botts* said that Mr Hay reasoned as though the Court had only to examine one side; it was desirable on the side of the defence, that they should examine their testimony, as they were desirous of going away Capt Bissell they wanted to bring forward to test the accuracy of Dunbaugh's testimony, and indeed to entire disqualify him

Chief Justice. Capt Bissell might be examined immediately if it should be thought proper

Mr *Burr* objected to the kind of testimony which the prosecution was about introducing, he wished them to mention the nature and object of their testimony.

Mr *Hay* said, that what they were about to bring now, was conversation amongst the parties, evincing their intention, in deed it was rather improperly called conversation, because it was rather communications, in which this Washita settlement was acknowledged to be a sham The Court has already permitted us to produce the evidence of persons who belonged to the meeting at that place, and now we ask to produce the very same sort of testimony from persons who were not present at that island, but who belonged to that meeting

Mr. *Wirt* The declaration now to be introduced are not loose and general conversations, detached from the expedition, but fact preparatory and auxiliary to the expedition itself declarations respecting the engagement of persons in the thing itself

Mr *Burr* quoted M'Nally who stated that " counsel ought not to call witnesses without stating the object which they wished to examine them for " He objected to the introduction of persons to relate conversations merely, and those perhaps much previous to any meeting

The Court appeared to recommend an argument to be opened, which perhaps might eventually save time

Mr. *Botts* then spoke at considerable length in which he recapitulated much of the evidence, and took a general review of the transactions and its overthrow, so far as the evidence had gone. He also marked out the boundaries to which the evidence ought to go In the course of his speech he quoted 2 Hale 280 2 Washington's Rep 246 Foster 213, 5 St Tr. 37 Fries's Tr 19, 20. Sitgreaves's speech Willis's case 1710 8 St Tr 255 Foster 241. Berwick's case 17, 18 Foster 11, 12 Loft's Gilbert 812, 813. M'Nally 73, and 274 much of his observations and quotations related to the question whether the conversations of others who were now upon examination with him (Blannerhasset and Smith) ought to be heard whilst his case was under examination, and be applied in any way to him: particularly so, whilst there were two charges in topic. this, however, he objected to

The *Chief Justice* doubted whether the charge for a misdemeanor was before the Court, until Mr. Wirt informed him that it really was added in the application to the Court by a written statement, to which the Court then acquiesced.

Mr *Botts* said if that was the case they should propose a conclusive bar to it, because it never was made out The clerk having read the charge, he acquiesced. He observed that all which he had said in the treason case must apply, as far as it would to the case of misdemeanor. At some further time, however, it might be necessary to enlarge upon the application of the evidence and the connection in this charge

Mr *Wickham* also spoke at some length on the same subject : he referred to the opinion of the Court and quoted Hale and Foster in support of the positions

The *Chief Justice* refuted some observations which had been ascribed to him. Mr Wickham continued his observations He quoted and descanted on Salkeld 635 5 State Trial 37 and the evidence which has been delivered.

Mr *Martin* after that produced some authorities Fries's trial 86, 179, 197 Tucker's 4 Blackstone, 146 3 State Trial 775. *The strongest suspicions cannot be given in evidence in proof of trea-*

son 4 State Trial 191. *Stricter proof is requisite in treason than in any other criminal matter. The conduct of persons, wherever it should be considered doubtful, is always taken in the most favorable point of view.* Again, 3 State Trial 56 and 744, Hawkin's book 2, chapter 40, section 4. Leech's edition

Mr. *Burr* also spoke at some length.

Mr *Hay* said it was not their intention to make any reply,—not because the argument was unmaterial, but because they conceived the decision of the Court had already settled the question. If there had been a doubt, they would not have objected to meet it.

Chief Justice. I have certainly from the beginning stated that I considered myself merely as an examining magistrate. and it is my opinion, that, in the previous stages, there is a material difference as to what is now admissible, and what would be on trial. I think that the argument which has been offered goes rather more to the *sufficiency* of evidence than an examining magistrate ought to hear. The admissibility of this sort of testimony on trial, is a doubt to me, but I should suppose that it was proper to be heard by an examining magistrate, because he must proceed upon general ground.

I doubted, when I first heard this kind of testimony, upon the ground, principally, that the intention was not communicated to the whole · and whether the object charged at Cumberland was a common object. If it was not a common object, I doubted whether it could be called levying war or not. I ultimately determined however to hear all the evidence, because I considered myself as merely an examining magistrate. It appears to me the same now.

It is very true that the present impression I have on the subject, (and I think it results from the opinion already given) that the declarations of Blannerhasset in this case, would not affect any body but Blannerhasset. Now if it will affect him only, (the order being given to hear evidence respecting the whole three at the same time) it certainly is proper to hear this testimony.

Mr *Hay* How far that can be regarded as affecting the whole, might remain until the discussion on the testimony takes place. Their being connected and engaged in the same enterprize, might be proved, and I do not see that your opinion prevents us from making out that connection.

Chief Justice I should have no difficulty in hearing any argument on that point. I have not formed a determinate opinion on it, but if I have given any opinion toward it, it must have been given in the misdemeanor case and not in the treason. That is, that the confession, or declarations of Blannerhasset did not affect others. This is a point, however, upon which I am willing to hear any observations.

The testimony again proceeded

Alexander Henderson was sworn

Mr *Hay* Mr Henderson, please to state to the Court all that you know of this transaction.

Mr *Henderson.* About the last of August or 1st of September, 1806, Mr *Blannerhasset* wrote to me, that he and Mrs. *Blannerhasset* intended to visit my family in the course of a few days

On the day appointed he and Mrs Blannerhasset came in company with my brother John After taking some refreshment, Mr Blannerhasset entered into some conversation about the severance of the union he mentioned the advantages that would arise to the people in the western country from a separation, that we were paying three or four million dollars towards the support of the present government, when with one hundred thousand, we might support a government of our own · He mentioned Col Burr's name, as a man of brilliant or splendid talents as well as of great goodness of heart, (or some expression of that sort) that he had made the fortunes of hundreds without at all advancing his own; he mentioned as an instance, the Manhattan Bank and Company. *This* conversation took place before dinner After dinner a walk was proposed to my mill I objected to it. as I was weak and not able to walk Mr Blannerhasset mentioned that I was as well able to walk as himself, and insisted that I should go along with my brother and himself Shortly after we got into the meadow, Mr. Blannerhasset mentioned that he had a great deal of confidence in my brother and myself We assured him that we should not betray it, and that it was not misplaced. He then mentioned that under the auspices (I think that was the expression) of Col Burr, a separation of the union was contemplated, that no particular line of division had as yet been fixed on, whether it was to be the Alleghany, or whether or not the South Branch of the Potowmac, (I well recollect that he mentioned the rich settlement on the South branch was to be included, that New Orleans was to be seized; the bank or banks of New Orleans, to be seized, that all the military stores in that country were to be seized, that a park of artillery, at or near New Orleans, which were said to belong to the French (I think 50 pieces) and which Mr Jefferson was too œconomical to purchase, was also to be seized, and that country revolutionized in the course of 9 months He mentioned that the principal characters throughout the union were acquainted with or concerned (I do not recollect which) in the enterprize, that the officers of the army and navy were secured He mentioned General Eaton as being engaged, Mr. John Graham; Mr Alston, Col Burr's son-in-law, as enamoured of the scheme He mentioned other names, I think, but I cannot recollect any, except Robert G. Harper, who was either concerned or engaged. My brother asked Mr Blannerhasset what kind of government was intended to be established Mr Blannerhasset mentioned that it was not yet determined on, but a more energetic than the present was contemplated My brother asked him if any foreign power was to be engaged in it. He said that there was not. My brother asked him if John Randolph, member of Congress was acquainted with and engaged in it Did I mention that Mr Blannerhasset said, that he himself had embarked in the scheme ? Mr Blannerhasset replied, that Mr Randolph was not. He mentioned the great advantages that would arise to those who took an early and active part in the enterprize. Mr. Blannerhasset then mentioned his own property (Mr. *Wirt* What it was worth ?) A Yes He mentioned that he was a partner of the firm of Dudley Woodbridge and Co —that he had property in the funds of Great Bri tain He mentioned that he had five thousand dollars, (I think such was his statement) in the hands of a gentleman in Philadelphia or New York; that he had a suit against Mr Woodbridge's father in Marietta, for some five or ten thousand dollars, I do not remember which. He valued his property on the island at fifty thousand dollars—I do not recollect of any other particular communication from Mr. Blannerhasset

Mr *Hay* With what view did you understand this detail of his property was made? A Shall I tell you my impressions? I have omitted one particular expression of his as relating to his English funds. "that they could not get at them"

Mr *Wirt* Did he say who *they* were? A He did not, but I supposed the government of the United States in case of hostilities

Mr *M'Rae* Did you understand with what view it was, he spoke of his other property.

Mr *Martin* objected to any such interrogatories about the impressions or inferences of a witness. If the publication of this trial goes to Europe, what a contemptible opinion will it afford of our judiciary proceedings?

Chief Justice Was there any thing else besides what you have stated, from which you made this inference? A. Nothing else

Mr *M'Rae.* Was there any thing calculated to make a particular impression on your mind? A My impression from his statement was, that he intended to show, if he risked so much property that we might surely risk the little we had.

Mr *Wirt* Will you state the answer you made to this application? A. We did not positively tell Mr Blannerhasset that we would not join in the enterprize, but that we must take time to consider, that we had relations on this side the mountains whom we must consult

Mr *Wirt* Did Mr Blannerhasset mention the effect this revolution would have on Wood county? A. He said that it would not long remain neutral, and that we must take an active part for or against

Mr *Blannerhasset* Do you mean Wood county? A I mean that part of the country

Mr *Wirt* Could you understand why your brother enquired whether John Randolph was not concerned? A. Because Mr Blannerhasset had mentioned that the leading characters in the union were concerned, and we considered John Randolph as a man of a great character, and a very leading man Mr Wirt Did you understand whether he said any thing of Mr. Jefferson? A Mr Blannerhasset said, if Mr. Jefferson was any ways impertinent, that Col Burr would tie him neck and heels, and throw him into the Potomac. Q What did he say of his means of opposition to the government? A He mentioned that with 3 pieces of artillery and three hundred sharp shooters, he could defend any pass in the Allegany mountains that he had seen, against any force the government could send against him. Mr Wirt Did he show you any compositions he was about to publish? A He showed me the first and second numbers of the *Querist*, which he intended to publish; at all events he shewed me one, which he read to me and then gave it to me to read it over night. I kept it all night and returned it next morning

Mr *Hay* Did he say that he had written those pieces? A. So I understood.

Mr *Wirt* Did he say that he was going to publish them? A He said, that he was going to Marietta next day to attend to the publication? for that the printer was a timid man and required to be backed. Q What did you inform him about your own intentions? A We informed him that we knew not whether we could or could not join in the scheme We however told Mr. Blanner hasset that he must not consider us as in any way committed. Mr Wirt. Do you recollect he told you, what particular circum stances would prevent your long remaining neutral, was it any commercial arrangement? A. I think he said, that being in possession of the New Orleans country and the mouth of the river, we could not long remain neutral Q. Do you carry your produce to market through that channel? A We do not

Mr *Hay* He said that Mr Graham was engaged, had you seen Mr Graham on the subject? A I had not seen Mr Graham for 8 or 10 years before but I saw him a short time after this interview On the 20th November, I received a letter from Mr Graham, earnestly requesting an interview with me at the mouth of little Kanawha I met him there on the 22d I must confess, that I had every inclination to disclose this secret to him, when I first met him, but I did not conceive myself justifiable, because I had promised to keep this communication secret Considering however that Mr Blannerhasset had positively assured me that Mr Graham was positively concerned it, I asked him first, if he was concerned in any scheme with Col Burr down the river He said that he was not, and moreover that he was authorized to prevent and arrest any such illegal proceedings I did then conceive myself justified in communicating to him the substance of the schemes Before this time, about the 1st of October, we had determined to oppose the scheme; and went down to the mouth of Kanawha to inform Mr Blannerhasset of our in tentions, but he was gone down to Kentucky perhaps with Mr and Mrs Alston; and we then sent a message to that effect to Mr Blannerhasset that they might not be deceived as to our in tentions. At the same time my brother and myself proposed a meeting of the citizens of Wood county, in order to obtain the sense of the people, on what course they ought to pursue

Mr Hay And was there a meeting; A There was Q Did you come to any resolutions? A We did

Mr *M Rae.* What were the substance of them? A. That we were determined to support the constituted authorities of our country

Mr *Martin* And were the resolutions published? A They were, I think in a paper published in Morgan Town

Mr *Hay* Do you know Blannerhasset's writing? A. I am not certain Q Did you ever see him write? A I do not recollect Q Did you receive *these two* letters from him? A. I did

Mr *Hay* This letter dated on the 31st August, mentions his intentions to visit you.

Witness It may not be improper to state, what gave occasion to that second letter. Mrs Blannerhasset insisting on taking my little boy home two or three weeks with her family, I agreed to reluctantly Three or four days after they had left us, I sent my overseer for my boy, who brought the child with that second letter from Mr Blannerhasset This second letter covered an extract from a Marietta paper, signed Querist, relative to the " Western World," and referred to in that letter

Mr *Wirt.* Do you know Peter Taylor? What is his character? A I have heard no one speak of him but Mr Blannerhasset, and he spoke of him in very high terms. Q. What is your brother's name? John G Henderson? A Yes Q. Did he not represent Wood county? A He did some years ago

Cross-examined

Mr *Blannerhasset* Have you not been a representative of Wood County? A. Yes Q You lived in Wood County some time before I knew you? A I did. Q Had you any reason for not cultivating my acquaintance sooner? A I had the reasons were partly private and partly political —I have no objections to state those reasons. The political reason, that you were a democrat, and was opposed to the present administration Q Do you not recollect that I opposed the election of your brother, G Henderson and that my vote was refused? A I do, for then I personated my brother. Q Do you not recollect it was refused because I had at that time no deed for my land? A. I do. Q Do you not recollect that I had the honour of voting for you on a subsequent occasion, A I do Q Was it not after that election, that our acquaintance was formed? A It was Before that election, I do not recollect to have known you

THURSDAY, September 24

Conclusion of Alexander Henderson's Cross examination

Mr *Blannerhasset* Do you recollect at the time of the conversation, you expressed any personal dislike of Colonel Burr? Did you not express a sense of hostility towards him? A I am sorry that the gentleman has put the question I am sorry to wound any man's feelings wantonly —But I always thought him a dangerous man, and the late occurrences have not at all changed my opinion

Mr *Martin* How long has your opinion of him been formed? A Ten or fifteen years ago, when he was making the tour of Virginia Mr *Martin.* Not when he was said to be fixing means to overturn the federal administration? A I do not recollect, but I heard much at that time of Colonel Burr

Mr *Hay* here wished to identify the two letters, which Mr Henderson had presented to the Court, from Mr Blannerhasset Mr Botts however admitted them They were then read by Mr Hay, but they contain nothing important The examination proceeded

Mr. Hay Did you, Sir, read the *Querist?* A. I read the first No in manuscript—It was signed *Querist* Q I think you said yesterday, that Mr Blannerhasset confessed that he was the author and was going to Marietta to publish it? Mr *Blannerhasset* rose and objected to reading these publications on such evidence

He observed, that some body may have written under the same signature on the very same subject and that there was a lacuna or chasm which was required to be filled up. Mr *Hay*. We will fill up that chasm. Mr Neale copied it

Mr Neale was then called into Court and sworn. Mr *Hay*. Will you state to the Judge, what you know of the publication in the Marietta Gazette, under the signature of *Querist* ? A. About first of September Mr Blannerhasset sent for me and told me that he had something to copy about the division of the states, and that the printer had met with some difficulty in understanding the writing of the first Number. I copied the second and third Numbers, and carried them to Fairlamb, the printer at Marietta and gave them to him. Q. Did you read the papers as they came out? A. Yes, Mr Blannerhasset supplied me with the whole. Q. Did they correspond with the manuscript? A. Yes, the very same I think. The Court accepted them, but on the suggestion of Mr Hay, the reading was waved and they were to be put into the possession of the Chief Justice.

At Mr Hay's suggestion the witnesses who had been examined, were agreed to be discharged, except General Eaton. He declared that he did not " wish to go "

John G. Henderson was sworn.

Mr *Hay*. Please state to the Court all you know of this transaction

Mr *Henderson*. I rode with Mr Blannerhasset and his wife to my brother's house on the second Monday in September last. When we got near to my brother's house, Mr Blannerhasset introduced the subject of the separation of the union. He stated, I think, that it was to be conducted under the auspices of Col Burr. He mentioned that there were many eminent characters in the eastern and western states concerned. He mentioned the names of Gen Eaton and Mr John Graham, perhaps others at that time, I do not recollect. I do not believe that any thing more passed between us, till we arrived at my brother's. When we got to my brother's we took some refreshment (dinner). I was not much in company with Mr Blannerhasset till dinner, and I do not know whether his conversation led to that subject or not. After dinner we walked into the meadow, my brother, Mr Blannerhasset and myself. The subject was then renewed, under injunctions of secrecy, which we agreed to observe. Mr. Blannerhasset observed that it was a subject of great importance. He stated that the object was the separation of the union, he mentioned characters who were concerned in it; observed that Col Burr was at the head of it, or words to that effect. He spoke very much in praise of Col Burr, mentioned an instance of his goodness of heart with respect to the Manhattan company, and making the fortunes of many without benefiting himself. Gen Eaton's and Mr Graham's names were mentioned, and a number of others, whom I do not recollect, that were acquainted with it; among the rest was Mr Harper, and Mr Alston's name was mentioned, as being highly pleased with the scheme. In the course of conversation, Mr Blannerhasset observed, that New Orleans would be seized. He mentioned that the park of French artillery at New Orleans which Mr Jefferson was too economical to purchase, was to be procured, whether seized or obtained in any other way, I do not recollect. He stated that the people in the lower country were displeased with the present government, on account of their interests not being protected or attended to. He seemed to apprehend no opposition in that quarter. He said, the attempt will be made in less than nine months, that he himself had embarked in it. He observed, that it would be a favorable juncture for effecting the object, owing to a want of energy in the administration; I am not, however, certain, whether he or which of us made the observation, we all three concurred in it. I think Mr Blannerhasset observed, that he hoped he should see my brother at the head of a regiment of horse, at some time, but I do not recollect. He seemed anxious for us to join. Some time in the course of conversation, the name of Mr Grainger was mentioned, I thought in a threatening style, as if he would have cause to repent his having made use of an expression sometime before published, importing that danger was threatening in the west. I do not know whether my brother was present during this observation. Mr. Blannerhasset said, that we must take an active part one way or the other, as we could not remain neutral. He mentioned an expression of Col Burr's, respecting the people in the city, or the administration, if that they were any ways impertinent, he would tie them neck and heels, and throw them into the Potomac.

Mr. *Hay.* Did I understand you to say, that this was an expression quoted from Col Burr? A. Yes. We desired Mr. Blannerhasset, just before he left my brother's, not to consider us as committed, that it was a subject which required reflection, and that we must consult our friends on this side the mountain, who were interested in that country. I mentioned it to my father under the same injunctions, on which I had received it from Mr Blannerhasset. I recollect having asked Mr Blannerhasset, when he spoke of the leading characters of the union, whether John Randolph had been made acquainted with it. He answered, no.

Mr *Wirt.* Why did you put that question? A. Because Mr. Blannerhasset had said, that the *leading* characters of the country were concerned. I asked Mr Blannerhasset what kind of a government he would establish in the western country. He said, that this was not yet determined; but that a more energetic one than the present would be adopted. I asked Mr Blannerhasset also, if any foreign power was concerned. He assured me there was not.

Mr *Hay.* You asked him what form of government was to be established? A. Yes. Q. Where did you suppose the seat of this energetic government was to be? A. He did not mention, but I supposed it was some central place.

Mr. *M'Rae.* Did he mention the line of division? A. He did not particularly, but he said that the people in the south branch would be in an awkward situation. Q. Did he mention the Alleghany? A. I do not recollect. Q. Did he mention any thing about commanding the passes of the Alleghany? A. Yes he said, that with a few cannon and a few sharp shooters, he could defend any pass in the Alleghany. Q. Did he mention the *Quænist* in your presence? A. He did Q. What did he say of it? A. He read one number of it. The first words in it were "universal history every where teaches or informs," or some such expressions. Q Do you remember what was the object of those pieces? A I understood that it was to promote the separation of the nation. Mr M'Rae Do you recollect any observations about Blannerhasset's property? A I think he estimated his property on the island at fifty thousand dollars, and besides he had a small fund in Europe, which he said would be safe He said they could not touch that Mr M'Rae What did he mean by " they?" A I do not know his allusion but I suppose he meant the government

Mr *Wirt* Do you recollect any observations about the expence of supporting government? A He said that we were contributing three or four millions to the present government, when one hundred thousand would be sufficient for a government of our own *Witness* I have omitted to state, that after my brother received his last letter from Mr Blannerhasset, my brother and myself went down to inform him of our decided opposition to his plan He and Mr Alston were gone down the river, and we directed the overseer to inform Mrs Blannerhasset of our intentions. There was a subsequent meeting of the people of Wood county on this subject, and resolutions were adopted in opposition to the scheme And a month afterwards, the militia volunteered their services to suppress it Shortly after I left that county for Dumfries.

Cross examined

Mr *Wickham* Was this conversation in earnest or jocular? A Perfectly serious. Q. Did you hold any conversation with Mr. Blannerhasset before this, which led to it? Were you in the habit of expressing opinions adverse to the union? A I *never* was opposed to the union Q Is it talked of in that country? A It has been talked of as an event that would take place in half a century or a century Q Was your deposition ever taken? A. It never was Q At whose instance did the meeting of the people you spoke of take place? A Several of us called it, and among the rest my brother and myself Q And they passed resolutions about this plan? A They did Q How were they informed of this scheme? A From reports in the county Q. Did you communicate any information to this meeting? A No; nor my brother, any thing but general observations Q What was the purport of these resolutions? A. Nothing but to prepare for the danger which was to be apprehended. One of the resolutions alluded particularly to Col Burr Q Was Mr Blannerhasset's name ever mentioned? A A proposition was made to insert Mr Blannerhasset's name in one of the resolutions, I opposed it. Q Did you communicate on this subject with Mr. Graham? A I had left the country at that time.

Mr *Martin* What were your politics? A They were federal and are so still

Mr *M'Rae* What have you considered Mr. Blannerhasset's politics to be? A. Democratic.

Chief Justice Did you understand that this separation was to be effected by political means quietly or by force? A I understood him to mean, that if the lower country was in their possession, it would bring the upper country along with it

Mr *M'Rae* And he conceived the lower country to be dissatisfied with the government? A He did.

Mr *Wirt* Did Mr Blannerhasset state the manner in which this revolution was to be brought about? A No; he did not Q did the meeting in Wood county arise from any of Mr Blannerhasett's declarations, or from the movements on the Ohio? A I suspect the last.

Mr *Blannerhasset* What movements? A I did not myself use that word I alluded to the building of the boats and kiln drying meal

The Counsel for the defendant called in Alexander Henderson

Question by Mr *Wickham* —To whom did you communicate this conversation with Mr Blannerhasset? A To Mr *Graham* Q At what time? A On the twenty second of November Q What led to this communication, did Mr. Graham make any enquiries of you? A No I received a letter on the twentieth requesting an interview. Q Did he state any reasons for wishing that interview? A I think he did say that he had heard that there was something going on in the Western Country inimical to the government, and that he was authorized to enquire into it, Q Why did he apply to you, do you know? A I think he got information from my brother James

Mr *M'Rae* What encouragement did he give you to induce your acquiescence in his plans besides? A He said that he hoped in less than two years he should see me at the head of a regiment of horse Q Had you ever changed your politics? A No Sir Q Are you what is denominated a Federalist? A Most decidedly

Chief Justice Did Blannerhasset say that this change was to be effected by force? A I do not recollect that he did

Here the Counsel for the prosecution read the articles from the Ohio Gazette termed the " Querist" They consist of an interlocutory essay, whose decided object appears to have been to demonstrate to western people, the advantages that would result to them by separating from the Atlantic States, and stating their contitutional right to adopt the expedient, in justice to themselves " Every line of them breathes the spirit of discontent, dissatisfaction, and revolution."

Mr *M'Rae* to Mr Henderson. Did you, or did you not yesterday speak of Mr Burr's seizing on New Orleans? This question was objected to, but was afterwards answered A I think that he said an attempt at revolutionizing that country would be made in less than nine months.

Richard Neale's testimony.

In a conversation which I had with Mr. Blannerhasset he stated his object to be a decision of the union. It was to go by the back bone, and take in Kentucky, Tennessee and Georgia into the western part, and a seperate government was to be established there by which means, he said, the money would be kept among the people there that was now paid for the sale of lands. I asked him where he was to have the Capital he said he expected at Lexington in Kentucky I asked him if Congress would not be opposed to it he said he expected not But he said if they were one cannon on the mountain, it would be sufficient to oppose all the force they could send. I left Wood County on the twentieth of October, for Alexandria.

Mr *Hay* Do you know Peter Taylor, and if so, relate what character he had and what character Mr Blannerhasset gave of him to you? A. I have heard him speak in very high terms of him, both as to his honesty and fidelity he said that he thought it impossible that the creature could tell falshood, and that he had great confidence in him Q Do you know Jacob Albright's character? A I have very little acquaintance with him, but I have always understood that he was a sober industrious man He has worked with my son a little, and he was punctual and honest

Cross examination.

Mr. *Wickham* You say that Mr Blannerhasset spoke to you on the subject of keeping secrets, what secrets do you mean? A Why he said that he had some writings he wanted published and he told me he was the author of them (the Querist) Q What pursuits does Albright follow for his livelihood? A Why, Sir, he is working about, I understand he is an industrious sober man who lives by his labour Q Where did Blannerhasset engage Taylor? A I do not know He was there when I came there I have not been living there quite two years I believe he was in Blannerhassets service three or four years

Chief Justice Did Mr Blannerhasset tell you what means he had in view to complete this expedition? A. I was hard of hearing and weak of understanding, and I did not ask the question

Mr *Burr* Were you present at the taking of Albright's deposition? A. Yes Q Who examined him? A. John G Jackson Q Had he any printed paper? A. Not that I know of Q Did you understand that he said, that the men had levelled their guns at Poole, (instead of Tupper?) A I do not recollect it

Mr *Hay*. Do you know whether Mr Burr was at the island in September? A I never saw him there, but I understood that he was there a little before I got there

Mr *Wirt* to the Court " It is remarkable that Colonel Burr was at the island on the first of September, and the first number of the *Querist* is dated on the fourth "

Mr. *John Henderson* returned to supply an omission in his evidence, that Blannerhasset informed him, that the officers of the army and navy were disgusted with the administration, and disposed to join. Mr. Blannerhasset also mentioned in the course of the day, that General Moreau was expected to reside near Pittsburg

John Graham was sworn.

Mr *Hay*. Please Sir to state what you know of this transaction

Mr *Graham* —In the latter end of October last I received a letter from Mr. Madison, requesting that I would pass through the western country, on my *return* to New Orleans I know not whether it be proper to assign to the Court the reasons of this wish. It may serve however to explain my conduct in the western country.—Mr Madison stated to me as a reason of this request, that government had received information from various quarters, that a project was on foot to sever the union, or to invade the territory of Spain

Mr *Wickham* objected to this explanation

Witness It was to show that I had acted in obedience to my duty as an officer of the government

Mr *Wickham* What office did you hold? A I was secretary of the Orleans territory When I arrived at Marietta about the middle of November, I made enquiries, and heard, what it may not perhaps, be proper to state Mr Duval called on me and informed me that Mr Blannerhasset had just arrived with him and would wait upon me After passing the usual compliments, and expressing his pleasure at seeing me, he begged leave to read to me certain letters. which he had received by Captain Elliot of the western country, who had just returned from Pittsburgh Mr Blannerhasset made many enquiries relative to Comfort Tyler, Dean and Butler, and the preparations which they were making for their expedition down the river, what number of men and settlers they had obtained. Mr Elliot gave him to understand that there would be more settlers than there would be boats for them. When Mr Blannerhasset received this information he observed, that they could descend in his boats, as he had more boats than men. Before Captain Elliot quitted the room, Mr Blannerhasset handed me a letter, which he said he had received a few days before from Colonel Burr in Kentucky. Shall I state my recollection of the contents of that letter?

Mr *M'Rae.* Do you believe the letter to have been Colonel Burr's? A I believed it was Colonel Burr's writing; for though I had never seen Colonel Burr write, yet I had seen many letters said to be written by Colonel Burr. I merely mention this letter to show that it gave rise to a conversation between Mr. Blannerhasset and myself, relative to the contents of this letter. The conversation was somewhat desultory, nor do I particularly recollect the order in which the several topics were introduced. In general I recollect, that Mr. Blannerhasset animadverted upon the conduct pursued towards Colonel Burr at Frankfort; stating however his belief that this conduct was not authorized by the government. He mentioned that Col Burr had purchased from Col Lynch, I think a certain part of baron Bastrop's grant in the territory of Orleans He stated also, that he was to have an interest in this purchase, and seemed desirous of impressing on my mind a belief, that the object of his preparations was the settlement of this land, but I cannot now recollect that in the course of conversation he did positively avow it His object seemed to be to avoid an explicit avowal; but he said, that they avowed that this was their object, that it was a legal one, and government would have no right to interfere, until it was ascertained, that they (meaning Col. Burr and himself, as I understood) had an terior object He contended that he had a right to go towards this object with just such preparations as they thought proper This was an opinion in which I did not acquiesce I made few enquiries; but he admitted in the course of conversation, that he was building boats for the expedition in which he was engaged with Colonel Burr, that he was engaging young men single and without families to go down armed, he said they would have no cannon, but they would have rifles He stated in the course of conversation the use to which these rifles might be applied to resist the Indians and Spaniards or kill game—It is justice to Mr Blannerhasset to add, that he said, that he did not solicit men to go, that he took such only as pleased to go, and that he did not expect more than three hundred men would go with him. He stated also that he was engaging provisions for this same expedition From what I had heard after my arrival at Marietta, and from the manner in which Mr Blannerhasset entered my room and made these communications, I was rather induced to believe that he conceived me to be one of the party Q Why from his manner? A. My acquaintance with him before was slight, and yet he was extremely polite to me, and expressed how happy he would be at seeing me in his own house For reasons which it is unnecessary to take up the time of the Court with, I was anxious to undeceive Mr Blannerhasset I asked him, if he *had* stated that I was one of the party. He said that he had, and that he had understood so from Colonel Burr When I assured him I was not, he expressed considerable surprize, not by verbal declarations, but the by marked air of his countenance He observed to me, that I did not know Colonel Burr, and passed some eulogiums upon him, and asked me in a very impressive manner whether I had not heard of an association in New Orleans for the invasion of Mexico. I told him that I had not, and I ventured to assure him that there was no such association there. He told me that there certainly was, and that about three hundred men had signed to such an association I think *that* was his expression, for the purpose of invading Mexico After I had repeated my thorough conviction that there was none such, and assigned the fact of his being deceived about me as a presumptive reason why he should be deceived about others, he told me that he had obtained this information from Mr. Bradford

Considering Mr Blannerhasset at that time as a deluded man, I endeavored to draw him off from the undertaking in which he was engaged; and considering that it was more the policy of the government to prevent than to punish such enterprizes on the Ohio, I informed him, that so far from being concerned in the plan, I was an agent of the government, authorized to enquire into the facts relative to this enterprize in the western country, and to take such steps as might be necessary for repressing it. I then stated to him, from reasons drawn from Col. Burr's visit to New Orleans in the preceding summer, from the information which government had received, and from the nature of the preparations which Mr Blannerhasset himself was then making, why I believed that the object of Col. Burr was either to attack the territories of the United States, or those of Spain. I assured him at the same time, that any collection or combination of armed men on the Ohio, would under these circumstances be consi dered as a violation of the laws and repressed accordingly. He again contended that they had a right to go down the river, as they thought proper, inasmuch as they avowed the settlement of the Ouachita which was a legal object. Though we could not agree on this point, he asked me whether there would be any ob jection or opposition made to those men, if they went down in in small parties I gave him to understand, that this would de pend upon circumstances, but that when they were collected, they would be arrested, and the enterprize would end in the ruin and disgrace of all those who were concerned in it.

During this conversation, I stated to Mr. Blannerhasset point edly, that I knew not the opinions of Mr. Jefferson or Mr Madi son; that these were my own opinions, and that I had power to act under the government of the United States, as circumstances required; that I was authorized to call on the constituted autho rities of the country, if the constitution was about to be violated. I wish the Court to understand, that I was to consider the mov ing down the Ohio as a violation of the law, and I was then to call on the constituted authority. When I spoke of the reasons which influenced my belief as to Col Burr's plans, Mr Blanner hasset observed to me, that however acute the opinions of gen tlemen might be, he and Col Burr were as well acquainted with the constitution and the laws as the administration itself, and that they knew very well what they were about Q. What pro duced this remark? A. I do not recollect, but perhaps it may have been the arguments which I had used to show that the ex pedition was a violation of the laws Mr. Blannerhasset said, that he had joined his friends in this undertaking, and could not abandon them, unless they consented to give the thing up; and asked me, if he was at liberty to communicate to Col Burr the information I had given him I told him, he was. I do not re collect whether I have mentioned the opinion I expressed to Mr Blannerhasset of the validity of Bastrop's grant I told him all that I knew of the title, and that Col Burr would have no title to it, and that if he had, the Orleans land could be no object with Mr. Blannerhasset

Mr *Wirt* How came you, sir, informed about this title? A I had been at New Orleans, where the subject was much talked of Q Have there been any judicial proceedings about it? A I told Mr Blannerhasset that Mr. Lynch claimed under Mr. E. Liv ingston, that this was a considerable purchase; and that Mr Livingston had invalidated this contract in Court.

Mr *Burr* I deny that this is a fact

The next day, perhaps that afternoon, I met Mr. Blannerhasset at another house, in company with gentlemen, most of them strangers to me Mr. Blannerhasset was speaking and avowing that Mr. Burr had a great many friends in Kentucky. I obser ved, that this would much depend upon his object; if to settle Ouachita lands, that the people would wish him well; but if it was to attack the territories of Spain, or those of the United States, he would have very few friends In reply, Mr Blanner hasset observed, that whatever was his object, he either had or would have a great number of friends. This was in a publi room, in a tavern, several gentlemen were present; I recollect particularly a Major Sproat. Either on that evening or the evening of the next day, Mr. Blannerhasset said, he was writing to Colonel Burr. He invited me to his room, and wished to know how much of our conversation he might communicate to Colonel Burr. I told him the whole, if he chose, that the information was intended for him, but that he might communicate it to Col. Burr. During this time, and for a few days afterwards, the intercourse between us was friendly, but after I had had a conversation with Mr. Henderson, I had no farther communications with him, save dining with him one day at the same table, and he rose immediately after dinner, and I did not see him again until we met in the Mississippi territory.

Mr *Hay*. Had you any communications with Mr Burr? A. I had; and in the Mississippi territory too. In consequence of the information I had received from Mr Henderson and others, I lodged information with the governor of Ohio, and a law was passed, and I was also instrumental at Frankfort in Kentucky in the passage of a similar law. Their object was to put an end to these expeditions.

When I arrived at the little town of Washington in the Mississippi territory, about the latter end of January or beginning of February, I heard that Colonel Burr was in the house.

Mr. *Hay*. Where is Washington? on the Mississippi river? A. No, it is ten miles from it, and seven miles back of Natchez. It is the seat of government of the Mississippi territory. I waited on Colonel Burr principally with a view to ascertain whether the information I had given to Mr Blannerhasset had been communicated to him. I asked him whether Mr. Blannerhasset had communicated our conversation to him. He said that he had. I told him on entering his room, that I had just arrived from the upper country, and perhaps he might be anxious to hear the news. He told me that Mr. Blannerhasset had accused me of a breach of hospitality. I replied, that I never was in his house in my life. He spoke of his protested bills drawn in Lexington, and seemed to attribute their protest to the measures adopted by the government. I told him that just before I left Lexington, the merchants there had received information that they would be paid. He said that they ought to be paid, as the man on whom they were drawn had the funds to pay them with. He then spoke of the measures pursued by government as ruinous and rigorous (I am not certain which was his expression), that they had detained his people. Q. Was this before or after his trial? A. It was before; he had then entered into recognizance. He said, that he had invited investigation into his conduct, he spoke of the measures of the military, and his determination to resist them. I understood him to mean the military of the United States; he either said that he had, or that he would order his people to resist them. He said, that he had claimed the protection of the civil authority, and thought *that* protection would be adequate to his safety. He spoke too of the Ouachita settlement, I believe he told me that he should send his people there, but did not know whether he should venture into the territory himself; intimating, as I thought, an apprehension of General Wilkinson.

He asked me if I knew what had given rise to the president's proclamation. I told him that I did not, unless it was General Eaton's communication. The Court will see from the date of the proclamation, that any information I could have imparted had not then reached the seat of government Col Burr observed, that the machinations of his enemies had led to these proceedings, and that facts did not support and justify them. I assured him that those who were alarmed and agitated were not his enemies, at least this was the idea I intended to convey, and after stating to him the alarm extending through the western country, I proposed to him that he should make some public declaration as to his real object His reply to this was, that he was a party concerned, and that no declaration of his could have any effect He seemed disposed to ridicule the idea of his bringing about a separation of the union by physical force, that it was to be produced by moral, not physical causes I mentioned to Col Burr that I had heard in the western country of a considerable number of men, perhaps two thousand, being collected for the purpose of invading Mexico His reply was, that he supposed *that* event was in case of a war with Spain I told him, no, that I had not understood it as depending on that condition He then said something about the Ouachita lands, and replied, that perhaps when they had a separate government, something of that sort might be attempted (meaning, as I understood, the invasion of Mexico) Soon after this, or at least before I had heard any explanation of what he meant by " a separate government," a gentleman of his family came in, and I took my leave. I had no further conversation with Mr Burr or Mr Blannerhasset I lodged an information against Mr Blannerhasset, and was with him before a magistrate

Mr *Hay.* Did you make particular observations to Mr Blannerhasset about the sort of preparations he was making? A He spoke of the settlement of the Ouchita as their object He never positively told me it was, but he said they avowed it as their object I observed to him, as a reason why I should not think it was, that young men without families or without any of the implements of husbandry were engaged to go He said that their arms were to kill turkies or Indians. He then launched out into an abuse of the administration, their neglect of the army and navy, &c I forgot to state this circumstance When Mr Blannerhasset met me to know how far he was at liberty to communicate my opinions to Col Burr, I urged to him the impropriety of his engaging in these objects, he said it was impossible that Colonel Burr could have so much deceived him and his son-in-law, Mr Alston

Mr. *Wirt* Was this remark after you had announced yourself as the agent of government? A It was

Mr. Wirt Did he say any thing to your objection about the want of implements of husbandry? A He did say something about the opening of roads But he never did tell me the real object Q Do you know any thing of the Ouachita land? A I never was on it Q What is its character? A. Some say it is good; and some say it is bad. I believe the greater part of it is covered with water, and there is some very fine land

Cross-examined.

Mr *Burr*. Did you ever see Bastrop's patent? A Never. Q. Did you read it? A No, I always understood, that there never was one

Mr *Burr* You have said that the greater part was water; I will assure the Court that it was to be laid out without any water Were you ever examined before? A. Yes I made a deposition, when I lodged information before the legislature of Ohio. Q. Were you examined on any other occasion. A I was before the Grand Jury. Q Did you say any thing then of a conversation you had with Gen Neville? A. Yes I told General Neville that I had come to make some enquiries into this affair. General Neville informed me what had passed in his conversation with Mr Morgans He said the people had apprehended that your object was a seperation of the United States, but that if it was the invasion of Mexico, you would be better received on your return than you ever had been Q Did you not speak of the boats? A I did Q Did you not say, they were unfit to go up the stream? A I so understood at that time Q Do you not know they were seized by the government to send troops up the stream? A I did not hear of it before I came here Q Did I give you a welcome reception? A I was not acquainted with your manner It was cold but I thought respectful Q Have you not heard Governor Williams, Mead, and Rodney say, that they would not suffer the military to take me? A I most certainly recollect, that I both thought and said that it was improper to take you by military authority; and I heard Governor Williams say, if the attempt was made, he was not authorized to sanction it Q Had you not heard of the stipulations made to me by Williams and Mead? A I knew not of Governor Williams's stipulating with you I heard of Mr. Mead's doing it. Q. Was there no law to arrest me? A. I mentioned to Governor Williams that if the laws were not sufficiently energetic to meet such occurrences, it was better to provide one But I never saw the law. Q Did you not hear of an officer being there to arrest me? A I had a conversation with a Lieutenant Peter, who was lately in this place, relative to this subject The *counsel* for the prosecution objected to this course of examination on this subject.

Chief Justice If Mr Burr means to alledge these measures as an excuse for his own military preparations, he may press these enquiries Mr *Burr* I did suppose from the sort of duties which Mr Graham discharged in that country, that he must have known of the stipulations of Mead and Williams, and that in direct violation of these a party of officers in disguise (that is without their uniform) and with concealed weapons, as dirks and pistols were there to seize me. Mr Graham certainly knows something

Mr *Graham* I can speak of my conversation with Governor Williams and Lieutenant Peter, for with no others did I communicate on this subject Governor Williams told me, that Doctor Carmichael had been authorized to come to the Mississippi territory and seize you; whether this was before or after your trial, I know not. He said that he was extremely unwilling to have any such thing done. I observed that it was extremely improper to suffer a person to be seized, who was then in the c dy of the law He said that he had remonstrated with Dr. Carmichael, that Dr. C had given it up and returned.

Mr *Burr* Did Carmichael belong to the army? A No—to the Mississippi territory—I was proceeding to state that the night Colonel Burr left Washington, I heard some of the officers in the room, in which I slept, conversing about him, and one of them observed, that if Colonel Burr was not arrested on that night he would make his escape—The gentlemen left the room, and I afterwards understood from Lieutenant Peter, that an application had been or was about to be made, to Governor Williams for permission to arrest Colonel Burr—Lieutenant Peter having understood that I had heard a part of this conversation, informed me, that he had come with other officers to arrest Colonel Burr, and I advised him to do nothing that would violate the laws of his country—He gave me to understand, that at that moment he felt himself bound to obey the orders of his General, like a good soldier I urged every consideration I could suggest against the exercise of military authority, and I did then understand that it was not his intention to proceed against Colonel Burr Indeed I understood that Colonel Burr had made his escape I advised Governor Williams to make such an arrangement with him as would send him on to Washington for trial, or to detain him in that territory for trial

Mr *Blannerhasset.* You stated that you had given information against me, and led to a prosecution? A I did not say that I had led to a prosecution, but only that I had given information against you, that you might be taken to the district where the expedition had been fitted out Q Why did you prefer Judge Toulman to Judge Rodney; the last being the senior Judge? A I made no choice?

Q Did you not understand that Judge Toulman was the Judge of the Tombigbee county? A I understood that he was Judge of the Mississippi territory, and Judge Toulman still insists upon it that he possesses this authority Q Did you not apply to the attorney general of that territory? A Certainly not Judge Toulman would have interfered, but Judge Rodney issued a writ of habeas corpus Q Was it by direction or request of the government, that you informed against me for the misdemeanor? A By neither Q Do you not expect to pay the one thousand dollars? A I expect not Q To whom are you to pay it? Mr Graham here addressed the Court he said that Judge Rodney had refused to send Mr Blannerhasset round for trial, but had held him to bail; that he himself had been recognized, that the Court was to sit some time in May, the Judge considered the Supreme Court as the proper tribunal, the attorney general thought otherwise, that before the Court met he had besides been indisposed, and had obtained the certificate of his physician that he could not attend the Court

Mr. *Burr* Are you still secretary of the Orleans territory? A. I am not. Q Do you now hold any office under the government, and what is it? A. I am Chief Clerk in the office of the Secretary of State
Was there any arrangement made to seize Col. Burr after judicial proceedings against him? A Governor Williams

and myself both agreed that his trial in the Mississippi territory was a mere farce, and that something ought to be done. *He proposed* to see Col Burr, and make some arrangements with him to come on to the city of Washington for his trial. Colonel Burr informed him, that he was merely going to ride to Colonel Osborne's for that night. Governor Williams informed me that he received a great coat at the suburbs of the town and disappeared.

Mr Wirt Was not Colonel Burr held in recognizance? A Yes Q Did you see such a recognizance? A Yes I saw it myself in the clerk's office

Mr Burr If it is there, I pronounce it to be a forgery

Mr Hay observed that the truth would appear in time. Mr. Hay. Were any legal proceedings pending at the time of his departure?

The *Witness* asked the Court if this was a proper question?

Chief Justice It is a mere difference of opinion about a fact—Colonel Burr contended that his recognizance had been complied with—Governor Williams says not

Mr Hay Was his departure from Washington sudden? A It was certainly sudden, as Governor Williams told me, he had been promised with a call from Colonel Burr

Mr. Burr Are you still Secretary of that territory? A No Q What office do you hold—if any A I am at present Chief clerk of the department of state

Mr Blannerhasset Do you know any thing of the warrants that were issued against me by Governor Tiffin? A No, I do not—I understand that there were warrants issued against you. Q Did you advise or suggest such a measure? A I certainly did not

Mr. Wirt What was Governor Williams's opinion and your own respecting Burr's going off? A Why, sir, we thought that the trial in the Mississippi territory was a perfect farce We agreed that something was necessary to be done Governor Williams then thought it best to propose to Colonel Burr to come on to Washington, to have a full examination into the circumstance and that if he refused to come on, (knowing that he had not power to send him,) he would take steps to detain him until witnesses could be obtained there Directly after, he disappeared, with Colonel Osborne's great coat, and never was seen there afterwards Q Did you see the recognizance he entered into here? A Yes

Mr Hay Was there any proceedings in Court going on against Mr Burr at the time of his departure?

Chief Justice In order to get at this, a copy of the record might be produced.

Mr Burr There was no recognizance filed: I was not bound to attend in that Court after the Grand Jury had given in their return, and they had nothing to do with me; therefore, if there is a recognizance produced by Judge Rodney, I pronounce it a forgery.

Mr Graham I was present at the trial.

Mr Hay. I want to know whether Colonel Burr's departure was sudden and unexpected.

Mr. *Graham* It certainly was unexpected Gov. William told me that he had received a promise from Col. Burr of a call on him and he did not call

Stephen S Welsh was again called.

He was asked to relate what farther he knew of the transaction

Witness. I was told by the Court to relate all that I knew, but there was some part of the conversation that passed between Blannerhasset and me in September, as we were coming down the river with Mr. Alston and his lady, that was not related. Mr Blannerhasset asked me how I should like to go to a new country? My reply was, that I should like it very well, if there was a prospect of making any thing He said there was a prospect of getting plenty of land I asked him what part of the country? He either then said it was Florida, or asked me how I should like to go to Florida I then made answer that I should like to go to that country very well I told him I would go

Mr Hay You went down the river with him, did you? A Yes Q Was there any thing in your knowledge about the concealment of arms? A I recollect that one evening there was a search for arms (after dark) There were arms taken out of Floyd's and Berry's boats, and I understand that a search was to be made next morning

Chief Justice How many arms were there—do you know? A I do not, but I think there were about nine musquets with bayonets taken out of Berry's boat

Parley Howe and *David C Wallace* were called to testify to the character of *Albright* They spoke of him, and of *Taylor* also, in high terms as to honesty and respectability of character.

Charles Duval was called

Mr *Hay* What do you know as to any communications you had with Colonel Burr. Mr Blannerhasset and others *Witness* never saw Colonel Burr but once, and that was in New Orleans two years ago last November, but I have had frequent communications with Mr Blannerhasset The first time I ever had any, was at Marietta, in Sept 1806, when I had flour to sell asked him whether he did not want to buy flour, and engaged twenty barrels, he did not however receive more than five or six barrels of it. I mentioned to him that I had understood from Mrs Blannerhasset, that he was going down the river and a number of my acquaintances were going with him, and that I did not know, but that I too would go, if I knew what he was going for He told me that Colonel Burr and himself and others had purchased large tracts of land, and wanted settlers to go on it. I told him that I had land enough at home and that I did not want to go to settle land. He then represented as though there was something else in view; but he did not tell me at that time He said a number of people were going who had never asked what they were going for—they believed it to be something worth going for —they were leaving their plantations, their neighbours, every thing He said he was going to leave his, I might surely leave mine, and that I might suppose it was for something very handsome I mentioned something about his leaving his own plantation a man who was so well situated. He said that what he had there he did not regard as a straw, in comparison of the object which he had ahead. I had a great many interviews with him on the subject, sometimes he told me one thing, and sometimes another. I told him that Mrs Blannerhasset had informed me that Mr Graham was one of the party——Mr Blannerhasset agreed that it was so. The Court will be pleased to notice that Mr Graham and myself had once travelled to New O leans together. He mentioned, if I would go with him, could I arm myself with a gun? I told him I had a rifle that I could take with me, that I never had used a musket. He said that that would answer. He asked me if the young men on the Muskingum who were like to go with me, had arms or could get them? I told him it was probable they all had arms, as they belonged to the militia. He said if they would find arms he would find ammunition. Just before M. Blannerhasset's boat went off, Mr Graham came to Marietta, and Mr Blannerhasset was that night at my father's house. My father told me that my old friend Mr Graham was in town, and Mr Blannerhasset told my mother that she had better not let me go to see Mr Graham, for Mr Graham would certainly persuade me to go down the river.

Mr *Hay*. Will you state the different objects which Mr. Blannerhasset held out to you?

A He mentioned to me that he was going out into the Spanish territory, about the same time that he spoke of my arming and said, he supposed we should have a little fighting to do; but the Spaniards were cowards and would soon run.

M. *Hay* Did you understand where you were to fight the Spaniards? A Somewhere about the Ouachita lands, that they might be troublesome and that he wanted men of my description to do it.

M *Hay* Did he profess, any other object? A. My father asked him what he wanted me for, if to work, that I would not work at home. He said he did not want all to work. He wanted men of my description, he did not care if he had one thousand such.

When he was bringing up this kiln-dried meal I asked him what it was for. He said it was to take down the river—I asked him why he did not get flour? Because he said, they were going into the Spanish country, and flour would not keep as well. He told me he wanted us to get knapsacks to carry eight or ten days provision for marching—I mentioned that I was a poor traveller, and I would get me a Spanish horse and ride. He said he was going out among the Spaniards an ignorant set of men, and he wanted clever young men to go and take command of them · to have a commission and some office too . I mentioned to him that I would not hesitate to go there and stay two or three years, if I could make my fortune. He said if I once got there, he'd warrant that I never would return, I would be so fond of the place. I told him I never wished to go to a place, whence I could not return to visit my friends. He said I should like the country so well, that I would be contented to stay there. He told me that, when we got to the mouth of Cumberland river, we should be joined by Colonel Burr and the whole party, when the whole secret would be divulged, and if I did not like it he would bear my expences back to Marietta I told him that if I went down and a number of my friends were going also, I should like to have choice of my boat's crew He said if it was so, I must still expect to be under the same regulations as regular troops, that was, that we might have the privilege of choosing our own officers, till we got to the mouth of Cumberland, there we were to meet Colonel Burr, and we must then submit to such regulations as Colonel Burr thought proper My motive for making this proposition as to my friends was, that a number of strangers were going and I did not wish to be with them I recollect nothing farther of any great importance

Mr Duval's further examination was postponed, and the Court adjourned till to morrow.

FRIDAY, September 25.

Charles Duval continued with his testimony We were to be under the command of Mr Blannerhasset until we got to the mouth of Cumberland.

Mr *Hay* Do you recollect any conversation respecting the temper and disposition of the people at New Orleans? A He told me that the citizens of New Orleans were very much dissatisfied with their government, and that they spoke very much against Gov Claiborne Q Do you recollect his mentioning any farther about the expedition? A Yes, he said that they must be at New Orleans by Christmas Q What was the general character of Albright? A Why, the first time I ever saw Albright, he came up to my fathers' mill with this kiln-dried corn He appeared to be a very hard working man the people generally said that he was a very steady honest Dutchman, and that they would as soon take his word as Gen Tupper's.

Mr *Wickham* It is a very great pity that the gentleman had not thought proper to compose Gen Tupper's evidence with Mr Albright's whilst he was here

Chief Justice It is a much greater pity that the evidence could not keep to the circumstances

Mr *Hay* I beg pardon of the Court for thus diverging, but I thought it proper to support the character of this poor man, who has nothing but his honest character to carry him through life, by enquiring what it was, since he has been so violently attacked at every turn of his testimony

Mr *Wickham* All that I said was not affecting the character of the man I only said that he contradicted himself, and therefore was not a proper witness

Mr Duval continued his testimony I agreed to go to New Orleans with Mr Blannerhasset, and when I got there, if I did not like their plan, I might go and see Mr Graham, who was a particular friend of mine, and, no doubt, he would put me into some way of business. Q Was this before you saw Mr Graham? A No, it was after Mr Graham had told me the consequences. he said that if I had a notion to go down the river, it would be more to my credit to go some other way Q Do you know any thing respecting the kiln-dried meal A Yes, I know it was ground and packed at my fathers' about sixty bar rels, besides about thirty barrels that was not kiln-dried. **Q.** The boats were stopped were they not? **A** Yes, about half way between where they were built by Col Barker, and Marietta They were to have gone down after dark Mr. Blannerhasset said that if the boats were not all done by such a time, he would take what were done, and start off Col Barker got all the hands he could, to get them ready by that time. I do not particularly recollect what day it was

Cross examination

Mr *Wickham* Was there any think said concerning a war with Spain? **A** Yes Mr Blannerhasset mentioned to me that he expected there would be one **Q** Was it pretty generally expected in that country? **A** I believe it was **Q** Was it pretty generally wished for? **A** No, I cannot say it was **Q** Did you ever give in affidavit on this subject? **A** No, Sir, never **Q** Did you lodge any information with Gov Tiffin or any one else? **A** No, with no person in the world **Q** Did you ever go to Chilicothe on account of this business? **A** I went there once **Q** Who did you go in company with? **A** Mr Graham **Q** Did you go at his request? **A** No, I had business out there **Q** What has become of this flour, the kiln-dried meal and those boats? **Q** I do not know, but I believe Gen Buel took it by order of the government **Q** How do you know that it was taken by order of the government? **A** I do not know certainly that it was **Q** What became of the boats? **A** Why they were taken up into a creek near Marietta, some got broke up, some were repaired, and sent down with troops to the Mississippi I believe to St Louis, so it was said

Testimony of *David C. Wallace*

Mr *Hay.* State to the Court what you know of this transaction

In the fall of 1806, Mr. Blannerhasset informed me, that he was engaged in a plan with a number of persons, which he thought would be highly advantageous, and that he was authorized to offer me the appointment of *Surgeon General* I enquired, Surgeon General of what? And he replied, he was not at liberty to explain until I had engaged in the expedition He used various arguments to induce me to join. He said that I should be in very excellent company, that the association would consist of respectable individuals, and particularized Colonel Burr. He thought that after so long an intimacy, I might rely on his friendship. The conversation ended with my peremptory refusal to join in any expedition, the nature and plan of which I was not fully informed of, and approved I heard Mr. Blannerhasset make proposals to several individuals to join; offering one hundred acres of land : each man to furnish himself with a rifle and blanket He stated, that when they got to the mouth of Cumberland, the plan was to be disclosed . all those who did not like it were at liberty to return Some of the men engaged ; others took time to consider the proposition fully. At this time the boats building up the Muskingum were nearly completed, and a general rumor prevailed that Burr. Blannerhasset & Co were preparing an expedition to dissever the states, and to carry the war into Mexico When Mr. Blannerhasset again asked me to join, I replied, that the same objections continued, and that I was not yet informed of the objects of the expedition. To which he replied, " you have heard what we were about ;"—which I understood as assenting to the truth of these reports. I told Mr. Blannerhasset that I expected they would be stopped descending the river, to which he replied, that " he did not believe that the country would be able to stop them, that he would have five hundred men from Marietta, he would have seven boats at that place, and they would be joined by others from above " I remarked, that the people in the western country were excellent marksmen, and that the woods on the banks of the river would afford them an excellent covering to firing upon those who were descending the river He replied that " in that case, he would land a party and set fire to every house and town " I rode with Mr. Blannerhasset to see the boats that were building up the Muskingum, where he shewed the builder and myself the articles by which the men under his command, as he called it, were to be governed on descending the river Each boats' crew was to choose the captain, until they joined Colonel Burr at the mouth of Cumberland, where he was to direct their proceedings. At the boat yard, he directed the builder to have an apartment fitted up in his boat for Colonel Burr, as he expected the Colonel, when he joined him at the mouth of Cumberland, would sometimes wish to stay with him During the ride I observed to Mr Blannerhasset, that I did not believe the plan would succeed, as the people generally detested and execrated it To which he replied, " if the people could not see their *interest*, we will not cram the measure down their throats " Mr Blannerhasset shewed me some letters he had received from Colonel Burr, about the period—[Mr *Wirt* At which time was it? A Between September and the going down the river]—in one of which he admonished him not to be alarmed at the rumors respecting his arrest in Kentucky ; as he apprehended no danger but delay to return the intended settlement on the Ouachita A person present (Captain Elliot) enquired, whether Colonel Burr had mentioned any thing about the expedition To which he replied, " Nonothing comes to us on that subject by the mail." Mr Blannerhasset spoke to me to furnish them a quantity of medicines, and such directions for using them as were calculated for a military expedition In a conversation with Colonel Burr in 1805, he expatiated on the situation of the western country ; on its being compelled to pay large sums, for the sale of lands, which were spent in the Atlantic states ; and on the three millions of dollars which he said were paid for tax. These observations made by Colonel Burr induced me to believe—[Mr. *Botts* objected to the witness stating any of his own inferences]—Colonel Burr observed that this same money would vastly improve the commerce of the western country

Mr *Hay* Did you ever read the *Querist*? A. I read the first and second numbers at Cincinnati Q. Did the observations in these recall to your recollection your conversation with Mr Burr A. They did When I saw these papers, I was asked my opinion about the author. I said, that in my opinion, Colonel Burr had suggested the ideas, and Mr. Blannerhasset had put them into words. Q. Were the rumors that you spoke of general? A. They were so. they were in every man's mouth.

Cross-examined.

Mr *Wickham*. Have you had a medical education? A Yes, I received it in the University of Pennsylvania Q Had you ever performed any surgical operation? A I had not I never practiced physic, nor did I ever intend it Q Was this conversation before or after your refusal to join? A All these conversations were after that Q Did any of the men applied to by Mr. Blannerhasset in your presence, go? A I do not know Q What was the tenor of these rumors? A That this party intended to effect a separation of the union, and to carry an expedition into Mexico Q When the offer of Surgeon General was made to you, did you believe it to be serious? A I cannot be certain of Mr Blannerhasset's motive for making this proposition, but supposed that his object was to induce me to join, although I had not practiced physic

Mr *Martin* Were you in the habit of curing gun-shot wounds or cutting off limbs? A. No, sir, nor did I wish it

Mr. *Wickham*. When were you in Philadelphia? A. In 1799 and 1800. Q Whose lectures did you attend? A I attended Drs Woodhouse's, Rush's, Wistar's, and Barton's Wistar was joint professor of anatomy and surgery with Shippen. Q Did you attend all the lectures? A Yes, sir

Mr *Hay*. How long were you engaged in the study of medicine? A Seven years. Q Did Mr. Blannerhasset know of this? A He did.

Mr *Wirt*. Did you attend any surgical operations in the Hospital? A I did one winter

Mr. *Wickham* Who did you study with? A I studied about three years with Dr White of Philadelphia.

Mr. *Hay* Was this the same as Dr. White of Baltimore? "No," said Mr *Martin*, "he was then in Ireland" *Witness*. What, Dr White of Philadelphia? Mr. *Martin*. Oh! no, Mr Hay and myself understand each other.

Testimony of Robert Wallace.

Q Where do you live? A. I live in Marietta Sometime last fall, in November, I believe, I received a message from Mr Blannerhasset to come down to the island I went. It was soon after Mr. Blannerhasset returned from Kentucky After I had been there some time, Mr Blannerhasset took me into a small room, and said he wished to speak to me privately. He then asked me if I had not heard he was going down the river I told him that I had He asked me if I would go with him He said he was not then at liberty to reveal the object entirely, but, if I would depend on his friendship, he would do well for me He spoke of the settlement of the Ouachita land; but intimated that there was something else in view. In the same evening, there were several young men at Mr. Blan-

nerhasset's house, from Belpre They were all requested to join
the expedition, and go down with him They were all to fur
nish themselves with a rifle and blanket. The next morning I
had some more conversation with Mr. and Mrs. Blannerhasset.
Among other things, I asked whether the government counte
nanced this expedition· I had heard something from Captain
Elliot, the evening before, that this was an expedition intended
against Mexico. Mr Blannerhasset replied, that it was a mat
ter of no importance whether the government aided it or not
government was weak, and that they would have nothing to do
with them, unless the government attempted to suppres them:
in that case they would make resistance. Mr Blannerhasset
laughed at my staying at home, and spending my life behind a
counter he said it was a dull life, and if I were to go with him,
I should have an opportunity to distinguish myself, but at home,
I should spend my life in obscurity.

On the next day I rode to Marietta with Mr Blannerhasset
On the way, he was engaging several young men to go down the
river with him, offering them lands Among the rest was one
Rathbone, a schoolmaster I told him that he was a great drunk
ard, and he would be of no service to him in making of a settle
ment He said it was no matter such fellows would be good sol
diers, and that his allowance would not be sufficient to enable
him to get drunk, when he is brought under good discipline Mr
Blannerhasset was then going up the Muskingum to hurry for
ward the building of Burr's boats No farther conversation pass
ed then He was at my father's once afterwards, (I was in the
room) He then offered my brother the post of Surgeon General
if he would go with him

Mr *Wickham* When was that ? A. That was in the month of
November, I think soon after my father returned from Cincinnati
My father told him that he had better give up the enterprize en
tirely, and stay at home at his island, for he was as well off as
he could be any where, that he could not possibly succeed; his
force was too small and the Spaniards were too strong. That
might be possible, he answered, but General Wilkinson and his
army would join them, and then they should be able to go through
When I was at the island, Mr Blannerhasset told me, that if I
were to go out there, I might have a little fighting with the Spa
niards, but that they were great cowards, that they would soon
run, and we should be sure to overcome them

In the month of August, I think it was, Mr Blannerhasset was
at my father's house, when he made use of several arguments to
prove how much it would be to the interest of the western States
to separate themselves from the union.

Mr *Wirt* Did you see any provisions ? A I know there was a
kiln when I was on the island, drying some corn Q. Did Blan
nerhasset speak of Burr at any time ? A Yes—he generally men
tioned that Mr Burr belonged to the expedition, and I believe
he was the leader of it I understood him to say that he was at
their head, I remember once particularly asking him, whether
Colonel Burr was concerned in the expedition : he said that he
was one of the leaders He also mentioned General Eaton, and
several other men in the State. Q. Did he say nothing about the

result to yourself, if you were to go? A Yes, he said that my fortune would be made if they were to succeed, but that if they did not he was a ruined man Q Do you recollect any observations from him, as to the course to be pursued, in case they were opposed by any party? A I was present when he talked to my father about landing of men, and burning houses in case they were opposed in going down the river He did not say they *would* do it, but that they *could* do it Q What arms did you see on the island? A There were two blunderbusses, two or three guns, three brace of pistols, a sword, a dirk, a keg of powder, some bullets, and some lead I believe he had owned these arms for a long time.

Cross-examination.

Mr *Wickham* Did you ever agree to go with Mr Blannerhasset? A No, it was left undetermined, I wished to consult with my father, and so did Mr Blannerhasset, he had too much esteem for my father to take such a step without his consent Q Was there any talk about a war with Spain at that time? A I do not know, but Mr Blannerhasset did give some hints about it, but I am not certain.

Mr. D Woodbridge came into Court to explain an observation which had been used on a former occasion He said that the partnership accounts between Mr Blannerhasset had been settled, from which it might be inferred, that all their accounts had been settled The truth, however, was, that though the partnership was dissolved, their private accounts were not yet adjusted.

Return J Meigs Junior, was then introduced He enquired whether he should state any thing about the seizing of the boats Mr. *Hay.* No, Sir, I wish you to state particularly what passed between General Tupper and yourself Mr *Burr* And what is that enquiry to the Court? It is to fortify Jacob Albright's testimony I presume that such will be the conclusion, if it appears that General Tupper has told Mr Meigs the very things which Albright has substantially related Mr *Hay.* Has not General Tupper left his affidavit? Mr *Wickham* I know not, But when that shall be produced to the Court, it will then be time enough to introduce Mr. Meigs Mr *Hay*, We have Mr Meigs' *affidavit* and if it be necessary, we shall introduce it. Mr. Meigs was discharged from farther attendance

Edmund P Dana, Sworn.

I never saw Colonel Burr but once previous to my seeing him in this place.

In November last Mr. and Mrs. Blannerhasset came to my house in Belpre his object was to purchase cyder. In the course of our conversation he said that he was going down the river; that he had been purchasing land in the west, in company with Mr. Burr and others, and that he was going down to settle it. This was about the middle of the day, and my father gave them an invitation to stay to dinner They stayed and there was a good deal of conversation at dinner on these subjects. Mr. Blannerhasset stated the particular advantage of the Ouachita land above the rest of the country that it was near the market, and calculated for the raising of cotton He said, there was a large association for this purpose, and that he wanted young men to go. Those who embarked early, if they succeeded in the undertaking would no doubt make their fortunes I observed to my brother, who was sitting with us, that if fortunes were so easily made he had better go Mr. Blannerhasset replied, that he wanted such men as we were He said he did not want to carry us without my fathers consent. My father observed, that we were own men, and might act as we thought proper. I think Mr. Blannerhasset bargained for five or six barrels of cyder, which he said he was going to carry down the river with him He invited us to the island, where he would give us more particular information of his design.

A short time after, I was in the orchard gathering apples. Mr. Blannerhasset came to me to talk more about the enterprize down the river. He asked me if I had any serious intentions of going. I said. I was unsettled I would embrace any favorable opportunity of bettering my situation and if I knew the object of this enterprize , I could better tell whether I would go or not. I observed that there were some rumors that the plan was unfavorable to the government, and if it was, that I would have nothing to do with it. He pledged his most sacred honor to me, and swore on the honor of a gentleman, that the plan was not hostile to the government; and he went on to name several characters, who he said were concerned, that the association was very extensive, spreading from Maine to Georgia I asked him to name them He said, that if the plan was a lawful one, it was a good one, from the high opinion I had formed of his talents. He said that Gen Wilkinson was to join with his army. He mentioned Gen. Jackson of Tennessee, who was then preparing a body of militia, (two or three hundred I think,) and who was ready to join them He mentioned Gen Dayton I think I asked him, if the Swartwouts of New York were not concerned.) There was a gentleman then at our house by that name.) He said they were. He named a number of other characters, whom I do not recollect

Mr *Hay* Were you on the island, on the night of their departure? A I was Mr. Blannerhasset told me, if I would come over to see him, he would show me a plan of the Ouachita country. Some few days after this, I went over to the island Mr Blannerhasset was at home, but engaged with some gentlemen who were there He made no further communications to me, seeming to doubt whether I was seriously disposed towards his plans. I staid only a few minutes. I now recollect that I have omitted a part of the conversation with him When he said that Gen. Wilkinson and Jackson were going to join with their troops, I asked him what this was for, if for the settlement of lands, they surely were not necessary He said, that there was a great many Indians and Spaniards in that country, whom they must go prepared to resist

I had no further conversation with him till the 9th or 10th of December, when he sent a servant to know whether he could get three or four horses to ride to Marietta. I said that he might have all that I had. About 12 o'clock in the day, several gendemen came; among them I think were Mr. Blannerhasset, Tyler and I think Mr Smith, there were six gentlemen. I understood they were going up the Muskingum after the boats. Sometime in the afternoon they returned They rode to the landing opposite the island and sent the horses down I understood from flying reports, that they expected opposition, and had returned Hearing that they were to start that evening. I felt anxious to see their departure, and to find out their object With two young men I went down the river; found a skiff at the landing, and passed over. We landed just above where Tyler's boats lay, went to the house into a large room, where a number of men were collected round the fire, and Colonel Tyler among them I told him that I understood they were about to start down the river We walked out into the north-wing of Mr. Blannerhasset's house together, and there a young man by the name of Bent observed to me, that he understood from Mr Blannerhasset, I had some intention to join

Mr *Botts.* You need not give any evidence of conversations which were out of Mr. Blannerhasset's hearing

Mr *Hay* That point is already decided the Court is to judge about it These conversations connect the chief leaders of the party

Mr *Burr* spoke. He said he had no concern in this testimony; but as it respected a question of *principle*, he would trouble the Court with a very few observations He remarked something about what had been said of the difference in this examination, and what it would have been, if it had been a case before a Jury He believed the principle to be uniform, and applicable at all times, and in all places and circumstances, and that a Judge was confined by rules of law Among those rules he recognized one, that there was no situation in which a Judge could divest himself, or overleap the rules of evidence If he could, by what limits was he to be governed? These rules are imperative because we have no others. There is a difference, to be sure, in different capacities for instance, a Court of Chancery will receive *ex parte* depositions and so will a Court in cases of contempt but still, the rule of law governs what is properly called legal testimony, and rejects illegal I submit this to the Court, lest the proper rules of evidence should be too lightly appreciated, when the effect will be nearly the same in their operation, although it is not before a Jury

Mr. *Hay* spoke at some length, and Mr *Botts* in answer

The *Chief Justice* said, that he was willing to hear such testimony, in his capacity of an examining magistrate, although he might not, perhaps, was a verdict pending. Indeed, he thought it proper to search into every circumstance that was attainable, to come at the whole transaction

Mr *Dana* continued his testimony —I then told Mr. Tyler, that when I knew the object, and liked it, I might possibly go along with them, but Mr Blannerhasset had told me a story about the settlement of some lands, in which I did not place much confidence. He said that it was a fact that they had made the purchase, but that they had other objects in view besides that I told him that I had my own opinion on the subject · that I thought their operations were intended against Mexico. At that time there was a strong prospect of a Spanish war, and I thought I should have no objection to go. He observed that I was not much mistaken in my opinion. I told him that since Mr. Blannerhasset had mentioned it to me, I had been at some pains in learning the geography of that country; that the people of Mexico were very numerous, and that with an handful of men, we should not be able to make any impression. He answered, that with five hundred well armed and disciplined men, he thought they should be able to overset it. I asked him, then, whether he was well acquainted with the different roads to that country? He answered that they were perfectly so; that they understood every cow path through the country. He said that they were not going to plunder and rapine, but to relieve the distressed citizens of Mexico, which they had been invited to do for five years past.

I think I then observed to him, that if they would avow *that* to be their object, they would get three to join them to where they would one, under the impression that now prevailed. I think that he answered, that it was impolitic to discover their object, lest the Spaniards might get information of it, and fortify themselves against it. I observed to him, that I wished them success; if I thought proper to join them, it would be somewhere down the river; for I was not ready then.

After Colonel Tyler and I had done our conversation, we went up to the hall chamber; there were a number of gentlemen there. Mr. Blannerhasset observed, that they were going to start that night down the river. He spoke of a law which the legislature of Ohio had passed, which he thought unconstitutional; but that if it was so, it would operate very much against him, and he wished to start as soon as possible. Some observations were dropped about his going away. He said that he was sorry, after living so long there, to leave it in the night; that he was conscious he had done nothing wrong; but that he was determined to go away, the season being very far advanced.

About nine o'clock I bid him farewell, and returned home. I saw Colonel Burr once before at a regimental review at Marietta, with Colonel Meigs, and several other military gentlemen, in 1805.

Cross-examination

Mr. *Botts.* Did Mr. Blannerhasset and Mr. Tyler speak of a Spanish war, as certainly in prospect to take place? A. I certainly think they did; and that there was a strong prospect of a Spanish war.

Testimony of David Gilmore.

Mr. Blannerhasset was in Marietta, in the latter end of October with General Tupper. Mr. Blannerhasset asked me if I was the person who taught school in Marietta. After a short introduction, he observed that he was about to descend the Ohio, and go up the Red river to make a settlement; that he supposed that the accumulations I might make were not adequate to what I might make with him. He would like to have me to go with him; that he was going to settle a new country, which would be advantageous to those who would volunteer to go round to that settlement. He mentioned the fertility of the country, the advantages of a market that was near to it, not far from New Orleans. He thought that the prospects were so promising and flattering that I could not hesitate a moment in determining in favor of going I said, if I knew the object was certain of benefitting myself, I would have no objections to going. He then observed, that Mr Belknap was a fine and promising young man, that he stood high in his estimation, and that he would give me the same privileges as Mr Belknap would derive. That evening he insisted very urgently upon my going down the river with him. I wanted time to consider, but, that if he would make any engagements on which I could rely, I was willing to join I said I would call at his island on the next Saturday We walked to Mr. Woodbridge's and he made enquiries, if I was acquainted with surveying—I said if I could get any thing that way I would go but I had heard of other objects being in view

Mr *Hay* Did you press him to disclose the *real* objects of this plan? A I did He referred me to Mr. Belknap, and if I concluded to go, he would let me know more when I called upon him. Q Did you see Mr Belknap? A I did, but I had not time enough to enter into the merits of the case Afterwards I visited Mr Blannerhasset, and he asked me whether I had determined to go down the river I told him that I had not yet had sufficient time to talk with Mr Belknap I asked him what were the prospects, and what were the discoveries of the objects, he would make to me, and then I would tell whether I would go or not. He said that I must engage first, and then he would tell me   Mr. Blannerhasset seemed wiling to say very little on the subject, and seemed rather to consider me as a spy. I wanted some assurances, and perhaps intimated, that I wanted every thing to be put on paper I told him that I had heard they would bear the expences of the people back, and I think, he said, that would be very unreasonable I made some enquiries as to their numbers, and he said, that some were coming down the river from Pittsburg, enough to furnish crews to the boats that were building on the Muskingum? I think he mentioned two hundred. He mentioned General Eaton as engaged I asked him whether he expected three or four thousand men down the river He said he could not tell. I asked him if he expected one thousand; he could not inform me. He observed that it was necessary for every person who descended the river to carry arms I asked him the reason, and he said, that there were a number of Spaniards or Indians on the Red river, who might attack them if they were not armed. He then observed that he would prefer rifles to common fowling pieces.

Cross-examined.

Q Did any person go from your part of the country but Mr. Blannerhasset? A No one from Marietta.

Mr. *Hay* Where is your present home? A. am going on to Mississippi. Q But where do you consider yourself at home? A. At Marietta

The affidavits of Mr. Phelps and Mr. Glover were here offered to the Court.

Mr. *Burr* objected to them, because the witnesses had been here, and might have given him permission to examine them by question; but no notice was given to him of any such examination.

Mr *Hay* answered. Several applications had been made to him from the witnesses, and it was possible that he might have permitted these men to go away; but he had certainly given notice to the Court, that, it not being possible to keep the witnesses, he must take their affidavits.

Mr *Botts* said, that he did not mean to contradict what Mr. Hay had said, but the most manifest injustice would attend the discharge of one of these witnesses particularly (Mr. Glover,) whose evidence they were prepared to rebut, and confound. His evidence could not, therefore, be received.

As to Phelps, he is a person of distinction in the western country, and was very active in the arrest of persons. We therefore suppose that they ought both to attend here. If these affidavits may be taken, so may be others.

Some conversation here occurred between Mr *Hay*, Mr *Wickham*, and Mr *M'Rae*. After which, the *Chief Justice* decided that the affidavits ought not to be read, because the witnesses might and ought to have been detained.

Mr *Hay* said, that the witnesses were not discharged.

The *Chief Justice* said, that he did not know how that would affect the case; but perhaps the other testimony might give all the evidence which was material.

After some conversation between Messrs. *Botts*, *Randolph* and *Hay*.

Mr *Hay* observed, that he had gone through all the testimony, except some additional of Gen. Eaton and Gen Wilkinson's. He understood that some objection would be made to the competency of Gen Eaton; he wished it now to be declared.

Mr *Burr*. I shall not now raise any objections: I shall take my own time. When Gen Eaton's name was first mentioned, I believe that I informed the Court that I believed it to be in my power to disqualify him from giving evidence. I have been since in search of it, but have not yet come to it, in consequence of the absence of some persons, and the unwillingness of others to do their duty.

Mr *John Graham* was called by Mr. *Wickham*. Some questions of little importance were asked him. Q As you have announced yourself to be authorized by the government, and we suppose expressed the wishes and opinions of the government, I would ask you whether you did countenance the military arrests that were made there? A I certainly did not. I understood that arrests had been made, but I understood that the powers had not been carried into effect. I stated to Lieut. Peter, that it would be improper to carry it into force.

Some conversation here occurred respecting the introduction of the evidence of Gen Eaton, which closed the session.

Mr. *Hay* said he wanted to ask Gen. Eaton a few questions,

SATURDAY, September 26.

The testimony of General William Eaton.

Mr Hay We only wish that part of your testimony which you have not yet delivered You recollect that there was a part of it which was excluded by the decision of the Court.

General Eaton. I know nothing concerning Blannerhasset and Smith I have no recollection that their names were mentioned to me, till after the prosecution was commenced. All that I know of Burr's project to dismember the union, is already before the Court. After Colonel Burr had expressed to me the intended projects, already related, and overcome my objections, he went so far as to assert, that he would erect his standard at the seat of government Mr Burr enquired of me, with what officers of the marine corps, and navy, I was acquainted. I told him with most of them. It is impossible for me to remember distinctly every adverb expressed to me in the course of conversation, but this I perfectly recollect, that if he could *gain* the marine corps and secure to his *interests*, the naval commanders, Truxton, Preble, and Decatur, he would turn Congress neck and heels out of doors, assassinate the President, or what amounted to that, and declare *himself* the protector of an *energetic* government If that distinct expression was not used, (though this impression is strong on my mind that it was used in the course of conversation) yet he used such expressions as these, " hang him," " throw him into the Potomac," " send him to Carter's mountain " Mr Burr proposed to me to endeavor to *gain* the marine corps, and to *sound* Preble and Decatur, with whom I had been in habits of intimacy, but I had not been so with Truxton.

A circumstance now recurs to my recollection. He also desired me to gain a Capt Davidson, a very brave man, and who is as honest as he is brave Mr. Burr seemed to select a Mr Reynolds, a Lieutenant of marines, a handsome and excellent officer, whom he wished to engage. He gave importance to the subject of the marine corps, and he asked me with some engagedness, how the marine corps stood I answered him " make yourself easy Sir, the marine corps *stand* as they *should* stand " Here I beg leave to observe, that I never felt myself prepared to insult the honor of either of these gentlemen, by making such propositions to them, and if I had thought them corruptible, I was not yet prepared. I remonstrated with Colonel Burr on the fallacy of his hopes to engage such men as Truxton, Preble and Decatur, in the projects he had conceived Observing that these gentlemen were clothed with well merited honors, independent in their circumstances, and that *such* were not the *materials* for a revolution This Mr Burr admitted; but observed, that they were, undoubtedly, like others, conscious of the imbecility of the government; and like military men, would prefer, (I think that was his expression) a government of more energy, where enterprize would be encouraged, and merit duly rewarded.

I stated obstacles to the project, then in speculation, such as I thought insurmountable. I asserted that it would be impossible to find a party of men in this country, who would support him in projects of such a treasonable, and I think I said, murderous nature. He observed, that he knew better the dispositions of the principal citizens of the United States than I did He made re ference I think to the political divisions of the people   At this distant moment however, I cannot be positive I recollect to have mentioned to Colonel Burr, that I had lately travelled from one extreme of the continent to the other; and though I found a diversity of political sentiment among the people, they appeared united at the most distant aspect of national danger. He again recurred to the weakness and want of energy of the administration and to his own resources; he seemed to make his project meritorious, as he said, the degraded situation of our country required more energy in the government. he said that the blow must be struck; and if he struck it at that time and place, he would be supported by the best blood of America I observed that one solitary word would destroy him. He asked me what word. I said, "USURPER." He smiled at my want of confidence, and quoted examples from ancient and modern story. in which, I think, were named Julius Cæsar, Cromwell, and Bonaparte. Much speculative conversation passed, which I cannot distinctly recollect; but which went to convince me of the unprepared state of the people of these U. States to defend them selves against an energetic blow, which conversation was pretty much closed by this observation of mine, that if he should succeed at the seat of government, his throat would be cut in six weeks by the Yankee militia.

Cross-examined.

Mr. *Baker*. At what time was this conversation held ? A Between the middle of February and last of March, 1806 Q. Can not you come nearer to the time ? A. We had frequent conversations I received various notes from Col B. requesting to see me Our conversations were commonly held at the house of Mr Wheaton, sergeant at arms, where Colonel Burr boarded. I frequently dined at that house with gentlemen in Congress, and we some times passed an hour or an half before dinner in conversation. We had interviews at other times when the subject was started

Mr *Botts*. At what particular period was it Sir, that you exclaimed against the views of Col. Burr ? A As to time I do not recollect Q I mean as to the stage of your communication? A. It was when he opened his views to me of overturning the government. But through the whole of our intercourse I used such strong expressions of disapprobation against his plans, that Col. Burr ought to have been satisfied, he had no right to use *my* name Q. Was there no particular expression by which you conveyed to him, your unwillingness to associate in his plans ? A I have already stated to the Court, that my expressions must have convinced Colonel Burr, that I was not disposed for the enterprize. Q Was there no particular objection you made, more distinguished than any other, by energy of language ? A. None more so, than I have already stated, I did not think it good policy to awaken the suspicions of Colonel Burr ? Q. Do you recollect the time when you threw off the mask ? A. It was when I told him that the people were not prepared for his usurpations, that the very name of *usurper* would put him down, and although he might calculate on the weakness of some quarters of the union, yet there was strength in the north which would cut him off. When Colonel Burr returned to the subject of dismembering the union, the central project seemed to have been abandoned

Mr. *Wickham* You said that it was not your policy to be more explicit? Will you explain what you meant by that observation? A I have already given you an explanation of that, before the Court and the Jury, but I will repeat it I knew not that Mr Burr had made communications to any one else, and if I had positively declared that I would oppose him, I doubted whether he would not turn the tables upon me I had a further view, had Mr Burr, by means unknown to me, got his outrage upon the government in motion, I should have endeavored to have been near him. Q Was your conversation about the marine corps, before or after your throwing off the mask? A I think it was previous. My memory as to time, is not the most accurate, and as it relates to the question of time, I cannot be positive on the subject.

Mr. *Botts* Did you say that your toast was printed in a Springfield paper? A I was about to observe, with the permission of the Court, on that subject I never meant to be positive on that point. I am impressed with the opinion, that this toast went through the hands of Stephen Pinchon of Brimfield, and through him to said paper The toasts have been given to the public, and it is more than possible I gave it more than once Q. Who was the printer of the Springfield paper? A I do not at this moment recollect his name, though he is among the number of my friends

Mr *Wickham* Or the title of the paper? A "The Spy"

Mr *Botts.* You have detailed a number of harsh expressions you used to Colonel Burr Did he keep in perfect good temper all this time? A. Col. Burr, sir, has a powerful command of his muscles I did not, at all times, find that they were unruffled. I could read in his countenance, sometimes concern, sometimes solicitude, and sometimes a disposition to make a trifle of my objections Q. I think you said that it was generally your intentions not to disclose in your intercourse with Colonel Burr, that you were inimical to his views? A You understood me correctly. Q. But that, nevertheless, his muscles were sometimes ruffled? A. They were Q Were your conversations then of a nature to ruffle him? A I spoke to Colonel Burr with much plainness: and even if I had been cordial in my approbation of his plans, I should have sounded my objections, that I might have tried his force. I have done the best that I could for my country I have attempted to exert all my wisdom. It was a painful ground on which I was taken. I took the advice of two intelligent gentlemen (whose names I am at liberty to disclose,) and they did not think it advisable for me to make a full disclosure to the government, for my solitary communication would not avail against the weight of Colonel Burr's character, for, with all the evidence, even now before the world, I still feel the weight of that character.

Mr. *Baker.* And who were the gentlemen that advised you? A. The Hon. Samuel Dana and John Cotton Smith.

Mr. *Burr* Had we any conversation before the month of January? A It recurs to me that I spoke to you in Philadelphia, between the 20th and 24th December. Q. On this subject? A. I had a communication with another gentleman at that time of a very indefinite nature At Philadephia you gave me no distinct nor well digested ideas of the project, but you spoke of a Spanish war

Mr. *Martin* We must have that gentleman's name ; who was it? A. Jonathan Dayton.

Mr *Burr*. Had you any expectations or promises of a military command from government? A It is true that the chief clerk in the department of war, (though in confidential terms,) asked me whether I would accept of a vacant rank of Lieutenant Colonel on the establishment I answered that I would take no rank on a peace establishment There were no other overtures to me on this subject, but when there was a prospect of war, you, and other men, who, I then thought of, as I thought of you, proposed a command to me in case of war It is true that a gentleman near the government asked me if I would take a command under the celebrated General Miranda I asked him if he was authorized by government to make this proposition? He said, no I then observed, the question requires no measure, as I found that too, to be a project of darkness I was determined to know to what it all tended.

Mr *Baker*. Who was that man? A Dr William Thornton. I will ask the indulgence of the Court to make one observation It has been asserted by Colonel Burr, that it was his intention to disqualify me for the stand which I now occupy I shall remain here a reasonable time to indulge him in the attempt. It will not avail him *Let him look through all the pages of my life, he may find some errors and extravagancies there, but he will find neither felony, nor fraud, nor neglect of duty*

Testimony of General James Wilkinson

Mr. *Hay*. Will you be so good as to state the written communications made to you by Colonel Burr, and the oral communications of Mr. Swartwout?

General *Wilkinson* On or about the 8th of October of the last year, (1806,) I was sitting, in the evening, with Colonel Cushing, at his quarters, and with him alone, when a gentleman entered

Mr. *Hay* At what place? A. At Natchitoches. The gentleman enquired for Colonel Cushing, who rose, and received him He presented a letter to the Colonel, who broke the seal and read it The gentleman then announced himself to be the Mr. Swartwout referred to in that letter, and Colonel Cushing introduced him to me as the friend of General Dayton ; handing me, at the same time, the letter, a copy of which I have, and the contents of which I well recollect —(See Appendix *I*)

Mr. Swartwout took his seat, and informed us, that being on his way down the Mississippi for New-Orleans, in company with a Mr. Ogden, they had heard, at fort Adams, of the impending operations against the Spaniards, which had induced him to ascend the Red river in order to join me, and volunteer his services

in the campaign , and that Mr. Ogden had proceeded on his jour
ney to New Orleans Colonel Cushing retired for a few minutes,
and pending that interval, Mr. Swartwout slipped from his side-
pocket a letter and packet, or envelope, which he said he was
charged by Colonel Burr to deliver to me. I hold the letter in my
hand, and it is a formal letter of introduction of Mr. Swartwout,
by Colonel Burr

Mr *Martin* observed, that if any letters were produced, they
should be lodged with the Clerk, that both parties might have an
opportunity of inspecting them

Chief Justice Not unless they are read.

[The letter was laid on the Clerk's table]

General Wilkinson I enquired of Mr Swartwout where Colonel
Burr was? He answered, that he was in Philadelphia, or that he
had left him there Colonel Cushing returned, and the conversation took a general course After some time, Mr. Swartwout
withdrew, and I retired to my chamber , and in the packet or
envelope, I found a letter addressed to me in cypher, from Col.
Burr

Chief Justice. I did not understand you How did you get that
letter ?

General Wilkinson It was in the packet or envelope. This letter was principally in cypher , the closing paragraph however
was in the ordinary script. I resorted to the key and attempted
an interpretation of the letter I did not complete it; but discovered enough, in the course of the evening, to satisfy me, that
there was some *illicit* project on foot. I rose early in the morning and called on Colonel Cushing, my second in command, and
adjutant inspector of the army I stated to him that Mr. Swartwout had borne me a letter, the nature of which I explained, and
observed to him, that Mr Swartwout's declarations that he had
come to volunteer in the campaign against the Spaniards, were
merely intended to cover his real design I then communicated
to Colonel Cushing the measures which I should pursue , enjoining on him at the same time to observe the strictest secrecy.—
Were it permissible to be read, here is a statement of the facts
sworn to by Colonel Cushing. [The General at this time held in
his hand the paper marked *(J)* See Appendix]

Mr *Wirt* This statement is signed by Colonel Cushing, with
a certificate of his qualification, in legal form, annexed.

Mr *Wickham* An affidavit, forming no part of the case before
the Court, cannot be introduced

Mr. *Hay* General Wilkinson states, that on the morning after
the letter was partly decyphered, he stated to Colonel Cushing
its contents, and communicated to him the measures which he
should pursue These are *facts* detailed in that deposition, and
if the gentlemen do not wish to see them, there is an end of the
controversy. [The General proceeded]

One paragraph of the letter I observed was in the ordinary script.
[Here the paragraph was read by General W in the following
words. " He is a man of inviolable honor, and perfect discretion
—formed to *execute* rather than to *project*—capable of relating
facts with fidelity, and incapable of relating them otherwise. He
is thoroughly informed of the plans and intentions of—————,

and will disclose to you as far as you enquire and no farther.— He has imbibed a reverence for your character, and may be embarrassed in your presence. Put him at his ease and he will satisfy you "] I determined to avail myself of this reference, to obtain from Mr. S. that information, which I could not discover from the letter; that is, the object to which Colonel Burr explicitly directed his views, and in the course of several days I obtained from him, substantially, the following facts: that he had left Colonel Burr in Philadelphia, occupied day and night almost, in an object which he had in contemplation, that he lived in a retired part of the city, in a small house, with several rooms, where he received persons with whom he had to transact business, and that he saw no two persons at the same time.

He observed to me, that *Commodore Truxton* was frequently with him, and zealously engaged in this enterprize. He observed at the same time, that a man who superintends the public buildings at Washington, was also zealously engaged. He did not recollect his name, but on my mentioning the name of Latrobe, he said, *that* was the man. He said that he had been dispatched by Colonel Burr from Philadelphia, and had traversed the States of Ohio and Kentucky. I so understood the gentleman at that time, but have since discovered that he descended the river.

[Mr *Botts*. By whom did you understand that he descended the river? *A*. By a man who informed me that he had rowed him down from Pittsburg.] Another reason why I may have been mistaken, was this. He informed me that he had passed to Frankfort in quest of General Adair, for whom he had dispatches from Colonel Burr; and not hearing of him there had returned back to Lexington in pursuit of him, where he was informed by Major Waggoner, that General Adair (being ill in health) had gone to some medical spring; and that if he would wait a few days he might see him, that he did so, and so had an interview with him without incurring any suspicion, at which time he delivered his dispatches. He said General Adair was zealously engaged in the enterprize, and observed, " tell him I will write to him, and that I expect to meet him at the place, that he may depend I will meet him at the spot," or words to that effect.

Mr Swartwout proceeded to inform me, that he came to Louisville, and felt himself at a loss how he should reach me with the most certainty, that a rumor had prevailed that I had descended the river. Finally on the advice of Mr Floyd, he had determined to go across the country, under an expectation of finding me at St Louis. Accompanied by Mr. Ogden, he prosecuted his journey to Kaskaskias. Finding that I had descended the river, he altered his route. He procured a skiff, employed hands, and followed me to fort Adams. At this point I asked him, whether the sudden change of route might not expose him to suspicions. He said that to guard against this, he had wounded his horse with his penknife, and informed the people that his intentions were to have visited St Louis, but having met with an accident, he should pursue his original destination; which was to descend the river to New Orleans. On arriving at fort Adams, and discovering that I had proceeded to Natchitoches, he determined to follow me, and his friend Mr. Ogden (pursuing his route) went on with dispatches from Colonel Burr to his friends in New Orleans. Mr Swartwout informed that Col Burr, supported by a numerous and powerful association, extending from New York to New Orleans, was about to levy an armed force of seven thousand men, with a view to carry an expedition against the Mexican provinces; that five hundred men would descend the river with Col. Swartwout, and a Major or Colonel Tyler, that the boats were already built He observed, that this territory would be revolutionized where the people were ready to join; and that some seizing, he supposed would be necessary at New Orleans; that they expected to make their embarkation about the first of February; that they proposed landing at La Vera Cruz, and marching from thence to Mexico I observed to him that there were large sums of money in the bank of New Orleans.

He replied, he knew that, full well I observed "surely you will not violate private property" He said, " We mean only to borrow and return it again; that they must equip themselves at New Orleans; that naval protection would be had of Great Britain; that Commodore Truxton and the officers of the navy were so disgusted with the government, that they were ready to join; and that pilot boat built schooners were contracted for, on the southern coast of the United States for the service"

He enquired of me, whether I had heard of Dr. Bollman, and on my replying in the negative, he expressed some surprize, observed, that Dr. Bollman and Mr. Alexander had been dispatched from Philadelphia, by sea, to New Orleans with dispatches from Colonel Burr to me, and that they must have arrived Mr. S informed me, that he was obliged to go to New Orleans, and was also under engagements to meet Colonel Burr and General Dayton at Nashville on the 20th of November. I think Mr S left Natchitoches about 18th of October, for New Orleans as I understood.

It may be proper in this stage of my testimony to say, that the envelope which contained the cyphered letter from Col Burr, covered also two other letters To save misapprehension, it may be also proper to say, that when I speak of an envelope, it is in contra-distinction to a sealed packet. It occurs to my recollection, that a letter addressed to John Peters, Esq of Nashville, was enclosed in the envelope; as well as another letter, from General Dayton, in cypher. (See Appendix *L*)

Mr *Baker*. Do you say that General Dayton's was enclosed in another letter? A. No. I say expressly the reverse. It came with it.

Mr *Wickham* objected to reading the letter from Gen Dayton. He said, that General Dayton being absent, he had no opportunity of consulting him, or of ascertaining his wishes respecting it. If, however, there be no other evidence that this letter was from General Dayton, except that a letter was received by General Wilkinson, purporting to be a letter from General Dayton, it surely may be read. If the letter by itself would not be evidence, its being connected with others could not make it so.

Mr. *Hay* On that distinction I mean to offer it. If General Dayton were before the Court, he might require some other evidence as to the authenticity of that letter. General Wilkinson is telling his whole story he is to give his whole narrative, and all the circumstances will bear upon each other

The *Chief Justice* at first said, that if General Wilkinson could say that the letter influenced his conduct, it might be read; but finally, he observed, that on the motion now before the Court, it might be improper to read it If it be the intention of General Wilkinson to state, that certain conduct of his was produced by that letter, he may state that such conduct was produced

General Wilkinson. I must say this letter materially influenced the measures which I pursued

Mr *Hay* There is certainly a wide difference between this case, (*a mere examination before a Judge,*) and a trial before a Jury This letter may identify General Dayton with the meeting at the mouth of Cumberland.

General *Wilkinson.* Here is the letter, addressed to J. Peters, Esq and signed " A Stephens " It appears to be in a disguised hand , but, I have no doubt, of its being in the hand-writing of Colonel Burr. (See Appendix M.)

I returned from the operations against the Spaniards, the 5th of November ; and on the following morning—

Chief Justice. To what place did you return ? A. To Natchitoches.

On the morning of the 6th of November, a small Frenchman, (whom I had never seen before, nor have I ever seen him since,) presented a packet to me, and took his leave. This I found to be a letter from Dr Bollman, covering a letter from Col. Burr. The letter from Dr. Bollman, in his proper hand-writing, bears date September 27th, 1806, from New Orleans (See Appendix, *N*)

Here is the cyphered letter, enclosed by Dr Bollman ; and I find it an exact duplicate, as it professes to be, of the one received by Mr. Swartwout, with this variation—"Doctor Bollman, equally confidential, better informed on the subject, and more intelligent, will hand this duplicate " [This letter was laid upon the Clerk's table.] That letter also inclosed one from General Dayton.

Mr. *M'Rae* Of the same tenor as the former ? A No ; quite different This letter from General Dayton is partly in cypher, and partly in common script (See Appendix, *O*)

Mr. *Wirt.* Are you acquainted with General Dayton's handwriting ? A Perfectly.

Mr *Hay* How did you become acquainted with it ? A. From a long and familiar correspondence. Here is a letter from Gen. Dayton to me, introducing his son, which will shew the similarity of the hand-writing. [Here the General produced the letter of introduction] On the same morning, I received the following information from Natchez, in a letter from James L. Donaldson, dated the 30th of November, 1806. [Here General Wilkinson offered to read the letter, but it was rejected by the Court.] (See Appendix, *P*) In consequence of the receipt of this letter from Mr. Donaldson, and my reflections on the letters from Colonel Burr, I determined to concentrate my whole force at New Orleans as soon as possible [Mr. *Hay* said that he was willing, in order to save time, to wave every thing which related

to the operations of the army; and requested that General Wilkinson would proceed to relate what occurred at New O. leans.]
I proceeded from Natchitoches to Natchez, and descending from that place, reached fort Adams on the 18th of November; where I found Mr Swartwout, who had been taken ill on his route from Natchitoches to New O leans; and, for his accommodation, was invited by some of the officers to that place. He informed me, that Mr Ogden had reached that place on his way to Tennessee; but, being alarmed by the rumors which prevailed in that part of the country, he was afraid to proceed, and had halted there. I enquired of Mr Swartwout, whether Mr. Ogden had borne any letters. He said, that he had not, but that Lieut. Spence of the navy, had been sent some time before from New O. leans, through the country, with letters from Colonel Burr. I proceeded on, and reached New O. leans on the 25th of November, in the evening; and, on the 26th in the morning, I received this letter from Doctor Bollman. [Here General Wilkinson produced the letter—See Appendix, Q] This letter reminds me of a circumstance which I had omitted. The morning after I had received the letter at Natchitoches, I acknowledged the receipt of it in a short note, and informed him that I should be in New Orleans about the 20th. I did not call on Doctor Bollman till the 30th. After the ordinary salutations, I enquired, whether he had heard of Colonel Burr since his arrival. He informed me that he had not. I asked him, if he had heard of Lieutenant Spence's arrival in Tennessee. He enquired how I came to know any thing of Lieutenant Spence. I informed him that it was through Mr. Swartwout. He assured me, he had sent dispatches for Colonel Burr, by Lieutenant Spence, and that he had heard of his arrival at Nashville. He then enquired what part I meant to take? I observed, that I felt myself delicately situated. It was impossible that I could take any part, while I held my commission; and I was so circumstanced, I could not get rid of it. He asked me, what I thought of the competency of the force for the undertaking. I observed, that it depended upon a variety of circumstances—such as winds, weather, composition, and appointment of the troops; skill in conduct, the resistance of their opponents; and other causes, on which the success of military operations depended. But, I gave it as my opinion, that I thought the force insufficient. He said, that Colonel Burr had gone too far to retract, that he had numerous and powerful friends in the United States, who stood pledged to support him with their fortunes, and that he must succeed. He then enquired of me as to the state of the magazines of provisions in New Orleans. I observed, that, if Colonel Burr descended with the force proposed, they would starve, unless they brought provisions along with them, for I had before ascertained precisely the quantity then on hand. He said, that it was his opinion also, that there would be a scarcity of provisions; that he had written to Colonel Burr on that subject; and that he expected a supply from New York and Norfolk, where Colonel Burr had many friends. He said that he had noticed in the public prints the sailing of some vessels with flour, and supposed that they might be designed for that place. I did not see Doctor Bollman

afterwards till the 5th of December, the day after the arrival of
the mail; and I called on him to enquire the news. He said that
he had seen a letter from Colonel Burr, of the 30th October, in
which he stated he should be at Natchez on the 20th December,
with two thousand men, to be followed by four thousand more;
and that he could have raised or levied twelve thousand men as
easily as six, if he had thought them necessary. I then informed
Doctor Bollman, that if Colonel Burr came to New Orleans, I
should oppose him. He replied, they must come there for pro
visions and equipments. He observed, that Colonel Burr had
great confidence in me, but he did not know what had passed be
tween us, and asked if I could not make such a defence as would
cover my reputation, and still permit him to come. I replied in
the negative, and we then parted. Some few mornings afterwards, he called at my quarters. There was a gentleman in the
room, and I took him into the piazza. He said that he wanted to
know my determination. I expressed my surprize, and told him
that he knew my determination.

Mr *Hay.* While you were thus exacting from Dr. Bollman the
secrets of his party, were you taken any measures for the security of New Orleans? A. Yes. My orders and instructions
will shew what measures I deemed it necessary to pursue. For
these, I am responsible to the executive of the United States.

Mr *Martin.* Are the cyphered letters filed? A. Yes. Q. Is
the key finished? A. Here it is.

Mr *Botts* mentioned the situation of Mr. Tazewell, who was
summoned as a witness on the part of Col. Burr. He said, that
Mr. Tazewell had represented the situation of his family to re
quire his immediate return home. Mr Botts observed, that al
though he had introduced the request of Mr. Tazewell to be dis
charged, he should be compelled to oppose it.

Mr. *Tazewell* stated, that he had been unexpectedly summoned
to answer enquiries, he well knew, as to certain proceedings be
fore the Grand Jury, that he had just been informed of an occurrence in his domestic affairs, which made it indispensably ne
cessary for him to return home immediately, that there were
many gentlemen of this place and vicinity, of the Grand Jury,
as well qualified as him, to give evidence on the points upon
which he should be called upon to depose, as he possibly could be,
and who should be subject to no kind of inconvenience in attending. If he was to be examined at all, he requested that it might
be done, for the situation of his family was such, that he should
be compelled to return.

The *Chief Justice* said to Mr Tazewell, that he knew full well
it was not in the power of the Court to discharge him.

Mr. *Botts* said it was impossible to examine Mr. Tazewell until the testimony of Gen. Wilkinson had been gone through with.
It was not possible to know the importance of his evidence, un
til Gen. Wilkinson was cross-examined.

Mr *Hay* observed, that it was an unprecedented measure, to
introduce any member of the Grand Jury to prove what had
passed in the Jury room.

Mr *Botts.* We have not said for what purpose we mean to introduce him.

Mr. *Hay*. I presume that I may be permitted to *presume* for what purpose

Mr *Baker* said, he meant to speak generally of the propriety and convenience of giving testimony of what passed in the Jury room One good effect, at least, would result from it, that by introducing witnesses to prove what had passed there, it would prevent people from giving evidence to the Grand Jury which they could not support elsewhere.

Mr *Botts* called for the key to the cyphered letters of Colonel Burr General Wilkinson handed him a small pocket dictionary, and a paper containing certain hyeroglyphics.

Mr. Botts In the duplicate received by Dr Bollman, there is an erazure. Will you be so good as to explain the cause of it?

Gen. *Wilkinson* That erazure was made by myself, and the words afterwards introduced by me I have a deposition which will be more satisfactory than my own explanation.

Mr. *Botts*. Whose deposition? A Mr Duncans.

Mr *Wirt* then read the deposition of Mr Duncan.

The deposition of A L Duncan, a witness in behalf of the United States against Aaron Burr, taken at the request of the said witness, and by the consent of George Hay esq attorney for the United States in the district of Virginia, and of the said Aaron Burr, to be read in evidence, if required, on all trials, motions or other proceedings in course of law in which the said Aaron Burr shall be concerned at the prosecution of the said United States.

I consent that this affidavit may be read in all cases in which the United States are concerned against Aaron Burr in the same manner as above expressed

(Signed,)   GEORGE HAY, A.U S *for the Vir. Di.,*

During the commotions excited in New Orleans last winter what was termed Col Burr's conspiracy, and his associates and accomplices in that place, I was called upon in my professional capacity by Gen. Wilkinson for counsel and advice in some measures which he was about to adopt The temper and disposition which I had discovered in New Orleans, and the reports which daily reached that city from above, induced the belief that half measures were not suited to the times, and that the public safety required the exertion of extraordinary energies, I therefore urged the General repeatedly to the seizure of suspected persons, and the declarations of martial law. When Bollman was seized, I suggested to the General the expediency of transmitting with him a statement of facts, on oath, to justify the step, and to warrant his commitment He then put the letters which he said were written to him by Col. Burr, and which he also said were transmitted to him by Swartwout and Bollman, into my hands, on which, together with some further information and knowledge of their views which the General possessed, I framed the deposition which accompanied Bollman, intentionally omitting every thing which was calculated to inculpate the General, or which might by exciting suspicion, have a tendency to weaken his testimony. Having prepared the deposition, I presented it to Gen. Wilkinson to be deposed, who strongly and repeatedly objected to the omissions I had made, and urged warmly that the whole should be introduced. He also desired that a declaration of Bollman, with which he frequently interlarded his conversations, should be entered, viz " 'That he had come to New Orleans with views " to the settlement of lands on the Ouachita, and was a mere " spectator." And it was only after a full exposition of the sole objects of the document, that I could prevail upon him to depose to it. It is idle and absurd to impute any sinister intention to the omission, because on any trial which might ensue, it was known the original documents must be introduced as they have been. I recollect, during the winter, General Wilkinson was called before the legislature of the territory to give an account of the state of public affairs, and he informed me he had intended to submit to their inspection Col Burr's duplicate, he having erazed such parts as had been intended to implicate him, as he knew several of the members, and particularly the Speaker, to be interested in opposition to his measures, and for the promotion of such a state of things as were best calculated to favor Col. Burr's enterprize I understand that the erazure made on this duplicate was but partial, the General having determined to give oral information to the legislature, which employed him two successive days, and that he considered the duplicate unimportant, (whilst the original has been preserved untouched) excepting the short paragraph relative to Bollman, which is preserved in its original state, and the only words erazed " Your letter post marked 13th May, is received," have been re-inserted in the General's own hand On or about the 15th of August, since my arrival in this city, Gen Wilkinson put in my hands, and those of J. L Donaldson, esq four or five letters, observing to us, " I submit " to you those letters which I have not examined since I left St. " Louis, they are from Col Burr, I do not recollect their particu- " lar contents, but having received them in confidence, and know- " ing they blend personalities with politics, I have not permitted " myself to re-examine them, because I feel an insuperable re- " pugnance to violate the trust of any man. I give them to you, " here is the cypher, decypher them, consider their contents well, " and then inform me whether their promulgation may be neces- sary to my honor." We did so, and we gave the General our opinion, that the promulgation might be necessary and proper. From an examination of those letters, and the General's evident surprize, and prompt declaration of his ignorance when we communicated certain passages of those letters, it was my own and Mr Donaldson's opinion that he had but partially decyphered them.

In answer to interrogatories on the part of Col Burr, I recollect to have solicited the command of a party to Natchez for the purpose of arresting Col Burr, and believed from the instructions which the General possessed, together with the state of things at that period, that the measure was warrantable; and having seen several communications from the government to Gen Wilkinson and particularly that in reply to this letter of the 2d of October, I had no doubt of the sanction of government to any measures which were calculated to defeat the views of Col. Burr. I have seen communications of a confidental nature from the president to Gen. Wilkinson, and I believe in reply to the General's letter of the 21st of October.

(Signed,)   A L DUNCAN.

City of Richmond, sct.

Sworn to and subscribed before me, ⸦
 this 5th day of September, 1807. ⸧

(Signed)   *Henry S Shore*

         A True Copy.

                   Teste

(Signed)   WILLIAM MARSHALL, *Clerk.*

Q Was the letter exhibited to the legislature? A It was introduced; but I confined myself to oral communications Q. What was the occasion of the erazure? A To put it out of the power of a certain faction in the legislature, to whom, at that time, I intended to submit the paper, to conceal it from that faction who were opposed to my measures, and who, I believe, were inimical to the true interests of their country, and were labouring to excite suspicions that I was connected with Col Burr, in order to destroy the public confidence in me, and thus to defeat my measures At the head of this faction I considered John Watkins, Esq the speaker Having determined not to submit the letter, I restored the words Q Did you prepare any translation to submit to the legislature? A. No I only made notes Q Did you make a translation for any other purpose? A Only a partial and imperfect one Q For what purpose? A. To understand it Q Was there any other occasion for which a translation was made? A No Q. Did you make any translation for the executive? A. No. Q. Were those words, "your's post-marked 13th of May is received," erazed? A Yes. Q Where is the copy of your letter, covering a copy of that of Colonel Burr, and your deposition to the president of the United States? A It is among my papers.

Mr *Hay* Do I understand you correctly, when I suppose you to say, that the translation intended for the legislature of New-Orleans, was sent to the president? A. No (Mr Hay immediately observed that, on recollecting dates, he perceived that he had misunderstood General Wilkinson, that the letter was sent to, the president before the session of the legislature of New Orleans.)

Mr *Botts.* Do I understand you to say that this was your translation of the letter which was intended for the legislature of New Orleans? A. No It was Mr Duncan's

Mr Botts. Have you ever sworn that this was a true translation? A. No Only substantially so. (General Wilkinson. May I be permitted to offer a few words of explanation?) When Dr. Bollman was arrested, I will confess to you that I was so little acquainted with judicial proceedings, that I did not know it was necessary to do more than accompany him with a letter of advice I was about to send him off in this way, when Mr. Duncan suggested to me the propriety of sending forward a deposition to justify his commitment. I put the letter into the hands of Mr. Duncan, with the key, and he made out the interpretation. When Mr. Duncan presented the translation to me, I stated my objections to the omissions He urged me to sign the deposition. The time was urgent, the express waiting, and I confess that I feared a rescue. This did not give me much time to consult my understanding If I had, it is probable that I should have resisted the signing of the deposition, with those omissions, notwithstanding my confidence in the judgment and integrity of my counsel. I was, also, at the time, oppressed by domestic afflictions; and my mind was hurried and agitated by the painful and interesting scenes which surrounded me

Mr. Botts Were there variations between this original letter in cypher, and that sent on to the president? A Yes Mr Botts. Were they noticed by you, or by Mr Duncan in your presence? A. I suppose so, because I objected generally to the omissions Mr. Botts How was the cypher formed? A. It consisted of an American edition of Entick's dictionary, and of Hieroglyphics. Mr Botts Which was formed first? A The dictionary Mr Botts When was that formed? (Here General Wilkinson referred to a letter, without a signature dated in 1800, and said he presumed it must have been formed about that time) Mr. Botts, Do you know the time of the year? A I presume it was October.

Mr Baker To whom was that letter addressed? A. To myself Q By the same By whom was it written? A By Colonel Burr (General Wilkinson observed that it was a private letter, to which he had referred merely to refresh his memory, the concluding paragraph of which is, " when I receive your cypher and your address, you shall hear from me" Mr. Wickham insisted upon seeing the letter General Wilkinson refused; but said it was at the disposal of Colonel Burr, and handed it to him) Mr Botts With whom was the cypher formed? A Colonel Burr and myself, Mr Botts When were the Hieroglyphics agreed upon? A To the best of my recollection, the Hieroglyphics which refer to the alphabet were formed about the change of the administration, after the induction of the president The Hieroglyphics are divided into two parts, one part relates to the alphabet and figures, and the other part to arbitrary names of designations Mr. Botts When were the arbitrary names established? A I think in the year 1795 or 1796, but not delivered to Colonel Burr at that time. Mr Botts Who originally devised the cypher? A That you hold in your hand (the Hieroglyphics) was devised partly by myself, and partly by Captain Campbell Smith Mr Botts. Are you sure it was in 1796, in which that part was devised? A I think I said in 1795 or 1796, but could not ascertain which But, adverting to the motives which induced me to form it, I think it was in 1794 Mr Botts Are there no circumstances which can enable you to ascertain the time? A. I could have proved with certainty, the time, if a witness whom I had summoned had attended. Here is another cypher made by captain Smith in 1791; and the Hieroglyphics representing the president and vice-president are the same with those used in the cypher with Colonel Burr.

Colonel Burr. What was the mode adopted by you of sending round the prisoners? By public vessels? A No My plan was to engage passages on board private vessels, and to lay in a double stock of stores for their accommodation.

Colonel Burr. When did your dispatches go on board the vessels? Can you ascertain the time? A Not without recurring to my correspondence.

Mr *Wirt*. You had been for many years in habits of intimate correspondence with colonel Burr? A Yes

---

MONDAY, *September 28*

The Court did not proceed in the examination, in consequence of Colonel Burr's being unwell

---

TUESDAY, *September 29*.

The examination of witnesses was resumed, on the part of the united States, although Colonel Burr was still unable to attend on account of his indisposition.

Mr *Graham* observed, that when he was before the Court the other day, he had omitted he believed, to detail part of a conversation which he had with Mr. Blannerhasset. He was also apprehensive, that he had not been so explicit, in relation to his conversation with General Neville, as he could have wished He therefore requested permission of the Court to add a few observations by way of explanation

He said that Mr Blannerhasset observed, in the course of their conversation, that both Col Burr and himself believed that the people of the western country would be benefitted by a separation of the union, but they had found, that they were not ripe for the measure, and as they had no personal views, they were not disposed to hasten the event. I understood him to mean that the people of the western country were not ripe for the measure. I think Mr. Blannerhasset went on to say, that this was an event which must happen; but of this I am not so certain This conversation took place at Marietta.

Mr. *Hay* At what period of the conversation?

A. At the first conversation Indeed I had but one conversation with him Our subsequent interviews and conversations were merely casual.

Mr. *Hay* Was it at the first part of your conversation with him? A No. Towards the close, and after I had informed him that I was an accredited agent of the government.

I have some reason to believe that I may have been misunderstood with respect to what I said relative to General Nevill. Col. Burr had asked before, what conversation I had about a gentleman in the neighborhood of Pittsburg, before the Grand Jury, without mentioning his name The allusion was understood to be Gen. Nevill, and whenever I mention the name of a gentleman is my wish to state every circumstance which occurred as nearas possible. My recollection of the conversation with General Nevill is this After detailing the conversations which he had had with others, he said that there had been a strong prejudice against Colonel Burr about Pittsburg, that the people there were attached to the union, and they believed that Colonel Burr had intended to separate it. Afterwards he said there was reason to believe that the expedition was meditated against the Spaniards, and his visits might be more welcome.

General Eaton requested permission to introduce a letter which he had just received from *Stephen Pynchon*, esq of Brimfield, Massachusetts, stating with precision several circumstances with respect to a subject, of which he had before spoken doubtfully. See the letter at the end of General Eaton's evidence.

Mr *Wickham* I must protest against such a course of proceeding.

Mr. *Hay.* This letter I presume relates to the toast. The gentlemen have over and over again interrogated General Eaton, with respect to that toast; and now when he is able to state with accuracy, every material circumstance in relation to it, we are told that they do not wish to hear it.

General Eaton From this letter I am enabled to state, that when I passed through Washington in the month of December, 1805, on my way to the northward, there was some intimation that this project of separating the union was in embryo. A public dinner was given to Captain Decatur and myself in Georgetown; and I am pretty certain, that this toast was once given and originally there. As I passed through Philadelphia, sometime about the 20th of December, an application was made to me by a gentleman, whose name I presume I am not at liberty to mention here.

(Mr *Martin* We request his name. *Jonathan Dayton,* said General Eaton) He told me there was a project of a revolution in the western country, and hinted at a general revolution, and said he should introduce me to Colonel Burr. I had an interview with Colonel Burr, but he did not go so fully into the subject as General Dayton had done; he talked much of war and enterprize, and of an expedition against the Spaniards, and here the conversation ended at that time. I passed on to the northward, and entered the village in which I lived; and having received many civilities from my fellow citizens and neighbors, I gave an entertainment in return, at which I gave this toast. I was still ignorant of the extent of the project, nor did I positively know that Colonel Burr was then chief mover. On my return to the city of Washington, Colonel Burr laid open to me his whole views, as I have before stated. Then it was, that I wrote on for the paper containing this toast, for the purpose of laying it before Colonel Burr, and with it my sentiments of his project.

Copy of a letter from Stephen Pynchon to General Eaton, September 22, 1807.

My Dear Sir—The toast "palsey to the brain that shall plot to dismember, and leprosy to the hand, that will not draw to defend the (or our) union," about which Burr has asked questions, was as you have correctly stated, printed at Springfield. It was among other toasts, submitted to my discretion to publish, and was accordingly sent to Springfield, for that purpose in your absence. I sent you the paper, I think, containing the toast, when you were at Washington, in the spring or winter of 1806.

The sentiment was given by you, as a toast, at the time of your *entertainment* to the citizens of this place, as a compliment for what you termed *civilities* you had received from them.

I did think, and do still thing, that it was, when given, entirely new, and that it had never before been given by you to the public, in any other place. The sentiment was a bold and pleasing one to me, I accordingly selected it as one which would so appear to others I know not, that it may not have been published before. If it had been, that circumstance was unknown by me. At any rate it was published at Springfield by your permission, and given by you as a toast in my hearing in this place, and received my entire approbation; although I knew not the particular application of it, or the circumstance out of which I am certain it grew; I mean the conspiracy

I know not, Sir, whether this will ever reach you. If it should be so fortunate it may be serviceable I therefore send it

Your last letter, with its accompanying paper was enigmatic. I am, however, at no great loss to conjecture its meaning. I hope my conjecture of its import is correct At any rate no man can more cordially wish, that if it be correct, and an anticipated event take place God may be with you, and give you safe deliverence from evil

With him your friends must leave you, desire him to take charge of you, and conduct you to his happiness and glory No news. I therefore only add, farewell; and that I am very cordially, yours, &c.

S. PYNCHON.

Gen Eaton.

General *Wilkinson* addressing the Judge

From the rapidity with which the interrogatories were put, and the promptitude of my answers when last before you, I fear some misapprehension may have occurred; I therefore beg leave to explain the facts to which the interrogatories appeared to be pointed, which I trust I shall be able to do clearly, concisely and satisfactorily

The only explanation of the cyphered letter of Colonel Burr's, transmitted by Swartwout and Bollman which I have made, was done hastily and by piece-meal at Natchitoches: I think I have called this an imperfect interpretation, and I have done so, because, although it gave me their full sense, yet by omissions and abreviations, it could not be well understood by another.

On reflection, I think it was from this document, and not from notes, that the purport of Colonel Burr's letters were given to the legislative council and representatives of the territory of Orleans. I find the summons from the house bears date the 15th of January last, and I believe the examination commenced the 17th. It lasted two days, and therefore I cannot recollect the particular course or circumstances. I find by references to my papers, that certain documents were submitted to the Clerk to be read under restrictions, and it is probable I carried with me to the house, all the papers respecting the subject of inquiry.

I have some impression that this same document was proffered to the Grand Jury, to aid them in their interpretation of the cyphered letters of Colonel Burr, but I cannot speak with certainty This examination lasted several days, and like that before the legislative council and representatives of the territory of Orleans, was diffuse, desultory and complicated, and therefore it is impossible for me to charge my memory with minutiæ

The interpretation of Mr Duncan was made the 25th or 26th of December, 1806, twenty days before my examination by the legislative council and representatives of the territory of Orleans.

I did not transmit an interpretation of the cyphered letter to the president, but I well recollect explaining it to Mr. Isaac Briggs, the confidential messenger sent with my letter of the 12th Nov who was charged also to make oral communications to the president.

By reference to the original letter it will be found, that a deposition is attached to it; this was done preparatory to the transmittal of it to the president, as was my intention by a special messenger, but the fear that it might be lost changed my determination. I kept it in my possession, and brought it with me.

Referring to Colonel Burr's letter of the 10th of October, 1800, I have said that I believed the cypher depending on the book, was formed in that year, yet it may have been afterwards I perfectly remember, that about that period, Colonel Burr informed me he had to send one hundred and fifty miles for the counterpart of the book, and also in answer to a letter I wrote him from the frontier of Georgia, the Oconee river in the year 1802, he then being in Charleston, he informed me he could not write so free as he wished, as he had not the cypher with him

In accounting for the erazure of the duplicate of Col Burr's letters, I have mentioned the apprehension which had been exhibited of being an accomplice of Colonel Burr's, and that I was preparing for his reception This device had excited such alarm, and the friends of government were so incensed, that I was cautioned by Silas Dinsmore, Esq to take care how I moved, as I was in danger of being tar'd and feathered.

After General Wilkinson had finished his addresses to the Court, Mr. *Martin* asked him if he had the original translation of the cyphered letter of Colonel Burr? His answer was, I have not I have looked for it, but cannot find it

General *Wilkinson* then said, that he wished to present the deposition of Captain Walback, formerly a member of his family. It went to explain his very general habit of corresponding in cypher

Deposition of Captain J B Walback

I had the honor to become acquainted with General James Wilkinson some time in August, 1799; became attached to his military family in December, 1800, was appointed an aid-de-camp in the spring following, and continued in that capacity until the last of November, 1804.

During the above period, I have witnessed that General Wilkinson did employ cyphers of different kinds in his correspondence, among them was an English pocket dictionary. Several of the cyphers I have made myself; designed copies of some of them are still in my possession, and others I have recognized since my arrival at the city of Richmond, Particularly one to the late General James Jackson, another to the late Major General Alexander Hamilton, a third to a Mr. Hulings, then at New Orleans, a fourth to Colonel Cushing, a fifth to Mr Silas Dinsmore, and one to myself. Several of those were projected in 1802 and 1803, at the time the port of New Orleans was shut, and for the purpose of procuring and conveying intelligence to the government

Q Did you ever observe in General Wilkinson any act, or disposition, which marked inattention to his duty, as to the zealous and faithful discharge of the trust reposed in him as an officer of the United States? A From my own observation and experience, (being now nearly twenty-six years in military life,) I can declare that I have never known any officer more zealously devoted to the service in which he was engaged, and I can safely declare, that I have never seen an officer of General Wilkinson's rank, voluntarily and cheerfully expose himself to such privations, hardships and sufferings, in the course of his duty, as I have seen him meet with alacrity. Q Do you know the hand-writing of Captain C Smith? A I do. Q. Are these Hieroglyphics of his writing? A They are. Q. Are they the same which were employed by Colonel Burr in his correspondence with General Wilkinson? A They are the same which are employed in Colonel Burr's letters, shewn me since my arrival at the city of Richmond, and said to be delivered by Messrs. Swartwout and Bollman to General Wilkinson. Q. Do you recollect when Captain C Smith left General Wilkinson's family? A Some time in July, 1801. Q. Do you think General Wilkinson afterwards saw or was near him? A. I am certain not, because General Wilkinson did not return from the Mississippi until May, 1804, and Captain Smith resided in the state of Maryland, and died in the winter 1803 or 1804. Q Have you seen General Wilkinson employ the pocket dictionary, now presented to you in writing cypher? A I have. Q Will you say in what year? A. I am not positive as to the year, but it was during the period I was attached to his military family. Q Did you hear a sentiment from General Wilkinson, calculated to disaffect the troops, or to abate their zeal for its promotion? A No, on the contrary, I have witnessed that General Wilkinson always used his utmost endeavors to promote harmony, comfort and good order among the troops, and by his precepts as well as example, to insure subordination and patriotism.

(Signed)   J. B. WALBACK,
Capt Artillery.

I am content that the above shall be read as evidence in all cases between the United States and Colonel Burr, and that any thing that may be added by the affiant, by way of answer to interrogatories, may also be read.

(Signed)   GEO. HAY, Att'y U. S.
for the Richmond District

City of Richmond, set.

Sworn to and subscribed before me, an Alderman of the city aforesaid, this 5th day of September, 1807

Signed)   *Henry S. Shore*

Mr *Wickham*. Have you ever accurately decyphered the letter sent to the president? A. No. I have said before that the only interpretation I ever made, was hastily done at Natchitoches. Mr Wickham Then you are not able now to point out the differ ence between Mr. Duncan's translation and the original letter A. Specifically I cannot; *substantially* I can. Such parts were left out as were calculated to inculpate me for the reasons alrea dy stated. Mr Wickham. I observe one of the cyphers is in hie roglyphics designed in 1799 or 1801. A That is erroneous When the hieroglyphics were formed they were taken from a small slip of paper and annexed to that in your hand to prevent its being lost. Q. Can you tell when they were made A I cannot pre cisely. I have before stated the time as nearly as I can Q. Can you tell upon what occasion they were made? A For the pur pose of communicating with Colonel Burr Q. Do you recollect your having sent a letter to Colonel Burr, from St Louis, in May or June, 1806? I have such an impression, but have not the most distant recollection of its contents. [Mr. Wirt submitted it to the Court whether it could be proper for the opposite counsel to in terrogate General Wilkinson as to a letter which was in their own possession. If they meant to rely upon the letter as evidence they ought to produce it He considered it unfair to select such parts as might tend to inculpate General Wilkinson, and keep back those which would lead to an explanation of his conduct.] Mr Wickham said, it was their own paper, and they were not bound to produce it 'till they thought proper Their object was to cross examine the witness and see whether he was consistent with himself; this they had a right to do. The Chief Justice said, that the question would not be permitted to have any bearing on the cause unless the letter was produced Any thing drawn out of the letter would not be testimony unless the opposite party who had it in their possession would exhibit it to the Court But it was obvious that they had another object which was to ascer tain the consistency of the witness

Mr. *Wirt*. If the object be to shake the credibility of the wit ness, is it not fair to him and to the conduct of the cause to exhi bit the whole letter.

Mr *Baker* A very ingenious mode has been adopted by the gentlemen. We put the questions, and they undertake to furnish the answers, without leaving it to the witness to do it himself. We do intend to shake the credibility of General Wilkinson, and to make him produce the shake himself.

Mr. *M'Rae* I understand the Court to say that the examina tion as to the contents of the letter shall have no effect unless the letter itself be produced.

Chief Justice General Wilkinson says that he has no recollec tion of the contents of the letter. The subject matter of the letter cannot be established by the examination But the witness may be cross examined for the purposes avowed by the opposite coun sel

Mr. *Wickham*. Do you recollect that you did write to Colonel Burr in 1806? A. I have before stated that I have such an im pression; but I have no recollection of the contents of any com munication made to him, although I remember the motive which induced me to write

Mr *Wickham*. You have no recollection of any particular expression A. No. Except in a letter of October or November 1805—2. Q Have you any recollection of any expression or sentiment expressed in your letter of 1806. A. I have no recollection Q Was it your expression that we should have a war with Spain? A. It was my opinion, and there was a very general impression that we should have a war with that power Q. Do you not recollect writing any thing respecting the measures of the government, in relation to a war with Spain. Have you no recollection of any opinion expressed in a letter to Colonel Burr? A I do not recollect having expressed any opinion respecting the measures of the government The only expression I have any idea of, is one used in a letter of October or November 1805, in which, I believe I say " I fear Miranda has taken the bread out " of your mouth."

Mr Wickham There were letters published from you while in the neighborhood of the Spaniards Have you copies of those letters here? A I have the whole correspondence Mr Wickham We only want the letters of September and October, which state that war with Spain is inevitable

General Wilkinson. I think that I may have said so, and believe that I have papers here which throw some light on the subject Here are my instructions to the officer who commanded the troops when they left St. Louis [General Wilkinson handed to Mr Wickham copies of his instructions to Colonel Cushing]

Mr *M'Rae* What is the date of those instructions? A The 6th and 8th of May, 1806. General Wilkinson said that he would, with pleasure, submit the whole correspondence, if he could do it consistently with his own ideas of propriety. But there were contained in it, such secret military operations, as it might be improper to expose

Mr *Wickham* I think you state that at that time, the expectation of a war with Spain was very general? A. It was so. and if my instructions to Colonel Cushing can be read, they will shew my own impressions [Here Mr M'Rae read the instructions of General Wilkinson to Colonel Cushing of the 6th of May, 1806; for which, see Appendix, *R, S*]

Mr. Wickham I think you have said that there was an universal expectation of a war with Spain, about the time when the troops of that nation crossed the Sabine A. Yes I have said so I had made arrangements for a general attack. Mr. Wickham To what cause are we to ascribe the accommodation which took place between the two armies? A To a wish to spare the effusion of blood; and, perhaps, because on one side there was reluctance to fight Q. On which side? A On the side of Spain. Mr. Wickham. Can you tell the particular motives which induced them to re-cross the Sabine, and change their position? A I think I can explain them. Immediately on my arrival at Natchitoches on the 24th of September, I addressed a letter to Governor Cordero, whom I considered the Commander in Chief of the Spanish forces on that frontier. I communicated to him my orders from the president, and urged him, on the ground of right and of humanity, to withdraw his troops from the east of the Sabine and re-cross that river. Whether this or the vigorous preparations for the offensive opperations which I immediately commenced on my arrival at Natchitoches, produced the effect or not, I cannot tell. But the fact is, that the Spaniards about the 27th of the month, raised their camp at Bayou Pierre, marching by their right, intersecting the highway from Natchitoches to Nacogdoches, about twenty miles in front, pursued that route, and re-crossed the Sabine about the 29th or 30th.

Mr. Wickham. Was this after you had received the cyphered letter? A No. It was some time before. Mr. Wickham. Had you any correspondence with the Spanish commandant, on the subject of Colonel Burr's expedition against Mexico? A. None. The earliest communications which I made on that subject were after my return to Natchez. Mr Wickham Has the jurisdiction of the United States ever been exercised as far as the Sabine? A I cannot tell. Mr. Wickham Was it in consequence of instructions from the government that you concluded the convention with the Spanish commandant? A. No. Mr. Wickham. I do not recollect whether that convention has ever been published A Never Mr. Wickham Have you any copy of that convention? A Yes But until it shall be the pleasure of the government to publish it, I do not think myself at liberty to divulge its contents I do not think it reconcileable to the duty of a military commander to anticipate his government in the publication of official communications

Mr Wickham. Were there any secret articles in that convention? A None. There was but one article Mr Wickham Was there any sum of money agreed to be paid on either side? A. Not one cent Mr Wickham you note two letters to the president, one of the 21st of October, and the other of the 12th of November 1806 Have you a copy of that of the 12th of November, and will you give me leave to ask whether that letter was before the Grand Jury? A. It was submitted to the Grand Jury [Mr Wickham said that they called for a copy of that letter If the counsel on the other side thought proper to oppose it, they might do it at once

Mr *Hay* We shall certainly oppose the production of the letter. The president had been consulted on the subject; and he has excepted such parts as he thought it would be improper to produce The Chief Justice, remarked, that after the president had been consulted, he could not think of requiring from General Wilkinson the exhibition of those parts of the letter which the president was unwilling to disclose

Mr *Wickham* The whole letter having been before the Grand Jury, and acted upon by them, we certainly have a right to call for it also]

Mr Wickham Were the Spaniards in considerable force on the east side of the Sabine? A They were reputed to be so. Mr Wickham. What was the strength of the army of the United States? A About five hundred effective men. Mr Wickham. What orders did you receive from the government in the months of December and February last? A. I cannot say what particular orders I received during those months Owing to the frequent changes of my position, I was for more than six months without orders But it is impossible for me to answer the interrogatory to the extent in which it is put, without subjecting myself to severe military penalties. Nothing can be more improper or dishonorable than to divulge military orders of a secret or confidential nature.

[Mr. *Wickham*. There can be no doubt but under the sanction of the oath which General Wilkinson has taken, he may be compelled to give testimony as to the points on which he has been interrogated In England nothing is more common than for the most secret transactions to be disclosed in a Court of Justice. Considerations of delicacy in the witness have never been permitted to have any weight.

Mr *Hay*. There is a material difference Those were cases between individuals, this is a communication from the executive government. We are not at liberty to dive into the secrets of the executive department to know what orders they give to their agents, and to proclaim those orders to the world; orders which were given for the public good There can be no doubt but the public good does require that various orders of the government should forever remain a secret

Mr. *Wickham*. The gentleman did not understand my question I asked General Wilkinson what orders he had received from the government in relation to Col Burr]

Mr Wickham. Did you receive any orders to attack Colonel Burr and his party? A. That question may require some qualification Mr. Wickham Did you send any officer in disguise to take Col Burr? A I sent three Mr Wickham. Their names? [Mr Hay said, he did not think General Wilkinson was bound to answer such questions, that he was not bound to furnish evidence against himself or to subject himself to prosecution. Although he believed that the exigencies of the times would justify the measures with Gen. Wilkinson whether he would answer the question or not.] *General Wilkinson* If the question goes to criminate myself, I presume that I am not bound to answer it

Chief Justice. Would General Wilkinson be subjected to an action for sending to apprehend Colonel Burr, unless he had been seized.

Mr. *Hay*. It may go to criminate him as a military man. He may have acted without orders.

Mr *Wickham* I do not presume that he acted *without* orders; but under the orders of the government.

The *Chief Justice* said, that he could not perceive the application of the evidence, but, as evidence was introduced to shew the flight of Colonel Burr from Washington, this, he presumed, was intended to account for it.

Mr. *Wickham* Will you state the names of the officers sent to apprehend Colonel Burr? A Captain Hook, Lieutenant Peter, Lieutenant Mulford, Dr. Davidson of the army, and Dr. Carmichael of the Mississippi territory. Q. Did you direct them to go without uniform? A. I feel real delicacy in revealing my orders.

I think I did mention to them the propriety of going in the attire of private citizens to elude the vigilance of Burr's spies, many of whom were in New Orleans, and would give him notice of their departure from that place. It was also prudent to send them in that manner, that the jealousy of the Spaniards, through whose territories they had to pass, might not be excited.

They were sent privately, for the success of the enterprize depended upon it

Mr. *Wickham.* Did you give them written or oral instructions? A. Both. Q. Have you copies of the written instructions? A. Not here. Q. Will you furnish copies? [Mr. *Hay* objected to the production of those orders. He said that they had a right to impeach the credibility of the witness, but not to compel him to disclose the orders given to those under his command.] Q. Were these orders to seize Col. Burr wherever they could find him? A. They were sent on that service expressly. I think the orders were confined to Natchez, information having been received that Colonel Burr had taken up his quarters there. Q. Were there any orders to seize him even in Court? A. I cannot say, but presume there were not. Q. Were any private soldiers sent on this service? A. No. Q. Were any soldiers sent to Lieutenant Jones's gun boats? A. Infantry were furnished to supply the place of marines in all the gun boats. Q. Were any instructions sent by you that the men in Lieutenant Jones's gun boats should act? A. I gave Lieutenant Jones no orders, as he was not under my command. Q. Was Commodore Shaw considered under your authority? A. He was rather considered as co-operating with me, but he had a discretion of his own. Q. Was there a recommendation to Commodore Shaw to give directions to Lieutenant Jones to take any measures to apprehend Colonel Burr? A. I think the orders required him to do so. Q. What orders were given for the disposal of Colonel Burr? A. The orders were, that he should be put on board a vessel, and sent by the way of New Orleans to the city of Washington. Q. Were these orders written? A. I believe they were. Q. What orders had you from the government, or did you do it on your own authority? [Gen. Wilkinson took time till to-morrow to consider the subject and to examine his papers.] Q. When you were at New Orleans, were not letters addressed to other persons frequently brought you from the post-office. by whose orders were they delivered to you; were they opened, and with what view?

Mr. *Hay* thought that they had no right to ask such a question. It might be important between the United States and General Wilkinson. But it does not appear to be proper to interrogate him as to his conduct any where, unless it has some bearing on the cause; nor can a witness be asked any question, the answering of which might subject him to a prosecution. If we had introduced evidence on that point, they had a right to cross-examine him.

Mr. *Wickham.* We may suppose, without impeaching the credit of General Wilkinson, that he will give as favorable an account of his conduct as any man standing in his situation may be disposed to do. General Wilkinson has detailed a number of

very strong ground. We wish to shew that the General has the strongest possible motive to criminate Colonel Burr. We were permitted to ask him about sending officers in disguise to seize Colonel Burr : we wish now to prove some other seizures. This evidence has a direct reference to the case of Colonel Burr. If General Wilkinson took all these measures, it will surely have a tendency to weaken his testimony,

Mr. *Martin.* We mean to shew that General Wilkinson is identified with the government; and the government had declared they would justify him. We have a witness to prove the express declarations of the secretary at war, that General Wilkinson stood low with the government, till his energetic measures at New Orleans had raised him in the estimation of the president. They can only justify his acts by shewing an impropriety in the conduct of Colonel Burr. The more we shew that the constitution has been trampled on, and the rights of the citizens invaded, the more *they* will endeavor to shew the impropriety of the conduct of Colonel Burr, in order to justify it

Mr *Hay* Mr. Martin has avowed the motives of Colonel Burr's counsel to be, to identify General Wilkinson with the government. Admitting that General Dearborne had made the declarations ascribed to him, admitting that the president had formed that opinion of General Wilkinson, how can his answer to the question propounded, have any bearing on this case? Suppose General Wilkinson should say, that in consequence of the expected arrival of Colonel Burr, the agitated state of the country, and a knowledge that he was surrounded by the accomplices and partizans of Burr in New Orleans, he had taken letters from the post-office, (and he would only have done what he ought) how could it affect the present case? It is manifest that the answer of General Wilkinson must leave the question between the United States and Colonel Burr exactly where it was before.

Mr *Wickham.* When these questions were asked Mr. Murray before, they were thought proper, and he was even cross-examined by the counsel for the prosecution. The gentlemen. had ascribed to Colonel Burr improper acts. Now to impeach General Wilkinson's credibility, we shew that he has been guilty of violent acts. Is he not interested to shew the conduct of Col. Burr to be improper, in order to justify his own?

Mr. *Baker.* Suppose, says Mr. Hay, this declaration of General Dearborne to be true; suppose that Gen. Wilkinson did not deserve to stand high in the confidence of the government; would it not have any bearing on the cause, wou'd it not leave the question between the United States and Colonel Burr exactly where it was before? At one time the counsel on the other side seem willing to give the General up: now they stand forward as the champions of the worthy General. Suppose it be proved that he has thrust his hand, or directed others to do it, into the post-office and pillaged letters. Suppose it be proved that he has made erazures in letters, and then sworn that translations of them were true copies, which were as much like the originals as any other thing, and that he has sworn to this, that, and the other, whether true or false, will not all these things affect his credibilty?

Mr *Wickham* said, that it was a question entirely for the consideration of General Wilkinson himself. If he thought proper to answer the question, it was not the business of the prosecution, to interfere.

The *Chief Justice*, after making some remarks on the nature of the question, observed, that General Wilkinson was not bound to answer any question that might criminate himself.

[Some observations were made as to the extent of the opinion of the Court. Mr. Wirt supposed, from the decision of the Court in the case of Wyllie, that Gen Wilkinson could not be bound to answer the question. Mr. Wickham thought directly the reverse.]

Mr *Wickham* to General *Wilkinson* You have heard the opinion of the Court. Were or were not letters addressed to other persons frequently sent from the post-office to you, by whose orders, and were they opened, and with what view? Can you answer that question without criminating yourself? A I shall not answer that question. Mr Wickham Were orders sent to stop and examine travellers? A There were. These were the joint orders of Governor Claiborne and myself. At that time Colonel Burr was daily expected at Natchez with two thousand men, and I wished to cut off all communication between that place and New Orleans, in order to prevent him from receiving information from his adherents, and to gain time for strengthening our defences. The imperious circumstances which justified this measure I will relate. A general panic had seized the friends of government in New Orleans.

[Here General Wilkinson was interrupted by the counsel of Colonel Burr, who objected to his stating the motives which governed him.]

Mr. *Wirt* said, that if the witness were called on to accuse himself of arbitrary acts, he ought to explain the motives with which those acts were committed.

Mr. *Wickham* said, it was their wish to go on with the cause without being interrupted with the explanation of the witness; and after they had gone through, the counsel for the prosecution might ask for any further explanation which they deem proper.

Mr. *Wirt* observed, that he did not mean to interrupt the examination. But it was well known that the proceedings of each day are published; and it is important to the feelings of the witness, that he should state the grounds on which he proceeded.

Mr. *Martin* The proceedings have heretofore been published without regard to the feelings of Colonel Burr.

Mr *Wickham* to General *Wilkinson*. When did General Adair arrive in New Orleans? A. On the 14th of January. Mr. Wickham. Has your conduct in seizing Adair, Ogden, Swartwout and others, been approved or disapproved by the government? Have you received any communications from the government on that subject?

Mr *Hay*, It has been the constant effort of the counsel on the other side to identify General Wilkinson with the government. We have heard of the plundering of post offices, violating oaths, and prostrating private rights. Now it is asked if the government approved of these acts. Is it decorous, is it proper to pursue this course? They may ask questions to implicate General Wilkinson, but is it proper to endeavor to cast an imputation upon the government? I feel no solicitude on the subject; for when all the circumstances are considered, and the real situation of that country understood, though I will not say that the measures were strictly lawful, yet I will say the exigencies of the times called for them, and that the person who held the high and responsible situation of General Wilkinson, was bound to pursue the course which he did. General Wilkinson still retains the command of the army. If the gentlemen wish to infer from that circumstance, that the government approved of his conduct, let them do so

Mr *Wickham* It is not our object to criminate the government, but to obtain the truth We hope General Wilkinson will not say that his conduct has been approved by the government. Is this a State secret?

The *Chief Justice* said that he should be sorry to require an answer which would state the opinions of the government. He was sorry that an objection had been made to answering the question

Mr *Hay* said, he believed that the government knew nothing about it, and rather than that it should be supposed, that the administration directed measures which they were unwilling to avow; let them go on. He was willing that they should go on, and instead of making this an enquiry into the conduct of Colonel Burr and his accomplices, let it be solely, as it seemed to be, an enquiry into the conduct of the government.

Mr *Wickham* repeated the same question to General Wilkinson, whether his conduct in seizing Gen. Adair, Ogden, Swartwout, and others, had been approved or disapproved by the government, and whether he had received any communication from the government on the subject?

General Wilkinson said, he had no objection to answering the question, except so far as the answer might be considered, a disclosure of what might be deemed private instructions In the first instance, said General Wilkinson, I acted on my own responsibility. I have said that I was left six months without orders; but I seized no man under the orders of the President.

A conversation occurred on the subject.

General Wilkinson in answer to some interrogatories of Mr Wickham, respecting the arrest of Adair, Ogden, Bollman, Swartwout, &c. hesitated to answer, but not from any consciousness that he felt of having done wrong; he had no sort of objection to subject himself to the consequences; but as a military officer, and as a man of honor, he was bound to do that, which the interest of his country would demand.

In the first instance I acted on my own discretion I was left six months without orders, but accident produced the effects which have been seen, and the different transitions which have taken place.

Mr *Wickham*. Did I understand you to say, whether it was, or was not approved by the government?

General Wilkinson I should wish to be spared answering that question

Chief Justice Do you think that question interesting, or necessary? Unless that question shall be proved to have a direct bearing on this part of the case, I shall not persist

Mr *Wickham* The Court must see that it has a direct bearing on the character of General Wilkinson.

The answer was not pressed, and the Court adjourned.

WEDNESDAY, September 30.

On account of the indisposition of Mr Burr, there was no Court

THURSDAY, October 1

Chandler Lindsey was called by Mr Wickham

Q Have you had frequent conversations with Dunbaugh ? A Yes Q Have you lived in the house with him? A Yes, we have boarded together, since we have been at this place Q Have you had conversations with him, respecting his deposition ?

Mr *Wirt* objected to any answer being given till Dunbaugh would be present.

Thomas Hartley was then again called by Mr Wickham

Q What occupation were you following at the time you left Nashville ? A I was a taylor Q How came you to go down? A. I was to go down and work my passage Q Did you assist to cook, &c A Yes, always Q. Did you agree to go with him all the way to New Orleans ? A Yes, he told me that they were to wait at the mouth of Cumberland about two weeks

Mr. *Hay.* Who went with you ? A. Mr. Fort and Mr. Hopkins Q Did you know that they were of Burr's party? A. After I got to the mouth of Cumberland, not before.

Court Where did you come from ? A. I came down the Cumberland to the mouth of Cumberland, where we waited till the boats went off Q. Did the boat you come down in go off with them ? A. I do not know.

General Wilkinson was about to explain more fully some of the interrogatories put to him at his last examination, when he was interrupted by Mr Wickham, who declared that he felt no disposition to interfere with the explanations of the witness, but was very anxious to go on with the cause With respect to the motives with which any act was done, he knew nothing and cared nothing.

The *Chief Justice* declared, that General Wilkinson had a right to explain any interrogatories, and again repeated the substance of the opinion which he had before given

General Wilkinson proceeded—I have been asked, whether in October, 1806, I did not expect immediate hostilities with the Spaniards? I was required to account for the cause of the sudden change of position of the Spanish army? I was interrogated as to the convention with the Spanish commandant, and with peculiar delicacy I was asked, whether any money was received as a condition? also, whether I had not posted guards on the highways about New Orleans, to intercept travellers? To these interrogatories, quite unexpected I made such replies as I was then enabled to do from memory. By referring to my papers they will shew that I did expect a war with Spain, so early as September, 1806

(Here the General referred to an extract of his letter of the 8th of September, and his letter of the 4th of October, 1806, to the Secretary at war, which were read. See notes *T* and *V*)

On my advance to take command of the barrier post, I passed fort Adams on the 12th of September. There I found two letters from Colonel Cushing, detailing his correspondence with the Spanish commander, and was then asked for a copy of the convention. I am now about to do that, for which my country and gentlemen of my profession perhaps may condemn me. But under the charges and insinuations by which my character has been assailed, I flatter myself, that should I be guilty of any impropriety, the circumstances in which I am placed will excuse me.—Here are all the papers relative to that convention (General Wilkinson produced a number of letters, containing the correspondence between him and the Spanish commandants, about the time the troops of that nation re-crossed the Sabine)

Mr *Martin* said, they wished to have the papers, and hoped the Court would have no objection.

The *Chief Justice* observed, that he had no objection, but wished it to be distinctly understood, that he would not coerce the production of any paper, which related to a negociation between this country and any foreign government

Mr. *Martin* said, that would depend upon circumstances. He held it a sacred principle, that if the government thought proper to prosecute a citizen, they were bound to produce every paper which might be necessary for his defence, or give up the prosecution

Mr. *Hay* thought it would be improper to read the papers, because they related to a negociation with a foreign government, and because they had no relation to the subject before the Court. General Wilkinson had, indeed from the insinuations which had been made, been induced to produce those papers, but it was evidently done with a considerable degree of embarrassment, and would not justify the reading of them if it were otherwise improper.

Mr *Wickham*. I have asked for the convention with the Spanish commandant, but am told that it is a State secret. I concur with Mr. Martin, that when an individual is prosecuted by the government, no, State secrets should prevent the production of every paper necessary for his defence.

General Wilkinson said he wished it to be understood, that these were very imperfect translations of the letters of the original

Spanish, and therefore, that he could not deliver them but under the stipulation, that they should be accurately translated before publication, as he had discovered Governor Cordero, and Governor Herrara, to be officers of polished education from his correspondence with them. He had made this stipulation as a duty which military men owe to one another throughout the world.— These letters contain the convention; a convention without an article.

[The *Chief Justice* said, that he would not compel the production of the convention, unless its bearing on the case be shewn. Mr. *Martin* We have a right to it. I hope it will be noted that we have made a solemn demand of these papers.] General Wilkinson proceeded. The next question which was asked me, was whether I had not made private communications to Lieutenant Jones. I have said that I gave no orders to Lieutenant Jones but if I had, here are documents to shew, if not a justification of any conduct in all the measures, I presumed, at least an extenuation. [Here General Wilkinson presented several papers shewing the agitated state of New Orleans, and the dangers with which it was threatened. They were not read. See Appendix T. and W.

Mr *Wickham* to *General Wilkinson* Do you recollect the last question I put to you? has your conduct in seizing Swartwout Bollman, Ogden, and Adair, been approved or disapproved by the government, and have you received any communications from the government on this subject?

General Wilkinson said, he must refer to his honor, to know whether he was bound to answer that question.

[The *Chief Justice* declared, that it might be answered under the restrictions already laid down.]

General Wilkinson I can say that three of those persons, perhaps four, were seized on my own responsibility, without any orders from the government.

Mr. *Wickham* Which three? A. Bollman, Swartwout, Ogden and perhaps Adair.

Mr. *Wickham* Had you any orders then, or afterwards to seize them; had you any orders with respect to the seizure of Colonel Burr by military force? A. No—not at that time. Q. Had you any afterwards?

General Wilkinson That is a question of very great delicacy with me, (addressing himself to the Judge) can a question be fairly put and an answer coerced, which may destroy a man's honor?

Mr *Wickham* said, that there was no rule of law, which prevented a witness from giving an answer, unless it subjected him to a criminal prosecution. Mere sympathies were no cause of refusal. However unpleasant these questions might be to General Wilkinson, it would be a shameful dereliction of duty in the counsel of Colonel Burr not to put them. He said that he had not experienced any sympathies towards his client.

General Wilkinson to the *Judge* Is a trial before a Court Martial similar to criminal prosecution? I might be subjected to military punishment, to as severe punishment as could be inflicted by a civil tribunal for revealing my orders.

The *Chief Justice* said, that he was not sure that General Wilkinson could be required to answer that question.

Mr. *Wickham* contended that there could be no articles of war, which could punish a man for disclosing what he is called upon to declare in a Court of Justice. The Court had a right to require the disclosure, and would enforce its own authority.

Mr. *M'Rea* contended, that when the answer required would lead to the discovery of a fact, which might subject a man to a punishment, it was always deemed a good reason to withhold it. He understood the answer, which might be given by General Wilkinson to be of this nature. The question was calculated to extract from him a fact, the disclosure of which might tend to subject him to punishment. He could not say what would be done before a military tribunal, but it was possible that he might be punished if he answered in a particular way. Suppose he should say, that the government did not authorize him to seize the persons of Burr and his accomplices: and that he acted upon his own responsibility ; or suppose he should be acting under the authority of government, but upon examining his powers should find that he has transcended them ; would not a disclosure of this fact criminate him, and subject him to prosecution ?

The *Chief Justice* said, that the question did not lead to the fact of seizing those persons, but to the authority with which it was done. If General Wilkinson had committed the act with authority, he must shew his orders.

Mr *Wickham* said, he did not believe any thing which General Wilkinson could say would be legal evidence in the cause. It was not that kind of evidence which was admissible in prosecutions of this nature. But it was important to know what orders the government had given, and whether he had exceeded those orders.

Mr *Martin*. We wish to know the conduct and character of the government on this occasion. We wish to know whether any, and what orders were given by the government. Is there to be one rule as to the prosecution, who wish to take the life of a man away, and another rule as to the man whose life they seek to take ? Mr. Hay had no objection to an answer from General Wilkinson as to the conduct of the government throughout. He said that Mr Martin had disclosed his real object to be, to try the government, and not the accused. Will this ascertain the innocence or guilt of Colonel Burr ? The object evidently was to arraign the government before the bar of the public ; but he was perfectly satisfied that when the conduct of the government should be known, the people of the United States would think that the government had done exactly what it ought to have done.

[Mr. *Wickham*. In commenting on the evidence we shall endeavor to shew that a number of witnesses have been brought forward by the government who have taken a most decided part in the prosecution; and that their real object has been to render themselves acceptable to the government.] General *Wilkinson*. I had an order from the government.

Mr. Wickham. From what department ? A. From the administration. Q. From whom ? A. From Mr. Jefferson. Q. Have you any written order ? A. I have among my papers, but I will not produce it. I had rather go to jail. Mr Wickham demanded the production of the order; but said that if General Wilkinson required time to consider of the consequences of a refusal, he had no objection to allowing it to him General Wilkinson, (addressing the Judge) you are from professional experience more competent to decide on the propriety of revealing my orders, than I possibly can be The letter which conveys the particular order alluded to, may embrace a variety of other matter, many parts of which it would be highly criminal in me to divulge. I conceive I should forfeit my honor and the confidence of all military men, if I were to reveal my correspondence with the government, without the command of my superior. (Mr. Hay had no doubt, but the order was in strict conformity with law, but if there be private and confidential communications in the letter, it would not be required of General Wilkinson to produce it.

Chief Justice If the order be mingled with other things, private and confidential, the Court will not require its production) Mr. Wickham to General Wilkinson. Did you by letter or otherwise, request any person not of the army to seize Colonel Burr, and put him on board a vessel ? A I gave instructions to a gentleman who is now here, Silas Dinsmore, Esq and who is not of the army Q. Did you give such orders to others ? A I recollect Dr. Carmichael, but no other person, except the officers of the army. Q. Do you recollect expressing to any person that he would confer the highest obligation on the government by seizing Colonel Burr ? A. It is probable that I did, for those were my sentiments. My great object was to apprehend him, and deliver him over to the civil power for trial; and the City of Washington was the place to which I wished him sent But I had no idea of doing an injury to his person I recollect a German came to me and proffered to take Colonel Burr; but on coming to particulars, he said he would take him dead or alive I was shocked at the idea, and declined employing him. Q Have you the cypher No. 2d. A. I have not. Q Are you acquainted with a person by the name of Kibby ? A I am acquainted with two of that name ? Q Where do they reside ? where does Timothy Kibby reside ? A. In Louisiana. Q. Have you had any communication with him on the subject of an invasion of Mexico, and when ? A. I cannot recollect. I have seen a deposition ascribed to him, inserted in the public prints replete with falshoods. Q. You are not certain then whether you ever wrote to him on the subject ? A I am certain that I never wrote to him specifically on that subject He was an officer of the militia and I might have corresponded with him on some matters relating to his command I recollect to have received an order from the government to ascertain the strength of the militia in the territory, and I might have spoken or written to him on that subject. Q Can you say whether you did or did not ? A. I cannot Q Did you inform him of the object of Lieutenant Pike's expedition ? A. I think not, from the deposition I have seen. Here are my orders to Lieutenant Pike. [General Wilkinson produced his instructions to Lieutenant Pike. See Appendix *X. Y.*]

This is the information given by me to General Samuel Smith, which goes to illustrate my ideas of the state of our controverswith Spain [Here General Wilkinson read the extract of a letter, annexed, marked Z]

Mr *Wickham.* You mentioned that Swartwout was with you about the first of October? General *Wilkinson* I think about the 8th or 10th. I believe I have said the middle, because I marched on the 23d, and Swartwout had left me some days before

Mr *Wickham* Your letter to the government is of the 21st of October, will you assign a reason for so long delay? A I took time cautiously to draw from Mr Swartwout what information I could obtain, lest I should excite suspicion Another circumstance was, that I was busily engaged in making arrangements of the artillery transports, and other military equipments in order to take the field Mr *Wickham* You say in your letter to the president, that " you are not only uninformed of the prime mov-" er and ultimate objects of the daring enterprize, but you are ig-" norant of the foundation on which it rests, of the means by " which it is to be supported, and whether any immediate or col-" lateral protection, internal or external is expected ' I beg leave to ask, why you stated this to the president, after getting the information you did, from Swartwout? A. The answer is very plain, but the question is complex If you will dismember it, I can answer it Mr *Wickham* read an extract from the letter (being part of that just quoted) and said, I think this is different from the information you gave the Court General *Wilkinson.* I doubted the information I received from Swartwout. I could not suppose that Colonel Burr or any other individual would have the audacity or folly to undertake such an enterprize without the assistance of some foreign power. I could not, therefore, view him as the prime mover, but as the instrument I doubted Swartwout's declarations, and although they had an effect upon my mind, I could not place solid confidence in them He said that the people of the territory were ready to join He was a stranger in the country, and therefore could know nothing of their dispositions but from information I was acquainted with them, and had heard of no such disposition. Mr. *Wickham.* Then you doubted whether Swartwout was authorized to make these communications? A. I beg your pardon I believe that he was authorized, and instructed to deliver me lessons of falshood Mr *Wickham.* Then you say that you still doubted? A It is so expressed in the letter Mr *Wickham* These expressions, I understand, conveyed the true state of your mind at that time. General *Wilkinson* I wish you to understand me. When I contemplated the audacity, 'the iniquity and the folly of the enterprize, I did believe that Colonel Burr was stimulated by some foreign power. With respect to revolutionizing the territory, I could not place any solid confidence in it, until I received the communication of James L. Donaldson, esq when combining all the circumstances I wrote my letter of the 12th of November. Mr. *Wickham.* Then I understand you to say that this was the true state of your mind at that time? General *Wilkinson* Yes. Propounding this question brings to my recollection a subject not thought of before. I enquired of Mr. Swartwout from whence Colonel Burr derived his funds He said, from the aid of friends, and the sale of property, in which sale he had been employed I knew that Colonel Burr had no property. This declaration of Swartwout gave me less confidence in his communications Mr. *Wickham* I observe in your letter of the 21st of October, this expression, " my desire to avert a great national calamity " At that time you had doubts whether the enterprize might not be salutary ' Gener. l *Wilkin son* Would it be improper to assign my reasons why I supposed it might be salutary ' As I passed through Natchez, I understood that Mr. Meade, who exercised the functions of governor had spoken of an attack on the Spanish post of Baton Rouge, and I was informed by a Mr Dunlap and a Mr Smith, that he had said the government would connive at the measure

Mr. *Wickham.* The postcript on the letter Should Spain be disposed to war seriously with us, might not some plan be adopted to correct the destination of the associates, and by a suitable appeal to their patriotism, engage them in the service of their country ' I merely offer the suggestion as a possible expedient to prevent the horrors of a civil contest. And do believe, that with competent authority I could accomplish the object " Am I to understand that this postscript contains the true state of your mind at that time ' A. There is some uncertainty whether that postcript is a part of the original letter It is noted on the corner in my own hand writing, and not in that of Mr. Burling, who was then one of my aid-de camps, and by whom the copy was made [Mr. Baker It never was understood that a copy would be received by Colonel Burr Now we see the necessity of having the original] General *Wilkinson* I have no sort of hesitation to state what my feelings were If the Spaniards had been seriously disposed to war, I did believe that by a suitable appeal to the feelings and patriotism of the deluded citizens who might have descended with Colonel Burr, they would have been induced to join our standard, and oppose a foreign enemy sooner than enter into a conflict with their own countrymen. My idea was this, that the president would have forwarded to me blank commissions to be offered to influential leaders. Mr. *Wickham.* This postscrip says nothing as to leaders, but to the body in general. General *Wilkinson* I cannot give any definite idea of my sensations at the moment I think I could not have meant leader, but the leaders Mr *Wickham* If you were ignorant of the intentions of the leaders, why not as well apply the expression to the leader ? A. Because I did not think I could offer any thing to him which he would accept Mr *Wickham.* As to the postscript, you are uncertain whether it was written at the time of the original letter Mr *Wilkinson* Though I am uncertain of that, yet I believe contains a correct representation of my feelings. Mr. *Randolph* In case of actual hostilities were you authorized to accept the services of volunteers ' A I should certainly think I had Mr *Randolph* And to commission them? A. No But I might have mustered them. The president has no power to grant commissions, but with the approbation and consent of the senate. I recollect that during the administration of Washington, volunteers were accepted There were no commissions granted, but was ants of authority which were obligatory in those corps, but conferred no command over an officer of the line. Mr *Randolph*, My question is this, if hostilities had been determined on with the Spaniards, would general Wilkinson have been authorized to accept the services of volunteers? A. I think so at present; but a reference to my instructions will more fully shew. Mr. *Randolph* And to drive the Spaniards beyond the Sabine and pursue them into Mexico? A. Not to pursue them beyond the Sabine. Q. If the Spaniards had not made the convention and receded from their position on the east side of the Sabine, would you have attacked them? A. Yes. Q. From your own responsibility, or the orders of the government? A. from specific instructions. I had contemplated the possibility of such an event, and had given my orders accordingly. [These orders were not offered in evidence, but may be seen in Appendix, &]

Mr *Martin* Did you drive them beyond the Sabine? General *Wilkinson* (smiling) said it was a sort of driving.

Mr. *Wickham* You say that the first intimation you had of Colonel Burr's designs was from the cyphered letter? General *Wilkinson* I have said so. But I had received a number of ambiguous hints before. Q. In what way? A. By letter. Q. When did you communicate the contents of this cyphered letter to the government? A. You will observe in my letter of the 12th of November, reference is made to a confidential messenger, Mr Briggs, to whom I repeatedly read the cyphered letter, to enable him to communicate the contents to the president. Q. What communication did you make through Mr Briggs was it Mr. Duncan's translation? A. No. Mr. Briggs left Natchez immediately after the date of my letter of the 12th of November. Mr. Duncan's translation was made in New Orleans after I arrived there. Q. Have you the paper about you containing the instructions to Briggs? A. I gave no instructions to Briggs except verbal ones. Q. Have you the translation made by you? A. No. I have looked for it, but cannot find it. Q. Was it before the Grand Jury? A. Yes, it was an old worn out paper. Q. Was this information by Briggs an exposition of the whole contents? A. I read the heads to him, and verbally explained the contents. Q. Was the letter completely decyphered? A. I have said *no*, frequently. I have said that the only interpretation made by me was hastily done at Nachitoches. Mr. Wickham. Then you did not relate the whole contents to Briggs? A. I laid it before him, and explained the contents as already stated.

Mr *Randolph*. I think in this letter you say, " Miranda has taken the bread out of your mouth." A. No. You are quite mistaken. That letter was written, I believe, in October 1805. Mr. Randolph. Admitting it to have been so far back, how came it to be a matter of surprize to you, that an expedition was set on foot according with your own ideas; or that you should say Col. Burr's views were not distinctly known till you received the cyphered letter? A. I had received a number of ambiguous letters from Colonel Burr; and in a letter of mine to him, I made use of the expression " I fear Miranda has taken the bread out of your mouth," in order to draw from him his real object. Q. In what manner did you consider Miranda as taking the bread out of his mouth ? A If I can state the grounds of those opinions, I would say that they were derived from letters received from Colonel Burr ; which I am not at liberty to disclose. Mr Randolph. Was the position taken by the Spanish forces considered by the president as an invasion of our territories ? A. Certainly.

Mr M'Rae. I understood that opinion was founded upon what appeared in the public prints

General Wilkinson. The president's orders were explicit to drive them out of the territory claimed by the United States These orders I communicated to the Spanish commandants.

Mr Randolph. In the intercourse between you and the Spanish commandants, were all the forms of war observed? General Wilkinson. In what respect ? Mr. Randolph As to military interviews I considered this a state of war. A. Between Nachitoches and Nacogdoches, there was a constant intercourse Mr. Randolph. But in the relation of one army to another ? Gen. Wilkinson. I can state the situation I remember that the day on which I reached the Sabine, my advanced guard captured three Spaniards without arms on the left flank I had them returned to the Spanish commandant, and desired that he would not permit a repetition of the trespass.

Mr Wickham I think you said that you wrote to Colonel Burr from Nachitoches General Wilkinson When did I say so ? Mr. Wickham I thought I heard you say so. General Wilkinson. You guess well , but if I am not mistaken, you got that information from Swartwout. Q Did you write ? A. I did Q. What did you do with the letter ? A Destroyed it Q. Did it go out of your hands ? A It did. It was sent to Natchez ; to which place I followed, recovered and destroyed it. I will give you my reasons for doing so. After writing, I received the letter from Mr. Donaldson, dated the 30th of Oct. and conveying the information received from Myers Michael, which removed my doubts as to the extent of Mr. Burr's designs and their sinister nature. Mr Wickham Then I understand you to say, that Mr. Donaldson gave you the first correct information. A It excited very strong apprehensions in my mind, that some general and deep-rooted conspiracy had taken place above Mr Wickham You have no recollection of the letter of the 13th of May ? A. No I wish it could be produced It would release me from all obligation to withhold the confidential letters of Colonel Burr. Q. Did you write him any other letters? A. I have an impression on my mind that I wrote him two or three letters Mr. Wickham. The cyphered letter gave you the first idea of a plan of revolutionizing the western country? A The cyphered letter gave me no information on that subject. Mr. Wickham. Did you ever give the government any information before ? A. I had no definite idea of Colonel Burr's plans. I had received from him several letters of a very ambiguous cast, but they contained nothing treasonable. I wrote to a minister (Robert Smith) and in my letter say, " Burr is about something, but whether inter-" nal or external, I cannot discover. I think you should keep an " eye to him." Mr. Wickham. When was that letter written ? A I cannot tell when I wrote it. Q. When was Colonel Burr at St. Louis ? Colonel Burr was at St Louis on the 11th of September, 1805, and left that place on the morning of the 19th. In the interim he had been in that part of the country where Kibby lives, though I do not know that he saw him Q. Which Kibby? A The fellow who gave the deposition which has been published Q What is the date of your orders for descending the river? A. I cannot tell. Q. Have you those orders here? A. I am not certain; most of my papers are in Williamsburg, the troops descended in the beginning of May Q Did you authorize any officer to arrest any person after you descended? A. No I gave instructions to Lieutenant Peter, whom I had left at Natchez, and required him to give me regular information.

He read the following deposition of Lieutenant Peter

I arrived at Natchez about the 27th of October, from the Missouri, where I received a letter from Gen Wilkinson, dated Nachitoches, 23d October, 1806, directing me to dispatch an express with a return of my detachment, and to fall down to fort Adams and take the command of that post I arrived at fort Adams about the 3d November, and took command from Lieut. Sever, on my arrival I found a Mr. Swartwout confined in the doctor's quarters, with a violent attack of the billious fever I was introduced to him I think by Dr Davidson, who informed me that Mr Swartwout had been at Nachitoches, and on his return to the mouth of Red River, had been violently attacked, and sent up to the garrison for medical aid, that he had gone down to see him, and found him in a dreadful hovel, and had advised his embarking on board a barge, which was ascending to the fort, where he could be more comfortably situated, and have his constant attendance. On the 12th, I received letter No. 1, hereunto attached, dated, Nachitoches, 6th November, this was handed me by Lieut. Graham, who informed me of the termination of the expedition to the Sabine, and that the troops were then on their return   Letter No. 2, hereunto attached, informed me of the return of the General to Natchez, which created some anxiety in my mind in consequence of the orders exacting secrecy and ordering boats for the movement of all the military stores from fort Adams. On the 15th several of the officers arrived from Nachitoches and and visited their families, who were all at a loss to account for the rapid movement of the troops from Nachitoches to Orleans, and the embarkation of the military ordinance stores at fort Adams, confirmed us in the belief that danger was apprehended from some quarter, and that Orleans must be the point of attack. We continued in this situation until the morning of the 18th, when the General arrived and requested me to walk with him to the battery, where he communicated to me the designs of Colonel Burr, informing me that he had received several letters from Colonel Burr through one of his agents (Mr. Swartwout) and that Burr's principal attack would be upon Orleans; I was never more astonished, not having heard that any suspicions were entertained against him; I informed the General the situation in which I had found Mr. Swartwout on my arrival, and requested leave to arrest him. The General refused, saying that he expected to get much more out of him, that he had held out to Swartwout the idea of his not opposing Col. Burr, and that he should assemble his whole force at Orleans, to enable him to defend that place and defeat the whole plan I was directed to continue my civilities as before, for fear that Mr. Swartwout might get alarmed at the movement of the troops and military stores. On the 19th I received orders to proceed with my command to Natchez, with instructions to take the necessary measures to ascertain the approach of a body of armed men from the Ohio country and to give the General the earliest information by express, of every movement from that quarter, either at Natchez or by sending a confidential party up the river above the Yazou, in the disguise of hunters, and I accordingly communicated regularly every information I could collect. About the last of December, I saw two letters, one from the post-master of Nashville, to Henry Turner of Natchez, dated the 18th December, stating that Col Burr was then in Nashville, and that he meant to proceed, on the 20th, to the mouth of Cumberland, where report said, he would have assembled from five to eight thousand men, and that it was generally believed that he intended a visit to Mexico. The other letter to a Mr. Wood from Nashville, spoke of Col. Burr's being in Nashville; that two of his proselytes had left town that morning for Orleans by land, from the best of my recollection the above statement of the letters to Turner and Wood is correct, and Col. Burr's arrival every day expected, by all persons at Natchez. For my own part I did not doubt it, and considering this information as all important to the General, I proceeded for Orleans, arrived there on the second January, and communicated it to him Soon after this information was corroborated by the arrival of Bradford, the printer of the Gazette Orleans.

GEORGE PETER

County of Washington, Sct.

On this 19th day of September, 1807, George Peter came before me, a Justice of the peace for the county aforesaid, and made oath on the Holy Evangelist of Almighty God, that the facts stated in the foregoing, are true as stated.

THOMAS CORCORAN

At the time I descended the river we had no posts except the Chickasaw Bluff on the Mississippi, and Massac, near the mouth of the Ohio, except a small party at the Arkansaw, and another opposite to Cincinnati.

Mr *Hay* Was there any post between the Chickasaw Bluffs and Massac ? A. No Q. Was there any military posts between Pittsburg and New Orleans. A. None except those which I have mentioned.

Mr. *Wickham* asked General Wilkinson, for his alphabetical cypher, who went to his lodgings for it.

In the mean time, the Court examined GABRIEL G VAN HORNE.

Witness.—I was at the Chickasaw Bluffs, at the time of Colonel Burr's descent down the river. On the 4th day of January, 1807, Lieutenant Jacob Jackson, came to the United States' factory, at fort Pickering, accompanied by a gentleman, whom he introduced to Thomas Peterkin, United States' factor, Peter

Morgan and myself as clerks to said factory, as Colonel A
Burr. After some conversation, Colonel Burr and Lieutenant
Jackson left the factory and went to the garrison. Shortly after,
one of the soldiers of the garrison came to the factory, with an
order signed, A. Burr, for thirty weight of lead, twenty-eight
pounds were delivered to the solider. In the space of about four
hours the soldier returned to the factory, with a number of musket balls in his hat, saying he wanted to have them weighed, to
know how much the original quantity had lost in running the
balls. After his having them weighed, he took them away in his
hat. In the course of the day some boats came to the Bluffs, and
the men came up to the factory. Colonel Burr requested Mr. Peterkin to let the men have goods and he would pay for them. Colonel Burr was frequently at the factory in the course of the
day, and often had conversations with Mr. Peterkin.

In the evening Mr. Peterkin, Mr Morgan and myself, went to
the garrison where we found Colonel Burr I took notice that
Colonel Burr was frequently called to the door by the men that
had arrived in the boats, to have private conversation with him.
Lieutenant Jackson asked Colonel Burr when Mr Blannerhasset would be there? To which Colonel Burr replied, that he was
then floating by and could not land his boat. In the morning
Colonel Burr came to the factory and demanded a bill for the
articles which his men had got the day before. The bill was
made out amounting to sixty or seventy dollars, which he paid.
The only articles I can remember, were, the lead, three dozen
tomahawks, and three bear skins. After paying the bill, Colonel
Burr departed and I saw him no more.

Cross-examined.

Mr. *Burr* What kind of tomahawks were these; were they
intended for war or for more peaceable purposes? A. They
were such as were used for shingling.

Mr. *M'Rae.* Would they do well for fighting? A. They would
answer very well.

Mr. Wickham to General Wilkinson, after his return to Court,
Can you ascertain when the hieroglyphic cypher was made? A.
The arbitrary characters, were designed I think, in 1794; but I
do not say it was given to Colonel Burr at that time.

Mr. Wickham Will you give me leave to ask upon what occasion it was formed?

General *Wilkinson.* I will with pleasure. Pending the Indian
war, we had unhappily much dissention in the army. I felt myself extremely oppressed and persecuted, and I had reason to believe that every artifice was put in operation to injure my standing with the government, and to have me removed from service if
possible; and there were many who shared my persecution. In
the autumn and winter of the year alluded to, a number of officers retired from the army, either on furlough or by resignation, among whom was that most gallant officer, Captain Leonard
Covington, since a member of Congress. At this time my quarters were embosomed in a wilderness and remote from any post
office, and we had no regular mail. The cypher was therefore designed to secure safety to a free correspondence, and an unreserv-

ed interchange of sentiment respecting public men and public measures, particularly such as related to the army

Mr Wickham I think you say that it was formed in 1794? A Yes, and I will give you my reasons I have another cypher in which the hieroglyphics respecting the President and Vice-President are the same as in that now before the Court, which was designed by Captain Smith, for Captain Covington, in the year 1794; at the time he retired from the army [See an extract of a letter from Captain Covington to General Wilkinson, Appendix, A a]

Mr. Wickham. I observe the word *republican* is presented in the hieroglyphic by '76, *aristocratic* by '89, *navy* by '96, *city of Washington* by a single house and that an indifferent one Pray why was that, as the seat of government was not removed till many years afterwards? I observe the city of Washington, but not Philadelphia, nor any place mentioned as the seat of government? A. The cypher was formed by my aid-de-camp, Captain Smith, and the designations originated in his caprice, without my privity or participation

Mr. Wickham. Do you recollect for what purpose New Orleans was designated in the hieroglyphics? A I can probably account for it If you will refer to those periods you will discover, that we were in an equivocal situation with all the maratime powers, more particularly with England and Spain The navigation of the Mississippi had been a subject of much discussion, and one in which the western people felt a considerable degree of interest. The Ohio is also designated. That is probably confined to mere locality. We were then engaged in a war with the Indians, and were in the woods on the waters of the Ohio, I have before said, that I could not account for the various designations, but I offer these as circumstances which may have influenced Captain Smith in forming them

Mr Wickham Do you recollect when the alphabet in cypher was put on this paper, (alluding to a paper on which the hieroglyphics were written, which he then held in his hand?) A. Last winter, I believe, they were put on to prevent them from being lost.

Mr. Wickham have you brought up the letter or communication from the government, which we wished to have here to look at? A. I have not.

Mr. *Hay* I think you said there was no military post between Pittsburg and New Orleans, but fort Massac, the Chickasaw Bluffs and one at Cincinnati. A. Yes That at Cincinnati was established by the government after the flight of Blannerhasset

Mr. *Hay.* Was there none at Natchez? A There were only Lieutenant Peter and a few men left at that place to keep a look out, and give me regular information.

Mr *Hay* then begged leave to introduce the testimony of George Poindexter, esq who was accordingly examined.

George Poindexter, esq.

Mr *Hay* Is this the original agreement entered into between Cowles Meade, acting Governor, of the Mississippi territory and Aaron Burr ? A. Yes. If it is proper, I will state the circumstances which led to the agreement, and Colonel Burr's surrender to the civil authority of the Mississippi territory.

Chief Justice. Proceed Sir.

Witness On the day preceding the date of this agreement, I was appointed by the Hon Cowles Meade, then the acting governor of the Mississippi territory, an honorary aid-de camp, for the express purpose of visiting Colonel Burr at the boats near the mouth of Bayou Pierre, on the western margin of the river Mississippi ; which I did in company with Major William B. Shields The object of this visit was to gain correct information as to the situation of Burr, to ascertain his views so far as he would communicate them, and to procure his pacific surrender to the civil authority. We were accompanied by a Mr Ralston, one of Burr's party, who had called on Judge Rodney to give his deposition. We arrived that night at Judge Bruin's, who resides near the mouth of Bayou Pierre. The next morning we proceeded down the river till we came opposite to Colonel Burr's boats, and Ralston gave a signal for a boat, which was immediately sent over for us. Before we embarked, we were joined by Colonel Thomas Fitzpatrick. Several persons, then unknown to me, but whose names I have since understood, came on horseback to the bank of the river and crossed with us ; I supposed them to be agents, sent by Burr into the country, to collect information respecting the public sentiment concerning him, and to induce the citizens to believe his plans were laudable and sanctioned by government. When we reached the western bank of the river, we were met by Colonel Burr, to whom Major Shields handed a letter, of which he was the bearer from Mr Meade, acquainting Colonel Burr with the object of our visit In the letter there was a sentence relating to the restoration of tranquility in the territory, which sentence Burr repeated once or twice with a sneer, adding, that "he had no intention to injure the citizens of the United States" Colonel Burr then expressed himself to this effect : " As to any projects or plans which may have been formed between General Wilkinson and myself heretofore, they are now completely frustrated by the perfidious conduct of Wilkinson, and the world must pronounce him a perfidious villain." Burr also, in speaking of Wilkinson, said, " If I am sacrificed, my Port Folio will prove him to be a villain." He further stated, that so far from having any designs hostile to the citizens of the United States, he had intended to have met Mr Meade at Gibson Port, on the day of a general muster, which happened at that place about the time of his arrival at Bayou Pierre, but was deterred from doing so, by a belief that he would be assassinated, were he seen passing through the territory He then pointed to his boats and asked, if there was any thing military in their appearance. I told him it was true his men did not appear to be armed, but they were just such persons as I should expect to see about a camp ; they did not seem to be in a situation to settle themselves on farms. I also remarked to Colonel Burr, that I had no hesitation in giving him the most perfect assurance of personal safety while in the territory, until he should be disposed of, according to the laws of his country ; that the object of Mr Meade in calling out the militia was to preserve inviolate, the laws and constitution of the United States; that if that object could be secured without the employment of force, it would be preferable, but assured him that force would be used if necessary, for which purpose the militia were then on their march to arrest his progress   Colonel Burr declared his willingness to submit to the civil authority, and proposed that an interview should take place between himself and the acting governor, on the next day, at some convenient place in the territory, that we should guarantee his person from actual violence in the meantime, and restore him to his boats, if Mr Meade should not accept his surrender to the civil authority, that his boats and people should keep the position they then occupied until after the proposed interview took place, and that in the meantime, *his people* (as he called them) should commit no breach of the peace, nor violate any law of the United States or of the Mississippi territory.   The place designated at which Colonel Burr should meet the executive, was the house of Thomas Calvit, a respectable citizen of the Mississippi territory, who resides near the mouth of Coles Creek, where the detachment of militia which had descended the river were stationed.   The substance of these propositions was committed to writing, at the request of Colonel Burr, and copies interchanged; the copy given to Colonel Burr is in the hand-writing of Major Shields, and that which remained in our possession, is in the hand-writing of Colonel Burr, subscribed by him in my presence, and also by the witness, Colonel Thomas Fitzpatrick   Colonel Burr, according to stipulation, descended the river on the 17th day of January last, (the day after the agreement was entered into,) as far as the mouth of Coles Creek, in company with Colonel Fitzpatrick, who directed him to be taken in charge by Captain Davidson's company of dragoons, and conducted to the house of Mr Calvit.   In a short time after Colonel Burr's arrival, Mr. Meade and himself commenced a conversation on the subject of his surrender to the civil authority of the territory   I do not know every thing that passed between them, but understood the following terms were offered to Colonel Burr by Mr. Meade. 1. That the agreement entered into for the purpose of procuring that interview, should be declared void. 2 That Burr should surrender himself unconditionally to the civil authority, and proceed directly to the town of Washington. 3 That his boats should be searched, and all military apparatus found on board of them to be disposed of as the executive should think fit.   To these terms Mr. Meade required Colonel Burr's unequivocal reply, as I understood, in fifteen minutes, and if not agreed to, Burr was to be instantly returned to his boats, and the militia ordered to seize the whole party by force.   The terms were agreed to, and carried into effect   Colonel Burr declared himself unwilling to fall into the power of General Wilkinson, and requested that if any attempt should be made to seize him by a military force from New Orleans, that it might be opposed.   I was myself of opinion, that General Wilkinson would make no such attempt, as it would tend to subvert the laws and constitution of the United States, and also the municipal regulations of the territory.   Had such an effort been made, while Mr. Meade was the acting governor, I have reason to believe, that he would have maintained the empire of the law and the rights of the civil authority by force, if necessary Major Shields and myself attended Colonel Burr to the town of Washington, where he was delivered over to the custody of the law, and the examination of the witnesses immediately commenced before Judge Rodney A committee of five gentlemen, as well as I recollect, was appointed to examine the boats, who proceeded up the river for that purpose, and I believe made their report to the executive.

I was then called on in my official capacity, as attorney general, to give a written opinion as to the course which ought to be pursued with Colonel Burr. I did so, and that opinion, I believe, was filed in the office of the secretary of the Mississippi territory My opinion was, that we had no evidence to convict Colonel Burr of any offence in the Mississippi territory, that the Supreme Court of the territory to which a Jury was about to be summoned, had no original jurisdiction of any prosecution, and could only take cognizance of points of law reserved at the trial in the Circuit Court; that therefore Burr ought to be sent, under a sufficient guard, directed to the city of Washington, where the Supreme Court of the United States would be in session, and the Judges attending from every part of the union, could direct the accused to be tried in the district where, from the evidence, it might appear that an overt act of treason had been committed. But Judge Rodney thought differently, and a *venire facias* was issued, requiring the attendance of seventy-six Jurors at an adjourned session, of the Supreme Court of the Mississippi territory, held in February last. From the number of Jurors attending, a Grand Jury of twenty-three persons was selected, who received a charge from Judge Rodney, and adjourned until the next day. At the meeting of the Court the next morning, I moved to discharge the Grand Jury, 1. Because the Court did not possess original jurisdiction in any case 2. Because the depositions, submitted to my inspection, did not furnish sufficient evidence to convict Colonel Burr of the offences with which he was charged, so as to bring them within the Mississippi territory. 3. That a warrant might issue, transmitting the accused to a Court, having competent jurisdiction to try and punish him, if guilty of the crimes alledged against him. The Court being divided on this motion, it was overruled. The Grand Jury then retired. I determined to prefer no indictment, and left the Court. In the evening while I was engaged in the legislature, a message was sent me by the Court, requesting my attendance I immediately repaired to the Court-room, and was desired to look at the presentments of the Grand Jury. I perused them, and found that the Grand Jury had presented the acting governor for calling out the militia; the manner in which Colonel Burr had surrendered to the civil authority; the proceedings at Orleans; and, I believe, the general government itself, did not escape. I felt, and declared my astonishment at such unwarrantable proceedings, and informed the Court that I should take no further notice of the presentments, and retired. Judge Rodney, I believe likewise, censured the conduct of the

Grand Jury. It may be proper to mention, that a respectable proportion of the Jury withheld their signatures from these presentments. Colonel Burr that evening went to the house of Col. Osmun, and disappeared. I afterwards attended the Court, and had a judgment *nisi* entered on the recognizance given by Burr, and his securities, Lyman Huding and Banijah Osmun, a *scire facias* was issued and served on the securities, which is now depending before the Supreme Court of the Mississippi territory. What happened after Colonel Burr withdrew, I know not except from hearsay.

Cross-examined

Question by Mr. *Martin*. Have you a copy of the recognizance said to have been entered into by Colonel Burr? A. I have not, but have seen a copy in the hands of Mr Hay. Q. Were you present when it was executed? A. No.

Mr. *Martin*. You said that the Judges ordered seventy-six jurors to be summoned. Who were the Judges? A. Bruin and Rodney.

Mr *Wickham*. Do you know any thing of military men sent from New-Orleans, to seize Colonel Burr? A. I understood that there were, and that a Dr. Carmichael, who resides in the Mississippi Territory was one.

Mr. Wickham. Was there an expectation in that part of the country that General Wilkinson had sent men for that purpose, and that Colonel Burr would be seized? A. It was talked of, and generally disapproved. Q. Where was Colonel Burr at the time of his entering into the convention on the west side of the Mississippi? A. He was in the territory of Orleans, and, in pursuance of his agreement came over to the Mississippi territory.

Mr. Wickham. Did Colonel Burr seem to be apprehensive of military force? A. He did not, except that he was particularly unwilling to fall into the hands of Gen. Wilkinson. He enquired of Colonel Fitzpatrick, Major Shields and myself, whether there was any pass or way above Natchez through which he could get to Ouachita, and wished to know whether there was any person who could be employed to pilot him. We gave him no satisfactory answer. the subject. My own impression was that he wanted to establish himself on the Ouachita, as a place of rendezvous to which his men might rally.

Mr. Wickham. Have you understood that an officer of the army was sent by General Wilkinson to take Colonel Burr? A. I heard a lieutenant of the army (but I had rather not mention his name) say that he was one of the persons employed for that purpose.

Here Mr. Hay offered to read the recognizance entered into by Colonel Burr in the Mississippi territory. Mr. *Martin* objected to its being read and declared it to be a forgery. He said he was willing to answer the consequences to Judge Rodney, and to give it under his hand that it was a forgery.

Mr. *Hay*. Judge Rodney is so *near* Mr. Martin that you can answer for it with perfect *safety*.

Mr. *Poindexter*. Mr. Harding, one of the securities in the recognizance, said that the recognizance returned by Judge Rodney was not the one entered into by Colonel Burr. Mr. Osmun and himself. But I do not think it was believed by one honest man in the territory.

Mr *Hay*. Did the paper of which this is an authentic copy, bear any mark of erazure? A. Not that I recollect. It was in the usual form in which Judge Rodney took other recognizances; that the person bound should attend from day to day until discharged by the Court. The recognizances of Blanuerhasset and others taken on the same occasion, were in the same form. Judge Rodney informed me that Mr. Harding sat down to draw the recognizance, and, after beginning it, said it was useless to go through with it, that they would acknowledge themselves bound before him, and he might make out the recognizance in due form at his leisure.

Mr. *Wickham*. Then you understood Mr Rodney to say that the recognizance was not reduced to writing until the departure of Colonel Burr from his presence? A I so understood him.

Mr. *Wickham*. Then it was no recognizance at all

Mr. *Poindexter*. That is a question of law.

Mr *Hay*. As something has been said about Mr Rodney, what is his general character? A One of the most honest men under Heaven, and an old revolutionary patriot.

Mr Hay And this is the man who has been charged with forgery by Mr. Martin!

Mr. *Martin*. Let him be who he will, I charge him with having returned a different recognizance from that which was entered into before him

Mr. *Wickham* called on Gen Wilkinson to produce the president's letter, approving his measures.

Gen. Wilkinson. By referring to my papers, I discover I have made a mistake. I find I have no orders from the president, directing the seizure of Col. Burr; the order is from the Secretary of War, and has been already published, directing me to seize the principles in the enterprize. I did believe I had an order from the president specifically directing the arrest of Colonel Burr This mistake arose from my misapprehension of the tenor of a letter from the President, of February, which blends public communications with private affairs

Mr. *Wickham*. Have you no letter from the Secretary of War, approving your conduct in general terms? A. I never had such a letter from him. The approval of my conduct is expressed in qualified terms

Mr. *Wickham*. You wrote to the president about these transactions—was the letter to which you referred an answer to those communications? A. That letter in its public relation, merely acknowledges the receipt of two letters from me, and the arrival of a confidential messenger I sent to to the president. It gives some directions, but generally, conveys information merely.

Mr. *Wickham* then applied for the production of this letter — it might be important to Colonel Burr in this point of view. General Wilkinson sends on certain communications by Mr. Briggs, and in this letter the president acknowledges the receipt of them

—So that by refering to that letter, it was easy to know what were the communications made to the President by Gen. Wilkinson.

Mr. *Martin.* We have a right to demand this letter.

Chief Justice It is easy to read the passage which refers to the two letters, and to Mr Briggs's communications.

Mr. *Martin* proposed to put the letter into the hands of the Chief Justice, who might mark such passages as he might think proper to be read

General Wilkinson. The letter is in the hands of the attorney for the United States.

Mr. *Hay* If the Court will state those subjects, to which the letter should relate to have any bearing on this case, I am ready to produce such passages

Mr *Burr* observed, that he knew but of one ground on which a public document should be withheld from a Court of Justice, which was, that it might contain something relative to foreign negociations, actually pending, and the public good required its concealment. But in the present case, the transactions referred to in the letter, might have passed over ; a letter too which is not a public document, but a private communication.

Mr. *Martin* No government ever dared to suppress information, which was necessary to an individual, against whom it had commenced a prosecution. There never was such an attempt to establish a new principle. as is done on the present occasion.

Mr *Hay* Mr Martin asserts, that there never was such an instance as the present, and that we are attempting to establish principles altogether new, I do not, Sir, attempt to establish new principles ; I do aver my confident opinion, that this paper does not, in the slightest degree relate to the present case. I will not say, that the gentlemen know this fact, nor do I say that they have other objects in view What effects they may have out of doors, what materials of declamation they may furnish to gentlemen of a certain way of thinking, I now not But I do assure gentlemen, that when this letter is produced, it will have a very different effect from what they may contemplate (Mr Hay then read the last paragraph of the letter)

Mr. *Burr.* If there be a single sentence in that letter relating to me, I have a right to demand it Why is a greater regard paid to the president's secrets than mine ? My papers have been fraudulently seized, and such passages only culled from them, as suited the purposes of my enemies.

Mr. *Hay.* I am placed in an embarrassing situation. I have no objection to the production of this paper ; but in my opinion it has not the smallest application to the present case If this letter is ever produced it will but place the conduct of the president on that high ground of propriety which has ever been contemplated, and assigned to him by the people of the United States. if gentlemen want this letter, let them state *how* it is relevant, I am content that you, Sir, (the Chief Justice) should read this letter, or that any other person should ; but I cannot consent to produce every paper, which gentlemen may think proper to ask for.

Mr *Wirt*. These gentlemen it seems are carrying on an impeachment against the president of the United States. What is their object in demanding this letter? It is no more than vainly to attempt to inculpate the president, and to gratify their spleen and resentment against him Is that the object? Is A. Burr more or less guilty, because he has approved or disapproved the measures of General Wilkinson? They want to ask you which is the most guilty, Thomas Jefferson, or Aaron Burr? Are *you* then trying the president? And even if you were, would you not have him here, and give him an opportunity of answering to his accusers? This letter Sir, if ever it is produced, will show that the motives of the administration, were as pure and as proper, as its friends could wish, or its enemies could fear; it will appear, that the reprobated conduct of General Wilkinson, in this instance, was such, as was justified by the circumstances of the case; and if the administration have approved it, they have approved of nothing but what was proper. We hope, that unless the Court be satisfied of the relevancy of this paper, they will not, unnecessarily, violate the sanctity of private correspondence.

Mr. *Wickham*. It has been said that we wish to inculpate the government No, Sir, our object is to defend ourselves, and if in doing this, we do inculpate the government, so much the worse for them When, Sir, the government have spent one hundred thousand dollars on this prosecution, when every quarter has been ransacked for evidence against us, is it not important for us to show from what motives this prosecution has been commenced? General Wilkinson has been under examination these two days He has produced documents which he has mutilated and then restored. Gentlemen say, that *he* is the pivot on which the prosecution turns—We wish, Sir, to examine how far this witness has been consistent with himself; and what credit it due to his declarations.

Mr *Martin*. It has been already decided in this Court, that the president has no morerights here than the man who walks the streets in rags. " What " says the gentleman, " will you then violate the sanctity of private correspondence ?" Sir, when that gentleman made this declaration, I looked at his face to see if it did not blush with shame, and even burst blood at expressing such a sentiment.

Mr. *Wirt*. I hope, Sir, the redness of a man's *face* is no evidence of his guilt. Mr. Martin mistakes me. I demanded whether, this Court would violate the sanctity of correspondence, unless there was an adequate necessity.

The argument was continued for some time in this desultory manner, after which,

The *Chief Justice* observed, that he much regretted, that any difficulty had occurred on the subject, that is was irksome to him, and it was with considerable reluctance, that he required the production of such a paper; but that he did only what his duty prescribed to him; that it was impossible for him to determine, even if he saw the letter, how much of it was relevant to the present case, because he could not anticipate what ground of de-

tence would be taken by the accused. He saw, however, no ne
cessity for reading it in public

Mr *Wickham* Let us see the letter, and then if we think it
relevant to the present case, we may read it in the cause, but no
copy need be taken

Mr *M Rae* I should rather, Sir, that it would be exhibited in
the most public form It is the only way to avert the misrepre
sentation of its contents

Mr *M'Rae* then read the letter marked, (*B b* ,

Mr *Wickham* demanded the production of the whole letter of
the 12th of November General Wilkinson. Did you lay it before
the Grand Jury A I did

Mr *Burr* The entire letter has been used against me before
the Grand Jury All idea of State secrets is therefore at an end,
and there can be no objection to produce the whole of it in Court,
I shall expect that General Wilkinson will bring the whole of it
in Court to-morrow.

Mr *Hay* I have nothing, Sir, to say on this subject.

Chief Justice The president has certified his reasons for com
municating only certain parts of that letter, and he believes that
the other parts have no application to the present prosecution

Mr. *Martin* I hope the Court has not already decided that
point Has not this Court already declared, that the president
has no more power here, than any other man ? If this be law, for
which gentlemen now contend, God forbid that I should remain
a citizen of the United States! And is Mr Jefferson to be a Judge
of the relevancy of evidence, in a prosecution in which he has ta
ken so active a part against the accused ? Mr Jefferson, Sir, is a
man of no great legal knowledge He was of no celebrity as a
lawyer before the revolution, and he has since been so much en
gaged in political pursuits, that he has had time enough to un
learn the little law he ever knew

Mr *Hay* The only end of this conversation is to abuse Mr
Jefferson

Mr *Martin* Sir, we shall so use Mr. Jefferaon, as not to abuse
him Remember that the life and liberty of Colonel Burr are
shown to be no longer dependent on Virginians , and therefore I
am freed from any restraint, in declaring what I think If Mr. Jef
ferson himself was here, would not this Court call him before it, and
make him disclose upon oath, the contents of that letter ? Suppose,
Sir, that in this letter Gen. Wilkinson had denounced Governor
Claiborne and Cowles Meade , suppose that he has represented all
the people of New Orleans as disaffected , suppose that he has at
tempted to throw every influential man but himself under the sus
picions of the government, in order that he may raise himself into
favor , is this a satisfactory reason why this letter should be res
pected or withheld ?

Mr *Burr* repeated that this letter had been laid before the
Grand Jury , and that it was therefore no longer a State secret
and that he had a *right* to ask for any thing which General Wil
kinson had shown or said to the Grand Jury

Chief Justice After such a certificate from the president of the
United States as has been received. I cannot direct the produc

tion of those parts of the letter, without sufficient evidence of their being relevant to the present prosecution. I should suppose, however, that the same source, which informed you of the existence of this paper, might inform you of the particular way in which it was relevant

Mr *Burr* In such a case, I ask no man's opinion but my own

Chief Justice I cannot assist you

M *Burr* Have not I a right to ask what any one said before the Grand Jury? Mr *Wickham* read certain parts of the *extracted and furnished* copy, to shew that from the context of those parts, *the omitted passages bore directly on the subject* The president of the United States might have had proper reasons on account of General Wilkinson, to withhold those parts, but General Wilkinson himself, has no right to withhold them, and if he produced *the whole letter* before the Grand Jury for the sake of criminating Colonel Burr, he may certainly be called upon, to lay it before this Court

General *Wilkinson* begged leave to correct the expression of the gentleman about his motives He did not produce this letter before the Grand Jury to criminate Colonel Burr, but to vindicate himself.

M. *Wickham* That is the very thing which I say. Why did he wish to vindicate himself, but to give greater effect to his crimination of Colonel Burr? General *Wilkinson* begged leave to state another consideration When he appeared before the Grand Jury, he recollects Mr Taylor of the Grand Jury enquired of him, whether he introduced certain papers to vindicate his own conduct, and that he replied in the affirmative, he remembers also, observing to the Grand Jury, that certain parts of his information involved such delicate personalities, that he would not willingly give it publicity, and therefore he hoped, what he said would be received in confidence, to which, a member (Mr Barbour) after some pause, replied, "whatever you say here, sir, is received in confidence"

Mr. *Hay*. Mr. Tazewell is here and will confirm the statement

Mr *Burr* Then they did a very improper thing, and I hope this Court will not countenance such a proceeding The gentleman must be mistaken, Sir The Grand Jury could not thus receive secret information Mr *Hay* observed, that gentlemen acted very precipitately in condemning the Grand Jury unheard, and appealed to Mr Tazewell for what he knew on this subject

Mr. *Burr*. They have no right to introduce a witness now, when we have one under examination. Mr *Wirt* supposed, that when the Grand Jury was thus charged by the accused or his counsel, they had a right to appear in vindication of their own conduct.

Mr. *Burr*. That may be a pleasant occupation to the Court *hereafter* But at present we have a witness under examination.

After a long and desultory argument, the *Chief Justice* determined that the correct course was, to leave the accused all the advantages which he might derive from the parts actually produced , and to allow him all the advantages of *supposing* that the omitted parts related to any particular point The accused may avail himself as much of them, as if they were actually produced

Mr *Wickham* We shall then insist in the course of argument, that our suppositions if not disproved, must be received as evidence.

Mr *Martin* And I shall take the liberty of stating what is actually contained in the omitted parts of the letter For I know what they are

Mr *Wirt* Mr Martin, Sir, is privileged to say what he pleases of any person or thing.

Mr. *Burr* to *General Wilkinson* Was there not an order given by you to seize the person of Mr Pintard ? A I have no recollection that I gave such orders, and I conclude from the circumstance of an explanation I made in the newspapers, that I did not.

Mr *Burr* I have seen an order said to have been from you, for seizing him? A. I do not recollect it ; but if any such is shown to me I shall certainly confess it. Q. Did you give any orders to arrest Daverzac? A. I gave general orders only I stationed a guard about two miles above New Orleans to stop boats and persons Q What were the orders given to that guard ? A. To stop all persons descending the river Q And to seize papers too ? A I do not recollect Q. Were the papers of Mr Pintard brought to you ? A They were , but they were immediately returned

Mr. *Hay* Is it the opinion of the Court, that General Wilkinson is to be interrogated about all his transactions at New Orleans ? I object not to hearing the truth ; but I cannot consent to this sacrifice and waste of time   I believe it to be a principle of law, that when a witness is introduced by the prosecution, he is only to be cross-examined about the points of his original testimony Is this prosecution never to end ? Or are we to wait to give the accused an opportunity of entrapping General Wilkinson, which they avow to be the object of those interrogatories ?

Mr. *Wickham* It is a novel idea, just started by the gentleman If such were the law, the prosecution need only to seize on the the most material witness on behalf of the accused, examine him only as to a few points, and then dismiss him. All his evidence in favor of the accused would consequently be lost

Mr *Hay*. The law is laid down in 2. Atkins. The *Chief Justice* overruled the objection and the examination proceeded

Mr. *Burr* What letters directed to me, did you take from Pintard or Daverzac ? A. None. Q. Did you return to those gentlemen, all the papers you took from them ? A I think I did not But I do not recollect what part of them I retained Q You have read the constitution By what authority did you seize private papers?

General Wilkinson to the Court Am I bound to answer questions which may criminate myself ?

Mr *Burr* To state the authority, by which he seized the papers, cannot criminate him, though the fact of seizing might

Chief Justice to General Wilkinson. When you discover any question may criminate you, you need not answer it.

Mr Baker And when he does resort to that expedient, he is to be understood as shuffling from the question, and is likely to criminate himself by his answers

Mr Wirt And it is also understood, that when called on in this manner, he may explain his conduct by drawing a picture of the defenceless condition in which he found New Orleans, and the necessity of resorting to such strong measures for its defence

Mr Baker And if he does give us a picture, it must be a true and faithful one

Chief Justice. I have stated to General Wilkinson, that he is at liberty to explain the motives of his conduct

General Wilkinson Then, Sir, I will explain and substantiate the motives of my placing this guard, and of my other measures Here is a paper, a letter of advice from General Jackson to Governor Claiborne, warning him of the approach of a large body of men to New Orleans, combined and engaged for unlawful purposes Here, Sir, is a deposition which goes to shew that Judge Prevost, the step son of Colonel Burr saluted a public officer in the streets of Orleans and congratulated him on the arrival of General John Adair as the second in command to Colonel Burr, at New Orleans Here is a deposition of Commodore Shaw, which shows that Bradford the printer, had reported a most terrific account of the movements in the upper country, of an armed brig being equipped, and even of 12,000 stands of arms being issued by Colonel Burr These were the reasons for my taking such decided steps; and so impressed was I with the dangerous situation of my country, that if I had omitted these precautionary measures, I should have deserved the severest denunciations of the government I was prompted by that pure patriotism which has always influenced my conduct, and my character for which I trust will never be tarnished I shall continue to defy the utmost art, fraud, deception and villainy, that my enemies can practise towards me

Mr. Wickham objected to the production of the depositions. After a desultory argument the *Chief Justice* determined that it was not correct to read them. If these affidavits had been made previous to the transactions at New Orleans, they might have been read as explanatory of the grounds of General Wilkinson's conduct ; but being taken since, they are objectionable, as every thing of that kind ought to be subjected to a cross-examination. General Wilkinson has stated the grounds of his own conduct, and very properly ; but he has no right to support his explanation by illegal evidence.

Mr Baker The Court having disposed of the depositions, the only question remaining, relates to the letter. On this question, two points occur. 1st. Whether this is a correct copy of a certain letter ; and 2dly Whether that letter was written by General Jackson.

Chief Justice to General Wilkinson Do you know the hand writing of General Jackson ? A. I know it only by comparison. I never saw him write

Mr Wickham. Did you compare this letter ? A. My clerk did, and he is here

Mr *M'Rae* Is it not your best belief, that this is a true copy of the original? A. I believe it to be a correct copy.

Mr M'Rae Did not this letter form the ground, in part, of your conduct? A It did certainly influence my conduct Mr *Wickham* objected to its being read, because it was only proved to be a true copy by the general recollection of the witnesses Some desultory discussion ensued

Chief Justice Both sides admit, that it is immaterial, whether General Wilkinson's impressions of the state of New Orleans were actually true or false Both sides admit that he may produce any letter, which is verified by himself. But this copy is not proved by him to be a true copy There is no objection to General Wilkinson's stating the contents of this letter, but that statement cannot be confirmed by the copy that is offered

Mr *Wickham* There is one thing more to be considered The Court has not come to any positive decision as to the letter of 12th November If General Wilkinson does not produce the omitted parts, by the rules of evidence we are at liberty to state and to use them, until they are disproved. General Wilkinson may if he pleases, produce the letter at any subsequent period

Mr. *Hay* The president of the United States has prescribed the course which should be pursued. It is he, and not General Wilkinson, who withholds the omitted parts Is it fair then, that the opposite counsel should supply these omissions as they please, and that their suppositions should be received as evidence?

Chief Justice I have already decided this question It is certainly fair to supply the omitted parts by suppositions, though such ought not to affect General Wilkinson's private character If this were a trial in chief, I should perhaps think myself bound to continue the cause, on account of the withholding the parts of this paper. and I certainly cannot exclude the inferences which gentlemen may draw from the omissions

General *Wilkinson*. I have to offer, Sir, a letter from James L. Donaldson, which Mr Martin called for yesterday Mr *Martin* This is only an extract General Wilkinson I had no other Mr *Martin*, (returning the paper) We take no extracts Mr *Wirt*, (in an under-key) Unless it be of molasses

General *Wilkinson* I have also another paper. It is the extract of a letter from Mr Covington, showing that the cypher was invented in 1794 Mr *Wickham*. Did you ever use these cyphers, or any of them, or any other cypher, in correspondence with the baron Carondelet? A No, but I must reflect on that question before I answer it decidedly.

Testimony of Commodore Shaw.

Mr. *Wickham* For what is Commodore Shaw introduced?

Mr *Hay* To authenticate the copy of a letter from General Jackson to Governor Claiborne, shewn to General Wilkinson.

Commodore *Shaw* I recollect to have seen the original

Mr. *Wickham*. You will please, Sir, to state its contents.

Commodore *Shaw* Governor Claiborne sent his servant to me with an invitation to dinner, adding, that he wished to see me on *public* business. I was unable to wait upon him that day, but

I saw him on a subsequent day, when he took a letter from his pocket, and shewed it to me. It was a letter from General Jackson to himself, and had been thrown into the office by some anonymous person. This letter gave Governor Claiborne a strong suspicion of General Wilkinson, and reminded him of the Ides of March, and insisted upon the necessity of placing New Orleans in a state of defence.

Chief Justice. When was this? A. Some time in December.
Q. Did report convey any information of troops approaching New Orleans? A. Yes—every day in December and January, rumours were arriving of troops approaching our south-west frontiers; and my impression was, that every thing should be done for the safety of the city; and that, if General Wilkinson had not taken the measure that he did, he would have deserved censure.

M. *M'Rae*, [looking in the letter in his hand] Do you recollect whether General Jackson recommended in his letter, that the Governor would use every possible means of defence?

M. *Wickham* objected to putting questions from the letter.

Chief Justice. You must not, Sir, take the letter in your hand, and propose questions from it. It is really of no consequence whether the letter is read or not. No doubt the substance of it has been stated.

Mr. *M'Rae.* Have I no right to read over the letter, and afterwards interrogate the witness as to its substance? It is my object, I confess, to draw out the substance of the original letter.

Mr. *Wickham.* In that letter, were there not strong suspicions expressed against General Wilkinson? A. There were. Mr. Wickham. I should suppose, then, that General Wilkinson might have easily judged of the correctness of the rumors, which were circulated about Colonel Burr.

Mr. *M'Rae.* State, Sir, what you know of these transactions.
Witness. The alarm in New Orleans in December and January was very considerable. We did not know when the enemy would advance upon us. There was an apprehension of an attack by sea, and I was then authorized to purchase a large ship, to be stationed at the Balize. The gun boats, which had been ordered to enter Lake Pontchartrain, were commanded to take a different position. Some time after, there was a report, that a fleet under English colours, were actually cruizing off the mouth of the Mississippi; and this increased the alarm.

Mr. *Burr.* Was it a fact, or not, that this fleet was there? A. I do not know; such was the report, and it was brought up in a packet that comes weekly from the Balize. It was not said to be a fleet of merchantmen, but of ships of war. The report was, I believe, on the counting-house books. Mr. Bradford, the printer, also made a communication to me on the 6th of January, which produced a considerable effect. He informed me, that he had spent some time in the city of Washington and Philadelphia, and from Philadelphia he had travelled to Pittsburgh, and from thence proceeded to New Orleans; that he had seen a number of men under arms at the mouth of Cumberland river, and two gun-boats building, which the men on board told him would be delivered up by Colonel Lyon to Colonel Burr, besides a number of small arms, and a thirty-two pounder, ready to go on board, and that this flotilla was to be under the command of Captain Talbot

Mr *M'Rae* Did this information reach General Wilkinson? A. Yes—I told him of it myself. The communication was made in the company of Mr. Hines and Major Spencer

Mr *Wirt* What was the situation of New Orleans at that time? Was it in a condition to defend itself against any attack by sea? A. It was in a very defenceless condition.

Mr *Wickham* Were these rumors before General Wilkinson's arrival at New Orleans, or afterwards? A. Afterwards. Gen Wilkinson made to me a full communication of all that he knew, I dare say a week before it was known to the public. He shewed the cyphered letter from General Dayton, with his signature to it. This enabled me the sooner to get my naval preparations ready.

Mr. *Hay* Did General Wilkinson give you this information under injunctions to keep it secret until the proper time for divulging it should arrive? A. He did, until he could obtain more complete information from some of Colonel Burr's agents then in town. Q Was Col Freeman then in New Orleans? A He was

Mr *Wirt* What was the strength of the garrison then in New Orleans? A. In the upper fort there were 3 pounders and one 2 pounder. All the guns in the lower fort were dismantled In the upper fort there were six men, and a corporal's guard I am sure there were not more than three guns there. Q What was the number of regular men in garrison? A It was a small garrison Generally, there were parts of four companies of regulars there Q. What was the precise number? A I do not recollect

Mr *Hay* Did not those who were responsible to the government for the safety of New Orleans, suspect many of disaffection? A I did suppose there were many in and near New Orleans who were inimical to the government of the United States

Mr. *Wirt.* Suppose an attack had been made by a fleet from below, and an army from above would the people of the city have resisted with proper spirit? A I thought, Sir, that the people were not as patriotic as they out to have been. Many endeavored to discourage a belief that there was any danger of an attack

Cross examined

Mr *Wickham* Did General Wilkinson shew you the cyphered letter? A Yes—in manuscript. Q Did he shew you the translation? A He did. Q Was it General Wilkinson's copy? A I so understood it Q A copy of the whole letter? A Yes, as the true copy of the whole letter, received by General Wilkinson, through Mr Swartwout Q Did you say there were four companies of regulars at New Orleans? A I said they were not full Q Was there any alarm before General Wilkinson got down? A None that I heard of. Q Did you suspect the people of New Orleans to be disaffected, because they would not hear these rumors? A No, not for that reason I believed them disaffected for other reasons? Q While these rumors prevailed, did the ordinary of flat-bottomed boats continue coming down the river? A It did. Q. Did the mails arrive as usual? A They were not regular in January, I thought some of my letters were detained, and I then determined to communicate with the government by water Q Did you obey any orders from General Wilkinson? A. No—our service was quite distinct But I had orders to co-operate with General Wilkinson, and he might send the squadron to what point he pleased.

Q Who gave you the orders to apprehend Colonel Burr? A They were from government, and I think, from general W. My orders from the government have been published, and I suppose, Colonel Burr may have seen them in Natchez The original orders are at my lodgings [Here Mr Hay produced a copy of these orders]

Mr *Burr* That is not the order, Commodore Shaw, which was published at Natchez? A (having read it) the very same Sir, *verbatim*. Q Did you not see an order in the newspapers directing my boats to be destroyed, &c? A I did not, Sir These orders (those in his hand) were put on the custom-house books.

Mr. *Burr*. Was there any qualification, " if attacked," in the order which was published? A There was Q Was it not an order to attack and destroy without any qualification? A Oh! no Sir.

Mr *Poindexter* was again called and farther examined.

Question by Col. *Burr* Do you recollect whether it was one of the stipulations between Mr Meade and me, that military authority should be laid aside? A You were not required to surrender yourself a prisoner of war, but you surrendered unconditionally to the civil authority.

Col Burr. Did not Mr Meade promise to disuse all military authority as to me? A I do not recollect to have heard Mr Meade say any such thing

Col *Burr* Did you not hear Mr Meade felicitate me on my fortunate escape from a party who were armed with knives and tomahawks for the purpose of coming on board my boat and massacreing me? A I was not present at any such felicitation Q Had Mr. Meade in his possession any document which would authorize him to issue any civil process against me? A Mr Meade was an executive officer, and could not issue a civil process in any case. Q, Did not Mr Meade declare to me that there was not any document in the territory to authorize the issuing of civil process against me? A I do not recollect to have heard any such declaration Q Had Judge Rodney any document before *him* that would authorize the issuing such process? A That is a matter of opinion. There were sundry depositions in his possession, some of which were given by persons belonging to your party, many of whom voluntarily came forward, and had their own depositions taken, in order to induce a belief that they had forsaken you. That was the general impression, as it appeared to me, and I believe it to be the fact In those depositions they stated nothing of importance against you Q Were not some persons seized by military force, and brought before Judge Rodney? A Not after your surrender to the civil authority, until the discovery of a paper which was said to have been taken out of the cape of a negro boy's coat There was then some seizure at Natchez by order of the executive; and the persons seized were detained under guard a short time, but whether they were brought before Judge Rodney or not, I do not know.

Here Mr *Poindexter* observed—One circumstance I omitted to mention yesterday which took place at the time when I visited Burr's boats. A boat commanded by a lieutenant Patterson of the militia, with between twenty and thirty armed men landed about two hundred yards below, on the west side of the Mississippi, for the purpose of ambuscading the men of Burr's party who were separated from their boats, and were amusing themselves in the woods. A person whom I did not know at that time, but whom I have since found to be Davis Floyd, approached Col. Burr, and asked him what was to be done; saying that a boat had landed a short distance below on the same side of the river, that he was not afraid to attack the boat, provided such were his directions. Colonel Burr immediately requested Colonel Fitzpatrick to interfere to prevent any attack from the boat; which he immediately did, and directed the lieutenant to return with his men to the mouth of Coles Creek.

Colonel *Burr*. Did you not hear Mr Meade say that, if Wilkinson should attempt to arrest me by military force, he would join me with the militia to prevent it? A. I never did, but I remember Mr Meade said that he would not permit any military force to come into the territory, and arrest you out of the hands of the civil authority, if he could prevent it. He kept some militia in readiness for the purpose of supporting the civil authority, and acting as circumstances might direct. We were of opinion that a majority of the people who were about the court-house at Washington at the time the Grand Jury made their presentments were the friends of Burr, consisted generally of persons who had come promiscuously into the territory, and it was supposed would interfere to rescue him, if necessary. My own impression was, and I believe it was the general impression that he wished the force immediately about himself to cut a diminutive figure, while a majority of his adherents were dispersed over the country for the purpose of making favorable impressions on the people concerning him.

Mr. *Hay* here produced the paper said to have been found in the cape of a negro boy's coat, which paper is in the following words: "If you are yet together, keep together, and I will join "you to morrow night. In the mean time, put all your arms in "perfect order. Ask the bearer no questions, but tell him all "you may think I wish to know. He does not know that this "is from me, nor where I am." Directed to C. T. and D. F.

Mr *Hay* asked Mr. Poindexter if that was the original paper said to have been found in the cape of the negro boy's coat. He answered yes.

Mr *Hay*. Who were supposed to be meant by C. T. and D. F. A. Comfort Tyler and Davis Floyd. Q. Is that paper in the hand writing of Colonel Burr? A. I believe it is.

Mr *Wickham*. Where did you first see that paper? A. In the hands of governor Williams.

Colonel *Burr.* How long were the persons who were seized at Natchez after that note was found, detained in custody? A. I do not recollect how long particularly, but one or two days I believe. Many of the young men arrested at Natchez declared that if Burr's designs were against the government of the U States, they would be the first men to turn against him, and cut his throat. There are a number of them now remaining in the territory, for he has supplied us with Schoolmasters, Singing masters, Dancing masters and Doctors in abundance.

Mr *Hay* Where was Colonel Burr at the time when this paper was found? A He had disappeared, and was generally supposed to be at a Doctor Cumming's, near Gibson Port

Witnesses on behalf of the Accused

Littleton W Tazewell was called to be sworn as a witness on the part of the accused

Witness I wish, before I am sworn, that the point should be determined by the Court whether, as a Grand Juror, I am bound to give evidence of what passed in the Grand Jury room. I do not wish that the community or the Grand Jury should lose any right they may have, by any acquiescence of mine, if by law, a Grand Jury-man ought not to be called upon to state what happened before the Grand Jury I submit myself to the Court, and will act according to its judgment

Chief Justice There is no doubt but it would be improper for a Grand Juror to be examined to establish facts as founded on the evidence given before the Grand Jury, because the statements sworn to before them, are only *ex parte* but as to what a witness now called upon, did say before the Grand Jury, evidence may be given by any Grand Juryman to prove the consistency or inconsistency of the witness As an individual, I cannot say but I approve of the original policy of the law, which prescribed in the oath of Grand Jurymen, a clause of secrecy; but when the legislature of my country have changed the laws, and struck out of the oath what relates to secrecy, it proves to me that the legislature thinks differently.

Mr *Hay* This circumstance has weight I thought we could not come to this question to-day, but it involves the most serious consequences The Grand Jurymen are called to establish some change, between the statement of General Wilkinson before the Grand Jury, and his statement made known in Court The Court ought to hesitate before they admit such testimony I have been told that the reason which induced the legislature to make the alteration in the oath of Grand Jurymen was this all presentments were to be made, on the knowledge of two of their own body, (or on other legal evidence) and as their oath required that they should keep secrecy, it was often impossible for the attorney who prosecuted for the Commonwealth, to prosecute with effect, as they could not know the names of the witnesses, and to remove this obstacle to public justice, the clause of secrecy was struck out If the opinion of the Court be not decidedly made up, I should wish to have an opportunity of reflecting on the subject, and shewing that this evidence ought not to be admitted

Mr *Wickham* observed, that the legislature had, no doubt, well weighed the policy of the clause requiring secrecy, and had determined against it, that there was no reason why they could and should not adhere to this legislative alteration, and that as to a witness any thing he had said any where, might be given in evidence against him, to shew his inconsistency.

Mr *Martin* A Grand Juryman can, like any other man, prove facts known to himself, independently of what the witness proved before the Grand Jury.

Mr *Hay* said, that Mr Martin did not understand him, and explained further that Mr Henning had informed him, that the legislature were induced to make the alteration in the oath, for the reasons already stated

Mr *Martin* observed, that the only reason that justified the Grand Jury's oath of secrecy, was to prevent offenders against the laws from getting information of inquiries made against them, and escaping—that this held no longer after the Grand Jury had been discharged—that while the Grand Jury were deliberating, it was proper to keep these proceedings secret and that those against whom presentments were to be made, should not have notice to make their escape, but that to prevent Grand Jurors from giving evidence after they are dispersed, was to lay the foundation for the most atrocious and most infamous perjuries—that any man might go before the Grand Jury, and charge another who was innocent with the most outrageous and enormous crimes in the world, and have him arrested and confined, and yet remain perfectly safe and secure from any punishment for his perjury

Chief Justice The question as to the policy or motive of the legislature in changing the oath is different from the question before the Court, which is, what is the legal effect of the changes. The original policy required the oath, but as the legislature have changed it, I cannot see how the inference can be avoided, that their opinion of the policy is altered

Mr *Wirt* If it should be discovered that in the original institution, secrecy was necessary, independently of the oath, the Court would not then receive the testimony, without the consent of both parties

After some few desultory remarks, relative to reserving their objection to Mr Tazewell's testimony, Mr *Burr* said, that gentlemen might submit to his testimony with a protestando The *Chief Justice* again stated, that the original policy of the institution which presented the oath of secrecy being changed, the testimony he supposed must be heard, and

Mr Tazewell was sworn.

Mr. *Burr* Can you state the questions you put to Gen Wilkinson in the Grand Jury, and his answers?

Mr. *Tazewell*. It would be perfectly impossible to state them all, from the length of time he was under examination; but I have notes of the facts stated by him, from which and my memory I may be able to answer any questions which gentlemen may be pleased to ask?

Mr Burr State what you recollect about the formation of the cypher

Mr Tazewell There are three kinds of cyphers. The original cypher was produced before the Grand Jury, in order to enable them to decypher the letter received from yourself, (addressing himself to Colonel Burr) It is the alphabetical cypher, framed from an edition of Entick's pocket dictionary, now before the Court but as proper names occurred, the dictionary could not answer the purpose, and arbitrary marks were invented to represent them. The hieroglyphics were stated by General Wilkinson himself, without any interrogatory put to him, to have been devised by Captain Campbell Smith, in the year 1794, the dictionary and arbitrary alphabet and arbitrary signs for units, were designed in 1799 or 1800

Colonel Burr Were there any objections made as to these dates? A There were objections as to these dates in my own mind The cypher was formed in 1794 On the face of the cypher these words occur "*Canada, Louisiana* and *New Orleans*" It seemed to me a circumstance somewhat singular, that as early as the year 1794, cyphers relative to those countries should have been adopted, when probably no individual in this country had the acquisition of Louisiana in contemplation, as it was not purchased till some years afterwards I asked him why he thought of a cypher expressive of that country, at that time? He said, that he could not explain the reason then, but that he would examine his papers and would tell us The next day Gen. Wilkinson, of his own accord, told us, that the treaty with Spain, about the free navigation of the Mississippi, was formed about the year 1794 But he had correspondence on the subject, which was of great moment to the western country That in the year 1794, I was an officer in the army which marched near Canada against the Indians, and thus, therefore, part of the cypher had relation to Canada He said that the cypher might have been formed in the year 1794, 1795 or 1796, but he believed in the year 1795. He was asked whether he could be more explicit as to the time, and he gave the same answer as he gave to-day in Court

M. Burr Did he assign any other reasons, why the cypher had relation to this country? A I do not recollect that he did, or whether we asked any further questions on the subject.

Mr Burr Did General Wilkinson say any thing about this letter to me? A It was a subject of great interest with the Grand Jury to understand the cypher and the contents of the cyphered letter After decyphering it, it excited a strong wish in them, to see the letter post marked the 13th of May, referred to in it, having been received from General Wilkinson by you, in the course of the correspondence between you. That wish was strengthened by the testimony of Mr Swartwout, who said, that he had seen a letter from General Wilkinson to yourself—that it was partly in common writing, and partly written in cypher And the letter contained these words: " *I am ready.*" Questions were then put to Gen. Wilkinson, whether he had written such a letter. He answered, that his impression was, that he had written one, perhaps two or three letters, that he was sure, but that his impression was, that he had written some let

ters   He was then interrogated as to the contents of those letters   He said he could not recollect them, but there was one expression which he wrote on that occasion, which he did recollect, and his object in writing it was. to discover Mr Burr's
real designs   That expression was, " *I fancy Miranda has*
" *taken the bread out of your mouth—and I shall be ready for the*
" *grand expedition before you are* "

Mr *Burr*   What motive did he assign for saying that Miranda would take the bread out of my mouth, and that he would be
ready for the grand expedition before I would? A   He said that he
had had an interview with you at St Louis; in which you stated
that you had some great project in contemplation, but whether
it was authorized by the government or not, he did not explain
nor did you then enquire   He said. this was all the information
he was possessed of at that time, of your designs—that he was
satisfied you had some great project in view, but had not expressed what that project was, that he was therefore anxious to
extract from you your real designs   That the object of the correspondence was to develope those designs   Mr Burr   Did he
assign any reason for wishing to develope my design? A   I do
not recollect that he did, or did not, but the avowed object was
to communicate them to the government

Mr. *Wickham* (holding in his hand a key to one of the cyphers
Has there been any addition or alteration in this paper, since you
saw it before the Grand Jury? A. I will state my impression-
Sir   I well recollect that this endorsement suggested one doubt
to the Grand Jury: " I solemnly swear, that the numbers and
hieroglyphics within, excepting those which denote the alphabet
and the units, " Burr" and " Wilkinson," were written by th
late Captain Campbell Smith in the year 1804, 5 or 6, then actin
as my aid-de-camp"   Mr Randolph and myself had both bee
acquainted with Captain C Smith, and supposed there was som
mistake in this date   I recollect putting this question to Gene
ral Wilkinson. " Do you think that this cypher could have bee
formed in 1804, 5 or 6, as Captain C Smith must have been dea
before that time?"   The General, after some consideration, sug
gested that there must be a mistake in the date, and that " 1794
was intended instead of 1804   I think also that the figures 1801
on the face of this paper, have been added since it was laid be
fore the Grand Jury   I suppose that General Wilkinson's me
mory has become refreshed and more correct since his examina
tion

Mr *Hay*   General Wilkinson was not interrogated *here* abou
th's alteration? Mr *Tazewell* General Wilkinson was asked
whether this was an affidavit which he intended to swear to? He
said that there was a mistake in the date specified in this endorse
ment, and that it ought to have been 1794, 5 and 6, (as it is no
put) instead of 1804, 5 and 6, (as it was *then* written) Mr *Hay*
This endorsement is not in General Wilkinson's hand-writing
General *Wilkinson*   It is in the hand of my clerk, Mr. Nau, wh
is here

Mr *Hay*. If Mr. Tazewell is introduced here merely to show
these variations, why was not General Wilkinson himself interrogated about them? He could have himself explained them

Mr Burr We have not heard of these variations before. **Q.** Was not the year 1798 first mentioned as the date of the cypher? **A** I do not recollect.

Mr Baker. Do you recollect when it was represented to him that it was impossible a certain date would be correct, that he immediately changed it? **A** I am not certain.

Mr Burr Did you not understand, that the motive of his holding a correspondence with me was to draw from me my views? **A** I am not certain that this was his language. **Q** Did you understand him to say, that his object was to communicate my views to the government? **A.** Such, Sir, is my impression. Indeed this inference from his answers was so palpable, that I did not think it necessary to ask the question.

General Wilkinson. Do you recollect, Sir, of any stipulation or acknowledgment, before the Grand Jury, that what passed *there* was in confidence? **A.** I have lately conversed with another Grand Juryman, and I have now reason to believe that something of the kind did pass. You had the letter of the 12th Nov. in your hand. You read a part, and then stopt, observing that, perhaps, you ought not to read the ballance. Mr. Barbe then said, from what you had said before the Grand Jury, you might do it with safety and in confidence.

Mr Martin You ought not to have entered into such engagement.

Mr Tazewell There was no stipulation or engagement entered into on the subject. But, now, Sir, as to this testimony, and particularly the subject of that letter, I beg you to understand, that when I heard the letter, I thought it improper, as a gentleman, to disclose its contents to any one, although I have often heard General Wilkinson's name mentioned, and I never shall, unless forced by law to do it.

General Wilkinson Do you recollect, Sir, when I mentioned to the Grand Jury that my object was to draw from Colonel Burr his real design whether that object anteceded the 13th of May spoken of, or not? **A** I do not recollect that you referred to any antecedent circumstance, particularly. You only spoke of letters of 1805 and 1806, as important. All the letters you spoke of, were subsequent to his visit to St Louis.

General Wilkinson thought it probable that he might have written such a letter, post-marked 13th May, but had no precise recollection.

Q *To witness* Do you recollect my assigning for a motive of drawing what I could from Burr of his designs, that if they were good, the government might participate in the advantages of his object, but if otherwise, I should do as I have done? **A** I believe you did. I recollect you said something of sinister views you thought he had, particularly in your reference to Judge Easton, which was a letter written in such mandatory terms as to offend you.

Mr. Burr. Then this was anterior to my visit to St. Louis? **A.** You had given General Wilkinson's letter of introduction to Judge Easton at Massac, which was delivered by an aid.

[Conversation and questions of little importance closed the sitting, and the Court adjourned till to morrow morning]

SATURDAY, October 3.

Chandler Lindsley was again called.

Colonel *Burr* Do you know whether Dunbaugh, after his examination, had an opportunity of seeing his deposition ? A I recollect sometime in June, he said he could recollect his affidavit given in New Orleans, verbatim. He said he had a copy of it Sometime afterwards he was in his chamber, and I was passing by, or was in the same room with him, and saw him on the bed with a paper in his hand. I asked him if it was a copy of his affidavit, and he said yes Q Did you afterwards see it in his hand ? A No

Mr *Martin* At what time did you see him with that paper ? A In the month of June, previous to his examination before the Grand Jury

Mr *Hay* Where do you reside ? A My former residence was in Connecticut Q Where is it now ? A I have no fixed place, but expect to return to Bristol, in Connecticut. Mr *Wirt* Is that the place of your nativity ? A. Yes

General Wilkinson's testimony concluded.

Mr *Martin* You offered an extract of your instructions to Lieutenant Pike yesterday We wish to see them

General Wilkinson I have now in my hand a complete copy of those instructions If they are admitted, I wish them to be read [They were received and deposited with the clerk] Mr. Martin had asked me yesterday respecting the information which Major Bruff had given to General Smith and Mr Read of the Senate. I have a copy of it Here it is

Mr *Martin* We only want to know when it was received ? A. I do not recollect It was dated on the 1st of March, 1807, at the city of Washington

Mr Martin Then it could not have influence on your conduct at New Orleans We do not want the paper [See note *A A*]

General Wilkinson said, that this same Major Bruff had been summoned here as a witness by Colonel Burr, to take revenge, as he had alledged, for past injuries. *Colonel Burr* asked whether this was offered as testimony ? *General Wilkinson* No, I only offer what I can prove *Colonel Burr* said that if General Wilkinson had any further evidence to give, he would go on with it But these appeared to be mere conversations, and he did not know whether dictated by passion or not *General Wilkinson*, addressing the Judge I stand here in a very complex character On the one hand, summoned as a witness on the part of the United States, on the other arraigned as an offender by Colonel Burr and his counsel. I therefore hope, should I commit any impropriety, it will be ascribed to the peculiarity of my situation

Mr *Wickham* I asked you if you had had any communications with Timothy Kibby, and whether you had ever made any propositions to him as to an invasion of Mexico A I cannot charge my recollection There was a very general idea that hostilities with Spain would certainly take place It is possible that I might have spoken to him, as an officer of the militia, with respect to the probable force which he could bring into the field in such an event

Mr Wickham Have you ever made any confidential communications to him or to any other person on that subject? A. I am not conscious that I ever did

General Wilkinson having been informed that there were no more questions to be propounded to him, addressed the Judge as follows Upon a former occasion you will recollect, Sir, that reference has been had to a certain letter of which so much has been said That letter is designated by the words said to be used in it "Yours post marked the 13th of May, has been received" Yet that letter has been withheld under the pretext of delicacy, while we have seen it employed in the most artful and insidious manner to injure my reputation and fame Sir, I demand the production of that letter I hope that a reputation acquired by nearly thirty years of service is not to be filched from me by the subtility, artifice or fraud of Colonel Burr and his counsel I hope that on Monday next, you will permit me to introduce a variety of letters and documents, explanatory of the insinuations and inuendoes which are calculated to implicate me as an accessary in his plans A member of the Grand Jury has been brought forward to state what my evidence was, which is an additional reason why I should be permitted to explain. It was my intention to have commenced my testimony by giving a regular detail of the proceedings of Colonel Burr from his first passage of the mountains, but I have been advised to confine myself to a narration of the occurrences which commenced at Natchitoches It is now my duty to go back to that period, and trace Colonel Burr, step by step

The *Chief Justice* said, that the Court could not sit to hear any thing except what related to the cause As to the intention with which General Wilkinson had done any particular act, he had been permitted to explain, in the whole course of his testimony. With respect to what has been drawn from Mr Tazewell, as he understood it, there was no variation between his statement, and that of General Wilkinson

The papers which General Wilkinson wished to refer to had as well appear before the public in any other way, as through the channel of this Court

Mr *M'Rae* said he did not know that General Wilkinson had gone so fully into an explanation of the various parts of his evidence as he intended He had understood the Court to say, that General Wilkinson might be permitted to explain himself as to any particular fact mentioned in the course of his testimony It is the wish of General Wilkinson, on every occasion, to explain the motives which governed him ; and if in some points, he has not been so full as he intended, he hoped that the Court would still hear him

Mr *Wickham.* General Wilkinson must necessarily stand in a very delicate situation Very heavy charges are brought against Colonel Burr, which are attempted to be established by the testimony of General Wilkinson. It must have been foreseen that the counsel of Colonel Burr, if they did their duty, would endeavor to impeach the credibility of General Wilkinson as a witness But this is a common case It is a thing which may happen in the case of every witness who is brought before the Court A witness is brought forward on whose testimony much reliance is placed He is, of course, cross-examined to see whether he be consistent with himself, or whether his credibility can be impeached. In the present case, I am certain that General Wilkinson has been treated with every degree of delicacy which the nature of the case would admit of With respect to myself, I am conscious of having done nothing but what my duty dictated, and of having used as much delicacy towards General Wilkinson, as his relation would justify. We do not see the necessity or propriety of General Wilkinson's entering into explanations If these are to be made, they had better be reserved for some other time, and some other place.

Colonel Burr General Wilkinson has been sworn to tell the truth, the whole truth and nothing but the truth If he has not told the truth, let him do it now ; and not by his explanations, interrupt the examination of other witnesses

General Wilkinson I have received, and have now in my possession a number of letters from Colonel Burr of a ambiguous nature, combining matters personal with matters political, but they contain nothing which would subject him to legal penalty or legal obstruction I have before observed, that under the circumstances in which these letters were received, I did not feel myself at liberty to divulge their contents without the permission of Colonel Burr I now ask that permission, for I feel that delicacy which others *profess* to feel. The letter post marked on the 13th of May has often been mentioned, and has been used to injure my character, and envelope it in doubts and suspicions This letter, if written at all, must have been in answer to one received from Colonel Burr. Why has it not been produced ? I challenge its production. for if it were brought forward, it would release me from all obligation to silence, and would enable me to exhibit to public view, the letters of Colonel Burr Sir, I am incapable of uttering an intentional falshood ; and under the solemnity of the oath which I have taken, I have no hesitation in saying, that the declarations of that gentleman (pointing to Colonel Burr) that he had put the letter beyond his power and with my knowledge, is totally destitute of truth.

(A A)

Washington, 1st March 1807

Major Bruff communicated to S. S. and Colonel Reed, that Judge Easton, (immediately after the first number of the Western World appeared) told him, (Bruff) that it was in his power to ruin Colonel Burr, that he had told him his plans ; that they were such as had made his hair stand an end, but he had gone so far, that he could not recede Bruff told him, that he owed it to himself as an honest man, to inform government That I cannot do, said, Easton, for I am under an oath of secrecy ; but, could

you had previously taken an oath paramount to any other to your country I cannot tell, said E but I will communicate the whole to you, if you will come under an oath of secrecy, indeed, continued he, Colonel Burr told me, that he had heard of you, that he had heard you was a brave man, had sense and firmness, and desired me to speak to you I am therefore, at liberty to tell you all the plans, if you will swear that you will keep the secret Burr refused, and advised Easton to act like a man of honor and a friend to his country, or he would hereafter repent

Examination of Matthew Ellis.

Mr *Burr*. What do you know of Dunbaugh? Did you see him at Baton Rouge? A I did He told me that he had just got out of prison for debt, by paying part of the debt and giving bail for the rest Q Bur what passed between you? A. When I met him, I was surprized to see him He said he had been arrested in Natchez by Lieutenant Romney Q For what cause? A As a deserter

Mr *M^c^Rae* At what time did you see him at Baton Rouge? A On Sunday the 28th of March

Mr *Burr* What further account did he give of himself? A. He said that he had been sent down the river, that he had made his escape and had demand protection of Governor Grand Pre, at Baton Rouge He said that he intended to stay there, till he had got his pardon from General Wilkinson, which he had written for

Mr Burr His pardon for what? A For desertion. He told me that he had descended the river with you at Captain Bissell's request, and that he had written to General Wilkinson, that if a pardon was sent to him he would come down and give information of all that he knew against you He also put a letter into my hands for Captain Bissell

Mr Burr What was the purport of that letter? A. To inform him that he repented leaving the garrison at Fort Massac in that manner, and to request him to support the statement he had made about leaving the fort When he gave me that letter he requested me to put it in the nearest post-office, and not to let Lieutenant Romney have it Q What did he propose to Captain Bissell in that letter? A I did not see that letter, and I know only what he told me He told me that his letter to Captain Bissell corroborated that to General Wilkinson

Cross-examined.

Mr *Hay* What State do you belong to? A. I belong to Pennsylvania but I came from Natchez to this place. Q When did you descend the river? A On the 20th of November. Q In what boat? A In my own. Q Are you the person who sold your boat to Blannerhasset at the mouth of Cumberland? A. I sold it to Mr Burr, but went down in her to Natchez. Q You came with certain articles? A Yes Q. On a general trading voyage? A Yes

Mr Wirt You went down in your own boat after you sold her to Burr ? A Yes, I was not to deliver her, till I got to Natchez

Mr M'Rae. What time did you pass Blannerhasset's island? A I do not exactly recollect, but some time in the latter end of November.

Mr Hay. Where did Blannerhasset and his squadron fall in with you ? A Not before I arrived at the mouth of Cumberland Q Did you sell your merchandize to Colonel Burr ? A the greater part Q What induced you to go down the river with them to Natchez, after your boat was sold ? A Because it was not paid for

Mr M'Rae What articles did you sell to Colonel Burr ? A A parcel of hoes, axes, iron and ploughs I was not to receive any pay, till I got to Natchez Q Were there any boats at the mouth of Cumberland ? Was Blannerhasset there ? A I believe he was Q Was Floyd ? A. Yes Q Tyler ? A Yes Q Israel Smith ? A. I expect he was Q You went down with Floyd a head ? A Not altogether under Floyd Q Why did you go a head. A I did not know Q When did you leave Natchez ? A About the first of March. Q. You were not sent to New Orleans by any body ? A No Q What carried you to New Orleans ? A Business of my own. Q Did you carry any thing for sale to New Orleans ? A. May be, I had a few deer skins and some Racoon skins left

Mr. Wirt How long did you remain in New Orleans ? A About 8 or 10 days. Q Did you see Colonel Burr on your return? A I did Q Where did you see him last ? A At Washington in the Mississippi territory, where I was at the trial of Colonel Burr. Q Were you there when the trial closed ? A No I went up several times to hear it, but the crowd was so great that I could not get in Q Why did you go to Washington ? A I went to see Colonel Burr for a settlement Q What claims had you on Colonel Burr ? A I do not exactly recollect the amount Q Any claims for your boat ? A. Colonel Burr consented I might take back my boat Q What other claims had you ? any for iron A Yes. and for apples and other articles Colonel Burr had told me not to part with the axes, mattocks, and ploughs at all events

Mr Hay Had you any previous acquaintance with Dunbaugh ? A No, but I had seen him once before

Mr M'Rae Were you never requested by any one to converse with Dunbaugh ? A No Q Were you acquainted with none of the party before you saw them at the mouth of Cumberland ? A None, I believe Q How came it to pass that you had the conversation with Jacob Dunbaugh ? A It was accidentally He came into the tavern where I was Q Where did you intend to go, when you left Pittsburg ? A To no particular place Q Did you understand nothing at the mouth of Cumberland, of the purpose for which those men were gathered together ? A I heard at the falls, that they were going to settle lands Q Were any propositions made to you to join the party ? A No I never conversed with any but Col Burr, and then only to make a bargain Q Were you to have waited at Natchez till the arrival of Col. Burr A Yes I got on the 5th of Jan The trial of Colonel Burr was in February Q What did you wait so long for ? A I had business with Mr Ponsonby. Q. Did that business detain you so long ? A No

I chose to remain. 'Twas partly curiosity and partly business that detained me. I might have finished my business in a day or so Q Did you get payment for the articles in the boat? A No I never have for any of them Q Did you deliver any of them? A. I did some of them

Mr *M'Rae.* Were you summoned here? A. Yes, Mr Ashley sent me word to be here Q Had Mr Ashley been down the river? A No. Mr Ashley was in the back part of the country. Q What reason had you to believe, that Mr Ashley had the power to summon you? A I was told that he was summoning others, and he sent me a verbal message to come, but I don't know by whom, I understood too from Captain Floyd that I should be wanting

Mr *M'Rae.* When did you receive a subpœna? A Not before I came here

Examination of Captain Bissell.

Mr *Burr* You have heard the testimony of Dunbaugh, I wish you to state every thing that came within your personal knowledge; how he came off; whether on my application, or by your direction Did you receive any message from me by Mr Hopkins? A None further than a billet you sent me on the morning of the 26th It was delivered at my quarters at fort Massac by Mr Hopkins He was introduced to me by Mr Fort, who had been previously introduced to me by a merchant of New-Haven Mr Fort walked up with him, and took breakfast with me I had then heard of Colonel Burr's acquittal in Kentucky, and I supposed he was peaceably descending the river

Mr *Wickham* read the billet in the following terms

(1)
Mouth of Cumberland, 25 Dec

DEAR SIR,
I avail myself of the opportunity of Mr Hopkins to offer you salutations and the compliments of the season

Having proposed to descend the river in a few days, I shall have the pleasure of paying my respects to you on my way, and of receiving your commands for the south.

I am Dr Sir,
Very respectfully,
Yr Obt St

A. BURR

Cap BISSELL, *commanding at Massac.*
Mr. *Hopkins*

Mr *Burr.* Did you receive any other letter from me besides that? A. None I had a little conversation with Mr Hopkins, none about Colonel Burr's passing the garrison On the evening of the 29th was the next information that I received. Mr. Tyler arrived with his barge They took supper with me. After supper, some of the gentlemen said they must return to Col Burr, who would stay in the bend above, all night. I invited some of the gentlemen to take a pallet with me, which they agreed to. Colonel Burr's boats, nevertheless, came down in the night. I had retired to bed, when my centry hailed aloud. I arose, and undressed, repaired to the fort. Some one said that Col Burr's boats were passing I thought this a singular thing, after I had been told that Colonel Burr would stay in the bend above His boats went down to the bend of Bayou, a mile below the fort When I returned to the house, I found that Tyler had gone to the boats

Mr *Burr* Is not the lower bend a good harbor? A It is Q. Is not the river just opposite to the garrison a bad one? A It is I have seen boats sometimes staved on the rocks in that part of the river I rose soon in the morning, to pay my respects to Col Burr I went down in my boat, and was introduced into his room I invited him to breakfast, which he declined, I invited him to dinner, but he declined all my civilities. He asked me if I had received any news from below I replied that I had not He then informed me that General Wilkinson had made a compromise with the Spaniards He said he was sorry for it, and that General Wilkinson ought to have fought them I observed, that I supposed General Wilkinson had acted by orders Mr *Burr* How came Dunbaugh to go? A After breakfast, while I was at my ice house, Dunbaugh came and asked for a furlough of twenty days He had previously asked me for a furlough to go down the river to do business. After a short time, I agreed that he should go; this happened while on parade, and not at the back of the fort, as his testimony states It is proper to mention that a boy had come up with two billets, one for Dunbaugh and the other for me Here is mine. When I was in Colonel Burr's boat, he had asked me if I knew of an opportunity to send to St Louis by the way of the lead mines, and whether he could procure an express I told him that I had reviewed my garrison, and that I had a thought of sending a messenger, and Dunbaugh to be that messenger, as he had a good horse, that if he would bear his expences, Dunbaugh might go M. *Burr* Is it not impossible to get an express in that part of the country? A It is There is no population in the neighborhood of the garrison The Indian title is just extinguished They are just surveying the land, but it is a mere military post

Mr. *Wickham* read the letter in the following terms

(C)

Jan 30

Sir,

If you will give Serjt Dunbar a furlough for 20 days, I engage that he shall conform to the terms of it

In this case, he will not go to the Lead mines

Very respectfully
Your obt. servt

A. BURR.

Mr *Burr* Was Dunbaugh inspected? A He was, and mustered too. Q Did he show his clothes? A He did Q Did you tell him to borrow any clothes in which he was to appear on parade? A I did not His own clothes were then there, and are now in his own box at fort Massac. He wanted to carry his clothes, but I forbade him. I gave him this furlough, with a pointed order to return at the end of twenty days

(3)

Sergeant Jacob Dunbaugh of my company has leave of absence for twenty days from date, at which time he is to return to this garrison

Fort Massac,
Decr. 31st. 1806
DAN BISSELL, Captain
1st Regt U S Infantry,
Commanding

(Endorsement)

Brunsburgh 23, January, Sergeant Jacob Dunbaugh having expressed a wish to return to his company at Fort Massac and there being no regular officer at this place I have, from a respect to the public service, on his application, to request that he may be permitted to join his company

BNJn. BRUIN.

Endorsed { On our way to Pety Gulph directed to Joseph
Calverts two miles from the Gulph.

When I handed him this furlough, I also delivered him a small billet for General Wilkinson, informing him of what I had done. Here is a copy of that letter

(4)

Fort Massac, December 31, 1806

Sir—Jacob Dunbaugh of my company having solicited the indulgence of a furlough for twenty days, and Colonel Burr pledging himself, that Dunbaugh shall conform to the terms of it, I have thought proper to grant the indulgence, and hope it may meet your approbation

Colonel Burr will inform you how I am and how situated Mrs. Bissell is still confined to the house, but I think recovering.

I am respectfully,
Your obedient servant,

DANIEL BISSEL, Capt.

General Wilkinson,
Pr. Col Burr

Mr *Burr* Do you remember sending me any message by Dunbaugh to the mouth of Cumberland? A I remember well that I sent him to buy a beef, and told him, if he saw Col Burr, he was to present my compliments to him. But I did not tell him to proffer my services to Colonel Burr nor to any one else. I am an officer of the United States only. That part of his evidence is false

Mr Burr Did you receive a letter from Dunbaugh while he was at Baton Rouge? A Yes on the eleventh June I received a letter which he wrote from Baton Rouge There is no date to it The post mark is Washington, Mississippi territory. I received it with other letters from New Orleans. Captain Bissel then read the following letter,:

(5)

Honored Sir—With sorrow I take Pen in hand to inform you
that I had to tell the officers that you sent me as a Spy against
Colonel Burr and had to make outt of what I new againg him I
wrote that you sent me on that Purpes the thought My Capt was
interrested I told them that he did not know what Burr's men
ing was to take some men down the River with him My Capt
thought as I had been down before him that I could find what
his intention was Lieut Roney took me up as a Diseerter and
put me on board the Schooner Revenge to send me to New Or
leans but I did not go he tuck my furlow from me I told Him if
He would give me my furlow that I would go to the General but he
would not

I should be thankful if my Capt would send me some money if
there is any for me and my Boots if my Detes air paid I wished
more than a thousand times I had staid at Fort Massac I have
nothing more but still remain your humble Serv't.

                                        J,, DUNBAUGH Sergt
(In the margin John Prechard is in due me 8 dollars)
Dan'l Bissell Capt
          commanding

I am at Baton Rouge, and will Remain untill I Get a pardon
   Mr *Burr* Had J Dunbaugh been discharged from service the
year before? A Dunbaugh had been a faithful Sergeant, but I
represented to General Wilkinson the propriety of permitting
him to find a substitute, who could do more service, as he had lost
the use of one of his fingers This defect is mentioned in the ad
vertisement of him as a deserter

   Mr B Has he yet been tried for desertion? A No I have not
yet preferred a charge against him Q Is he liable to a prosecu
tion? A. Yes, I suppose so Q Did you ever make him a present
of a breast plate? A I did, but not at the time he has stated It
was on a day when I lost a son Mr. Owens was about leaving the
garrison at that time, and presented me with a very handsome
breast plate—I gave my old one to my Sergeant This was about
the last of October or beginning of November Q Did you make
a report to the government which has been published? A I think
a letter of mine to the Secretary of war, has been published with
a letter of General Jackson's

Cross-examined.

Mr. *Hay*. Is this the furlough that you gave?
   A It is; but there is some endorsement on it of which I know
nothing
   Mr *Hay* Aye! that is some writing of Judge Brum's
   Mr *Burr* Have magistrates a right to enlarge furloughs? A
I know of no such thing in the articles of war
   Mr *Hay* Had you any previous acquaintance with Col Burr
A. Yes, I had seen him at fort Massac, in General Wilkinson's
quarters. Q Did you know that Dunbaugh was going down the
river A Yes, I gave him permission, and such was my confi
dence in Colonel Burr, and such my ignorance of his movements
in the western country, that had he asked me for a Sergeant

and six men I should have indulged him. Q. When you gave him his furlough, how far down the river did you expect him to go? A. I supposed not further than Madrid. However I do not recollect that I gave him any particular injunctions as to that point because he was to return at any time within twenty days

Mr Hay. You say he was your confidential Sergeant? A. He was, I raised him from a first Corporal. He was illiterate and I requested him to learn to write. Perhaps I had set copies for him myself. Q. You had a good opinion of him then till lately? A. I had.

Mr *Wirt*. You said that Colonel Burr wanted a messenger to go to St Louis? A. I did. Q. Do the lead mines lay on the land route to St Louis? A. They do.

Mr Wirt. I see in Burr's letter, that Dunbaugh was not to go by the lead mines? Did you understand he was going by them? A. Oh! no, I supposed that he was going down the river to New Madrid, perhaps to bring back letters. I knew nothing of Colonel Burr's movements. Q. Did you conceive that Col. B guaranteed his return? A. I had but a short conversation with Colonel Burr, for I was at that time busy. Dunbaugh applied to me for a furlough, but he had before applied to me for one to go to New Madrid. Q. Then I understand you did not rely on Burr's guarantee? A. I cannot say. When his billet was put into my hands, I was engaged on parade, and I believe I told Dunbaugh, that I would see about it.

Mr *M'Rae*. I think you said that you knew nothing of this expedition? A. I heard that Colonel Burr had been tried and acquitted in Kentucky, and I had heard it from travelling ignorant people, who could not give me much information. Q. Then you had received no such information as induced you to question the propriety of his movements? A. None. I was acquainted with his standing, when he left the Senate of the United States. I respected him as a former vice-president of the United States, and felt disposed to treat him with all the civility which was due to his rank. Q. When you granted this furlough to Dunbaugh, did you not advert to his engaging in Burr's service and exhort him to obey his orders? A. I did not, I only granted him a furlough for twenty days. Q. Did you speak at all with Dunbaugh when he applied for his furlough? A. I recollect to have told him, that Colonel Burr had also applied for him to go. I always speak to my men when they go on furlough, to enjoin on them propriety of conduct. I did not call him to my room and give him any private instructions, as his testimony states. I might have called him before me, and told him to treat Colonel Burr with politeness. I so felt towards him both at that time, and in eighteen hundred and e

Mr *Burr*. Have you the advertisement of the desertion? A. Yes. It is filed in Court. It was read.

(6)

TEN DOLLARS REWARD

Deserted on the 19th of January, 1807, when on the indulgence of a furlough, Jacob Dunbaugh. Sergeant in Captain D Bissell's

company, first United States regiment of infantry. He is of a
Dutch descent and is about 5 feet 8 1-2 inches high, brown hair,
blue eyes, fair complexion He is by trade a hatter. He has lost
the use of one of his fingers on the left hand, which stands crook
ed inward. Whoever will take up said deserter, and deliver him
up to any military post in the United States shall receive the
above reward and reasonable expences.

Fort Massac, January 19, 1807.

DANIEL BISSELL,
Captain commanding.

(Endorsement)

I do hereby certify, that the within advertisement among seve
ral others of the same tenor and date was handed to me by Capt
Daniel Bissell on the morning of my departure from fort Massac
first of February last, which I distributed in the territories of
Mississippi and Orleans I do further certify, that Captain Bisse
requested me to make use of every exertion in my power to hav
the within mentioned deserter apprehended

Given under my hand this 28th day of July, at Nashville, in th
year 1807

THOMAS A. CLAIBORNE

When Dunbaugh overstaid his time, I wrote to some of m
friends, among the rest to Lieutenant Hughes, requesting him t
report to General Wilkinson the desertion of Dunbaugh, I ex
pressed the great confidence I had in him, my anxiety lest h
should have been deluded away by the followers of Colonel Bur
or lest he should be sick, if he was sick, I requested Mr Cla
borne to furnish him with some money, if he was not to adver
tise him as a deserter.

Mr *Hay* Have you any objection to produce that letter? A
will look at it and then determine

I presume it would be necessary to state the civilities whic
have past to and from Colonel Burr On Butler's trial I was fre
quently with him in the morning He had been acquainted wit
Mrs Bissell from a child He had sent her a barrel of apples from
the mouth of Cumberland, and she returned some little thing o
other, such as preserves.

Examination of Judge Todd.

Col Burr Did Colonel Lynch submit to you for your opinion
the title of papers of Bastrop's grant? A Colonel Lynch shew
ed me the title papers on which he said the grant was founded
Q Did he say any thing about my having acquired an interes
in it? A No Q Did you give any opinion as to the title? I wa
not sufficiently informed of the laws of the territory to give an
decided opinion I discovered the grant as founded on a condi
tion, which it was said had not been complied with, and I wa
inclined to doubt its validity. Q. Were you in Kentucky, durin
the summer of the last year? A I was Q. Was there a goo
deal of alarm among the people? A There was. Q Was th
owing to any acts which I had done? A I saw publications i

the print stating, that preparations were making of boats and provisions in the state of Ohio a publication also appppeared, in the " Western World," under the signature of an " Observer," which excited a good deal of alarm Q How many years have you been a resident of Kentucky? A Ever since 1786. Q Can you state what has been the general reputation of Gen Wilkinson for the last four or five years? A For the last four or five years I have not seen General Wilkinson

Mr Wirt His reputation as to what?

Colonel Burr As to integrity and truth

I never heard that question d For the last twelve months there has been an unfavorable opinion against him owing to his official and public conduct There have been publications and republications circulated injurious to him, but whether true or false I cannot say

Mr Wirt Do you recollect what kind of an instrument Bastrop's grant is? A Not of the kind I have usually seen The instrument is from the Governor of New Orleans to Bastrop, granting him so much land, on condition that he would settle so many families upon it, the government of Spain to furnish them with provisions for such a length of time I understood from Colonel Lynch, that the government had not complied with the condition on its part

Mr Hay Do you recollect whether the time for the performance of the condition had elapsed? A Yes, it had elapsed. Q. Did Lynch shew you any thing deducing his title from Bastrop? A No, but he said his title was regularly deduced from Bastrop Q Was it the original or a copy of the grant you saw? A. It was the original in the Spanish language

Mr M'Rae Was the only evidence of Lynch's title his own declarations? Was there no other evidence of title to him? A No other evinced, deducing a title from Bastrop.

Mr Tazewell was again called by Col Burr, and asked whether he had observed any inconsitency in the evidence of Gen. Wil, inson Mr. Tazewell said it was not for him to state what his impressions were, arising from the whole tenor of Gen Wilkinson's evidence Indeed it was impossible for him to answer a question put in that way. if he were asked whether in any particular part of Gen Wilkinson's testimony he had observed a variance, he would answer the question He was then asked, whether he had observed any inconsistency or contradiction in the evidence delivered by Gen Wilkinson, before the Judge, and that given to the Grand Jury? His answer was, none at all But said Mr. Tazewell, as I have gone so far in speaking of my impressions, it may e proper for me to state what opinion I had formed. I must say, that I saw no good reason for Gen Wilkinson to invite Col Burr to the western country

Mr Hay. Do you recollect whether the testimony of Swartwout coincided with that of Gen Wilkinson? A. They could not e said to oppose each other in their testimony Mr Swartwout was examined first ; and many of the circumstances to which he deposed were unknown to Gen Wilkinson

Mr *Hay.* I speak as to the conversation between Swartwout and Gen Wilkinson

Mr *Tazewell* Perhaps there was this difference; Gen Wilkinson stated, that in the absence of Col Cushing, which was spoken of by both of them, Mr Swartwout slipped into his hand the ciphered letter from Col Burr Mr Swartwout, who discovered the utmost frankness and candor in his evidence, stated the transaction in a different manner. He declared that the letter was delivered openly, without any effort to conceal it.

Mr *Hay* But they both stated the fact to be the same, that it was delivered in the absence of Col Cushing? A. Yes. They both stated that fact in the same way. I would not be willing to be understood that I doubted any thing Mr Swartwout said Although he appeared before the Grand Jury, under very unfavorable circumstances, and my impressions were very strong against him; yet the very frank and candid manner in which he gave his testimony, I must confess, raised him very high in my estimation, and induced me to form a very different opinion of him, from that which I had before entertained.

Examination of Colonel McKee

Mr *Burr.* Did you see any persons seized in the Mississippi Territory? A At Natchez I saw upwards of 20 of your party seized Q When was this? A About the 18th of February Q Was it before or after my trial? A It was after the trial Q Did you see Mr Graham there? A. I saw the Governor, Colonel Claiborne, and Mr Graham Q Had you any conversation with either of those gentlemen about seizing me by military authority? A I did converse with Mr Graham on that subject. I expressed my regret at seeing you seized He told me that I should soon perceive the cause of it Q Did you know of any measures for seizing me by martial law? A I heard that some had been taken and these reports were still further confirmed by a letter which I received from General Wilkinson Q What was in the letter A The postscript stated that if I wished to make myself acceptable to the government, I must seize Burr, Blannerhasset, Smith, Tyler, Floyd, or Ralstone Q Who conveyed this letter to you? A Commodore Shaw Q " If you wished to make yourself acceptable to the government"? A If you wished to tax the government beyond denial, or some such expression.*

Q. Was any proposition made to you by General Wilkinson relative to the Spanish colonies? A There was Q. Was there an invitation to you in relation to these colonies? A. In 1805 about Christmas, I received a letter from General W asking me whether I could not raise a number of cavalry to follow his fortune

* *Copy of a Postscript to a letter of General James Wilkinson to John McKee, dated New Orleans, February 8th, 1807*

" If you want to distinguish yourself and tax the government beyond denial, go alone and seize Burr or Blannerhasset or Tyler or Ralstone or Floyd or all of them and deliver them to the flotilla."

on a crusade to Mexico   Q. Have you that letter?   A I have it not here, but on the Mississippi.   I do not particularly recollect its date   Q What number of cavalry was mentioned ? A. I know not

Mr *Blannerhasset*   At the time General Wilkinson wrote to desire you to seize me, was I in the hands of the civil authority? A So I understood.

Cross-examined.

Mr *M'Rae* You held an office under the general government? A I have not been in one for 4 years Q What office was it? A I was agent for Indian affairs to the Choctaw nation Q And when did your office cease? A I was removed by the president in 1802 Q Did you not receive a letter from Colonel Burr through the hand of Lieutenant Jackson. A. I did Q. Where is that letter? A It is destroyed Q State its principal contents? A It was written on the 6th of January 1807, and invited me to meet him at Bayou Pierre on the 13th. Q Do you recollect whether there was nothing more in this letter, besides the invitation A I recollect nothing more The letter itself I burnt

Mr. *Hay.* Was no particular object stated in this letter? A None Q And why, Sir, did you burn that letter? A Because I saw men arrested for a much less matter than carrying such a letter, and I put it out of my possession.

Mr. *Hay.* You say there was a postscript to a letter which you received from General Wilkinson, what did you understand was the purport of that letter? A. I did suppose, that we should go to war with the Spaniards. Q Did he state that the expedition was unauthorized by government? A He did not.

Mr. *Wirt.* He gave you then no impressions of an illicit object? A he did not at that time.

Mr. Wirt. You answered it? A. Yes   Q Where is your answer? A This is my answer Here Mr Hay read the following letter.

Chickasaws, February 22, 1806

Dear General,

Your kind remembrancer of 3 Dec I received, and had written to you immediately after at the Bluffs, but a French-Indian countryman who had promised to call on me for it went off without doing so I had written a great deal about recruiting in Tennessee, about cutting and slashing and packing dollars and enjoying orium cum dignitate. But " *all our differences amicably settled with Spain*" knocks all these Utopia to the devil and I am again awake to the painful anxiety attendant on a state of suspence. I have requested my friend Moore to press the Secretary to decide, and I expect his answer in less than a month. Whatever my fate may be, I must always feel myself deeply your debtor for the solicitude you have manifested for me

Has any news reached your capital from Captains Lewis and Clark? it is rumoured here that they have been killed, I hope sincerely there is nothing of it.

I have the honor to be,
With esteem and affection,
Your friend,

JOHN M'KEE.

His Excellency General Wilkinson

Mr. *Hay*. Is that also your writing dated as late as February last ? A. It is

Mr *Wirt*. At the time of this correspondence and before, did you consider General Wilkinson as your friend, whose agency you were willing to employ with the Secretary at war ? A I expected much less, Sir, from his interest than his disposition to serve me

Mr Wirt You considered him then as a friend. whom you would be willing to trust ? A I did. Q. Is this your writing ? A It is Here Mr. Wirt read the following letter

Chickasaws, August 1st, 1805

Dear Sir,

Your friendly *talk* from Pittsburg, 13 May, I had the pleasure to receive at this place a few days ago I thank you sincerely for your letter to the Secretary of War I hope it will have the effect at least of relieving me from the most painful suspence I have ever experienced —I had addressed him myself from Tennessee just before I set out and am now beginning to look for his answer—I would have written you sooner on the subject of my Expectations, but I thought them so well founded as not to require even mentioning to the Secretary; they were founded on a direct and unsolicited promise from himself to me that I should be provided for in Louisiana as soon as the government should be organized. This was confirmed to me afterwards through Col Moore and general Trigg, and last winter he repeated to several of my friends his continued disposition to serve me, but I remain as ignorant as I was two years ago in what way I hope it may be in your quarters—and soon, for a state of suspense is penance worse by far than fasting. I trust like a good Catholic that I am in a fair way for Heaven, even if I should have to pass through a jail

I think I understood from Mr Dinsmoor that he had written you at large, on the late successful negociations with this nation, he has to-day started to Natchez, from thence to the Choctaws, where about the beginning of Oct the commissioners are to meet that nation at *Mount Dexter* and make another attempt to treat for land—I have had some talk with both the White and Red Mingos about securing a tract of land to a Choctaw boy that has contrived to prattle himself into my affection—this is my business here—my prospects of success are not very flattering, as I find the business must be clogged with other negociations.

On the 28th ult Col Burr passed this on his return from Orleans to Nashville and I understood he intended (to) visit your government

If I am disappointed in the hope of going up the Mississippi, when I leave this, I will inform you of my course and prospects

With respect an esteem, I have the honor to be,

Your Excellency's
Obedient Servant,

JOHN M'KEE.

His Excellency General Wilkinson.

Mr *M'Rae* then also read the three following letters

Chickasaws, October 19, 1805.

Dear General,

    Your friendly letter of the 8th ult. received by post on the 15 instant, and from some cause or other it was the most acceptable I ever received, it found me here alone far gone in the blue devils, doubting whether I had not better expatriate myself and try my fortune amidst the storm now gathering in Europe You cannot think it strange that I feel extremely mortified when I tell you that I have a year past since May last been waiting in daily expectation of receiving orders to repair in a public capacity to some part of your government; this expectation was excited by the unsolicited promises of the Secretary of war. It is true he has still held out to my friends the idea that he intended to provide for me and it must be admitted that he has taken time enough to do it well In the mean time however I am suffering the most painful anxiety and my cash exhausted to a small sum. I have always suspected Claiborne of injuring me with the government, though he declared with uplifted hands to the contrary. I was informed that he had in 1801 made some representations to you and Col Hawkins founded on a report made to him by Colonel Joslyn, that I had abused him and the president in a conversation at Mr. M'In.ches in this nation in very severe and improper language, I have since seen Colonel Joslyn who gave me a certificate of which the enclosed is a copy. for what I said of Mr Claiborne a candidate for an office in the State of which I am a citizen. I certainly can be accountable only to him, not to the government that has since cloathed him with the mantle of its power If I had learned ornate et polite discere to a man whose head and heart were neither of them formed to my taste on the scale of great Mingo's, perhaps I might have been fitted with an office e'er this, however, nil desperandum, Teucro duce. I'll remain here till X'mas; the Choctaw treaty I fear will fall through this season and that will not be among my least disappointments, for I had some expectation of procuring at it a tract of land for my young Choctaw It is reported here from Cumberland that the Secretary of war has written that if the Choctaws wish to sell land they must send deputies to Washington.

    Cressite, &c is very catholic, but when, I proceeded father to 'bleach high'' I blushed to the fingers ends, but why, I would not tell you for all my hopes in the government, on paper I mean

With sincere respect and esteem I have the honor to be
      Your Excellency's
        Obedient Servant,

              JOHN M'KEE

His Excellency General Wilkinson

    The irregularity of the mail-carriers occasioned this to be a mail later than I expected. I am now informed by a letter from Mr Dinsmoor, that the commissioners will meet the Choctaws about the first of November, and this morning I set out with your friend General W. Colbert to Mount Dexter to attend the treaty.

              J M'KEE

CHICKASAW BLUFFS, *December 20*, 1806.

Dear General—So many oportunities present themselves here for conveying a letter towards Orleans, that I would be ungrateful to leave this without at least offering you the compliments of the season, and my hearty prayers for the success of your bark, on this tempestuous sea of liberty, for with all my confidence in her staunchness I cannot help feeling some anxiety on account of sunken rocks and the cursed pirates that infest her track.

I set out to-morrow morning for the Chickasaws, and if you should have leisure to inform me of your health by post, I will remain there long enough to receive it, and I hope not much longer.

I have the honor to be with very sincere respect and esteem,
    Dear General,
        Your obedient servant,

JOHN M'KEE

His Excellency General Wilkinson

NATCHEZ, *January 25*, 1807

Dear General—I wrote you a note from the Chickasaw Bluffs about X'mas Soon after I set out for this place, where I have been ten days, and will yet remain perhaps too weeks longer—just to laugh at the ridiculous scenes that are passing before us. There is a wide field for conjecture, and every man takes his own direction The *little mingo* here has assumed a *military attitude* to defend the alter and the throne as well against Colonel Burr as the encroachments of the army

I have little doubt that ere this you will have set me down as a Burrite, and as little that you will believe me when I assure you that as yet I am not; and I must know the object and the means better than I do before I can be. 'Tis true that having nothing to do and hearing that some great enterprize was on foot, pratronized by many great men, and wink'd at by the government, I came here to profit by any opportunity that might offer of bettering my situation by honorable enterprize As yet I see no way open, but in the face of my country's laws, and desperate as my fortune is, I will never deliberately do an act that will prevent me from returning to the spot where I was born.

I have lately received a letter from Mr Simpson, saying " your friend General Wilkinson wishes you were here. as he has it now in his power to serve you." This to me just now is very interesting information—and by return of the mail will be glad to hear from you.

Need I tell you, that considerable pains are taken and taking here to render your name unpopular, and by persons too, I am informed, who speak much of the laws and constituted authorities of the country.

Your friend Dinsmoor, Freeman, and M'Kee, occupy a room here and laugh at this puddle in a storm

I have the honor to be very respectfully,
    Your Excellency's
    Obedient servant

JOHN M'KEE

His Excellency General Wilkinson.

HUNSTON, *February* 16, 1807.

Dear General– I received a few days at Natchez, your favor of the 8th instant, and nothing could have given me more pleasure, for the strange distant reserve of some of my friends in this quarter, and an observation from Doctor Carmichael that my note from the Bluffs had excited some suspicions of me in a bosom, that shall never be justified in haboring any, had mortified me sorely, read that note again, and if it does not speak the language of a heart that loves you, I must have been very unfortunate in expressing myself.

I never was a *Burrite*, nor can I ever give myself up to schemes of lawless plunder—'tis certain that in my present situation I might have engaged in any honorable enterprize, however hazardous—but the late one such as it has been represented, is such as I hope no friend of mine will ever suspect me of favoring.

I have not means, and if I had, I have not at this moment the time to give you much information on the state of things in this country

May your purse keep pace with your heart and may you live a thousand years

Your affectionate friend,

JOHN M'KEE.

His Excellency General Wilkinson.

Mr *Burr* Did you make any reply to that postscript ? A. I did not, I answered the letter itself

Mr *Hay* complimented Colonel M'Kee's letters; declaring them to be excellent *models of the Epistolary style*

Mr. *Burr* observed, that a number of witnesses whom he had summoned, had gone away during his indisposition, and that he had but one more witness to produce, except to establish certain circumstances against General Eaton.

Mr *Blannerhasset* then requested that a Mr. Gates might be called in on his behalf.

Examination of Nathaniel Gates.

Mr *Blannerhasset* Will you state what you know about the seizing of the boats and provisions near Marietta ? A. I was present at the time of seizing the boats. There were a few barrels of kiln dried corn meal on board, and a few barrels of apples belonging to Mr Putnam Q. Did you see any officers on duty ? A. I saw militia officers; General Buel and his aid-de camp, Captain Clark. Q Were you a militia man ? A I told them they had no right to call upon me in that character, during my present capacity

Mr. *Blannerhasset* You had been used only to carry a fife and not a musket ? A. Yes. Q. Did they accept of your apology for not acting ? A They said, that if I would attend at twelve o'clock with my musket, I should be immediately discharged.

Mr. Blannerhasset. Did you see any authority under which General Buel acted ? A. Yes, he shewed me a paper, which he said was his authority from Governor Tiffin Q Did you see the boat that was built for my family ? What has become of it ? A The last time I saw it, it lay in a very uneasy posture near Marietta

Cross examined.

Mr. *Wirt* As far as I understand you, you were called on to attack the boats ? A Yes Q And you were called on to carry a musket ? A Yes. Q And you were unwilling to do it ? A I was Q That is, you were willing to whistle and not to fight ? A Yes.

The following deposition of *Charles Fenton Mercer*, was then offered on the part of the accused and read

City of Richmond, State of Virginia

Personally appeared before me Edward Carrington one of the magistrates for the city of Richmond aforesaid, Charles Fenton Mercer, of the county of Loudon and State aforesaid, a witness summoned to attend the trial of Aaron Burr, who being duly sworn on the holy Evangelists of Almighty God, deposed as followeth, viz That having been called to the neighborhood of Point Pleasant, at the mouth of the great Kanawha, between the 20th of September and 6th of December, 1800, to transact some business, relative to an estate which he has in the county of Mason, he became acquainted with Mr. Herman Blannerhasset through the introduction of Mr J. Alston, of South Carolina, once a fellow student of the deponents, in the college of New Jersey. This acquaintance commenced about the first of November, near an open boat on the Ohio, in which Mr. Alston, attended by his family with a carriage and pair of horses, and accompanied by Mr Blannerhasset was descending the river as far as Kentucky, from whence he expected to prosecute his journey home by land. The reputation which Mr. Blannerhasset had acquired for talents, learning, and taste, and an accentric and somewhat a romantic mode of life, rendered this unexpected interview one of the most interesting events which occurred to this deponent during his residence on the Ohio, and he accepted with much pleasure an invitation from Mr. Blannerhasset to visit his then beautiful and once much celebrated island. It is true, that about that perod, and for several weeks after, reports were in circulation, that Mr. Blannerhasset was engaged with Colonel Burr in some common enterprize, which many persons imputed a highly criminal design. But those reports, and especially the injurious suspicions often connected with them, seemed to have arisen from pre-existing prejudices against Col. Burr, which it was not difficult to trace to an origin very remote from the designs now ascribed to him , as the reports were believed and propogated by those who spoke of them with a conviction and a zeal proportioned to their ignorance, or malignity ; and as they were in themselves most improbable, absurd, and ridiculous, the deponent considered them entitled to no serious consideration About the middle of November the deponent again saw

Mr. *Blannerhasset* at the house of Colonel Andrew Lewis, on the Ohio, three miles from Point Pleasant, where he alighted from his horse for an hour or two, in his journey from Kentucky In a conversation which then occurred he adverted with much sensibility to the reports above mentioned which had then become more current, and to which every day was adding some new exaggeration, and declared them to be utterly false He was the last man in the world, he said, who would be disposed to disturb the peace or impair the prosperity of the United States Weary of political situations in his native country, he had sought, he added, and found an asylum in America, the tranquility of which, he could never violate. " He had indeed " he admitted, " united with Colonel Burr, (whom public rumor had injured as much as himself,) in the plan of colonizing and improving a large tract of country on the Red river, originally granted by the king of Spain to one Baron Bastrop, and lately purchased by Colonel Burr of a gentleman of Kentucky The tract contained eight hundred thousand acres, and the condition with Colonel Burr and himself were to pay, for it was, forty thousand dollars, but by distributing a part of it in hundred acre farms, among a number of emigrants, whom such an inducement, they expected, would invite to join them, they had no doubt on the most moderate estimate, of being able to raise the value of the remainder to more than one million of dollars Mr Blannerhasset declined the pressing invitation of Colonel Lewis to make a longer suspension of his journey, alledging as his reason for prosecuting it with greater rapidity, that the servant who accompanied him, had been sent to him in Kentucky by Mrs Blannerhasset to urge his immediate return home for the protection of his house from the fury of a mob who had threatened to burn it down. He added also, that he expected to leave the island in ten or twelve days after his return, as it was his intention to remove his family down the river before the severity of the approaching winter sat in, and renewing his former invitation to the deponent, politely hoped that he would commence his journey to the interior of Virginia within that period

Sometime after this conversation, on Saturday evening, the 8th day of December, the deponent arrived in the course of his journey home, at the shore of Ohio, opposite to the island of Mr Blannerhasset, and having first learnt, with some surprize, that Mr Blannerhasset was yet on the island, crossed over to his house in a violent storm of wind and rain That evening and the following day, he spent at the most elegant seat in Virginia, and in the society of Mr Blannerhasset and his lovely and accomplished lady. He saw no other persons on the island, except their two infant children, their servants, Mr. Neale, the clerk of the Court of Wood county, a Mr. Putnam, who had come from the Ohio side of the river, to rent the island of the proprietor, who was soon to abandon it, some young ladies who visited Mrs Blannerhasset on Sunday morning, and two or three of the inhabitants of the Virginia shore, who came to enquire of the deponent the price of some lands, which he had advertised in the adjoining county of Mason The deponent having expressed a desire which he felt on visiting the country the year before to become the purchaser of Mr Blannerhasset's farm, he had the godness to show him the plan and arrangement of his house. Every room in it was opened to his inspection As he walked through the different apartments, the proprietor frequently apologized for the confusion into which its furniture was thrown by his preparation for his leaving it, and observed that the greater part of his furniture, his musical instruments and his library containing several thousand volumes of books, were packed up for immediate removal His children were also habited in their habited dress Nothing he added, delayed his departure, except the unfinished condition of the boats which were to take him down the river

Finding that Mr Blannerhasset estimated his farm, containing one hundred and eighty acres of land, with its improvements, at fifty thousand dollars, which he remarked was ten thousand dollars less than they had cost him, the deponent abandoned all idea of becoming their purchaser, and the rest of the time which he spent at this beautiful seat, was employed in conversation with its proprietor and his family It turned upon his removal to the Ouachita, the name of his new purchase He pressed the deponent to become a participant in it, suggesting how much it would augment his fortune, and enforcing the inducement which he offered to his interest, by an assurance, that the society which he invited the deponent to join, would soon become the most select and agreeable in America He spoke of Colonel Burr as the moral head of it, and when the deponent expressed a doubt of the permanancy and happiness of an union, formed under such an auspices, and dwelt on such traits of the general character of Colonel Burr, as he deemed exceptionable Mr Blannerhasset vindicated him with the enthusiam of an ardent admirer and friend, and furnished the deponent with facts of which he had never before heard, and which he treasured up in his memory, as the foundation of further enquiry into the character of that gentleman. They related entirely to occurrences of ancient date, and on this side of the Allegany

Mr Blannerhasset having intended, before the deponent reached his house, to visit Marietta on Sunday evening, the deponent availed himself of a double motive to quit this attractive spot He did not leave it however, without regretting, that the engagements of its proprietor, and his own dreary journey but just begun in the commencement of winter, forbade him to prolong a visit, which, although so transient, had afforded him so much pleasure It is but a tribute of merited gratitude to add, that he left it in perfect good will to all its inhabitants. All that he had seen, heard, or felt, corresponded so little with the criminal designs imputed to Mr Blannerhasset, that if he could have visited him with unfavorable sentiments, they would have vanished before the light of a species of evidence, which if not reducible to the strict rules of legal testimony, hath nevertheless a potent influence over all sensible hearts, and which, though it do not possess the formal sanction, hath often more truth than oaths or affirmations! What! will a man, who weary of the agitations of the world, of its noise and vanity, has unambitiously retired to a solitary island, in the heart of a desert, and created a terrestrial paradise, the very flowers, and shrubs, and vines of which he has planted, nurtured and reared with his own hands: a man whose soul is accustomed to toil in the depths of science, and to repose beneath the bowers of literature, whose ear is formed to the harmony of sound, and whose touch and breath daily awaken it from a variety of melodious instruments—will such a man start up in the decline of life, from the pleasing dream of seven years slumber, to carry fire and sword to the peaceful habitations of men who have never done him wrong? Are his musical instruments and his library to be the equipage of a camp?—Will he expose a lovely and accomplished woman and two little children, to whom he seems so tenderly attached, to the guilt of treason and to the horrors of war, a treason so desperate? A war so unequal? Were not all his preparations, better adapted to the innocent and useful purpose which he avowed, rather than to the criminal and hazardous enterprize which was imputed to him. Whence arose those imputations? From his union with Colonel Burr. But it is evident, that he has been led to this union from his admiration of the genius, and confidence in the virtue and honor of the person with whom it has connected him. That which with a harsh judging world, is the foundation of a belief of his guilt, when thoroughly and candidly examined, carries on its face therefore, the stamp of his innocence. Such were the sentiments with which the deponent left the island of Mr Blannerhasset. He has only to add, that he reached Marietta, after a ride of fourteen miles, in company with that gentleman, at nine o'clock at night; that he slept at the same house with him and parted from him with much regret on Monday morning, at he house of Judge Woodbridge. Mr Blannerhasset on that day went up the Muskingum to visit his boats and the deponent prosecuted his journey home.

Given under my hand this 21st of September, 1807.

E. CARRINGTON.

Here Mr Wickham read the following affidavit.

The affidavit of JULIAN DEPESTRE, *of lawful age,*

Saith I have no knowledge of Col Burr ever entertaining any designs or intentions against the peace of the United States or against New Orleans, nor against any other part of the United States, Nor have I any knowledge of his having any designs against any part of the dominions of the king of Spain, so long as that power should keep at peace with the United States.

In the last days of July 1806, in one of my visits to Col Burr in Philadelphia, I communicated to him my desire to make a tour in the western country to seek for an advantageous situation for my family Col. Burr told me that if I would be ready, he would be glad to go to that country with me · and that if I could be at Bedford by the tenth of August, we would spend there a few days, and then proceed by Pittsburg, adding obligingly, that he would introduce me to some of his friends, who probably would be the most proper persons to direct me in some requisition ; I agreed, and the 11th of August I met Col. Burr at Connelsburg, and continued in his company till the second or third of September, that I left him a few miles the other side of Chilicothe

We spent about seven or eight days of the time I was with Col Burr at the springs of Bedford, then we went to Pittsburg where I was introduced by him to General O'Hara. The 22d of August we went to Mr Morgan's, half way we met with his two sons, the eldest and the youngest, who came, sent by their father to welcome Col Burr and accompany him to his house, there we dined and passed the night; next morning we went to breakfast at Washington. Mr Morgan's eldest son accompanied us, after breakfast we parted and continued our journey. When we travelled in the back part of Virginia and in the Ohio, I saw several men coming, some in their name and some in the name of several others to Col Burr, they generally told him that they had understood, that there would be a Spanish war, and that he was to have a command, in which case they came to offer themselves, manifesting the pleasure they would have to serve under his orders, Colonel Burr would always hear what they had to say, and answer them in my presence, and I must say that so long as I travelled with him he never avoided my presence to speak to any body; in general, his answers to them were, that there was no such thing as a war till now, and that he had no kind of commissions of government, but that if it happened that there should be a war, which he thought would be the case, that he would make every effort in his power to take an active part in it, and that if he succeeded, he would be very glad to command such brave men; I saw them all go back very well pleased with him: it was about that time on my observation to Colonel Burr, if he had really a mind to take a part in a Spanish war, if there was one, that he asked me if in that case I would accept service in the army of the United States, or, if the views of government should not extend to conquest, in a private enterprize, to be composed of volunteers, adding that such expeditions were permitted by the laws of the United States in case of war; I answered him all at once, that if he had credit to procure me such situation in the army as would suit me, I was very willing, he then replied that he understood it so.

We arrived at Marietta the 26th August, and the 27th, we went to visit Mr Blannerhasset on the island, we dined and passed the night there, the 28th, we came back to Marietta, and the 29th we took the road to Chilicothe, where we arrived the 31st

The 2d of September, I left Colonel Burr about twenty miles from Chilicothe, he pursued his journey to Cincinnati where I declined going with him, having an intention of visiting Upper Louisiana, and fearing my time was already too short from that time I have not seen him, (except a moment at Louisville,) where I had spent a few days with my friends, that was about the 10th of September. At my return, about the 20th of October, I found him again at Lexington, busy and much engaged with old papers and others, he told me he had made the purchase of the *Ouachita lands*, of which he had spoken to me and offered to accommodate me with as much as I pleased, for the same price it cost him   I acknowledged this mark of friendship, but told him I declined for the moment, because I wanted to go to see and provide for my family, he then asked me if I renounced to take a part in the Spanish war, if there was one, I told him there was none yet, that even it was my opinion, there would be none, but in case there should be one, if he pleased to send me word of it, and of the situation in the army, he would have obtained for me, I would be on the spot as soon as himself   He agreed that I was right, but told me he believed there would be war, and he hoped I would stay a day, to take his letters   I agreed, and the next day he sent me a letter for H B Latrobe, which I delivered on my passage at Washington city

The deponent, on cross examination, on the part of Colonel Burr, being asked the following questions, viz

Q Did you, when at Morgan's, hear Colonel Burr talk of any military expedition, or of a separation of the union? A No, except during the dinner, when old Mr Morgan began once or twice speaking about the rumors of a separation of the western from the eastern states, but Col Burr seemed not willing to engage in such conversation, and did all he could to get rid of it, seeming more pleased with the conversation of the ladies

Q Were you generally near Colonel Burr, or separately engaged? Did you see him engaged in particular conversation during that visit? A I heard the Morgans give their testimony, and I do not know for my part when such long conversations could take place   it was not before me, and Colonel Burr was but very little time absent from me   After dinner I left him with the company, and with old Mr Morgan in the garden, where Colonel Burr came and joined us with the ladies, about fifteen minutes after   We were together all the remainder of the day, in the walks we took, and visits we made, except when I was abed, Colonel Burr took the candle, and went out the doors for a few minutes, and then came back to his bed

Q Did you hear Colonel Burr, during the time you was with him, talk of a separation of the western from the eastern states? A Never, I only remember that in almost all the houses we stopped to, people would often engage a conversation with us upon that subject, but Colonel Burr would always laugh at the idea

Q Did it appear to you that he was or he was not seriously interested in making some new establishments in lands? A. His project of purchasing lands on the Ouachita was a more general topic of our conversation when we were travelling, and he seemed anxious to prevail upon me to engage in it

Q In what state of mind was then old Mr. Morgan? A We were told that he had been of late very sick, and he appeared to be quite in dotage.

(Signed)   JUL. DEPESTRE

City of Richmond, ss.

Personally appeared before me, Edward Carrington, a magistrate for said city, the above named Julian Depestre, and made oath that the foregoing affidavit by him subscribed is true.

Given under my hand, this 1st Oct 1807.

E. CARRINGTON

ELIJAH JONES *was then called on the part of Mr. Blannerhasset.*

Mr. *Wickham* Will you relate the conversations and trans actions, that passed between Mr Blannerhasset and yourself?— The counsel for the prosecution objected to this question Could the declarations of Mr Blannerhasset be considered as evidence?

Mr Wickham enquired, whether the declarations previous to the act alledged as an offence, might not be received as evidence?

Mr. *Blannerhasset* observed, that his declarations had been frequently quoted and urged *against* him, particularly in relation to the Hendersons Had he not the same right to quote his own declarations, when they were brought forward *for* his vindication?

Chief Justice And any person who accompanied Mr. Blannerhasset may be considered as a competent witness.

Mr. *Hay*. Did you then go down the river?

Witness. I did not Q. Did you agree to go with Mr Blannerhasset? A There were no articles of agreement between us, though I agreed to go There was however nothing binding and I did not go

Mr. *Hay* How easy would it have been for Mr. Blannerhasset to have made certain propositions to gentlemen, for the purpose of keeping his real object out of view.

Chief Justice. What prevented your going?

Witness. Because Mr Blannerhasset went off before the time that was appointed. If he had remained, if the boats had been finished and not stopped, I certainly should have gone.

Counsel Proceed with your evidence.

Witness In the fall of 1806, I called on Mr Blannerhasset, at Marietta, to know on what terms I could go down the river with him ——I informed him, that if we could agree on terms I would go with him He said, that I should be furnished with liquors and provisions, when going down the river, and that at the end of the journey I should receive one hundred acres of land, yet the engagement was to be no ways binding upon me, and I might leave him whenever I was dissatisfied. I mentioned there was a rumor in circulation that there was something else in view besides the settlement of the Ouachita, and that his designs were hostile to the U States; if so, he had better inform me at once, for if he took me with him under such circumstances, he would take an enemy. He said they were not hostile to the United States — I asked him if they were obstructed by a party in descending the river, whether they would defend themselves? He replied, that he would not resist the constituted authority, or persons lawfully authorized to stop him, but if they were not lawfully authorized, the laws of the United States would bear him out in resisting He observed that those who went on the first to settle lands, would have the most, as he would do the most help to them

Mr. *Wickham* Then your agreement was to leave Mr. Blannerhasset whenever you pleased? A It was Q. Was the president's proclamation received before their departure? A. I think it was not till afterwards, though I am not positive

Chief Justice. Mr. Woodbridge said it was not received till Friday afterwards.

Cross examined

Q At what time did he say he should leave the island? A. Different times were stated He intended to have started earlier than he did, but Colonel Barker did not finish the boats in time. He then said, that he should start as soon as they were finished Q Did he positively deny that he had any hostile designs against the United States? A. He did deny it I told him if he had any designs hostile to the United States, he had better tell me at once, and not to take me in, for if he did he would take an enemy. He lifted up his hands to heaven and said, he had not

Mr *M'Rae* Did he say that you should receive information of the object of the expedition at the mouth of Cumberland? A. Yes, that I should get such satisfactory information at the mouth of Cumberland, as would confirm me in my resolution to go on. I asked him if Colonel Burr was to meet him down the river.— He said it was probable, but he did not say where, but he seemed to speak of the mouth of Cumberland as being the place where he was to meet him.

Mr. *Blannerhasset* Did I not observe that information would also be given to you at Limestone, or the falls, and at other places down the river? A. Yes; you said that I would get better information than I had received at Marietta.

Mr Blannerhasset Did you not understand that the farther you went down the river, and the nearer you got to the Ouachita land, the better information you would receive about that land?

I understood from you, that I would receive such satisfactory information down the river, as should determine me to go on

Thomas Bodley

Mr. *Burr* Do you know of my purchases of land of Colonel Lynch? A I do—I think in the month of September, 1806, while Colonel Burr was in Kentucky, he and Colonel Lynch came to my office I was clerk of the Circuit Court in Kentucky, and mine was an office of record They stated to me, that they were making a contract for land, and asked me to draft a decree for them As at that time much engaged myself, I made a memorandum of the terms which they explained to me, and directed one of the young men in the office to draft a deed. That deed did not please them and another was drafted, which was recorded in the office of William Todd, notary public. After the decree was drafted, they showed me the plots of land, and Colonel Lynch told me, that he sold his interest or part of his interest in the Ouachita grant, and Colonel Burr had settled a part of the purchase money with Mr E Livingston, and had received the balance in Kentucky bank bills and drafts on New York A part of the bills I myself received from Colonel Lynch in payment of a debt.

Mr *Burr.* About that time was there no great deal of conversation about a Spanish war? A There was a great deal. Q.

Were not expeditions against the Spanish territories a very common topic? A. The Spanish was frequently mentioned at musters. War was considered as inevitable, and it was said to be stated in letters from the commander in chief on the Sabine.

Mr. Burr. Was there not a general ardor on the subject, especially among the younger part of the community? A. There was There was a great deal of zeal in some parts of the country — A great many expressed a willingness to join in a war. There are many young men in Kentucky, at any time ready to engage in a war that is authorized by the government, and particularly in one with Spain.

Cross-examined

Mr. Hay. Is it customary in that country to have deeds recorded in a notarial office? A. It is, when the deed is to go to a different state. Mr. Hay asked Mr. Wickham if there was any copy of that paper in Court. Mr. Wickham replied that there was not.

Mr. Hay. As the paper has been mentioned, it is better to produce it in Court.

Mr. Burr. A gentleman had said that my purchase of Ouachita land was all pretence, I wished to show that money had been paid on that transaction. I did not come here with my deed to establish a title. Mr. M'Rae to Mr. Bodley. Did you see the deed? I saw the original. It is now on record, and I recollect its contents. Q. How much land was this deed for? A. I am not certain about the number of acres, but the impression on my mind is, that it was for 300,000 acres.

Mr. Hay. Did you not understand from the parties that the period had expired for complying with the conditions of Bastrop's grant? I understood that it had been so from a default of the government, but that it had afterwards renewed the grant. Q. Was this transaction with you before or after Judge Todd was consulted? A. It was one or two years after the consultation.

Mr. Wirt. Did you see the original Spanish grant? A. I am not certain. I saw many papers recorded in my office, but I am not certain whether that was among them. I saw a copy in the hands of Colonel Lynch.

Mr. Hay. Did Colonel Lynch ever show any grant transferring Bastrop's title to him? A. I do not think he did.

Mr. Wirt. On whom were the drafts on New-York drawn? A. On George M. Ogden.

Mr. Burr. Had we any conversations about a Mexican expedition? A. Yes, frequently and frequently he spoke about Spanish war. He spoke several times on this subject to me and others. He thought if there was any war with Spain, that was the interest of the United States to carry an expedition into Mexico. He said, that he himself would willingly engage, and asked me, whether men could be got in Kentucky to embark in it. I told him, I thought they could.

Mr. Hay. Did you make any contract with Colonel Burr for flour? A. He said that he expected to settle the Ouachita land and in the event of a war, he would stipulate with his men to go against the Spaniards, and that then he would take from me any quantity of flour, not exceeding two boat loads.

Colonel Charles Lynch.

Mr. Burr. Will you relate whether I purchased any land of you, and how much? A. Yes—You purchased my interest in Bastrop's grant, wherein was about three hundred and fifty thousand acres. Q. Did I pay you any money? A Yes—about four or five thousand dollars Q. Did you suppose the three hundred and fifty thousand acres was exclusive of Livingston's claim? A I will explain. I claimed under Morehouse, and also purchased a mortgage of Stephen Wartz I found that Edward Livingston had also purchased the same mortgage I commenced a writ against Morehouse, and was about to commence one against Livingston, but I purchased him out Under that compromise I was entitled to about seven hundred thousand acres. The survey was made and marked upon the grant I was entitled to six-tenths and he to four-tenths of the whole grant of twelve hundred thousand acres Q. Was it a separate or joint interest of mine? A A joint interest Q Was I to settle what you owed to Livingston? A That was my object in selling

Mr. Hay. Had you a suit with Livingston? A No I was about to commence a suit, but we compromised I agreed to give him thirty thousand dollars for his interest. Then I sued Morehouse. Colonel Burr was to pay Livingston the amount of my purchase of him; he also paid me four or five thousand dollars in money, and was to take up certain paper which I valued at thirty thousand dollars more.

Mr M'Rae. Did you receive any drafts from Colonel Burr? A. Yes Q On whom were they drawn? A. On Mr. Ogden of New-York. Q. Had you any grant conveying an absolute title? A. In 1796, the petition was presented by Bastrop. in 1797, Bastrop was to furnish five hundred families, the government to find them in provisions for six months, but it being inconvenient to the government to furnish the provisions, a letter of office was granted to Bastrop by the baron de Carondolet, to dispense with the necessity of introducing the families Q. Will you state the various proceedings which have taken place on this grant? A. First, there was the petition, then the survey, upon that the patent, and then the letter of office.

Mr. *Burr* Did you get the opinion of James Brown as to the validity of Bastrop's grant? A Yes, and of Mr. Gurley too. They both said the title was good

Mr. *M'Rae* Do you suppose that there is no necessity to carry families there, now, for the purpose of saving the title? A. No, not now.

Colonel *Burr* Have you any account of the nature of the soil and the value of the land included in the grant? A. I have been on the land, and spent several days in exploring it. I have a certificate with me signed by several respectable gentlemen, stating it to be very valuable [Here Colonel Lynch produced the certificate]

Mr *Hay.* What is your own opinion of its value? A I think it very valuable Q. How far is it situated up the Red river from its mouth? A. About two hundred miles. It lies on the Ouachita river, and extends towards the Mississippi, from which in a direct line, it is not more than twenty or thirty-five miles.

Mr *Burr* Was your contract with me in consideration of money only, or upon condition of settlements? A. I considered the condition of settlement the principal consideration.

Mr. *M'Rae* What is the date of your contract with Colonel Burr? A. Last fall. The first thing I did was to contract with Colonel Burr after his arrival in Kentucky

Colonel *Burr* Was there any thing said about corn which you were to furnish me with? A. Yes, I was to furnish you with a quantity of corn. I received a letter from Colonel Burr about when he was at the mouth of Cumberland. He wrote from the mouth of Cumberland, that he should want more than I had agreed to furnish him with. He stated that he was then going on with a few friends to the land on the Ouachita, and wished me to send him some more corn and some utensils. Q. What kind of utensils? A. To clear two roads from the Mississippi. By cutting a road twenty-five miles, three hundred may be saved

Mr *Burr* What proportion of the land is prairie? A. I do not know precisely, but I suppose about one hundred thousand acres. Colonel *Burr* What is the character of that kind of land? A. It is esteemed among the French and Spaniards the most valuable, because it is fit for immediate cultivation

Mr *Hay* You spoke of a letter from baron de Carondelet, dispensing with the settlement of the land, was that before the cession to the United States? A. Yes; in 1797. All the transactions about it were in 1797. I have got letters stating that the commissioners appointed to adjust the claims to lands in this territory, thought it as good a title as any in Kentucky

Mr *Wirt.* Have you got a copy of your deed? A. No. Did it contain a general or a special warranty? A. In every conveyance of the kind, there is always a clause, providing case of an interference by Congress

---

MONDAY, October 5

Examination of Evidence.

This day Mr. *Burr* proceeded to put into execution his threat against General Eaton

Mr. *Burr* addressed the Court. I have understood, Sir, that there are certain proceedings of a Court Martial, of which General Eaton is the subject, and in which he was charged with offence that would disqualify him as a witness. After a satisfactory search, I find that the papers were burnt in the war-office. I have procured a deposition of the chief clerk in the war office, to show that such is the fact. This is to establish the loss of the papers, with a view to let in oral testimony.

Mr. *Hay* objected to this proceeding. Suppose that this deposition did actually establish the fact for which it was produced, yet why establish it in this Court? Mr Hay said he should object to the production of the records of a Court Martial. He presumed that General Eaton's trial was of a military nature, for some neglect or violation of military duty; and not for a charge of a civil nature. Taking this fact for granted, he put

sumed that the Court would not permit the introduction of the original records. The accused was at liberty to go into evidence as to the general character of a witness, but not as to any particular fact. Under such circumstances it was unnecessary to occupy the time of the Court either with this affidavit or with parol evidence.

Mr. *Burr.* The affidavit proves that such papers were burnt in the war-office. We shall prove by a witness, that such a Court Martial was held, and that General Eaton was found guilty of certain crimes, which would disqualify him as a witness in a Court of Justice. We shall prove that he has been convicted by a Court Martial of *crimen falsi*, and that the records of these proceedings were transmitted to the war-office, where they were burnt. We shall then produce a witness to prove these charges. Then will arise a novel question, how far a man convicted of a crime, not in a Court of common law jurisdiction, is disqualified from serving as a witness in a Court of common law, if it be such a crime as would amount to such a disqualification in a Court of common law. When the Court shall hear the proof, the question will then arise as to General Eaton's credibility and competency. We shall urge it as to both these points. We shall show, that the crimes were great enough to affect his competency, and if they were of an inferior dye, they would affect his credibility.

Mr. *Hay* presumed that evidence might be at any time brought up to affect the *competency* of a witness, but that if it was intended to impeach his *credibility*, it could only be done on the ground of general character; and that no witness' credibility could be attacked by any particular charge, unless he had received previous notice, and was permitted to prepare for his defence.

After some discussion, the *Chief Justice* over-ruled Mr. Hay's objection.

Mr. *Baker* then read the following affidavit.

District of Columbia, Washington County, ss.

Personally appeared before me, one of the Justices of the Peace of the United States in and for the county of Washington in the district of Columbia, John Smith, chief clerk in the war-office, who being duly sworn, deposeth and saith, that having searched the records and papers in the war-office, there are no records of proceedings of Courts Martial, or any papers or proceedings relative to the same, previous to the year one thousand eight hundred and one, and that he hath understood and verily believes, that all records and proceedings of Courts Martial, which were deposited in said office previous to the   day of November, in the year one thousand eight hundred and one, were burned with the office and a number of other papers on that day.—That having come into the office since the above date, he never saw any record or proceedings of a Court Martial held on William Eaton, and that there is no record or proceeding of such Court Martial now in the war-office to the best of this deponent's knowledge and belief.

Sworn before me, this 24th day of September, A. D. 1807.
RICHARD PARROTT.

[Annexed is the certificate of James Madison, Secretary of State, that the above R. Parrott is a Justice of the Peace as above stated.]

Colonel Henry Gaither.

Mr. *Burr* Are you acquainted with General Eaton? A. I am Early in '93.

General *Eaton* I presume I have a right to know what is to be proved by this witness

Mr *Wickham.* With respect to General Eaton's right, that is out of the question He forgets that this is a case between the United States and Mr *Burr*

Mr *Burr.* I have stated twice, that Colonel Gaither is to prove certain proceedings of a Court Martial We shall prove the conviction of General Eaton for certain crimes, and we may perhaps go further, and say, something as to his general character.

General *Eaton* I am willing, Sir, that the most minute acts of my life should be enquired into But, Sir, I have been taken by surprize. I did not suppose that the tombs were to be ransacked, to establish things which happened beyond the flood But, the records of that Court Martial should be produced here. The law in every case requires the best evidence

Mr *Wickham.* It is unfortunate that General Eaton did not know that the records were burnt.

General *Eaton* You, Sir, know that there are always three copies of the proceedings of a Court Martial This man who arrested me, if he has done his duty, ought to have kept one copy, the Judge Advocate another, and a triplicate copy of them is filed in the department of war But, Sir, if all these copies are lost, I will supply them, and though my copy may not be *verbatim* and minute, I will furnish the general contents I wave my demand for the copy of the record, and if testimony be now introduced, I shall only claim the privilege of explaining, after the witness has concluded.

After a few remarks from the bench, Colonel *Gaither* proceeded

In the early part of 1796, my acquaintance with Capt Eaton commenced on the river St Mary's, at a fort then building, called fort Pickering, where he then commanded. I commanded the troops of the United States on the Oconee On the information of Captain Dunscomb, I had Captain Eaton arrested, and had a Court Martial The trial was held

Mr. *Burr.* What offences were charged? A I do not recollect. I was not present at the Court Martial. Mr. *Burr.* State then as far as you do know Witness There was something about dealing in the soldiers' rations, and something about selling the public corn to the inhabitants of that part of the country. Mr *Burr.* For his own profit? A. So the report ran The number of charges against him I do not recollect, but he was found guilty of some one, or perhaps the whole I had the proceedings signed by the President of the Court, Captain Freeman, and Captain Eaton was suspended from command either for three or six months Mr *Burr.* What did you do with these proceedings?

A They were sent on to the Secretary at war. They were upwards of one hundred pages I do not know whether I confirmed the sentence or not There were some letters from Captain Eaton, requesting me not to send them on.

General *Eaton* I wish those letters produced

Mr *Burr*. And what did you do with Eaton? Did you send him on? A He was to be under arrest for some months, after the confirmation of these proceedings Many things were laid against him. Major Commandant Freeman complained of his quarters being stoned in the night, and supposed Captain Eaton was the cause of it. I thought it best in consequence of these complaints, to send him on to the Secretary of war, he being of no use there so long as he was suspended.

Mr *Wirt* Was the sentence ever confirmed by the Secretary at war? A I do not know, I never heard

Mr. *Hay* Will you be pleased to say, what charges you do recollect? A I cannot repeat the charges. There was something about selling public corn to the inhabitants, and clothing his soldiers with nankeens which he had brought from Philadelphia, and on which he made a profit However, I never attended the Court I only arrested him

Mr Hay Can you form any conjecture as to the number of charges? A I cannot The whole record was not filled up with the charges; but they also contained the proceedings and Capt Eaton's defence

Mr Hay. Do you know whether you confirmed the sentence or not? A. I do not recollect But I believe I did not; from having received some letters from Captain Eaton insinuating that I would not do justice, at which I was much hurt. Q And you do not know whether the Secretary at war confirmed the sentence? A I do not I never heard any thing more about it, until I heard of his being sent as Consul to Tunis

Mr *Wirt*. Then he was appointed to Tunis after all these proceedings?

Mr *M‘Rae*. When an officer is convicted of a crime, is it not customary to cashier him? A. It depends on the nature of the offence I have seen them sometimes cashiered and sometimes rebuked.

Mr M‘Rae Was it not regular for you first to have acted on this sentence? A By the rules and Articles of war, I might have done it, and so far indeed, until it touched his commission.

General *Eaton* Are you positive that the suspension of the Court was for three or six months? A I do not say, that the sentence ran for three or six months. There was a suspension for months or years Mr M‘Rae. For years? There is a very great difference between years and months.

Chief Justice. That is of no importance.

Mr *M‘Rae*. It certainly shows the incorrectness of the witness's memory. Q. Did you say that General Eaton wrote you not to send the records to the Secretary at war? A. So I understood from his letters. He wanted a conference with me.

General *Eaton* Are you confident whether this request was made before or after the trial? A. I am not confident. It has been a great while ago.

Mr. *Hay* Is it customary for the Secretary at war to send an answer, when a sentence is sent to him for confirmation? A Yes——but many letters from him to me never arrived and some that arrived were broke open Q. And you sent General Eaton to the Secretary at war? A Yes; a vessel was going from St. Mary's to Philadelphia I wrote to Captain Eaton to come down, and sent him on to Philadelphia for further instructions.

Mr. *M Rae* Did you hear from General Eaton afterwards? A Just before he shipped himself off to Tunis, he wrote to me

Mr. *Martin.* Did the complaints cease, after he went to Philadelphia? A Yes We were perfectly tranquil

Mr *Wickham,* Do you recollect any charge of putting an infant on the Muster Roll and drawing rations for him? A No Q A little boy? A Yes, after I thought it improper to have two filers and a drummer on the roll

Mr *Wickham* What was his name? A Donaldson or Daniel son

Mr *Hay* Was this one of the charges before the Court Martial? A No

Mr Hay Then you will answer no questions as to that

Mr *Wirt* How long did you remain in the army after this A. Till June 1802

Mr Wirt Did you resign then? A. I got a letter from the Secretary at war, revoking my commission

Mr *Hay* Were you not yourself under arrest? A. Yes, by the civil authority, and then by the military Q At what time A In 1802 Q Was nothing done in the military arrest? A I considered my dismission as giving me liberty to withdraw, and I came off Q By whom were you arrested? A By General Wilkinson

Mr *Wirt* What officers composed the Court Martial, that tried General Eaton? A Major Commandant Freeman, President Captain S Tinsley, Captain Nichol, and some other officers. I am not certain whether Captain Davidson and Ensign M'Call were the other members

General *Eaton* They were Ensign M'Call and Lieutenant Thompson.

Mr *Wirt* Did they remain in service? A. Freeman is now a Major, Thompson is dead, M'Call, I think is in service

Captain Samuel Tinsley

Mr. *Burr* You were a member of the Court Martial that was held over General Eaton at St Mary's? A. I was Q What were the charges? A I recollect but one Q And what was that? A For speculation When General Eaton went there, he had brought round with him some nankeens, which he had made up into summer coats, and furnished to his men on a profit, it was supposed Q Was he found guilty on these charges? A He was suspended from his command.

Mr *Hay.* Do you recollect, to which charge the sentence of the Court applied? A. I do not

Mr. *Wirt.* Do you know whether that sentence was ever confirmed? A I never heard.

Mr Wickham. What was the general character of General Eaton in the garrison? Was he generally respected? A. He was not generally liked by the officers. Do you recollect any charge about public corn? A. I cannot distinctly. There was something said about it. I understood that there was some corn sold by General Eaton.

General Eaton That is true.

Mr Wickham. We are asking the witness

General Eaton I will save you that trouble, Sir

Mr Baer. The question is, were the avails applied to his private profit? A. It was said.

Mr M'Rae. No Sir. Do you know any thing of it? A. I do not.

Mr M'Rae. How long was General Eaton suspended? A. For three or six months.

Mr Hay You stated that the corn was sold by General Eaton's order, was it publicly sold? A. I do not recollect

General Eaton Was not the corn sold by the acting Commissary of the garrison, Thompson, was it not sold through the Quarter-Master's department? A. I cannot tell

Mr M'Rae Was it sold secretly? A. I will state what I heard, that a part of the corn was sold and applied to the use of part of General Eaton's family. So Thompson said

General Eaton rose to speak

[*Mr Burr* Before General Eaton, goes on, I wish to know how he stands before the Court, whether as giving testimony or as a party. If he is to be considered as giving testimony we may ask him some question. If the Court thinks proper to indulge him in any observations I have no objection]

General Eaton I understood by the opinion of the Court expressed a few days ago, that explanations, in the situation in which I am placed are admissible.

Chief Justice But you will confine yourself to explanations only

General Eaton proceeded In the fall of the year 1795, I received an order from the Secretary at war to take a command on the St Mary's, being then a Captain on the military peace establishment Colonel Gathier at that time commanded the regulars on that station, and James Seagroves was Indian agent for the Southern nations Reports from these gentlemen represented to the Government of the United States, the people of Georgia as disaffected, insurrectious and disorganizing —That they were, in the back country under the command of General Clarke preparing an expedition against East Florida. They represented General James Jackson as the head or patron of this discription of citizens. They described the Indians as hostilely disposed and the Spaniards as balancing between dispositions of war and peace. [Did I state that my orders from the Secretary at war were distinct, and special.—I accepted the command with distinct and special instructions from the Secretary at war] These same reports recommended the establishment of a trading factory on the waters of the St Mary's, and also recommended that a military post be stationed there, with a view of over awing the Indians or arresting them if necessary, of keeping the Spaniards in check, and an eye of vigilence towards any disorderly citizens of Georgia, who might attempt to make aggressions on the territory of a friendly neighbor. Early in the month of January 1796—I arrived at Coleraine, a post on the waters of the St Mary's with directions and special instructions from the Secretary at war pointing directly towards these objects and shortly after, took my post at the head of three companies of infantry. I ought to mention that in passing through Savannah I waited on General Jackson, and communicated to him the two first objects of my command. He apprehended no danger, but said that in case of need, he would order to my assistance any number of militia, which circumstances should require. This, I confess, surprised me not a little, and gave me reason to suspect the accuracy of the information of Seagroves and Gaither. But I still concealed from General Jackson one of the objects of my command, which was to keep a watchful eye on the citizens of Georgia. I much disliked the position assigned to us by Seagroves, on the waters of the St Mary's, as a military post. The trading house, in freshes, was below high water mark. There were no military sites near it, and the circumjacent country was a low, pitch pine barren. The water was bad, being that of the river St Mary's.

Though there had been some commotions on that frontier, yet I found the Indians friendly, the Spaniards peaceable, and the citizens of Georgia tranquil, except some external discontents concerning the Yazoo grants.

The post at Coleraine was designated by Seagroves as the best military position on the waters of the St Mary's. I reconnoitred the country up and down the river, and nine miles above by that post, by land, I found an elevated site, good encamping ground, and fair springs of running water. The reports which my duty required me to make, contrasted these relative positions, and relative facts, and were so diametrically opposite to what had before been represented, that I soon found myself in collision with Seagroves. I had discovered that the position recommended by Seagroves was his own private property, and that he owned thirty thousand acres of land adjoining, and I was told (but this I do not assert as a fact) that Colonel Gaither was in partnership with him. Colonel Gaither visited me at my post in the month of February, I think, and, among other friendly things, offered me a partnership, in a purchase which he had made in the Yazoo grants, on advantageous terms. This I declined, as I disliked that business in all its shapes. It occurred to me also that Seagroves, about the same time, proposed to me, as an inducement to remove my family and settle in Cambden county, to accept as a compliment four or five thousand acres of land in the neighborhood of Coleraine. I told him, jocosely, but suppose he understood me, that he did not bid high enough.

In the summer following, whether in July or August, I cannot say, commissioners arrived who were appointed by the government of the United States to treat with the Indians, to settle certain boundaries, and disputes about boundaries which had not before been adjusted. About that time the misunderstanding between Col. Gaither and Mr. Seagroves and myself became very distinct and visible. there was not much intercourse between us;

I know their labors and their understanding to be competent to the discovery of such a case, if it existed. But, if it cannot be done, it is removed beyond the possibility of a doubt that this case cannot be warranted in law.

I shall have occasion to shew, that cases have occurred where such a motion might have been made with as much propriety as the present is; but neither the learned counsel in Great Britain or America thought of such an expedient. They really do surprize me; but this is not the first time, for at the very commencement of this case, we had to encounter difficulties which were never known in this, or any other country. I refer to the challenges made to grand jurors. It never was a matter of much solicitude with me; and I never thought it worth while to trouble myself about that; but this following after, I cannot avoid mentioning the dangerous tendency of this unprecedented effort to stop the evidence from being heard. It is dangerous as a precedent, because, if ever this Court should ever determine that they have the power to take upon themselves the question of fact, the trial by Jury is gone! you break down one of the greatest bulwarks of civil liberty! Mr. Wickham observed that as a citizen, and as a father, he felt an extreme solicitude; but he will excuse me if I say that his solicitude was directed to the wrong point. It is of infinitely more importance that an erroneous construction should be put upon the law by giving the power of decision on a part of the evidence to the Court, concerning treason, than that the whole case should be intrusted, as it is to a Jury. It may, here and there produce perjury, a victim, as they please to call it, may be here and there offered up, perhaps. I know that the gentleman does feel (as we all ought to feel) for the preservation of our liberties, and for those principles which ought daily to be felt in every part of the community; we know that we are all daily witnesses of encroachment on those systems which are intended to serve our community. I am sure that if the gentleman had manifested a support to the doctrines for which I now contend, and had exhibited the same learning, ingenuity and talents which he has displayed on the other side, he could have satisfied this Court, and every man, that the principles which have been advocated lately within these walls, are fraught with more terrible mischief than can be easily conceived. In this light the subject has always been viewed by me, and I call upon the gentleman to produce a contrary testimony, or a contrary case. No case, Sir, ever existed till the present moment, and according to the doctrines of law, the inference must be, that no such law is existing; and no such motion ought ever to be made.

I will observe to the Court, before I enter into Mr. Wickham's train of reasoning, that this great and leading proposition of his, is founded on the insufficiency of the evidence to prove the overt act. Here he has assumed a fact which he had no right to assume; he has no right to say that the evidence which we are about to advance will not prove the fact. He might say that so or so was said at the bar, and produce his contrary authorities; and on the contrary, I have no objection to declare that the prisoner was guilty of the fact alleged by a strong constructive presence. Nay, I shall not object to declare, that the evidence which I am about to bring, will prove the actual presence of the accused at the time charged. How, then, can the gentleman object to evidence which is about to be introduced, upon the assumption that the facts which are about to be produced will be insufficient to obtain a verdict of guilty upon the indictment?

Chief Justice The argument has gone on, and the Court have so understood it, upon the idea that the fact was admitted in Court, that the accused was absent, and in the state of Kentucky at the time charged

Mr Wickham He did state plainly to the Court, that he had no evidence to prove that Col Burr was present. However, if he means to retract, let him now come forward and prove that he was present

Mr. Burr The gentleman had reason to know that I was not present, but that I was on my way to Tennessee

Mr Hay I do not know that I shall be precluded of the right to produce my evidence of facts from any admission which I might make, though the gentleman may have a right to take it for granted that he was not there, from the statement I have made.

Mr Burr I disclaim it altogether he is not able to prove my presence, and therefore I wish him to use his utmost to produce evidence upon this point

Mr Hay I do not expect to prove that he was upon the island at the time indeed the evidence leads to the conclusion that he was not there they have no right however to take it for granted that we cannot prove any such fact Lest the gentlemen should suppose it inconsistent with candour, I will drop any further discussion on this subject, with the remarks which have been made

But, suppose it to be formally, officially, and regularly admitted, that the accused was not on the island then, Sir, comes on the great question, " What will be the result?" The counsel say that " there will be no end to the prosecution, for all other evidence must inevitably be irrelevent, and therefore must be arrested, you have failed in an essential point, and it will be impossible for you to proceed one inch!" Now, as the gentleman knows full well that such a position would not be readily acceded to, he thought proper to use the utmost effort of his talents upon it, and it was supported with as much learning and ingenuity as perhaps was ever displayed within these walls

This argument was used under four distinct heads First, as Mr. Burr was not present, he was merely an accessory, and not a principal, and that being the case, an accessory in treason is not an offence punishable under our constitution and laws. Secondly, That if he be a principal in the treason, he must be a principal in the second degree, whose guilt therefore, in consequence of his being absent, is, in itself, derivative; and, therefore, no parole testimony can be given. Thirdly Because the facts must be proved as laid; and as the indictment charges the prisoner with levying war on Blannerhassett's island, and the evidence does not prove him to have been there, all the other evidence is inapplicable, and therefore ought not to be heard. Fourthly: Because no parole evidence can be given to connect the prisoner with the transactions on the island, until we shew an act of treason to have been committed there, and the assemblage there to have met for a treasonable purpose

The doctrine to be maintained, on the part of the United States, in opposition, has already been stated with such perspicuity, and illustrated with such ability, that it would really seem unnecessary for me to say a word on the subject. I shall not, therefore, say much, except it be in relation to the coincidence of the opinion of the Judge who presided at the examination; and the opinion of the Supreme Court, whose authority has been so strongly denied.

Besides these four leading points, there were two others of minor importance, which I merely mention, in order to let the Court see that they do not go unnoticed. I shall not trouble the Court on them—because one of them is abandoned by the gentlemen themselves, and because the other was not much pressed by them. However, in the earnestness of his zeal, commendable zeal, no doubt, he did make these two positions in support of his argument. The fifth position was, that Mr. Burr was charged, in the indictment, to be concerned with persons unknown, when the evidence proved that they were known. and sixth, that the indictment stated, that there was a war, when the evidence shews that there was no public war.

These reasons Sir, constituted the main pillars of the mighty edifice which the gentlemen had raised, upon which to build the defence of their client. Now, if that was the only object they had in view, or if they could attain their object without doing injury to the community, I should not feel a solicitude, such as I now do, to oppose their structure. but whilst they are erecting this mighty edifice for him, they are erecting a more mighty fortress, by which they will destroy the temple itself. and they cannot complete their edifice, without obtaining means to ruin the temple. I shall examine this; I shall endeavour to shew you that they have no foundation, and that the materials of which their temple is made, are rotten. and will not stand.

In doing so, I am sensible that it is a disagreeable task; and, I can assure the gentlemen, that I do not mean to press one principle which I do not most sincerely believe to be correct, however they may suppose otherwise. I consider it to be the duty of a prosecutor in behalf of the United States, to expound the laws with *honor* and *candor*; and I can assure the Court, that I shall do it with integrity and impartiality too, whatever views may be taken of my official capacity. Nay, I will say, that I will do it with independence. It is possible, and, perhaps probable, that I may not be suspected of that state of purity which it may be my desire to maintain. It is possible, nay, probable, that the feelings which have been excited in this case, and which the gentlemen themselves have produced, may have excited feelings in my mind extremely well calculated to mislead me. I can inform the Court, however, that I have endeavoured, and shall still endeavour to avoid all those painful sensations which would have any tendency to bias my mind towards desiring that any innocent person should be convicted.

Before I follow Mr Wickham through his devious, perplexing, and eccentric course of argument, I will examine the general result. Where does he mean to carry us? Is it in the straight road of common sense? Is that supposition deducible from his arguments? No, Sir, the consequence inevitably is, that the evidence which would bear most strongly upon the issue, is to be cut off: all relevant evidence is to be all at once arrested and suppressed, in the middle of the proceeding, and we are to hear no more it, because it is said that we have not proved the "overt act," and therefore, the prosecution must fall to the ground

Now admit, for a moment, that he was not present, but that he had a powerful government of those transactions; it certainly would prostrate every principle of justice, to hold him in any other light than that of a principal. It would be a violation of justice in this or any other country, and especially would it be contrary to the system of jurisprudence held sacred in that country from whence we draw our code. We say, that *actual presence* is not necessary, according to the statute laws of this country, nor according to the common law of England, provided the accused is leagued in the general conspiracy, and performs a part in that conspiracy—"however remote," or "however minute." This is a position which we are authorized by the supreme court to take, sec 6 The law is clear and perspicuous, authorizing the very position which we have taken, and in the very terms which we have introduced it to the Court I hope, therefore, that it will not be repeated, that the gentlemen who advocate this position, dishonor themselves, because, they surely have good authority to support them

If such then be case, as we can easily contend it is, ought we not to have it in our power to submit all the evidence which is connected with the transaction, to the jury? It is a great question of law and fact under the constitution, whether he has been guilty of the overt act of levying war against the United States, or not: and this is a question for the consideration of the jury, and not of the Court We say, Sir, and confidently believe, that whether the accused was present at the moment, or whether he was at any other place, is totally immaterial It cannot have any effect upon the weight of the evidence respecting him, and the case cannot be taken out of the hands of the jury without a most flagrant violation of the best of principles, and the destruction of every security connected with civil liberty Sir, you have already decided this question, long before this elaborate argument commenced, and before you could have anticipated such an extraordinary motion You have said, Sir, that this was a question of *fact* and not of *law*, and, therefore, it must be decided by the jury "The opinion of the Court on any point of law may be asked and given to the jury, and even after that, the jury, upon a whole view of the case, may give their verdict in direct opposition to the opinion of the Court. The court leave the facts to the jury, but if they please, they may decide upon *law* and *fact* Littleton, 368; Co. Lit. 355 Upon these, and all other authorities, it is clear, that the evidence ought not to be cut in two Every thing that bears upon the point in controversy, must be admitted;

and no Judge ever dared to withhold such evidence from the jury. I call upon the gentleman (again) to produce an authority, if such there be.

I feel not the danger which such a doctrine as that for which we contend can produce, whatever they may think. I feel infinitely more about their principle, than I do about a mis-construction of the Constitution in the way they apprehend, because, I do not think there is danger of a traitor being wrongly convicted, or, that our construction can affect the vital liberties or civil rights of traitors. The doctrine of jury trial *ought* to be viewed with the utmost reverence. When a Judge is about taking a step which may lead him beyond the line of his authority, he ought to advance towards that line with the utmost caution. A good Judge would rather stop a mile on the safe side of that line, than go one hair's breadth beyond it, lest he sap the foundation of our inestimable Constitution and civil liberty, and establish a dangerous or oppressive precedent. And it is owing to this care which has always been taken by the bench, that the gentleman, with all the learning he possesses, and all the laborious research which he has used, has not been able to produce one solitary case where such a decision has been made, nor even one solitary case, where counsel have had the temerity to bring such a question before a Court. They have not even pretended that they could support their motion by reference to direct authority, in black and white. But they think that they have accomplished their point, by producing one or two cases, which they suppose would warrant such an inference. Let us examine these cases which are supposed to justify this motion to exclude further evidence.

They say, that where a man is indicted as an accessary, you must produce the record of conviction of the principal person concerned. They produce this argument with a view of calling upon us to prove first, the conviction of the persons who were upon Blannerhassett's island, and then, say they, you may go on with the evidence. This argument, Sir, is not law, and if it were, it would not bear the inference which they would draw from it. If it is not law, all the investigation we can give it, will not make it so. The gentlemen seem to have taken it for granted, that this bold assertion of their's would pass, if not unnoticed, at least uncontradicted · and, therefore, inferred that they might have the liberty to exclude enquiry whenever they pleased. Now, the real doctrine is this. If a man be indicted as an accessary, he is at liberty to state, *before his trial*, that he does not choose to be tried until the principal shall have been convicted. The Judge, knowing all this to be his right, suspends the prosecution until the principal is convicted. It is a principle which the law of England allows, to require the conviction of the principal first : but it never was heard of, in England or here, that the accessary was at liberty, *after the jury were sworn*, and a part of the evidence produced—when he finds that it begins to bear heavy upon him, to move to stop the remainder from being brought forward. This is supported in 1 Hale, P. C. 623. The gentleman took a part of this authority. I will choose to take the whole of it; from which it will appear, that the basis of the position laid down is not law. But, if he be considered as an accessary, how is it possible to put an end to the trial, and discharge the jury without their examing all the premises of the case? There is no inference that can be drawn, which will support the motion upon legal principles. These remote precedents which they produce, are not analogous to this case; and many of them are assumed as law, when they are not. In whatever capacity it may be supposed that the party is indicted, the decision must be made upon the facts, and, therefore, whether the Court or the Jury decide upon the question of fact, then inference must be erroneous, when they think the evidence ought not to be heard. Here is a particular fact charged on Blannerhassett's island, we offer evidence to support the charge of that fact; the accused says he was only an accessary, not being present there; and, therefore, under the law and constitution of this country, he is not punishable. Now, does not this amount precisely to the question before a jury? Is not the defence which he now makes, identically the same as though it was made before the jury? What is the plea made before the jury? "Not guilty." He supports this, by saying, that he was an accessary; and the Court are called upon to decide the identical issue which has been already referred to the jury; and what is worse, they are to decide that issue without hearing more than one-fifth of the evidence! Of all the novelties which have ever been presented to the contemplation of a Court, this is the most strange; and of all doctrines that ever have been contended for, this is the most unprecedented. I call upon the united learning and labor of all the gentlemen, to discover from all the volumes within their research, a precedent. They draw inferences to be sure, but I think it has been plainly shewn that they draw erroneous ones.

But, Sir, to press this point a little farther. I must confess that I feel greatly interested in it, infinitely more than I do about any other part of the case. I repeat my argument. If the Court undertake to decide, do they not decide that he, not being present, can, at most, be but an accessary; or even that he is not an accessary, and, therefore, he is not guilty. This is a question the jury, only, are sworn to decide. We have an indisputable and sacred right, to lay before the jury all the evidence which is relevent. This is what I wish to do, and this is what the prisoner is anxious to prevent. The Court have recognized this doctrine, in speaking upon another point the other day. The Court did say, that they would give no decision as to the point of levying war. Will they, then, undertake to decide the whole case, and say, that, in consequence of the absence of the accused, he is not guilty? Will they say, that evidence relating to the case, in consequence of his absence, shall not be heard? Sir, it is a question of law and fact, whether the accused did levy war or not. We charge him with levying war, and he denies it. The rule which has uniformly governed all proceedings from time immemorial to the present is, that all evidence bearing upon the point shall be received. The other day, Mr. Martin furnished a case from 4 St. Tr. 661, to support the doctrine which he supposed would give the Court a power to decide upon questions of fact. There might, perhaps, be something in that long case of 40 or 50 folio pages, that might favor some of his doctrines; but there is certainly one point argued and decided there, very similar to this, and which must destroy the position. The counsel thought the overt act was not proved by two witnesses, but, Sir, *no motion* was made to stop the enquiry; on the contrary, Lord Holt, in giving his opinion, says, that whether the facts were or were not proved, was not for *him* to decide—*that* was the province of the jury. 2 Dallas, 356, is a similar case. There was one witness who swore to the overt act; another said, " it ran in his head" that it was so and so, and that he had seen the accused at the place of rendezvous. Though it was contended, in that case, that the fact was not made to appear by two witnesses, yet no motion was ever made to exclude the testimony which remained. Now, how came it about that the learned and able counsel in those cases, did not take the course which has been recently discovered by the accused here? Had the counsel for Rookwood, A. D. 1696, or the counsel for Mitchel, A. D. 1781, less talents than those who now appear here? They were gentlemen of great talents, learning, and character, and had as much zeal for their clients as they ought to have possessed, but, I must confess, not equal zeal to that manifested here. But it never entered into their minds, that, because the prosecution had not proved a particular point of enquiry, that the whole case was to stop before the evidence was all given.

I will trouble the Court with one other remark. The gentleman said that it was laid down in the books, that after proving the overt act in the county where it is laid, you may then go on to prove other overt acts in other counties. To support this, he referred you to Hawkins, 125, 126. From this, it is inferred, that the *Court* must decide upon the question, whether the overt act laid, is proved or not, before the admission of any collateral evidence, and that, if the overt act be not first proved, the other evidence must be rejected. Now, Sir, I conceive that the real rule is this. After introducing and examining the evidence as to the overt act laid, you may then give evidence of overt acts in other places. But by this, the Court do not decide upon any fact whatever. According to my exposition, it is the rule of the Court, only to say to the prosecutors, " gentlemen, introduce your evidence relative to levying war on Blannerhasset's island *first* " If there is no evidence of any facts there, and the witnesses should be relating other things, then the Court have power to restrain, and require relevent testimony only to be given. "The party is charged so and so, introduce first your evidence upon the point of the indictment, and then you may introduce evidence from other counties, which may be collateral, and therefore relevent." If the decision may be made upon the proof of the facts first, I must declare it contrary to all maxims and trials in law, and in direct opposition to your own solemn decision at another time. I admit, that it may be stopped until the principal facts are introduced, because, till that is brought, the other can have no bearing on the case. This affair of difficulty will not present so formidable a face, if we consider that some trifling mistake may have crept into some one of the authorities. Even intelligent writers, and able speakers are not always able to extricate themselves from the errors which a want of precaution might let slip. Sometimes a word might be twice repeated in a very small compass, and other errors occur unobserved.—Now, let us apply this to East, and substitute the word "evidence" in place of the word "proof," and then it resolves the authority to exactly what I say.—1 East. 125. He might well do it, in order to avoid what might be termed an unpleasant repetition. This will make their mighty argument vanish to nothing; because their mighty Colossus would have nothing to rest upon. By this trifling expedient, every difficulty will be removed.

But there is another difficulty, if this rule is to be taken literally, which will demonstrate the absurdity of it. After "proof" of the overt act, of which the Court are to judge, the gentlemen say, "you may produce collateral evidence." Now, they say we cannot do it, because we have not proved the overt act; and whenever it is admissible, the Court lets it in on the ground of the overt act being first proved. What is the result of this? Why, that after the overt act is completely proved, the Court say that you shall have the *privilege* of bringing in other evidence to prove it! Now, would there be any thing like sense in this? If there is, I am not competent to discern it, I must confess. These ideas were advanced by Judge Peters in Fries' trial, 175, and certainly it is a difficulty which no human ingenuity can surmount; because it goes to transfer a power which has never been exercised by a court of law from the creation to the present day; and such a doctrine must merit our highest indignation.

The argument now about to be introduced, was advanced by Mr Botts, in the course of his ingenious, droll, and learned address, from 1 East. 96, 97. The general principle contained here, is—that if you are trying A for a particular act, you cannot bring against him the acts or confessions of B, unless the connection between A and B is proved—and then it might be relevant. This you must do, before you can bring evidence respecting B's guilt; but the moment that the connection is proved, you may go through with your evidence. This is all very true, but the important question is, who is to judge respecting the connection? East says the Court must judge! Now, I will ask who made East a judge in this case? There is no reference to any authority whatever. What does he get his law from? Not from any express authority. I presume he got it from inference and deductions made with the same sort of ingenuity as Mr Botts drew his conclusions. It is a great undertaking for a man to write a great book; and it is not to be wondered, if expressions should escape without much notice. Sometimes Hale, Foster, Blackstone and others, have been guilty of it, and such is the infirmity of the human mind, even in great men. Surely the gentleman will not require that we should take the *dictum* of East, when that *dictum* is unprecedented; and, especially when we turn over two more pages of his book, and there discover what danger doctrines may lead us if we quit the plain principles of *common sense*. That is a *terra firma* where we can rest without danger. But, when we get on the great ocean of

With respect to the last arrest of the partisans of Colonel Burr, when a considerable number were arrested, it arose from the following circumstance. In a few days after Colonel Burr had left the town of Washington, and was said to have escaped, and after the governor's proclamation for his apprehension had issued, as I understood, a negro boy was discovered near the mouth of Coles Creek, (opposite to which Colonel Burr's boats were stationed), riding on a horse which had belonged to Colonel Burr, and having on his surtout coat, as I heard. These circumstances created a suspicion, the boy was searched, and there was found, sewed up in the cape of his coat, a paper in these words:—" If you are " yet together, keep together, and I will join you to-morrow night " In the mean time, put all your arms in perfect order. Ask the " bearer no questions, but tell him all you may think I wish to " know He does not know that this is from me, nor where I am " C. T. and D. E." This paper was proved to be in the hand-writing of Colonel Burr, by a Colonel Fitzpatrick, as I understood In consequence of this discovery, a number of men, (perhaps twenty or thirty), said to be the adherents of Colonel Burr, were arrested, and put under guard. They were not in close confinement, when I saw them, nor did I ever hear of them being in that situation They were only guarded 'till the alarm was over. I saw several of them going to their lodgings to dinner ; and, as I understood, they were usually put on their honor to return at a particular time and place.

LEMUEL HENRY

Hanico Coun'n. &c

Sworn to before me, in due form agreeable to law, 14th October, 1807.

DANIEL L. HYLTON

TUESDAY, October 6

Major *Bruff* was offered as a witness on behalf of the accused

Mr *Martin* Relate to the Court if you had any conversation with General Wilkinson about the time and circumstances, of his return to St. Louis

Mr *Hay* interrupted, by wishing the object of the questions to be known, as had been so frequently asked of him, respecting witnesses which he introduced.

Mr *Martin* The object is to prove similar conversations as those stated by Kibby, as to the great schemes, and making fortunes, proposed by Wilkinson

Mr *Hay* denied any knowledge of what Kibby could relate of him, although he had seen an affidavit of Kibby's to the paper. But what could be the object of Major Bruff's testimony ? It might be to prove that General Wilkinson had, in some period or other of his life, formed some schemes similar to what was now charged to Burr If that was the case, could there be any propriety in bringing forward conversations held with one single witness a principle which was before refused ?

When the evidence of a witness is to be impeached, it is to be on his general character, or upon the ground of his having been formerly convicted of some offence, so as to render him incompetent as a witness in law A man must, to be sure, who has lived long in society, have some, who will disapprove of his conduct; and, perhaps, from misunderstanding his actions and motives, might have a number of enemies; and that, often for want of a due explanation and appreciation of that character for no man could be prepared to explain *every action* of his life.

Besides, there was another, and material objection, which was that it was not in the least connected with the question before the Court. Burr is charged with treason, in levying war against the United States, and with misdemeanor, in forming designs to invade the Spanish provinces. A defence is set up, among the rest, by the introduction of the present witness, who is produced to prove, that a similar attempt was intended to be made against the Spanish provinces at some time passed. Could this be counter evidence?

Mr. *Martin.* I had supposed, that, by the argument which the gentleman formerly used, (" this Court being only an examining Court,") any thing might go to the Judge. but I trust that we shall be able to shew this to be *good* evidence. General Wilkinson has declared, that he had no knowledge of Burr's designs, until that cyphered letter was known. now, a part of Burr's testimony is, that Wilkinson had a knowledge of his views, and a participation (in part) with them.

Again, Sir, we shall prove that he turned traitor to Colonel Burr, and violated his engagement with him, by endeavouring to sacrifice him to the government. Sir, we mean to contradict General Wilkinson's own testimony by the introduction of this, and to prove, that not only Colonel Burr's conduct was perfectly innocent, but that, if he was guilty, General Wilkinson was also guilty. But, in any conversations of secret expeditions between them, they were both perfectly innocent.

Mr *Wickham* proceeded in comparing the ideas supported by the prosecution, and now denied by them as to the applicability of testimony. It was a little singular that the rule should so suddenly differ. He really could not think the gentleman to be serious in his diversifications: for surely any evidence might be brought to shew the inconsistency of a witness.

He went on in some severe strictures on the truth of General Wilkinson's testimony, and insisted upon his coincidence in the primeval, and some of the subsequent transactions, as would be proved by the witness now offered.

General *Wilkinson*. May I be permitted to make one observation? I am not in the smallest degree surprized at the language which has upon this, and several other occasions been used by the counsel of Colonel Burr, men who are hired to misrepresent.

Mr *Wickham.* I will not submit to such language from any man in Court.

The *Chief Justice* declared the style of General Wilkinson to be improper, and that he had heard too much of such language in Court.

General *Wilkinson* apologized. He said that it was impossible he could offer any intentional disrespect to the Court, but he could not remain silent when he heard himself called a traitor. General Wilkinson proceeded. I am astonished at the explana tion of the objects for which this witness is called. Had I known the purpose for which he *volunteered* his services, (for he was not summoned), I should have been able to produce documents to shew the long, the implacable hatred which he has borne towards me

Mr *Wickham* said that Major Bruff was under the protection of the Court

General *Wilkinson.* I pray that his testimony may be introduced

Mr. *Hay* observed, that he had no doubt of the law, as to the right to impeach the credibility of a witness, by shewing an inconsistency in his testimony. He admitted that, if Maj. Bruff's evidence were introduced for that purpose, it was proper; but if for any other purpose, it was improper. They had no right to interrogate him for the purpose avowed by Mr. Martin, to shew that General Wilkinson entertained the same views as Colonel Burr. However, as General Wilkinson was content that Major Bruff should proceed, he would not object

The *Chief Justice* declared that he would not hear the witness as to any *particular* allegations against General Wilkinson, but with respect to any inconsistency in his testimony, he must hear him

Major Bruff proceeded

My testimony will arise from a number of conversations with General Wilkinson

In four of these conversations, General Wilkinson took me aside, in three of which he locked me up in his room. The first hint I had of a connexion between General Wilkinson and Col. Burr, was drawn from two paragraphs in Kentucky newspapers, in the spring 1805, before General Wilkinson reached St Louis The first alluded to the old plan to form a separate government west of the Alleghany, and ascribed it to General Wilkinson and his associates, and doubting whether that scheme had yet been abandoned The next was an extract of a letter from fort Massac, published in the papers, which stated that Colonel Burr had been several days there with General Wilkinson, probably giving the General lessons on government, or digesting a new code or constitution for the government of Louisiana. These hints, with information received from Captain Stoddard immediately from fort Massac, and who assured me that Colonel Burr was, or had been there, closely engaged with General Wilkinson, and that he had or was about to furnish him with a barge and scow, to descend the river into New Orleans

Mr *Wirt* You have not said when A. In June, 1805 These circumstances put me on my guard, and determined me to watch the motions of General Wilkinson and Burr

As the General approached St. Louis, ascending the Mississippi from fort Massac, he dispatched a light barge ahead with directions for me to meet him six or eight miles below. I obeyed. We met, landed and ascended the bank. The General took me into the woods. As we walked on, the General observed, that he had been informed the territory was divided by parties, (I mean upper Louisiana) which he attributed to the

Americans, and said he would crush party, or perish in the at tempt. I observed, that there had been some party business a bout the time of the convention and these memorials to Con gress, but none since, except an aversion the French had to the expence, delay and uncertainty of our laws, and the introduc tion of lawyers. He then asked me how I stood with the French inhabitants, for he had heard there was some misunderstanding or coolness between us, occasioned by my observations about antedated concessions and fraudulent debts. I observed, that some uneasiness had been excited by a report I had made to the Secretary at war, respecting private surveys which were in public property, but I believe they were then satisfied I had merely done my duty. He observed, that he had witnessed their many attempts in the lower country to defraud the public, (the Orleans and Mississippi territories) but he knew them and man kind generally, and if I would place my dependence upon him, we would manage them for me.

Mr. *Hay.* He would manage them for you? A. Yes, it allud ed to the French. About this time some Frenchmen from St. Louis had found us out, and were rushing through the bushes on us. He damned them for their intrusion.

Mr. *Hay.* To their faces? A. No, to me; said he had some thing of importance to communicate, hoped to have had an op portunity there, but that he would take the first opportunity after he had got settled.

A day or two after his arrival at St. Louis, his orderly came to me. I attended. I was taken into his parlour, and he locked the door.

Mr. *M'Rae.* What time? A. About the last of June or first or second day of July. Mr. M'Rae. Can you name the day? A. I cannot.

General *Wilkinson.* Can you come within five days? A. No. I cannot. We commenced walking. The General appeared to be ruminating, and after two or three turns, he asked me what sort of government would suit Louisiana. Without hesitation I replied, a representative republic would meet both the wishes and expectations of the people. He answered that he was sur prized to hear me say so, for the French could not understand its principle, or be brought to attend elections, that the Ameri can inhabitants were a turbulent set, the mere emptyings of jails, or fugitives from justice, and did not deserve a free gov ernment, that a military government was best for these people and no other was contemplated for them.

Here Mr. *Hay*, observing that Major Bruff retired to a table on which several papers were laid, asked him when he had made the statement of his testimony, which he was then giving. On being answered, that it was recently done, and since his arrival here, Mr. Hay requested that he would not again look at it. Major Bruff said, that his statement was drawn from a number of letters which he had written to his friends about the time of the transactions alluded to; and from an intended publication against the General. That the politics of the United States had undergone a great change: that the honest and wise had united to save the federal constitution, and prevent a division of pro perty, which the democrats aimed at; that the democratic party in Congress had split and dwindled, and that John Randolph, Nicholson and Leib, had lost their influence both in Congress and with the executive I observed that he attributed principles and motives to the republicans which they abhorred

Mr *Hay* To which part, did you belong ? A To the democratic

Mr *Martin* Were you not then a democrat, and did not Gen Wilkinson know you to belong to that party. A Yes On this subject we had a good deal of conversation, I remarked on the folly to suppose that John Randolph would consent to throw his property into the public stock, in order to have a scramble for a part of it However, the General observed, that the object of the democrats was to produce a state of anarchy and confusion, to seize on the property of the federalists, and divide it among themselves, and this too he told me with a very serious face I will make one observation here it is, that these conversations which I had with the General, were at different times, and it is possible that I may not have classed them precisely in point of time, but I am certain that they did happen, and nearly as I have stated, and if the General will be candid, he will acknowledge it

General *Wilkinson* Indeed I will not

Witness. He said that Pennsylvania was convulsed by the democrats; yet they would not succeed in turning out M'Kean, or introducing their arbitrary system I think that this ended the conversation We got warm, and the General threw open the door, and I walked out

After dinner his orderly came for me again I attended: was taken into his room, and the door fastened He assumed a milder manner, and assured me that the politics not only of the United States, but of the executive, had changed, that the difference between the present and former administration was merely in name; that parties were kept alive by the cunning, in order to help them to office, or to keep them in, that the people mistook the character of Mr Jefferson, that a want of energy was no part of it, but rather obstinacy Here he observed that the French had not been enough attended to in the territorial appointments; that they were the natives, and the Americans were ungrateful intruders; and now railed against a king and government which had raised them from ashes

Mr *Wirt* To whom did he allude? A I considered that he pointed his remarks to Mr Austin particularly It was the Spanish king and government to which I alluded. He then observed that Governor Claiborne, a miserable thing or tool, had distributed the appointments in the lower country among his American followers and dependents, and had neglected the French, for which he was execrated, despised and forsaken by every person of talents and honor, except by a Dr Watkins, who no doubt had some personal views. I observed that in the lower country the great body of the people were French, but that in the upper country, there were more than two Americans for one Frenchman, and that the disproportion encreased daily by emigration, and would soon entitle us to elections He replied,

God forbid that you should ever see an election in Louisiana, and then observed that it was the intention of the government to depopulate that country, except the villages of St. Louis, St Geneva, and St. Charles, and a small district of country around each, merely sufficient to support them; the land would be offered to the inhabitants on the east side of the Mississippi, which if they refused to remove to, they would be pushed over on the point of the bayonet and that I should be employed in that business. As I found that my replies only irritated the General and kept back the important communications, I therefore determined when I could not acquiesce in sentiment with the General, I would endeavor to be silent till I got the *important secret* But I found I had already gone too far The General appeared to be vexed and disappointed, threw open the door, and I walked out

The next morning his orderly came for me again I attended; and we had another parlor conversation with closed doors He assumed a friendly manner and begged me to recollect that it was some time since I left the Atlantic States, and assured me that public opinion had undergone a great change in favor of energetic governments and measures, that if I persisted in exploded notions, they would injure me with my government, that democratic notions produced licentiousness; and that the very existence of an army and democracy were incompatible; that republics were ungrateful, jealous of armies and military merit, and made no provision for the superannuated and worn out officers, but who were left to starve In these latter opinions I agreed with him The General seemed pleased that I should assent to one of his opinions He was now silent While we walked the floor one or two turns with his eyes down on the floor and seemed to be musing, he then observed, that he was fertile in schemes, had made fortunes for many who did not then thank him for it I smiled. He said, " perhaps you think I had better have made my own fortune—True, but I have now a *grand scheme* in contemplation, that will not only make my fortune, but the fortunes of all concerned," he paused as if waiting for my answer I was silent had nothing to say, but wanted him to explain and go into the detail After walking the floor several times, during which he appeared much agitated and vexed, he threw open the door and I walked out, with only this glimpse of the *secret*, which he had so long been preparing me for.

As I attended daily for orders until the arrival of Colonel Cushing, the next morning I found the General rather distant and reserved He observed, that he had yet enemies in the army, and among them some from his own State; that he either hated or loved Marylanders more than others Presuming this intended for me, I replied, I suppose you take me for a Marylander " Why, are you not?" I answered no, I was born in Jersey, but had the good luck to be brought young to Maryland, of which State my father, grand father, and great grand father were natives " Born in Jersey, (replied the General,) a second cousin to a yankee and a damned cunning fellow I suspect." This was the first *rude* thing he had said to me, for before this I was treated with respect, and had received many friendly letters from him; I therefore attributed this to my declining to join him in his scheme to make fortunes. Some time after the troops moved to Cold Water, an officer informed me, that they were encamped on a low damp bottom, subject to be overflowed.

Mr *Hay* objected to the course of the testimony pursued by the witness.

Col. Burr said, that he did not know the whole extent of his testimony, but that he had been introduced to shew palpable contradictions in the evidence of General Wilkinson.

Witness. The Missouri was on the one side, and a marsh or bog on the other, and the whole cantonment commanded by a high second bank, or hill in its rear. I observed the situation was not only unmilitary, but would probably become the grave of the troops, if they were not removed. At that time I did not know the General had contracted for the ground as private property—"a snug fixture where he might hang up his sword." The morning after this conversation I was sent for by the General, and severely and rudely reprimanded before two strangers, and forbid to interfere with his *plans* and *measures.* I replied it was my duty and inclination to obey his military arrangements, but should I discover any *plans* or *measures* which put to hazard the peace and safety of the United States I would not keep silence, be the consequences what they might. He understood me, and from that moment I believe my ruin was determined on.

Colonel Burr arrived a little while after this at St. Louis.

Mr *Wirt.* At what time?

A. I believe in August, 1805. A Judge Easton who appeared to think very highly of Colonel Burr, and boasted of possessing a part of his confidence, informed me, that Colonel Burr had enquired of him, whether there was an officer of experience and enterprize, who could be trusted with the command of an expedition to Santa Fee, and gave me a very inquisitive look. I demanded by what authority Colonel Burr made the enquiry, or in what light I was to view it. He replied, that Colonel Burr at that time held no public office, but that he had powerful friends, and would probably be in a very exalted situation before long; that I had been well spoken of to Colonel Burr, (I suppose by himself) and he advised me to make him my friend. I answered, that the enquiry was a suspicious one, for if government chose to employ me in that or any other way, it had a right to command my services, for I was in service at that time. We dropt the subject.

Mr *Martin* Was Easton at St. Louis? A. Yes. Q. Was he in great habits of intimacy with General Wilkinson. A. Yes, there appeared to be a good understanding between the three.

Witness. But as General Wilkinson some time before had wrote to me that " every information of the road to Santa Fee would be highly acceptable," and recently sounded my inclination towards energetic governments, and his *grand scheme* to make fortunes. I no longer doubted of their connection.

Mr *Martin* How long was Colonel Burr at St. Louis, how was he treated by General Wilkinson, and how was he sent across the river? A. When he arrived I was not in town, but understood that the Gen. had rode out with him to the cantonment to view the troops I saw the Colonel on the evening he returned — The Colonel strictured the situation, and laughed at the General's military notions

Mr *Wirt* At Cold Water?

A Yes at Cold Water, and christened afterwards Belle Fontaine

Mr *Wirt* How far from St Louis? A Twelve or fourteen miles

Mr *Martin* When Colonel Burr was there, how was he treated? A. The General made a dinner, it was understood for Col Burr I was invited, the Colonel did not attend, but was said to be sick. When Colonel Burr was leaving St Louis, I was about to cross the river to my plantation on the opposite side. The baggage was brought to the ferry boat, when I saw the General's barge getting ready, with colors and a complete crew in uniform I afterwards saw the Colonel pass my farm on his journey in company with Doctor Brown only, Easton was not with him

Some time after Colonel Burr left St. Louis, General Wilkinson and Easton fell out Easton complained the General persecuted him, and often talked in a dark mysterious manner about a western empire Captain Stoddart also hinted to me, after his return from fort Massac, that some great scheme was in agitation between Colonel Burr and General Wilkinson, but did not say what Easton positively stated that there was a connection between General Wilkinson and Colonel Burr He complained that the General persecuted him I observed, that it was very strange that he should be the common friend of Colonel Burr and General Wilkinson, and yet they should misunderstand one another about him, that I rather suspected the General, finding him unpopular with the French, and that he would not answer their purpose, had persuaded Colonel Burr to shake him off Easton replied, that Colonel Burr was in his power, and that he dared not to treat him in a deceitful manner I replied, that I did not know Col Burr but that his enemies represented him as an artful intriguer Some time afterwards Mr Easton came to me and observed, that he believed my conjectures about Colonel Burr were true, and that he was to be made a sacrifice of, that he should go on to the seat of government and try what he could do for himself Easton was then a Judge appointed by the President, but not confirmed by the Senate, and he was apprehensive it would not, that General Wilkinson was using his influence to prevent the confirmation But observed, ~~Colonel Burr~~ was much in his power, for that he had made him proposals which made the hair rise upon his head, astonished and confounded him so that he was struck dumb.

General Wilkinson. Were these his very words? A. Yes; that Colonel Burr observing this, would have retracted, but it was too late I urged him to explain the nature of the proposals. He said he was under an obligation of secrecy, but no obligation should hold him if he found Colonel Burr false to him I observed that he well knew that any obligation which led him to conceal or commit a crime, could not be binding He observed, he was going on to the seat of government, and should see Colonel Burr and then he should take his measures. I saw Easton after his re-

turn I urged him to explain the business which he had mentioned before; but he pretended to have forgot that such a
conversation had ever passed between us [Mr. Hay. Was his
appointment confirmed? A No. He lost his appointment and
had seen Colonel Burr.] About this time a paper called the Western World made its appearance, one of which was, I believe directed to the General, weekly.

Mr. Hay. After the return of Easton? A Yes. It roundly ac
cused General Wilkinson of the old plan, of being concerned
with Miranda, and connected with Colonel Burr I observed to
Easton, that I believed I should get the whole story from the
Western World without being under any obligations to him,
that if he had done his duty, he might have served himself and
his country, and perhaps prevented the effusion of blood. He ob
served, that he had once attempted to make a disclosure to government, but instead of being countenanced he got a reprimand.
I demanded the instance He said, that he had wrote to a Sena-
tor in Congress, either from Vermont or New York, that he
could prove General Wilkinson to be the projector of Miranda's
expedition The gentleman acknowledged the receipt of his letter, but informed him he had burnt it, and advised him to mind
his own business, and take care how he meddled with men high
in power and office.

Mr. Martin. Had General Wilkinson any conversation with
you with respect to the appointment of a certain John Smith of
Louisiana? A. I had a conversation with him about John Smith:
I remember going into the General's office, when he handed me
two letters, one from Major Hunt, the civil and military commandant, and the other from Smith. who complained that the
commandant had ordered him off the mineral lands The General censured the order, and he asked me if I knew who John Smith
was I replied no, but had been informed he was one of Cox's
Captains. So Maj. Hunt insiduously observes, replied the Gene-
neral, but *that* does not *lessen him in my esteem* He added, that
Smith was brother-in-law to Mr. Early, a member of Congress, who had brought forward a resolution to reduce the army,
and dispense with his services as General, that there were many
of his stamp in Congress—therefore they must be attended to and
kept in good humour, or we shall be turned to the right about.

Mr. Martin Did you appear before the Secretary at war, in
order to make a statement as to the conduct of General Wilkinson, which you considered endangered the United States, and
what was his reply?

Mr. Hay objected to the question, as it had no relation to the
subject.

Mr. Wickham said, that General Wilkinson had been interrogated by them, and required to say, whether his conduct was
approved or disapproved by the government; that the government had taken the most active part in this prosecution, and it
was right and proper that the sentiments of the government
should be known.

The *Chief Justice* said, the difference is this. The evidence of
General Wilkinson arose from communications officially made
directly from the government. This is a different case. The evi-

dence here offered, consists of conversations with the officers of the government.

Mr. *Martin* said, that the Secretary at war was applied to in his official character, and in his official character, he had said, that General Wilkinson must and would be supported; that he had stood low in the estimation of government before his energetic measures at New Orleans, but now he stood very high.

Mr *Hay* was about to make some observations in opposition to the introduction of such evidence, when Gen. Wilkinson consented that the witness should go on.

In March, 1807, a few days before the rising of Congress, I was in the city of Washington and waited on the Secretary of war, and the subject which gave rise to this visit and conversation between the Secretary at war, the Attorney General and myself, was an appeal from the sentence of a general Court Martial, whose proceedings, I contended, had been arbitrary and oppressive, and sentence illegal and unjust.

Mr. *Wirt.* Against whom? A. Myself, and that I was not arrested till after General Wilkinson had sounded, and found I would not answer his purpose; and I believed for fear I might penetrate his plans, and be a spy on his actions, he determined to put me aside. The Secretary at war replied, that there had been a time when General Wilkinson did not stand well with the executive, but his energetic measures at New Orleans had regained him his confidence, and he would support him.

Mr *Wirt.* Who? A. I mean the President. I asked if an enquiry into the conduct of General Wilkinson, his oppressions, and illegal acts, and his connection with Colonel Burr, might be expected? He answered there might be an enquiry after the present bustle was over, but at present, he must and would be supported. I then observed, that if an inquiry might be expected in a reasonable time, I would ask a furlough and wait, but if not, I should resign immediately. He observed, that I must not calculate on a speedy enquiry; but if I was determined not to serve under General Wilkinson, my only resort was to resign immediately.

Mr *Martin.* Who said so—General Dearborn? A. Yes, General Dearborn. He however recommended me to draw up a short statement of facts for the President, respecting my trial and sentence. I replied, that if I did, I should certainly charge General Wilkinson with having been connected with Colonel Burr, and with having made attempts to bring me over to his grand scheme of making fortunes. He replied, if these are your impressions you will be correct in stating them. This was the first conversation I had with the Secretary at war.

I had a second conversation with the Secretary at war, in which I insisted that General Wilkinson was acquainted with Burr's plans; that I would produce proof, that he had been concerned, and did not cecede, till he found that Colonel Burr had commenced the enterprize with a handful of men, that the country was alarmed, and the project was a desperate one. I then had a conversation with the Attorney General on the legality of restoring my pay and emoluments, which had been suspended by the sentence of the Court Martial. I informed him that a con-

cation between General Wilkinson and Colonel Burr could certainly be proved. He observed, that the General had been low with the President, but at that time stood high, and would be supported. He observed however, that there was a great deal of mystery in the allusions of Colonel Burr's letter to General Wilkinson, as well as their making use of a cypher. He advised me not to resign, but to wait events, for the Secretary at war had informed him, that I was the only republican field officer in the service, and that public opinion was very fluctuating and whimsical.

After this, I had a conversation with the Secretary at war and the Attorney General together. I think that Captain Clark, the companion of Lewis, was also present. The Secretary at war shut the doors. We had some previous conversation, as after the Attorney General came in, the Secretary at war introduced it again, by observing, that he had been informed, Colonel Burr had accompanied General Wilkinson to the western country, spent several days with him at Massac, and then furnished the Colonel with a barge and men to descend the Mississippi to New Orleans. I replied, that this was one among many reasons to suspect a good understanding, connection and co-operation between the General and Colonel, that I imagined both of them were well informed of the old plan attributed to the General and his associates, to form a separate government west of the Alleginy, under the auspices of Spain or England, of his famous memorial, which it is said procured him exclusive privileges from the Spanish government, and the extraordinary visit Colonel Connelly from Canada paid him in Kentucky, but there were recent events which were not without suspicion: Such as his having spent the last winter of Colonel Burr's vice presidency at Washington, their great intimacy, the interest made to get General Wilkinson appointed and confirmed Governor of Upper Louisiana, with Burr's brother-in-law Secretary to the territory, and many of his friends to places of trust and influence. General Wilkinson's drawing several hundred troops into a cantonment near the mouth of the Missouri, his connections with Colonel Burr, General Adair, John Brown of Kentucky, John Smith of Ohio, and several others, since implicated or suspected of being concerned with Colonel Burr, to procure a charter for cutting a canal on the Indiana side of Ohio, on which charter a bank was ingrafted, and would have produced those funds, the want of which, seems first to have made the General to hesitate—alluding to a paragraph in the cyphered letter. I then stated Colonel Burr's visit to New Orleans, in a barge furnished by General Wilkinson; and that after visiting the lower country, he came to St. Louis. I then stated the conversation with Judge Easton, as before mentioned, and the intimacy of those three persons, and that when Colonel Burr was about leaving St. Louis, the General had a barge got ready with much parade to put him over the Mississippi, that some time after Col. Burr's return to the Atlantic states, Miranda's expedition got ready and sailed, which a gentleman promised, if called on, to come forward and prove General Wilkinson to be the projector of (that gentleman is Judge Easton.) I then observed, that it was not easy to suppose, that Colonel Burr, who knew Wilkinson's character, his former attempts and desperate fortune, should spend so much time with him at Washington, where the scheme seems to have been first projected, pass through the country where Colonel Burr must commence his enterprize, where Wilkinson was well acquainted, and where Burr wanted agents (alluding to the Ohio) and partizans, yet never found him to make proposals, but wait till all was ready, and then make his first overtures in a letter, and before he knew the success of that letter in converting a patriot General into a traitor, should throw himself and his best friends, his *choice spirits*, into the power of a General, he had so much insulted, that the General's measures in Upper Louisiana certainly had a tendency to disgust the people with the change of government, and to prepare them for a revolt, that I did not know the General's attempts upon other officers, but he certainly had tried me, but if, on the contrary, Col Burr did communicate his plans to the General, either at Washington, at Massac, or at St Louis, and the General did not immediately inform his government, he has not only grossly imposed on them, and the public at large, but has been guilty of misprision of treason, and perjury. The Attorney General, after I had gone through my statement and information, in substance and order, nearly as related, asked me what would be the result if *all* this should be proven?—why just what the federalists and the enemies of the present administration wish—it would turn the indignation of the people from Burr on Wilkinson; Burr would escape, and Wilkinson take his place. I observed, that it possibly might be the event, but justice and honor required that the whole truth should be known, let it operate as it might

I then left the Attorney General and Secretary at war together, and stepping down to the Post-Office, found letters from St Louis, detailing the operations of Colonel Burr; and of a party from St Louis, and St Geneva, the common friends of Wilkinson and Burr. who attempted to join him with twelve thousand weight of lead

[Mr *Wirt* Who was the letter from? A Samuel Hammond.]

That letter offered proof, that the party, sent by General Wilkinson to Santa Fee, was connected with, and a part of Colonel Burr's plans. As that letter related to the subject which we had been talking on, I sent it to the Secretary at war and the Attorney General, and another letter to the same point which came on with it from Judge Easton They wrote, that Major Westcott and Dr Stell had left St. Louis, and were joined by a Mr. Smith, Dodge, &c from St Geneva,—who attempted to join Colonel Burr near the mouth of the Ohio. The Secretary at war returned the letters, and thanked me; but I have been surprized, that, after offering proof, that none of them were summoned before the Grand Jury Major Bruff was here asked who those gentlemen were He mentioned General Adair, Judge Easton, and Major Kibby. who would prove the object of the expedition to Santa Fee; also Mr Provinchiere He then stated, that he had seen a letter from General Wilkinson to General Adair, in which General Wilkinson urged him to *come on*; said that HE could not go without him; and then asked if he was ashamed to serve under a Spanish conspirator.

General Wilkinson. When was that letter dated? A I do not recollect when. General Adair read it to me, and he offered me a copy, which made me the less particular about its date. Q. Where was the letter received? Was it at Washington in March last? A. It was the letter, which, as he said, induced General Adair to go to New-Orleans

General Wilkinson pressed him to come on, said that thirty thousand troops would be sufficient to effect their purpose, as they would have little more to do than to take possession of the country that they were to divide them into three columns, and General Adair was to have the command of one of them

Mr M'Rae What country were they to take possession of? A I cannot say, but my impression was, the Spanish country

The General then chided him for the caution he used in writing, asked him if he was afraid to trust his friend, or ashamed to serve under a Spanish conspirator. At the bottom of the letter were these words —" We shall certainly have a Spanish war."

Chief Justice Do you know the hand writing of General Wilkinson? A I do, very well I sit by General Adair when he read the letter, and it appeared to be the hand writing of General Wilkinson —But I did not take it up to compare it.

Mr. *Martin* Do you remember the date? A I cannot tell the date, or the place from which it was written.

Mr *Hay* Did it appear to be of a recent date? A. Yes. Gen-Adair complained bitterly, he said that this letter had induced him to go to New Orleans, where he was seized by General Wilkinson

Mr *Wirt.* Will you name all the witnesses who could give evidence of the connection between Burr and Wilkinson? A Judge Easton, to prove that General Wilkinson was the projector of Miranda's expedition, and to prove his connection with Colonel Burr; Major Timothy Kibby, the person whose deposition has been circulated, and Pierre Provinchiere, who could prove the connection between General Wilkinson and Colonel Burr, and who was the common friend of both; Colonel Samuel Hammond, with whom General Wilkinson had a conversation nearly similar with the one held with me, and Samuel Hammond jun

I believe I did not mention Colonel Dupiester, to prove the designs of the party as to the establishment of a western empire I think Colonel Dupiester was mentioned as the friend of Colorel Burr, and, as I am informed, came to St Louis as his agent, and brought with him commissions and proclamations

Mr, *M'Rae.* Did you see him at St. Louis? A A Colonel's commission it was said was offered to Colonel Chouteau, who attempted to throw it into the fire.

Mr *Hay.* From whom did the proclamations and commissions come? A They were said to be from Colonel Burr Q Who was to have commanded the horse? A Mr Delany, who had been an officer of the horse in the French service (it was said) was offered a distinguished command in Colonel Burr's army A Colonel Dupiestre, it was said, brought on letters,—one to Provinchiere, and another to Timothy Kibby, the common friend of Colonel Burr and General Wilkinson.

Chief Justice Did you see these letters? A. We had a little democratic club, intended to counteract those gentlemen A Mr,

Wherry, to whom Provenchiere shewed the letter, took a copy, and brought it down to us

Mr. *Wirt*. What was in the letter? A. Something to this purport "He was ready, hoped they would be ready; and hoped the expedition would begin to move about the 15th of November"

Mr *Martin* How long have you been in the American service? A I bore arms in 1775, against the tories, had a second Lieutenancy in '76, and continued in service throughout the war Q Have you been in the service ever since? A I entered the service again in '04, under an expectation of bearing arms against the British, for I had been taken a prisoner during the war, and had not been well treated by them Q What was your grade when you left the army? A Major of artillery

Mr *Wickham*. Did you see such a deposition as that of Timothy Kibby, in the hands of the Attorney General or Secretary at war A. No I gave them the letter already spoken of, and I expected that all the gentlemen whose names I have mentioned would have been summoned It has been said, that I came on here as a volunteer I certainly should have came on in any event, but I was surprized that those gentlemen were not summoned, and that the enquiry was to be on one side only.

Mr *Wirt* Is the Samuel Hammond you have mentioned, the same person who had a commission in the time of Genet? A The very same.

Mr *Hay*. I think you said it was in June, 1805, that General Wilkinson disclosed to you this important secret? A Not in June Sometime in the summer: I think in July Q What was the impression on your mind at the time? Did you suppose it was a project hostile to the United States? A I did suspect that he had some grand project in view I expected that he would have made the disclosure without my saying I wished him to make my fortune, I did not intend to come under any obligation, or to commit myself. Q. When was the first time you made any communication to the government or any of its officers, with respect to these projects? A I have a letter here, dated January 8th. 1806, in which I say, " I have no confidence in the patriotism of General Wilkinson, " and, as a man, I think of him with horror."

Mr. *Wirt* To whom is that letter addressed? A To the Secretary at war

Gen *Wilkinson* Were you under arrest at that time? A. No —I was not [looking at his papers] It does not appear from this letter that I was under arrest at that time-

Mr *Hay* I want to know the *fact*, whether you were then under arrest or not? A. I was not Q What was the interval between your arrest, and the trial by Court Martial? A. I believe eight or ten days, but am not certain.

Mr *M'Rae* Had you not been in expectation of an arrest? A I had expected it for some time. In a conversation with the general, about my saying he would not be in office six months, he got very warm, and said—" This is sedition " I replied—" then arrest me "

Mr *Hay*. At what time did this conversation take place about Cold Water, when you stated in your evidence your ruin was decided on? A I think in September, 1805 Then commenced a system of persecution which terminated in my arrest. I was charged, among other things, with contempt to the General . that I never denied. I was found *not guilty* of all the other charges, except that one Major Bruff then said, that the sentence of the Court Martial had been reversed by the President of the United States and his pay and emoluments, which had been suspended by the sentence restored

Gen *Wilkinson* I understood that was by stipulation. What is the date of the President's reversal ? A. I believe it was on the twelfth of March last ? and my pay and emoluments being restored, is equivalent to a reversal

Major *Bruff* proceeded The Secretary at war, observed, that the President was disposed to do me justice ? but it was a delicate point, and there was no precedent, where a sentence had been confirmed by a commander in chief, and afterwards reversed by the President I answered, I thought it was not very delicate in General Wilkinson to approve a sentence which was a mere personal thing between us. I understood it was about the fifteenth of November, the expedition was to have commenced, and the Mexican *standard*, [an emblem of the sun,] to have been *raised* This delayed my departure from St Louis. expected to have seen knights of the sun, and lords of Mexico among the chiefs of those *chosen spirits*.

Mr. *Martin* Whose property is the place called Cold Water ? A. I understand the greater part belongs to Gen Wilkinson. About four acres of it, is deeded to the United States for a factory He wrote on for me to purchase such a place It was about this place that Gen Wilkinson made the rude attack upon me, which I have before mentioned , but, I believe, the true source was, that I had said to an Officer in the confidence of Gen Wilkinson that he would not be in office six months. I knew that Congress was about to meet, and that it was contrary to the genius of our government that he should hold the two offices General and Governor of Louisiana.

General *Wilkinson* When did you receive the first intimation of my intention to retire from service ? A This is intimated in a letter from you, dated April 5th, 1805 [See Note *A*] Q. Did I not reiterate this intention after I came to St Louis ? A. I believe you did Q Do you recollect at what period after I got to St Louis; whether late or early ? A I cannot recollect. You often mentioned the subject. Q. Were you subpoenaed to attend this place ? A. I was. I saw a subpoena in the hands of a gentleman for me ; and Mr Martin had told me in Baltimore here was one ordered , and, therefore, I considered myself as subpoenaed from Queen Ann's county, in Maryland. Q Then you had a conference with Mr Martin ? A. I had. Q Do you recollect to have said that you were reluctant to come, but Mr. Martin had promised to lash me into tortures ? A. I have said, that from a conversation of Mr Martin's, I had reason to believe that your letter post-marked " 13th May," would be produced ; but, that I should have came in any event. [See Note *B*] The first intimation I had of this, was from a letter written by a gentleman of the Grand Jury to a friend of mine, stricturing the testimony of General Wilkinson given before that body That part of the letter was confidentially read to me

[Major Bruff was about to state a conversation with Mr Martin, when he was interrupted by Colonel *Burr*, who said he could not consent to a narration of the conversations which had been held with his counsel.]

General *Wilkinson*. Did you not say that you believed Burr was guilty; but that I had done you a serious injury, and you thought this a good time to seek redress? A I have said, that I believed Colonel Burr concerned in that expedition with you I have said so, and I think so still

Mr. *M'Rae*. Will you state the character of Judge Easton? A I have accused him of endeavoring to cheat out of half the land we purchased in common, on which an arbitration is now depending

General *Wilkinson* Had you no land speculations with Easton? A No, I had no *speculations*, but we made a purchase of a single tract of land together. Perhaps you call *that* land speculations Q You said, that when Colonel Burr arrived at St. Louis, Easton and myself were intimate? A I thought so Q Did you not know, that about that time, I did not suffer him to come into my house? A I heard him say, after Colonel Burr had left St Louis some little time, that you were persecuting him.

General *Wilkinson* I hope I may be allowed until to-morrow morning to select the letters of this gentleman, which I shall offer in opposition to some small matters which the Court have heard. I have also some testimony to offer, which may go to invalidate the credibility of this witness I have many questions to propose to him.

Commodore Shaw was again called.

Mr *Hay* Did you travel in the stage with Major Bruff as he was coming to this place? A. I did. Q. Will you state the conversation which passed?

General *Wilkinson*. Be so good as to say what impression the conversation had on you, respecting myself.

Mr *Burr* No, Sir, state facts, and not conversations. The witness *must* relate *facts*.

Witness The conversations were between this place and Fredericksburg, and were addressed to Captain Gaines and Lieutenant Swearingen, and not to me, but I understood, as Major Bruff stated, that he was convinced of this plot in the western country, and that he had kept a watchful eye over them for a considerable time. I recollect his saying, that he was coming on without being subpœnæd, except from what he understood from Mr. Martin, and that he was come on to tell a long story

Major *Bruff* Do you recollect I sat still a great while A Yes. It was after we dined.

Mr. *M'Rae* You cannot give a detail of the conversation? A No, Sir; but I thought he intended to injure General Wilkinson; as he said, that the General done him serious injury before.

Major *Bruff*. INJURE, says the witness? A. That was the impression that I had. I did not know at that time that you were in the army, or had been at all. I supposed that he had done you an injury, and that you were come forward to retaliate.

The *Chief Justice*, on some objection being made to the relation of " *impressions*," observed, that if a witness could not recollect the exact words, he might state their import as near as he could; but not strictly to call them impressions

Mr *M‘Rae*. State, as nearly as you can, the substance of the words

Witness. I have stated what I understood to be their substance Major Bruff said, that the subpœna was in Baltimore, that he was come on to tell a long story, that he had a good right to know that such a conspiracy existed, and that he had been looking out for it a long time.

Mr *M‘Rae* to Major *Bruff* I understood you to have said, that you were summoned from Queen Ann's county, in Maryland did you ever see the subpœna there? A. No. Q. What induced you then to think that you were summoned there? A I own property in Queen Ann's county, where I had been making arrangements for my return from the western country. I went to Baltimore to transact some business, where I met with Mr Martin. He told me, that if I had not come to Baltimore, he should have gone to see me. I asked him, if the letter postmarked " 13th of May," would be produced. He said, he believed it would; and informed me that I might consider myself summoned, for that he should order a subpœna for me

Colonel *Burr* I desired that no conversations with any of my counsel might be mentioned.

Major *Bruff* When I came here, about the 10th, the gentleman who was included with me in the summons, shewed me a copy of my subpœna, but it was not served

Mr *Hay* You said, that you saw what kind of a Court Martial there was in that part of the country A My impression was, that my trial was not a legal one. I challenged some of the members of the Court, and offered to prove that they were prejudiced. As to the stage. I did not ride in the stage with the gentleman from Fredericksburg to this place. He must be mistaken, for we left him at Fredericksburg. From Alexandria to Fredericksburg he did ride with us.

Commodore *Shaw*. I possibly might have been in an error as to the place when the conversation took place.

Captain *Daniel Bissell* was again called.

General *Wilkinson*. Were you a member of the Court Martial that sat on the trial of Major Bruff? A. I was. Q. By whom was Major Bruff arrested? A. By Captain Richmond. He preferred the charges, and solicited the arrest. Q. How many members composed the Court, their names, and rank? A. Col. Thomas Hunt, President; Colonels Cushing and Kingsbury; Captains Lockwood, Bissell, Strong, and Many; Lieutenants Peters, Mulford, Carson, Whitlock, Richardson and Kimble. Q Was the Court unanimous in their sentence? [Some *doubt* arose about the propriety of answering this question consistently with the articles of war. It was waved for the present.]

Vor 3 Y y

Mr. *Martin* Was it not some short time before the Court Martial, that an address was handed about, and signed by most of the officers? A. I believe it was. Q. Did Major Bruff sign it? A. I do not know that he did. I did not see his name to it. Q. Did not the officers impugn the honor of the members who did not sign it? A. It has been more than two years since the address was circulated, and I cannot recollect what were the impressions of the moment. Major Bruff said, he had seen a mutilated copy of the address published in the papers. The address was to the President: the object of which, was to continue General Wilkinson in the office of commander in chief, while he was Governor of Louisiana. It says a great many handsome things about his services from Canada to Florida, and the sufferings which he had undergone in the cause of his country.

The following is the address referred to in Capt. Bissell's testimony.

To his Excellency,

THOMAS JEFFERSON,

President of the United States.

Sir,

It does not comport with the pride of a soldier, tacitly to behold his General assailed by unmerited slanders, or to suffer the veteran, with whom we have run a *long* course of hardships and perils, to fall a sacrifice to undeserved calumnies. The spirit of a soldier revolts against such apathy, and every man of sensibility would condemn such cold-heartedness.

We mean not to offend, by this offering of a just tribute to merit, nor to derogate from the worth of the living or dead by those expressions of our sentiments.

We have seen with horror, and have felt with indignation, the various attempts which have been made to blast the character of General James Wilkinson. Some of us have served under his command twelve years, and have followed him from Canada to Florida, and all have been habituated to his command for many years; during which period, we have seen him encountering almost every vicissitude to which military life is incident. Generous, benevolent and humane—his heart, his hand and his purse, are ever open and ready to succor distress and relieve misfortune. Hardy, enterprizing, daring and brave, he encounters obstacles with alacrity, and is most exalted when pressed by difficulties. The ice, snow, and wintry blasts of the North; the arid sands and burning sun of the South, wild mountains and morasses, present no impediments to his course, when duty calls. Ready to take the lead in every extremity, he never exacts from others what he is not willing himself to perform. Daring, yet vigilant and cautious, he is provident in warding dangers, and resourceful in mastering them.

Let him be judged by his orders and arrangements, and military men will honor his principles and practices. Rigid in his discipline, exact in his policy, and indefatigable in every branch of service; he delights to comfort and cherish the sick soldier, and pays a sacred respect to the laws of his country, and the rights of his fellow citizens, of which numerous instances could be given.

With him for a leader, we shall neither fear danger nor fore see difficulty, but shall march to battle with the assurance of victory.

The subscribers, composing the whole of the officers present at the cantonment, and St Louis, would suffer martyrdom sooner than profess what they do not believe, or proffer homage where it is not due; and with these sentiments, they hesitate not to declare, that they have offered the opinions of every man of honor who carries the sword of the United States.

Signed by

Thomas Hunt, Colonel 1st United Regiment Infantry
Thomas Cushing, Lt. Col Adj. and Inspector Army.
Jacob Kingsbury, Lt Colonel 1st Regiment Infantry.
B Lockwood, Captain 1st Regiment Infantry
Elijah Strong, Captain 1st Regiment Infantry.
Daniel Bissell, Captain 1st Regiment Infantry
James Richmond, Captain 1st Regiment Infantry
James B Many, Captain Artillerists
George Peters, 1st Lieutenant Regiment Artillery.
Clarence Mulford, Lieutenant, Regiment Artillery.
William Carson, Lieutenant 1st Regiment Infantry.
A Whitlock, Lieutenant 1st Regiment Infantry.
William Richardson, 2d Lt and Adj 1st Reg Infantry
Joseph Kimble, Lieutenant Adjutant
William King, Surgeon's Mate
A Sangrain Surgeon's Mate
Jonathan M. Robinson, Acting Surgeon's Mate.

[A]

CONFIDENTIAL.

I am desirous like yourself, to make a snug fixture, and hang up my sword Our soil, we may thank God, is not favorable to military pursuits, and the profession of arms has become disreputable in our free and peaceful country. Will you look out for a handsome spot for me, five or six miles from St Louis of one thousand acres more or less; rich, well timbered, and lying well for cultivation, with excellent water and and a mill-seat. I want such a spot. Will you have the goodness to look for one without speaking, and, if a bargain presents, you make in your own name a provisional contract, to be off, or on, in six months Pardon the freedom I take with, and the trouble I offer you

With esteem and respect,
Your obedient servant,
JAMES WILKINSON.

Major Bruff
April 5th, 1807.

[B.]

Colonel Meig's Certificate.

Richmond, *September 23d, 1807.*

I certify, that at Richmond, during the trial of Colonel Burr for treason, Major James Bruff informed me that he was attending as a witness for Colonel Burr, for which he was sorry. That Luther Martin had promised him, that if he would attend as a witness, he (Martin) would expose the character of General Wilkinson, by introducing into Court a certain letter written by General Wilkinson to Aaron Burr, which letter Colonel Burr had declined submitting to the Grand Jury; and that Mr. Martin declared that he would lash General Wilkinson into tortures, and upon those promises he came.

Signed,

RETURN J. MEIGS, jun.

WEDNESDAY, October 7.

Mr. *M'Rae* requested, that on account of the extreme indisposition of one of Mr. Wirt's children, which prevented him from attending, the Court might be adjourned till to-morrow. Independent of this circumstance, General Wilkinson, whose feelings had been severely wounded by the testimony of a witness yesterday, was in the course of preparations to remove those unjust imputations. He hoped that no objections would be made to the adjournment.

Mr *Hay* said, that by an arrangement of the counsel of the United States, the principal part of the reply would devolve upon Mr. Wirt. It was, therefore, important that he should be present to know what ground had been occupied by the counsel who preceded him. He did not expect any inconveniences would result from the proposed adjournment, and hoped it would not be opposed.

The adjournment was opposed by Colonel *Burr*, who stated that one of his counsel had been placed in the same situation as Mr Wirt, and no indulgence was asked of the Court on that account. He also mentioned, that the Court had, at his own request, proceeded with the examination, when he was too much indisposed to attend.

Major Bruff begged leave to correct an error in part of his evidence given yesterday, in a point not material. This respected his attendance at the office of General Wilkinson every day. After his remark about Cold Water, and his saying that " should he " discover plans and measures which put to risk the peace and " safety of the United States, he would not keep silence, be the " consequences what it might " General Wilkinson was not visible to him for several days. Other officers attended, said Major Bruff; but I was not permitted to his presence. I wrote to the General, and I received an answer which I have not got here. It however stated, that I should receive such attention as my conduct and rank entitled me to.

John Brokenbrough and Joseph C. Cabell, members of the Grand Jury, were called by Colonel *Burr*.

Colonel *Burr*. I will ask you both, gentlemen, whether General Wilkinson before the Grand Jury acknowledged that in any of his letters he had made use of the words, " he was ready."

Mr *Brokenbrough*. I recollect that General Wilkinson acknowledged that in the winter 1805, 6, he had written to you several

letters; in one of which he used the expression " what has become of the grand expedition. I fear Miranda has taken the
" bread out of your mouth I shall be ready before you." He also
assigned as a reason for writing such a letter, that he had done it
with a view of drawing from you a full disclosure of your project ;
if it should be correct and patriotic, that he might unite in it ; if
improper, that he might reject it. I asked General Wilkinson
whether he had written the letter post-marked, " 13th of May."
He said, that he did not recollect

Colonel Burr. What period was assigned to that letter just quoted ? A The winter of 1805, 6

Mr *Cabell* being requested by Colonel Burr to state his recollection of the evidence of General Wilkinson as to the points
above mentioned, proceeded in substance as follows General
Wilkinson had stated, that he had an interview with you at St.
Louis, at which, you mentioned a grand project , but that you did
not enter into particulars He remarked that he had made some
enquiries as to the nature of the enterprize ; but, you observed,
it was unnecessary to enter into particulars, for it was possible
it might never be carried into effect After Colonel Burr left St
Louis, General Wilkinson remarked, that he had revolved in his
mind the conversation which had passed between him and Col.
Burr, when he spoke of a western enterprize, and concluded, that
an attack on Mexico was contemplated ; which was to be carried
on by the aid of a British fleet through the Gulph of Mexico.
That he had written several letters or notes to Colonel Burr, with
a view to ascertain his real design, between the time of their in
terview at St. Louis, and the commencement of the following summer ; but did not appear to be positive as to the number or nature of those letters. But he remarked, that his object was to
draw from Colonel Burr a disclosure of the nature of the enterprize , if it were proper, that he might participate in it ; if not,
that he might make a disclosure to the government General Wilkinson on being interrogated as to the contents of his letters, answered, that he could not recollect precisely the terms, and but
only these expressions, which he used in one of them ; " I fear
" Miranda has taken the bread out of your mouth , I shall be rea-
" dy for the grand expedition before you are." I must repeat,
that General Wilkinson did not appear positive as to the dates,
number, or contents of these letters, but only these expressions.
With respect to the letter post-marked " 13th May," General
Wilkinson on being interrogated, was not positive of having written it ; but, said, he believed he had.

Mr *Wickham* Do you recollect whether General Wilkinson
produced a copy of the cyphered letter, which, he said, was a true
copy ? A I do not recollect. I recollect General Wilkinson ten-
dered a copy. Q. To Mr. *Brockenbrough.* Do you recollect whether General Wilkinson produced any fair copy of the cyphered
letter to the Grand Jury ? A. I recollect we had a newspaper in
which it was published , and as we decyphered the original, we
often compared our translation with that copy, and found some
variations.

Mr. *Hay* Have you a copy of the cyphered letter as translated by the Grand Jury ? A. I have

Mr. *Wickham.* State that there were material and essential variations between the translation made by the Grand Jury and that published.

Mr *Cabell* said, he begged leave to observe, that Gen. Wilkinson was one out of fifty witnesses examined by the Grand Jury; that his examination took up four days, and that such circumstances were treasured up, as were deemed material.

Mr *M'Rae* Have you attended to the examination of Gen Wilkinson before the Judge? will you state whether his testimony correspond with that before the Grand Jury? A That is a very extensive one, and which it is impossible to answer During the examination of Gen. Wilkinson before the Judge, my attention was often called off, and therefore I cannot pretend to say, whether his testimony corresponded throughout, with that before the Jury If you will state any part of his testimony, I will endeavour to state whether it corresponded

In general, as far as I have attended to the evidence of General Wilkinson given before the Judge, the narrative is very much the same with that given before the Grand Jury, with some slight variations. For instance, I understood that General Wilkinson said before the Court, that but *one* letter passed between him and Colonel Burr, from their interview at St Louis to the commencement of the next summer, before the Grand Jury, I understood him to have said *some* letters or notes

The circumstances of the packet being slipped from the side pocket of Mr Swartwout, and thrust into the hands of General Wilkinson in the absence of Colonel Cushing, at the interview at Nachitoches, was mentioned to the Grand Jury, if it was not mentioned in Court, that makes another variation

Mr *M'Rae* It was mentioned

Mr *Cabell* Then, Sir, I stand corrected, I have already stated, that I could not recollect accurately all Gen Wilkinson's testimony before the Court

Mr. *Wickham* to Mr *Brokenbrough* Do you recollect any variation between the evidence of Mr Swartwout and General Wilkinson? A As to the delivery of the letter there was no difference; but, in the details of their conversations, there was a very important one

Here some desultory conversation took place, between the counsel on both sides, and the Court, on the subject of Mr. Tazewell's reply to the question propounded to Dr Brokenbrough The Counsel for the prosecution and the Chief Justice disagreed in their notes

Mr. *Wickham* asked Mr Cabell the same general question Mr Cabell answered, that the statement of Mr Tazewell had appeared to him very plain and correct, and had been delivered with his usual ability

Being called on to state how far Gen Wilkinson and Mr Swartwout agreed in their testimony before the Grand Jury, in relation to their conversations at Nachitoches, answered, I must say, that they coincided in some respects and differed in others The material variance is this. Swartwout most positively denied that he had made any criminal communications whatever; and denied his having said any thing about seizing. According to

General Wilkinson the communications of Swartwout, were criminal; according to Mr. Swartwout they were perfectly innocent and honorable.

As I have spoken in such high terms of Mr. Tazewell's statement, I must beg leave to except from that sentiment, the inference which he drew from the manner in which Mr. Swartwout delivered his testimony before the Grand Jury. The manner of Mr. Swartwout, was certainly that of conscious innocence. But there is other testimony in the case. I chuse to suspend my opinion of characters till this investigation shall have terminated.

THURSDAY, October 8

Mr. Bodley was called, and asked whether there was any contract in the deed to send a number of settlers to the land? He answered, that there was not in the deed, he never saw the original contract between Colonel Burr and Colonel Lynch. He had the memorandum on which the deed was to be drawn, but there was no such thing in it. He stated the terms of the memorandum, as much as before recited.

Questions by Mr. Martin and Mr. Burr were asked, as to his having seen or known any thing of the original contract or agreement. He answered that he had not—he had heard them speak of former contract and agreement, but had never seen it. He had heard both of them speak of a settlement on the Washita grant, but whether it was a stipulation between them or not, he could not say, but there was no such thing in the deed.

Mr. Hay. Do you know Ephraim Kibby. A. I do. Q. In what capacity did he serve under General Wayne and at what period? A. He had the command of a party of spies or rangers in the year 1793, and in 1794, he had the command of another party.

Some questions were here asked by Mr. M'Rae, as to the assistance that was to be afforded by him to Burr, in his intended enterprize.

The Witness declared, that there were no measures taken by him, or intended towards the enlistment of men, but what must proceed under the sanction of the government of the United States.

After some desultory conversation, Mr. Hay said, that he was ready to go on with the argument of the cause, but he would not do it unless directed by the Court. An attack had been made on General Wilkinson by Major Bruff, which it was the right and the duty of General Wilkinson to explain. Not a word in the long and labored narrative of Major Bruff, was testimony applicable to the case before the Court. But having made such serious charges against General Wilkinson—justice requires that the General should be heard in explanation.

Gen. Wilkinson. I have several matters to submit to the Court which have been brought to my recollection by the occurrences of yesterday and the day before.

Grand Jurors have been brought forward to contrast my evi
dence before that body, with what I have said here in the wide
range of testimony, which has been permitted ; a witness may be
readily misconceived by others, or misunderstand himself. In
the case of Mr. Tazewell, your honors sense of his testimony,
was in direct opposition to that of Mr Burr's counsel ; and in the
case of Mr. Cabell, one of the most correct men in the world, he
had misconceived or did not understand me, respecting the mode
in which Swartwout delivered Mr. Burr's letter to me. It is
with deep regret I trespass on the time of the Court ; but, when
every art is employed, and evidence is drawn from every quarter,
to rip up the remotest transactions of my life, t effect my credi
bility ; to wound my fame, and rob me of my reputation

Here Mr. *Wickham* interrupted General Wilkinson, and said
he must object to the course which he was about to pursue. Gen
Wilkinson stands here on the same ground as any other witness.
Let his explanations apply to his evidence, but let him not go into
other subjects.

Mr. *M'Rae* hoped, that the same indulgence which had been
granted to others, would be extended to General Wilkinson It
will be recollected with what patience their witness, Maj Brof
had been heard for six hours, while he was merely indulging
himself in the carnage of General Wilkinson's reputation. Gen
Wilkinson who had been listening with the most exemplary pa
tience, now comes forward to explain, and in the midst of a very
short and respectful evidence, he is interrupted by the counsel
on the other side.

The *Chief Justice* said, there could be no doubt as to the dis
position of the Court, to hear as full an explanation as General
Wilkinson might please to make, but he being merely in the cha
racter of a witness, would confine himself to a narrative of facts
and resort to arguments as little as possible.

Mr *Hay* hoped that something of argument would be permit
ted General Wilkinson had been assailed vitally, intentionally
and deliberately by Major Brof, and his explanations could not
be so well understood, unless he should, in some instances, resort
to argument

The *General* resumed When I was first brought before the
Court, it was my intention to have commenced with Colonel Burr
at Washington, and to have traced him, step by step, from his
passage over the mountains, until his return. But I was confined
to such facts as were deemed immediately relevant to the question
before the Court, and therefore I commenced with the receipt of
his letter at Natchitoches

Now, Sir, find myself obliged to adopt this course, in order to
explain certain observations, which have come from the Grand
Jurors, and also, the inuendoes and insinuations of Major Brof
who having charged me with a sinister connection with Col. Burr
has travelled from Washington to St Louis, in order to find mat
ter for the justification of the imputation He has laid some stress
on the interest, which he said was made, (by Mr. Burr and his
friends,) to procure me the government of Louisiana. I am under
no obligation to explain how I procured that government

were, I could say, a tender was made to me of it by the President
before they had any idea of the circumstance

I am charged with having invited Col. Burr to the western
country Herein I have been misunderstood, for the thing is not
so. A few days after Colonel Burr descended from the Vice-
Presidential chair, an enquiry was made by me, as to the course
he intended to pursue. He told me he intended to visit New Orleans, I remember his very words were, " I have a few thousand
dollars left, and I will not go to work until they are spent." I was
solicitous to see him reinstated in the councils of his country;
and speaking to the honorable John Fowler, then a member of
Congress, on the subject, he informed me that Mr. M. Lyon had
suggested to him the idea of Mr Burr's going to Tennessee, to
procure his election to a seat in Congress, as residence was not a
necessary qualification to election in that State, and requested
me to speak to Burr on the subject I did so and I think he said,
it was a luminous idea, appeared to be delighted with the plan,
and in concert with Mr Fowler and Mr. Lyon, I then understood.
and have since been assured by the former, who is now in town,
the plan was digested without my presence, or participation at
any interview

Mr Burr soon after proceeded to Philadelphia He wrote me
on the 20th of March, requesting a letter of introduction to General Adair, and informing me that he should set out for the
western country about the tenth of April The next letter I received from him was at Pittsburg, dated the 30th of April, in
which he told me he was to sail that day for the lower country,
and was sorry he could not see me. At Louisville I received a
third letter, dated the 19th of May, in which he deeply regrets
he could not see me there ; and begs me to forward the letters of
introduction, I had promised him for New Orleans, to that city
he proceeded from Louisville to Frankfort ; and I am authorized to say, did there apply to John Brown esq to aid him in his
proposed election in Tennessee, and to that end, requested letters
from Mr Brown to his friends there. He then proceeded to Nashville, where it appears he remained beyond his calculation. I fell
down the river to Massac, where Colonel Burr arrived on the 8th
of June ; and instead of spending *several days* in giving me lessons
in government, and preparing a new code or constitution for
Louisiana, he the *next day* prosecuted his voyage for New Orleans, in company with several officers of the army, who had been
ordered to that city on a general Court Martial, and it will
be proven, that I furnished him with neither barge nor crew.
I heard no more from Mr Burr until the 30th of July, when I
received a letter from him at the crossing of the Tennessee river, in which he informed me, he was on his way to Lexington
and hoped to be with me at St. Louis about the first of September. He arrived at St. Louis on the 11th of that month, in the
evening ; expressed a wish to visit St. Charles ; and I accompanied him in his route to the cantonments of the troops, about
seven miles distant, from whence he proceeded without me, and
crossed the Missouri to St. Charles ; from thence passed over the
portage des Sioux to the Mississippi, and descended that river in
a canoe to St. Louis. I think it was in our ride to the cantonment,

that Mr. Burr, speaking of the imbecility of the government, said it would moulder to pieces—die a natural death, or words to that effect, adding, that the people of the western country were ready to revolt. To this I recollect replying, that if he had not profited more by his journey in other respects, he had better have remained in Washington or Philadelphia—for surely said I, my friend, no person was ever more mistaken! The western people dis affected to the government! They are bigoted to Jefferson and democracy. And the conversation dropt. Mr Burr on the same ride, I think, spoke to me of purchasing an estate in that country, observing, that he had received advice of a sum of money which he should receive on his return to the eastward, and asked me if I would resign my government to him in the course of the winter if he should desire it. This I rejected on account of the emoluments, which was two thousand dollars per annum (for I was disgusted with the government,) and he offered to indemnity me.

Nothing particular passed between us after this, until the afternoon before his departure, which was on the 19th of September in the morning. He informed me, that he wished to have some conversation with me, and I invited him to my house for the purpose. In the course of this interview, he asked me, " whether I could be content to vegitate or moulder in that " d—'d government?" meaning the government of Louisiana. I expressed my satisfaction with the situation, observing, that " I was making arrangements to retire to private life; that I " was tired of the erratic life I had long led; and that the deli- " cate situation of my wife, to whom I owed more than I could " render, made it necessary." After some pause, he asked me if my energies or enterprize were lost or dead, to which I replied, " that my energies and enterprize had profited me lit " tle else through life, than to expose me to perils and hard- " ships." He then observed, " but suppose some grand enter- " prize should present, which would lead direct to fame and for- " tune." To this I replied, with indifference at first, remarking, that " I had been so long under expectations for something of the kind, " that I had given them up as vain." but added, after a short pause, " if the government should think proper to direct any " thing of the kind, it would not find that my energies or enter " prize were lost." " Surely." replied he, " under the authori- " ty of the government," and naming a minister, asked me " if " an order from him would satisfy me." I answered, that " an " order from any minister was obligatory on me, as they all " were the organs of the presidential will." " Will!" said he; " such a measure has been thought of, but it is unnecessary to go " into the details of a project which may never be carried into " effect," and I replied, that " I had no curiosity to hear" And here you have a knowledge of as much of his designs as I possess.

It has been observed, that I had no idea of any project of Col. Burr before the receipt of his letter by Mr. Swartwout. This I deny. I have said, I had no idea of any *illicit* design, such as would subject him to legal penalty, or legal obstruction. Between the period of Mr. Burr's leaving St. Louis, and May

1806, I received six letters from him. I have said, that those letters blended matters personal, with matters political. I have considered those letters confidential; they were so received, and I will not expose them, but in the last extremity, without Colonel Burr's permission: but, if I have that permission, I will do it now. I have asked it, and do again ask it. Those letters were of an ambiguous aspect, speaking of some enterprize, without designating any; and were calculated to inculpate me, should they be exposed. I have said, I made a communication to a public minister, (the Secretary of the navy) to the following effect "Burr is about something; but whether internal or external, I cannot discover." It has been made a question, how I could, feeling the friendship I professed for Colonel Burr, make such a communication, when unapprized of any criminal intention, and I reply, that I justify it from a sense of public duty, paramount to all other obligations, from the consciousness, that if Burr intended no harm, the communication could do him none, as it was confidential, and on the ground of self-security against future events

In the course of Wednesday, *Thomas Bodley* was again called into Court at the request of the Attorney for the prosecution.

Question by Mr *M'Rae* You mentioned in your testimony on Saturday last, that a memorandum was given you to write the deed by, from Colonel Lynch to Mr Burr Was there any thing in that memorandum about corn, cutting roads, or making settlements? A. There was not, it was simply a memorandum stating the quantity of land to be conveyed, the description of it, and the consideration: the deed was wrote agreeable to the memorandum. I never saw the original contract, but was informed by the parties, there were other stipulations in their agreement. Q Was there any thing of corn, cutting roads, &c mentioned in the deed? A. There was not

Mr. *Hay* Do you know Ephraim Kibby? A I do Q In what capacity did he act in General Wayne's army? A. In the year 1793, he had command of a small party of spies or rangers, in 1794, he had command of a larger party, and in both years was called Captain Kibby.

Mr. *Bodley* As I am again before the Court, I beg leave to observe on part of my testimony more fully. I stated, that "I made a conditional contract with Colonel Burr for flour" I did engage two boat loads of flour with a view of letting him have it, but before the boats were sent off, the President's proclamation came to hand, and no part of it was ever delivered to Col Burr, or to any person for him. When Colonel Burr enquired of me if men could be got to go to Mexico in case of a war, I gave it as my opinion, they could. I gave him the names of a number of young men, who I thought would probably engage, and made him acquainted with some of them. Having heard it remarked since I gave my testimony, that I must have had some knowledge of Colonel Burr's plans, I think it my duty to state, that in every conversation I had with Colonel Burr. his remarks relative to an enterprize against Mexico, were predicated on a war with Spain, and never did I hear him or any other person with whom he had conversed in Kentucky, intimate that he had any thing in vi inimical to the United States, or that his views were in any respect treasonable

I hope that the Court will indulge me with one further observation I have been charged by the editors of the *Western World*, (which paper I consider one of the most scurrilous, abusive and unprincipled ever published) with being a partizan of Colonel Burr I have been represented in that paper in different capacities, from the *foot pad* to the *aid* of Colonel Burr. I avail myself of this opportunity, under the solemnity of an oath in the presence of this Court and before the whole world, to declare, that I never have, either directly, or indirectly, been engaged in any act of treason against my country, or in any misdemeanor in violation of the laws of the United States I am firmly attached to the federal government, and will do my utmost to support it whenever my services may be required

General Wilkinson's evidence continued

I had formed several opinions of Mr Burr's views: sometimes I thought them chimerical, and the most definite idea I had ever attached to them was, that he had formed some connection with the British government, that he was to operate with an expedition by the Gulph against the Mexican provinces, and that the United States were, in case of a war, which was every where expected, to co-operate by the Mississippi. I recollect well this impression, from the circumstance of my having mentioned to several persons, that if they would shew me the embarkation of any army in England, equipt for a southern climate, I would tell them we should have a war with the Spanish provinces, and from this impression, my idea respecting Miranda's " taking the bread out of his mouth," must have sprung. I beg it may be remembered at this time, that Colonel Burr descended from the vice-presidential chair with great eclat, and I did believe he was not only re-ascending in the public confidence, but in the confidence of the executive—and for these reasons. His step-son, Judge Prevost, had been appointed district Judge to the territory of Orleans. The republican body of the Senate had addressed Governor Bloomfield to enter a *nolle prosequi* on his behalf, in a case of great hardship and delicacy. The Senate had addressed him in the most flattering terms, and Dr. Browne, the gentleman who had married his wife's sister, had been appointed (solely on the recommendation of Colonel Burr) Secretary to the territory of which I had been appointed Governor

Frequent reference has been made to the letter said to be " post-marked 13th of May." I have said, I do not recollect whether I wrote Colonel Burr such a letter or not, and of course I can have no recollection of the contents, but I have said, I believed I had written him three letters after he left St Louis, and this was my idea; but I recollect no particulars, except the expression relating to Miranda, though I remember perfectly the motives with which I did write him. I now find from his letter of the 16th of April, that he had received no letter from me after October or November 1805, and therefore I conclude I wrote him but two letters, from the period he left me at St

Louis to the present day I again require that the letter imputed to me, " post-marked 18th of May," should be produced. I think it was in the letter I wrote in October or November 1805, that I make mention of Miranda, and I now believe it was after the receipt of a letter from him of the 24th of December 1805, that I warned the Secretary of the navy against him It has been said by one of the Grand Jury, that I declared I had employed language in my notes or letters, to draw from Col Burr his real objects, that I might, in case they were commendable, partake of them, and if otherwise, report him to government I acknowledge the first motive, but I do not recollect the alternative If his plans had been vicious, I should have done my duty; if they had been innocent, I should not have reported him I find by reference to my correspondence, that I received no orders to leave St. Louis until the 11th of June 1806, the troops had sailed the 8th of May, and I was left to exercise the functions of civil Governor, God knows without any idea of leaving the country, until the order arrived, and the much talked of letter, bears " post-mark 13th May," a month before I received my orders.

Mr *Hay*. Will you state what passed between yourself and Major Bruff when he descended the river to meet you on your approach to St Louis? A I will. But I can state before you, Sir, (addressing the Judge,) and before God, (turning up his eyes to Heaven, and placing his hands on his heart,) that his whole narrative is either a vile fabrication, or a distortion of facts, and I will shew why this man above all others in the world, should not be in my confidence On my arrival at fort Massac, I met a number of officers under orders to attend a general Court Martial at New Orleans, among whom, was Captain Stoddart, who had taken possession of Louisiana on the part of the United States and preceded Maj. Bruff in the command of St Louis, and had acted as civil Commandant of the country, 'till he had been superceded by the appointment of Gov Harrison, who had acted as Gov of Indiana and also of Louisiana, until I was appointed to that territory In the course of my enquiries of Captain Stoddart relative to the state of the territory ; he informed me that Major Bruff had by his conduct made himself very unpopular with the inhabitants. In ascending the Mississippi I halted at Kaskaskias, where I received a letter from Governor Harrison by the hands of a Mr Wallace, or a Captain Prince, who were in company; of which letter I hold an extract in my hand. [The reading of this extract was opposed by the counsel of Colonel Burr. The *Chief Justice* declared that General Wilkinson might either read the extract or state its contents *General Wilkinson* read the extract See Note No D] The letter is dated the 7th of June 1805, and was received the 29th or 30th of the same month, and I met Major Bruff on the 3d of July. At the same place I received by a dispatch boat an invitation to dine on the day of my arrival at St Louis with Mr Augustus Chouteau, who I understood was the senior magistrate of the district, and as good a man as there is in that or any other country. As I approached St Louis I sent a light barge ahead and requested Major Bruff to meet me, for he also had invited me to dine with him on the day of my arrival Knowing the jealousy of his disposition and being desirous to conciliate and prevent exception, I wished to explain to him my motives for giving a preference to Mr Chouteau's invitation : which I did when we met, by stating to him that approaching the territory in my capacity of Governor, the first respect was due to the Civil Magistrate ; that I gave Mr Chouteau the preference on this ground and hoped he would excuse it I met Major Bruff on the beach under a steep bank I did not take him into the woods, nor had any conversation with him of the import he has stated We ascended the river about a mile, and were hailed from the shore. The boats landed, and I was met I think, by three gentlemen, Mr Augustus Chouteau Mr Anthony Souland, and Mr Charles Gratiot, who were introduced to me on board my barge and invited me to land and take horse to St. Louis ; to which I consented, and debarking I was received by a troop consisting of fifty or sixty dragoons, commanded by Captain P. Chouteau, the brother of Mr Augustus Chouteau These, I presume, were the Frenchmen who hunted us up in the woods I mounted a horse which had been provided for me, and was escorted to St Louis These are the facts so far as they related to the interview with Major Bruff I dined with Mr Chouteau, but found that Major Bruff had anticipated Mr Chouteau, and had engaged every officer to dine with him I was left alone.

Mr *Hay.* Had you those other conversations mentioned by Major Bruff, in which he states you to have been ruminating about a grand project, which was to make the fortunes of all concerned A It is impossible for me to say what conversations I had with the officers of the garrison, especially the one whom I found in command ; but from the circumstances already stated, it is impossible I should have had those conversations with Major Bruff mentioned by him The Major, in order to substantiate his tale has affected an air of mystery, and his imagination has furnished the scenery ; for this purpose he takes me into the woods, has us hunted up by Frenchmen, then locks a door where there was no lock, it being fastened by hooks and staples , nor was it necessary to shut it at all, as the ordinary guard at head quarters gave the sentinels for its protection This locking of the door betrays some concert : for I well remember that a few days ago, one of the counsel of Colonel Burr (Mr Martin) demanded of me emphatically, whether I did not recollect being locked up in a room with a gentleman and having a long conversation with him.

Mr. *Hay* Did you ever select Major Bruff for the purpose of making confidential communications ; or state to him any thing about the prospect of making fortunes ? A No, never

Col. *Burr* Are you acquainted with a Mr Bon Ami, a magistrate of New Orleans ? A I have no recollection of any person of that name. [Mr Wickham called for the production of the original letter of Governor Harrison to General Wilkinson from which an extract had been read. The counsel of Col. Burr contended that as an extract had been read from it, they had a right to the whole letter, as the best evidence. They were answered by the counsel for the United States, that there was not a word in the letter which had any relation to Major Bruff except the paragraph which had been read, and that the latter was entirely private and confidential   After some further debate the Chief Justice declared that he felt great repugnance at the idea of producing the letter, as it was entirely private and confidential, and he was certain that neither the letter nor the extract could be evidence in the cause, but it was a rule of law, that when an extract was read, the whole paper must be read if demanded   In the present case the whole letter must be produced, or the extract be withdrawn,

Mr. *Hay* remarked, that Gen Wilkinson had been drawn into the production of the extract by the opinion of the Court.

Gen *Wilkinson* addressed the Judge, and declared that he had produced the extract by his permission, and that without that permission he would not have produced it, that he held the letter sacredly confidential, and would go to jail rather than produce it.

The *Chief Justice* directed, that the extract should be withdrawn, and requested that all those who took notes of the proceedings would erase every thing which had been said about the letter or the extract

Mr. *Martin* hoped that they would erase the impression from the public mind.

Mr *Wickham* You have said something about dining; did you not write to Major Bruff from Kaskaskias excusing yourself for not dining with him? A. I cannot recollect   Mr *Wickham.* Are you certain the door had no lock? A. I have my clerk here who can prove that it had no lock, it was fastened with hooks and bolts after the French manner

Mr Wickham. Do you recollect what gentleman went down in the barge with Major Bruff? A. I cannot.

Mr. Wickham. Do you recollect whether Mr. Gratiot came with him? A. I have said that Mr Gratiot, Mr Chouteau and Mr Soulard met me; but whether they came with MajorBruff, I cannot say

Mr. Wickham. Will you say whether you first met Mr Chouteau and Mr. Soulard in the woods? A I have already stated the circumstance of their going out of the boat with me, and accompanying me to St. Louis

Major Bruff was called in and *cross examined* by the prosecution.

Mr *Hay*   I think you said that you had taken up some impressions of Gen Wilkinson's connexion with Col Burr, previous to to his arrival at St. Louis? A I had. Q Do you recollect having any conversation with an officer, stating that your reasons for inviting Gen. Wilkinson to dine with you, were on account of the injuries which had been done to his character? A No, but I have argued that the cropping order was perfectly a military one, and that he had a right to issue it; but I said nothing of his moral character. Nor have I justified his persecution of Colonel Butler   I have also said that he had some good military notions, though I do not know how, or in what service he acquired them   Q Do you recollect having any conversation with Gen. Wilkinson in presence of Colonel Cushing? A. What conversation do you allude to?

Mr. Hay. There had been a coolness between you, long anterior to the arrival of Gen. Wilkinson? A. Yes. I had long been persecuted by the General, but wished to bury the hatchet. I had been confined to a garrison without the liberty of going out of it, except by the permission of a superior officer who was posted three hundred miles distance. Here is a postscript to a letter which proves an order to that effect from Gen Wilkinson (See note E.) (Read it)

Mr *Martin* Where did this superior officer live ? A At Norfolk, and I was stationed about thirty miles from Wilmington in North Carolina

Mr *M'Rae* What was your construction of that order, is it possible that you could take it literally and suppose that you were to be constantly confined within the walls of the garrison. A. The order shews the intention; but the place had no walls—it was therefore nugatory—yet I considered the intention to confine me to the spot—nor did I leave it till I had permission. General Wilkinson ought to have known the situation, but it appeared he did not I wrote to the Secretary at war or Colonel Burbeck, from whom I received orders that admitted of my occasionally leaving the works and place

Mr *Hay* Will you state whether General Wilkinson wrote to you to purchase some land ? A I have a letter here of the 5th of April, 1805, which speaks of that subject. Q When did General Wilkinson speak to you about his intention to quit the army and retire to private life? A I have had a number of conversations with General Wilkinson, and in my evidence, I have endeavored to throw them into as much order as possible, but it is difficult to state any precise time when he mentioned to me that subject Q Was it at St Louis? A Yes, but the letter before mentioned gives a full explanation of his intention Q. Did he continue in this style of conversation after his arrival at St Louis? A He did Q But your suspicions still continued of his connections with Col Burr? A I have stated that my suspicions arose from two paragraphs in two separate Kentucky paper

Mr. *Hay* You stated in your evidence the other day, that you made a communication to the Secretary at war, and said to him that you could prove General Wilkinson's connexion with Col Burr Will you state why you said so ? A. In one of my conversations I named witnesses, who I believed could prove it, and insisted it was susceptible of proof I not only thought so then, but I think so still, and shall make it my duty to collect and exhibit proofs.

Mr. *M'Rae* Did you say that General Wilkinson's having dined with Mr Chouteau filled you with indignation ? A. I have said that I thought it an indignity offered me, and it was so thought of by the officers. But let me here say, that General W. having denied our interviews in the woods and rooms, are incorrect And I can completely prove it on my return to St. Louis. Q. Did you not recommend Cold Water as a suitable spot for a cantonment ? A While General Wilkinson was at Washington I received several letters from him, in one of which he, stated that a cantonment was wanting for five hundred men He directed me to select a spot near Kahokia He described the kind of position he wished. I reported several situations answering his instructions, but I do not recollect that I mentioned Cold Water among them—although I had viewed it and thought it offered a good military position, (but not in *the bottom*) which the General fixed on—nor did I conceive it was contemplated to have a cantonment in the midst of the settlements.

Mr. *M'Rae*. Were you not in treaty for it yourself? A. I was. I wanted it for a farm and mill seat and not for a military post. Q Do you know whether that place is occupied as a military post, or used merely for the convenience of the soldiers while stationed there? A. I think it a very unmilitary position The troops were posted in a thick wood, which they had to cut down, dig up by the roots, and grub up the bushes for a parade It may hereafter make a good meadow or field, when they are ordered on Q Is there a factory there? A Yes Q Good water? A There is a good spring and a handsome marsh next to the second bank.—— There is also a commanding situation for a cantonment within the purchase, but not at that spot Q Are you certain that there was a good understanding between General Wilkinson, Colonel Burr and Judge Easton? A I believe there was. Easton often visited him, and endeavored to reconcile us after we fell out, and the General has sometimes read to me paragraphs from letters he received from Colonel Burr, about the probability of a war with Spain, and a change of politics in the United States — he has also read others from Dayton and John Smith of Ohio, &c. Q Have you any reason to believe there was an intimacy between General Wilkinson and Judge Easton? A. I have said I believed there was—Easton has told me so. Q Have you any other reason? A. Easton was almost every day with the General ? At what period? A. On General Wilkinson's arrival previous to the fourth of July and for some time after, Easton was frequently in the General's office, and spoke of him in the highest terms Q Was there any intimacy previous to the General's arrival? A I never saw them together previous to the General's arrival Q Did Major Kibby reside on the frontiers previous to the arrival of General Wilkinson? A I believe he did. have seen him, and understood he lived near St Charles. I esteemed him as a man of honor, whose word and oath would be taken, where perhaps General Wilkinson's would be shaken Q. When Major Kibby made the deposition which has been mentioned, was it not reported and believed, that Lieutenant Pike and his party had been destroyed? A I cannot tell when he made the deposition Q. When you heard of the deposition was it not reported that Pike and his party were killed? A On recollection I think I have seen an account in some newspapers of their having been destroyed, but the only report which I deemed correct was, that they were taken by the Spaniards and conducted Santa Fee Q Did not Major Kibby quit our government and become a subject of the king of Spain? A. That is my presumption I found him in that territory when I arrived there; but as did not review the possession, it is mere conjecture. Q When Judge Easton mentioned to you that Colonel Burr had made certain proposals, did he speak of any particular newspaper? Not that I recollect Q. You have said there once seemed be a good understanding between Gen. Wilkinson and Burr; y should Burr apply through Easton for a man of enterprize, not immediately to General Wilkinson himself? A. The Colonel can best answer this question, but if I may be allowed to conjecture, it was because the General had tried me before, and found I was too much of a democrat to be made a traitor of. Q But will you say how came Burr to apply to Easton? A You had better ask Colonel Burr that question, he may answer it Q Were you and General Wilkinson about that time at variance- A Yes He had before reprimanded me about the freedom with which I spoke of his military position at Cold Water, mea sures and plans. Q. Did Easton know it? A. I presume he did Q. You said that you had informed some of the heads of departments, that Judge Easton could prove General Wilkinson to be the projector of Miranda's expedition will you state when you gave that information? A In March last? Q When did you first obtain it? A Just before I left St. Louis, in November last

Mr. M'Rae. Then you received it in November and communicated it in March?

Major Bruff I left St Louis in November, for the seat of government, but was detained on the way, so that I did not arrive till about February.

Mr. M'Rae. Did I understand you that in August 1805, you suspected an improper connection between Burr and Wilkinson? A I have said that the first hint I had, was from two paragraphs in two separate newspapers This was afterwards strengthened by the information of Captain Stoddart, of Burr's being at fort Massac, and the attempt of General W. to sound me. Q. I speak of the time when the impressions were formed. Did that suspicion exist in August 1805? A Yes. That they were connected in some plan? Q. Believing as you did, why did you not communicate your suspicions to some of the officers of the government? A. I do not always communicate my suspicions; I was waiting for acts My letters will show the nature of the communication I made. I Have a copy of one with me Q. When is the first letter dated which communicates those hints? A The one I have with me is dated the 8th of January, 1806.

Mr. M'Rae Did you state in that letter all the various circumstances you have mentioned, such as General Wilkinson taking you into the bushes, your b. surprized by a party of Frenchmen, and his having mentioned to you the plan of a grand project, by which all concerned were to make their fortunes?

Major Bruff. What will be the consequence if I read a part of that letter—will the letter itself be demanded?

Chief Justice certainly, but you may state from recollection

Mr. Hay You said, that it was your intention to state facts and I wish to know whether these facts were stated. Now here are important facts.

Major Bruff. Hints were thrown out in the letter of the 8 of January, 1806, but nothing communicated till March 180 that can be regarded as a statement of facts. I however think had given hints before, but have not the letters with me to re fresh my memory—nor can I read what I intended as hints, from the I one have with me.

Mr Hay I assure you that I shall not call for it if you say is a confidential letter.

Major Bruff. Then I will say generally, that I did give hints, about which, I expected, the Secretary at war would have called for explanations and demanded proofs. I also made a communication to Captain Lewis, immediately after his return, and related to him the conversations between Judge Easton and myself. [Q What Captain Lewis?—the one who explored the waters of the Missouri and Columbia rivers, and the western part of the continent as far as the Pacific Ocean? A The same.]

Mr *Hay* But did you tell him of the conversations which passed between General Wilkinson and yourself, did you inform him that General Wilkinson had mentioned to you the grand expedition? A I believe that I hinted something of that nature

Mr *M'Rae* Will you say whether you made a disclosure to the Secretary at war, before the 8th of January 1806? A I have said over and over, that I believe I had hinted suspicions of Wilkinson's measures in previous letters, but have not those letters with me I did think that Wilkinson and Burr were connected, and acting in concert, and under this impression remained in that country till the 15th of November, 1806. In order to counteract and oppose their attempts, and pull down their standard.

Mr *M'Rae* Did you write prior to the 8th of January, 1806? A. I was in the habit of writing to Joseph H Nicholson and other public characters Q Had you written letters to them injuriously to General Wilkinson, before the 8th of January, 1806? A My letters detailed Wilkinson's measures, which I considered suspicious and hostile to the interest of the United States and of Louisiana I also stated that Gen. Wilkinson appeared to consider me as a spy on his conduct, and had deprived me of all command, and intercourse with the troops, and had prejudiced the officers against me Q But had you written to any of the heads of departments prior to the 8th of January, 1806? A How often will you ask me this question? I have repeated over and over that I have not the correspondence with me What do you wish me to say? I will repeat that my impressions are, that I gave the government hints before that time, that Wilkinson's conduct was suspicious

Mr *Hay.* Did you think it was incumbent on you to state to the Secretary at war your suspicions of the patriotism of General Wilkinson, if they had been well founded, and your ideas of the views of Col Burr? A I was waiting for something unequivocal. I expected it to happen every day.

Mr *M'Rea.* Did you say the other day that the Secretary at war had declared that General Wilkinson would be supported by the government? A. I did The Secretary at war appeared angry and frowned when I denounced Wilkinson, and said, he must and would be supported Q At what time did Judge Easton leave the territory for the seat of government? A I think in November 1805

Mr. M'Rae Did you not give Easton special letters of introduction to your friends? A. I believe I did, or if I did not, I ought to have done so. He was then denouncing Burr and Wilkinson. Q. Was that after you suspected him of treasonable designs? A. It was after he mentioned the treasonable designs of Burr and Wilkinson. Q. Did you not write to your friends, particularly recommending Easton? A. I wrote to Mr. Robert Wright and General Samuel Smith, as to the state of the territory, and that Judge Easton was persecuted by Wilkinson, and was united with us to penetrate and defeat their designs Q As far back as November 1805, was there a public denunciation? A I gave the conversations with Judge Easton the day before yesterday Q When did Judge Easton swindle you? A. My information was long since that conversation. Q Are you on terms of intimacy with him now? A. No; at variance We have an arbitration depending.

Captain Edmund Pendleton Gaines

Mr M'Rae. We wish Captain Gaines to state the conversations of Major Bruff, as he came on to this place in the stage.

Captain Gaines Sometime in the beginning of August, I passed in the mail stage from Alexandria to this place, and a little after day-light of the first morning after we had left Alexandria, I found Major Bruff, and Lieutenant Swearingen, were passengers. They got into conversation about Burr's trial I paid very little attention to it, for indeed I did not calculate on its ever being noticed again; but my curiosity was at length excited, by his saying, that he was informed by Luther Martin of Baltimore, that a subpœna was out for him, and hearing of it, he had come on voluntarily for the purpose of giving evidence against General Wilkinson I remarked to him, that as he had volunteered his services, it was presumable he had something of importance to communicate, and enquired what it was He mentioned several things which he has already stated to the Court, and among others, a communication from Judge Easton, in which, he, (Easton) observed, that he had written a letter to a member of Congress offering to prove General Wilkinson to be the projector of Miranda's expedition. This appearing to be the principal evidence which he had to offer against General Wilkinson, I expressed my surprize that he should come for that purpose, as it could not be considered legal evidence. It appeared to me from the whole tenor of his conversation, that he considered himself injured by General Wilkinson, and spoke particularly of his arrest. He stated, that General Wilkinson had done him a considerable injury, and that the communications which he had now to make would bear very heavily on the General, or would do him as great an injury

Mr Hay Do you recollect any particular expressions? A The substance of the conversation was as I have already detailed it, that General Wilkinson had done him a serious injury in the case before the Court Martial, and now he would have it in his power to give evidence which would bear hard upon the General or do him as serious an injury

Captain Daniel Bissell

Mr M'Rae It will be recollected that Captain Bissell was a member of the Court Martial which sat on the trial of Major Bruff, and has been partly examined. We wish now to ask some further information from him.

Mr. M'Rae to Captain Bissell   Was the Court unanimous in the sentence passed upon Major Bruff? A. There was a legal majority in favor of the sentence, some were for one more severe, but none for a milder one.   Mr M'Rae What was the character of Major Bruff among his brother officers and the people at large? A I have been but little acquainted with Major Bruff. I had received letters from him, and written in answer, on public business, before I became personally acquainted with him   On my return to St Louis in 1805, I found Major Bruff in great disrepute among his brother officers   He had been charged with being a partizan, and of having excited jealousies among the officers   He did not visit General Wilkinson, and a great many things were said of him , but I did not enquire into the particulars I had never spoken to General Wilkinson about him, but made enquiries of Captain Richmond and many others, and found that they united in an opinion very unfavorable to the Major   Mr M'Rae What is your opinion of the cantonment of Cold Water, as to healthiness, and the convenience of wood and water? A There is a great abundance of wood, and the best water in that part of the country   The cantonment is on the first bank, and in a sandy and dry situation   It is not a commanding situation, because a hill runs parallel with the river, about half a mile distant from the cantonment. I was informed by my brother, Captain Russel Bissell, who was for some time stationed there, that the troops were very healthy   They were very healthy, when I was there on the Court Martial, and have been reputed to be very healthy ever since.   Mr. M'Rae Was that situation chosen for a place of rendezvous or a permanent position? A. I cannot say what was the object of the station It is very convenient as a place of rendezvous, and also for the collection and transportation of provisions and military stores   Q What is the general character of Judge Easton? A I have generally understood he bore an infamous character   Q. Did Major Bruff give Judge Easton a room in the quarters furnished by the public to Major Bruff? A. That I know nothing of

Mr. Martin Is that the Judge Easton who was commissioned by Mr Jefferson? A I suppose so.

Mr. M'Rae Did General Wilkinson furnish a barge to Col Burr when he left St Louis? A The barge and men which Col Burr had, were furnished by myself I received no orders from Gen Wilkinson on the subject It was my own private barge, and the men belonged to my company, who were going down the river on public duty about the same time It was an accommodation to Col. Burr and no injury to myself. General Wilkinson never gave me either verbal or written orders, to my recollection, to furnish a barge and men to Col. Burr

Mr Randolph. I am requested to ask you whether on the Court Martial for the trial of Major Bruff, General Wilkinson was not a witness against him; and whether Major Bruff did not put a question to him about the conversation in the woods below Corondelet? A. I have no recollection of any such question, the affair lasted very long, and a number of questions were asked which I cannot possibly recollect Q During the Court Martial did not the officers invite Major Bruff to dine with them? A I re collect having dined with him at two places, perhaps more. Q. Do you recollect General Wilkinson saying, in answer to some question, that he did not keep a memorandum of small conversations? A I recollect such an answer of General Wilkinson, but I do not recollect the question

Major Bruff As my character has been brought in question, I beg leave to submit extracts of several letters from the General himself, who ought to know more of me than any other officer present [Here Major Bruff read the extracts marked F & G.] The proceedings of the Court Martial have been furnished me, and among the documents is note 3d of October, 1805, which he read

Mr. *M'Rae* Did you return an answer to that note? A I had an interview with the General

Major Bruff here read an extract of a letter from General Wilkinson, of the 4th of August 1797, G and another shortly after the death of General Wayne, stricturing the character of that officer, dated June 18th, 1797

Lieutenant Colonel Hulford

Mr *M'Rae* Are you well acquainted with Major Bruff? A I served under him Q What was his general character? A That is a very delicate question Unfortunately for Major Bruff he had not many friends either among the citizens or officers

Chief Justice What was the character of Major Bruff as a man of truth? A I never heard it called in question

Mr *M'Rae* What was his general character before the arrival of Gen Wilkinson, as a man of integrity and truth I say his *general character,* for I never will enquire as to every *particular act of a man's life?* A I cannot say. I do not know how he was esteemed as a man of integrity and truth I never heard it impeached, but think the General had more friends than he It now he was not liked as the commandant of the post Q What kind of a position is Cold Water; is it a desirable one? A I thought it the most desirable one I ever saw, as to healthiness, wood, water and the convenience with which provisions and military stores might be collected Q. Were you placed there for the accommodation of the troops as for any military operations? A that place was selected for a cantonment, and for that purpose it is the most eligible I ever saw. Q. What is Judge Easton's general character? A It is not good Q. Did Major Bruff accommodate Judge Easton with quarters in the garrison, which had been furnished to the Major by the public? A He did When I speak of Major Bruff as not a good commandant of a post, I mean as to his not agreeing with the officers As to his military skill I say nought

Colonel Henry Gaither was called in and interrogated as to the character and conduct of Major Bruff during the revolutionary war

Colonel Gaither As to Major Bruff's standing in the continental service, he was very young when he entered into it, he was a very active, brave enterprizing officer, he was sundry times badly wounded, and as soon as he was able, always returned to duty, he stood very high among the officers

Mr Martin. Was his reputation high among the officers? A He stood high with the officers of the higher grades, particularly with General Otho H Williams, Colonel Smith and the rest of the field officers

Mr Martin As to his character in private life? A I frequently met with him in the society of Cincinnati, and have long known him in private life, and never heard any thing illegal against him His character, as far as I have ever known or heard, has always stood fair

Major Bruff I was never arrested, or even reprimanded during the whole course of the revolutionary war, and services since, but on the contrary have had many flattering things said to and of me throughout my military life, till General Wilkinson differed with me Captain Richmond, the officer who signed the charges and solicited my arrest, I considered as my friend, he was at my house almost every day before the troops moved to Cold Water, and on terms of intimacy till the moment of my arrest As to any disagreement with the officers of the garrison at St Louis, I had none, except about duty When I arrived, the garrison was in the most wretched order Not an officer understood the manuel or artillery exercise They did not even know how to post the men to the pieces or the priming and loading motions I therefore kept the officers to close duty, and it was for that cause, if any, that they complained and were dissatisfied, the inhabitants noticed and applauded the difference in the police and appearances of the men Respecting the French, I had no personal difference with any one of them, nor did I ever injure any in their person or property If I was unpopular with them, t must have arose from loose observations I may have made about antedated concessions and surveys that took in the public fraudulent grants works The Judges, military commandants and lawyers (except Donaldson) were opposed to the General's measures, and friendly to me and the bar volunteered their services in my Court Martial, and the principal part of the Americans were on my side of the question But I did not visit the cantonment, and on being upbraided with my unsociable deposition on that account, I observed that they did not want democrats there, alluding to General Wilkinson's arrangements to keep me from it and mixing with the officers

Lieutenant Mulford being asked whether a majority of the people were friends to Major Bruff or General Wilkinson, observed, I fully believe that by far the greater part of the people, both French and Americans were the friends of Gen Wilkinson.

Major Bruff replied, that the President of the United States was the best judge of that, the only instance in which we tried our strength, was in a petition respecting the removal of General Wilkinson from that government and the appointment of his successor.

———

(D No 1)

Extract of a letter from Gov Wm Harrison to Gen James Wilkinson

" VINCENNES, June 9th, 1805.

" Receive I pray you no impressions relative to the people of St Louis from Major Bruff for reasons that I will hereafter give plain. The bare idea of his being in your confidence, would frighten some of them out of their senses.'

(E)

Extract of a letter from General Wilkinson, dated
"*Head Quarters, City of Washington,*
15th October, 1806.

' Your residence will necessarily be within the walls of the place, and you are not to absent yourself from it, without permission from your superior officer, who under such indulgence must be responsible for consequences.

"JAMES WILKINSON."

" *Captain Bruff.*'

———

(F)

Extract of a letter from General James Wilkinson, dated
" DETROIT, August 4th, 1797.

" Your ideas touching the association of talents and duty are familiar to me, and will always have influence on my conduct, and from the specimens of your intelligence which have fallen under my observation, it is but justice for me to declare, that I take pride in such an officer, and that I shall feel pleasure in serving and obliging the man.

With much consideration,
I am respectfully, Sir
Your most obedient Servant,
JAMES WILKINSON."

" *Captain Bruff.*'

———

Extract of a letter from General Wilkinson, dated

" *Head Quarters, Fort Wayne,*
June 18, 1797.

" The neglect of which you complain, and which I make no doubt are well founded, are by no means partial. The condition of that part of the army stationed in this quarter, is truly deplorable, and at this moment presents a frightful picture to the scientific soldier. Ignorance and licentiousness have been fostered, while intelligence and virtue have been persecuted and exiled the consequences were, that factions have been generated to sanction enormity, and it followed that all ideas of system, œconomy, order, subordination and discipline, were banished, and that disorder, vice, absurdity and abuse infected every member of the corps militaire. To clear this Augean stable of anarchy and confusion, to extract order from chaos, to incorporate the shattered parts of companies and of regiments, and to attach responsibility to its proper subjects, have employed my days and my nights for two months, and my work is not yet half finished, tho' with the zealous co-operation of the intelligent and honorable part of my officers, I despair not of the final result.

I am, Sir,
Your most obedient servant,
JAS. WILKINSON.

' *Captain Bruff.*"

" Your request for personal accommodation, as far as it depends on me, shall be strictly respected. For I find no pleasure in life equal to that of serving an old meritorious soldier of the revolution."

———

" It is necessary that you should descend the river and take the temporary command of fort Adams, on special service, which have strong claims to your skill and experience "

(G)

War Department, March 18, 1807

SIR,

Your letter of the 17th instant has been received. It is with regret that I find myself compelled by the principles established in this department, as well as by a sense of official duty, to accept your resignation, and it is hereby accordingly accepted, to take effect on the 30th of June next. In the mean time, you are at liberty to attend to your private affairs. That the remainder of your life, a great part of which you have spent in the service of your country, may be as happy as the lot of humanity admits, is my sincere wish

I am very respectfully, Sir,
Your obedient servant,

H DEARBORN.

Major James Bruff

———

It was announced on both sides that there was no other evidence to produce. The argument on the evidence was then opened by Mr. *Hay*, who moved the Court to commit Aaron Burr, Herman Blannerhasset, and Israel Smith to prison, on the charge of treason committed against the United States, in levying war against the same, at the mouth of Cumberland

Upon the first point, he contended that the *intention* of the leaders of the parties charged, was treason by the erection of a separate government at New Orleans, and by the division of the western country. He quoted Fries's Tr 81, 172, 1 East. 131; M'Nally 270, 361, and the opinion of the Supreme Court on the subject of *actual* war He next proceeded to the examination of the true qualifications of a witness from the authorities. First objection general bad character. Mr. M'Nally, 322, 324, Peake's evidence 84. 2d objection conviction of an infamous crime. M'Nally, 258 Peake, 88. 3d objection, difference of statements. He then took a review of laws and precedents of the English Courts, 25 Edward 3, 4 St. Tr 86, M'Nally 611, 1 East. 97. On the subject of *accessories*, he quoted the Earl of Southampton's case, A. D. 1600 1 St. Tr 190, and as authority that ignorance was no excuse, read 5 East 59, 70, 97, 102

Mr. *Randolph* said, that he observed Mr Hay had not touched the charge of misdemeanor

Mr *Hay* said that he considered it of so little importance, as to be willing to leave the case with the Court. He would, however, on that subject refer to the deposition of Capt Walbeck; and the testimony of Judge Todd, Col. Dinsmore, &c. &c. The whole testimony being given, there could be no doubt but the Court would from the voluminous notes it had taken, be sufficiently able to designate the crime, and the place where it was committed.

Mr *Randolph* commenced in answer, and objection to the motion for commitment, by urging the plea of former acquittal He spoke upon the four points which had been laid down, upon which the prosecutor rested the conviction of Col Burr, to wit The general theory or prediction that the western country would at some time be seperated 2dly, That it was indicated from Mr Burr's expressions that he had attempted to instigate and accomplish in time this separation 3dly It was supposed that his acts in that country had a strong tendency to the accomplishment of this object 4thly It was supposed that he was implicated by and in whatever was spoken by others on the subject of a separation of the union He took a review of the evidence concerning these points—the Morgan's, Gen Easton's, Com. Truxton's, &c &c Gen Wilkinson's testimony, he denominated as interested, on account of his connection, the bias of whose situation necessarily rendered his evidence weak He read M'Nally, 54 referring to Loft s Gilbert, 223. Mr. R then went into a review of Gen Wilkinson's testimony, the cyphered letter, the introduction of Mr Swartwout, Col Cushing's testimony, &c &c during which he made some remarks on the conduct of the government, and of Gen Wilkinson He laid down some principles and elucidations of law What Mr Hay had called " communications," he contended were to be viewed in the light of *declarations* or *confessions*, which could only be received in open Court—Foster 253; stat. Ed 3d, and 5 Ed. 6, stat 7 Wm 3, 1 M'Nally, 373, Foster 244 Again The private declarations of an individual, not appearing to have been communicated to the body at large, or at all adopted by it, could not be received as evidence against the prisoner—2 M'Nally, 625, Ridgeway's report of Leary's trial 105 This referred to what was called Mr Blannerhasset's confessions to the Hendersons, Wallaces, Graham's, &c

He then enquired what was the *conspiracy* ? (so termed,) and referred to the evidence touching what passed at Cumberland He concluded with some remarks respecting the misdemeanor (as charged), and insisted that there was, from every account which had come to public knowledge, an invasion in our territory by the incursion of the Spanish troops across the Sabine— whether they again reticated or not, and whatever might be the cause of that retreat.

MONDAY, October 12.

Mr *Martin* commenced an elaborate argument He first drew a picture of the evidence as exhibited by the gentlemen who favored the prosecution in the infancy of the transaction, in which he spoke of the purchase of the Washita lands, and of those engaged to settle thereon, from the evidence produced upon that subject He called the attention of the Court to the President's message of the 2d December to Congress, referring to the proclamation, &c —to the evidence of the Morgans, Eaton, Wilkinson, Dunbaugh and Albright As to the general inapplicability of conversations Mr. Martin read M'Nally, 518. 12 Vi ner's abridgement 68, Placita 46. On General Wilkinson's testimony compared with Mr. Duncan's affidavit, he quoted 2 Lot't's Gilbert 661.

TUESDAY, October 13

The deposition of *Benjamin Stoddert* was offered by the prosecution, but was objected to by the defendants. On which Mr Hay moved process to issue to bring Mr Stoddert into Court to give evidence. Some conversation ensued. Mr Stoddert had attended the Court, and had returned to his home, (George Town, Columbia). The Court ordered the attachment to issue.

Mr *Martin* recommenced his argument by reading Mr Duplestie's affidavit, and Mr Burr's letter of July 26, [p 13, Appendix] upon which he made his inferences. He then referred to the deposition of James L. Donaldson, whom he called General Wilkinson's confidential friend. Some objection was made to its production; but on explanation, it was agreed that it should be read. [It was introduced in the Supreme Court in the case of Bolman and Swartwout]

It was read.

Deposition of James L Donaldson.

In open Court, personally appears James Lowry Donaldson, who being duly sworn, deposeth and saith, that he was in the city of New Orleans, in the Orleans territory, and the environs of said city, from the 15th of October to the 10th day of December, 1806, that during the latter part of this time he was frequently in the company of General James Wilkinson, and visited the General the day after his arrival at New Orleans. On this occasion this deponent received in confidence from General Wilkinson, information to the following purport. That the General had undoubted and indisputable evidence of a treasonable design formed by Aaron Burr and others to dismember the union, by a separation of the western States and territories from the Atlantic States; that New Orleans was in immediate danger, and that he had concluded a hasty compromise with the Spaniards, so as to be able to withdraw his troops instantly to this the immediate object of attack and great vulnerable point. That he had received a letter from Burr, holding forth great inducements to him to become a party, of which he shewed me the original in cypher, and another written paper, purporting to be a decyphered copy of the letter. He expressed great indignation at the plot, and surprise that one so well acquainted with him as Burr, should dare to make to him so degrading a proposal, and declared his determination of defeating the enterprize, or perishing in the attempt. He observed in addition, that there were many agents of Mr Burr then in the town, who had already been assiduous in their visits, and towards whom he was determined to act with cautious ambiguity; so as at the same time to become possessed of the whole extent of the plan, the persons engaged, and the time of its execution; and also to prevent any attempt on his person, of which he declared he had serious apprehensions. Of the number of these agents he was not aware, but mentioned the name of two of whom he was certain, Messrs Bollman and Alexander From time to time, as this deponent had interviews with General Wilkinson he informed this deponent that he had received additional information respecting the movements and designs of Burr by means of these agents, of whom he considered Bollman as the principal In the course of these transactions, this deponent was employed by General Wilkinson in the copying of certain papers and documents, and preparing certain dispatches for the general government, which the General intended to forward by the brig Thetis While thus employed at the General's lodgings, this deponent has remarked upon two different occasions, a person knock for admittance at a door with a window in it, opposite the table where this deponent was sitting ; who this deponent was informed by General Wilkinson was Dr Bollman Upon these occasions the General has suddenly risen from his seat, and accompanied this person in a number of turns up and down a balcony in the front of the house, apparently engaged in deep conversation Upon the latter of these occasions the General on his return into the chamber said to this deponent, " that is Dr Bollman, his " infatuation is truly extraordinary, he persists in his belief that " I am with Burr, and has this moment shewn me a letter from " the latter, in which he says that he is to be at Natchez on the " 20th December with two thousand men ; that four thousand will " follow in the course of a few days, and that he cou   with the " same ease have procured double that number " General Wilkinson then observed that he had obtained all the information he wanted, and that the affair would not be kept much longer a secret from the public

When this deponent left the city of New Orleans, the inhabitants of that city were in a state of great alarm, and apprehended a serious attack from Mr Burr and his confederates This deponent understood that mercantile business was much embarrassed, an great fears were entertained of considerable commercial failures in consequence of the embargo which had been imposed that General Wilkinson was taking strong measures of defence, and that four hundred persons were then actually engaged in the fortifications of the city

And further this deponent saith not.

JAS L DONALDSON

Sworn to in open Court

Wᴹ BRENT Clerk.
City of Washington.

January 26, 1807.

Mr *Martin* then proceeded to examine General Wilkinson's deposition, and the cyphered letter—also the communication to Congress, [L and H Appendix], upon which he made some remarks He afterwards took up Dunbaugh's testimony, and remarked on his supposed variance with Captain Bissell's respecting the gorget—the cyphered letter—the borrowed clothes—his desertion, &c [The public can judge from the evidence]. This closed the day.

WEDNESDAY, October 14

This day's proceedings commenced with the evidence of Captain *Stephen Decatur*, (of the navy of the U States) He stated that in Dec 1805, in Philadelphia, a conversation occurred with Col Burr, respecting the certainty of a war with Spain, when Mr. Burr observed, that the *navy* was not a place for a man of enterprize to distinguish himself, but that an *army* was, and that he would in confidence tell him, that he intended to *carry an expedition into Mexico* He wanted seven thousand men for that purpose, but the principal object was to get officers That the government knew of the expedition, and Gen. Wilkinson was concerned with him

Mr Hay Were there any particular propositions made to you to join this plan, or did you only infer the object from what you heard?

Witness Yes Mr Burr proposed to me to join with his plan, but I did not, because I thought I could be more useful in the navy, in which I had been brought up, and was accustomed to Q Did he offer you any particular situation? A No, he did not

Mr Wirt Did he offer you any inducement to engage in his plans? A No other than his impressions that there would be a greater opportunity in the army to distinguish myself than I could have in the navy.

Cross-examination

Mr. *Burr* Can you with any certainty say, whether I told you that government had been made acquainted with it?

Witness I cannot at this time particularly recollect, but my impressions were, that government knew of your plans, but I do not know that you stated how or when they knew of it. I do not recollect your precise form of expression Q Then you do not know whether I said, that they *were*, or *would be* informed of it? A My impressions were that the government knew it (from what you said) I have no distinct recollection as to the means by which they became acquainted with it, or the precise object

Mr *Martin* What time was this? A In December 1805 This was the first time ever I had seen Col Burr

Mr *Hay* Do you know whether you put the question, whether the government knew of it or not? A No I do not, but from the conversation, I understood that it did

Mr *Martin* then continued He first examined the letter dated, 3d January, 1807—See Appendix [B b] after which he compared the *oral* and *communicated* events from Blannerhasset's island, down the river

He next read the deposition of Lieutenant George Pete s, [See Appendix &] to prove that the officers who went in pursuit of Burr were out of uniform, and had received orders so to act for the seizure of Burr This he considered a most important paper to clear Col Burr from the character attributed to him, of having flinched from the examination into his conduct at Washington, Mississippi territory—and to prove the subserviency of the civil authority to the military, even in their disguise.

Mr Martin then referred to the testimony of Captain Shaw, respecting Lieutenant Jones, who had nobly refused, he said, to execute the orders given to him. He said he had sent a summons for Lieutenant Jones, but he had received no other return to it than an answer that he was under arrest. He next quoted Gov Williams's proclamation [Ap *E.*] respecting the seizure of Burr; but he asked, what could be the inference, when it appeared indisputably, that it was not to avoid any civil authority, but to avoid being seized by the arbitrary power of a military, and to avoid being placed where he had no reason to believe that his life would be safe, that he deemed it a proper step to put his safety out of their hands. And yet, Governor Williams had hazarded his character, by issuing this proclamation, which was not founded nor supported by facts or appearances. As long as the history of this transaction should remain, it must throw an indelible reproach and infamy on him for his unjustifiable conduct

The next evidence of note, was Mr Poindexter, and in it, the conduct of Judge Rodney, whose situation, he said, was well known [Here Mr Martin went into a very desultory review of the transactions of the Court and Grand Jury in that territory]

But it seems that we have, by that gentleman, a little bit of paper produced, in the hand-writing of somebody; I cannot tell who, but he *believes* it to be the hand-writing of Colonel Burr How he knew any thing of Colonel Burr's hand-writing, however, I cannot tell, nor is it of any consequence However, the history of this circumstance is, that a Negro boy had come with this billet pinned, or sewed, or someway fastened to his great coat! How it came there, or how it came into the hands of the government, I cannot tell; but somehow or other it was brought into view, be it what it will

Here Mr *Poindexter* explained the circumstance The paper was brought by the gentleman who took it out of the *cape* of the Negro's coat I saw it in the hands of Governor Williams The truth of it is, that it came from Colonel Burr, to the best of my belief, from what I know of his hand writing

Mr *Wirt.* The boy did not know who it came from, it appears

Mr *Poindexter.* It was from the hand-writing, and from the stile, that we formed an opinion who was the writer; indeed, I had no doubt on the subject.

Some strictures from Mr. Martin on this note, drew forth from Mr Poindexter some farther evidence, that he had seen his (Mr Burr's) writing, and he had no hesitation to express his firm belief that the note was written by him.

Mr *Martin* I have seen him write many times, but I do not see the least similarity to his hand in this note.

Some desultory conversation here ensued

Mr *Martin* then drew some inferences from the conduct of Cowles Meade, respecting the negociation of Burr, on the general state of the country, and on the presentment; from which he drew a general inference, that there could nothing criminal be discovered in the whole transaction, as the Grand Jury had amply testified There could be no other object than to prevent persons who had not a legal authority, from exercising a spirit of persecution and assault, under the impression of the laudability of their measures, or else with a view to procure the favor of the government. Trusting to the honor of Mr Meade, however, Colonel Burr thought himself secure, but he afterwards found it to be otherwise, for the moment Governor Williams arrived, the honor of Meade was superceded by Williams's authority, for he united with Burr's enemies, and acted so as to attempt (with Wilkinson) to take him out of the civil power!

Mr *Burr*. As the gentleman has mentioned Cowles Meade's name, it is but due to him to say, that I shall never charge him with a violation of the agreement made between us. This agreement was made by him in his capacity of Governor, but the obligation must equally devolve on Williams, as to compliance. Governor Williams did actually agree to protect me from any unlawful seizure, conformable to the form a contract. But what occurred afterwards is well known. Governor Williams did actually encourage a party to seize me, and it would have been executed if he had had his will.

Mr *Wirt* called Mr *Poindexter* on this subject, of whom Mr. Martin made an enquiry, whether Mr. Meade had disavowed of the treaty made between him and Burr?

Mr *Poindexter*. The Court will recollect my original testimony. I can only repeat it.

Mr *Martin*. But this Cowles Meade disavowed

Witness. I said that he came to Calvit's, that the military were very much enraged, and that, very probably, they would commit an outrage on Colonel Burr and others. It was understood that many respectable young men were engaged, but I never understood that those who were engaged to stop their intended progress (whatever it might be) would violate the laws of the union in their zeal. In conformity to this stipulation with Mr. Meade, he went to Mr Calvit's. It was understood between Mr. Meade and myself, that this agreement should last no longer than the interview, but notwithstanding, when Colonel Burr arrived, he had several conversations with Mr Meade and myself, separately. What advantage he got by it, I know not. I went to bed, but Colonel Burr came into my room with Major Shields, when it was expressly declared that the writing should be void. Major Shields proposed to destroy it, but I did not approve of it. We went together after that to Washington.

Mr *Burr*. Do you not know that I told Mr Meade that I would go there with my own attendants? Do you consider yourself in any respect as my guard, or as any way acting for my security in the country? A. I went with you to the town of Washington in the character of aid-de-camp to Mr. Meade: and I did not not consider myself as divested of that station until I had delivered you over to the civil authority. Q. How did you deliver me over? A. Why, by informing the Judge, and I understood you waited on the Judge to enter into recognizance. Q. Did I enter into recognizance? A. You did, and the conditions were, that you should await the pleasure of the Judge. Q. Do you recollect my asking you whether there was any civil authority in that district to issue civil process? A. I do not know.

Q Do you recollect Judge Rodney saying, that he could not is. sue? A No, I do not, but I believe that he said he had many de positions in his possession, sufficient to warrant your arrest, as well as some others It was the determination of Judge Rodney to have the investigation before his own Court, otherwise you would have been sent off immediately It was a mere matter of opinion in the Judge whether there was probable cause, in any matter that came before him, to commit you for trial Mr Ralston called and gave a voluntary deposition on the subject my idea was, that he might then be at liberty to go round thro' the country, and sound the situation of the country and the opinions of the people

Mr Bur If you saw the deposition, I would ask whether there was any thing in it which would tend to criminate any body A I do not recollect, and cannot say Q Do you recollect that it was ever asked of him? A I do not know that, but I know it was declared in your presence to have been done with your consent

Q Were there not two copies of the agreement with C Meade? A There were Q Was the copy ever asked for? A I do not recollect that it was Q Did not Mr Meade frequently pledge himself to protect me against the military authority under Wilk- inson? A I do not know that I was present at any such pledge being expressed, but I do recollect his saying that he would pro tect you against any military force being sent into the territory Q Was it not a protection from Gen Wilkinson? A Why it was understood so Q Do you not recollect my remonstrating strong- ly against a guard that came into the town? A I do not Q But do you not recollect his saying to me, by way of apology, that the guard was come there merely to keep the peace A No Q But what did you hear him say was there not an apology communi- cated to me? A Not to my knowledge The guard was placed there and kept in order to be in readiness to transport you to the city of Washington, in case the civil authority could not Q Did you see the venue? A No I did not I know that I issued a foreign warrant to get you to some place, where you ought to be tried I thought Kentucky, and I advised the Judge not to have a Jury on you there Q Is your name to the venue? A No Q Is it sign- ed by both the Judges? A I believe it was

Mr Burr I refer your honor to that sentence in the agreement with Cowles Meade, that the military should not come nearer than Coles Creek but you will observe, Sir, what this gentleman says

Mr Martin then recommenced his speech by attacking the pro ceedings at the Mississippi territory. He referred to the agree ment, with some strictures and on the subsequent proceedings related by Mr Poindexter He scrutinized the conduct of Judge Rodney, who he said well knew the will of the government, and was answerable for his acquiescence thereto He did not blame Mr Meade for any violation of plighted faith His honor was liberal- ly pledged by Mr. Poindexter and Mr Shields Had they power to pledge his honor? If they had not, why did they do it? If they had, and it was violated, it was no longer binding. His honor was pledged, that whilst they remained in the territory, Col Burr.

the people who were with him, and his boats &c. should remain unmolested, but there was not an act of power to commit any of them there

Mr Martin went on to the testimony of Silas Dinsmore, who was at New Orleans before, and after the alarm and the arrival of Gen Wilkinson, in which examination he referred to what Capt Shaw said about the letter of Gen Wilkinson of Nov 12 This was merely a recital and comparison of the testimony of these two gentlemen He called to view the letter of White to Burke, in order with the others, to compare dates, so as to know what might have influenced Gen Wilkinson's return so rapidly

Mr Martin next referred to the offer made to Col Dinsmore of five hundred dollars to take Burr, and to the encouraging letters held out to Colonel M Kee of February 8, 1807 He next called the attention of the Court to the evidence of the two Hendersons respecting the " Querist," under which head he drew the evidence of Mr D C Wallace, Mr Graham and Mr Henry, respecting the origin and progress of the expedition, and made suitable inferences, at the same time taking in all other relative evidence, so as to prove the expedition merely speculative, which character he incessantly attached to it, and upon the plausibility of which, he as forcibly reasoned, under all the contracts and engagements that had been entered into, whether for men or for land

Here he commenced his observations on Major Bruff's testimony, and remarked on the closetting of the Major with General Wilkinson, &c &c Mr. Martin then reviewed Mr Hay's opinion, that a combination of this sort was to be considered in the light of a conspiracy, in which case the conversations and acts of others were to be brought against Colonel Burr Upon which some conversation occurred, and Mr. Hay explained, that a man may be indicted for conspiring and acting in levying war in the same count Mr Martin said, that there must be proof that the person himself was engaged with the conspirators, and to the extent of that conspiracy, before the declarations or acts of others could be testimony in Court —M'Nally, 612, on Hardy's trial. 1 vol p. 345, 246, 347 He then went into a review of Southampton's case, 1 St. Tr 107, as to the *intention* of injuring the queen.

He then contended that the *most favorable* interpretation was to be given, where the charge was of such immense magnitude. He quoted Captain Blade's case, 3 St Tr 739, and mentioned the expressions attributed of driving the President into the Potomac, &c in Mr. Eaton's testimony. The cases of Dean and Wedderburn, and Fries, he said were quite different, because they were found with the party and assisting in the transactions, which Colonel Burr never was. In cases where declarations were made, as in the case of Demarree and Purchase, they accompanied the criminal acts themselves Now whether as to *intention* or *action*, for ought which had appeared, he contended that nothing could be proved against the defendant.

He concluded with some severe reflections on the conduct of the President in his communication to Congress, upon the bare evidence of the letters from General Wilkinson, the information

Vol   C . c c

en by the Morgan family, and General Eaton's disclosure. How far he had a right to call Col. Burr a suspicious character, he knew not, unless it was his determination to view every thing in its worst light, and at the same time approve and applaud General Wilkinson as the saviour of his country. Yes, he said he had made a hasty peace on the Sabine, to signalize his patriotism! Mr Martin made some concluding remarks on the conduct of the administration in its measures in searching for facts to establish the charge now made; and, as he said, to screen Gen Wilkinson.

' He said he had examined into the case of Cochrane, who was a Romish priest at Lisbon, and had declared there, that he would kill the king of Great Britain if ever he met with him. This was in July. In August he was found in England and taken up. The declaration was the treason, and the coming into England was the overt act laid. This was in 9 Ch. t Keyling, p. 18. This relates to where words alone are sufficient to be denominated imagining the king's death. Hale and Foster however think that words alone cannot be treason.

Again, as to war. Is a declaration of war necessary to be denominated war, if, de facto, there is war? Upon this he read 1 Hale, P. C. 100, 103, 104, Tooke 219, Vattel B. 3, Ch. 4, sect. 57, Puffendorff, Ch. 6, Grotius, B. 3, Ch. 3, sect. 6, p. 553, Patterson's opinion in Smith and Ogden's trial, 84, 85, 86. The opinions he read to shew the constituent parts of war, and in illustration of the arguments he had used to prove the position that in this case there was no war, and consequently no war under our constitution. He also contended upon these premises, that the Spanish measures on this side of the Sabine was war de facto, though no blow was struck.

Mr Hay denied this last position. There was an essential difference between invasion and actual war. The merely occupying land claimed by another party is not invasion, since they may do it under the impression that it is their own property. When hostility commences, then there is war de facto.

Mr Burr here read the proceedings of the Superior Court at New Orleans, which he presented merely to read the return made by General Wilkinson as to the arrest of Dr. Bollman. Three days after this, General Wilkinson sent off Dr Bollman. The object of this reference was to prove to the Court, that the city of New Orleans was under the exclusive and entire direction and control of General Wilkinson.

Mr. Wickham commenced his observations by declaring that he should not trouble the Court much with the law on this case; but he should go largely into the evidence. Equivocal acts and open acts of war, however, he declared to be materially different. On this ground, he presumed the intention must be plainly proved, which only could be inferred from the action of the body at the time.—Thus, an act apparently lawful, never could be made criminal unless the principal act charged was proved to be unlawful. In the presence or sight of God an act might be criminal in thought, but a Court of Justice requires the will and the act to constitute a crime. He enlarged on this position, and took a review of the evidence of Dunbaugh and Captain Bissell upon the ground of opposition of testimony [The testimony can be compared]. Then he took up General Eaton's, Commodore Truxton's, the Morgan's and the Hendersons. In his inferences he quoted the opinion of the Court September 14. Captain Bissell in opposition to Dunbaugh; the cyphered letter, &c which he dwelt upon to some length. He still contended that Burr had no other project in view than the invasion of Mexico in the case of a war, and endeavored to square all his positions and arguments to support that point; and to bring every piece of testimony thither, by arguing that nothing was said or done to the contrary, and that his declarations was conditionally directed to that point wherever he went, under the idea, at least, that encroachments were made and measures were taken by the Spaniards tending to promote a war;—indeed every body expected a war with Spain, and without it, he contended not fifty men could have been gotten on any account to appear in hostility. War or peace, however, depended on General Wilkinson, and all the witnesses proved that Colonel Burr did expect a war.

Mr. Wickham then made a few concluding remarks on the part the government had taken in the prosecution of this case. He hoped it was now closed forever.

FRIDAY, October 10.

Mr. M'Rae made reply to the charges made by the counsel of Colonel Burr respecting the measures of the government, the conduct and character of the witnesses (as charged) and particularly the measures of Gen. Wilkinson in producing the witnesses at New Orleans to the Court. He contended for the principle that "probable cause" was sufficient to govern an examining magistrate in his determination on commitment. He then called the attention of the Court to the nature of the proof wherever the motion was founded. First. The proof consists of acts done by Aaron Burr himself. Secondly. It consists of his declarations, made at various times and places. Thirdly. The acts and declarations of others, his accomplices.

To support the first, he referred to the evidence respecting the arms, which the nature of the evidence would prove to have been possessed at Cumberland, by the party of whom Aaron Burr was head; and there the overt act was laid against him. Deacon's Wedderburn's, Roach's, Layer's and other cases in state trials he proved would fully amplify this doctrine; and that, after proof of the overt act, they might travel any where to shew the complexion of the act. On the second point he reasoned at some length and with much perspicuity, after which, he quoted 1 East 133 to 135 M'Nally 377 1 Hall P C 506 and 114, to 116. 1 Dallas 39 2 Dallas 86, 87. These authorities, to be sure, related to *confession*, which was an acknowledgement of guilt for something done; but here nothing was done as to the disclosures made to General Eaton, it must be rather the nature of an act than of a confession, because it was an attempt to excite and prepare towards the doing of an act.

On the third species of evidence Mr M'Rae read 1 East 96 to 100, which, upon an examination of the light in which Mr. Burr had viewed these persons as "his people" he contended was not answered by Mr. Randolph's quotation from M·Nally 625 The coincidence and connexion were too striking to be affected by any rules contained in the books

Mr. M'Rae then commenced his review of the evidence, and first as to the *intention* of the accused He first critically review ed General Eaton's testimony, in which he vindicated the General against the attempt to charge him with fraud &c under the evidence of Colonel Gaither But, however it might be supposed by others who had not received it, he contended that, in its principal parts it was supported (under all its pressures) by the Morgans, the Hendersons, and even by Commodore Truxton, however much of the marvellous might be attributed to it Captain Decatur indeed had received communications not very dissimilar After some observations on which he remarked on Mr Woodbridge's, Taylors, Duval's, Wallace's, Gilmore's and Graham's principally to prove, that from the declarations of Mr. Blannerhasset it was understood that the accused was to command the expedition, to prove the measures they took, and the object they had in view, all which, instead of proving that they awaited the movements of government to go against Spain proved that they would oppose and resist the government, if there should be any attempt to check them He then made some observations on the enlisting of men for 6 months, which he said was no proof that they were to clear the land. He also refer red to the evidence of Mr. Henry, and Mr Poindexter, as to what passed in the Mississippi territory Next he took up the acts and the means at the mouth of Cumberland upon the evi dence of Mr Fisk, Love and others, upon which he made some remarks, as well as to display the feasibility of taking Orleans, even with one hundred men, from the state of military opposi tion in that quarter at that time He reviewed the progress of the party down the river, their military appearance and the command which Burr had of them, by the evidence of Welsh, Love, Moxley, Allen, Fisk, Lindsley, M'Dowel and Dunbaugh, all of whom were of the party.

As to the evidence of Gen. Wilkinson, although it would otherwise be all-important, yet, as it had been so strongly at tacked, and as there must evidently appear to be sufficient testi mony to support the motion without it, he could not deem it of vast importance to enter into it. The character and politeness however of that gentleman before the Court, and his willingness to open a disclosure of *every* thing, ought not to be disregarded notwithstanding Major Bruffs most ardent attempts to invalidate it Indeed, from the unprecedented and unprovoked attacks which the general had been doomed to receive, he and every one must consider him as a persecuted man. On the vindication of General Wilkinson, Mr. M'Rae continued at some length, and as to his measures in New Orleans, under the general report that was circulated in all quarters, no doubt could be entertained of their efficacious and useful promptitude Approbation and ad vice was given by men of rectitude and character, such as Com modore Shaw, and Mr. Dinsmore, and indeed every good citizen

Mr. *M'Rae* concluded, by assigning the true motives for engaging in this prosecution to be patriotism, and a desire, humble and weak as his talents were, to exert them in the cause of justice and his country's good. If the defendant was innocent, he hoped he would be acquitted; but, if guilty, he thought the interest of society demanded a conviction. At all events, he wished him to enjoy a fair trial.

SATURDAY, *October* 17

Mr. Lemuel Henry was again called

Mr *Burr* observed, that when Mr Poindexter was under examination, there was something spoken of respecting an armistice or agreement between Mr Meade and himself, which might receive some light by this witness. He wished therefore to ask him a few questions.

Mr *Burr*. Mr Henry, were you at the town of Washington when I came there? A. Yes Q Was there a guard established in the street, and about the house in which I lodged? What message did I send to Cowles Meade concerning it? And what was his answer? A. There was a guard stationed as you mentioned, but Mr. Meade said it was intended as much for the protection of your person as for the public safety Q. Did I desire you to remonstrate with Mr. Meade against the establishment of that guard as a violation of our treaty or agreement? A You desired me to remonstrate with him about it, and I understood you to complain of it as a violation of his agreement with you I mentioned this to him, and he said that the guard was necessary for your protection, as well as for the public safety

Mr *M'Rae* Do you know any thing about that armistice? A Only from report. Q Any thing from Cowles Meade? A Not at all.

Mr *Power* was then introduced.

Mr *Burr* This witness is to be examined for two purposes First, to verify certain papers. Secondly, to prove that General Wilkinson was at a certain period in the pay of the Spanish government, and then, by other witnesses, we shall prove that his pay has continued, and that he has frequently been in the habit of receiving large sums of Spanish silver The object is to impeach his credibility, by proving the falshood of his declaration that he had not corresponded with the Baron de Carondelet.

Mr *M'Rae* said it was not regular to offer proof of any particular crime to impeach the credibility of a witness No rule of evidence is more clear, than that the general character of the witness is all that should be investigated for that purpose; since every man ought to have notice to enable him to defend himself against any specific charge. He observed that General Wilkinson had heretofore been slanderously accused of being a pensioner of Spain; that being desirous of giving his calumniators an opportunity of proving their charges against him, he had once requested General Washington, when he was President, and afterwards Mr. Adams, to direct a Court Martial for his trial, but they (satisfied of his innocence) refused his request General Hamilton also declared that he thought the charge a slander, and a trial unnecessary

Mr *Wickham* Receiving money from the king of Spain is not an indictable offence Our ground of defence is, that Mr. Burr's expedition was in concurrence with General Wilkinson, against the dominions of the king of Spain, in case of a war If we prove that at the time Wilkinson was pretending to favor Burr's expedition, and secretly determined to defeat it, he was receiving a Spanish pension, this will explain his conduct He defeated the enterprize of Burr by hatching a charge of treason against the United States, on purpose to serve the king whose money he was receiving

Mr *Martin* I am not surprized that gentlemen should have so much feeling on this subject, especially the gentleman who made this objection There can be no prosecution against a man for receiving Spanish money Mr Benjamin Sebastian, in Kentucky, was indeed accused of this as an offence, and it was proved upon him, but I have not heard, though he voluntarily resigned his office of Judge, that any prosecution was instituted against him For my part *I wish there was a little more Spanish money among us I should like to have some of it myself* We wish to shew that General Wilkinson is interested in the destruction of Mr Burr, that he has placed himself in such a situation, he must hang Mr Burr, or be himself eternally detested He offered to be tried by a Court Martial, because he knew that the only witness against him was out of the power of the process of the United States—being in the dominions of the king of Spain

Mr *M'Rae* The gentlemen have heretofore been arguing that the United States were in fact at war with Spain If so, it would have been a great crime in Wilkinson, an officer in the United States, to receive a pension from the king of Spain

Mr M'Rae also read a part of the 9th section of article I of the Constitution of the United States, which declares that " no " person, holding any office of profit or trust under them, shall, " without the consent of Congress, accept of any present, emolu- " ment, office, or title of any kind whatever, from any king, " prince or foreign state " Would it not then, said Mr M'Rae, be a crime in General Wilkinson, holding a commission under the Government of the United States, to violate the constitution by receiving a present from the king of Spain? Being admitted to be a crime, it cannot, under the rule of law which I mentioned, be offered in evidence. If, in fact, any money was received by him, it might have been in commercial intercourse with some Spanish officer, and, if he had been informed in time of the accusation against him, he might have explained the circumstance, and shown that such was the case.

Mr M'Rae also remarked the inconsistency of the arguments of the counsel for Mr Burr, then insisting that his intentions were perfectly innocent, (being merely the settlement of Washita lands,) and yet attempting to brand General Wilkinson with guilt, for being a participator in these intentions If they were both equally guilty, this would not render Aaron Burr less criminal

Mr *Wickham* We never said that General Wilkinson and Mr Burr were equally guilty. What I said was, that both were engaged in an honorable enterprize in the event of a war with

Spain. What we charge General Wilkinson with, is having unit-ed with Mr Burr, and then deserting him—turning traitor—and representing the case quite differently from the truth.

The *Chief Justice.* It is absolutely necessary to hear the testi-mony to judge of the fact. The only difficulty is, that it does not appear, under the impressions I now have, what effect it can have. If it was proved that General Wilkinson had been a pensioner of the Court of Spain, it could have no influence on the case.

Mr *Wickham.* We say that Gen. Wilkinson had an interest with the king of Spain, and in order to preserve the dominions of that monarch, which he knew were about to be attacked, he withdrew from Burr, and represented an enterprize which was perfectly in-nocent and eventual, as one highly criminal.

Mr *Martin.* General Wilkinson by betraying Colonel Burr had a double motive, the one was to acquire favor with his own go-vernment, the other with the king of Spain.

The *Chief Justice.* I do not understand it to be your object to prove a continuing pension.

Mr *Burr.* Our object is to prove the receipt of fourteen thou-sand and odd dollars at one time, and some knowledge of the payment of other sums of money to General Wilkinson.

Mr *Burr to Mr Power.* Are you acquainted with Alexis Bon Ami? A. Yes. Q. Do you know his signature? A. I think I do. Q. Is he a Justice of the peace in New Orleans? A. Yes. [Here Mr Burr produced a certificate from the office of the Secretary of State, shewing that Mr Bon Ami was a Justice of the peace for New Orleans.]

Mr *Burr.* Are you acquainted with the signatures of Messrs Derbigny and Mercier? A. With both very well.

Mr *Burr.* Will you look at those papers, (shewing him their depositions, signed by them respectively, and attested by Bon Ami, a Justice of the peace for New Orleans.)

Mr *Power* said, he believed the signatures to those depositions, were in the hand writing of the persons whose names were an-nexed to them.

Mr *Burr.* Do you know whether M Mercier was subpœnæd to attend here? A. I believe he was. I heard him say he was subpœnæd; but the afflictions of his family were such, arising from the death of his father-in-law, that he could not possibly attend.

Mr *Burr.* Do you know why M Derbigny is not here—do you know whether he was subpœnæd? A. I heard him say he was. Q. Why did he not attend? A. I heard him say it would be the utter ruin of his family, if he were to take such a long and expensive journey, and in the meantime neglect his busi-ness.

Mr *Burr.* Is he a man upon whose personal exertions his fa-mily depend for a subsistence? A. I believe so.

Mr *Burr.* Do you know of any correspondence in cypher by General Wilkinson with Baron Carondelet?

Mr *Hay* objected to the question on the grounds before stated; and because the answer, whether it be in the negative, or affirm-ative, could have no influence on the case.

Mr *Wickham* said, that General Wilkinson in the course of his examination had been asked, whether he had been in the habit of corresponding with the Baron Carondelet in cypher, and had answered " No," but immediately after he said " he did not recollect" He admitted that the answer of General Wilkinson was hastily given, but still if we are able to prove, that he had been in the habit of corresponding with the Baron Carondelet in cypher, his saying that he did not recollect such a correspondence, will have a direct tendency to weaken his testimony. If a witness has sworn to a particular fact, although immaterial to the cause, the opposite party may falsify that part for the purpose of impeaching the credibility of the witness

Mr. *Burr* repeated the last question to Mr Power. Do you know of any correspondence in cypher by Gen Wilkinson with the Baron Carondelet?

Mr *Power*. (addressing the Judge) I beg the Court will indulge me with the liberty of making a brief statement of certain circumstances, that will shew the peculiar delicacy and and hardship of my situation I shall begin by observing, that I have to boast of being a Spanish born subject, and that for several years past, I have had the honor to be, and still am an officer in the service of his catholic majesty It is true that my domicile is, and has been in New Orleans, ever since the cession of Louisiana to the United States But I have resided there in the character of a Spaniard, under sanction of a stipulation in one of the articles of the treaty, by which the full enjoyment of all the civilization, and privileges of an American citizen is guaranteed and secured to every and all Spanish subjects, for the space of twelve years — Under this safe-guard I was living in peace and perfect security, little dreaming, that so long as I did not violate the laws of the land, I should ever be disturbed or molested for doings, to which I was a perfect stranger

On the sixteenth of August, being Sunday, a Subpœna was handed to me by the attorney or agent of Mr Burr, by which I was cited to appear before this Court, to give testimony on behalf of said Mr Burr's in the present trial.——I made some objections to receiving the subpæna, alledging that it was irregular and illegal, for these two reasons :—the first, that I had always understood that no writ could be served on a citizen on a Sunday , the second, that the proper channel through which it ought to have come, was through the hands of the Marshal of the district But I was soon convinced that my objections were nugatory and of no weight—a few days after I was informed that several other gentlemen were subpœnæd as well as myself, but that they were dispensed from appearing before this Court, by giving their affidavits I immediately offered to do the same, and declare that I knew nothing of Colonel Burr's projects This was not admitted, and on my manifesting some reluctance, and a disposition not to obey the summon, I was given to understand, that the same authority by which, in similar circumstances a certain Mr Knox was committed to the common jail and confined among malefactors in Orleans, and from thence scandalously hurried off, and put on board of ship, would be exercised against me. I instantly submitted to this powerful and irresistible tie argument, which more than all their logic convinced me of the propriety and justice of the measure

Mr Burr Are you about to object to answering the question? A I am, Sir That I have been an agent of the Spanish government in the western country, for several years prior to the running of the boundary line between the United States and the two Floridas, is a circumstance of such a notoriety, it is so well, so generally known, that it would be idle and absurd, and altogether useless for me to deny it I do candidly confess, that I have been sent, on several occasions, into that country, and employed there in negociations of importance, as an officer possessing the confidence of his sovereign I therefore, as such, consider myself bound by the strongest ties that can fasten on a man of principle and honor, not to answer any interrogatories that may have any relation to any transactions or operations of the Spanish government, that may be proposed to me by any tribunal upon earth, except such, as may be duly established and authorized to that effect by the king my master.

Mr Hay. Are you going to answer the question as to the correspondence? A I am about to shew my situation to be so delicate, that I cannot consistently with honor answer it, nor can I answer any question which may operate against the king my master.

Mr Burr Had you any mercantile connexion with General Wilkinson? A I had not Mr Burr said that he did not think there had been any pretext offered which would justify an evasion of the question

Mr. Power What would be the amount of the deposition of a man, who in the very act of deposing, was breaking his most sacred engagements, and pronouncing himself a perjured villain?

Mr Burr Are you under the obligation of an oath, as to the transaction? A I am under the obligation of the *honor* of an officer, an obligation of the highest dignity, which was imposed upon me when I accepted the badge of my office I never did repeat any set form of words, the mere formulary of an oath was never proposed to me, and my superior officer knew my sentiments too well to offer me such an insult Such a proposition I should have rejected with disdain and indignation

Mr Wickham said, that however unpleasant it might be to Mr. Power to answer the question, or whatever his ideas might be as to his honorary engagements, still it was necessary, for the sake of justice, that the question should be answered. Mr Power's being an officer of the king of Spain, could not release him from the obligation to give evidence in a Court of Justice He was now here, within the power of the Court, and would be dealt with as any other citizen of the United States

The *Chief Justice* said, the question must be answered, though he was very sorry that the necessity existed The objection to answer was not a valid one

Mr. Power I have already said, that when the interest of the king my master is implicated, I will not answer. The Court may take what measures it pleases (Addressing Mr Burr)—Place yourself in my situation, Colonel Burr, put your hand upon your own bosom, and say, what you would do yourself

Mr *Martin* begged Mr. Power to recollect that the life of a man was at stake ; a man who was prosecuted with rigor by his own government. He must recollect the importance and neces sity of calling in the aid of all the evidence which can be procur ed to exempt him from unmerited punishment

Mr *Power* I feel full well the situation of Colonel Burr. But I have more at stake than Colonel Burr. I have my honor, my reputation, which are more dear to me than life or property What would my family, my children, do with property, if these were violated ?

Mr *Wickham* said, he would not press the answer at that time, nor apply to the Court to take the necessary measures to enforce it , but would give Mr Power a few hours to reflect He will be expected to attend here at three o'clock, at which time the same question will be repeated

Mr Power attended a little after three o'clock, and remained for several minutes after But Mr Wirt being then in the midst of his argument, he was not called till after he had left the Court room He was again introduced on Monday.

Mr. *Burr* offered to read the depositions of Messrs Mercier and Derbigny

Mr *Hay* objected both, because it was improper to read depo sitions where the witnesses might be had , and because they con tained matter improper to be given in evidence He instanced the deposition of Mr Stoddart, which the Court would not suffer to be read, although, besides being subpœnæd, he (Mr Hay) had written him several letters pressing his attendance He said that the absence of the witnesses could not be justified on the grounds stated by them The excuse offered by one was nothing but the death of his father-in-law , and by the other was, that the distance and expence attending the journey, and the loss of his personal exertions for a subsistence to his family, would produce utter ruin to them, if he were to attend. Many other witnesses had attended under circumstances much more oppressive

The counsel for Mr Burr contended, that there was a wide difference between the case of Mr. Stoddart and that of these witnesses Mr Stoddart was convenient to the Court, and his attendance might be enforced Besides, they did not understand the deposition of Mr Stoddart to be absolutely, but only provi sionally rejected , and that it might be read, if his attendance could not be procured

The *Chief Justice* decided that the depositions might be read, if they contained no matter which was improper to be given in evidence It was finally agreed that the Judge should take the depositions and select such parts as were legal evidence

Mr *Wirt* commenced an elaborate and elegant speech upon the evidence, and in answer to the observations which had been made in opposition to the motion On the subject of locality, Mr Wirt read Kelyng 16, Sir Henry Vane's case It was resolved, " that in this case, the treason laid in the indictment, being the " compassing of the king's death, which was in the county of " Middlesex, yet a war levied by him in Surry, might be given " in evidence, for *being not laid as the treason, but only as the overt* " *act to prove the compassing. it is a transitory thing, which may be*

" proved in another county But if an indictment be for levying
" war, and that made the treason for which the party is indicted, in
" that case it is local, and must be laid in the county where in
" truth it was " Under this restriction he said it was, that Hawkins b, 2, ch 35, sect 3, laid down his doctrine.

After some elucidatory remarks on the nature of the motion,
M. Wirt observed that two questions arose which must be resolved by the evidence 1st Was the assemblage in question a levying war against the United States? 2nd Was it a preparation against the provinces of Spain, then, and now, at peace
with the United States? It would have been well if all the evidence and argument had been simply confined to these two questions, for these, and these only could affect the case But a la-
byrinth and thicket of briars had every where been opposed to
any thing like a straight course

The first question, Mr. Wirt observed, diverged itself in to two
subordinate ones Was the assemblage in a warlike posture?
Was it destined against the United States? The first question the
Court has decided. " It is apparent that Judge Foster alludes to
" an assemblage in force, or as Judge Hale terms it, in a warlike
" posture—that is in a condition to attempt or proceed in the treason
" which had been contemplated " He enquired into their condition,
means, and strength from the evidence, as well as the condition
and strength of the forts down to New Orleans On the subject
of levying war, which was declared to necessarily embrace
" actual force," he read and descanted on Vaughan's case The
positions taken by the gentlemen, included every thing but actual battle, and yet they wanted to reduce the crime below a common riot Intimidation was not necessary. If it were, it was exhibited on the Ohio by the marching of the Wood county militia,
the rapid movement of the troops from the Sabine to New Orleans, &c This was not a secret but a public or open assemblage
and undoubtedly an unlawful assembly, which is amply defined
in 4 Blackstone, 146 Applying these rules to the positions laid
down, it would be only a riot to seize and hold New Orleans, but
applying the evidence to the law, the Court would then judge
whether it was not treason He proceeded in the definition at
some length, and read Foster 219 He took a view of the design
of the assemblage from the transactions, and from extensive circumstances He reviewed the movements from Beaver downward,
and the mantle of mystery which attended them Four objects
had been assigned for the assemblage The settlement of the
Washita land, and the invasion of the Spanish provinces in case
of war. These two were innocent, but there were two others
which would well account for Burr's silence at Cumberland &c
That invasion in time of peace, and the dismemberment of the union.
Indeed the conduct of both Burr and the party with him evinced
not only the design, but the act of treason or misdemeanor, or both
He referred to p 100, 101, 110, 148 of Fries's trial; where the
very same objections now made by the counsel for the accused
were then made by Fries's counsel, (Messrs. Dallas and Lewis)
but all which were over-ruled by the Court, p 171, 174-5

On the point of confessions, Mr. Wirt read Judge Iredell's opinion in Fries's Tr and 1 M·Nally 361, on the authority of 2 Hawk.

P C ch 46; 2 St Tr 105, 1 Hale P C 116 Fost 202, 1 Hale 114.

As to the features of the acts themselves, he contended that they were not equivocal, but evident acts of guilt The rule from M'Nally was general *Whatever a man has said at any time* relative to the matter in issue is admissible, without any discrimination as to the *prima facia* guilt, equivocality or innocence of the act to which they relate But an act even innocent, upon the face of it, has been converted into a guilty one by antecedent declarations Crohagan's case, Croke Charle's 821 He read 1 Hale P C 114 to 116, with Sergeant Wilson's notes, Kelyng 13, with Chief Justice Holt's notes, and Browne's, and the review of the whole by Foster 200 to 204 His coming to England was the act, and his words were received merely as explanatory of that act

He did not admit of that great distinction which had been contended for, between the treasons of compassing the king's death and levying war, as described in the books The *act* and the *intention* are the component parts of the crime, of whatever description it might be Why then should it not apply to one species of treason as well as another? In Chrohagan's case his words might have been the effect of acrimony and haste, and they occurred upwards of two years before the overt act but Burr and his party, instead of being under the direction of haste and passion, were calm, deliberate, and in the promotion of their plan But there was also a chain of conversations from 1805 down to 1806 In Kelyng, he said, there was a case where words were admissible, not merely in an act which was equivocal or innocent, but where no act at all was done by the accused In Fries's case also, the charge was "levying war," but the Judge admitted the explanatory evidence of conversations And yet, on this subject, gentlemen are continually holding up the idea of distinction between compassing the king's death and levying war Such evidence was perpetually received in the case of Hardy and Tooke, and the reason of the rule of law applies it with equal aptitude to levying war 1 East, 96, 7, speaks of treason generally—he read the rule, &c. and observed, that there was nothing then to enquire, but to know whether the case was founded on conspiracy. He then proceeded to prove, that the conspiracy was proved in one of the ways at least laid down by East—first, by the acts of Burr himself—or secondly, by his own acts and those of Blannerhasset, concurring at the same time and to the same purpose; his domestication in the family of Blannerhasset, his being with him in the contract at Marietta, the letter that Taylor took to him at Lexington; his reception of Blannerhasset at the mouth of Cumberland; and above all, his referring his men to Blannerhasset for information of the plan, were evidences of the act being *his* Under the 2nd head, the connection and identity of the object was proved by the same scheme being known to both Read Eaton's and Henderson's testimony, compare the same, adding the Morgans, with the numbers signed " Querist," as to the separation of the western from the eastern country Read the incentive held out by Burr to Truxton and others, and that of Blannerhasset to Hendersons, Wallaces, &c —the reciprocity, and union of motive

and means   Burr spoke of turning Congress out of doors, &c.
Blannerhasset did the same.   Then expression of the parties
connected, &c. were the same   And lastly, the constant declarations of Blannerhasset that, he was embarked in Burr's enterprize, and his joining him at Cumberland, all were demonstra-
tive in the highest degree that they were as one, and that their
conversations on that subject were equally applicable to both.

So he said stood the case with Burr and Blannerhasset   As
to Smith, he was at the mouth of Cumberland, and evidently one
of the principal men in the plot

MONDAY, October 19.

Mr _Hay_ continued his argument by vindicating the competency of the witnesses, which had so seriously and so frequently been attacked   First, General Eaton, as attacked by Colonel
Gaither.   He believed it was not expected that General Eaton was so well prepared to " roll the torrent back upon its
source," as he did to the utter confusion of the witness, and of
those who brought him   He next spoke of the testimony of the
Morgans, of Dunbaugh's of Captain Bissell's ; and of the respect
for, and confidence he reposed in Dunbaugh, and of his situation after his desertion. But who, he asked, committed the greatest crime; the denunciator who caused it to be committed, (Burr),
or the poor deluded instrument ? But happily the evidence of
this man, as to hiding the musquets, was corroborated by S. S
Welsh, who patched the augur holes through which the ropes
passed to suspend these guns   In Burr's acknowledgment of the
cyphered letter to him, he is supported by Mr Poindexter   And
in Burr's solicitude to get men to desert, &c. as related by Dunbaugh, he will be supported by Lieutenant Jackson

General Wilkinson. Mr Wirt next proceeded to vindicate ;
next to which he spoke of the Washita lands, and of Mr. Blannerhasset's great earnestness to go to the enjoyment of these
unpeopled woods from his terrestrial paradise on the island   He
then proceeded to enquire the natural character of Col. Burr,
and traced his aspiring genius through life ; and his disappointed aim at the presidency, his ambition mocked and baffled forever, " _even in that point, in which he had treasured up his soul_ "
Would it be surprizing if a man like him " liked the rocking of
the battlements?" Proud, bold and adventurous, what was not
to be expected from him ? The " pride of atchievement," the
blaze and roar of battle, and the shout of victory ; a diadem
sketched in bright perspective, and seen beyond the smoke of
glorious war, were his attractive objects, and not the dull settlement of Washita

As to the witnesses—their testimony to different conversations
—the only particular communication of the prisoner to each—
their being stopt at every point of their narration—enabled the
gentlemen, as availing of the better ground, to rely on what they
called contradictions   Doubtless Aaron Burr knew too well to

make a disclosure of one kind to any two witnesses But Mr
Wirt said they had principally relied on one witness, (Commodore Truxton, who was truly eulogized) but who stopped Burr,
before he had half disclosed himself, to prove that he meant no
more, or otherwise that he had spoken to his confident and friend
He quoted the principal features of the Commodore's testimony,
and made several observations on it—comparing it with the corroborative of General Eaton's, and Blannerhasset's disclosure
to the Hendersons. From Eaton's he read at some length, and
drew in the corroborative evidence of the Morgans, as to his attempts to execute the aforesaid project by exciting enlisting of
" fine fellows," " officers," &c and inveighing the spirit of dissention among them, (but generally in vain) During all this time
however, Mr W. begged it to be remembered, that there was no
sign of war The "Querist," he said, breathed a separation of
the union as desirable; but what were the moral causes suggested by Mr. Blannerhasset as instruments? The auspicies of Col
Burr—the park of artillery at New Orleans, ten thousand soldiers on the western waters—the plunder of the bank, and military stores, and the seizing of the shipping at New Orleans, and
the violent obstruction of the Mississippi by blocking up its
mouth. This is the *ultima ratio regum !*

True to his appointment, in December he attended at the rendezvous at Cumberland, and descended the river with *his* men
From Thomas Hartley's testimony, it appeared, that two men
were recruited at Madrid, who were to drop down with the boat
to be delivered to Aaron Burr, and to go to New Orleans on a
service of six months, for which they were to receive the pay of
twelve and a half dollars per month, and one hundred acres of land !

In the interview with Mr. Poindexter, Mr Wirt said, he considered that a perfect acknowledgment of General Wilkinson's
statement was made in these words " as to any projects or plans
which may have been formed between General Wilkinson and
myself heretofore, they are now completely frustrated by the perfidious conduct of Wilkinson " This was after Gen Wilkinson had
blown the scheme by promulgating the cyphered letter, and was a
plain acknowledgement that it was *his.* Assuming therefore the
character of an independent prince, he entered into formal *capitulation* with Mr. Meade.

As to the peaceable disposition of these men, of which so much
had been said, Mr Wirt referred to the evidence of Mr Poindexter respecting Davis Floyd ; and to the note found in the cape of
the boy's coat in these words " if you are yet together, keep together, and I will join you to-morrow night *in the mean time put
all your arms in perfect order* Ask the bearer no questions, but
tell him all you may think I wish to know He does not know that
this is from me, nor where I am ' This was directed to C T
and D F, and was said to be from Burr He again contended
that treason had been committed, although the party who were
with Burr might not have known the precise object, but their ignorance did not purge away the guilt of those who had treasonable designs, nor did it even exculpate those who were ignorant

of the design, much less their *leaders*. Although Mr. Martin had said that the Earl of Southampton knew of Essex's design, and made inferences on it, yet by 1 St. Tr p 206, he explicitly avows his ignorance of them, and so Hale considered it 1 Hale, p ch 133, 139, so Kelyng 77 Although these men knew not even the intention, they were the victims of the imputed sin of the Earl of Essex He insisted upon the similarity between the men of the Earl, who knew not his particular object, and those who followed Burr in ignorance, But the guilt of Burr and the other leaders was now the subject of investigation

In addition to the evidence produced Mr Wirt called the attention of the Court to the cyphered letter, [Appendix p. 19] The authenticity of that letter did not rest on General Wilkinson—it bore date 29th July, During that month it would be observed, that Burr announced to Commodore Truxton, that he was about dispatching two couriers to Wilkinson with letters The two couriers, Bollman and Swartwout, carried duplicates of this letter to Wilkinson Indeed Burr acknowledged this letter to Danbaugh and to Mr Poindexter Six months provisions are spoken of there as contracted for—here is a key to the *six months* engagement of the men Mr W then applied this letter to the charge for misdemeanor, in which he was supported by the opinion of the Supreme Court [Appendix p 26] Indeed there could be no doubt of probable cause upon that charge

Colonel Burr said that he did not like the character of his land, or his title to it to be impeached He would therefore offer certificates which Colonel Lynch had left, from several persons who authenticated it

All the gentlemen had spoken of *probable cause* as the ground for commitment in this case He believed that not even probable cause had been shewn When gentlemen talked of what a Judge or a Court should think or feel, he thought he had a right to demand that nothing but legal evidence should be heard, and that nothing but legal conclusions and inferences should be permitted to bias the mind of the Court

There had been for some time, he said, filed in the Court, three depositions made at Alexandria on the 25th March last, where General Eaton spoke of him in the highest terms of respect and confidence One by Dr Dick, another by Mr Dalton and another by his daughter Mrs Deblois He could wish them to be read The professional engagements of one of the gentlemen, the age of another of the deponents and the sex of the other, he presumed, would be a sufficient apology to the Court for their not personally appearing in Court

Mr *Hay* objected If these depositions related to the conduct of the accused himself, he would not object, but he did not wish the characters of others to be canvassed

Mr *Burr*, There is not a single word of disrespect to the character of General Eaton included in the whole of them

General Eaton If the object of these depositions is to prove that I have not spoken disrespectful of Colonel Burr or that I have spoken respectfully of him after the communication he made to me, I am ready to admit the fact. It never was my disposition to hurt Colonel Burr's character, and perhaps in promiscuous conversation I might have spoken well of him

Lieutenant JACOB JACKSON was then called and sworn, on the part of the prosecution.

Evidence of Lieutenant Jacob Jackson, delivered in Court, on Monday, the 19th of October, 1807, which evidence was revised and again sworn to by him, on Tuesday, the 20th of the same month, in the form of a deposition

I, Jacob Jackson, a second Lieut. in the regiment of artillerists, do certify and say, that on the 3d or 4th day of Jan. 1807, *Aaron Burr* arrived at the Chickasaw Bluffs in the night time, with one boat, and sent to the commanding officer of the garrison, wishing to know whether he could have quarters in the garrison during the night Being the commanding and only officer there, I informed the messenger that the said Burr could be accomodated Accordingly, he came to the garrison in company with several other gentlemen, and the next morning he asked me whether I had heard of the attempts made in Kentucky to prosecute him, under an apprehension that he was about to invade the Spanish dominions I answered that I had not. He then went on to observe, that he had been prosecuted, but that nothing could be made out against him ; that he was going on a project which many wished to know, but that from their inquisitiveness, he was not disposed to gratify them " It was a project, however, said " he, which was honorable to myself, and which would be the " making of those who should follow me, provided they survived " the undertaking " He continued to observe that the subjects of Spain were in a very distressed situation, and that his project would tend to relieve them from the tyranny of their government. I was then asked by him, what I thought the opinion of my brother (a member of Congress*) was on the subject. I answered that I did not know He then asked what I thought of such a project myself? I answered, that if the United States were going to war with Spain, I should be very glad to embark in the enterprize on which he remarked that the leading characters in the United States did not mean openly to carry on a war against the Spaniards, but that they secretly favored his views I then told him that, if such was the case, I was willing to engage in the enterprize, and after telling me again that the leading men in the United States (by which I supposed he meant to include the heads of departments) approved his measures, he remarked that he wished to engage young men, that he wished *me* to go with him for one ; and that in case I complied, he would give me a Captain's commission. Fully believing from the conversation and high standing of said Aaron Burr, that a war was secretly to be

---

* John G Jackson, Harrison county, (*Virginia*)

carried on by the United States against some of the territories of Spain, I finally consented to engage under him. He then observed that I might probably want some money to raise a company. I replied, that I did not want more than was sufficient to take me home ; and mentioned one hundred and fifty dollars He enquir-ed whether I could not let him have some arms and ammunition I replied that I had a small supply of these articles, but that I did not think myself authorized to furnish him ; on which he ob-served, that he had got some at another garrison, and that I should be justified in supplying him . to which I replied, that I did not wish to implicate myself He then requested me to let some of my men prepare two or three muskets, and run him some balls, (the lead he procured at the public factory) as he wanted them in descending the Mississippi, to kill game for the use of himself, and the residue of his men who were behind , and I ac-cordingly suffered the muskets to be repaired, and the balls to be run In the course of various conversations, he frequently re-quested me to let him have some soldiers to go with him ; which I as often refused at last he wished me to let him have a soldier to carry a letter to Colonel *John M Kee*, in the Chickasaw nation ; and, on my refusal, he requested me to give one of my soldiers a pass for twenty days , and observed, that if he did not return, I could not be blamable , this I also refused In the course of this conversation, he asked me whether I could not *then* go with him, or soon follow him, and take with me the soldiery under my command—In answer to which I remarked, (being somewhat alarmed at his propositions) that I was about to send in my resig-nation, and that as soon as I was discharged from the service, I had no objection to following him ; but that I could not under-take to seduce the soldiery from their duty while I held a com-mission I also observed, that my family was respectable, and that I would not do any thing to injure the feelings of my rela-tions, or to wound my reputation as an officer ; and that, whate-ver might be his projects, I did not wish to hear any thing more about them, unless they were honorable ; to which he replied, that his views were honorable, and that by my complying with his re-quest, I should not incur any blame , that many of the officers of the army were actually engaged with him, and that he expected to derive great assistance from the present military force ; that General Eaton was coming round with the navy, and that he expected soon to receive ten thousand stand of arms He moreo-ver observed, that, as he was acquainted with my father, he should like to have me join him, and the sooner I did it the better I replied that it might be some time before I could receive an ans-wer to my resignation—but that when I did, I would follow him, provided I found him patronized by the United States. He then observed that it would not do to delay business, and would there fore furnish me with money to raise a company. He asked me the expence of a man to carry a letter to Colonel *M'Kee* in the Chickasaw nation. I replied about fifteen dollars he then asked me how many Indians I thought Colonel *M'Kee* could raise in the Choctaw nation: My reply was, that I did not know; but that Colonel *M'Kee* had resided there some time, and his influ-ence was probably considerable. On the morning of the 6th of the said January, just before he started down the Mississippi, on my entering the room where the said *Burr* was, he said to me, there is something for you on the mantle-tree-piece over the fire on which I took from thence one hundred and fifty dollars in pink notes and a draft on *John Smith* for five hundred dollars, he at the same time presented me, observing, that a draft was easier carried than money; that, as to a receipt for the money, he should not take any; and that in case I disliked his plan, he relied on my honor to return it This money and draft were given me by the said *Burr* for the express purpose of raising a company of men to join him, and for building a boat calculated to ascend currents, particular instructions about which he gave me. He further observed, that he *intended to fix himself in the Spanish dominions, and there proclaim his intentions*, that if I was not informed of them before I left the Bluffs, he wished me on my way to Virginia to call on General *Tupper* at Marietta, to whom he should communicate his intentions, as soon as he had fixed himself in the Spanish dominions, and that *he* would communicate them to me, and at the same time he gave me a letter to said *Tupper*, which I burned as soon as I received the President's proclamation and, on his leaving the Bluffs, he pressed me to leave the garrison in fifteen days, and not to wait for the acceptance of my resignation, and on my way down the Mississippi, to endeavor to get as many of the soldiers at the Bluffs to accompany me as possible. And further this deponent saith not.

JACOB JACKSON.

Lieut Reg't. of Artillerists.

Jefferson county, ss.

Sworn to before me in due form, agreeable to law, this 20th October, 1807

Dan'l L Hylton, *Justice of the Peace for the said county.*

Cross Questioned

By Mr. *Burr*. Did you ever see me before that night? A. Yes, but I had no acquaintance with you Q Did you not complain of your situation, that it was an irksome one, and that you were going to leave it? A. I told you, that I intended to resign Q Did you not complain that you wanted money, and that you could not get a horse to carry you home? A I did not Q What became of the money? A I was robbed in three weeks after of two hundred dollars Q What did you do with the order on Mr Smith? A I have it here in my trunk Q Did you ever receive any money upon it? A I did not. Q Did you deliver the letter to Mr Smith? A No Q What did you do with it? A Soon after I received the President's proclamation, I burnt it. Q. Did you read it? A. No Q Are you not under arrest? A. Yes. Q On what charges? A. Because it was suspected that I was connected with you. I believe that this was the principal cause. Q. Were you summoned here? A Yes. Q Where were you arrested? A. At fort Adams Q Were you told what to say here? A I was not I was summoned by the Sheriff of Jefferson county Q Did you receive permission from any authority to come round here? A After I was summoned, I was not permitted by any officer I served with Colonel Cushing Q Did you give my affidavit? A Yes Q Who drew it up? A Captain Stoddart

Mr M'Rae Was there any spot designated for you to carry the men to? A I was to have ascended the Red River some distance, and there get instructions

Evidence of Colonel Cushing

Mr Hay said, that his object in bringing forward Col Cushing was to prove the accuracy of the statement made by Gen Wilkinson.

Q Do you recollect the arrival of Swartwout at Natchitoches? A Yes, I do, and have made an affidavit on that subject. [See Appendix p 27] but without refreshing my memory with it. I might not now recite the facts which occurred, in the particular order in which it then occurred to me The substance of it was, to give the first conversation which was held with General Wilkinson on the subject of the visit of Mr. Swartwout, if it was proper for me to read that affidavit, my memory would be refreshed so as to answer any question that might be asked

Mr Hay Relate it as nearly as you can recollect

Here Col Cushing related the facts without any deviation from what is published in his affidavit--[See Appendix J]

Mr Hay On the morning after Mr. Swartwout's arrival, Gen. Wilkinson made a communication to you on the subject—did he A did, and he mentioned that he should also inform Captain Burling He bound me to secrecy, but desired me to commit the communication to memory The reason of this injunction was that he wished to get still more of the designs of Col Burr, as on that point the cyphered letter was not sufficiently communicative Q Did he shew you the cyphered letter? A I saw it in his room

There was no cross-examination

Mr Hay expressed his wish to hear Wylie, (Mr Burr's secretary) in Court, to prove that he wrote that cyphered letter, which was spoken of, by the direction of Mr. Burr

Wylie was sworn and examined, but he said that it was not his hand writing, nor did he know who wrote it

Mr Wirt wished that the letter from Mr Burr, dated January, 1806, wherein he stated that there would be no war with Spain, and that it was not the policy of this country that there should be a war, might be produced

After some conversation, it was agreed, that after Mr Burr had inspected it, it might be given to the Court for private inspection

Mr Burr then mentioned a circumstance, which had come to his knowledge since the examination of Mr Power, which gave him reason to believe that a sum of money was paid to General Wilkinson for a specific object He did not want to enquire what that object was, because it appeared that it could not be obtained. But it must operate as a conviction to the Court first, to shew something of his motive for what had been done ; and next, to destroy his evidence Thus said he, if I shall be able to prove that I was averse to the object of division, it must operate to my advantage. Again. As to opposing the sovereign of Mr. Power, it was natural for him to endeavor to criminate me, in order to ingratiate himself with the king of Spain, his master The bearing therefore of this evidence on the case, might be duly appreciated if it be heard.

Chief Justice It is not material that I should determine a question of this sort, as there is not a Jury on the case. I am not satisfied that the evidence is admissible, even in any state It is not necessary to enquire into the point, even if full testimony could be given , because if General Wilkinson did receive money from the king of Spain, it could in no wise affect the opinion which I shall give on the question now presented.

Mr *Burr* I beg leave to make a single remark on the situation of Lieutenant Jackson.——He is brought before this Court standing in the same situation as a person under an indictment, (he being under arrest, which in military law is equivalent.) In civil law it is thought illegal to produce such a witness; and therefore it must affect his competency. A young officer in such a situation certainly must look forward with some anxiety to the judgment of the Court Martial, and he must be as much in the power of his superior officers as a man in *any* situation can be — Now, Sir, when my commitment in some degree might depend upon his evidence, I consider it of importance to enquire whether his testimony ought to be attended to? I have no doubt but if he was free from bias, he would give very different evidence from what he now might be expected to give I think the government ought in consideration of its own honor, before they bring forward witnesses so circumstanced, to at least discharge them from prosecution. We have two instances of this kind in view. Serg Dunbaugh and Lieutenant Jackson. I do not mean however to bring them to a level. The probability however of his evidence will be judged by yourself as to Gen Tupper, and as to his recruiting service It is not probable that I should have communicated to him an unlawful plan, and then he to go into Virginia to make his election after some months, whether he would execute it or not

Mr. *Hay.* It appears to me that the narrative has been clearly and consistently given in all its parts. He did not say that Gen Tupper knew of the plan of Burr, nor could it be supposed that he did. As to the arrest under which Mr Jackson may be, I can hardly suppose that the Court will say, that it will have the slightest effect upon him Any man who looks at the situation in which this young man was placed, could easily turn his apologist every thing speaks in his favor. The young man was displeased with his situation at that post, and was disinclined to stay there: he was therefore a fit object for the prey of Col Burr.

When we consider the testimony of Dunbaugh as to what passed at this fort, there appears too near a coincidence to doubt the recital They both speak of the attempt of Burr to delude the soldiers , and here an attempt was made to delude the officer from his duty too, and bring the soldiers along with him '

Mr *Martin* If what he said was ever so true, it does not prove that Colonel Burr had any criminal object in view.

Mr *Hay.* If he took an officer from his station, and attempted to seduce any soldiers from the allegiance which they had sworn to keep, it certainly is strong proof toward treason

Mr. Power appeared in Court.

Mr *Burr.* How far are you willing to answer the enquiries made of you on Saturday?

Mr *Power.* I shall trouble the Court with two or three observations

The gentlemen were good enough to allow me time to consult upon the matter, and get counsel. Grateful as I feel for this indulgence, I must confess I have not, nay, could not avail myself of it. It is pretty well known, that I am an utter stranger in this place; without a single friend to take any interest in my situation, not even any acquaintance, and without the knowledge of any gentleman of law from whom I could procure counsel. However, I have understood that the Court have a right to resort to coercive and rigorous measures to extort from me that, which my ideas of correctness and propriety—that, which my conscience, my sense of duty and honor, forbid me to reveal

And should the Court think proper to adopt such measures—well—I must submit to my fate with patience and resignation, congratulating myself that I am in a country where the rack and torture are not in use, and where I do not run the risk of being put to the question. I shall also have the consolation that flows from a consciousness of not having departed from my duty. I will again openly avow it. This is my motto "Fidelity to my king." This I consider my first, my most essential duty, this is an obligation paramount to every other, and to which every other must bend. This language, probably, is new within these walls, and, I make no doubt, perfectly unintelligible to many. But some, I trust, interiorly, applaud the principle; and possibly, would be proud to have an opportunity to display it.

The counsel for Mr Burr insisted that he should be compelled to state all that he knew concerning a correspondence between General Wilkinson and the Baron de Carondelet

The *Chief Justice* observed, that the existence of such a correspondence could be of importance in the present case no farther than it might be considered as discrediting General Wilkinson's declaration, that he did not recollect his having carried on a correspondence with the Baron de Carondelet, in a cypher similar to that which was used by Mr Burr. He said that the object of that correspondence would, if explained, have no effect on his decision relative to the motion now before him. He therefore required Mr Power to answer questions as to the existence of such a correspondence, but not as to its objects.

Mr. *Power.* I apprehended that, without any violation or breach of my most sacred duties, I can satisfy the gentlemen. I can gratify their curiosity, and give them the information they appear so obstinately bent upon getting. for I confess I do not see any thing criminal or deserving of blame in gentlemen's carrying on a correspondence in cypher with the Baron de Carondelet, or any other Baron or Governor of Louisiana, or any pro vince, and more particularly in General Wilkinson, who I have every reason to believe has been in the habits of corresponding in cypher with several of his acquaintance—witness Gen. Dayton. I can even quote myself—also a very excellent and worthy friend of mine, Mr R. R. Keene, of New Orleans, who has shewn me a cypher he had from General Wilkinson, so that I feel myself perfectly at ease on this point, as it does not in any shape affect or throw any light on the political concerns of my government.

As the Colonel has also said something about monies, neither shall I feel any reluctance in declaring what I may know concerning any sums of money said to have been received by General Wilkinson. For it is pretty well known that the Spanish government, at a former period, did contract with the General, and I believe with some other gentlemen of Kentucky, for considerable supplies of tobacco. If the gentlemen will confine themselves within these limits, in their interrogatories, they shall find me ready to satisfy them. But beyond these I declare I will not step.

Mr *Burr* then asked Captain Power, if he knew that General Wilkinson had corresponded in cypher with the Baron de Carondelet, to which he replied, that he did not know that General Wilkinson had carried on a correspondence in cypher with the Baron, that as far as he recollected, the cypher was complicated, and that a small pocket dictionary was also used.

Mr *Hay* enquired for Mr. Swartwout, to ask him a single question.

Samuel Swartwout—sworn

Mr. *Hay*. Did you deliver a packet to General Wilkinson? A. I did; but I did not know its contents, nor did I receive it from Colonel Burr. I have looked at that cyphered letter, but my opinion is, that it is not Colonel Burr's hand writing. Q. Had you any conversations with General Wilkinson? A. I had. Q. Was any one present? A. No, it seemed to be the General's wish to have no one near us. Q. How did *you* receive this packet? A. From Mr Ogden. Q. Did you receive no letter from Col Burr at that time? A. Yes; but I do not think he made any reference to the cyphered letter. I supposed however that this cyphered letter came from Col Burr.

Mr *M'Rae.* Would you not have objected to a public disclosure of your communications with General Wilkinson? A. I would have spoken in presence of confidential persons. Q. Would you have done it, except in the most confidential manner? A. I would not.

Mr *Burr.* Did you hear General Wilkinson's testimony? A. A part I heard, and have read the rest. Q. Did you tell him any thing about revolutionizing the western country; when did you first hear of it? A. I heard it for the first time in Court —. When it was mentioned on my trial at Washington, I spoke to my counsel, Messrs. Harper and Key, and wished to refute it on my oath. The General has said that I talked about seizing New Orleans, and the banks there. Now I did not know at that time there were any banks in New Orleans, nor did I know of it until

I got to Fort Adams. I spoke to the General however about another country.

Mr. *Burr*. What was that? A. Mexico.

Q. Did you make any enquiry about the progress of the war with the Spaniards? A. Yes; I was authorized to bring you an account of the war, and of the state of the preparations. General Wilkinson declared to me, that he hoped the severance of the union was Colonel Burr's object, and that he would be glad of it. He spoke some very hard words of the President. Q. Had you reason to believe that a severance of the union was Colonel Burr's object? A. I can say this. I had free access to his papers while at Philadelphia? and I never saw or heard of any thing from Colonel Burr, that was the least derogatory to patriotism.

Mr. *Wirt*. Did you hear of a body of men prepared by Colonel Burr to go to Mexico? A. I did not. Several of the officers of the United States told me, that they thought there would be a war with Spain, and I then offered my services. But I will candidly say, that I was ready to forget the law of Congress passed to repress private enterprizes, and that I would have gone, whether war or not.

Mr. *Wirt*. Was it the object of the project then, to go beyond the boundaries of the United States, *into* Mexico? A. Oh! yes, *that* was avowed.

The evidence and argument being now entirely closed, the Court adjourned to the next day to deliver the opinion.

TUESDAY, October 20.

The *Chief Justice* delivered the following opinion on the motion for commitment, which closed this long case.

Much of the difficulty of the present case arises from its being attended by circumstances entirely opposite to those which are usually founded in motions of a similar description.

An examining magistrate commits, and ought to commit on probable cause. In defining his duty, after stating that he may arrest either upon his own suspicion or that of others, Blackstone adds, " but in both cases it is fitting to examine upon oath the party requiring a warrant, as well as to ascertain that there is a felony or other crime actually committed, without which no warrant should be granted ; as also to prove the cause and probability of suspecting the party against whom the warrant is prayed "

But although the existence of a fact as the foundation of the charge must be proved before a magistrate can legally imprison a citizen, it is not believed to be true that the same necessity exists for ascertaining with equal clearness the full legal character of that fact, or the degree of guilt which the law attaches to it. On a charge of murder, for example, the homicide must be proved; but the enquiry whether it be justifiable or otherwise, is seldom made by an examining magistrate. He could not refuse to commit unless it was perfectly clear that the act was innocent. An opinion that a Jury ought to acquit, would not warrant a refusal on his part to take the steps which might bring the accused before a Jury.

In cases where the legal effect of the act alledged to be criminal is in any degree doubtful, it would greatly derange the regular course of justice, and enable many offenders to escape, should a magistrate refuse to arrest until he had received full proof of guilt. If the fact be of such a character as perhaps to be construed into a high and dangerous crime with the aid of other testimony which the nature of the case admits, it would seem to be a duty to secure the person, in order to abide the judgment of the law.

Among the many reasons which may be enumerated for committing in a doubtful case, are

1st. That upon a considerable portion of a criminal charge, it is the peculiar province of a Jury to decide

2d. That additional testimony is to be expected ; and

3dly. That the person most commonly making the commitment is a Justice of the peace, not authorized finally to try the offender, and who, consequently, whatever may be the fact, is not presumed to be so competent a judge of the law of the case as he is, to whom the power of deciding it is confided.

Had these proceedings commenced with the present motion founded on testimony such as is now adduced, I certainly should have felt no difficulty in deciding on it. But the proceedings are not now commencing. The persons against whom this motion is made, have been arrested, one in the Mississippi territory, one in Kentucky, and one in the western parts of Pennsylvania or New York, and brought to this place for trial. An immense number of witnesses have been assembled, and a very extensive investigation of the transactions alledged to be criminal, has taken place. The result has been the acquittal of one of the accused upon the principle, that the offence, if committed any where, was committed out of the jurisdiction of this Court, and a *nolle prosequi* has been entered with respect to the others. The witnesses intended to establish the charge before a Jury, have been examined, and the probability of obtaining testimony which can materially vary the case, is admitted to be very remote. The great personal and pecuniary sufferings already sustained, must be allowed also to furnish some motives for requiring rather stronger testimony to transmit the accused to a distant state for trial, than would be required in the first instance. It may likewise be added as a consideration of some weight, that the Judge who hears the motion, though sitting as an examining magistrate, is one of those who is by law entrusted with the power of deciding finally on the case and there seems to be on that account the less reason for referring the party to a distinct tribunal on a point, on which a sligh doubt may exist.

I do not believe that in England, whence our legal system is derived, a Justice of *assise* and *nisi prius*, after hearing the whole testimony, would commit for trial in another county, a man who had been tried in an improper county, unless the probable cause was much stronger than would be required on ordinary occasions

These conflicting considerations, certainly render the questions to be decided, more intricate than they would be in a different state of things. After weighing them, I have conceived to be my duty not to commit on slight ground, but at the same time I cannot permit myself to be governed by the same rules which would regulate my conduct on a trial in chief

There are certain principles attached to the different characters of a Judge sitting as an examining magistrate and on a trial in chief which must essentially influence his conduct even under circumstances like those which attend the present case. It is a maxim universally in theory, though sometimes neglected in practice, that if in criminal prosecutions, there be doubts either as to fact or law, the decision ought to be in favor of the accused. This principle must be reversed on a question of commitment. In a case like the present, if the Judge has formed a clear opinion on the law or fact, which there is not much reason to suppose additional testimony might be obtained to change, it would be injustice to the public, to the accused, and to that host of witnesses who must be drawn from their private avocations to the trial, should he take a step which in his judgment could produce only vexation and expence; but if he entertains serious doubts as to the law or fact, it is, I think, his duty even in a case like this, not to discharge, but to commit.

The charges against the accused are

1st. That they have levied war against the United States at the mouth of Cumberland river in Kentucky; and

2dly. That they have begun and provided the means for a military expedition against a nation with which the United States were at peace.

With respect to one of the accused, a preliminary defence is made in the nature of a plea of *autrefois acquit.*

If the question raised by this defence was one on which my judgment was completely formed in favor of the person by whom it is made, it would certainly be improper for me to commit him; but if my judgment is not absolutely and decidedly formed upon it, there would be a manifest impropriety in undertaking now to determine it. This does not arise from my fear to meet a great question whenever my situation shall require me to meet it, but from a belief that I ought as well to avoid the intrusion of my opinions on my brethren in cases where duty does not enjoin it on me to give them, as the withholding of those opinions where my situation may demand them. The question whether *autrefois acquit* will be a good plea in this case, is of great magnitude and ought to be settled by the united wisdom of all the Judges. Were it brought before me on a trial in chief I would, if in my power, carry it before the Supreme Court, when brought before me merely as an examining magistrate, I should deem myself inexcusable were I to decide, while a single doubt remained respecting the correctness of that decision

To settle new and important questions in our criminal code especially where those questions are constitutional, is a task upon which a single Judge will at any time enter with reluctance; certainly, he would not willingly engage in it while acting as an examining magistrate. There is a decent fitness which all must feel in bringing such questions, if practicable, before all the Judges. In England, trials which are expected to involve questions of great magnitude, are seldom assigned to one or two Judges. At that interesting crisis when Hardy, Tooke, Thelwall and others were indicted for treason, Chief Justice Eyre was aided and supported by four associate Judges of high talents and character. It would, I have no doubt, in that country be a matter of surprize if any person, whatever might be his station in the judiciary, should undertake to settle a great and novel point on a question of commitment. Although, in the United States, our system does not admit of a commission authorizing a majority of the Judges to constitute a Court for the trial of special criminal cases, yet it does admit of carrying a doubtful and important point before the Supreme Court, and I should not feel myself justified were I now to give an opinion, anticipating such a measure.

I shall therefore consider this motion as if no verdict had been rendered for either of the parties.

Both charges are supported by the same transaction and the same testimony. The assemblage at the mouth of Cumberland is considered as an act of levying war against the United States, and as a military armament collected for the invasion of a neighboring power with whom the United States were at peace.

From the evidence which details that transaction it appears, that from sixty to one hundred men who were collected from the upper parts of the Ohio under the direction of Tyler and Floyd, had descended the river and reached the mouth of Cumberland about the 25th of December, 1806. The next day they went on shore, and formed a line, represented by some as somewhat circular, to receive Colonel Burr, who was introduced to them, and who said that he had intended to impart something to them, or that he had intended to communicate to them his views, but that reasons of his own had induced him to postpone this communication, or, as others say, that there were then too many byestanders to admit of a communication of his objects.

The men assembled at the mouth of Cumberland appear to have considered Colonel Burr as their chief. Whatever might be the point towards which they were moving, they seem to have looked upon him as their conductor.

They demeaned themselves in a peaceable and orderly manner. No act of violence was committed, nor was any outrage on the laws practised. There was no act of disobedience to the civil authority, nor were there any military appearances. There were some arms and some boxes which might or might not contain arms. There were also some implements of husbandry, but they were purchased at the place. These men assembled under contracts to settle a tract of country on the Red River. No hostile objects were avowed, and, after continuing a day or two on an island in the mouth of the river, the party proceeded down the Ohio.

There are some circumstances in this transaction, which are calculated to excite attention and to awaken suspicion. If the exclusive object of those who composed this meeting was to settle lands, it would naturally form the subject of public conversation, and there would most probably have been no impediment to a free communication respecting it. The course of the human mind would naturally lead to such communications. The silence observed by the leaders on this subject, connected with hints of ulterior views, seemed calculated to impress on the minds of the people themselves, that some other project was contemplated, and was probably designed to make that impression

That the men should have been armed with rifles was to be expected, had their single object been to plant themselves in the Ouachita; but the musket and bayonet are perhaps not the species of arms which are most usually found in our frontier settlements, nor were the individuals, who were assembled, of that description of persons who would most naturally be employed for such a purpose. The engagement for six months too is a stipulation for which it is difficult to account upon the principle, that a settlement of lands was the sole or principal object in contemplation.

These are circumstances which excite suspicion. How far they may be accounted for by saying, that ulterior eventual objects were entertained, and that the event on which those objects depended was believed to be certain or nearly certain, I need not determine; but I can scarcely suppose it possible that it would be contended by any person, that the transactions at the mouth of Cumberland do, in themselves, amount to an act of levying war. There was neither an act of hostility committed, nor any intention to commit such act avowed

Very early in the proceedings which preceded this motion, I declared the opinion that war might be levied without a battle, or the actual application of force to the object on which it was designed to act; that a body of men assembled for the purpose of war, and being in a posture of war, do levy war; and from that opinion I have certainly felt no disposition to recede. But the intention is an indispensable ingredient in the composition of the fact, and if war may be levied without striking the blow, the intention to strike must be plainly proved

To prove this intention, the prosecutor for the United States offers evidence of conversations held by the accused, or some of them, with various individuals at different times, relative to the views which were entertained and the plans which had been formed, and of certain facts which took place after leaving the mouth of Cumberland. For although it was decided not to be within the power of this Court to commit for trial in a territory of the United States, yet every transaction within a territory has been given in evidence in the expectation, that such testimony might serve to explain the meeting at the mouth of Cumberland, and because it was believed to be proper for an examining magistrate to receive it.

That conversations or actions at a different time and place might be given in evidence as corroborative of the overt act of levying war, after that had been proved in such a manner as to be left to a jury, I never doubted for an instant. But that in a case where the intent could not be inferred from the fact, and was not proved by declarations connected with the fact, among which I should include the terms under which those who composed the assemblage were convened together, this defect could be entirely supplied by extrinsic testimony, not applying the intent conclusively to the particular fact is a point on which I have entertained doubts which are not yet entirely removed. The opinion of Judge Iredell in the case of Fries, according to my understanding of it when read at the bar, appears to bear strongly on this point, and that opinion would be conclusive with me, at least while acting as an examining magistrate. I have not reviewed it particularly, because my decision will not depend on the propriety of admitting this mode of proving the intent.

It has also been made a question, whether after proving a connection between the accused for some general object, the conversations of one of them may be given in evidence against any other than himself for the purpose of proving what that object was. On the part of the United States it is insisted, that such conversations may be given in evidence on an indictment for treason in levying war. By the defense it is contended, that such evidence is only admissible on indictments for a conspiracy, or on indictments where a conspiracy may be laid as an overt act.

The principle that one man shall not be criminated by the declarations of another, not assented to by him, nor made in due course of law, constitutes a rule of evidence, which ought not unreflectingly to be invaded.

It is one of those principles on which I do not think myself required to decide, because I am not sure that its decision, however interesting it might be on a trial in chief, would essentially affect the question of commitment, nor am I confident that its decision as argued on the part of the United States, would introduce the testimony it was designed to introduce. In the English books generally, the position that the declarations of a person not on trial, may be given in evidence against a man proved to have been connected with him, is laid down only in cases of conspiracy, where the crime is completed without any other open deed. The position is certainly not laid down with respect to such cases, in terms which exclude its application to others, but it is not laid down in general terms, and is affirmed to apply to those particular cases, without being affirmed to apply others. From this general observation relative to the English books, East is to be excepted. He states the proposition generally. Yet it may well be doubted, whether this general statement was not with a view to the law in that treason, which, in England, almost swallows up every other.

But admitting the law to be the same in treason by levying war, as in cases of conspiracy, how far does it extend?

The doctrine on this subject was reviewed in the cases of Hardy and Tooke. On the part of the crown, a letter of Thelwall containing seditious songs composed by himself and sung in the society, was offered as evidence against Hardy, who was connected with Thelwall. This testimony was rejected because it was not a part of the transaction itself, but an account of that transaction given by Thelwall to a person not engaged in the conspiracy. The Court was divided, three for rejecting and two for admitting the evidence.

A letter addressed by one conspirator to another, but not proved to have been received, was then offered and admitted against the opinion of the Chief Justice, who thought that such a letter did not amount to an act done which might be evidence, but only to a relation of that act, which could not be evidence. He was overruled because a letter from one conspirator to another on the conspiracy, was a complete act in that conspirator

The next paper offered was a letter from a society in the conspiracy, which was found in the possession of one of the conspirators, and this was unanimously admitted

The principle which appears to be established by these decisions, is, that a letter from one conspirator to another on the subject of the conspiracy, is evidence against all, but that a letter from a conspirator to a person not connected with him, stating facts relative to the conspiracy, is only evidence against himself. How far a conversation held with a stranger for the purpose of bringing him into the plot, may be considered as a transaction, and therefore, testimony to show the general conspiracy, does not appear from these decisions.

This species of evidence is received to show the general object of the conspiracy, but can affect no individual further than his assent to that object can be proved by such testimony as is admissible in ordinary cases

I notice this point for the purpose of observing, that I do not decide it on the present motion.

The first question which arises on the evidence, is,

With what objects did those men convene who assembled at the mouth of Cumberland?

Was it to separate the western from the eastern states by seizing and holding New Orleans?

Was it to carry on an expedition against Mexico, making the embarkation at New Orleans?

Was this expedition to depend on a war with Spain?

The conversation held by Colonel Burr with Commodore Decatur, stated his object to be an expedition against Mexico, which would be undertaken, as the Commodore understood, with the approbation of government in the event of war.

To General Eaton, he unfolded his various conversations, plans for invading Mexico, and also for severing the western from the Atlantic states

To Commodore Truxton, he spoke of the invasion and conquest of Mexico in the event of a war, as a plan which he had digested in concert with General Wilkinson, and into which he was extremely desirous to draw the Commodore. A circumstance is narrated by this witness, which has been noticed by the counsel for the United States, and deserves consideration. It is, the declaration of Colonel Burr, that he was about to dispatch two couriers with letters to General Wilkinson relative to the expedition. It was at this time that Messrs Bollman and Swartwout are said to have left Philadelphia, carrying each a copy of the cyphered letter, which has constituted so important a document in the various motions that have been made on this occasion. This letter, though expressed in terms of some ambiguity, has been understood by the Supreme Court, and is understood by me, to relate to a military expedition against the territories of a foreign prince. In this sense, the testimony offered on the part of the United States, shows it to have been also understood by Bollman, by Swartwout, and by General W.

kinson. The inference is very strong, that this letter is the same to which Colonel Burr alluded in his conversation with Commodore Truxton, and strengthens the idea that the accused gave to that gentleman a true statement of the real object, so far at least as relates to the point against which his preparations were to be directed. All the conversation relative to an expedition by sea would be equally inapplicable to any attempt on the territories of the United States, and to the settlement of lands.

His conversations with the Messrs. Morgans, certainly indicate that his mind was strongly directed to military objects, that he was not friendly to the present administration, and that he contemplated a separation of the union as an event which would take place at no very distant day.

His conversation with Lieutenant Jackson points in express terms to hostility against Spain.

The conversations of Mr. Blannerhasset, evince dispositions unfriendly to the union, and his writings are obviously intended to disaffect the western people, and to excite in their bosoms strong prejudices against their Atlantic brethren. That the object of these writings was to prepare the western states for a dismemberment, is apparent on the face of them, and was frequently avowed by himself. In a conversation with the Messrs. Hendersons, which derives additional importance from the solemnity with which his communications were made, he laid open a plan for dismembering the union, under the auspices of Mr. Burr. To others at subsequent times, he spoke of the invasion of Mexico as the particular object to which the preparations then making were directed. In all those whom he sought to engage in the expedition, the idea was excited, that though the Wachita was its avowed object, it covered something more splendid, and the allusions to Mexico, when not directed, were scarcely to be misunderstood.

The language of Comfort Tyler also tends to prove that the enterprize was designed against Mexico.

The communications made to Gen. Wilkinson deserve much consideration in marking the real intention of the parties, because it is obvious that Col. Burr, whether with or without reason, calculated on his co-operation with the army which he commanded, and that on this co-operation, the execution of his plan greatly, if not absolutely depended. To General Wilkinson, both the cyphered letter and the explanations made by Bollman and Swartwout, declared the expedition to be military and to be intended against Mexico.

I do not think the authenticity of this letter can now be questioned. When to the circumstances enumerated by the counsel on the part of the United States, are added the testimony of Mr. Swartwout, and its being written in a cypher previously established between General Wilkinson and Colonel Burr. I think it sufficiently proved at least for the present, although not in the hand writing of the person to whom it is ascribed.

The conversation stated by Gen. Wilkinson, as passing between Mr. Swartwout and himself, so far as it is contradicted by that gentleman, cannot affect Mr. Burr for this plain reason, the person alledged to have made these declarations avers not only that he never made them, but that he was never authorized to make them, that he never heard from Mr Burr any sentiment indicating designs against any part of the United States, and never even suspected him of such designs. If then Gen Wilkinson be correct, I must consider the observations he narrates, as the conjectures of Mr Swartwout, not authorized by Mr Burr.

It is also a circumstance of some weight, that Mr. Burr's declarations at the mouth of Cumberland, furnish strong reasons for the opinion that he did not wish those to whom he addressed himself to consider the Ouachita as his real ultimate object, and the reference to further information from their particular leaders would naturally induce the expectation, that without any open avowal their minds would be gradually conducted to the point to which their assent was to be obtained. We find there were rumors among them of attacking Baton Rouge, of attacking other parts of the Spanish dominions, but not a suggestion was heard of hostility against the United States.

On comparing the testimony adduced by the United States with itself, this is observable. That which relates to treason indicates the general design, while that which relates to misdemeanor points to the particular expedition which was actually commenced. Weighing the whole of this testimony, it appears to me to preponderate in favor of the opinion, that the enterprize was really designed against Mexico.

But there is strong reason to suppose that the embarkation was to be made at New Orleans, and this, it is said, could not take place without subverting for a time the government of the territory, which, it is aledged, would be treason. The supreme Court has said that to revolutionize a territory by force, although merely as a step to or a mean of executing some greater projects, is treason. But an embarkation of troops against a foreign country may be made without revolutionizing the government of the place and without subverting the legitimate authority. It is true that violence might probably result from such an attempt and treason might be the consequence of its execution, but this treason would arise incidentally and would not be the direct object for which the men originally assembled. This treason would attach to those who committed it, but would not, I am inclined to think, infect a previous assemblage convened for a distinct purpose. If the object of the assemblage at the mouth of Cumberland was to embark at New Orleans for the purpose of invading Mexico, the law relative to that assemblage would be essentially different from what it might be if their direct object was to subvert the government of New Orleans by force. If in prosecuting their purpose at New Orleans war should be levied, this would be treason at New Orleans when the fact was committed, but it could not I think be said to be treason by levying war at the mouth of Cumberland, where the fact was neither committed nor intended. It might be otherwise if at the mouth of Cumberland, the determination to subvert the government of a territory by force, had been formed.

This opinion may be in some degree illustrated by the doctrine of the English books. Levying of war is an overt act of compassing the king's death. So is a conspiracy to levy war, provided the conspiracy be direct against the king or his government. But if it be a conspiracy to do an act of constructive treason, which act if done, would support an indictment for compassing the king's death ; the conspiracy without the act will not support the indictment. So in this case if the object be embarkation of a body of men against a foreign country, in the execution of which, war may or may not be levied, the fact becomes necessary to constitute the treason.

It is also a circumstance of considerable weight with me, that the proof exhibited by the United States to establish a general design to dismember the union, applies only to Colonel Burr and Mr Blannerhasset. It is not proved to have been ever communicated even to Tyler or Floyd. There is not only a failure to prove that such a design was communicated to, or even entertained by the men who were assembled at the mouth of Cumberland, but the contrary is in full evidence. The United States have adduced several witnesses belonging to that assemblage, who concur in declaring, that they heard nothing, that they suspected nothing, and that they would have executed nothing hostile to the United States. This testimony cannot be disregarded for it is uncontradicted, and is offered by the prosecution. How then can this assemblage be said to have levied war against the United States?

Had Burr and Blannerhasset constituted this meeting, no man could have construed it into an act of levying war, whatever might have been their purpose. Their being joined by others having no hostile intentions against the United States, who were attached to them with other views, and who would not permit themselves to be employed in the execution of such intentions, does not seem to me to alter the case. The reason why men, in a posture of war, may be said to levy war before a blow is struck, is, that they are ready to strike, and war consists in the various movements of a military force, as well as in actual fighting. But these men were not ready nor willing to strike, nor could their chief be ready to strike without them. He had yet to prevail upon them to come into his measures. This is not a meeting for the purpose of executing a formal design, but a meeting for the purpose of forming a design. It is therefore more in the nature of conspiracy than actual war.

Suppose Mr Burr had, at the mouth of Cumberland declared his object to be, to seize upon New Orleans and dismember the union, and that upon this declaration his men had universally abandoned him, could this have been denominated an act of levying war ? If we forget the constitution and laws of our country, if we suppose treason, like moral guilt, to consist in the intention, and that it may be legally evidenced by the words declaring that intention, the answer to this question may be in the affirmative, but it can consist only in an open deed of levying war. I confess myself unable to perceive how such a proposition can be construed into such a deed.

The case does not appear to me, to be essentially varied by the circumstance, that this design was not avowed, and that the men followed Colonel Burr with other views. Upon general principles it appears to me, that unless some act be committed, from which a treasonable intent may be inferred, that the treasonable intent must be proved in the assemblage, where that assemblage is composed of free agents, as well as in the person who convenes them, before the law considers war as being actually levied

This opinion is supposed, to be contrary to the decision in the case of the Earl of Essex and Southampton I have examined that case as reported in the Sate trials, and do not think it in any respect contradictory to the ideas I have delivered

The design of the Earl of Essex was to force his way into the palace and to remove certain counsellors from the queen, who were his enemies, but he intended no hurt to the person of the queen. For the purpose of executing this design he assembled a large body of armed men at his own house, who continued embodied, after being ordered by the proper authority to disperse, and he also entered the city of London for the purpose of raising the citizens in order further to aid him in the execution of his plan. Several consultations had been previously held at which the Earl of Southampton assisted, and it is not alledged in the case, that he was not fully informed of these projects. He believed that no design was entertained against the person of the queen, and therefore that his acts were not treasonable, but in the law he was mistaken. In fact, no particular design against her person was entertained, and Essex as little suspected as Southampton that they were committing treason They were ignorant that the law pronounced those facts to be treason, but they were neither ignorant of the facts themselves nor of the real intention with which those facts were committed

In this case, the Judges delivered their opinion of the law on two points The one, "that in case where a subject attempteth to put himself into such strength as the king should not be able to resist him, and to force and compel the king to govern otherwise than according to his own royal authority and direction, it is manifest rebellion The other, " that in every rebellion the law intendeth as a consequent the compassing the death and deprivation of the king, as foreseeing that the rebel will never suffer that king to live or reign who might punish or take revenge of his treason or rebellion."

Under this law opinion of the Judges, Essex and Southampton were condemned and executed The only difference between them was, that the quarrel was the quarrel of Essex, and Southampton only adhered to him, but he adhered to him knowing what he did and the intention with which he acted.

Believing then the weight of testimony to be in favor of the opinion, that the real and direct object of the expedition was Mexico, and inclining also to the opinion, that in law, either acts of hostility and resistance to the government, or a hostile intention in the body asssembled, is necessary to convert a meeting of men with ordinary appearances into an act of leving war, it would, in my judgment, be improper in me to commit the accused on the charge of treason

It is contended that they are not guilty of a misdemeanor, on one of these grounds. Either the United States were actually at war with Spain, or the expedition was dependent on war, and in the event of peace, was to be converted into a settlement on the Ouachita.

It is alledged that we were at war with Spain, because a Spanish army had crossed the Sabine, and entered the territory of the United States.

That a nation may be put in a state of war by the unequivocal aggressions of others, without any act of its own, is a proposition which I am not disposed to controvert, but I cannot concede this to be such an act. The boundaries claimed by the United States to their recent purchase of Louisiana, are contested by Spain Now if either nation takes possession of the contested territory as its own, it is an act which the opposite government may elect to consider either as an act of war or otherwise, and only the government can make that election. No citizen is at liberty to make it, or to anticipate his government

But it is alledged, that war, if not absolutely made, appeared to be inevitable, and that the prosecution of the expedition depended on its taking place. That the probability of war was great may be admitted, and this may extenuate the offence; but it still remains an offence which is punishable by law. If the expedition was really eventual, and was not to take place in the time of peace, then certainly preparations might be made for it without infracting any law; but this is a fact proper for the exclusive consideration of the Jury, and I shall make no comment upon it which might, the one way or the other, influence their judgment

I shall commit Aaron Burr and Herman Blannerhasset, for preparing and providing the means for a military expedition against the territories of a foreign prince, with whom the United States were at peace. If those whose province and duty it is, to prosecute offenders against the laws of the United States, shall be of opinion, that a crime of a deeper die has been committed, it is at their choice to act in conformity with that opinion

Israel Smith is not proved to have provided or prepared any means whatever, and therefore I shall not commit him If he has really offended against the laws, he may be prosecuted for the treason in Kentucky, or for the misdemeanor in his own State, where, (if any where,) his offence has been committed

After the delivery of the opinion of the Court the Chief Justice observed, that he had not specified, (in that opinion) the particular district to which the monitor were to be committed He thought it best that there should be only one trial for them; but if Burr was sent to Kentucky Blannerhasset could not, because he had provided no means for the expedition but in the district of Ohio

Mr HAY *Then moved for their commitment to Ohio, which was ordered.*

Mr. *Wickham* then moved for an attachment against Mr Benjamin Hawkins, an Indian agent, for detaining Dr Cummings, witness in this prosecution, and breaking open certain *papers* his care, belonging to Mr. Blannerhasset, one of the accused *rule ordered.*

Messrs. Burr and Blannerhasset were admitted to bail, in the sum of three thousand dollars each. Luther Martin and Dr. Cummings, securities for A. Burr. Dr. Cummings and Israel Smith for H. Blannerhasset.

The Court then adjourned.

APPENDIX.

[The Publishers subjoin the following communications and documents, collected by their Reporter, as an Appendix to the important Trial just closed It will preserve, for the reader, a connection of the most prominent measures taken by the Executive, and the information in its possession, on which they were founded already furnished through the medium of Newspapers, but perhaps forgotten]

(A)

BY THE PRESIDENT OF THE U STATES OF AMERICA,
A PROCLAMATION.

WHEREAS, information has been received, that sundry persons, citizens of the United States, or residents within the same, are conspiring and confederating together, to begin and set on foot, provide and prepare the means for a military expedition or enterprize against the dominions of Spain, that for this purpose they are fitting out and arming vessels in the Western waters of the United States, collecting provisions, arms, military stores, and other means, are deceiving and seducing honest and well meaning citizens, under various pretences, to engage in their criminal enterprizes; are organizing officers, and arming themselves for the same, contrary to the laws in such cases made and provided I have therefore thought fit to issue this my PROCLAMATION, warning and enjoining all faithful citizens who have been led without due knowledge or consideration to participate in the said unlawful enterprizes, to withdraw from the same without delay; and commanding all persons whatsoever, engaged or concerned in the same, to cease all further proceedings therein, as they will answer the contrary at their peril; and incur prosecution with all the rigors of the law. And I hereby enjoin and require all officers, civil and military, of the United States, or of any of the states or territories, and especially all governors and other executive authorities, all judges, justices and other officers of the peace, all military officers of the army or navy of the United States, and officers of the militia, to be vigilant, each within his respective department, and according to his functions, in searching out, and bringing to condign punishment, all persons engaged, or concerned in such enterprize, in seizing and retaining, subject to the dispositions of the law, all vessels, arms, military stores, or other means provided or providing for the same, and in general, in preventing the carrying on such expedition or enterprize, by all the lawful means within their power, and I require all good and faithful citizens and others within the U

States, to be aiding and assisting herein, and especially in the discovery, apprehension, and bringing to justice of all such offenders, in preventing the execution of their unlawful designs, and in giving information against them to the proper authorities

In testimony whereof, I have caused the seal of the United States to be affixed to these presents, and have signed the same with my hand Given at the City of Washington, on the twenty-seventh day of November, one thousand eight hundred and six, and in the year of the sovereignty and independence of the United States, the thirty-first.
Signed,   TH. JEFFERSON.
By the President,
        Signed,   JAMES MADISON
                                    Secretary of State.

(B)
By COWLES MEAD,
Executing the powers and performing the duties of Governor of the Mississippi Territory,

A PROCLAMATION.

WHEREAS, information from various sources, as well by affidavits as otherwise, has been communicated to me, of the designs of an association, whose object is the dismemberment of this and the neighbouring countries from the government of the United States · And, whereas, every attempt of this kind must be ruinous and destructive of the numerous blessings which we now enjoy, under the auspices of a government founded on the grand principles of political equality and indiscriminate justice And, whereas, this conspiracy is directed by men of secret and profound intrigue, for the aggrandizement of themselves and their minions, to the oppression of the great mass of the people whom they are endeavoring to dupe and inveigle from the foregoing cause, I have thought proper to issue this my Proclamation, for the purpose of guarding the good people of this Territory against the agents of this diabolical plot, and warn them of their danger from that quarter; and I do hereby solemnly call on and enjoin the officers, both civil and military, and the citizens of this Territory to perform their sacred duty to their country, by aiding and abetting in the detection of any agents employed in this country, and if found, to be brought without delay before proper tribunals of the country, that they may receive their trials for such high offences against the peace and happiness of the Mississippi Territory, and dignity and sovereignty of the United States. And I do further enjoin and require the officers and citizens of the Territory, to be on the alert and prove their patriotism by giving such assistance for the developement of this traitorous project as their respective situations will afford

And whereas, I am aware of the influence of intrigue and misrepresentation, and that men of pure intentions may sometimes be deluded I do therefore invite all of this description to return to the bosom of their country and the confidence of their government

And, whereas, I have reasons to believe, that many of the officers of this government have not taken the oaths required by the ordinance of Congress and the statutes of this Territory, I do in consequence thereof, require all officers who have not taken the said oaths, to come forward and take the same in the course of fifteen days from the date of this Proclamation, and in default thereof, I do hereby revoke all the powers civil or military which they possess, and their commissions are hereby vacated and annulled.   COWLES MEAD,

Dated 23d December, 1806

———

(C)

Copy of Colonel Burr's Letter to the Secretary, acting as Governor of the Mississippi Territory

BAYOU PIERRE, 12th January, 1807

SIR—Being on my way down the river, with a number of my friends, who are disposed to emigrate with me, I am greatly surprized to hear, that my views have been grossly misrepresented, and that my approach has been made the subject of alarm to the country.

The reports which charge me with designs unfriendly to the peace and welfare of this and the adjacent territory, are utterly false, and are in themselves absurd, and are the inventions of wicked men for evil purposes I do assure you, Sir, that I have no such designs, nor any other, which can tend to interrupt the peace and welfare of my fellow citizens, and that I harbour neither the wish nor intention to intermeddle with their government or concerns · on the contrary, my pursuits are not only justifiable but laudable , tending to the happiness and benefit of my country, and such as every good citizen and virtuous man ought to promote. These pursuits have very recently been the subject of investigation before an enlightened Grand Jury in Kentucky, whose report is herewith enclosed

If the alarm which has been excited for the most mischievous purpose, should not be appeased by this declaration, I invite my fellow citizens to visit me at this place, and to receive from me in person such further explanations as may be necessary to their satisfaction ; presuming that when my views are understood, they will receive the countenance and support of all good men

It is hoped, Sir, that you'll not suffer yourself to be made the instrument of arming citizen against citizen, and of involving the country into the horrors of a civil war, without some better foundation than the suggestion of rumour, or the vile fabrications of a man notoriously the pensioner of a foreign government.

Having understood that the militia of this neighbourhood were to be reviewed this day, I thought it a fit occasion to undeceive my fellow citizens, and relieve their apprehensions, and you the proper medium of communication ; and to this end I pray, Sir, that you will cause this letter to be read to the militia, when assembled ; and I hope from your candour, that you will confirm the sincerity of the declarations, by remarks derived from your personal knowledge of me, and to be inferred from the whole tenor of my conduct, as well in public as in private life.

I have the honour to be your obedient servant,

Signed,   A BURR

To his Excellency Cowles Mead, Esq

(D)

NATCHEZ, *February* 10

Col. Burr—On Monday the second inst an adjourned session of the Supreme Court of the Mississippi territory, was held in the town of Washington, to which Aaron Burr was recognized to appear, and answer such bill of indictment as might then and there be exhibited against him Col. Burr appeared on the day mentioned in his recognizance, attended by his counsel William B Shield and Lyman Harding, esqrs. Agreeable to *venire facias* issued by the honorable Thomas Rodney and Peter B Bruin, a Jury of seventy-two freeholders appeared in Court, and on the day following twenty-three of their number were selected by the Court as a grand inquest The honorable Thomas Rodney then delivered to them a comprehensive and impressive charge, and the Court was adjourned till ten o'clock the succeeding day, at which time Mr Poindexter, the attorney general, moved the Court to discharge the Grand Jury He stated that after examining the depositions submitted to him by the Court, he did not discover any testimony which brought the offence charged against Col. Burr, within the jurisdiction of the Courts of the Mississippi territory, and that the Supreme Court of the Mississippi territory, was not a Court of original jurisdiction, either criminal or civil, and could take cognizance only of points reserved at the trial in their respective Circuit Courts, where all criminal prosecutions must originate, according to the statutes of the territory He further observed that in order to secure the public safety, the territorial Judges ought immediately to convey the accused to a tribunal competent to try and punish him, (if guilty of the charges alledged against him) which they might legally do, and hereby effectually prevent the contemplated military expedition against Mexico, and maintain inviolate the constitution of the United States He therefore hoped that insomuch as the attorney prosecuting for the United States had no bills for the consideration of the Grand Jury, that they would be discharged.

Col Burr made several observations against the motion, and remarked, that if the attorney general had no business for the Grand Jury, *he had*, and therefore they ought not to be dismissed On this motion the Court was divided Judge Bruin declared himself opposed to discharging the Grand Jury, unless Colonel Burr was also instantly discharged from his recognizance

The attorney general then withdrew, and the Grand Jury were directed to retire to their room, who in the course of the day returned with sundry presentments

---

At a Supreme Court held for the Mississippi territory, at the town of Washington, on Tuesday the 3d of February, 1807

The Grand Jury of the Mississippi territory, on a due investigation of the evidence brought before them, are of opinion that Aaron Burr has not been guilty of any crime or misdemeanor against the laws of the United States, or of this territory, or given any just occasion for alarm or inquietude to the good people of this territory.

The Grand Jury present as a grievance the late military expedition unnecessarily, as they conceive, fitted out against the person and property of said Aaron Burr, where no resistance had been made to the ordinary civil authority

The G and Jury also present as highly derogatory to the dignity of this government, the armistice (so called) concluded between the secretary, acting as governor, and the said Aaron Burr.

The Grand Jury also present as a grievance destructive of personal liberty, the late military arrests, made without warrant and as they conceive, without other lawful authority; and they do seriously regret that so much cause has been given to the enemies of our glorious constitution, to rejoice at such measures being adopted in a neighboring territory, as if sanctioned by the executive of our country, must sap the vitals of our political existence, and crumble this glorious fabric in the dust.

P Smith, foreman,	Lewis Evans,
Ebenezer Rees,	James Spain,
James Andrews,	John Brooks,
Love Baker,	J. Guion,
George Overakes,	H Turnep,
John Rabb,	Nathl Hoggatt,
L Newman,	James Dunbar
John Wood	

On Wednesday evening, the Grand Jury were discharged, and Col Burr demanded his release from his recognizance—this the Court refused He did not appear in Court, on Tuesday morning, it was reduced to a certainty that he had made his escape

We understand that his excellency governor Williams, intended to seize on the person of Col Burr, the moment he was discharged by the judicial authority.

(E)
BY ROBERT WILLIAMS,
GOVERNOR OF THE MISSISSIPPI TERRITORY
A PROCLAMATION.

WHEREAS *Aaron Burr,* esq late Vice President of the United States, was bound in recognizance to appear at the Supreme Court of this territory, himself in the sum of five thousand dollars, and two securities in the sum of two thousand five hundred dollars each, " to answer any bills of indictment that might be found against him, and to continue to appear from day to day until dismissed by the said Court," which he has failed to comply with, and as it appears, has made his escape.

I do therefore, issue my proclamation for apprehending the said Aaron Burr, esq and by the powers and authorities which I possess, will pay, or cause to be paid, to any person or persons, who will take the person of said Aaron Burr, and cause him to be delivered to me at this place, or to the President of the United States, the sum of *two thousand dollars.*

Given under my hand, at the town of Washington, this 6th day of February, 1807.

ROBERT WILLIAMS.

(F)

The following letters appear in the late Mississippi papers, as having passed between Col. Burr and governor Williams

---

[*No Date*]

Sir—The vindictive temper and unprincipled conduct of Judge Rodney, having induced me to withdraw for the present from public view, I nevertheless continue in the disposition which has been uniformly manifested, of submitting to civil authority, so long as I can be assured, that it will be exercised towards me within the limits prescribed for other citizens.

It is proper however, before again surrendering, that I be informed of the cause or charge, if any, for which it is proposed to arrest me. whether bail be received, the tenor of recognizance and the sum in which security will be required. I ask further your assurance, that no attempt to send me out of the territory will be countenanced or permitted, and that my person shall not be subjected to any military arrest

I have the honor to be, &c

A BURR

His excellency governor Williams

12th February, 1807

Sir—I have seen your proclamation. It was unworthy of you to lend your sanction to a falshood. The recognizance on which I was bound, was on condition that I should appear in case an indictment should be found against me, and not otherwise. This special form was agreed on by Judge Rodney, after nearly half an hour's discussion, between him, Mr. Harding, and myself drawn up at his request by Mr Harding, and signed by the Judge in our presence, and in that of Col. Osmun, and will be found in the hand writing of Mr Harding, so signed, unless for fraudulent purposes, the Judge shall have destroyed it If he shall deny these facts, he must be as lost to shame as to principle If he shall admit them or they shall be otherwise established to your satisfaction, it is hoped that you will feel it to be your duty by a public manifesto, to cancel your proclamation, and to acknowledge the error on which it has been founded

A BURR

His excellency governor Williams.

Washington, *February* 13, 1807

Sir—Your two notes, the one without date and the other under that of yesterday, I have this moment received. Without any madverting on the usual style which you have permitted to yourself, I can only say, that from the judicial proceedings in the territory. you cannot be considered in any other light than as fugitive from the laws of your country; with these you are to well acquainted not to know, that it belongs to a department different from mine, to determine as to the nature of your offence and to decide as to the manner in which you are to be treated Hence you must see, it would be as improper, as it would be undignified in me, to enter into any stipulations as to your surrender In justice to myself however, I will observe, that so long as have the honor to preside in this territory, I shall never use the military, except in aid of the civil authority, and that if you submit yourself to this, you may be assured, that it shall "be exercised towards you within the limits prescribed for other citizens," similarly situated

I have the honor to be; &c

ROBERT WILLIAMS

Col. Aaron Burr.

(G)

WASHINGTON CITY, *January 22*

To the Senate and House of Representatives of the United States.

Agreeably to the request of the house of representatives, communicated in their resolution of the 16th inst. I proceed to state under the reserve therein expressed, information received touching an illegal combination of private individuals against the peace and safety of the union, and a military expedition planned by them against the territories of a power in amity with the United States, with the measures I have pursued for suppressing the same.

I had, for some time, been in the constant expectation of receiving such further information as would have enabled me to lay before the legislature the termination, at the beginning and progress of this scene of depravity, so far as it has been acted on the Ohio and its waters. From this the state of safety of the lower country might have been estimated on probable grounds, and the delay was indulged the rather, because no circumstance had yet made it necessary to call in the aid of the legislative functions. Information now recently communicated, has brought us nearly to the period contemplated. The mass of what I have received in the course of these transactions is voluminous: but little has been given under the sanction of an oath, so as to constitute formal and legal evidence. It is chiefly in the form of letters, often containing such a mixture of rumors, conjectures and suspicions as render it difficult to sift out the real facts, and unadviseable to hazard more than general outlines, strengthened by concurrent information, or the particular credulity of the relator. In this state of the evidence, delivered sometimes too under the restriction of private confidence, neither safety nor justice will permit the exposing names, except that of the principal actor, whose guilt is placed beyond question.

Some time in the latter part of September, I received intimations that designs were in agitation in the western country, unlawful and unfriendly to the peace of the union: and that the prime mover in these, was Aaron Burr, heretofore distinguished by the favor of this country. The grounds of the intimations being inconclusive, the objects uncertain and the fidelity of that country known to be firm, the only measures taken was to urge the informants to use their best endeavors to get further insight into the designs and proceedings of the suspected persons, and to communicate them to me.

It was not till the latter part of October that the objects of the conspiracy began to be perceived, but still so blended and involved in mistery that nothing distinct could be singled out for pursuit. In this state of uncertainty, as to the crime contemplated the acts done, and the legal course to be pursued, I thought it best to send to the scene, where these things were principally in transaction, a person in whose integrity, understanding and discretion, entire confidence could be reposed, with instructions to investigate the plots going on, to enter into conference (for which he had sufficient credentials) with the governors, and all other officers, civil and military, and with their aid, to do on the spot whatever should be necessary, to discover the designs of the conspirators, arrest their means, bring their persons to punishment, and to call out the force of the country to suppress any unlawful enterprize, in which it should be found they were engaged. By this time it was known that many boats were under preparation, stores of provisions collecting, and an unusual number of suspicious characters in motion on the Ohio, and its waters. Besides dispatching the confidential agent to that quarter, orders were at the same time sent to the governors of the Orleans and Mississippi territories, and to the commanders of the land and naval forces there, to be on their guard against surprize, and in constant readiness to resist any enterprize which might be attempted on the vessels, ports or other objects under their care. and on the 8th of November, instructions were forwarded to Gen. Wilkinson to hasten an accommodation with the Spanish commandant on the Sabine, and, as soon as that was effected, to fall back with his principal force to the hither bank of the Mississippi, for the defence of the interesting points on that river. By a letter received from that officer of the 25th of November, but dated October 21st, we learnt that a confidential agent of Aaron Burr had been deputed to him with communications, partly written in cypher, and partly oral, explaining his designs, exaggerating his resources, and making such offers of emolument and command, to engage him and the army in his unlawful enterprize, as he had flattered himself would be successful. The general, with the honor of a soldier, and fidelity of a good citizen, immediately dispatched a trusty officer to me with information of what had passed, proceeded to establish such an understanding with the Spanish commandant on the Sabine as permitted him, to withdraw his force across the Mississippi, and to enter on measures for opposing the projected enterprize.

The general's letters which came to hand on the 25th of November, as has been mentioned, and some other information received a few days earlier, when brought together, developed Burr's general designs, different parts of which only had been revealed to different informants. It appeared that he contemplated two distinct objects, which might be carried on either jointly or separately, and either the one or the other first, as circumstances should direct. One of these was the severance of the union of these States by the Allegany mountains, the other an attack on Mexico. A third object was provided, merely ostensible, to wit, the settlement of the pretended purchase of a tract of country on the Washita, claimed by a baron Bastrop. This was to serve as the pretext for all his preparations, an allurement for such followers as really wished to acquire settlements in that country, and a cover under which to retreat in the event of a final discomfiture of both branches of his real design.

He found at once that the attachment of the Western country to the present union was not to be shaken, that its dissolution could not be effected with the consent of its inhabitants; and that his resources were inadequate, as yet, to effect it by force.—He took his course then at once, determined to seize on New Orleans, plunder the bank there, possess himself of the military and naval stores, and proceed on his expedition to Mexico, and to this object all his means and preparations were now directed. He collected from all the quarters where himself or his agents possessed influence, all the ardent, restless, desperate and disaffected persons who were ready for any enterprize analogous to their characters. He seduced good and well meaning citizens, some by assurances that he possessed the confidence of the government, and was acting under its secret patronage, a pretence which procured some credit from the state of our differences with Spain; and others by offers of land in Bastrop's claim on the Washita.

This was the state of my information on his proceedings about the last of November, at which time therefore it was first possible to take specific measures to meet them. The proclamation of November 27, two days after the receipt of General Wilkinson's information, was now issued. Orders were dispatched to every interesting point on the Ohio and Mississippi, from Pittsburgh to New Orleans for the employment of such force, either of the regulars or of the militia, and of such proceedings also of the civil authorities, as might enable them to seize on all boats and stores provided for the enterprize, to arrest the persons concerned, and to suppress effectually the further progress of the enterprize. A little before the receipt of these orders in the state of Ohio, our confidential agent, who had been diligently employed investigating the conspiracy, had acquired sufficient information to open himself to the governor of that state, and to apply for the immediate exertion of the authority and power of the state to crush the combination. Governor Tiffin and the legislature, with the promptitude, and energy, and patriotic zeal, which entitle them to a distinguished place in the affection of their sister states, effected the seizure of all the boats, provisions and other preparations within their reach, and thus gave a first blow, materially disabling the enterprize in its outset.

In Kentucky a premature attempt to bring Burr to justice without sufficient evidence for his conviction, had produced a popular impression in his favour, and a general disbelief of his guilt.—This gave him an unfortunate opportunity of hastening his equipments. The arrival of the proclamation and orders, and the application and information of our confidential agent, at length awakened the authorities of that state to the truth, and then produced the same promptitude and energy of which the neighboring state had set the example. Under an act of their legislature of December 23, militia was instantly ordered to different important points, and measures taken for doing whatever could yet be done. Some boats (accounts vary from five to double or treble that number) and persons (differently estimated from one to three hundred) had in the mean time passed the falls of the

Ohio to rendezvous at the mouth of Cumberland, with others expected down that river. Not apprised till very late that any boats were building on Cumberland, the effect of the proclamation had been trusted to for some time in the state of Tennessee. But on the 19th of December, similar communications and instructions, with those of the neighboring states, were dispatched by express to the Governor, and a general officer of the western division of the state; and on the 23d of December our confidential agent left Frankfort for Nashville, to put into activity the means of that state also. But by information received yesterday, I learn that on the 22d of December, Mr Burr descended the Cumberland with two boats, merely of accommodation, carrying with him from that state no quota towards his unlawful enterprize. Whether after the arrival of the proclamation, of the orders, or of our agent, any exertion which could be made by that state, or the orders of the Governor of Kentucky for calling out the militia at the mouth of Cumberland, would be in time to arrest those boats, and those from the falls of Ohio, is still doubtful.

On the whole, the fugitives from the Ohio, with their associates from Cumberland, or any other place in that quarter, cannot threaten serious danger to the city of New-Orleans.

By the same express of December 19, orders were sent to the Governors of Orleans and Mississippi, supplementary to those which had been given on the 25th of November, to hold the militia of their territories in readiness to co-operate for their defence with the regular troops and armed vessels then under command of general Wilkinson. Great alarm indeed was excited at New-Orleans by the exaggerated accounts of Mr Burr, disseminated through his emissaries, of the armies and navies he was to assemble there. General Wilkinson had arrived there himself on the 24th of November, and had immediately put into activity the resources of the place for the purpose of its defence, and on the 10th of December he was joined by his troops from the Sabine. Great zeal was shewn by the inhabitants generally, the merchants of the place readily agreeing to the most laudable exertions and sacrifices for manning the armed vessels with their seamen; and the other citizens manifesting unequivocal fidelity to the union, and a spirit of determined resistance to their expected assailants.

Surmises have been hazarded that this enterprize is to receive aid from certain foreign powers. But these surmises are without proof or probability. The wisdom of the measures sanctioned by congress at its last session, has placed us in the paths of peace and justice with the only powers with whom we had any differences; and nothing has happened since, which makes it either their interest or ours to pursue another course. No change of measures has taken place on our part, none ought to take place at this time. With the one, friendly arrangement was proposed, and the law, deemed necessary on the failure of that, was suspended to give time for a fair trial of the issue. With the same power friendly arrangement is now proceeding, under good expectations, and the same law deemed necessary, on the failure of that is still suspended, to give time for a fair trial of the issue.

With the other, negociation was in like manner preferred, and provisional measures only taken to meet the event of rupture — While therefore we do not deflect in the slightest degree from the course we then assumed, and are still pursuing, with mutual consent, to restore a good understanding, we are not to impute to them practices as irreconcileable to interest as to good faith, and changing necessarily the relations of peace and justice between us to those of war. These surmises are therefore to be imputed to the vauntings of the author of this enterprize to multiply his partizans, by magnifying the belief of his prospects and support

By letters from Gen. Wilkinson of the 14th, and 18th of December, which came to hand two days after the date of the resolution of the house of representatives, that is to say, on the morning of the 18th inst I received the important affidavit, a copy of which I now communicate, with extracts of so much of the letters as come within the scope of the resolution. By these it will be seen that of three of the principal emissaries of Mr Burr, whom the general had caused to be apprehended, one had been liberated by Habeas Corpus, and two others being those particularly employed in the endeavour to corrupt the General and army of the United States, have been embarked by him for ports in the Atlantic States, probably on the consideration that an impartial trial could not be expected during the present agitations of New-Orleans, and that that city was not yet a safe place of confinement. As soon as these persons shall arrive, they will be delivered to the custody of the law, and left to such course of trial, both as to place and process, as its functionaries may direct. The presence of the highest judicial authorities, to be assembled at this place within a few days, the means of pursuing a sounder course of proceedings here than elsewhere, and the aid of the executive means, should the judges have occasion to use them, render it equally desirable for the criminal, as for the public, that being already removed from the place where they were first apprehended, the first regular arrest should take place here, and the course of proceedings receive here their proper direction.

TH. JEFFERSON

January 22, 1807.

Extract of a letter from General James Wilkinson, dated,
NEW-ORLEANS, *December* 14, 1806

" After several consultations with the governor and judges, touching the arrest and confinement of certain known agents and emissaries of Col Burr, in this city and territory, whose intrigues and machinations were to be apprehended, it is with their privity and approbation that I have caused three of them to be arrested. viz Doctor Erick Bollman, Samuel Swartwout, and Peter V Ogden, against who possess strong facts, and I have recommended to the governor to have James Alexander, esq. taken up on the grounds of strong suspicion. These persons and all others, who, by their character and deportment may be considered hostile to the interests of the United States, or dangerous to this feeble frontier under the menacing aspect of things from above, will, if my influence can prevail, be seized and sent by sea to the United States, subject to the disposition of government, and accompanied by such information as may justify their confinement, and furnish a clue to the developement of the grounds, progress and projectors of the treasonable enterprize in which they are engaged

" This letter will accompany Doc'or Bollman, who is to be this day embarked in a vessel bound for Charleston, under the charge of Lieut Wilson, of the artillery, who has orders to land with his prisoner, at Fort Johnson, or Fort Moultrie, to forward this dispatch by mail and to wait the orders of the executive Mr Swartwout will be sent to Baltimore by a vessel which will sail some time the ensuing week in custody of another subaltern, who will be the bearer of strong testimony against him and also Col Burr, and the others will follow under due precautions, by the earliest opportunities which may present

" I deem it essential to keep these prisoners apart, to prevent the adjustment of correspondent answers or confessions. to any examination which may ensue, and I hope the measures of the executive may be so prompt and efficient, as to relieve the officers in charge of them from their trust, before the interposition of the friends of the prisoners may effect their liberation

" By this procedure we may intimidate the confederates, who are unquestionably numerous in this as well as the adjacent territory, disconcert their arrangements and possibly destroy their intrigues, and I hope the zeal which directs the measure may be justified and approved. for whilst the glow of patriotism actuates my conduct, and I am willing to offer myself a martyr to the Constitution of my country, I should indeed be most grievously disappointed did I incur its censure

" Here Sir, we find the key to western states, and here we must form one grand depository and place of arms—combine to this disposition a river fleet competent to its occlusion and post it thirty or forty leagues above the Yazoo river, and we may repose in security, for the discontent and sufferings of our insurgent citizens which must immediately ensue, will soon open their eyes to the wickedness of their leaders and work a radical reformation without blood-shed This is my plan for resisting an internal attack—for external defence, gun-boats and bomb ketches with floating batteries at the mouths of the Mississippi and the passes from Lake Ponchartrain will be necessary

—

Extract of a letter from General James Wilkinson, dated,
NEW-ORLEANS, *December* 18, 1806

SIR—Since my last of the 14th inst writs of habeas corpus have been issued for the bodies of Bollman, Swartwout and Ogden, the two latter by judge Workman. who is strongly suspected for being connected with Burr in his conspiracy, as I have proof, this man declared some time since, that " the republican who possessed power and did not employ it to establish a despotism was a fool " His writ for Ogden was served on captain Shaw of the navy who had him in charge at my request, on board the Etna bomb ketch, and delivered him up. and Mr Workman discharged him without giving me a word of information although he knew he was confined by my order for a treasonable combination with Burr, and Mr. Ogden now struts at large. Swartwout I have sent off and shall so report, holding myself ready for consequences. Bollman was required by the Superior Court, but I have got rid of that affair also, under the usual liability for damages, in which case I shall look to our country for protection.

—

I, James Wilkinson, brigadier general and commander in chief of the army of the United States, to warrant the arrest of Dr Erick Bollman on a charge of treason, misprison of treason, or such other offence against the government and laws of the United States, as the following facts may legally charge him with—on my honor as a soldier, and on the Holy Evangelists of Almighty God, do declare and swear, that on the sixth day of November last, when in command at Natchitoches, I received by the hands of a Frenchman, a stranger to me, a letter from Doctor Erick Bollman, of which the following is a correct copy

"NEW-ORLEANS, *September* 27, 1806.
"SIR—I have the honor to forward to your excellency the *enclosed letters*, which I was charged to deliver to you by our mutual friend. I shall remain for some time at this place, and should be glad to learn where and when I may have the pleasure of an interview with you. Have the goodness to inform me of it, and please to direct your letter to me, care of———, or enclose it under cover to them. I have the honor to be with great respect, Sir,

Your excellency's most obedient servant,
    Signed,   ERICK BOLLMAN."
General Wilkinson

—

Covering a communication in cypher from Colonel Aaron Burr, of which the following is substantially as fair an interpretation as I have heretofore been able to make, the original of which I hold in my possession

"I (Aaron Burr) have obtained funds and have actually commenced the enterprize—detachments from different points and under different pretences will rendezvous on the Ohio 1st November—every thing internal and external favors views—Protection of England is secured—*T———is gone to Jamaica to arrange with the admiral on that station and will meet at the Mississippi——England——Navy of the United States are ready to join and final orders are given to my friends and followers—it will be an host of choice spirits——Wilkinson shall be second to Burr only—Wilkinson shall dictate the rank and promotion of his officers—Burr will proceed westward 1st August -never to return—with him go his daughter—the husband will follow in October with a *corps of worthies*—send forthwith an intelligent and confidential friend with whom Burr may confer. He shall return immediately with further interesting details—this is essential to concert harmony of movement.——Send a list of all persons known to Wilkinson west of the mountains, who could be useful, with a note delineating the characters. By your messenger send me four or five of the commissions of your officers which you can borrow under any

* *Truxton*

pretence you please —They shall be returned faithfully—Already are orders to the contractor given to forward six months provisions to points Wilkinson may name—this shall not be used until the last moment, and then under proper injunctions—the project is brought to the points so long desired—Burr guarantees the result with his life and honor—the lives, the honor and fortunes of hundreds, the best blood of our country—Burr's plan of operations is to move down rapidly from the falls on the 15th of November with the first five hundred or one thousand men in light boats now constructing for that purpose—to be at Natchez between the 5th and 15th of December—then to meet Wilkinson—then to determine whether it will be expedient in the first instance to seize on or pass by Baton Rouge—on receipt of this, send Burr an answer—draw on Burr for all expences &c The people of the country to which we are going, are prepared to receive us—their agents now with Burr say, that if we will protect their religion and will not subject them to a foreign power, that in three weeks all will be settled. The Gods invite to glory and fortune—it remains to be seen whether we deserve the boon The bearer of this goes express to you—he will hand a formal letter of introduction to you from Burr, a copy of which is hereunto subjoined, he is a man of inviolable honor and perfect discretion—formed to excute rather than project—capable of relating facts with fidelity and incapable of relating them otherwise He is thoroughly informed of the plans and intentions of————, and will disclose to you as far as you enquire and no further—he has imbibed a reverence for your character and may be embarrassed in your presence—put him at ease and he will satisfy you Doctor Bollman, equally confidential, better informed on the subject and more intelligent will hand this duplicate—29th July "

The day after my arrival at this city, the 26th of November last, I received another letter from the doctor, of which the following is a correct copy.

NEW ORLEANS, *November 25,* 1806

SIR,—" Your letter of the 6th inst has been duly received
" Supposing that you will be much engaged this morning I defer
" waiting on your excellency till you will be pleased to inform me
" of the time when it will be convenient to you to see me. I re
" main with great respect

" Your excellency's most
" obedient servant,

Signed,   ERICK BOLLMAN "

His excellency
Gen. Wilkinson, Fauxbourg

Marigny, the house between Madame Treigne and M. Macarty.

On the 30th of the same month I waited in person on doctor E Bollman, when he informed me that he had not heard from Col Burr since his arrival here—that he (the said doctor E Bollman) had sent dispatches to Col Burr, by a lieutenant Spence of the navy, and that he had been advised of Spence's arrival at Nashville, in the state of Tennessee—and observed, that Col. Burr had proceeded too far to retreat, that he (Col. Burr) had

numerous and powerful friends in the United States, who stood
pledged to support him with their fortunes, and that he must succeed That he, the said Dr E Bollman, had written to Col Burr
on the subject of provisions, and that he expected a supply would
be sent from New-York, and also from Norfolk, where Col Burr
had strong connections. I did not see or hear from the Doctor
again until the 5th inst. when I called on him the second time.
The mail having arrived the day before, I asked him whether he
had received any intelligence from Col Burr He informed me
that he had seen a letter from Col. Burr of the 30th October, in
which he (Colonel Burr) gave assurances that he should be at
Natchez with two thousand men on the 20th of December inst.
where he should wait until he heard from this place. That he
would be followed by four thousand more, and that he (Col. Burr)
if he had chosen, could have raised or got twelve thousand as
easy as six thousand, but that he did not think that number necessary—confiding fully in this information I became indifferent
about further disguise I then told the Doctor that I should most
certainly oppose Col Burr if he came this way. He replied,
they must come here for equipments and shipping, and observed
that he did not know what had passed between Col Burr and
myself, obliqued as a sham defence and waved the subject.

From the documents in my possession, and the several communications, verbal as well as written, from the said Doctor Erick
Bollman on this subject, I feel no hesitation in declaring under the
solemn obligation of an oath, that he has committed misprison of
treason against the government of the United States

Signed,   JAMES WILKINSON
Signed and sworn to this 14th day of December, 1806, before
me, one of the justices of this peace of this county

Signed,   I CARRICK.

PHILADELPHIA, *July 25*, 1806.
DEAR SIR—Mr Swartwout, the brother of Col. S. of New
York, being on his way down the Mississippi, and presuming
that he may pass you at some post on the river, has requested
of me a letter of introduction, which I give with pleasure, as he is a
most amiable young man, and highly respectable from his character and connections. I pray you to afford him any friendly offices
which his situation may require, and beg you to pardon the trouble which this may give you.

With entire respect,
Your friend and obedient servant,

A BURR.

His excellency General Wilkinson.

(H)

The following MESSAGE, containing a further developement
of the CONSPIRACY, was communicated to the two houses of
of Congress on Monday.

To the Senate and House of Representatives of the United States.
I received from General Wilkinson, on the 23d instant, his
affidavit, charging Samuel Swartwout, Peter V. Ogden, and

James Alexander, with the crimes described in the affidavit, a copy of which is now communicated to both houses of Congress

---

It was announced to me at the same time, that Swartwout and Bollman, two of the persons apprehended by him, were arrived in this city, in custody each of a military officer I immediately delivered to the attorney of the United States in this district, the evidence received against them, with instructions to lay the same before the Judges, and apply for their process to bring the accused to justice, and I put into his hands orders to the officers having them in custody, to deliver them to the marshal on his application

TH JEFFERSON,

January 26, 1807

I James Wilkinson, brigadier General, and commander in chief of the army of the United States, to warrant the arrest of Samuel Swartwout, James Alexander, esq and Peter V Ogden, on a charge of treason, misprison of treason, or such other offence against the government and laws of the United States, as the following facts may legally charge them with, on the honor of a soldier, and the holy evangelists of almighty God—do declare and swear, that in the beginning of the month of October last, when in command at Natchitoches, a stranger was introduced to me by Col Cushing, by the name of Swartwout, who a few minutes after the Col. retired from the room, slipt into my hand a letter of formal introduction from Col Burr, of which the following is a correct copy.

PHILADELPHIA, *July 25, 1806.*

DEAR SIR—Mr. Swartwout, the brother of Col S of New York, being on his way down the Mississippi, and presuming he may pass you at some post on the river, has requested of me a letter of introduction, which I give with pleasure, as he is a most amiable young man, and highly respectable from his character and connections. I pray you to afford him any friendly offices which his situation may require, and beg you to pardon the trouble which this may give you.

With entire respect,

Your friend and obedient servant.

A BURR

His excellency General Wilkinson

Together with a packet which he informed me, he was charged by the same person to deliver to me in private This packet contained a letter in cypher, from Col Burr, of which the following is substantially as fair an interpretation as I have heretofore been able to make, the original of which I hold in my possession.

" I (Aaron Burr) have obtained funds and have actually commenced the enterprize——detachments from different points and under different pretences will rendezvous on the Ohio, 1st Nov——every thing internal and external favors views—Protection of

England is secured—T—— is going to Jamaica to arrange with the admiral on that station; it will meet on the Mississippi ——England——Navy of the United States are ready to join and final orders are given to my friends and followers—it will be an host of choice spirits—Wilkinson shall be second to Burr only,—Wilkinson shall dictate the rank and promotion of his officers—*Burr* will proceed westward 1st August—never to return—with him go his daughter—the husband will follow in October with a *corps* of *worthies*—send forth—with an intelligent and confidential friend with whom Burr may confer He shall return immediately with further interesting details—this is essential to concert an harmony of movement Send a list of all persons known to Wilkinson, west of the mountains, who may be useful, with a note delineating their characters By your messenger send me four or five of the commissions of your officers which you can borrow under any pretence you please—They shall be returned faithfully——Already are orders to the contractor given to forward six months provisions to points Wilkinson may name—this shall not be used until the last moment, and then under proper injunctions—the project is brought to the point so long desired—Burr guarantees the result with his life and honor—with the lives, the honor, and fortunes of hundreds the best blood of our country—Burr's plan of operations is to move down rapidly, from the falls on the 15th of November with the first five hundred or one thousand men, in light boats, now constructing for that purpose—to be at Natchez between the 5th and 15th of December—there to meet Wilkinson—there to determine whether it will be expedient, in the first instance to seize on or pass by Baton Rouge—on receipt of this send Burr an answer,—draw on Burr for all expenses, &c. The people of the country to which we are going are prepared to receive us—their agents, now with Burr, say that if we will protect their religion, and will not subject them to a foreign power, that in three weeks all will be settled The Gods invite to glory and fortune—it remains to be seen whether we deserve the boon The bearer of this goes express to you—he will hand a formal letter of introduction to you from Burr, he is a man of inviolable honor and perfect discretion—formed to execute rather than to project—capable of relating facts with fidelity, and incapable of relating them otherwise. He is thoroughly informed of the plans and intentions of————, and will disclose to you as far as you enquire and no further—he has imbibed a reverence for your character, and may be embarrassed in your presence—put him at ease and he will satisfy you —July 29 "

I instantly resolved to avail myself of the reference made to the bearer, and in the course of some days drew from him, (the said Swartwout) the following disclosure—" That he had been
" dispatched by Col Burr from Philadelphia, had passed through
" the States of Ohio and Kentucky, and proceeded from Louis-
" ville for St. Louis, where he expected to find me, but disco-
" vering at Kaskaskias, that I had descended the river, he pro-
" cured a skiff, hired hands, and followed me down the Mis-
" sissippi to fort Adams, and from thence set for Natchitoches,
" in company with captains Sparks and Hooke, under the pre-
" tence of a disposition to take part in the campaign against the

C

" Spaniards, then depending. That Col. Burr with the support of
" a powerful association, extending from New York to New Or-
" leans, was levying an armed body of seven thousand men from
" the state of New York and the western states, and territories,
' with a view to carry an expedition against the Mexican pro-
" vinces, and that five hundred men under Col. Swartwout, and
" a Col or Maj Tyler were to descend the Allegany, for
' whose accommodation light boats had been built and were rea
" dy" I enquired what would be their course. He said " This
" territory would be revolutionized, where the people were ready
" to join them, and that there would be some seizing he sup-
" posed at New Orleans—that they expected to be ready to em-
" bark about the first of February and intended to land at Vera
" Cruz, and to march from thence to Mexico." I observed that
there were several millions of dollars in the bank at this place,
to which he replied, "We know it full well," and on my re
marking, that they certainly did not mean to violate private
property, he said, " they merely meant to borrow and would
" return it, that they must equip themselves in New Orleans,
" that they expected naval protection from Great Britian—That
" the captain——and the officers of our navy were so disgusted
" with the government that they were ready to join—that similar
" disgust prevailed throughout the western country, where the
' people were zealous in favor of the enterprize, and that pilot
' boat built schooners were contracted for, along our southern
" coast for their service—that he had been accompanied from
" the falls of Ohio, to Kaskaskias, and from thence to fort Adams
" by a Mr Ogden, who had proceeded on to N Orleans with let
" ters from Col Burr to his friends there" Swartwout asked me
whether I had heard from Dr Bollman, and on my answering
in the negative, he expressed great surprize, and observed—
" that the Doctor and a Mr Alexander had left Philadelphia
before him with dispatches for me, and that they were to pro
ceed by sea to New Orleans where he said they must have ar
rived`

Though determined to deceive him if possible, I could not re
frain telling Mr Swartwout, it was impossible that I could ever
dishonor my commission and I believe I duped him by my ad
miration of the plan, and by observing—" That although I could
not join in the expedition—the engagements which the Spaniards
had prepared for me in my front, might prevent my opposing it'
Yet I did, the moment I had decyphered the letter, put it into
the hands of Col Cushing, my adjutant and inspector, making
the declaration, that I should oppose the lawless enterprize with
my utmost force Mr Swartwout informed me he was under engagements to meet Col Burr at Nashville the 20th of November
and requested of me to write him, which I declined, and on his
leaving Natchitoches about the 15th of October, I immediately
employed lieutenant T A Smith, to convey the information in
substance to the President, without the commitment of names,
for from the extraordinary nature of the project, and the more
extraordinary appeal to me, I could but doubt its reality, notwithstanding the testimony before me, and I did not attach solid
belief to Mr Swartwout's reports respecting their intentions ou

this territory and city, until I received confirmatory advice from St Louis

After my return from the Sabine, I crossed the country to Natchez, and on my descent of the Mississippi from that place, I found Swartwout and Peter V. Ogden at Fort Adams; with the latter I held no communication, but was informed by Swart wout, that he (Ogden) had returned so far from New Orleans on his route to Tennessee, but had been so much alarmed by certain reports in circulation, that he was afraid to proceed I enquired, whether he bore letters with him from New Orleans, and was informed by Swartwout that he did not, but that a Mr. Spence had been sent from New Orleans through the country to Nashville, with letters for Col Burr,

I reached this city the 25th ult and on the next morning James Alexander, esq visited me, he enquired of me aside, whether I had seen Doctor Bollman, and on my answering in the negative, he asked me whether I would suffer him to conduct Bollman to me, which I refused He appeared desirous to communicate something, but I felt no inclination to inculpate this young man, and he left me A few days after, he paid me a second visit, and seemed desirous to communicate, which I avoided, until he had risen to take leave, I then raised my finger and observed, " take care, you are playing a dangerous game," he answered—" it will succeed"—I again observed—" take care"—and he replied with a strong affirmation—" Burr will be here by the beginning of next month " In addition to these corroborating circumstances against Alexander, I beg leave to refer to the accompanying documents, A. and B.—from all which I feel no hesitation in declaring, under the solemn obligation of an oath, that I do believe the said Swartwout, Alexander, and Ogden, have been parties to, and have been concerned in the insurrection, formed or forming in the States and Territories on the Ohio and Mississippi rivers, against the laws and Constitution of the United States

Signed,   JAMES WILKINSON.

Sworn to and subscribed, before me, this twenty-sixth day of December, in the year of our Lord one thousand eight hundred and six   GEORGE POLLOCK,

Justice of the Peace for the County of Orleans

---

(1)

SUPREME COURT OF THE UNITED STATES.

February Term, 1807

THE UNITED STATES *vs.* BOLLMAN AND SWARTWOUT.

Habeas Corpus on a commitment for Treason

Chief Justice MARSHALL, *on the twenty first instant, delivered the following opinion of the Court*

The prisoners having been brought before this Court on a writ of Habeas Corpus, and the testimony on which they were committed having been fully examined, and attentively considered, the Court is now to declare the law upon the case

1 This being a mere enquiry which, without declaring upon guilt, precedes the institution of a prosecution, the question to be determined is, whether the accused shall be discharged or held

to trial, and in the latter, in what place they have to be tried, and whether they shall be confined or admitted to bail. " If," says the very learned and accurate commentator, " upon this enquiry it manifestly appears that no such crime has been committed, or that the suspicion entertained of the prisoner was wholly groundless, in such cases only it is lawfully totally to discharge him   Otherwise he must either be committed to prison or give bail "

2   The specific charges brought against the prisoners is treason in levying war against the United States.

3.   As there is no crime which can more excite and agitate the passions of men than treason, no charge demands more from the tribunal before which it is made than a temperate and deliberate enquiry   Whether this enquiry be directed to the fact or to the law, none can be more solemn, none more important to the citizens or to the government, none can more affect the safety of both

4   To prevent the possibility of those calamities which result from the extension of treason to offences of minor importance, that great fundamental law which defines and limits the various departments of our government, has given a rule on the subject, both to the legislature and the courts of America which neither can be permitted to transcend

5   " *Treason against the United States shall consist only in levying war against them, or in adhering to their enemies, giving them aid and comfort* '   To constitute that specific crime for which the prisoners now before the Court have been committed, war must be actually levied against the United States   However flagitious may be the crime of conspiring to subvert the government of our country, such conspiracy is not treason   To conspire to levy war, and actually levying war, are two distinct offences   The first must be brought into operation by the assemblage of men for a purpose treasonable in itself   or the fact of levying war cannot be committed. So far has this principle been carried, that in a case reported by Ventris, and mentioned in some modern treatise on criminal law, it has been determined that the actual enlistment of men to serve against the government does not amount to levying war   It is true, that in that case the soldiers enlisted were to serve without the realm, but they were enlisted within it, and if the enlistment for a treasonable purpose could amount to levying war, then war had been actually levied

6.   It is not the intention of the Court to say, that no individual has been guilty of the crime who has not appeared in arms against his country   On the contrary, if war be actually levied, that is, if a body of men be actually assembled for the purpose of effecting by force, a treasonable purpose, all those who perform any part, however minute, and however remote from the scene of action, and who are actually leagued in the general conspiracy, are to be considered as traitors   But there must be an actual assembling of men for the treasonable purpose, to constitute the levying of war.

7.   Crimes so atrocious as those which have for their object the subversion by violence of those laws and those institutions which

have been ordained in order to secure the peace and happiness of society, are not to escape punishment because they have not ripened into treason. The wisdom of the legislature is competent to provide for the case, and the framers of our Constitution, who not only defined and limited the crime, but with jealous circumspection, attempted to protect their limitation, by providing that no person should be convicted by it, unless on the testimony of two witnesses, to the same overt act, or on confession in open Court, must have conceived it more safe that punishment in such cases should be ordained by general laws, formed upon deliberation, under the influence of no resentments, and without knowing on whom they were to operate, than that it should be inflicted under the influence of those passions which the occasion seldom fails to excite, and which a flexible definition of the crime, or a construction which would render it flexible, might bring into operation. It is, therefore, more safe, as well as consonant to the principles of our Constitution, that the crime of treason should not be extended by construction to doubtful cases, and that crimes, not clearly within the constitutional definition, should receive such punishment as the legislature in its wisdom may provide.

8. To contemplate the crime of levying war against the U. States, there must be an actual assemblage of men for the purpose of executing a treasonable design. In the case now before the Court, a design to overturn the government of the U. States, in New Orleans, by force, would have been, unquestionably, a design which, if carried into execution, would have been treason; and the assemblage of a body of men for this purpose, of carrying it into execution, would amount to levying war against the United States, but no conspiracy for the object, no enlistment of men to effect it, would be an actual levying of war.

9. In conformity with the principles now laid down, have been the decisions heretofore made by the Judges of the United States.

9. The opinions given by Judge Patterson and Judge Iredell, in cases before them, imply an actual assemblage of men, though rather designed for remark on the purpose to which the force was to be applied, than on the nature of the force itself. Their opinions however, contemplate the actual employing of force.

11. Judge Chase, in the trial of Fries was more explicit, p. 107.

12. He stated the opinion of the Court to be, " that if a body of people conspire, and meditate an insurrection to resist or oppose the execution of any statute of the United States, by force, they are only guilty of a high misdemeanor; but if they proceed to carry such intention into execution by force, that they are guilty of the treason of levying war; and the *quantum* of force employed, neither lessens nor increases the crime; whether by one hundred or one thousand persons, is wholly immaterial — ' The Court are opinion," continued Judge Chase, on that occasion, " that a combination or conspiracy to levy war against the United States is not treason, unless combined with an attempt to carry such combination or conspiracy into execution; some actual force or violence must be used in pursuance of such design to levy war; but it is altogether immaterial whether the

force used is sufficient to effectuate the object, any force connected with the intention, will constitute the crime of levying war."

13. The application of these general principles to the particular case before the Court, will depend on the testimony which has been exhibited against the accused.

14. The first deposition to be considered is that of General Eaton This gentleman connects in one statement, the purport of numerous conversations held with Col Burr throughout the last winter. In the course of these conversations were communicated various criminal projects, which seem to have been revolving in the mind of the projector. An expedition against Mexico seems to have been the first and most matured part of his plan, if indeed, it did not constitute a distinct and separate plan, upon the success of which other schemes still more culpable, but not yet well digested, might depend Maps and other information preparatory to its execution, and which would rather indicate that it was the immediate object, had been procured; and for a considerable time, in repeated conversations, the whole efforts of Col Burr were directed to prove to the witness, who was to have held a high command under him, the practicability of the enterprize, and in explaining to him the means by which it was to be effected.

15 This deposition exhibits the various schemes of Col Burr, and its materiality depends on connecting the prisoners at the bar in such of those schemes as were treasonable For this purpose the affidavit of General Wilkinson, comprehending in its body the substance of a letter from Col Burr, has been offered, and was received by the Circuit Court To the admission of this testimony, great and serious objections have been made It has been urged, that it is a voluntary, or rather, an extra-judicial affidavit, made before a person not appearing to be a magistrate and contains the substance only of a letter, of which the original is retained by the person who made the affidavit.

16 The objection, that the affidavit is extra-judicial, resolves itself into the question, whether one magistrate may commit, on an affidavit taken before another magistrate? For if he may, an affidavit made as the foundation of a commitment, ceases to be extra-judicial, and the person who makes it would be as liable to a prosecution for perjury as if the warrant of commitment had been issued by the magistrate before whom the affidavit was made.

17 To decide that an affidavit made before one magistrate, would not justify a commitment by another, might in many cases be productive of great inconvenience, and does not appear susceptible of abuse, if the verity of the certificate be established Such an affidavit seems admissible, on the principle that before the accused is put upon his trial, all the proceedings are *exparte* The Court, therefore, overruled this objection

18 That which questions the character of the person, who has on this occasion administered the oath, is next to be considered

19. The certificate from the office of the department of State has been deemed insufficient by the counsel for the prisoners,

because the law does not require the appointment of magistrates for the territory of New Orleans, to be certified to that office, because the certificate is in itself informal, and because it does not appear that the magistrate had taken the oath required by the act of Congress.

20. The first of these objections is not supported by the law of the case, and the second may be so readily corrected that the Court has proceeded to consider the subject, as if it were corrected, retaining, however, any final decision, (if against the prisoners) until the correction shall be made

21 With regard to the third, the magistrate must be presumed to have taken the requisite oaths, since he is found acting as a magistrate

22. On the admissibility of that part of the affidavit which purports to be as near the substance of the letter from Col Burr to General Wilkinson, as the latter could interpret it, a division of opinion has taken place in the Court. Two Judges are of opinion, that as such testimony, delivered in the presence of the prisoner on his trial, would be totally inadmissible, neither can it be considered as a foundation for a commitment Although in making a commitment, the magistrate does not decide on the guilt of the prisoner, yet he does decide on the probable cause, and a long and painful imprisonment may be the consequence of his decision The probable cause, therefore, ought to be proved by testimony in itself legal, and which, though from the nature of the case, it must be *ex parte*, ought in most other respects, to be such as a Court and Jury might hear

23 Two Judges are of opinion, that in this incipient stage of the prosecution, an affidavit stating the general purport of a letter may be read, particularly where the person in possession of it is at too great a distance to admit of its being obtained, and that a commitment may be founded on it.

24 On this embarrassment it was deemed necessary to look into the affidavit, for the purpose of discovering whether, if admitted, it contains matter which would justify the commitment of the prisoners at the bar, on the charge of treason.

25 That the letter from Col Burr to Gen Wilkinson, relates to a military enterprize, meditated by the former, has not been questioned If this expedition was against Mexico, it would amount to high misdemeanor, if against any of the territories of the United States, or if in its progress, the subversion of the government of the United States, in any of their territories, was a mean clearly and necessarily to be employed, if such mean formed a substantive part of the plan, the assemblage of a body of men to effect it, would be levying war against the United States

26 The letter is in language which furnishes no distinct view of the design of the writer The co-operation, however, which is stated to have been secured, points strongly to some expedition against the Territories of Spain. After making these general statements, the writer becomes rather more explicit, and says, " Burr's plan of operations is to move down rapidly from the falls on the 15th of Nov with the first five hundred or a thousand men, in light boats, now constructing for that purpose, to be at Natchez

between the 5th and 15th of December, there to meet Wilkinson, then to determine whether it will be expedient, in the first instance, to seize on, or to pass by Baton Rouge The people of the country to which we are going, are prepared to receive us Their agents, now with Burr, say, that if we will protect their religion, and not subject them to a foreign power, in three weeks all will be settled "

27 There is no expression in these sentences which would justify a suspicion that any territory of the United States was the object of the expedition

28. For what purpose seize on Baton Rouge? why engage Spain against this enterprize, if it was designed against the U States?

29 " The people of the country to which we are going are prepared to receive us." This language is peculiarly appropriate to a foreign country It will not be contended that the terms would be inapplicable to a territory of the United States, but other terms would more aptly convey the idea, and Burr seems to consider himself as giving information of which Wilkinson was not possessed When it is recollected, that he was the Governor of a territory adjoining that which must have been threatened (if a territory of the United States was threatened) and that he commanded the army, a part of which was stationed in that Territory, the probability, that the information communicated related to a foreign country, it must be admitted, gains strength

30 " Their agents, now with Burr, say, that if we will protect their religion, and will not subject them to a foreign power, in three weeks all will be settled "

31 This is apparently the language of a people who, from the contemplated change of their political situation, feared for their religion, and feared that they would be made the subject of a foreign power That the Mexicans should entertain these apprehensions was natural, and would readily be believed. They were, if the representation made of their dispositions be correct, about to place themselves much in the power of men who professed a faith different from theirs, and who, by making them dependent on England or the United States, would subject them to a foreign power.

32 That the people of New Orleans, as a people, if really engaged in the conspiracy, should feel the same apprehensions, and require assurances on the same points, is by no means so obvious

33 There certainly is not, in the letter delivered to General Wilkinson, so far as that letter is laid before the Court, one syllable, which has a necessary or a natural reference to any enterprize against any Territory of the United States

34 That the bearer of this letter is to be considered as acquainted with its contents, is not to be controverted. The letter and his own declarations, evince the fact

35 After stating, himself, to have passed through New York and the Western States and territories, without insinuating that he had performed on his rout any act whatever, which was

connected with the enterprize, he states, their object to be " to carry an expedition to the Mexican provinces "

36 This statement may be considered as explanatory of the letter of Col Burr, if the expressions of that letter could be thought ambiguous

37 But there are other declarations made by Mr Swartwout, which constitute the difficulty of the case On an enquiry from General Wilkinson, he said, " this territory would be revolutionized where the people were ready to join them, and that there would be some seizing, he supposed, at New Orleans "

38 If these words import, that the government established by the United States in any of its territories, was to be revolutionized by force, although merely as a step to, or a mean of executing some greater projects, the design was unquestionably treasonable, and any assemblage of men for that purpose, would amount to levying war ; but on the import of the words, a difference of opinion exists. Some of the Judges suppose they refer to the territory against which the expedition was intended — others to that in which the conversation was held Some consider the words, if even applicable to a territory of the United States, as alluding to a revolution to be effected by the people, rather than by the party conducted by Col Burr

39. But whether this treasonable intention be really imputable to the plan or not, it is admitted that it must have been carried into execution by an open assemblage of men for that purpose, previous to the arrest of the prisoner, in order to consummate the crime as to him, and a majority of the Court is of opinion, that the conversation of Mr. Swartwout affords no sufficient proof of such assembling

40 The prisoner stated, that " Col. Burr, with the support of a powerful association, extending from New York to New Orleans, was levying an armed body of seven thousand men, from the State of New York, and the Western States and territories, with a view to carry an expedition to the Mexican territories."

41 That the association, whatever may be its purpose, is not treason, has been already stated. That levying an army, may or may not be treason, and that this depends on the intention with which it is levied, and on the point to which the parties have advanced, has also been stated The mere enlisting of men without assembling them, is not levying war The question then is, whether this evidence proves Col Burr to have advanced so far in levying an army, as actually to have assembled them

42 It is argued that since it cannot be necessary that the whole seven thousand men should have assembled, their commencing their march by detachments to the place of rendezvous, must be sufficient to constitute the crime

43 The position is correct, with some qualification It cannot be necessary that the whole army should assemble, and that the various parts which are to compose it, should have combined — But it is necessary that there should be an actual assemblage, and therefore, the evidence would make the fact unequivocal.

44 The travelling of individuals to the place of rendezvous would perhaps, not be sufficient. This would be an equivocal act, and has no warlike appearance The meeting of particular

D

bodies of men, and their marching from places of partial, to places of general rendezvous, would be such an assemblage.

45 The particular words used by Mr Swartwout, are, that " Col Burr was levying an armed body of seven thousand men." If the term *"levying"* in this place, imports that they were assembled, then such fact would amount, if the intention be against the United States, to levying war. If it barely imports that he was enlisting or engaging them in his service, the fact would not amount to levying war

46 It is thought sufficiently apparent, that the latter is the sense in which the term is used. The fact alluded to, if taken in the former sense, is of a nature so to force itself upon the public view, that if the army had actually been assembled, either together or in detachments, some evidence of such assembling would have been laid before the Court

47 The words used by the prisoner in reference to the seizing at New Orleans, and borrowing by force from the bank, though indicating a design to rob, and consequently importing a high offence, do not designate the specific crime of levying war against the United States.

48 It is therefore the opinion of a majority of the Court, that in the case of Samuel Swartwout, there is not sufficient evidence of his having levied war against the United States, to justify a commitment on the charge of treason

49 Against Erick Bollman there is still less testimony. Nothing has been said by him to support the charge, that the enterprize in which he was engaged had any other object than was stated in the letter of Col Burr. Against him therefore there is no evidence to support a charge of treason

50 That both the prisoners were engaged in a most culpable enterprize against the dominions of a foreign power at peace with the United States, those who admit the affidavit of general Wilkinson, cannot doubt, but that no part of this crime was committed in the district of Columbia, is apparent. It is therefore the unanimous opinion of the Court, that they cannot be tried in this district

51. The law read on the part of the prosecution, is understood to apply only to offences committed on the high seas, or in any river, haven, bason, or bay, not within the jurisdiction of any particular State. In these cases there is no Court which has particular cognizance of the crime, and therefore the place in which the criminal shall be apprehended, or if he be apprehended where no Court has exclusive jurisdiction, that to which he is first brought shall be substituted for the place in which the offence was committed.

52 But in this case a tribunal for the trial of the offence where it may have been committed, had been provided by Congress, and at the place where the prisoners were seized by the authority of the commander in chief, there exists such a tribunal. It would be too extremely dangerous to say, that because the prisoners were apprehended, not by a civil magistrate, but by the military power, there could be given, by law, a right to try the persons so seized in any place which the general might select, and to which he might direct them to be carried.

53. The act of Congress which the prisoners are supposed to have violated, describes as offenders, those who begin to set on foot, or provide or prepare the means for any military expedition, or enterprize to be carried on from thence against the dominions of a foreign prince or State, with whom the United States are at peace.

54 There is a want of precision in the description of the offence, which might produce some difficulty in deciding what cases would come within it, but several other questions arise, which a Court consisting of four Judges finds itself unable to decide; and therefore, as the crime with which the prisoners stand charged has not been committed, the Court can only direct them to be discharged This is done with less reluctance, because the discharge does not acquit them from the offence which there is probable cause for supposing they have been committed on. and if those whose duty it is to protect the nation by prosecuting the offenders against the laws, shall suppose those who have been charged with treason to be proper objects for punishment, they will, when possessed of less exceptionable testimony, and when able to to say at what place the offence has been committed, institute fresh proceedings against them

------

(I)
Deposition of Colonel Cushing.

On or about the 8th of October, 1806, I was sitting at the dining table in my quarters at Natchitoches with General Wilkinson, when a gentleman entered the room and enquired for Col. Cushing I rose to receive him, and he presented to me the letter from General Dayton, of which the following is an exact copy, viz —

ELIZABETH-TOWN, N. J *July 27, 1806.*

" DEAR SIR—This will be presented to you by my nephew, a son of the late General Matthias Ogden, who commanded one of the Jersey Regiments in the Revolutionary War, and whom you probably relcollect. He is on his way to New Orleans, and is advised by me to call at your post, if it should be fort Adams, or elsewhere upon the Mississippi, as I am told it is. His merits and the esteem in which he is held by me, make me anxious to procure for him a welcome reception, even for the short stay of a few hours, that he will be able to make with you

"Any instance of friendly attention or assistance shewn to him, and his very worthy companion Mr Swartwout, will be gratefully acknowledged, and regarded as a favor conferred on" Dear Sir,
     Your sincere friend,

     And very humble servant,
          (Signed)   JONATHAN DAYTON.
Colonel Cushing.

(K)
PHILADELPHIA, *July 25, 1806.*

DEAR SIR—Mr. Swartwout, the brother of Colonel Swartwout of New York, being on his way down the Mississippi. and presuming he may pass you at same post on the river, has requested of me a letter of introduction, which I give with pleasure, as he is a most amiable young man, and highly respectable from his character and connections. I pray you to afford him any friendly of fices which his situation may require, and beg you to pardon the trouble which this may give you

With entire respect.

Your friend and obedient servant,

A. BURR

His Excellency General Wilkinson
Mr Swartwout.

(L)

Copy of a letter from General Dayton to General Wilkinson, written in cypher, except those parts printed in *Italicks* This cypher was designed by Gen Dayton, and founded on the Hieroglyphics known to Gen Wilkinson and Col Burr.

July 24th, 1806.

X Λ! ᐧ)-☉~*I*~⌒ᐧV ᐧ~☉-*IΛ*"
* []

It is now well ascertained that you are to be displaced in the next session Jefferson will affect to yield reluctantly to the public sentiment, but yield he will Prepare yourself therefore for it you know the rest.

You are not a man to despair or even despond, especially when such prospects offer in another quarter Are you ready ? Are your numerous associates ready ? wealth and glory, Louisiana and Mexico—*I shall have time to receive a letter from you before I set out for Ohio* —OHIO *Address one to me here, and another to me in Cincinnati Receive and treat my nephew affectionately as you would receive your friend.*

DAYTON.

FROM THE RICHMOND ENQUIRER.

Cyphers —In compliance with a previous promise, we present our readers with the following account of the *cyphers*, which have been exhibited to the Court during the late trial. They may serve to gratify their curiosity, and afford some amusement for an idle hour.

General Wilkinson and Burr began their correspondence in cypher, about the year 1800, or 1801, and near the period at which the latter ascended the chair of the Vice-Presidency. For this purpose they adopted three different cyphers The first of these is called the *hieroglyphic cypher,* and was invented by General Wilkinson and Captain Campbell Smith, as long ago as the year 1794, '95, or 96, for the purpose of communicating confidentially with General Wilkinson's officers in the western country. (Another cypher of a somewhat similar construction, was devised by Capt Smith in 1791, in which the hieroglyphics representing the President and Vice-President, are the same with those used in the cypher with Col Burr) The second is denominated the *arbitrary alphabet cypher,* and was formed by Burr and Wilkinson, in the year 1799, or 1800. The third is styled *the Dictionary cypher,* and was adopted by them in the year 1800 The famous letter from Burr to General Wilkinson, of 22d July, 1806, delivered by Swartwout at Natchitoches, and its duplicate of 29th of the same month, conveyed by Bollman, were written partly in each of those cyphers, and partly in English.

The following is a specimen of the hæroplyphic cypher:

President,   O
Vice-President,   ⊙
Secretary of State,   &c

These characters representing the opposite words, whenever they occur in a letter.

The arbitrary alphabet cypher, was in fact, nothing more than a substitution of other characters in the place of the letters, which actually compose the alphabet, and instead of the figures from 1 to 10

Thus A B C D E &c 1 2 . &c

With these new signs words were composed, and numbers represented at discretion.

The dictionary cypher, was of the following description. The Wilmington edition of the year 1800, of Entick's pocket dictionary, served as the key, by which such parts of the letters as were written in figures, were to be interpreted. For example, if the figures 3, 4, were used, the figure 3 pointed to the page in the book, and the 4 to the number of the word intended, counting from the top, in the first or second column on the page · which latter circumstance was also indicated by a slight mark above or below the 4

Gen 'Dayton's letters of 16th and 24th July, which were forwarded in company with Burr's, by Swartwout and Bollman, were written partly in the hieroglyphic and arbitrary alphabet cyphers above described, partly in English, but principally in Dayton's own cypher, called the cypher of which the key-word is France

It is composed in the following manner: the letters of the alphabet are numbered thus ·

· 1 2 3 4 5 . &c
 A · B · C · D · E · &c

In order to decypher a letter, or passages of a letter written in cypher take the first letter of the key-word F, fix on that letter in the series of the alphabet; count forward from that letter, as many letters as are equal to the first figure in the cyphered letter; as 8 for example, which will give I; and I will be the first letter of the first word. Then take the second letter of the key-word, as R; and in the same manner, as in the first instance, count forward as many letters as are equal to the second figure, as 2, which will give the second letter, T, which completes the first word, IT, continue in the same way with the ensuing letters of the key-word, till they are finshed; and then begin again: thus going through the key-word again and again till the letter is completed.

In the cyphered letter, the figures, or aggregates of figures, representing words, are separated by commas.

There was another cypher in use among some of the accomplices in this enterprize, the *key-word* of which was CUBA. The use of this cypher may be understood from the following scheme and explanations

	C	U	B	A
1	C	U	B	A
2	d	v	c	b
3	e	w	d	c
4	f	x	e	d
5	g	y	f	e
6	h	z	g	f
7	i	a	h	g
8	j	b	i	h
9	k	c	j	i
10	l	d	k	j
11	m	e	l	k
12	n	f	m	l
13	o	g	n	m
14	p	h	o	n
15	q	i	p	o
16	r	j	q	p
17	s	k	r	q
18	t	l	s	r
19	u	m	t	s
20	v	n	u	t
21	w	o	v	u
22	x	p	w	v
23	y	q	x	w
24	z	r	y	x
25	a	s	z	y
26	b	t	a	z

In order to compose a letter in this species of cypher, find in the column under the first letter in the key word, the first letter of the word which you wish to write, and the figure opposite to this letter represents the first letter of that word. To find the figure expressive of the second letter, look for that letter in the second column, and the figure opposite to that letter, represents the second letter in the word. Continue in the same way, with respect to the other two columns, if it be a word of three or four letters. But if it contains more than four letters, you must return to the first column, and proceed in the same manner; that is, the fifth letter of the word is to be found in the first column under C, the sixth letter in the second column, and so on. Thus, if *Hope* was the first word in the epistle, look for the letter H in the first column under C, which is opposite to the figure 6, as the representative of the first letter, the letter O is to be sought for in the second column, and is represented by the number 21, and so on with the letters P and E.

In the cyphered letter, the figures representing letters are separated by commas; the words are separated by periods.

The reader will immediately perceive, that besides *France* and *Cuba*, any other words might be used as the key-words of these cyphers, according to the discretion of the writer and his correspondent. The difficulty of discovering the key to one of these cyphered letters, would be still further augmented by the writer's shifting his key word for different epistles, according to some rule previously agreed upon 'The difficulty would be incalculably increased, if the writer not only continues to shift his key word, but the cypher itself'

There was another cypher in use, the key-word ALSTON; of the principle of which we have not yet received an explanation.

(M)

Sir—I have concluded to undertake the land *purchose* which we *talket* of last winter and *determet* to go on the lands this fall, any number of settlers could be had on this side the mountains, but I should *prefor* to have the gieater part from the western country—you promised to write about the horses, but have heard nothing from you, and suppose there will be no difficulty on that head—The money for the first payment is now ready—I shall be *att* Frankfort *abouth* the 15th *Augus* and hope then to meet you and Col Lynch there—It is quite necessary that I should see Lynch as I shall be provided with cash to go on vigorously with our speculation—Some of the concerned are now on their way to see you and will be with you nearly as soon as this letter—Please to encourage them and give them a good acount of things.

Your humble servant,
(Signed)   A. STEPHENS
Johnn Peters, esq —Nashville.

(N)

Letter from fiom Doctor Bollman to General Wilkinson, of the 27th September, 1806.

New Orleans, *September* 27, 1806.

Sir—I have the honor to forward to your excellency, the enclosed letters, which I am charged to deliver to you by our mutual friend.

I shall remain for some time at this place, and shall be glad to learn where and when I may have the pleasure of an interview with you Have the goodness to inform me of it, and please to direct your letters to me to the care of Messis Chew and Relf, or enclose under cover to them

I have the honor to be,
With great iespect, Sir,
Your excellency's most obedient servant.

(Signed)   ERICK BOLLMAN
Gen. Wilkinson

(O)

July 16th, 1807

My Dear Friend—As you are said to have removed your head quarteis down the river, and there is a report that the Spaniards intercept our mails, which pass necessarily through the territory occupied by them, in order to reach you, I think proper to address you in cypher, that the contents may be concealed from the Dons, if they make so free as to open the letter. Take

the following for the catch-word or check-word, (and you m'
very readily decypher the figures) viz in your own hieroglyphic
[ ], but in your own alphabet thus, [hieroglyphics.]
    V⌒—O I A

Every thing, and even heaven itself appears to have conspired
to prepare the train for a grand explosion, are you also ready?
For I know you flinch not when a great object is in view—Your
present is more favorable than your late position, and as you can
retain it without suspicion or alarm, you ought by no means to
retire from it until your friends join you in December somewhere
on the river Mississippi. Under the auspicies of Burr and
Wilkinson I shall be happy to engage, and when the time arrives
you will find me near you.

Write and inform me by first mail what may be expected from
you and your associates In an enterprize of such moment, considerations even stronger than those of affection impel me to de
sire your cordial co-operation and active support

                                                   DAYTON.

    Wealth and honor,   ⎤
Adieu,   ⎬   Burr and Wilkinson
    Courage and union   ⎦

Let me hear from you by mail, as well as by the first good private conveyance, and believe me with the best wishes for your
prosperity and happiness most truly,

    Your friend and servant,

                                 JONA DAYTON.

If you write in cypher, ⎫ [Hieroglyphics]
use the same words, viz ⎬   V⌒—O—I A

Note The key word to this letter in cypher is *France*

_____

(P)

*Extract of a letter from James L. Donaldson, esq. to General James
Wilkinson, dated Natchez, October 30, 1806.*

" Michael Myers, arrived here to day in fifteen days from St.
Louis, on his way to New Orleans He made a communication to
me with permission to transmit to you, which might stagger even
credulity, of this information *he says he is certain,* and most
firmly believes in the intelligence he communicates. This is
neither more nor less, than a plan to revolutionize the western
country has been formed, matured, and is ready to explode, that
kentucky, Ohio, Tennessee, Orleans and Indiana are combined
to declare themselves independent on the 15th of November.—
That proposals have been made to some of the most influential
characters at St Louis, by an accredited agent of the conspiracy
to join the plan. That this person, whose name Myers refuses
to reveal, is in a most respectable line of life, and had the most
unquestionable vouchers of his mission in French and English.
That he declared, if *money* was necessary, that it might be commanded to any extent. It is proper to add, that the persons thus
applied to at St. Louis, altogether refused to concur in any plan
of the kind, saying, that it should be only superior force, that
should dispense with their oath of fidelity to the United States.

" This may all appear to a person as well acquainted as you
" are with the politics of the western country, as *a second Spanish conspiracy*, and as such be ridiculed, and such is my im-
" pression of the wonderful plan   But Myers so firmly believed
" it, that having set forth on his journey by land to the United
" States, he was induced by his fears hastily to return to arrange
" his business at all events, and prepare for an explosion. He
" most solemnly protests the truth of the communication, and
" declares there are only four persons in St. Louis who are privy
" to the disclosure made by the secret agent   It is not improba-
" ble that this may be a " Ruse de guerre," a stratagem set on
" foot by the patrons of the Western World, to foster and keep
" alive the dissention, which, excited by the pretended exposi-
" tion of ancient conspiracies, may be fanned into a flame by
" spreading an alarm of an immediately and pressing treasonable
" combination. This I am apt to believe is the case, and in or-
" der more fully to succeed, they may study and affect mystery,
" as better calculated to excite suspicion, and that they may have
" the honor of a *New Discovery*   However, be the matter as it
" may, I communicate it to you as I received it, and have only
" to regret, that you had it not in person from Myer's informa-
" tion, of which, whatever your judgment might pronounce, the
" solemnity of his assertion and his certainty of the plan (altho'
" he was not at liberty to divulge the means) must have stagger-
" ed the mind *capable of believing it* "

(Q.)

Sir,

Your letter of the 6th inst. has been duly received. Supposing that you will be much engaged this morning, I defer waiting
on your excellency, till you will be pleased to inform me of the
time when it will be convenient to you to see me.

I remain with great respect,
Your Excellency's
Most obedient Servant,

(Signed)   ERICK BOLLMAN

New-Orleans, 25th Nov. 1806
His Excellency General Wilkinson, Fauxbourg, Marigny, the house between Ma-
dam Trevigne & Malle M'Carty.

St. Louis, *May 6th*, 1806.

Sir,

You are to embark to-morrow, and will sail early the next
morning with Lockwood's and Strong's Cos for fort Adams,
and on arriving there, you are to add Campbell's company to
your detachment, and must proceed without a moment's unnecessary delay up Red river, to Nachitoches, where you are to
take the command.

The point of your destination being deemed at present a critical one, it is desirable your companies should be kept complete ;
to the establishment and for this purpose, you are to make such
disposition of the recruits ordered from Tennessee or elsewhere,
as may be found necessary.

Vol. 3   E

Your remote position from the posts east of the Mississippi, renders it convenient and necessary that they should, as heretofore, report directly to and receive orders from head quarters, but the commandants are to report to you monthly, and will be liable to your orders as senior officers of the district, whenever the public service may require the interposition of your authority, which should be made with due caution to avoid clashing with the arrangements which may issue from head quarters

The posts west of the Mississippi are subject to your immediate command, and are to be governed accordingly. You are to appoint General Courts Martial within the limits of your district, and are to decide on all sentences which may not affect a commissioned officer agreeably to the rules and articles of war

At the distance which separates us, it would be vain and presumptuous to prescribe precise rules for your conduct in command, where the occurrence of incidents and change of circumstances may be so unexpected and variable as to baffle anticipation and to render positive orders destructive to the interests of the country. You are therefore to meet the public service with a sound discretion, and will be held responsible for events The trust is a high and important one; but it is with singular pleasure I can observe, that my long experience of your judgment and capacity, leaves no doubts on my mind, the result will justify the public confidence, and prove honorable to your name and profession.

I will therefore submit one observation only to your consideration, it is, that you should not fail to employ the force confided to your command, wherever it may be found most necessary, to protect or defend the rights and interests of our country within the sphere of your authority

With the warmest wishes for your fame and happiness,

  I am, Sir,

   Your faithful friend,

    and obedient servant,

     JAMES WILKINSON

Colonel TH : CUSHING, }
2nd Reg't Infantry. }

(S)

Instructions from General Wilkinson to Colonel Cushing

   ST LOUIS, May 8, 1806
    1 o'clock, A M

SIR,

Advice yesterday received from Major Porter, makes it my duty to direct the acceleration of your movements by every practicable means, and I trust that in the present state of the waters, you may reach fort Adams on the 20th inst.

On arriving at that post, the information you may receive, must determine the course of your conduct. should the Spaniards have resumed their positions east of the Sabine, or assumed a menacing aspect at Nacogdoches, you must add to your command every man at fort Adams, excepting a mere *locum tenens*, leaving orders at that place for Lt Col. Kingsbury to fall down to the mouth of Red river, and there wait the return of a sufficient number of your barges for his transport to the high grounds, from whence it may become expedient for you to march the whole of your command excepting the boats crews.

I hope Major Porter may have taken the precaution to transmit the executive a copy of the information he has forwarded to me, and that you may receive from that source, at an early period, decisive instructions for your government; in the mean time, *tho' war be our trade*, it is not only opposite to the genius and disposition of our country, but also to its substantial interests. The sword must not, therefore, be drawn but in the last extremity, to punish outrage, to resist invasion, or repel an attack

Should indications justify it, (and you must take measures to ascertain, if possible, the designs of *your neighbors*) you are to call to your aid every man who can be safely spared from the garrison, under your orders, and will employ every pains and exertion to put them in the highest state of fitness for offensive operations

You will find in the hands of Major Porter an order from the Secretary at war, which might justify you in pushing your neighbors beyond the Sabine river, should they have re-crossed it to the eastward. But as it appears from the public prints, that a pacific negociation has, on our part, ensued these orders, you must not strain their construction to favor the effusion of blood, and involve our country in the certain calamities and uncertain events of war

Learn with all possible precision, the force, composition and station of the troops opposed to you be yourself prepared for combat, and if a conflict must ensue, having previously animated your men by a strong exhortation, and sworn your officers, in their presence, to fall or conquer, make your onset with the bayonet, and your own glory the honor of our arms, and the interests of the nation, will be ensured and maintained

Wishing you life and laurels,
health and fame,
I am,
your faithful friend,
and fellow soldier,
JAMES WILKINSON

Col T H Cushing, 1st Reg U S Infantry

P S You are to take with you from fort Adams an 8 inch howitzer, which you will find there properly equipt and amply ammunitioned.

———

(*T*)

Extract of a letter from General James Wilkinson to the Honorable Henry Dearbourn, Secretary of war, dated Natchez, September 8th, 1806.

" I arrived at this place last evening at six o'clock and addressed a note to the Secretary of the territory (Gov Williams being absent,) of which you have a copy under cover with his answer ; this morning I waited on him, and have seen the plan adopted by Governor Claiborne and himself, the first article of which appears to be in direct opposition to your order respecting the removal of the Spaniards from Bayou Pierre, to which place I understand, they have fallen back, from the vicinity of Adayes and I hope they may continue there until my arrival at Nachitoches; for which place I shall commence my journey the moment after I have arranged with the Secretary of the territory for such auxilary force of militia, as may eventually become necessary from his jurisdiction; Governor Claiborne has, I understand, arrayed the militia in the western countries of the territory of Orleans, but I shall discourage their march, until I have penetrated the designs of the Spaniards, and may find him deaf to the solemn appeal which I shall make to his undertaking, his interests and duty

Let the President be assured, Sir, I shall drain the cup of conciliation to maintain the peace of our country, and the sword shall now be drawn, but in the last extremity, after reason and remonstrance have failed to preserve inviolate our territory east of the Sabine, but at the same time, that an awful responsibility retains the inclinations and ambition of the soldiers in this temperate course of conduct, in opposition to the order which I think I discern in the executive offices, of these territories. I will pledge my life to him that no act shall be suffered within my knowledge to tarnish the national honor or offect the lustre of his administration.

If the precautions furnished by my instructions to Col. Cushing, of which I transmitted you a copy from St Louis, have prevented the effusion of blood. I must believe I have done some good to the State, because the retrospection of the Spaniards has rendered the ultimate appeal unnecessary at least for the present, and nothing can be lost and every thing may be gained by a little delay, it seems better the opportunity for exciting hostilities should have escaped rather than it should have been seized on to let slip the dogs of war, before the effect of conciliatory measures had been duly trusted.

The retrograde of the Spaniards are not accounted for but may be ascribed to three causes, the unhealthiness of the troops, the want of forage for the immense cavalcade with which they are incumbered, or the failure of provisions, but as they would scarcely have made so formidable and bold an advance in the face of the prohibition uttered by Major Porter, without positive orders from the competent authority, it is reasonable to presume when the cause of their retrogression has been removed, they may resume their former position, for which events some preparatory arrangements must be commenced. The Spaniards who have approached Nachitoches being all mounted and without artillery, and each private being obliged too keep up four horses and a mule for service, out of his pay of an hundred dollars per month, it will be impossible for them to maintain a fortification but the same circumstance will enable them to refuse, or to give battle to our infantry at their discretion; to remedy this disadvantage and enable me, should I be forced to appeal to arms to drive them effectually beyond the Sabine or to cut them up, shall endeavor to procure about four or five hundred dragoons and mounted militia from the two territories, unless I should fin them so incautious as to enable me, by ...ced march of the established troops, to surprize their camp under cover of the night; but this is scarcely to be expected, if the commanding officer possesses a spark of military knowledge or experience.

A blow once struck, it would appear expedient that we should make every advantage of it, and if men and means are furnished, I will soon plant our standards on the left bank of Grand River. But I must beg leave to remark to you, that for distant operations, or the protection of our western frontier against the predatory incursions of the Spanish cavalry, a body of mounted men is absolutely indispensible

———

Copy of a letter from General Wilkinson to the Secretary at War.

Head Quarters, Natchitoches, October 4, 1806.

Sir—I yesterday morning received Governor Cordero's answer to my address of the 24th ult copies of which you have under cover The varied style of this letter, when contrasted with those of Governor Herrara and Colonel Cushing, and Governor Claiborne, combined to the circumstances of the Spanish troops having recrossed the Sabine to a man, has induced me on the ground of economy and expediency also to discharge the militia who had reached this place, and to countermand those under march, excepting about one hundred dragoons and mounted infantry, whom I shall retain in service, until I am apprized of the determination of the Captain General Salcedo, to watch the movements of our neighbors, to prevent their sinister intrigues with our disaffected citizens, and should they re-enter our territory, to aid the established troops in expelling them.

The Spaniards raised his camp at Bayou Pierre on the 27th ultimo; traversed the country to the high way, leading from this place to Nacogdoches, which he intersected on the 29th; about twenty-six miles in my front, and on the 30th crossed the Sabine and took post on the right bank, where Colonel Cushing left him the first inst. But notwithstanding I have been determined to diminish my force, as the pretensions of Governor Herrara have not been retracted, nor our jurisdiction acknowledged, and as the position taken on the right bank of the Sabine, is a material departure from the state of things at the surrender of the province to us, and exposes our territory to immediate invasion, I shall continue my preparations for defence and offence, and to wipe off the species of stigma which cavalliers may attach to the Spanish repossession of the ground, from whence we had driven them; to give confidence to our friends, to confirm the wavering and the disaffected; and above all, to assert unequivocally the pretentions of the government, I have taken post within the limits claimed by the officers of Spain, and in a few days shall move forward to the east bank of the Sabine, where I shall wait the arrival of Captain General Salcedo. Were I required to justify this step, I should reply, that the U.S having forced a Spanish guard to retire from a position within their acquired territory, that power protested against the act, denied their pretensions and armed for the avowed purpose of recovering the ground from which they had been driven. That a Spanish commander of respectable rank, at the head of a considerable force in military array, did not only recover the ground, but took a position much nearer to our barrier, and far within our limits. That this officer claimed the jurisdiction of the country east of the Sabine, to the Arroyo Hondo, and in behalf of his master the king of Spain, and declared his determination to protect and defend it as such. Were you to suffer such outrages upon the national sovereignty to pass over without notice, injurious interpretations might be levelled at our military character, and our forbearance might be construed into a tacit dereliction of our claims.

Under these circumstances, and to do away the shadow of right which the Spaniards may endeavor to found on their posterior occupancy, I feel it incumbent on me to take possession of the controverted tract to its utmost verge, where my conduct will be regulated by that of my neighbors, who the last evening occupied the spot where Colonel Cushing left him on the first instant, with his advanced guard mounted immediately on the bank of the river, but you may rest assured nothing shall be done on my part to excite unreasonable jealousies or provoke hostilities, and therefore to prevent the misinterpretation of my movements, I have taken the precaution to write Governor Cordero this day, warning him of my intentions, and the motives by which I am actuated agreeably to the copy now transmitted to you. Of the militia from this territory, about four hundred have turned out, which was more than I expected. From the Mississippi territory I have not yet heard, and therefore cannot say in what force they are advancing, I have hope from the aspect of Mr. Cordero's letter, and the actual state of their military at this moment, of which I have acquired the most clear and particular knowledge, that our differences here may be adjusted on honorable terms and without bloodshed. I shall however be prepared for events, and will keep you regularly advised of every material occurrence

With great consideration and respect,

I am Sir,

Your obedient servant,

JAS. WILKINSON

The Honorable Henry Dearborn, Secretary of War.

(U)

Letter from General Andrew Jackson, to his Excellency William C. C. Claiborne.

Sir —Although it is a long time since I wrote you, still that friendship that once existed, remains bright on my part, and although since I have had the pleasure of seeing you, I have waded through difficult and disagreeable scenes, still I have all that fondness for my old and former friends that I ever had, and their memory has been more endeared to me by the treachery I have experienced since I saw you, by some newly acquired ones. Indeed I fear treachery has become the order of the day. This induces me to write you. Put your town in a state of defence, organize your militia, and defend your city as well against internal enemies as external : my knowledge does not extend so far as to authorize me to go into detail, but I fear you will meet with an attack from quarters you do not at present expect. Be upon the alert; keep a watchful eye upon our General and beware of an attack, as well from our own country as Spain I fear there is something rotten in the state of Denmark You have enemies within your own city, that may try to subvert your government, and try to separate it from the union You know I never hazard ideas without good grounds—you will keep these hints to yourself But I say again, be upon the alert, your government I fear is in danger I fear there are plans on foot inimical to the union, whether they will be attempted to be carried into effect or not I cannot say, but rest assured they are in operation or I calculate boldly. Beware of the month of December I love my country and government—I hate the Dons, I would delight to see Mexico reduced, but I will die in the last ditch before I would yield a foot to the Dons, or see the union disunited This I write for your own eye and for your own safety, profit by it, and the Ides of March remember

  With sincere respect, I am as usual,

   Your sincere friend,

    (Signed)   ANDREW JACKSON

November 12, 1806

(W)

Copy of a letter from William White, to Col Andrew Burk, of New Orleans

    MIDDLETON, *December* 22, 1806.

DEAR SIR—Expect a large military force to take possession of of your city—should it not happen before this reaches you, you may look out with hourly expectation of seeing it headed by Col Burr

 This is intended, should you see it in time, to apprize, in order that you may be in readiness to take your advantages of the times —A number of persons from this neighborhood are engaged in this expedition, among the number is your old acquaintance Mr A. Ralston.

 Believe me to be, though much disappointed, still respectfully, yours.

    (Signed)   Wm WHITE.

Col. Andrew Burk, New Orleans.

(X)

Instruction to Lieutenant Pike

    ST LEWIS, June 24th, 1806

SIR,

  You are to proceed without delay to the cantonment on the Missouri, where you are to embark the late Osage captives, and the deputation recently returned from Washington, with their presents and baggage, and are to transport the whole up the Missouri and Osage rivers to the town of the Grand Osage.

 The safe delivery of this charge at the point of destination, constitutes the primary object of your expedition, and therefore you are to move with such caution as may prevent surprize from any hostile band, and are to repel with your utmost force any outrage which may be attempted.

Having safely deposited your passengers and their property, you are to turn your attention to the accomplishment of a permanent peace between the Canzus and Osage nations, for which purpose you must effect a meeting between the head chiefs of those nations, and are to employ such arguments, deduced from their own obvious interests, as well as the inclinations, desires, and commands of the President of the United States, as may facilitate your purpose and accomplish the end.

A third object of considerable magnitude will then claim your consideration It is to effect an interview and establish a good understanding with the Ya.r,tans, 1,c,tans, or Cammanchees

For this purpose you must interest Whitehair of the Grand Osage, with whom and a suitable deputation you will visit the Panis Republique, where you may find Interpreters, and inform yourself of the most feasible plan, by which to bring the Cammanchees to a conference —Should you succeed in this attempt; and no pains must be spared to effect it—you will endeavor to make peace between that distant powerful nation, and the nations which inhabit the country between us and them, particularly the Osage, and finally you will endeavor to induce eight or ten of their distinguished chiefs, to make a visit to the seat of government next September, and you may attach to this deputation four or five Panis, and the same number of Canzes Chiefs. As your interview with the Cammanchees will probably lead you to the head branches of the Arkansaw and Red Rivers, you may find yourself approximated to the settlements of New Mexico, and therefore it will be necessary you should move with great circumspection, to keep clear of any hunting or reconnoitreing parties from that province, and to prevent alarm or offence ; because the affair of Spain and the United States, appear to be on the point of amicable adjustment, and moreover it is the desire of the President, to cultivate the friendship and harmonious intercourse of all the nations of the earth, and particularly our near neighbors the Spaniards.

In the course of your tour, you are to remark particularly upon the geographical structure, the natural history and population of the country through which you may pass, taking particular care to collect and preserve specimens of every thing curious in the mineral or Botanical worlds, which can be preserved and are portable. Let your courses be regulated by your compass, and your distances by your watch, to be noted in a field book, and I would advise you when circumstances permit, to protract and lay down in a seperate book the march of the day at every evening's halt

The instruments, which I have furnished you, will enable you to ascertain the variation of the Magnetic Needle and the latitude with exactitude ; and at every remarkable point, I wish you to employ your telescope in observing the eclipses of Jupiter's Satelites, having previously regulated and adjusted your watch by your quadrant, taking care to note with great nicety the periods of immersions and emersions of the eclipsed Satelites These observations may enable us after your return by applica tion to the appropriate tables, which I cannot now furnish you, to ascertain the longitude.

It is an object of much interest with the executive, to ascertain the direction, extent and navigation of the Arkansaw, and Red River ; as far therefore as may be compatible with these instructions and practicable to the means you may command, I wish you to carry your views to those subjects, and should circumstances conspire to favor the enterprize, that you may detach a party with a few Osage to descend the Arkansaw under the orders of Lieutenant Wilkinson, or Sergeant Ballinger, properly instructed and equipped to take the courses and distances, to remark on the soil, timber, &c. &c. and to note the tributary streams. This party will, after reaching our post on the Arkansaw descend to fort Adams and there wait further orders, and you yourself may descend the Red River accompanied by a party of the most respectable Cammanchees to the post of Natchitoches and there receive further orders

To disburse your necessary expences and to aid your negotiations, you are herewith furnished six hundred dollars worth of goods, for the appropriation of which, you are to render a stric account, vouched by documents to be attested by one of your party.

Wishing you a safe and successful expedition,
I am Sir,

With much respect and esteem,
Your obedient servant,
JAMES WILKINSON.

(Signed)
Lieutenant Z. M Pike.

———

(*Y*)
Additional instructions to Lieutenant Pike.
Cantonment, Missouri, July 12th, 1806.

SIR,

The health of the Osages being now generaly restored, and all hopes of the speedy recovery of their prisoners, from the hands of the Powatomies, being at an end, they have become desirous to commence their journey for their villages, you are therefore to proceed to-morrow.

In addition to the instructions given y u on the 24th ultimo, I must request you to have the Talks under cover delivered to White Hair and the Grand Peste, the Chief of the Osage Band, which is settled on the waters of the Arkansaw, together with the belts which accompany them. You will also receive herewith a small belt for the Parris and a large one for the I,e,tans or Commanchees.

Should you find it necessary, you are to give orders to Mongrain the resident interpreter at the Grand Osage to attend you.

I beg you to take measures for the security and safe return of your boats from the Grand Osage to this place.

Doctor Robinson will accompany you as a volunteer. He will be furnished medicines, and for the accommodations which you give him, he is bound to attend your sick.

Should you discover any unlicensed traders in your route, or any person from this territory, or from the United States, without a proper licence or passport, you are to arrest such person or persons and dispose of their property as the law directs

My confidence in your caution and discretion, has prevented my urging you to be vigilant in guarding against the stratagems and treachery of the Indians, holding yourself above alarm or surprize, the composition of your party, though it be small, will secure to you the respect of an host of nntutored savages.

You are to communicate from the Grand Osage and from every other practicable point, directly to the Secretary of war, transmitting your letters to this place under cover, to the commanding officer, or by any more convenient route.

I wish you health and a successful and honorable enterprize, and am,

Yours with friendship,
JAMES WILKINSON.

Lieutenant Z M Pike.

(Z)

Extract of a letter from General Wilkinson to Gen S Smith, dated FORT ADAMS, 12th September, 1806

" At this moment thus stands the account between us and the Spaniards on the side of Texhas, we dishonor the armies of Spain and (as they alledge) violate their territory, by forcing their advanced post, and compelling their officer to fall back many miles (See General Dearborne's order to Potter) In consequence the Spaniard reinforces, advances, resumes his former ground and braves us. We remonstrate and menace, but he keeps possession of the disputed tract. Is not the balance against us? it is, my friend, and I will restore what we have—I trust in Heaven without blood-shed—but at all events "

------

(8)

GENERAL MORNING ORDERS,

Head Quarters, Camp La Piedra,
26 *miles from Natchitoches, October 28th,* 1806

PAROLE, }
C SIGN }

The depending movement of the troops, is not to seek an enemy, but to assert a right of sovereignty; this right is denied by the Spanish commander in our front, who has recently warned the General, that he considers his advance an act of hostility, which his orders compel him to resist Whatever then may be the calculation of the result, the safety and honor of the corps and the national interests require, that every individual attached to the expedition, should move and act as if an engagement was certain and inevitable We are obliged to wait the attack, and our opponents being all mounted, may give or refuse themselves at their discretion; and of consequence will avail themselves of any advantage we may offer them

The signal to prepare for action, when encamped, will be a gun from the left, on which every man who bears arms will take his place in the line, and the whole wait orders. The signal to form when under march, will be a gun from the front. The Infantry,

with their field pieces, will immediately form two lines with two
hundred yards interval, and on the flanks of the road; Farrar's
dragoons will retire by the road to the rear, and form column
prepared to charge; Major Welch's mounted infantry will skir-
mish and fall back, on the right or left of the front line, as the
ground and other circumstances may render most advantageous.
The moment the signal is given, the rear guard, Pioneers, and
every man of the line are to join their corps, leaving their packs
and teams in the charge of Mr Rogan and the engagers of the Quarter Master's and Contractor's departments Should an attempt
be made to turn our flanks, which is probable, the infantry will
form the hollow square, and the artillery take post on the angles
to enfilade the enemy with grape and canister Major Welch's
men to retire towards the rear and endeavor to out flank our assailants, keeping up as quick and deadly a fire as possible An
officer to each division of the infantry will take post with the
front rank, every other officer will be in the rear, to see the men
do not throw away their fire, and if one should be found so das-
tardly as to give back, to put him to instant death.

Under all circumstances the artillery will receive orders when
to fire; but the infantry, with shouldered arms, are to wait the
approach of the enemy, until within forty yards, when the front
rank is to present, level well, fire and charge bayonet If the
enemy are not broken or staggered, the second rank are to take
aim at their breasts, and when at fifteen yards are to pour in their
fire, and should they still come on, are to be received by both
ranks with doubtless resolution on their bayonets The dragoons
are reserved for a critical effort, and will receive orders when
and where to make it The gentlemen will bear in mind that
whatever may be the order of the charge, the instant they close
with the enemy, the action will become pell mell : They should
be careful to level their blows at the neck, rather horizontally
than perpendicularly, and in general to cut and pass from man
to man.

The Spanish force is greatly superior, and all mounted, but is
undisciplined. Their attack will be made in great disorder and
probably with velocity and an air of boldness, because they will
depend more on noise and appearance than the solid shock. It
will be our part to present a rampart of bayonets, whenever attacked Let the officers be attentive to their men, and the men
be silent and obedient to their officers. Let each individual put
confidence in his own strength and the co-operation of his flank
files. Above all, let us avoid hurry, which always produces confusion; and superiority of numbers will serve but to augment our
triumph, and encrease the honor of our arms.

(A a)
Extract of a letter from Leonard Covington to Gen Wilkinson.

MAY, 15th, '07.

You well know how much has been said and insinuated about
the memorable cyphered letter, handed you by Swartwout, and
of the means by which you unlocked the cypher, and altho' this
circumstance has never been explained by yourself or the admi-

nistration, and has been seized upon by your enemies as matter for crimination and ground for suspicion, yet I have never been at a loss, in my own mind, for the satisfactory explanation. You may not, perhaps, recollect, that in the year 1794, when I left the western country, (army,) that you requested me to interchange with you a cypher for the purpose of corresponding thereby; and at the time you informed me that you had practised that method with many of your friends. This circumstance coming to my recollection, I have examined amongst my old papers, and found the cypher, which is at your service, if it, and the circumstances connected therewith, can in any way advantage you. Pray snatch one moment, if possible, and let your friends here know how you feel and are situated, &c &c. Your favors by Mr J Johnson, all came safely to hand, and have warmed the feelings of your friends in this quarter. I pray God to keep you in his holy protection; and that he may make "thine enemies thy footstool." Farewell

L. COVINGTON.

Gen. JAS. WILKINSON.

———

(B b)
[DUPLICATE.]

Washington, Jan. 8, '07.

DEAR SIR,

I had intended yesterday to recommend to General Dearborne the writing to you weekly by post, to convey information of our western affairs as long as they are interesting; because it is possible, though not probable, you might sometimes get the information quicker this way than down the river, but the General received yesterday information of the death of his son in the E. Indies, and of course cannot now attend to business. I therefore write you a hasty line for the present week, and send it in duplicate by the Athens and Nashville routes.

The information in the enclosed paper as to proceedings in the state of Ohio, is correct. Blannerhasset's flotilla of fifteen boats and two hundred barrels of provisions, is seized, and there can be no doubt that Tyler's flotilla is also taken, because on the 17th December we know there was a sufficient force assembled at Cincinnati to intercept it there, and another party was in pursuit of it on the river above. We are assured that these two flotillas composed the whole of the boats provided. Blannerhasset and Tyler had fled down the river. I do not believe that the number of persons engaged for Burr has ever amounted to five hundred, though some have carried them to one thousand or fifteen hundred. A part of these were engaged as settlers of Bastrop's land, but the greater part were engaged under the express assurance that the projected enterprize was against Mexico, and secretly authorized by this government. Many were expressly enlisted in the name of the United States. The proclamation, which reached Pittsburg Dec. 2, and the other parts of the river successively, undeceived both these classes, and of course drew them off; and I have never seen any proof of their having assembled more than forty men in two boats from Beaver, fifty in Tyler's flotilla, and the boatmen of Blannerhasset's. I believe therefore that the enterprize may be considered as crushed, but we are not to relax in our attentions until we hear what has passed at Louisville. If every thing from that place upwards be successfully arrested, there is nothing from below that (is) to be feared. Be assured that Tennessee, and particularly General Jackson are faithful The orders lodged at Massac and the Chickasaw Bluffs will probably secure the interception of such fugitives from justice as may escape from Louisville, so that I think you will never see one of them. Still I would not wish, till we hear from Louisville, that this information should relax your preparations in the least, except so far as to dispense with the militia of Mississippi and Orleans leaving their homes, under our orders of November 25. Only let them consider themselves under requisition, and be in a state of readiness, should any force, too great for your regulars, escape down the river. You will have been sensible, that those orders were given while we supposed you were on the Sabine, and the supposed crisis did not admit the formality of their being passed through you. We had considered fort Adams as the place to make a stand, because it covered the mouth of Red River. You have preferred New Orleans, on the apprehension of a fleet from the West Indies Be assured, there is not any foundation for such an expectation, but the lying exaggerations of these traitors to impose on others and swell their pretended means The very man whom they represented to you as gone to Jamaica and to bring the fleet, has never been from home and has regularly communicated to me every thing which had passed between Burr and him No such proposition was ever hazarded to him. France or Spain would not send a fleet to take Vera Cruz; and though one of the expeditions, now near arriving from England, is probably for Vera Cruz, and perhaps already there, yet the state of things between us renders it impossible they should countenance an enterprize unauthorized by us. Still I repeat that these grounds of security must not stop our proceedings or preparations, until they are further confirmed Go on therefore with your works for the defence of New Orleans, because they will always be useful, only looking to what should be permanent rather than means merely temporary. You may expect further information as we receive it, and though I expect it will be such as will place us at our ease, yet we must not place ourselves so, until we be certain, but act on the possibility that the resources of our enemy may be greater and deeper than we are yet informed.

Your two confidential messengers delivered their charges safely One arrived yesterday, only with your letter of November 12 The oral communications he made me are truly important. I beseech you to take the most special care of the two letters which he mentioned to me, the one in cypher, the other from another of the conspirators of high standing, and send them to me by the first conveyance you can trust. It is necessary that all important testimony should be brought to one centre, in order that the guilty may be convicted, and the innocent left untroubled. Accept my friendly salutations and assurances of great esteem and respect.

TH: JEFFERSON.

*Copy of a postscript to a letter of General James Wilkinson, to John
M'Kee, dated New Orleans, Feb. 6, 1807.*

' If you want to distinguish yourself and tax the government
beyond denial, go alone and seize Burr, or Blannerhasset, or
Tyler or Raulstone, or Floyd, or any of them, and deliver them
to the flotilla "

———

CHICKASAWS, *February* 26, 1806

DEAR GENERAL—Your kind remembrancer of the 3d December, I received, and had written to you immediately after at the
Bluffs, but a French Indian countryman, who had promised to
call on me for it went off without doing so. I had written a great
deal about recruiting in Tennessee, about cutting and slashing,
and packing dollars, and enjoying otium cum dignitate. But
" *all our differences are amicably settled with Spain*" knocks all
these Utopia to the devil, and I am again awake to the painful
anxiety attendant on a state of suspense I have requested my
friend Moore to press the Secretary to decide, and I expect his
answer in less than a month Whatever my fate may be, I must
always feel myself deeply your debtor for the solicitude you have
manifested for me.

Has any news reached your capital from Captains Lewis and
Clark ? It is reported here that they have been killed, and I hope
sincerely there is nothing of it.

I have the honor to be,
    With esteem and affection,
        Your friend,

                                JOHN M'KEE

His excellency General Wilkinson

Mr. *Hay* Is that also your writing dated as late as February
last ? A It is.

Mr. *Wirt* At the time of this correspondence and before, did .
you consider General Wilkinson your friend, whose agency you
were willing to employ with the Secretary at war? A. I expected much less, Sir, from his interest than his disposition to serve
me

Mr. *Wirt* You cons   ed him then as a friend whom you
would be willing to trust? A. I did Q. Is this your writing?
A It is.

[Here Mr *Wirt* read the following letter]

———

CHICKASAWS, *August* 1, 1805.

DEAR SIR—Your friendly *talk* from Pittsburg. 13 May, I had
the pleasure to receive at this place a few days ago I thank you
sincerely for your letter to the Secretary of war. I hope it will
have the effect at least of relieving me from the most painful
suspense I have ever experienced. I had addressed him myself
from Tennessee, just before I set out, and am now beginning to
look out for his answer. I would have written you sooner on
the subject of my expectations, but I thought them so well founded as not to require even mentioning to the Secretary ; they were
founded on a direct and unsolicited promise, from himself to me,
that I should be provided for in Louisiana as soon as the govern-

ment should be organized. This was confirmed to me afterwards through Colonel Moore and General Trigg, and last winter he repeated to several of my friends his continued disposition to serve me, but I remained as ignorant as I was two years ago in that way. I hope it may be in your quarter, and soon, for a state of suspense is penance worse by far than fasting. I trust like a good Catholic, that I am in a fair way for heaven, even if I should pass through a jail. I think I understood from Mr Dinsmoor, that he had written you at large, on the late successful negotiations with this nation—he has to day started to Natchez, from thence to the Choctaws, where about the beginning of October the commissioners are to meet that nation at *Mount Dexter* and make another attempt to treat for land. I have had some talk with both the white and red Mingos about securing a tract of land to a Choctaw boy that has contrived to prattle himself into my affection—this is my business here—my prospects of success are not very flattering, as I find the business must be clogged with other negociations

On the 28th ult Colonel Burr passed this on his return from Orleans to Nashville, and I understood he intended (to) visit your government.

If I am disappointed in the hope of going up the Mississippi, when I leave this, I will inform you of my course and prospects.

With sincere respect and esteem,

I have the honor to be,

Your excellency's obedient servant,

JOHN M'KEE.

His excellency General Wilkinson

Mr. *M'Rae* then also read the three following letters

—

CHICKASAWS, October 19, 1805

DEAR GENERAL,

Your friendly letter of the 8th ultimo, I received by post on the 15th instant, and from some cause or other it was the most acceptable I ever received; it found me here alone far gone in the blue devils, doubting whether I had not better expatriate myself and try my fortune amidst the storm now gathering in Europe. You cannot think it strange that I feel extremely mortified when I tell you that I have a year past since May last, been waiting in daily expectation of receiving orders to repair in a public capacity to some part of your government, this expectation was excited by the unsolicited promises ♦the Secretary of war. It is true he has still held out to my friends the idea that he intended to provide for me and it must be admitted he has taken time enough to do it well. In the mean time however I am suffering the most painful anxiety and my cash exhausted to a small sum. I have always suspected Claiborne of injuring me with the government, though he declared with uplifted hands to the contrary, I was informed that he had in 1801 made some representations to you and Colonel Joslyn. that I had abused him and the President in a conversation at Mr. M'Intosh's in this nation in very severe and improper language. I have since seen Colonel

Joslyn who gave me a certificate of which the enclosed is a copy; for what I said of Mr. Claiborne a candidate for an office in the state of which I am a citizen, I certainly can be accountable only to him, not to the government that has since clothed him with the mantle of its power. If I had learned ornate et polite dicere to a man whose head and heart were neither of them formed to my tase on the scale of great Mingo's, perhaps I might have been fitted with an office e'er this, however, nil desperandum, Teucro duce. I'll remain here 'till X'mas. The Choctaw treaty I fear will fall through this season and that will not be among my least disappointments, for I had some expectation of procuring at it a tract of land for my young Choctaw. It is reported here from Cumberland that the Secretary of war has written that if the Choctaws wish to sell land they must send deputies to Washington

Cressite, &c is very catholic, but when I proceeded further to "bleach high" I blushed to the finger's ends, but why, I would not tell you for all my hopes in the government, on paper I mean.

With sincere respect and esteem I have the honor to be,

Your excellency's obedient servant,

JOHN M'KEE.

His excellency General Wilkinson.

The irregularity of the mail carriers occasioned this to be a mail later than I expected. I am now informed by a letter from Mr Dinsmoore that the commissioners will meet the Choctaws about the 1st of November, and this morning I set out with your friend General W Colbert to Mount Dexter to attend the treaty.

J. M'K.

CHICKASAW BLUFFS, December 26, 1806.

DEAR GENERAL,

So many opportunities present themselves here for conveying a letter towards Orleans that I would be ungrateful to leave this without at least offering you the compliments of the season, and my hearty prayers for the success of your bark on this tempestuous sea of liberty ; for with all my confidence in her staunchness I cannot help feeling some anxiety on account of sunken rocks and the cursed pirates that infest her track

I set out to-morrow morning for the Chickasaws, and if you should have liesure to inform me of your health by post I will remain there long enough to receive it, and I hope not much longer.

I have the honor to be

With very sincere respect and esteem,

Dear General, your obedient servant,

JOHN M'KEE.

His excellency General Wilkinson

NATCHEZ, January 26, 1807.

DEAR GENERAL,

I wrote you a note from the Chickasaw Bluffs about X'mas. Soon after I set out for this place, where I have been for ten days and will yet remain perhaps two weeks longer ; just to laugh at the ridiculous scenes that are passing before us. There is a wide field for conjecture and every man takes his own direction. The *little mingo* here has assumed *a military attitude* to defend the altar and the throne as well against Colonel Burr as the encroach-ments of the army

I have little doubt that ere this you will have set me down as a Burrite and as little that you will believe me, when I assure, that as yet I am not · and must know the object and the means better than I do, before I can be. 'Tis true, that having nothing to do, and hearing that some great enterprize was on foot, pa-tronized by many great men, and wink'd at by the government, I came here to profit of any opportunity that might offer of bet-tering my situation by honorable enterprize As yet I see no way open, but in the face of my country's laws, and desperate as my fortune is, I will never deliberately do an act that will prevent me from returning to the spot where I was born

I have lately received a letter from Mr Simpson, saying, "your friend General W wishes you were here, as he has it now in his power to serve you" This to me, just now, is very inter-esting information and by return of the mail will be glad to hear from you.

Need I tell you, that considerable pains are taken and taking here, to render you name unpopular ; and by persons too I am in-formed who speak much of the laws and constituted authorities of the country

Your friends, Dinsmore, Freeman and M'Kee, occupy a room here, and laugh at the puddle in a storm.
· I have the honor to be,
Very respectfully,
Your excellency's obedient servant,
JOHN M'KEE

His Excellency, General Wilkinson

—

HUNSTON, *February* 16, 1807.
DEAR GENERAL —I received a few days ago at Natchez your favor of the 8th instant, and nothing could have given me more pleasure . for the strange distant reserve of some of my friends in this quarter, and an observation from Dr. Carmichael, that my note from the Bluffs had excited some supicions of me in a breast which shall never be justified in harboring any, had mortified me sorely, read that note again, and if it does not speak the language of a heart that loves you, I must have been very unfortunate in ex pressing myself

I never was a *Burrite*, nor can I ever give up myself to schemes of lawless plunder. It is certain that in my present situation I might have engaged in any honorable enterprize, however ha-zardous, but the late one, such as it has been represented, is such as I hope no friend of mine will ever surpect me of favoring.

I have not the means, and if I had, I have not at this moment the time to give you much information of the state of things in this country.

May your purse keep pace with your heart, and may you live a thousand years
Your affectionate friend,

JOHN M'KEE

His excellency General Wilkinson.
G

(Dd)

District of Columbia, } ss.
Washington county. }

Personally appeared before me, one of the justices of the peace of the United States, in and for the county of Washington, in the District of Columbia. John Smith, chief clerk in the war office, who being duly sworn, deposeth and saith, that having searched the records and papers in the war office, there are no records of proceedings of Courts Martial, or any papers or proceedings relative to the same, previous to the year one thousand eight hundred and one, and that he hath understood and verily believes, that all records and proceedings of Courts Martial, which were deposited in said office previous to the   day of November, in the year one thousand eight hundred and one, were burned with the office and a number of other papers on that day. That having come into the office since the above date, he never saw any records or proceedings of a Court martial held on William Eaton, and that there is no record or proceeding of any such Court Martial now in the war office to the best of this deponent's knowledge and belief.

Sworn before me this 24th day of September, A. D. 1807

RICHARD PARROTT.

[Annexed is a certificate of James Madison, Secretary of State, that the above R. Parrott, is a justice of the peace as above stated]

INDEX.

[The following Index comprizes the whole of the volumes of this trial. It was intended, when this report was first commenced, to print it in small volumes; but on account of the unforeseen magnitude of the work, it was rendered necessary to increase the size. The 1st volume, therefore, is in two divisions which is distinguished by " part 1, and part 2," in *italic*]

Index.

Index.

Index.